C65511

S0-BIG-647

Historical Documents of Canada

General Editor: C. P. Stacey
Associate General Editor: Ramsay Cook

Historical Documents of Canada

General Editor: C. P. Stacey

Associate General Editor: Ramsay Cook

The following is a complete list of the volumes in the series;
those marked* are already published.

General Preface

Historical Documents of Canada is an attempt to do something never done in Canada before. There have been a certain number of collections of documents dealing with specific and limited areas of Canadian history: the late Professor W. P. M. Kennedy's *Statutes, Treaties and Documents of the Canadian Constitution*, once famous and still valuable, comes instantly to mind. The Government of Canada has lately begun to make an important contribution with its *Documents on Canadian External Relations*. There have also been, increasingly in recent years, general sourcebooks, books of "readings," and documentary publications, some of them excellent; but many of these are elementary in approach and are in varying degrees limited in size and scope. The present series has for its aim to present documentary coverage of the whole of Canadian history from the beginning down to a quite recent date; to deal to some extent at least with every important topic in that history; and to do this in a manner and on a scale suitable for university study up to the graduate level.

The task before the editors has not been easy. The documents that can be included, even in six large volumes, are very few by comparison with the enormous number available. We have tried not to omit any of the relatively few which informed opinion would universally regard as fundamental and unquestionable; beyond that, we have sought to make the best possible selection of individual papers of genuine significance; beyond that again, we have concentrated upon choosing representative documents which illustrate important situations, movements and problems. Many of the papers included are necessarily old and familiar friends. Many others, it will be found, have never been printed before.

All the papers printed in these volumes are contemporary documents. The only exception, if it can be called an exception, is the inclusion of certain statistical tables whose value to the student is obvious.

It has seemed to the general and volume editors neither necessary nor desirable to provide narrative introductions to the volumes or sections. There are now plenty of general histories of Canada available for the guidance of readers. Nor have we provided bibliographies, which are likewise not difficult to find elsewhere. We considered that the space that would have been required for this apparatus was better employed in printing additional documents. We hope that the explanatory notes preceding the individual documents, which normally include references to the most important relevant books, will give the student the sort of help he most requires.

To make the series as useful as possible to students, it has seemed desirable to present all documents in one language. French documents are accordingly printed in English translation. In due course we hope to arrange for a French-language edition in which English documents are translated into French.

Those concerned with this enterprise hope that these volumes, in addition to being an important aid for advanced students, will be helpful to teachers at all levels and a useful tool for reference. The General Editor, indeed, is optimistic enough to believe that almost everyone who is attracted by or concerned with the history of Canada will find them serviceable in some degree.

C.P.S.

Historical Documents of Canada
Volume V: 1914-1945

Historical Documents of Canada

Volume V

The Arts of War and Peace
1914-1945

Edited by

C. P. Stacey

Professor of History, University of Toronto
Late Director, Historical Section, Canadian Army

St. Martin's Press
New York

ISBN 7705-0861-8

Library of Congress Catalogue Card
No. 77-179356

Design by Robert Burgess Garbutt

Printed in Canada for
The Macmillan Company of Canada Limited
70 Bond Street, Toronto, Ontario.

Contents

2. The General Election of 1921

3. The General Election of 1925

4. The General Election of 1926

5. The General Election of 1930

6. The General Election of 1935

7. The General Election of 1940

III: Law, Justice and Police

A. Criminal Justice

B. Police Organization

IV: Social Life and Institutions

A. Population and the Growth of Cities

B. Trade Unionism and Labour Policy

C. The Aftermath of the First World War

D. Social Security and Welfare

E. Prohibition: Ontario as an Example

F. Immigration

G. Abandonment of Titles

H. The Status of Women

V: Economic Life and Policy

A. Trade and Commerce

1. The Bennett Tariff Policy, 1930-1931

2. The Pattern of Trade Agreements, 1932-1938

3. Restraint of Trade: Anti-Combines Legislation

H. The Depression After 1929

I. The Depression Robs Newfoundland of Responsible Government, 1933

J. Stevens, Bennett and Economic Reform, 1934-1935

VI: Northern Development and the Mining Frontier

VII: Religious and Cultural Development

A. Religious Organization: Church Union

B. Education and Cultural Conflict

C. The Arts

D. The Sciences

E. Control of Radio Broadcasting

VIII: External Affairs and Defence

A. The Commonwealth and National Independence

1. The First World War, 1914-1918: Constitutional Developments

2. The Paris Peace Conference, 1919

3. The Imperial Conference of 1921 and Imperial Foreign Policy

4. The Chanak Incident, 1922

E. Canada and the United Nations, 1943-1945

IX: War

A. The First World War

1. The Outbreak of War

2. Command and Control of the Forces and Conduct of the War

3. On the Battlefield and Above It

4. The Conflict over Manpower and Conscription

5. The Industrial Effort

6. Special and Emergency Legislation

B. The Second World War

1. The Outbreak of War

Introduction
to Volume V

This volume deals with a recent and very crowded period of Canada's history, including what may be considered that history's greatest events—the two world wars. To select a few score documents summarizing and illustrating this period is a very difficult task. As in all countries, Canadian documentation has accumulated enormously in the twentieth century. Mr. Eccles in the first volume of this series has to consider more papers than many people would believe; yet the total would be measured at most in hundreds of thousands, whereas in the years treated here one deals in millions. Fortunately, most of the millions have little or no historical value; yet their mere existence greatly complicates the historian's problem and, moreover, the papers actually possessing some historical value are far more numerous than at earlier times.

Of these significant papers, furthermore, a proportion are not yet available. Although public records policy has lately been liberalized, official scruples and the concern of families and individuals still keep some papers for this period closed to the student. It is fair to assume that when the archives are fully opened documents will come to light which ought to be included in this volume but cannot be so under present conditions. It is probably equally fair to assume, however, that we already have before us the vast majority of the significant records of the period.

In performing the task of selection it has been difficult to maintain an acceptable balance between topics and fields—the more so as no two historians would agree upon precisely what that balance should be. But it seems to me evident that there is an irreducible core of political and constitutional history which in a project like this must receive due attention. It is clear too that in economic and, still more, social matters one could go on publishing documents almost *ad infinitum* without exhausting either the supply of papers or the interest of the subjects. To my regret, on a great many topics I have had to limit myself, choosing representative papers to indicate the nature and the importance of a development without being able to explore it fully. This has been the case in particular with respect to the two world wars, on which thousands of relevant documents are easily available; I have been able to print only a few dozen. I should add that it has seemed impracticable to deal with provincial politics, except where there is a definite impingement upon the national scene.

This volume is heavily weighed down with government documents. Since my period has been a time of great legislative activity, I have been forced, in particular, to include a large number of statutes. In general these have been abbreviated by including only the more important sections. I have tried to leaven the lump of official papers with many private documents. I have drawn freely upon the daily press, and I believe that newspaper extracts have enabled me to give the reader at least a few clear glimpses of how Canadians lived, and how fundamentally their lives were changed, during these disturbed and hectic decades after 1914.

I have many helpers to thank. At different times during the long task Mr. Gerald Panting and Mr. Norman Hillmer acted as research assistants, and I have good reason to be grateful to them both. Three of my colleagues at the University of Toronto, Messrs. Craig Brown, Michael Bliss and Michael Cross, kindly helped me over various stiles. I am especially grateful to my brother-in-law, Professor Harcourt Brown, who has advised me in matters of French translation. The following institutions have been particularly generous: the Directorate of History, Canadian Forces Headquarters, Ottawa; the Historical Division of the Department of External Affairs, Ottawa; the Public Archives of Canada, Ottawa; the University of Toronto Library; and the Metropolitan Central Library, Toronto, including the Business Library. The University of Toronto twice made research grants to assist my work. Finally, my publishers, The Macmillan Company of Canada Limited, have been very patient and understanding, and I am especially grateful to Mrs. Diane Mew for her judicious editorial assistance.

C.P.S.

Historical Documents of Canada
Volume V: 1914-1945

I.
Constitution and Government

A.
The Crown and the Office of Governor General

1. The Controversy over the Dissolution of Parliament, 1926

The famous collision between Lord Byng of Vimy, then Governor General, and Mr. William Lyon Mackenzie King over the former's refusal of a dissolution of Parliament to the latter, and Byng's subsequent invitation to Mr. Arthur Meighen to form a government, was an important issue in the general election of 1926, and in that connection is dealt with below (**33-35**). Byng seems to have been moved chiefly by the feeling that Meighen, who had won the largest group in the Commons in the general election of 1925 (below, p. 78) had been unfairly treated in not being given a chance to form a government. The rather more important consideration that King, in asking a dissolution, was seeking to avoid censure by the House of Commons over the Customs scandal, was less prominent in his mind. The British government was not a party to the dispute — Byng had acted the part of an independent constitutional monarch — yet because he was an Englishman and a British appointee there was a widespread, if ill-founded, feeling that Canada had been treated like a colony. This influenced the Progressives in Parliament in voting against Meighen's "acting" ministers. One of the most extraordinary features of the affair was the autonomist King's unsuccessful attempt to get Byng to seek advice from the Dominions Secretary in London. See E.A. Forsey, *The Royal Power of Dissolution of Parliament in the British Commonwealth* (Toronto, 1943); H. Blair Neatby, *William Lyon Mackenzie King*, II: *The Lonely Heights* (Toronto, 1963); Roger Graham, *Arthur Meighen*, II: *And Fortune Fled* (Toronto, 1963); and R. MacG. Dawson, *Constitutional Issues in Canada, 1900-1931* (London, 1933). A larger selection of documents than is given here is in Roger Graham, ed., *The King-Byng Affair, 1926: A Question of Responsible Government* (Toronto, 1967).

2

1. Mr. King to Lord Byng, 28 June 1926

(King Papers, Public Archives of Canada) (hereafter P.A.C.)

Your Excellency having declined to accept my advice to place your signature to the Order-in-Council with reference to a dissolution of parliament, which I have placed before you to-day, I hereby tender to Your Excellency my resignation as Prime Minister of Canada.

Your Excellency will recall that in our recent conversations relative to dissolution I have on each occasion suggested to Your Excellency, as I have again urged this morning, that having regard to the possible very serious consequences of a refusal of the advice of your First Minister to dissolve parliament you should, before definitely deciding on this step, cable the Secretary of State for the Dominions asking the British Government, from whom you have come to Canada under instructions, what, in the opinion of the Secretary of State for the Dominions, your course should be in the event of the Prime Minister presenting you with an Order-in-Council having reference to a dissolution.

As a refusal by a Governor-General to accept the advice of a Prime Minister is a serious step at any time, and most serious under existing conditions in all parts of the British Empire to-day, there will be raised, I fear, by the refusal on Your Excellency's part to accept the advice tendered a grave constitutional question without precedent in the history of Great Britain for a century, and in the history of Canada since Confederation.

If there is anything which, having regard to my responsibilities as Prime Minister, I can even yet do to avert such a deplorable and, possibly, far-reaching crisis, I shall be glad to do so, and shall be pleased to have my resignation withheld at Your Excellency's request pending the time it may be necessary for Your Excellency to communicate with the Secretary of State for the Dominions.

2. Lord Byng to Mr. King, 29 June 1926

(King Papers, P.A.C.)

I must acknowledge on paper, with many thanks, the receipt of your letter handed to me at our meeting yesterday.

In trying to condense all that has passed between us during the past week, it seems to my mind that there is really only one point at issue.

You advise me "that as, in your opinion, Mr. Meighen is unable to govern the country, there should be another election with the present machinery to enable the people to decide". My contention is that Mr. Meighen has not been given a chance of trying to govern, or saying that he cannot do so, and that all reasonable expedients should be tried before resorting to another Election.

Permit me to say once more that, before deciding on my constitutional course on this matter, I gave the subject the most fair-minded and painstaking consideration which it was in my power to apply.

I can only add how sincerely I regret the severance of our official companionship, and how gratefully I acknowledge the help of your counsel and co-operation.

3. Lord Byng to the Secretary of State for Dominion Affairs, London, 30 June 1926

(Copy in P.A.C.)

Secret

As already telegraphed, Mr. Mackenzie King asked me to grant him dissolution. I refused. Thereupon he resigned and I asked Mr. Meighen to form a Government, which has been done.

Now this constitutional or unconstitutional act of mine seems to resolve itself into these salient features. A Governor General has the absolute right of granting dissolution or refusing it. The refusal is a very dangerous decision, it embodies the rejection of the advice of the accredited Minister, which is the bed-rock of Constitutional Government. Therefore nine times out of ten a Governor General should take the Prime Minister's advice on this as on other matters. But if the advice offered is considered by the Governor General to be wrong and unfair, and not for the welfare of the people, it behoves him to act in what he considers the best interests of the country.

This is naturally the point of view I have taken and expressed it in my reply to Mr. King (text of which is being telegraphed later).

You will notice that the letter in question is an acknowledgement of a letter from Mr. King (text of which is also being telegraphed later) appealing that I should consult the Government in London. While recognising to the full the help that this might afford me, I flatly refused, telling Mr. King that to ask advice from London, where the conditions of Canada were not as well known as they were to me, was to put the British Government in the unfortunate position of having to offer solution which might give people out here the feeling of a participation in their politics, which is to be strongly deprecated.

There seemed to me to be one person, and one alone, who was responsible for the decision and that was myself. I should feel that the relationship of the Dominion to the Old Country would be liable to be seriously jeopardised by involving the Home Government; whereas the incompetent and unwise action of a Governor General can only involve himself.

I am glad to say that to the end I was able to maintain a friendly feeling with my late Prime Minister. Had it been otherwise, I should have offered my resignation at once. This point of view has been uppermost in my mind ever since he determined on retaining the reins of office (against my private advice) last November.* It has not been always easy but it was imperative that a Governor General and a Prime Minister could not allow a divergent view-point to wreck their relationship without the greatest detriment to the country.

Mr. King, whose bitterness was very marked Monday, will probably take a very vitriolic line against myself — that seems only natural. But I have to wait the verdict of history to prove my having adopted a wrong course and this I do with an easy conscience that, right or wrong, I have acted in the interests of Canada, and have implicated no one else in my decision.

I would only add that at our last three interviews I appealed to Mr. King not to put the Governor General in the position of having to make a controversial decision. He refused and it appeared that I could do no more.

4. The Secretary of State for Dominion Affairs (Mr. L. S. Amery) to Lord Byng, 3 July 1926

(Copy in P.A.C.)

Private and Personal

I am truly sorry that at the close of your wonderfully successful term in Canada you should have had to face so difficult and unpleasant a situation as that which Mackenzie King's behaviour has created for you. It is not for me from here to attempt to judge the weight of all

*I.e., after the general election of 1925 (below, p. 78).

the factors which determined your decision that the possibilities of the Parliamentary situation were not exhausted and that you ought to give Meighen a chance of trying his hand. It was a courageous decision and a difficult one, and it is enough for me that you took it. I imagine that will be enough for the people of Canada too, who know quite well that no party or personal motive, nothing but your conviction of the public interest, could have influenced you. I can only add that it was no less wise than courageous of you to refuse flatly Mackenzie King's preposterous suggestion that you should cable to me for advice or instructions. He, of all people, should have been the last to try and invoke, in his personal interest, that dependence of Canada upon an outside authority which he has always so strenuously denounced in public. He has cut a contemptible figure in the whole business. His letter to you, with its threat of an Empire wide agitation, was scandalous and nothing could have been better than your reply. Nor can I imagine that his public denunciation of you, with its talk of Crown Colony Government etc. will do him anything but harm in the greater part of the country. . . .

5. Mr. King to Lord Byng, 3 July 1926

(King Papers, P.A.C.)

I duly received Your Excellency's letter of June 29th, for which I desire to thank Your Excellency.

Paragraph three of Your Excellency's letter reads as follows:

> You advise me "that as, in your opinion, Mr. Meighen is unable to govern the country, there should be another Election with the present machinery to enable the people to decide".

Also:

> My contention is that Mr. Meighen has not been given a chance of trying to govern, or saying that he cannot do so, and that all reasonable expedients should be tried before resorting to another Election.

To the accuracy of the statement of Your Excellency's contention as set forth in this paragraph, I have no exception to take. Inasmuch, however, as what purports to have been my advice to Your

Excellency appears in Your Excellency's letter within quotation marks, and might therefore be assumed to be words of mine as expressed in conversation with Your Excellency in tendering advice, may I respectfully say that the words "with the present machinery" — apart from the context in which they are to be found being set forth as a quotation — are quite misleading, as no such words were used or referred to by me in any advice tendered. Fortunately, the text of the quotation clearly indicates that the words taken as a whole could not have come from me as quoted.

I advised Your Excellency that, in my opinion, the existing situation in the House of Commons demanded a dissolution of parliament, and that there should be another election to enable the people to decide upon a new House of Commons.

In reply to Your Excellency's contention that Mr. Meighen had not been given a chance of trying to govern, or saying that he could not do so, I said that I could not advise Your Excellency to send for Mr. Meighen to form an administration, as I did not believe Mr. Meighen could form an administration which would command the confidence of the House. As to Mr. Meighen not having been given a chance of trying to govern, I pointed out that at the commencement of the Session it had been left to the people's representatives in parliament to decide as to who was to advise Your Excellency, and that Mr. Meighen's chances to obtain the support of the Commons had been quite as good as my own; that the House of Commons having declined to express any confidence in Mr. Meighen throughout the entire session, I could not see wherein there was any probability of the House giving him the support which would enable him to carry on the Government, and that therefore I could not assume the responsibility of advising Your Excellency to send for him. As there was still less probability of any other Hon. Member of the House being able to command its confidence, dissolution, to be followed by a general election, in which the people would be given an opportunity to decide, appeared to me the only course which I could advise, and I advised accordingly. . . .

6. Lord Byng to Mr. King, 5 July 1926

(King Papers, P.A.C.)

Many thanks for your letter of July 3. The letter in question was written entirely from the wish on my part to express my sincere gratitude for the help and co-operation you have given me during your tenure of the Premiership. The quotations in it are by no means intended to recall words used at our meetings, and in that connexion I would ask you to read the preceding paragraph.

I was stating my impression as to the one point at issue, and endeavouring to put it in a condensed form. . . .

7. Lord Byng Writes to an Old Friend, 6 July 1926

(A.M.J. Hyatt, ed., "The King-Byng Episode: A Footnote to History," *Dalhousie Review*, Winter 1963-64)

This letter was written to Byng's old comrade-in-arms, Sir Arthur Currie, who had succeeded him as commander of the Canadian Corps in France in 1917 and in 1926 was Principal of McGill University.

My dear old Arthur,

It is letters like yours that make this situation easy for me. Thank you Old Boy.

I want to tell you the whole story but I had better wait till we meet. I begged Mr. King not to put the King's Representative in the position of having to make a controversial decision and offered him two ways out of it. He refused and then told me (1) I was ruining the constitution (2) Breaking up the Empire (3) Putting Canada back in a colonial status. I replied that he put me in the position of being either (1) an inefficient and unconstitutional Govn Genl or (2) A moral coward — and that I chose the former and left the verdict to history.

But there! Nuff said! — I will tell you the whole story when we meet. I don't think I let Canada down, or the Corps, or my friends. Of course it will all blow over and of course my Canadian pals have been magnificent. I knew they would be.

Bless you Arthur my old friend and lots of love to her Ladyship and Marjorie from us both.

Yrs. ever

Bungo

2. The Crown and Canada after 1931

8. An Act Respecting Alteration in the Law Touching the Succession to the Throne, 1937

(1 George VI, Chap. 16)

> King Edward VIII abdicated in December 1936, in order to marry a twice-divorced lady whom neither the United Kingdom government nor the governments of the Dominions were prepared to recognize as Queen. In the light of the Statute of Westminster of 1931 (below, **185**), legislative action by the Canadian Parliament seemed required to confirm the action taken by the British Parliament by which the member of the royal family next in succession succeeded to the Throne as King George VI.

(Assented to 31st March, 1937)

Whereas his former Majesty, King Edward VIII, by His Royal Message of the tenth day of December, in the year of Our Lord one thousand nine hundred and thirty-six, was pleased to declare that He was irrevocably determined to renounce the Throne for Himself and his descendants, and that He had for that purpose executed the Instrument of Abdication, which is set out in Schedule One to this Act, and signified his desire that effect thereto should be given immediately:

And whereas, following upon communication to His Majesty's Government in Canada of his former Majesty's said declaration and desire, the request and consent of Canada, pursuant to the provisions of section four of the Statute of Westminster, 1931, to the enactment of His Majesty's Declaration of Abdication Act, 1936, which is set out in Schedule Two to this Act, was communicated to His Majesty's Government in the United Kingdom:

And whereas the following recital is set forth in the preamble to the statute of Westminster, 1931:

> "And whereas it is meet and proper to set out by way of preamble to this Act that, inasmuch as the Crown is the symbol of the free association of the members of the British Commonwealth of Nations, and as they are united by a common allegiance to the Crown, it would be in accord with the established constitutional position of all the mem-

bers of the Commonwealth in relation to one another that any alteration in the law touching the Succession to the Throne or the Royal Style and Titles shall hereafter require the assent as well of the Parliaments of all the Dominions as of the Parliament of the United Kingdom";*

and accordingly it becomes necessary to declare the Assent of the Parliament of Canada to the alteration in the law touching the Succession to the Throne set forth in His Majesty's Declaration of Abdication Act, 1936.

Now, therefore, His Majesty by and with the advice and consent of the Senate and House of Commons of Canada, enacts as follows: —

1. The alteration in the law touching the Succession to the Throne set forth in the Act of the Parliament of the United Kingdom intituled "His Majesty's Declaration of Abdication Act, 1936" is hereby assented to.

[Schedule One, King Edward VIII's Instrument of Abdication, and Schedule Two, the text of the British Parliament's His Majesty's Declaration of Abdication Act, 1936, are here omitted.]

9. The Royal Visit of 1939: Proceedings in Parliament

(*Debates, House of Commons*, 19 May 1939)

In May and June 1939, almost on the eve of the Second World War, a reigning British sovereign visited Canada for the first time. King George VI and Queen Elizabeth visited every province and were received with the warmest affection, not least in Quebec. In Ottawa the King, as King of Canada, met his Parliament and personally gave the royal assent to legislation.

THE ROYAL ASSENT

A message from His Majesty the King was delivered by Major A. R. Thompson, Gentleman Usher of the Black Rod, the house standing:

Mr. Speaker, the King commands this honourable house to attend

---

*Note nevertheless that the British Parliament's Act, though its preamble recites that Canada (meaning that country's executive government) has "requested and consented to" enactment of the Act, and Australia, New Zealand and South Africa have assented thereto, makes no reference to any requirement for action by the Dominion parliaments.

His Majesty immediately in the chamber of the honourable the Senate.

Accordingly Mr. Speaker, with the house, went up to the senate chamber to attend His Majesty.

And being returned:

Mr. Speaker reported that when the house did attend His Majesty the King in the senate chamber, His Majesty was graciously pleased to give his royal assent to the following bills:

An Act respecting a certain Trade Agreement between Canada and the United States of America. . . .

An Act to provide for the Training of Young People to fit them for gainful employment.

To these bills the royal assent was pronounced by the Clerk of the Senate in the following words:

His Majesty the King doth assent to these bills.

Then the honourable the Speaker of the House of Commons addressed His Majesty the King as follows:

May it please Your Majesty:

The Commons of Canada have voted supplies required to enable the government to defray certain expenses of the public service.

In the name of the Commons I present to Your Majesty the following bill:

"An act for granting to His Majesty certain sums of money for the public service of the financial years ending the 31st March, 1939, and the 31st March, 1940, respectively."

To which bill I humbly request Your Majesty's assent.

To this bill the Clerk of the Senate, by command of His Majesty the King, did thereupon say:

His Majesty the King thanks his loyal subjects, accepts their benevolence, and assents to this bill.

After which His Majesty was pleased to make a most gracious speech from the throne to both houses of parliament, as followeth:

HIS MAJESTY'S SPEECH

Honourable Members of the Senate:

Members of the House of Commons:

I thank you sincerely for your addresses received on my arrival at Quebec. The queen and I deeply appreciate your loyal and affectionate messages.

I am very happy that my visit to Canada affords me the opportunity of meeting, in parliament assembled, the members of both houses. No ceremony could more completely symbolize the free and equal association of the nations of our commonwealth. As my father said, on the occasion of his silver jubilee, the unity of the British empire is no longer expressed by the supremacy of the time-honoured parliament that sits at Westminster. It finds expression to-day in the free association of nations enjoying common principles of government, a common attachment to ideals of peace and freedom, and bound together by a common allegiance to the crown.

The queen and I have been deeply touched by the warmth of the welcome accorded us since our arrival in Canada. We are greatly looking forward to visiting each of the provinces, and, before our return, to paying a brief visit to the United States.

It is my earnest hope that my present visit may give my Canadian people a deeper conception of their unity as a nation. I hope also that my visit to the United States will help to maintain the very friendly relations existing between that great country and the nations of the commonwealth.

These visits, like the one recently made by the queen and myself to the continent of Europe, will, we trust, be viewed as an expression of the spirit of our peoples which seek ardently for closer friendship and better relations not only with our kith and kin but with the peoples of all nations and races.

Honourable Members of the Senate:

Members of the House of Commons:

May the blessing of Divine Providence rest upon your labours and upon my realm of Canada.

B.
The British North America Acts and the Process of Amendment

1. *The British North America Acts, 1915-43*

During the period covered by this volume, six statutes were passed specifically amending in some respects the British North America Act of 1867 (the most important written portion of the Canadian constitution) or acts later passed modifying it. All of these were acts of the British Parliament, including the Statute Law Revision Act of 1927 which repealed the B.N.A. Act of 1916 and a small part of that of 1915 (measures of merely temporary effect). All the British North America Acts passed during this period were the result of Canadian requests expressed in joint addresses to the Crown passed by the Canadian House of Commons and Senate. See R. MacG. Dawson, *The Government of Canada*, 4th ed. revised by Norman Ward (Toronto, 1963), and M. Ollivier, ed., *British North America Acts and Selected Statutes, 1867-1962* (Ottawa, n.d.).

10. The British North America Act, 1915

(5-6 George V, Chap. 45) (British statute)

The senatorial representation of the original four provinces of Confederation, and also (prospectively) of Prince Edward Island and Newfoundland, was settled by the British North America Act, 1867 (see Volume III). That of British Columbia was settled by the Imperial order in council of 1871 which admitted the province to the union, and that of Manitoba, Alberta and Saskatchewan by the Canadian statutes constituting these provinces (Volume IV), which also dealt with representation in the House of Commons. This Act of 1915 increased the representation of the western provinces in the Senate and placed it upon a uniform basis. Subsection vii of section 1 (1), and section 1 (2), were inserted in the Address to the Crown on the insistence of the Liberal-dominated Senate. See *House of Commons Debates*, 25 March and 10 April, 1915. Section 2 was primarily for the protection of Prince Edward Island.

(Assented to 19th May, 1915)

Be it enacted by the King's Most Excellent Majesty, by and with the advice of the Lords Spiritual and Temporal, and Commons, in this present Parliament assembled, and by the authority of the same, as follows: —

1. (1) Notwithstanding anything in the British North America Act, 1867, or in any Act amending the same, or in any Order in Council or terms or conditions of union made or approved under the said Acts or in any Act of the Canadian Parliament —

    (i) The number of senators provided for under section twenty-one of the British North America Act, 1867, is increased from seventy-two to ninety-six:

    (ii) The Divisions of Canada in relation to the constitution of the Senate provided for by section twenty-two of the said Act are increased from three to four, the Fourth Division to comprise the Western Provinces of Manitoba, British Columbia, Saskatchewan, and Alberta, which four Divisions shall (subject to the provisions of the said Act and of this Act) be equally represented in the Senate, as follows: — Ontario by twenty-four senators; Quebec by twenty-four senators; the Maritime Provinces and Prince Edward Island by twenty-four senators, ten thereof representing Nova Scotia, ten thereof representing New Brunswick, and four thereof representing Prince Edward Island; the Western Provinces by twenty-four senators, six thereof representing Manitoba, six thereof representing British Columbia, six thereof representing Saskatchewan, and six thereof representing Alberta:

    (iii) The number of persons whom by section twenty-six of the said Act the Governor General of Canada may, upon the direction of His Majesty the King, add to the Senate is increased from three or six to four or eight, representing equally the four divisions of Canada:

    (iv) In case of such addition being at any time made the Governor General of Canada shall not summon any person to the Senate except upon a further like direction by His Majesty the King on the like recommendation to represent one of the four Divisions until such Division is represented by twenty-four senators and no more:

(v) The number of senators shall not at any time exceed one hundred and four:

(vi) The representation in the Senate to which by section one hundred and forty-seven of the British North America Act, 1867, Newfoundland would be entitled in case of its admission to the Union is increased from four to six members, and in case of the admission of Newfoundland into the Union, notwithstanding anything in the said Act or in this Act, the normal number of senators shall be one hundred and two, and their maximum number one hundred and ten:

(vii) Nothing herein contained shall affect the powers of the Canadian Parliament under the British North America Act, 1886.*

(2) Paragraphs (i) to (vi) inclusive of subsection (1) of this section shall not take effect before the termination of the now existing Canadian Parliament.

2. The British North America Act, 1867, is amended by adding thereto the following section immediately after section fifty-one of the said Act: —

"51A. Notwithstanding anything in this Act a province shall always be entitled to a number of members in the House of Commons not less than the number of senators representing such province."

3. This Act may be cited as the British North America Act, 1915, and the British North America Acts, 1867 to 1886, and this Act may be cited together as the British North America Acts, 1867 to 1915.

11. The British North America Act, 1916

(6-7 George V, Chap. 19) (British statute)

The resolution for the address to the King which originated this one-year wartime extension of the life of a parliament was passed unanimously by the Canadian House of Commons (8 February 1916). It was moved by Sir Robert Borden and supported in an eloquent speech by

*Volume IV.

the Leader of the Opposition, Sir Wilfrid Laurier, who however stated that he would have strongly opposed any proposal to extend the existing Parliament's life for the duration of the war.

(Assented to 1st June, 1916)

1. Notwithstanding anything in the British North America Act, 1867, or in any Act amending the same, or in any Order in Council, or terms or conditions of Union, made or approved under the said Act, or under any Act of the Canadian Parliament, the term of the Twelfth Parliament of Canada is hereby extended until the seventh day of October, nineteen hundred and seventeen. . . .

12. The British North America Act, 1940*

(3-4 George VI, Chap. 36) (British statute)

The Employment and Social Insurance Act, 1935, part of the Bennett government's "New Deal" (below, p. 310) was held by the Judicial Committee of the Privy Council in 1937 to be *ultra vires* the Dominion Parliament. The King government sought the provinces' concurrence in an amendment to the British North America Act permitting Parliament to legislate on the subject, but three provinces, New Brunswick, Quebec and Alberta, delayed their consent until 1940. The Address to the Crown on which this Act was based was then agreed to by the Canadian Commons and Senate, the British Parliament promptly passed this Act, and the new Unemployment Insurance Act (below, **72**) was enacted before the end of the 1940 session.

(Assented to 10th July, 1940)

Whereas the Senate and Commons of Canada in Parliament assembled have submitted an address to His Majesty praying that His Majesty may graciously be pleased to cause a Bill to be laid before the Parliament of the United Kingdom for the enactment of the provisions hereinafter set forth:

*The British North America Act, 1930 (20-21 George V, Chap. 26), a British statute omitted here, was passed to give effect to agreements between the Dominion government and the provinces of Manitoba, British Columbia, Alberta and Saskatchewan concerning the transfer of control of natural resources to those provinces (below, **120**). This was the first of the B.N.A. Acts to mention that the Canadian Senate and Commons had submitted an Address asking for the measure.

Be it therefore enacted by the King's Most Excellent Majesty, by and with the advice and consent of the Lords Spiritual and Temporal, and Commons, in this present Parliament assembled, and by the authority of the same, as follows:

1. Section ninety-one of the British North America Act, 1867, is amended by inserting therein, after item 2 "The regulation of trade and commerce", the following item:

"2A. Unemployment insurance.". . .

13. The British North America Act, 1943

(7 George VI, Chap. 30) (British statute)

This measure originated in the feeling that a redistribution of Commons seats based on the wartime census of 1941 would be unfair to provinces (especially the western provinces) which had lost population as a result of war conditions. There was no consultation with the provinces, but the Quebec legislature passed a protest against the proposal unanimously and nine members of the Commons, all from Quebec, voted against the Address on which it was based. See the discussion (*Debates, House of Commons*, 5 July 1943), and Dawson, *The Government of Canada* (ed. 1947), pp. 145-6.

(Assented to 22nd July, 1943)

1. Notwithstanding anything in the British North America Acts, 1867 to 1940, it shall not be necessary that the representation of the provinces in the House of Commons of Canada be readjusted, in consequence of the completion of the decennial census taken in the year one thousand nine hundred and forty-one, until the first session of the Parliament of Canada commencing after the cessation of hostilities between Canada and the German Reich, the Kingdom of Italy and the Empire of Japan. . . .

2. Discussions on the Process of Amendment

14. Report of Special Committee of the House of Commons on the British North America Act, 1935

(*Debates, House of Commons,* 19 June 1935)

This report represents an attempt to solve the problem of amending the British North America Act which was inspired primarily by economic difficulties rendered worse by the world Depression. In accordance with it, the matter was considered by the Dominion-Provincial Conference held in December 1935, which set up a con-tinuing committee on it; this in turn constituted a sub-committee which reported a method of amendment along the broad lines suggested by Dr. Ollivier in this document, but in the absence of general agreement the matter was dropped (see the statement of the Prime Minister, Mr. St. Laurent, *Debates, House of Commons,* 17 October 1949). For full text of evidence taken, see *Special Committee on British North America Act: Minutes of Proceedings and Evidence* (Ottawa, 1935).

HOUSE OF COMMONS,

June 19, 1935.

SECOND REPORT

The Special Committee of the House of Commons, appointed to study and report on the best method by which the British North America Act may be amended so that while safeguarding the existing rights of racial and religious minorities and legitimate provincial claims to autonomy, the Dominion Government may be given adequate power to deal effectively with urgent economic problems which are essentially national in scope, begs leave to present the following as its second and final report.

Your Committee has held ten sessions and has heard the opinions of a number of witnesses.

Under the instructions of the Committee, telegrams were sent to the respective Attorneys General of the nine provinces in the follow-ing terms: —

The Special Committee of the House of Commons on the Brit-ish North America Act desires to have the views of your Government with respect to methods of securing amendments to said Act. The Resolution referred to the Committee follows. "Resolved, that in the opinion of this House a Special Committee should be set up to study and report on the best method by which the British North America Act may be amended so that while safeguarding the existing rights of racial and religious minorities and legitimate provincial claims to autonomy, the Dominion Government may be given adequate power to deal effectively with urgent economic problems which are essentially national in scope." While the Committee does not object to the personal attendance of a representative of your Government it was thought less costly to ask for a written submission. Copies of proceedings have been sent you, please intimate when we may expect to receive your submission. The following answers were received: —

Prince Edward Island. — "Your wire March twenty-seventh Government of Prince Edward Island is of opinion that Dominion Government should formulate its plan and policy for the purposes intended and that this should be submitted to the Provincial Governments and afterwards discussed at a conference of representatives of the Provinces and the Dominion. Signed by H. F. MacPhee, Attorney-General."

New Brunswick. — "Will wire views as soon as available. Delay unavoidable. Signed by W. H. Harrison, Attorney-General." (New Brunswick views not yet received.)

Nova Scotia. — "Our legislature now in session and most difficult to attend to matter of this kind now in way you suggest. We feel matter should be approached by conference between representatives of Provinces and Dominion, where each would have the views of the other and ample time to discuss the matter. Signed by J. H. MacQuarrie, Attorney-General."

Quebec. — "Your telegram received. Surely the committee cannot expect that the views of the province of Quebec will be discussed by a change of telegrams or letters. In a matter of such importance I suggest that a conference of the Dominion and the provinces should be held. Signed by L. A. Taschereau, Attorney-General."

Ontario. — "Province of Ontario does not desire to make any representation before your committee *re* British North America Act amendment, as no good purpose will be served by attempting to advise Dominion Government at this time. Signed by A. W. [*sic*] Roebuck, Attorney-General."

Manitoba. — "With further reference to your telegram of the 27th March to the Attorney-General and to his reply of the 5th instant, the government have now had an opportunity of giving consideration to the suggestion that it should make a written submission regarding the subject matter that is before your committee.

"The government of Manitoba is of the opinion that the subject matter referred to in the resolution is one of such importance that no written submission, setting out our views in reference to it, should be made without a conference with the other provinces and the Dominion Government. We would be willing to attend such a conference at any time, with a view to arriving at a definite method of procedure for making amendments to the British North America Act. Signed by John Bracken."

Saskatchewan. — "Referring to your telegram of the 27th day of March wherein you request the government of the province to make representations either orally or by written memoranda as to the methods of procedure which this province would suggest in connection with amendments to the Canadian constitution, I would say that I have been following with intense interest the proceedings of your committee. The question of what, if any, provision is to be made for amendment of the Canadian constitution from time to time is a question which ultimately must be decided by conferences between the governments of the provinces and the government of Canada with the possibility of a previous preliminary inter-provincial conference. In view of this fact it would appear to be unwise for the provinces to be giving their views before a committee of the House of Commons. With due deference, might I be permitted to suggest that the proper procedure is for your committee to pursue its present inquiry and to make a report to the House of Commons, which I presume will either be accepted or amended or merely received without binding the government to accept the proposals of the committee and with this report available the provinces could then give consideration as to what attitude they desired to take and perhaps discuss the matter amongst themselves and thereafter join with the Federal government in a general conference. The report of your committee would serve as a basis of discussion around which would take place the ultimate solution of this problem. We realize that the question is one of great national importance and should be decided in the welfare of Canada free of all political considerations, and we are certainly prepared to do our share towards the facilitating of a solution, but we feel that we must look after the interests of the province and think that the procedure I have outlined would be the proper course for us to adopt at this time. Signed by T. C. Davis, Attorney-General."

Alberta. — "*Re* amendment British North America Act. Alberta Government appreciates desire of committee to have views of all provinces before it on this very vital question but considers approach to question should be through interchange of views at inter-provincial conference. Signed by Mr. Lymburn."

British Columbia. — "Reference your wire twenty-seventh to Attorney-General requesting written submission from the government of this province to your committee it is the opinion of the government that amendment of the constitution is too important a matter to be dealt with in manner suggested. It is not thought that satisfactory conclusions can be reached either federally or provincially until a conference of the provinces and the dominion is held when full discussion may be had and matters properly debated. Other than stating that the right should be secured to amend our constitution in Canada this province respectfully declines to make submission to your committee, neither will it feel bound by any report which may be made by your committee. Signed by T. D. Pattullo."

In no case did the authorities of these provinces signify any desire to present their views to your committee, either in writing or orally.

The committee recognizes that there is a divergence of opinion with respect to the question of whether or not the British North America Act is a statutory recognition of a compact among the four original provinces of the Dominion and as to the necessity or otherwise of provincial concurrence in amendments. Without expressing any opinion upon that question, the Committee feels that in the present case and at the present time it is advisable in the interest of harmony and unity that there should be consultation with the provinces with respect to the adoption of a definite mode of amendment or the enactment of amending legislation which might seriously alter the legislative jurisdiction of the provinces and the dominion.

Many interesting suggestions were made. Dr. [W. P. M.] Kennedy,

Professor of Law at Toronto University, suggested that a Royal Commission should be appointed to study the workings of the Act, with a view to recommending a rearrangement of powers if thought necessary.

Dr. [M.] Olivier [sic], Joint Clerk of the House of Commons, suggested that:

(a) Obsolete sections should be dropped;
(b) Certain sections should be subject to amendment without consultation of the provinces;
(c) Certain sections should be amended only with the concurrence of a majority of the provinces;
(d) Certain sections might be amended with the consent of one province only;
(e) Other sections should be amended only on consent of all the provinces.

Dr. [F. R.] Scott, Professor of Civil Law at McGill University, expressed the view that as the Dominion Parliament represented the population of the provinces, ordinary amendments should be made upon a majority vote of both Houses and amendments affecting minority rights should be approved in addition by all provincial legislatures, in order to become law.

Professor [N. McL.] Rogers, Professor of Political Science at Queens University, suggested that a Dominion-Provincial Conference or a National Convention might appoint a committee to draft an amended constitution to be thereafter approved by the conference or convention and subsequently by the Dominion and provincial legislatures. He was of the opinion that the question of consulting the provinces was a matter of political expediency rather than one of legal right.

Dr. [A.] Beauchesne, K.C., C.M.G., LL.D., Clerk of the House of Commons, would have a new constitution drafted by a constituent assembly composed of delegates representing the various provinces and the Dominion, made up of all classes of people. The constitution so drafted would be thereafter adopted by the Dominion and the provinces, approved by the King, and the present act thereupon repealed.

The committee recognizes the urgent necessity for prompt consideration of amendments to the British North America Act with reference to a redistribution of legislative power and to clarify the field of taxation.

It is further of opinion that the conference hereafter proposed should carefully consider the adoption of a recognized yet flexible method of amendment.

In view of the fact that the several provinces did not feel it advisable to give the committee the benefit of their views with respect to the method of procedure to be followed in amending the constitution, the committee is of the opinion that before any decision upon the subject matter of the resolution is finally made, that the opinions of the provinces should be obtained otherwise if at all possible and for that reason recommends that a Dominion-Provincial Conference be held as early as possible in the present year to study the subject matter of the resolution. The proposed conference should have ample time in which to study every phase of the question.

In view of the above recommendation the committee expressly refrains from recommending any form of procedure for amendment so as to leave the proposed conference entirely free in its study of the question, except that the committee is definitely of the opinion that minority rights agreed upon and granted under the provisions of the British North America Act should not be interfered with. . . .

C.
The Electoral Franchise

15. An Act to Confer the Electoral Franchise upon Women, 1918

(8-9 George V, Chap. 20)

At the beginning of the period covered by this volume Dominion elections were conducted on the provincial franchises (see Volume IV). This arrangement was modified in 1917 by the Military Voters Act and the War-time Elections Act (below, **232, 233**). This Act, a wartime measure but passed after the 1917 general election, generalizes the limited franchise granted women by the War-time Elections Act.

(Assented to 24th May, 1918)

1. (1) Every female person shall be entitled to vote at a Dominion election who, —

(*a*) is a British subject;

(*b*) is of the full age of twenty-one years and upwards;

(*c*) possesses the qualifications which would entitle a male person to vote at a Dominion election in the province in which said female person seeks to vote: Provided that a married woman or an unmarried daughter living with her father or mother shall be deemed to have any necessary qualification as to property or income if the husband or either of the parents is so qualified.

(2) For the purposes of this Act a female person shall be deemed to be a British subject, —

(*a*) if she was born a British subject and is unmarried or is married to a British subject, and has not become a subject of any foreign power; or,

(*b*) if she has herself been personally naturalized as a British subject and has not since become the subject of a foreign power; or,

(*c*) if she has become a British subject by marriage, or by the naturalization as a British subject of her parent while she was a minor, and in either case has done nothing (other than in the second case by marriage) to forfeit or lose her status as a British subject, and obtains and presents to the official or officials in charge of the preparation or revision of the voters' lists of the constituency while he is so engaged in such preparation or revision a certificate under the signature of a judge of any court of record or of any superior court, under the seal of the said court, certifying that such female person is of the full age of twenty-one years, has resided in Canada a sufficient length of time, and is possessed of all requirements necessary to entitle her, if unmarried, to become naturalized as a British subject, and that she has taken the oath of allegiance to His Majesty; or,

(d) if, notwithstanding she is married to an alien, she was at the time of such marriage a British subject by birth and has not herself sworn allegiance to any foreign power: Provided, however, that this section shall not apply to the wife of an alien enemy. . . .

16. The Dominion Elections Act, 1920

(10-11 George V, Chap. 46)

This Act again set up a Dominion franchise for Dominion elections, a principle maintained ever since. It amounted to a complete code for the conduct and control of elections, but only its most important sections are given here. It provided for virtually universal franchise at the age of twenty-one. It also clearly established the right of women to sit in the House of Commons. This had been first stated in the Dominion By-Elections Act, 1919 (9-10 George V, Chap. 48, 7 July 1919), in the same words included in this statute as section 38. The first woman to enter the Commons was Miss Agnes Macphail, elected in the 1921 general election as a candidate of the United Farmers of Ontario.

(Assented to 1st July, 1920)

. . . 29. (1) Save as in this Act otherwise provided, every person, male or female, shall be qualified to vote at the election of a member, who, not being an Indian ordinarily resident on an Indian reservation,—

(a) is a British subject by birth or naturalization; and,

(b) is of the full age of twenty-one years; and,

(c) has ordinarily resided in Canada for at least twelve months and in the electoral district wherein such person seeks to vote for at least two months immediately preceding the issue of the writ of election.

(d) provided, however, that any Indian who has served in the Naval, Military or Air forces of Canada in the late war shall be qualified to vote, unless such Indian is otherwise disqualified under paragraphs (a), (b) and (c) of this section. . . .

38. Except as in this Act otherwise provided any British subject, male or female, who is of the full age of twenty-one years, may be a candidate at a Dominion election. . . .

D.
National Symbols

The delays and difficulties encountered in adopting a national flag reveal much about Canada's internal divisions. The documents printed here reflect Mackenzie King's cautious approach towards giving official status to the Red Ensign, for which he had a personal preference. In March 1944 he almost reached the point of asking for "a resolution of Parliament" approving it — but not quite (J. W. Pickersgill, *The Mackenzie King Record*, I (Toronto, 1960), 655). The nettle was not to be grasped until 1964, by which time conditions had changed and a quite different flag was adopted.

17. Order in Council on the Red Ensign, 1924

(Certified copy of a Minute of a Meeting of the Committee of the Privy Council, approved by His Excellency the Governor General on the 26th January, 1924 [P.C. 134])

PRIVY COUNCIL

The Committee of the Privy Council have had before them a Report, dated 23rd January, 1924, from the Right Honourable W. L. Mackenzie King, Prime Minister and Secretary of State for External Affairs, submitting that he has recently had his attention drawn to the practice which prevails of flying the Blue Ensign with the Canadian Arms in the fly over the offices of the High Commissioner for Canada in London. This flag was authorized by a despatch from the Secretary of State for the Colonies dated 16th July, 1870, to be flown by Canadian Government vessels, and its use on land in the heart of London is manifestly irregular. The reason offered for this variation from the Union Jack, which is flown over all Canadian Government buildings in Canada, is to be found in the need very generally felt by Canadians in London for a distinctive emblem which will afford a ready means of distinguishing the character of the buildings over which it floats, and the portion of the Empire to which they belong.

The Prime Minister considers that this purpose would be served by the employment in this connection of the Red Ensign with the

27

Canadian Arms in the fly, which, though originally authorized by the Admiralty to be flown over vessels of the Canadian Mercantile Marine, has come to serve a wider application, having been displayed in times past from the Government buildings in Ottawa, and quite generally throughout the country, where it is still often spoken of as the "Canadian Flag", meaning thereby, the distinctive emblem of Canada.

The Prime Minister therefore, recommends, without contemplating any variation from the present practice regulating the flying of flags from the Government buildings within the Dominion of Canada, and assuming that no local regulation would be violated thereby, that the requisite authority be given for displaying the Red Ensign with the Canadian Arms in the fly, on suitable occasions from all buildings owned or occupied by the Canadian Government, and situated without Canada.

The Committee concur in the foregoing and submit the same for Your Excellency's approval.

18. Canadian Army Routine Order, 1944

22nd January, 1944

4021 — FLYING OF FLAGS AT CANADIAN ARMY STATIONS

The Canadian Red Ensign with the Shield of the Coat of Arms of Canada in the fly is to be flown at all units of the Canadian Army serving with forces of other nations.

19. Order in Council on the Red Ensign, 1945

(P.C. 5888)

AT THE GOVERNMENT HOUSE AT OTTAWA

Wednesday, the 5th day of September 1945.

Present:

His Excellency
The Governor General in Council:
Whereas the Right Honourable W. L. Mackenzie King, the Prime Minister, reports that by Order in Council P.C. 134 of January

26th, 1924, authority is given for displaying the Red Ensign with the shield of the Coat of Arms of Canada in the fly (commonly known as " the Canadian Red Ensign") on suitable occasions from all buildings owned or occupied by the Canadian Government and situated without Canada;

That the Canadian Red Ensign was employed by Canadian forces during the present war; and

That, until such time as action is taken by Parliament for the formal adoption of a national flag, it is desirable to authorize the flying of the Canadian Red Ensign on Federal government buildings within as well as without Canada, and to remove any doubt as to the propriety of flying the Canadian Red Ensign wherever place or occasion may make it desirable to fly a distinctive Canadian flag;

Therefore, His Excellency the Governor General in Council, on the recommendation of the Prime Minister, is pleased to order and doth hereby order that the Red Ensign with the Shield of the Coat of Arms of Canada in the fly (hereinafter referred to as "the Canadian Red Ensign") may be flown from buildings owned or occupied by the Federal government within and without Canada.

His Excellency in Council, on the same recommendation, is further pleased to declare and doth hereby declare that it shall be appropriate to fly the Canadian Red Ensign within and without Canada wherever place or occasion may make it desirable to fly a distinctive Canadian flag.

Nothing herein shall be deemed to alter in any way the provisions now in force with respect to the flying of the Blue Ensign with the shield of the Coat of Arms of Canada in the fly on Canadian Naval vessels and other government vessels, nor with respect to the flying of the Canadian Red Ensign on Canadian Merchant vessels.

II.
Politics

A.
Parties
and Platforms

What follows is a selection of the most important party platforms in the period covered by this volume. For a more complete collection, with many platforms of minor parties, including the Communists, see D. Owen Carrigan, comp., *Canadian Party Platforms, 1867-1968* (Toronto, 1968).

20. Platform of the Farmers' Party, 1918

(Liberal *Speakers' Handbook* [1921])

This western farmers' radical program with its core of low-tariff doctrine had its origin in demands presented to the Dominion government by the Canadian Council of Agriculture in 1910; it was revised in 1916 and adopted in the form here given by a meeting of the Council at Winnipeg on 29 November 1918. So far as the Progressives can be said to have conducted a national campaign in the general election of 1921, this was the basis of it. See W. L. Morton, *The Progressive Party in Canada* (Toronto, 1950).

1. A League of Nations as an international organization to give permanence to the world's peace by removing old causes of conflict.

2. We believe that the further development of the British Empire should be sought along the lines of partnership between nations free and equal, under the present governmental system of British constitutional authority. We are strongly opposed to any attempt to centralize imperial control. Any attempt to set up an independent authority with power to bind the Dominions, whether this authority be termed parliament, council or cabinet, would hamper the growth of responsible and informed democracy in the Dominions.

The Tariff

3. WHEREAS Canada is now confronted with a huge national war

32

debt and other greatly increased financial obligations, which can be most readily and effectively reduced by the development of our natural resources, chief of which is agricultural lands;

AND WHEREAS it is desirable that an agricultural career should be made attractive to our returned soldiers and the large anticipated immigration, and owing to the fact that this can best be accomplished by the development of a national policy which will reduce to a minimum the cost of living and the cost of production;

AND WHEREAS the war has revealed the amazing financial strength of Great Britain, which has enabled her to finance, not only her own part in the struggle, but also to assist in financing her Allies to the extent of hundreds of millions of pounds, this enviable position being due to the free trade policy which has enabled her to draw her supplies freely from every quarter of the globe and consequently to undersell her competitors on the world's market, and because this policy has not only been profitable to Great Britain, but has greatly strengthened the bonds of Empire by facilitating trade between the Motherland and her overseas dominions — we believe that the best interests of the Empire and of Canada would be served by reciprocal action on the part of Canada through gradual reductions of the tariff on British imports, having for its objects closer union and a better understanding between Canada and the Motherland and at the same time bring about a great reduction in the cost of living to our Canadian people;

Fosters Combines

AND WHEREAS the Protective Tariff has fostered combines, trusts and "gentlemen's agreements" in almost every line of Canadian industrial enterprise, by means of which the people of Canada — both urban and rural — have been shamefully exploited through the elimination of competition, the ruination of many of our smaller industries and the advancement of prices on practically all manufactured goods to the full extent permitted by the tariff;

AND WHEREAS agriculture — the basic industry upon which the success of all other industries primarily depends — is unduly handicapped throughout Canada as shown by the declining rural population in both Eastern and Western Canada, due largely to the greatly increased cost of agricultural implements and machinery, clothing, boots and shoes, building material and practically everything the farmer has to buy, caused by the Protective Tariff, so that it is becoming impossible for farmers generally, under normal conditions, to carry on farming operations profitably;

AND WHEREAS the Protective Tariff is the most wasteful, and costly method ever designed for raising national revenue because for every dollar obtained thereby for the public treasury at least three dollars pass into the pockets of the protected interests, thereby building up a privileged class at the expense of the masses, thus making the rich richer and the poor poorer;

AND WHEREAS the Protective Tariff has been and is a chief corrupting influence in our national life because the protected interests, in order to maintain their unjust privileges, have contributed lavishly to political and campaign funds, thus encouraging both political parties to look to them for support thereby lowering the standard of public morality.

Definite Tariff Demands

Therefore be it resolved that the Canadian Council of Agriculture, representing the organized farmers of Canada, urges that, as a means of remedying these evils and bringing about much needed social and economic reforms, our tariff laws should be amended as follows: —

(a) By an immediate and substantial all-round reduction of the customs tariff.

(b) By reducing the customs duty on goods imported from Great Britain to one-half the rates charged under the general tariff, and that further gradual, uniform reductions be made in the remaining tariff on British imports that will ensure complete Free Trade between Great Britain and Canada in five years.

(c) That the Reciprocity Agreement of 1911 which still remains on the United States statute books, be accepted by the parliament of Canada.

(d) That all food stuff not included in the Reciprocity Agreement be placed on the free list.

(e) That agricultural implements, farm machinery, vehicles, fertilizers, coal, lumber, cement, illuminating, fuel and lubricating oils be placed on the free list, and that all raw materials and machinery used in their manufacture also be placed on the free list.

(f) That all tariff concessions granted to other countries be immediately extended to Great Britain.

(g) That all corporations engaged in the manufacture of products protected by the customs tariff be obliged to publish annually comprehensive and accurate statements of their earnings.

(h) That every claim for tariff protection by any industry should be heard publicly before a special committee of parliament.

Taxation Proposals

4. As these tariff reductions may very considerably reduce the national revenue from that source, the Canadian Council of Agriculture would recommend that, in order to provide the necessary additional revenue for carrying on the government of the country and for the bearing of the cost of the war, direct taxation be imposed in the following manner: —

(a) By a direct tax on unimproved land values including all natural resources.

(b) By a graduated personal income tax.

(c) By a graduated inheritance tax on large estates.

(d) By a graduated income tax on the profits of corporations.

(e) That in levying and collecting the business profits tax, the Dominion Government should insist that it be absolutely upon the basis of the actual cash invested in the business and that no considerations be allowed for what is popularly known as watered stock.

(f) That no more natural resources be alienated from the Crown, but brought into use only under short-term leases, in which the interests of the public shall be properly safeguarded, such leases to be granted only by public auction. . . .

Land Settlement

7. A land settlement scheme based on a regulating influence in the selling price of land. Owners of idle areas should be obliged to file a selling price on their lands, that price also to be regarded as an assessable value for purposes of taxation.

8. Extension of co-operative agencies in agriculture to cover the whole field of marketing, including arrangements with consumers' societies for the supplying of foodstuffs at the lowest rates and with the minimum of middleman handling.

9. Public ownership and control of railway, water and aerial transportation, telephone, telegraph and express systems, all projects in the development of natural power, and of the coal mining industry.

Other Democratic Reforms

10. To bring about a greater measure of democracy in government, we recommend: —

(a) The immediate repeal of the War Time Elections Act.

(b) The discontinuance of the practice of conferring titles upon citizens of Canada.

(c) The reform of the federal senate.

(d) An immediate check upon the growth of government by order-in-council, and increased responsibility of individual members of parliament in all legislation.

(e) The complete abolition of the patronage system.

(f) The publication of contributions and expenditures both before and after election campaigns.

(g) The removal of press censorship upon the restoration of peace and the immediate restoration of the rights of free speech.

(h) The setting forth by daily newspapers and periodical publications, of the facts of their ownership and control.

(i) Proportional representation.

(j) The establishment of measures of direct legislation through the initiative, referendum and recall.

(k) The opening of seats in parliament to women on the same terms as men.

21. The Liberal Platform, 1919

(Liberal *Speakers' Handbook* [1921])

This platform was adopted by the same National Liberal Convention (Ottawa, 5-7 August 1919) which chose William Lyon Mackenzie King as party leader. King was largely responsible for the resolutions on labour and industry. Not the least interesting features of the program are its similarity at some points to the Farmers' Platform (above, **20**), and its dissimilarity at others. To emphasize their essential sympathy with Progressive aims the Liberals published the Farmers' Platform as well as their own in their *Speakers' Handbook* for the general election of 1921. See R. MacG. Dawson, *William Lyon Mackenzie King: A Political Biography, I: 1874-1923* (Toronto, 1958), and the same author's *Constitutional Issues in Canada, 1900-1931*.

Resolution on "The Tariff"

THAT the best interests of Canada demand that substantial reductions of the burdens of Customs taxation be made with a view to the accomplishing of two purposes of the highest importance: First: diminishing the very high cost of living which presses so severely on the masses of the people; Second: reducing the cost of the instruments of production in the industries based on the natural resources of the Dominion, the vigorous development of which is essential to the progress and prosperity of our country.

That, to these ends, wheat, wheat flour and all products of wheat; the principal articles of food; farm implements and machinery; farm tractors, mining, flour and saw-mill machinery and repair parts thereof; rough and partly dressed lumber; gasoline, illuminating, lubricating and fuel oils; nets, net-twines and fishermen's equipments; cements and fertilizers, should be free from Customs duties, as well as the raw material entering into the same.

That a revision downwards of the tariff should be made whereby substantial reductions should be effected in the duties on wearing apparel and footwear, and on other articles of general consumption (other than luxuries), as well as on the raw material entering into the manufacture of the same.

That the British preference be increased to 50 per cent of the general tariff.

And the Liberal Party hereby pledges itself to implement by legislation the provision of this resolution when returned to power.

Resolution on "Reciprocity"

THAT the Reciprocity Agreement negotiated with the United States by the Liberal Government of Canada, in 1911, was a measure which realized the hopes that had been entertained and efforts made for better trade relations between Canada and the neighbouring Republic, by the statesmen of both political parties in the Dominion, from the beginning of the Dominion's history.

That the Agreement was fair and just to both countries and well calculated to promote the good relations so desirable;

That the action of the Conservative party under the leadership of Mr. (now Sir) Robert Borden in opposing and defeating the Agreement was a sacrifice of the best interests of Canada for distinctly partisan ends.

That the insincerity of the movement of the Conservative leaders on that question has been abundantly evidenced by the fact that, after coming into office, they proceeded to make some of the very tariff changes, a denunciation of which was their chief ground in the elections of 1911.

That the action of the Conservative leaders in preventing the consummation of so excellent an arrangement between the two countries deserves and should still receive, whenever the opportunity occurs, the severe condemnation of the Canadian people.

That the Reciprocity Agreement was approved in 1911 by the Congress of the United States, and the law giving such approval still remains on the American statute book.

That, if the proposal lately made in the Congress to repeal the said law be carried out, the people of Canada will have no cause to complain, since the Americans have kept the law unimpaired for the long term of eight years during which Canada has made no move to avail herself of its provisions.

That while, for these reasons, this Convention can take no exception to the proposal so made at Washington, we as Liberals again place on record our appreciation of the object of the said Agreement and our faith in the principles of friendly international relations underlying it, and we express our earnest hope that in both countries such principles will be upheld, and that a favorable moment may come when there will be a renewed manifestation by the two Governments of a desire to make some similar arrangement.

Resolution on "Encouragement to Agriculture"

IN the interest of agricultural production and development it is expedient to encourage co-operation and induce greater investment in farming; therefore, it is deemed expedient to utilize the national credit to assist co-operative Agricultural Credit Associations to provide capital for agriculture at the lowest possible rates.

With the object of reducing the high cost of living by eliminating as far as possible the waste and expense in handling food products between the producer and consumer, it is expedient to extend the principle and system of Canadian Government Elevators and to provide interior and terminal cold storage warehouses equipped for the assembling, assorting, preparing, storing and grading of food products in order that co-operative organizations and others may have available to them reliable modern equipment, for the distribution of farm products in superior condition and at lessened cost either for domestic consumption or for export. And that cold storage transportation facilities should be provided, at the cost of operation, for the shipment of food products throughout Canada and for the carrying to the markets of the world the surplus farm products of this country and delivering them in such condition that will make Canadian foodstuffs a standard of quality for the world's market.

That, in the interests of agriculture, in aid of greater production on the land, and for the conservation of the soil in Canada, it is expedient for the Government to arrange for the distribution of fertilizers at the lowest possible cost.

Your Committee on Agriculture begs to recommend that a Special Committee be appointed to prepare a resolution upon the banking system of Canada and the adapting of said system to satisfactory loans in connection with land and live stock, and to present such resolution to your Committee.

Resolution on "Labour and Industry"

RESOLVED that the Committee recommends that the National Liberal Convention accept in their entirety as a part of the Liberal Platform, in the spirit they have been framed and in so far as the special circumstances of the country will permit, the terms of the Labour Convention and General Principles associated with the League of Nations and incorporated in the Conditions of Peace.

These methods and principles for regulating labour conditions so set forth in the Treaty are as follows:

First. — The guiding principle that labour should not be regarded merely as a commodity or article of commerce.

Second. — The right of association for all lawful purposes by the employed as well as by the employers.

Third. — The payment to the employed of a wage adequate to maintain a reasonable standard of life as this is understood in their time and country.

Fourth. — The adoption of an 8-hour day or a 48-hour week as the standard to be aimed at where it has not already been attained.

Fifth. — The adoption of a weekly rest of at least twenty-four hours, which should include Sunday wherever practicable.

Sixth. — The abolition of child labour and the imposition of such limitations on the labour of young persons as shall permit the continuation of their education and assure their proper physical development.

Seventh. — The principle that men and women should receive equal remuneration for work of equal value.

Eighth. — The standard set by law in each country with respect to the conditions of labour should have due regard to the equitable economic treatment of all workers lawfully resident therein.

Ninth. — Each state should make provision for a system of inspection in which women should take part, in order to ensure the enforcement of the laws and regulations for the protection of the employed.

AND FURTHER RESOLVED:

1. That the introduction into the government of industry or principles of representation whereby labour and the community, as well as capital, may be represented in industrial control, and their interests

safeguarded and promoted in the shaping of industrial policies.

2. That in so far as may be practicable, having regard for Canada's financial position, an adequate system of insurance against unemployment, sickness, dependence in old age, and other disability, which would include old age pensions, widows' pensions, and maternity benefits, should be instituted by the Federal Government in conjunction with the Governments of the several provinces; and that on matters pertaining to industrial and social legislation an effort should be made to overcome any question of jurisdiction between the Dominion and the provinces by effective co-operation between the several Governments.

3. The representation of labour on federal commissions pertaining to labour matters.

4. Effective legislation for the conservation of human life and health.

5. The representation of labour on the Board of Directors of the Canadian National Railways.

6. That the system of re-training soldiers, unfitted for their past work because of physical injuries, be extended to disabled workers in industry.

7. More effective restriction of Chinese immigration.

8. The federal incorporation of co-operative associations.

9. The acceptance of the principle of proportional representation.

10. Immediate and drastic action by the Government with respect to the high cost of living and profiteering.

11. Restoration of the control of the executive by Parliament, and of Parliament, by the people through a discontinuance of government by Order in Council and a just franchise and its exercise under free conditions.

Resolution on "Conservation and Improvement of Physical Standards of Canadians"

WHEREAS the Great War and the greater epidemic* have taken an appalling toll of Canadian life; and

WHEREAS human life and physical efficiency are the Nation's greatest assets; and

---

*Of "Spanish" influenza. The epidemic is said to have killed six million people across the world in three months of 1918 (*Canadian Annual Review, 1918*, pp. 574-5).

WHEREAS the conservation and improvement thereof should be the Country's first care;

THEREFORE this gathering of Liberals in convention assembled pledges itself to a vigorous prosecution of the measures best calculated to conserve the life and improve the physical standard of our Canadian citizenship. . . .

Resolution on "Railways and Development of Natural Resources"

WHEREAS the construction of the National Transcontinental Railway wholly upon Canadian soil, including terminal facilities, and in the completion of the project steamship connection with Europe and the Far East, thus affording the best possible transportation between the Orient and the Mother Country and opening up a large portion of Canada not before developed, and providing for lowering of the freight rates, was undertaken by the Liberal Government and Parliament of Canada; and

WHEREAS the accomplishment of the purpose for which this transportation system was designed has been thwarted by the studied hostility of the Borden Administration, this Convention expresses its opinion that only by the defeat of the present Government can the beneficial results which should accrue from the construction of this great national transcontinental route be secured; and

WHEREAS the Government by its policy in dealing with the Canadian Northern Railway system, which, in addition to granting of subsidies and guaranteeing of bonds, also made large loans of the public monies and thus involved the Dominion of Canada in financial obligations which resulted in the Government assuming the ownership of the said system; and

WHEREAS in addition to assuming the enormous liabilities incurred by the purchase of the Canadian Northern Railway system the Borden Government forced through Parliament, in contravention of legislation already on the statute book, an Act under which $10,000,000 was paid to C.N.R. interests, the identity of whom has never been disclosed, this Convention condemns with all possible vigour this entire unbusiness-like transaction and demands full investigation into the conditions surrounding the purchase of the C.N.R. and the destination of the monies paid.

The Government now owns and operates some 16,000 miles of railway. We believe that the present system of management by a Board, the majority of the members of which devote but a small portion of their time to this work, is unwieldy, inefficient and extravagant, and that under it and the present administration public ownership and operation will not receive a fair trial.

Adequate facilities and tonnage for ocean traffic are a vital concern to the commerce of Canada and the utter lack of foresight on the part of the Government in neglecting to see that such facilities and tonnage were provided for the immediate After-the-War period is not only humiliating to the Canadian people, but is materially impairing our export trade.

At this time when the country should be in a position to take full advantage of the opportunities to secure its proper share of the export business on which the financial, industrial, and agricultural future of Canada depends, we are confronted with the lamentable situation that no adequate provision has been made for the transportation of the products of the farm, the factory and the forest to the markets of the world. With the knowledge of the enormous destruction of tonnage by the havoc of war in its possession, the failure of the Government to protect the trade of Canada against the condition that now confronts it shows an absence of business ability which merits the severest condemnation of the people of Canada.

This Convention declares its fullest confidence in the future of Canada, believing that a wise and economical development of our natural resources, and a judicious and vigorous immigration and colonization policy, coupled with stringent economy and efficient management in every department of Government, will solve the transportation and other difficult problems now confronting the country.

Resolution on "Canadian Autonomy"

RESOLVED that we are strongly opposed to centralized Imperial control and that no organic change in the Canadian Constitution in regard to the relation of Canada to the Empire ought to come into effect until, after being passed by Parliament, it has been ratified by vote of the Canadian people on a Referendum.

Resolution on "National Unity"

RECOGNIZING that the crown of Sir Wilfrid Laurier's life work and the dearest wish of his heart was the establishment of racial concord and national unity throughout the Dominion, the Liberal Party of Canada in National Convention assembled emphatically condemns all attempts to create racial discord and national disunion and would hold up as a lasting example to the Canadian people the inspiring ideal of that great Canadian—a united Canada in which all Canadians shall be on an equal footing, all working together in harmony and concord for the upbuilding and aggrandizement of their common country.

Resolution on "Control of Natural Resources by Provinces"

RESOLVED that the provinces of Manitoba, Saskatchewan and Alberta should be granted the ownership and control of the natural resources within their respective boundaries on terms that are fair and equitable, with reference to all other provinces of the Dominion. . . .

22. The Conservative Platform, 1927

(*Canadian Annual Review, 1927-28*)

This platform was adopted by the Conservative National Convention (Winnipeg, 10-12 October 1927) which chose R. B. Bennett as party leader. Additional portions of it may be found in Dawson, *Constitutional Issues in Canada, 1900-1931*.

The Tariff

This Convention desires to record its feeling of pride in the growth, progress and prosperity of Canada, under the historic fiscal policy of the Liberal-Conservative Party. It affirms its adherence to the principles of that policy in its declared objects of stimulating the development of the natural resources of the Dominion; preserving and enlarging the market for Canadian farm products; building up the industries of Canada, and thus creating employment for our workmen; promoting inter-provincial trade, and generally providing a diversified economic life which will be effectual in retaining Canada's sons and daughters within our own boundaries. This Convention affirms the principle that from time to time, as changing conditions require, the customs tariff should be revised and its rates adjusted and brought into conformity with such conditions. In such revisions, regard should be had not only to the objects of fiscal policy herein enumerated, but to the welfare of the consumer, and it is desirable in the national interest that in such revisions the cost of living and the cost of the implements used in production of whatever nature should be given special and attentive study, with a view to the reduction of such costs to the extent practicable. This Convention affirms the policy first introduced by the Liberal-Conservative Government in 1912, that with a view of having tariff rates under scientific investigation, a permanent tariff commission should be appointed, representative of the three great classes of Canadian industry — agriculture, labour and manufacturing — entrusted with the duty of studying tariff problems, and making such recommendations to the Government as it deems in the public interest with reasons therefor. Should it find that unfair advantage is being taken of tariff duties it shall make recommendations to be given effect to by the Government for reducing or removing tariff schedules or imposing special duties of excise upon products in respect of which such advantage has been taken, and its reports, findings and reasons therefor shall be laid before Parliament and made known to the public. And this Convention expresses the view that while strong effort should be directed towards the establishment of a system of preferential tariffs throughout the Empire no preference should be given at the expense of the Canadian farmer or workman, and all such preference should be conditional upon the use of Canadian ports.

Imperial Relations

This Convention re-affirms the traditional adherence of the Liberal-Conservative Party to the principle of loyalty to the Crown and to the maintenance of that integral connection of Canada with the British Empire, which is based upon full concurrence of the Canadian people. This Convention further expresses its satisfaction at the position attained by Canada as a nation within the British Empire, which was acknowledged at the close of the Great War by our participation in the Imperial Conference and Canada's signature affixed to the Treaty of Versailles, and also by Canada's admission with full status to the League of Nations. The Convention emphasizes the fact that the attainment of this position, which has been the result of the practical applications made by the leaders of the Conservative Party of the principles laid down by that Party, which was founded in the struggle for Confederation, and has continuously stood for the unity and equality of all Canadians and for the material, moral and spiritual development of Canada. This Convention rejoices in the powers and freedom of action which Canada as a nation has attained largely through the efforts and sacrifices of our soldiers, and pledges itself anew to the ideal of a united Canada.

This Convention emphasizes the fact that the Conservative Convention cherishes the traditions and purposes of the British family of nations, and believes that in the co-operation of the British nations will be found good for Canada and for the world.

Immigration

That Canada adopt an aggressive system of immigration based upon the selective principle and with that end in view efforts be directed to: (1) Repatriation of Canadians. (2) Securing a larger percentage of British settlers. (3) Taking full advantage of the assistance tendered by the British Government to promote Empire settlement. (4) Making arrangements between the two Governments to ensure proper training of the youth of the British Isles as agriculturists to better qualify them as Canadian settlers. (5) That in the selection and settlement of immigrants a sane classification and distribution should be made, taking into consideration the immigrant's previous occupation and adaptability and that in such distribution the needs of all Provinces should be given fullest consideration. (6) That in selecting new immigrants, relatives of present citizens of Canada should receive favourable consideration. (7) That special concessions be granted to Canadians to enable them to settle our vacant lands. (8) Oriental exclusion.*

Natural Resources of the Prairie Provinces

In the best interests of Confederation and the economic development of Western Canada the Provinces of Manitoba, Saskatchewan and Alberta should be granted their Natural Resources free from restrictions within the legislative competence of the Parliament of Canada, but with provision for the maintenance and administration of the school lands and school lands endowment for educational purposes according to the laws of the respective Provinces† and that the claims of these Provinces to compensation for loss for lands and resources alienated and the claims of any other Provinces in connection with this subject should be investigated with a view to satisfactory and equitable adjustment. . . .

*A "more courteous terminology" than this phrase was suggested in the Convention, but the phrase was ultimately allowed to stand (Canadian Annual Review, 1927-28, p. 53).
†The reference to school lands was inserted on the floor of the Convention (Canadian Annual Review, 1927-28, pp. 52-3).

Old Age Pensions*

Whereas all needy aged persons, wherever resident in Canada, qualified by residence have equal right to old age pensions; and

Whereas, the present federal pension law† is inadequate and unworkable;

Therefore, be it resolved that pension legislation should be the subject of federal legislation only.

Railway Policy

Whereas, the Canadian Pacific Railway owes its existence to the courage and vision of Conservative statesmen;

And whereas, the amalgamation of the different units now comprising the Canadian National Railways were achieved by the Conservative party;

And whereas, it is in the best interests of our country that both railway systems should remain separate and apart;

Be it resolved, therefore, that the Conservative Party pledges itself to maintain the Canadian National Railways as a publicly owned and operated utility and to make the directorate of that railway non-partisan and free from political interference. . . .

23. The "Regina Manifesto" of the C.C.F., 1933

(The Co-operative Commonwealth Federation Manifesto)
(leaflet, n.d., n.p.)

The Co-operative Commonwealth Federation was organized at Calgary in August 1932, at the very nadir of the Great Depression. This program (the first draft of which was written by F. H. Underhill, a University of Toronto history professor and president of the League for Social Reconstruction) was adopted at the C.C.F.'s first national convention, held at Regina on 19-21 July 1933. See Kenneth McNaught, *A Prophet in Politics: A Biography of J. S. Woodsworth* (Toronto, 1959). For Mr. Underhill's recollections of the occasion, see the introduction to his *In Search of Canadian Liberalism* (Toronto, 1960). The history of the C.C.F. is told in Walter D. Young, *The Anatomy of a Party: The National CCF, 1932-61* (Toronto, 1969).

*This and the following section are from the *Gazette*, Montreal, 12 October 1927.
†Below, **70**.

The C.C.F. is a federation of organizations whose purpose is the establishment in Canada of a Co-operative Commonwealth in which the principle regulating production, distribution and exchange will be the supplying of human needs and not the making of profits.

We aim to replace the present capitalist system, with its inherent injustice and inhumanity, by a social order from which the domination and exploitation of one class by another will be eliminated, in which economic planning will supersede unregulated private enterprise and competition, and in which genuine democratic self-government, based upon economic equality will be possible. The present order is marked by glaring inequalities of wealth and opportunity, by chaotic waste and instability; and in an age of plenty it condemns the great mass of the people to poverty and insecurity. Power has become more and more concentrated into the hands of a small irresponsible minority of financiers and industrialists and to their predatory interests the majority are habitually sacrificed. When private profit is the main stimulus to economic effort, our society oscillates between periods of feverish prosperity in which the main benefits go to speculators and profiteers and of catastrophic depression, in which the common man's normal state of insecurity and hardship is accentuated. We believe that these evils can be removed only in a planned and socialized economy in which our natural resources and the principal means of production and distribution are owned, controlled and operated by the people.

The new social order at which we aim is not one in which individuality will be crushed out by a system of regimentation. Nor shall we interfere with cultural rights of racial or religious minorities. What we seek is a proper collective organization of our economic resources such as will make possible a much greater degree of leisure and a much richer individual life for every citizen.

This social and economic transformation can be brought about by political action, through the election of a government inspired by the idea of a Co-operative Commonwealth and supported by a majority of the people. We do not believe in change by violence. We consider that both the old parties in Canada are the instruments of capitalist interests and cannot serve as agents of social reconstruction, and that whatever the superficial difference between them, they are bound to carry on government in accordance with the dictates of the big business interests who finance them. The C.C.F. aims at political power in order to put an end to this capitalist domination of our political life. It is a democratic movement, a federation of farmer, labour and socialist organizations, financed by its own members and seeking to achieve its end solely by constitutional methods. It appeals for support to all who believe that the time has come for a far-reaching reconstruction of our economic and political institutions and who are willing to work together for the carrying out of the following policies:

1. *Planning:* The establishment of a planned socialized economic order, in order to make possible the most efficient development of the national resources and the most equitable distribution of the national income.

The first step in this direction will be setting up of a National Planning Commission consisting of a small body of economists, engineers and statisticians assisted by an appropriate technical staff. . . .

2. *Socialization of finance:* Socialization of all financial machinery — banking, currency, credit, and insurance, to make possible the effective control of currency, credit and prices, and the supplying of new productive equipment for socially desirable purposes.

Planning by itself will be of little use if the public authority has not the power to carry its plans into effect. Such power will require the control of finance and of all those vital industries and services, which, if they remain in private hands, can be used to thwart or corrupt the will of the public authority. Control of finance is the first step in the control of the whole economy. The chartered banks must be socialized and removed from the control of private profit-seeking interests; and the national banking system thus established must have at its head a Central Bank to control the flow of credit and the general price level, and to regulate foreign exchange operations. A National Investment Board must also be set up, working in co-operation with the socialized banking system to mobilize and direct the unused surpluses of production for socially desired purposes as determined by the Planning Commission.

Insurance Companies, which provide one of the main channels for the investment of individual savings and which, under their present competitive organization, charge needlessly high premiums for the social services that they render, must also be socialized.

3. *Social ownership:* Socialization (Dominion, Provincial or Municipal) of transportation, communications, electric power and all other industries and services essential to social planning, and their operation under the general direction of the Planning Commission by competent managements freed from day to day political interference.

Public utilities must be operated for the public benefit and not for the private profit of a small group of owners or financial manipulators. Our natural resources must be developed by the same methods. Such a programme means the continuance and extension of the public ownership enterprises in which most governments in Canada have already gone some distance. Only by such public ownership, operated in a planned economy, can our main industries be saved from the wasteful competition of the ruinous over-development and over-capitalization which are the inevitable outcome of capitalism. Only in a regime of public ownership and operation will the full benefits accruing from centralized control and mass production be passed on to the consuming public.

Transportation, communications and electric power must come first in a list of industries to be socialized. Others, such as mining, pulp and paper and the distribution of milk, bread, coal and gasoline, in which exploitation, waste, or financial malpractices are particularly prominent must next be brought under social ownership and operation.

In restoring to the community its natural resources and in taking over industrial enterprises from private into public control we do not propose any policy of outright confiscation. What we desire is the most stable and equitable transition to the Co-operative Commonwealth. . . .

4. *Agriculture*: Security of tenure for the farmer upon his farm on conditions to be laid down by individual provinces; insurance against unavoidable crop failure; removal of the tariff burden from the operations of agriculture; encouragement of producers' and consumers' co-operatives; the restoration and maintenance of an equitable relationship between prices of agricultural products and those of other commodities and services; and improving the efficiency of export trade in farm products.

The security of tenure for the farmer upon his farm which is imperilled by the present disastrous situation of the whole industry, together with adequate social insurance, ought to be guaranteed under equitable conditions.

The prosperity of agriculture, the greatest Canadian industry, depends upon a rising volume of purchasing power of the masses in Canada for all farm goods consumed at home, and upon the maintenance of large scale exports of the stable commodities at satisfactory prices or equitable commodity exchange. . . .

5. *External trade*: The regulation in accordance with the National plan

of external trade through import and export boards.

Canada is dependent on external sources of supply for many of her essential requirements of raw materials and manufactured products. These she can obtain only by large exports of the goods she is best fitted to produce. The strangling of our export trade by insane protectionist policies must be brought to an end. But the old controversies between free traders and protectionists are now largely obsolete. In a world of nationally organized economies Canada must organize the buying and selling of her main imports and exports under public boards, and take steps to regulate the flow of less important commodities by a system of licences. . . .

6. *Co-operative institutions*: The encouragement by the public authority of both producers' and consumers' co-operative institutions.

7. *Labor Code*: A National Labor Code to secure for the worker maximum income and leisure, insurance covering illness, accident, old age, and unemployment, freedom of association and effective participation in the management of his industry or profession. . . .

8. *Socialized health services*: Publicly organized health, hospital and medical services.

With the advance of medical science the maintenance of a healthy population has become a function for which every civilized community should undertake responsibility. Health services should be made at least as freely available as are educational services today. . . .

9. *B.N.A. Act*: The amendment of the Canadian Constitution, without infringing upon racial or religious minority rights or upon legitimate provincial claims to autonomy, so as to give the Dominion Government adequate powers to deal effectively with urgent economic problems which are essentially national in scope; the abolition of the Canadian Senate. . . .

10. *External relations*: A Foreign Policy designed to obtain international economic co-operation and to promote disarmament and world peace.

Canada has a vital interest in world peace. We propose, therefore, to do everything in our power to advance the idea of international co-operation as represented by the League of Nations and the International Labor Organization. We would extend our diplomatic machinery for keeping in touch with the main centres of world interest. But we believe that genuine international co-operation is incompatible with the capitalist regime which is in force in most countries, and that strenuous efforts are needed to rescue the League from its present condition of being mainly a League of capitalist Great Powers. We stand resolutely against all participation in imperialist wars. Within the British Commonwealth, Canada must maintain her autonomy as a completely self-governing nation. We must resist all attempts to build up a new economic British Empire in place of the old political one, since such attempts readily lend themselves to the purposes of capitalist exploitation and may easily lead to further world wars. Canada must refuse to be entangled in any more wars fought to make the world safe for capitalism.

11. *Taxation and public finance:* A new taxation policy designed not only to raise public revenues but also to lessen the glaring inequalities of income and to provide funds for social services and the socialization of industry; the cessation of the debt-creating system of Public Finance. . . .

12. *Freedom:* Freedom of speech and assembly for all: repeal of Section 98 of the Criminal Code: amendment of the Immigration Act to prevent the present inhuman policy of deportation; equal treatment before the law of all residents of Canada irrespective of race, nationality or religious or political beliefs. . . .

13. *Social Justice:* The establishment of a commission composed of psychiatrists, psychologists, socially minded jurists and social workers, to deal with all matters pertaining to crime and punishment and the general administration of law, in order to humanize the law and to bring it into harmony with the needs of the people. . . .

14. *An Emergency Program:* The assumption by the Dominion Government of direct responsibility for dealing with the present critical unemployment situation and for tendering suitable work or adequate maintenance; the adoption of measures to relieve the extremity of the crisis such as a program of public spending on housing, and other enterprises that will increase the real wealth of Canada, to be financed by the issue of credit based on the national wealth.

The extent of unemployment and the widespread suffering which it has caused, creates a situation with which provincial and municipal governments have long been unable to cope, and forces upon the Dominion Government direct responsibility for dealing with the crisis as the only authority with financial resources adequate to meet the situation. Unemployed workers must be secured in the tenure of their homes, and the scale and methods of relief, at present altogether inadequate, must be such as to preserve decent human standards of living. . . .

Emergency measures, however, are of only temporary value, for the present depression is a sign of the mortal sickness of the whole capitalist system, and this sickness cannot be cured by the application of salves. These leave untouched the cancer which is eating at the heart of our society, namely, the economic system in which our natural resources and our principal means of production and distribution are owned, controlled and operated for the private profit of a small proportion of our population.

No C.C.F. Government will rest content until it has eradicated capitalism and put into operation the full program of socialized planning which will lead to the establishment in Canada of the Co-operative Commonwealth.

24. The Social Credit Gospel, 1935

(As quoted in John A. Irving, *The Social Credit Movement in Alberta*, Toronto, 1959, Appendix 1)

On this platform the Social Credit League of Alberta, led by William Aberhart, high school principal and evangelist, won a crushing victory in the provincial election of 22 August 1935. Social Credit in Alberta was a variation of the doctrines originated under that name by Major C. H. Douglas in England. Under Depression conditions, and as presented by Aberhart, it had a powerful appeal in the West. (On the West in the Depression, see below, pp. 289-91.) Social Credit went straight on into the federal political theatre, running 45 candidates in the four western provinces in the general election of 14 October 1935 and electing 17 — 15 in Alberta and two in Saskatchewan. The federal government disallowed the provincial legislation intended to implement this eccentric economic program; but Social Credit controlled the government of Alberta until August 1971.

1. FINANCE AND THE DISTRIBUTION OF GOODS

(*a*) The Cessation of Borrowing from Outside Sources and the creation of our own Credit, thus gradually eliminating heavy interest charges and retaining our own purchasing power. (*b*) The Distribution of Purchasing Power to bona fide citizens by means of Basic Dividends sufficient to secure the bare necessities of food, clothing and shelter. This distribution is to be based upon active willingness on the part of the individuals to co-operate in the welfare of the people of the Province. (c) The establishment of a Just Price on all goods and services, and the regulation of the price spread on all goods sold or transferred within the bounds of the Province. This Just Price is to be just and fair: 1. To the producers and to the distributors. They should not be required to sell goods for less than the cost of production or of import. 2. To the customers. They should not be exploited or unduly deprived of fair returns for their purchasing power. (d) The Establishment of an authority to deal with production loans.

2. THE PRESENT PROBLEM OF DEBT

(a) Private, or Mortgage and Tax Indebtedness. 1. The Distribution of Basic Dividends and the Establishment of a Just Price will at once begin to give our citizens the ability to cope with the Mortgage Indebtedness at present against their farms and their homes. 2. The Increase in Consumption will of necessity make a greater demand for services and that will produce wages to help settle these debts. 3. The Debt Adjustment Act will be amended to prevent hasty foreclosures on all property and adequately to meet the requirements of all classes of debtors. 4. Later, as prosperity returns under Social Credit, Interest-Free Loans may be granted to liquidate or refund the present interest-bearing mortgages. (b) The Municipal and the Provincial Debts. 1. Bonds could be offered to our citizens to liquidate this indebtedness at a lower rate of interest. 2. This would decrease the amount of taxes levied in proportion to the success of this proposition.

3. THE PROBLEM OF UNEMPLOYMENT

(a) Social Credit at once removes the demoralizing effect of Unemployment by the issuance of Monthly Dividends based on the Cultural Heritage of Citizenship. (b) The Increase in Consumption would of necessity result in increased employment. (c) The issuance of Basic Dividends would retain our young people longer in schools of training and thus prevent them from entering the Labor Market. The Increase in Dividends for people who have reached the age of 50 would tend to remove older men from productive employment. Thus, there would be more employment for those who were better able to perform it. (d) Every sympathetic consideration will be extended to those in immediate need.

4. THE PROBLEM OF EDUCATION

(An Eighteenth Century System can never handle a Twentieth Century Problem)

(a) Our schools should at once be made to supply the training that the New Social Order demands. Up to the present the University requirements for an Academic preparation has predominated our Educational System. Only a small percentage of our students ever enter University. (b) Further attempts should be made to bring the various Provincial Educational Systems into greater harmony. (c) The Basic Monthly Dividends will at once remove the hindrances to any student proceeding along any line of instruction that appeals to him.

5. THE BASIC INDUSTRY — AGRICULTURE

(a) The Just Price for all products will remove the necessity of selling under the cost of production. (b) The Marketing of Agricultural and Dairy products must be assisted: 1. By taking definite steps to find export markets. 2. By pressing for lower and more equitable freight rates. 3. By seeking a revision of the system of grading farm products. 4. By attending regularly to the Market Roads. 5. By encouraging the feeding, breeding, and finishing of better livestock in Alberta. (c) The Development of the Industry should be encouraged in the following ways: 1. By a careful investigation of the irrigation projects of the Province. 2. By an aggressive policy of Noxious Weeds eradication. 3. By a survey and the formation of a definite policy regarding the Drought Area of Alberta. 4. By improving the regulations regarding grazing and hay leases. 5. By amending the Homestead Laws to make it possible for settlers to establish homes for themselves. 6. We are heartily in favor of assisting in the continuance of Rural School Fairs, and Boys' and Girls' Club Work within the Province.

6. THE PUBLIC HEALTH PROBLEM

(a) Definite action should immediately be taken to provide satisfactory Health attention for the people in all parts of the Province, and any patient of a hospital should be permitted to secure any type of qualified, licensed practitioner he or she may desire. (b) We are favorable to the ultimate introduction of State Medicine into the Province.

7. THE ADMINISTRATION OF JUSTICE

(a) We favor the revision of the rules of court procedure, the reduc-

tion of costs, and the introduction of facilities for arbitration and conciliation. (*b*) We shall support the maintenance of Order and Law by
means of an efficient Police Force.

8. LABOR, INDUSTRY AND COMMUNICATION

(*a*) We shall encourage the establishment of essential industries
within our Province. (*b*) We favor a complete reorganization of the
Alberta Government Telephone System for the purpose of making it
efficient. (*c*) We will support and encourage an efficient inspection of
all industries to see that all laws for the health, safety and payment of
all labor and industry are safely guarded. (*d*) We favor the amendment of the present Compensation Act with a view to providing just
compensation to all workers.

9. GENERAL REORGANIZATION

(*a*) Every Department of the Government needs to be reorganized
and to be put on a business basis to eliminate the present enormous
waste of taxpayers' money.

10. PLANNING

(*a*) A thorough survey of Alberta's productive resources and the relationship of these resources to domestic consumption requirements
and export markets must be at once undertaken. (*b*) The methods of
taxation must be brought under immediate consideration for
revision and improvement. (*c*) The Social Credit Government when
in power will pass legislation to the effect that candidates submit to
the voters right of recall if they fail to carry out the proposals made
prior to election.

25. The Progressive Conservative War Platform, 1942

(Policy of the Progressive Conservative Party Adopted at the National Convention Held at Winnipeg December 9th, 10th and 11th, 1942) (Ottawa, n.d.)

This platform, marked by a new concern for social questions, and better thought out and expressed than most such documents, derives in
great part from the "Report of the Round Table on Canadian Policy"
drawn up at the "unofficial conference" of Conservatives held at Port
Hope, Ontario, on 5-7 September 1942. It was adopted by the same

convention that chose John Bracken as party leader and changed the party's name to "Progressive Conservative" at his behest. See J. L. Granatstein, *The Politics of Survival: The Conservative Party of Canada, 1939-1945* (Toronto, 1967).

Progressive Conservative Creed
"Freedom — Security — Opportunity and the British Partnership"

1. Freedom

Freedom is founded on a sense of responsibility to God and a belief that all men and women have been endowed by Him with individual worth and dignity. Being equal in importance before Him, they should be secured in equality of opportunity under the law and in the full exercise of the democratic liberties and rights which have become the heritage of free men.

2. Security

Freedom will be a reality when social security and human welfare become a fundamental objective of the nation. Freedom from want and freedom from fear are essential to a happy and normal family life. Want and fear must be banished and security brought within reach of all Canadians.

3. Opportunity

The prosperity of the Canadian people depends on our creative capacity, individual initiative, our energy, determination, and willingness to work. Gainful occupation for all is a primary objective of Progressive Conservative policy. We affirm our faith in the future of a United Canada. Our national resources under progressive development can be made to provide a high standard of living for all Canadians and for a larger population drawn from people whose intelligence and love of freedom will fit them for a democracy in the British tradition.

4. The British Partnership

We affirm our loyalty to the King and our faith in the British partnership. We accept the responsibilities together with the benefits of this partnership. The guarantee of freedom, security and opportunity for Canadians will be found in the strengthening of The British Commonwealth, its closer association with the United States of America and our other fighting Allies and in the application of the principles of the Atlantic Charter.

Progressive Conservative Policy
War

1. We proclaim our unswerving loyalty to His Majesty the King.

2. We affirm our belief that the future of this Dominion as a free nation can best be ensured as a member of the British Commonwealth of Nations.

3. We pledge to the men and women in the Services at home, abroad and at sea, support to the limit of our resources, to the end that they shall be adequately supplied with reinforcements, equipment and munitions of war in order that they can and shall be so employed in co-operation with our fighting Allies that Canada shall make her due and honourable contribution to a common and complete victory.

4. We favour the formation of an Empire War Council in which Canada and the other Dominions shall be represented.

5. Recognizing that the world struggle in which Canada is engaged requires a total war effort, we believe in Compulsory National Selective Service, and that all those selected to serve in the Armed Forces should be available for service wherever required. We believe in the effective total utilization and proper allocation for war, by compulsion where necessary, of all the resources of Canada, including agriculture, industry and finance, as well as manpower, and that our aim should be at all times to bring about so far as human means can achieve it, an equality in sacrifice.

6. All appointments and promotions in the Armed Forces of Canada should be based on efficiency only.

7. The cost-of-living bonus now provided for civilian employees should be extended to apply to pensions of veterans and to the dependents of men and women in the Armed Forces. In the event of any member of the Armed Forces being listed as missing there should be no interruption in the payment of separation allowance and assigned pay pending the definite establishment of a change of status of the member in question. . . .

11. Because the Canadian people are required to practice the most rigid economy to finance the cost of war, the departments of government including all those of national defence should practice similar economy.

12. Freedom of the person, of speech, of the press, the radio and other means of communication is essential to the well-being of the nation. When war makes limitation of this freedom necessary, safeguards should be provided against bureaucratic tyranny. . . .*

Reconstruction

1. Every person able and willing to work must be assured of gainful occupation with sufficient means to maintain a home and family. The objective is full employment at fair wages under progressively improving standards. We oppose relief as a substitute for work.

2. For the achievement of that objective — full employment at fair wages under progressively improving standards — and for the welfare and development of society, we strongly advocate the strengthening of the basic Canadian tradition of individual initiative and individual enterprise and opportunity, and the freeing of economic activities from bureaucratic controls. Government authority, however, should be maintained and exercised wherever necessary to protect primary producers, workers and consumers from exploitation through such abuses as price-fixing combines, monopolies and patent cartels. To those ends we believe that government should seek to create conditions under which the maximum volume of employment and the maximum national income may be assured through the initiative and enterprise of the people themselves.

3. It is the duty of the state:

(a) to maintain at high level the income and standard of living of the individual citizen, whose interests must always be paramount.

(b) To maintain the principle of private initiative and enterprise.

(c) To initiate, undertake and control projects of public and national benefit in those fields in which private enterprise is precluded from serving or is unable to serve the public interest.

4. Consideration should be given to the problems of the workers-on-their-own who comprise a large percentage of the people of this country and who lack the benefit of organization to protect their interests — the small retail merchant, the man or woman in services of various kinds, such as the carter, truck-driver and taximan, the odd-jobber, the handyman and the salesman on commission. Recognition must be given to their enterprise and initiative and to their threatened security and a way found by properly constituted authority to protect their interests as essential workers, consumers and taxpayers.

*Sections on War Veterans' Rehabilitation, Agriculture, Labour Relations, Natural Resources and Electoral Reform are omitted here.

5. (a) Youth should be educated, trained and given equal opportunity to equip themselves for life.

(b) Those of working age should be provided with ample opportunity for adult education.

6. We believe that the reconstruction of post-war Canadian economy must be based upon the following principle set forth in Section 5 of the Atlantic Charter:

"Fifth: They desire to bring about the fullest collaboration between all nations in the economic field with the object of securing for all, improved labour standards, economic advancement and social security."

A social security programme, the adoption of which we advocate, would include in a unified system:

(a) Unemployment insurance;

(b) Adequate payments for the maintenance of unemployables;

(c) Retirement insurance;

(d) The payment of increased Old Age pensions, at a reduced age, until such time as the retirement insurance scheme becomes fully operative;

(e) Adequate pensions for the blind;

(f) Adequate mothers' and widows' allowances.

7. We advocate the appointment of a Minister of Social Security and Reconstruction, charged with the administration of social security in this country.

8. The State's share of the cost of the social security system should be borne by the Dominion.

9. We recognize the obligation of government to make available to every citizen adequate medical, dental, nursing, hospital and pre-natal care, and to further advance public health and nutritional principles so that health may be safeguarded and preserved. This programme is to be financed under a contributory system supplemented by government assistance.

10. (a) Believing home ownership to be a solid foundation of our social and economic system, we advocate a national long-range low-cost housing plan, including home improvement, under-written by government, designed to make houses available on a lease-purchase basis to all families, whether urban or rural, who are in the lower income brackets.

(b) Slum clearance because of its social benefits and employment possibilities, should be undertaken as a government responsibility, in order to provide housing on a minimum cost basis, for those unable to pay the full cost.

The plan should be continuous but flexible, so as to provide employment, and stimulate construction as economic conditions may determine.

11. We advocate that there should be prepared forthwith a programme for the expansion, distribution and diversification of industry with particular reference to those provinces and areas where industry has so far not established itself on broad lines, and an immediate survey of war industry to ascertain to what extent it can be converted to supply peace-time requirements.

12. (a) Our resources are capable of progressive development and of providing a high standard of living for a greater population, and there is the obligation to provide opportunity for citizenship on equal terms to numbers of kindred-minded people from other lands.

(b) This policy of immigration should visualize and provide assurance of full employment and social security for our population regardless of racial origin.

(c) With a view to the perpetuation in Canada of a democracy in the British tradition, preference in immigration should be given to those whose political background, intelligence and love of freedom are likely to fit them for such a democracy.

(d) Immigration should be under the direct control of the government without any subsidiary arrangement with private interests.

(e) More attention should be devoted to immigrants in this country so as to ensure, as a condition of their naturalization, their full understanding of the privileges and their assumption of the responsibilities of Canadian citizenship.

13. We believe that a peace that is worth fighting for is worth preserving. We are opposed to the isolationist view that Canada can remain a world force, continue as a great trading country in the world and yet remain isolated from international policies that make for peace or war.

14. We regard the members of the British Commonwealth of Nations of which Canada is one, in partnership with the United States of America, as the most appropriate association of nations through which we in Canada should seek international co-operation.

15. We endorse the aims expressed in the Atlantic Charter and believe that Canada should join in the setting-up of effective international measures to give them practical application, correcting trade barriers, with a view to making the world's resources available without discrimination for the satisfaction of human needs.

16. We believe that the guiding principles of Canadian tariff policy should be:

    (a) To provide gainful occupation.

    (b) To maintain a high standard of living.

    (c) To ensure a fair price to the consumer.

17. The Government through a public corporation should establish a foreign trade advisory service to assist exporters, train men for foreign selling, and place them abroad in strategic places where they can facilitate the sale of Canadian goods and act as a medium for purchase of imports to aid export sales.

18. It is of the utmost importance that Canada should maintain control over and further develop her vital position in national and international air transportation.

19. We accept, without reservation, the full equality of women in the life of the nation. We believe that no opportunity in its service or work should be closed to them by reason only of sex; and we accept, as a natural corollary, that remuneration in all lines of production should rest on no other consideration than equal reward for tasks of equal value.

20. We deplore the decay of responsible government under the present administration. We demand the immediate restoration of the supremacy of Parliament.

Canadian Unity

We recall, with pride and gratitude, that our party rose to greatness through a fruitful partnership between two great races, English and French. We affirm our belief that the two cultures are part and parcel of our future development and that Canada's true greatness depends on sympathy and understanding between these two original races and all other races that have come to join in the building of our country.

Realizing the inherent greatness of Canada as a nation and recognizing the strength that can come only from unity of purpose, we believe that all the peoples of Canada should unite in fostering a common pride in Canadian achievement and institutions and a common loyalty to our ancestral traditions of equality, justice and toleration, and should seek, with due regard for constitutional rights, to achieve that profound sense of the importance of national interests which will ensure harmony and co-operation and that future for our country which was the aim of Confederation. . . .

B.
General Elections

For a survey of this subject at large, with details of the results of every general election from 1867 through 1968, see J. M. Beck, *Pendulum of Power: Canada's Federal Elections* (Scarborough, Ont., 1968).

1. The General Election of 1917

The general election held on 17 December 1917 resulted in a sweeping victory for the Union Government headed by Sir Robert Borden, which won 153 seats in the House of Commons while the Liberals loyal to Sir Wilfrid Laurier obtained only 82. Borden, however, took only three seats in the province of Quebec, the other 62 going to Laurier. See O. D. Skelton, *Life and Letters of Sir Wilfrid Laurier* (Toronto, 1921), and Henry Borden, ed., *Robert Laird Borden: His Memoirs* (Toronto, 1938).

26. Sir Wilfrid Laurier's Election Manifesto, 4 November 1917

(*Gazette*, Montreal, 5 November 1917)

A consultation of the people at short and regular periods is the right of a free people. The constitution provides accordingly for a general election every five years. It is undeniable that there has existed a strong desire in the community to avoid an election during the war.

An impression prevails that had I accepted the invitation of the Prime Minister to join his Government a new extension would have been possible. This impression is absolutely erroneous, the fact being that the invitation extended to me was coupled with the stipulation that the coalition Government would pass a conscription measure, and then appeal to the country, thus making an election unavoidable.

The Government as recently reconstituted, the Union Government so-called, is now appealing to the country for support. Six members of the Liberals, some of them close personal friends, have consented to become members of the Administration, and the programme which they intend to follow, has already been placed before the public; but in this programme no trace is to be found that the Liberal members of the Administration have succeeded in influencing their colleagues to the adoption of measures which they deemed essential, not only to win the war, but for the welfare of the country at all times. . . .

It was natural to expect that the re-constructed Government would give very serious attention to the economic situation of the country, which is admittedly critical. . . . The prices of all commodities have been steadily rising since the beginning of the war. The daily provisioning of the family table is from day to day becoming a more and more alarming problem. . . .

No measure to reduce the cost of living can be effective unless and until the tariff is reformed, and its pressure removed from those commodities in which there are "excessive profits," "hoardings," and "combinations for the increase of prices." Of this obvious, fundamental reform there is not a word in the Government manifesto. Indeed, members of the present Government have announced that all questions of tariff legislation must be relegated to after the war. . . .

In connection with the high cost of living, I would take drastic steps to bring under Government control all food-producing factories, so that food may be sold at a fixed price under the control of the Government, as has been done in Great Britain. . . .

One of the most important contributions towards winning the war is to put a stop to profiteering on war supplies. The Government has deliberately encouraged profiteering for the benefit of its partisan followers. . . . Should it be necessary, I would not hesitate, in order to immediately stop profiteering, to take control of the factories which are engaged in the supply of war materials, as has been done in Great Britain, and run them on the principle of reasonable return on investment for the owners, and reasonable legitimate profit. . . .

It cannot be said too often that this war could not have been avoided by the allies, and that it is a contest for the very existence of civilization. Of this the entrance of the United States into the conflict is further proof, if, indeed, further proof were needed. The American people long hoped that they would be spared that ordeal, but the ruthless violation by Germany of the most sacred canons of international law left them no option; they had to join in the fight against a power which has become the common enemy of mankind.

At the very beginning, impressed by the immensity of the struggle and of [sic] the necessity of bending all our efforts to the winning of the war, we of the Opposition gave to the Government every possible assistance. We assented to all their war measures, except when convinced that their measures would be detrimental rather than helpful.

This year the Government introduced a bill to make military service compulsory. With this policy I found it impossible to agree. If it be asked how this view is consistent with my oft-expressed determination to assist in winning the war, I answer without any hesitation that this sudden departure from the voluntary system was bound more to hinder than to help the war.

It should be remembered that, previous to the war, in all British countries, conscription was unknown. It was the pride of British peoples everywhere that compulsory military service, the bane of continental Europe, had never been thought of in Great Britain, and that even the gigantic struggle against Napoleon had been fought on the purely voluntary system.

At the same time it must be pointed out that, in Great Britain, for some years before the war, in view of the immensity of war preparations amongst all the nations of the continent, the question of conscription was seriously and increasingly discussed in Parliament and in the press, so that at last, when a measure to that effect was introduced by the Government, it came as no surprise. It found the people prepared, and yet even then strong protests were heard from many classes of the community.

Very different was the introduction of conscription in Canada. It came as a complete surprise. It never had been discussed in Parliament, and the voice of the press had been strong against it. . . .

No less emphatic had been the language of the Government. At the beginning of the session of 1916, in answer to my enquiry whether the promise recently made by the Prime Minister of enlisting 500,000 men meant conscription, he answered in these words:

"My right-honorable friend has alluded to conscription — to the idea in this country or elsewhere that there may be conscription in Canada. In speaking in the first two or three months of this war I made it clear to the people of Canada that we did not propose conscription. I repeat that announcement today, with emphasis."

Equally emphatic and unqualified were my own declarations on the subject. . . .

In combating the policy of conscription, all that I asked was that a measure of such moment should not be enforced by Parliament without an appeal to the people. I supported a referendum for the reason that the referendum is the most advanced and the most modern method of consultation of the people, without the complications inseparable from a general election. A referendum had also been asked on this very question by organized labor. My request was denied.

I appeal with great confidence to the fair judgment of the country that the introduction of conscription at this juncture and in the manner above described was a grave error, if it is remembered that the supreme object should have been, and still should be, to bring all classes of the community to hearty co-operation in the task which we assumed.

A fundamental objection to the Government's policy of conscription is that it conscripts human life only, and that it does not attempt to conscript wealth, resources or the services of any persons other than those who come within the age limit prescribed by the Military Service Act. This is manifestly unjust. The man who is prepared to volunteer his services and to risk his life in his country's defence is entitled to first consideration. Those dependent upon him, and who spare him from their midst, are the next most deserving of the state's solicitude and care. A policy which will accord first place to the soldier and the sailor in the concern of the state will, I believe, bring forth all the men necessary to fight its battles, without the need of recourse to conscription. If returned to power, I should adopt such a policy. My first duty will be to seek out the ablest men of the country, men of organizing capacity as well as men representative of all classes in the community, and invite them, irrespective of what it may involve in the way of sacrifice of their personal interests, to join with me in the formation of a cabinet whose first object will be to find the men, money and resources necessary to ensure the fullest measure of support to our heroic soldiers at the front, and to enable Canada to continue to the very end to do her splendid part to win the war.

As to the present Military Service Act, my policy will be not to proceed further under its provisions until the people have an opportunity to pronounce upon it by way of a referendum. I pledge myself to forthwith submit the Act to the people, and with my followers to carry out the wishes of the majority of the nation as thus expressed.

I would at the same time organize and carry out a strong appeal for voluntary recruiting. It is a fact that cannot be denied that the voluntary system, especially in Quebec, did not get a fair trial, and a fair trial would receive from a generous people a ready response which would bring men to the ranks, with good will and enthusiasm, and which would eliminate from our political life one of its most harrowing problems, as no loyal Canadian can view without the gravest apprehension a dispirited Canada at this critical hour of our history. . . .

Mr. Crothers, Minister of Labor, speaking recently at St. Thomas, declared that if "Quebec had done her duty, as the other provinces, we should never have required the Military Service Act." If enlisting in Quebec was not on a par with enlisting in the other provinces, on whom does the responsibility rest? On whom but the Borden Government, whose Quebec members, openly, strenuously and persistently preached the Nationalist doctrine of "no participation by Canada in Imperial wars outside her own territory."

That doctrine, first put forth in the riding of Drummond-Arthabasca in the autumn of 1910, by the whole Nationalist body, including two of the present Quebec ministers, won the election for them. In the general elections of 1911 reciprocity in Quebec was not the main issue; the main issue was the naval policy of the late administration, which was bitterly assailed by the same men on the same doctrine of "No participation by Canada in imperial wars outside her territory." And such doctrine, taught on the hustings, circulated by the Nationalist press at the expense of the Conservative organization, had a powerful influence in educating the public against the participation by Canada in Imperial wars outside her territory. The first result was at the polls, when the Liberals won 38 seats, and the Conservative-Nationalist alliance won 27, the popular vote being even more evenly divided, the Liberals polling 164,281 votes and the Conservatives-Nationalists alliance 159,299. The second result was when the war broke out, and a call made by the Government for volunteers. They reaped what they had sowed. There was one-half of the province which they had educated to reject such an appeal. . . .

In order to be effective, to satisfy the public conscience, and to secure that acquiescence in a verdict which should be the last word on all questions submitted to the people, a general election should be an appeal to the electorate such as it exists under the law.

The Government have discarded that fundamental principle of the institutions of a free people. They have designedly altered the sanctity of the franchise by choking discussion, by ruthlessly using the closure; they have deliberately manufactured a franchise with which they hope to win a victory at the polls, a permanent injury to the country. This Act known as the War Time Election Act, is a blot upon every instinct of justice, honesty and fair play. It takes away the franchise from certain denominations whose members, from ancient times, in English history, have been exempt from military service, and who in Great Britain never were, and are not now, denied their rights of citizenship. It takes away the franchise from men whom we invited to this country, to whom we promised all the rights and privileges of our citizenship, who trusted in our promises and who became under our laws, British subjects and Canadian citizens. . . .

It gives the franchise to some women and denies it to others. All those whose privilege it is to have near relatives among the soldiers, will be voters. The right will be refused to all those not so privileged, though their hearts are just as strong in the cause, and though they have worked incessantly for it. Moreover, in five provinces of the Dominion, namely, Ontario, Manitoba, Saskatchewan, Alberta and British Columbia, women have been admitted to the franchise. According to the terms of the Dominion law, which no sophistry can blur, being electors in the province, women are electors in the Dominion. The Act of last session snatches that right away from them. . . .

The Liberal members of the reconstructed Government have put the mantle of their respectability upon this nefarious Act, as well as upon the Canadian Northern Railway Act, and upon many others against which they strongly protested and from which their presence in the Government cannot remove the dangerous and indefensible character. . . .

A bold attempt is being made to silence the voice of the people by a systematic elimination of Liberal candidates from the field. It is my duty to appeal to all the friends of political freedom in every constituency to organize at once, in order to defeat such a conspiracy. Let the masses unite and select their own standard-bearers.

Should I be called upon to form a Government, I would hope to include in it representatives of business, of labor, and of agriculture, of the men whose sole object in dealing with the affairs of the country will be to devote the whole resources, wealth and energy of the country to the winning of the war. It can only be done by honest agreement amongst all the different elements and interests of the country. I would hope to have a Government representative of the masses of the people, the common people, whose guiding principle should be to defend them against organized privilege, which has heretofore had far too much control over the Government of the country. In this election it is my desire that the common people should have opportunity of expressing themselves in a free and untrammelled manner at the polls, so that their views may obtain in the new Parliament, and I trust that in every constituency candidates representative of this policy may be nominated, so that the people can vote for them. These considerations I now place before my fellow-countrymen of all creeds and of all origins for their appreciation and judgment. I have deemed it my duty more than ever, perhaps, in the course of my long public life, to speak frankly and unequivocally upon the problems that now confront us. The obtaining or the retention of office is at all times only a secondary consideration. In this election the supreme end is to assist in the tremendous struggle in which we are engaged, to maintain the unity of the nation, to avoid the divisions and discords which, for many years kept in check, are now unfortunately again looming up dangerous and threatening, to resolutely face the economic situation with the view of avoiding and lessening privations and sufferings, which should not exist in a country so richly endowed by nature as our country. Whatever may be the verdict at the polls, I will accept it, neither elated by victory, nor downhearted by defeat.

27. Sir Robert Borden's Election Manifesto, 11 November 1917

(*Gazette*, Montreal, 12 November 1917)

To the People of Canada:

The twelfth Parliament has been dissolved and it becomes the duty of the people to choose a new House of Commons. Under the constitution the mandate of those whom the constituencies returned in 1911 expired a year ago. But by agreement between the two parties in both the Commons and the Senate and with the clear sanction of public opinion, the duration of Parliament was, for causes strange and momentous in our history, extended for one year.

The circumstances and conditions under which and upon which the people must pronounce judgment are without precedent or parallel. Nearly three and a half years ago, in obedience to honourable alliances and out of regard for her very existence and the security of her dominions, Great Britain engaged in war with Germany. Canada, as became a partner nation in the British Commonwealth, entered the struggle by the decree of her Parliament. That decree was enacted without a single dissenting voice; and it gave true expression to the sentiment and determination of the people of this country. No Government could have lived and no Government would have deserved to live that did not give such instant effect to the popular will. . . . By voluntary enlistment an army of over four hundred thousand Canadian soldiers have gone overseas to service and sacrifice on the scarred fields of France and Flanders. Many thousands of them lie in graves hallowed by their blood and glorified by their suffering. Pride in their valour and their achievements mitigates the sorrow which possesses so many of our homes. Through what they have done we have a new revelation of patriotism. The nation is clothed with new dignity. But how meanly we shall stand at the bar of history if, through any neglect, or failure of ours, the cause for which they fell does not prevail. By the test which they met so steadily and bravely we shall be judged. If their living comrades in the trenches are not supported, shame and humiliation will be our portion. They will have paid a price for us beyond our deserts. What they sowed in honor we shall reap in dishonor.

When it became apparent that the voluntary system was not providing adequate reinforcements for the army, it became necessary to consider the provisions of the Military Service [Militia] Act empowering the Government to enforce compulsory military service upon all male citizens of Canada between the ages of eighteen and sixty inclusive. The selection under that law is to be made by ballot, that is, by chance. Under present conditions the public interest cannot be served by a chance selection, but it demands instead an intelligent selection, based upon a wise and careful consideration of the country's needs, both in the fighting line and at home. Accordingly, a new measure to authorize a selective draft of persons between the ages of twenty and forty-five was prepared and submitted to Parliament. Much care was taken to ensure that the measure would not be unfair or unjust in its provisions, that there would be no prejudicial interference with agriculture or industry, that there would be no preferences for groups, classes, sections or interests. The Military Service Act is a democratic measure, calling the rich as well as the poor—indeed, bearing more heavily on the rich in that it is more difficult for a young man of means to claim exemption on the ground that his labor is needed at home for the support of his relatives. It is eminently fair as between the provinces and as between those portions of our people who are of different racial origins, because it pays no attention whatsoever to provincial boundaries or racial groups, but calls up all young Canadians of the same circumstances wherever they may live. . . .

There was no thought of compulsion until compulsion became

imperative. There was no hesitation to seek authority for enrolment by selection when the necessity for greater reinforcements was indubitably established. It was the enemy — not the Government — which issued the call to arms and compelled a mobilization of all the resources of the Empire. The Government appeals to the people with confidence that the vigorous prosecution of the war is their immediate and supreme concern, and that the Military Service Act which authorized the selective draft is but a reflection of the temper and will of the nation.

The administration in whose name this appeal is made is not the agent or organ of any group, section or party. There are those among its members who must assume responsibility for the conduct of the war thus far; and such members do not seek to evade that responsibility. There are those also among its members who have no such responsibility. For the Military Service Act all assume the fullest responsibility, as do all for the future conduct of the war and for future measures of policy and acts of administration. It is not suggested that the Government which held office for six years is immune from criticism because a Union Government has been organized, but only that the war is the first consideration and that to its energetic and successful prosecution union among the people is as necessary as the coalition of political leaders. . . .

But there are other reasons why the Union Government should be entrusted with power. It has pledged itself to the extirpation of old abuses and to a wise and bold policy of constructive reform. The system of patronage in the distribution of contracts and offices which has prevailed in Canada for generations has been the root of many political evils. . . . It is believed that a Government derived from both political parties and strengthened by special representation of agriculture and organized labour, can act with greater freedom and independence than a Government which held office under the old conditions. Hence the resolution to abolish trading in patronage, to fill public offices by merit and not by favouritism, and to establish honest and open competition in awarding contracts and buying supplies.

It is not necessary to repeat in full the announcement of policy already made public. In carrying out these policies the Government engages to stop wasteful expenditure in unwise duplication of railways, and to arrange effective co-operation between the public and private railway systems. With the acquisition of the Canadian Northern Railway* the State becomes one of the chief carriers of pas-

* See below, **101**.

sengers and products. If public management is to be satisfactory, there must be vigor in administration and breadth and courage in outlook. Efficiency must be ensured. Considerations of personal or political patronage must be sternly ignored. Accommodation equal to that which the private companies afford must be provided. Measures must also be taken to ensure adequate ocean transportation under national or international regulations if extortionate charges are attempted. For many years in Canada railway policy was determined not so much by the needs of transportation as by the demands of rival groups of railway builders. As a result we have a great railway mileage, constructed at heavy cost, with long stretches of parallel lines where a single system could have handled all the traffic and at lower charges upon a smaller investment of capital. It is believed, however, that Canada will yet develop traffic in excess of present rail facilities; and in the meantime the Government will endeavor to co-ordinate existing services and improve and protect the national railways without injustice to private companies.

As old methods of railway building have to be abandoned, so old systems of taxation have to be revised. In order to meet the ever-increasing expenditure for war purposes and also to ensure that all shall share in common service and sacrifice, wealth will be conscripted by adequate taxation of war profits and increased taxation of income. . . . The franchise will be extended to women, not chiefly in recognition of devoted and capable service, in the war, but as a measure of justice too long delayed. . . .

The Government will strive to develop and stimulate a common patriotism in all elements of the people, and all portions of the Dominion. It inherits no baneful legacies. It cherishes no grievances or animosities. East and West are equal at the council table, and in the new Parliament all the provinces will have equal and adequate representation. In the electoral campaign it is greatly to be desired that reticence should be observed in the treatment of all questions in which smoulder the fires of old racial and religious quarrels and contentions. Those who gave their lives for us on far away fields of battle cherished the vision of a United Canada. To deny the vision would be treason to their memory.

The Government thoroughly realizes that in this National emergency there is imperative necessity for fulfilment of its policies with the least possible delay. It pledges itself to prosecute the war with ceaseless vigor, to strive for national unity, to administer the public departments with economy and efficiency, to devise measures of taxation which will regard social justice, and to neglect nothing that may be required to sustain the soldiers on service or to comfort those of their households whom they have left behind. Firmly convinced that these objects can best be achieved by a Government representing all parties, classes, creeds and interests, I appeal with confidence on its behalf for the sympathy and support of the Canadian people.

R. L. BORDEN.

2. The General Election of 1921

The general election of 6 December 1921 was a total disaster for the "National Liberal and Conservative Party" led by Arthur Meighen, but was less than a complete victory for the Liberals led by Mackenzie King. Meighen obtained only 50 seats while King took 117. Every seat in Quebec, Nova Scotia and Prince Edward Island went Liberal. As classified by the *Canadian Parliamentary Guide* the seats taken by the other parties were: Progressives, 64; Labour, 3; Independent, 1. The Liberals were thus just short of an absolute majority.

28. Arthur Meighen's Election Manifesto, 4 October 1921

(*Gazette*, Montreal, 5 October 1921)

To the people of Canada:

... I have been a member of the Government through eight eventful years and its leader for something more than one. The Government has conducted Canada's affairs through a devastating war. It has met and surmounted unprecedented difficulties, and survived the crises that such a war brings in its train. It has formulated policies by means of which the sufferings of the conflict have been and are being ameliorated and its loss and damage repaired. To the demands of those trying years it has devoted all its energies, and is prepared now with vigor undiminished to lead the way through the dangers and unsettlement which, in common with other countries, we are passing through. ...

The war is a memory, and a proud memory, but it is no longer an issue. Canada from 1914 to 1918, under the splendid leadership of Sir Robert Borden, passed through one of those crises that reshape the soul of a people. We must now face with courage the gigantic task of reconstruction. We must sustain and improve services already established for assisting those who especially suffered from the war; we must map out our course; we must choose policies that accord with our aspirations as a nation, that are suited to the present stage of our development, to our surroundings in the world, and to the troubled age in which we live.

By tradition, by the sense of common inheritance and of common ideals, the Dominion of Canada aspires to one destiny and one only — a destiny than which there is no nobler — nationhood within the British Empire. I am convinced there is no single thing more vital to the best interests of the world than that the British Empire as at present constituted should be maintained. We enjoy the fullest autonomy, and that autonomy is not challenged and never shall be changed. For the maintenance of the British Empire as a league of autonomous nations, there are common burdens that all must share, but these burdens are light, and the advantages abundant, in comparison with either the burdens or the advantages of any other destiny that can be conceived. Sentiment and interest are in accord in upholding British connection.

Forty-two years ago Canada accepted and ever since has consistently maintained a protective tariff. At the time the Canadian people decided on this policy experience had driven home two very important conclusions.

1. Our nearness to the United States was tending to drain the natural resources of our younger country into the larger manufacturing establishments of the republic, there to employ American workmen in their development, and American railways and other commercial interests in their distribution and sale. Hundreds of thousands of Canadians, workmen and others, were accordingly compelled to emigrate.

2. After this process had continued, a change in the American policy resulting in the imposition of a high protective tariff against us threw Canada into a state of reaction and depression, and to escape this penalty there was strong temptation to assume a submissive or dependent relationship towards the United States.

Acting in the light of these experiences, the Canadian people decided to build up an industrial system of their own. To thus develop our own resources and keep our people here earning wages and salaries and profits therefrom, a protective tariff was essential. A study of the last forty years will clearly show that the conclusions drawn by our fathers in 1878 were sound and right conclusions.

Those years have been years of continuous development through good times and ill; the markets of our towns and cities have become more and more the reliance of our agricultural producers. The value of our manufacturing, mineral and agricultural production has multiplied many times over. Being able to depend so largely on an ever-expanding home market, we have produced upon a scale that enabled us to enter markets abroad, and so successful have we been that the trade of Canada has multiplied over and over again. Our exports last year were fourteen times in value what they were in 1890 and four times what they were as late as 1910. Our total trade is now over seven times what it was twenty years ago. Indeed, the per capita trade of Canada stands in the front of the larger nations of the world, and has stood as high as 2½ times the per capita trade of the United States.

We have taken the strong self-reliant course, and have been able to pursue that course and maintain our prosperity regardless of the policy of any other nation.

For some years past, and very emphatically in recent years, a determined movement has been on foot seeking to reverse the tariff policy of the Dominion. The official Opposition in the House of Commons, now led by Hon. Mackenzie King, has made repeated and varied demands in Parliament for the wiping out of tariff schedules. Finally, that party was called into convention in August, 1919, which convention unanimously passed the following resolution:

"That the best interests of Canada demand that substantial reductions of the burdens of customs taxation be made. . . .

"And the Liberal party hereby pledges itself to implement by legislation the provisions of this resolution when returned to power."*

This resolution, though frequently evaded and more often avoided, sometimes paraded to entice allies, sometimes entombed to conciliate friends, nevertheless stands as the solemnly-recorded unanimous pledge of the Hon. Mackenzie King and his party. It is not a declaration of principle, but a concrete binding commitment to specific acts.

But a stronger and more menacing enemy has arisen. For some years past there has been growing up, first on the prairies of the west and later through selected parts of eastern Canada, a party backed by a costly and persistent propaganda, the purpose of which is to reverse the tariff policy of this country. This movement, led by the Hon. T. A. Crerar and Mr. H. W. Wood, has also set down its immediate tariff demands in black and white. They need not be here

* See above, **21**.

repeated. The resolution of the Liberal convention quoted above substantially embodies, indeed was modelled upon, the platform of the Wood-Crerar party. The latter, however, demand also the free entry of coal and vehicles, unrestricted reciprocity with the United States and free trade with England within five years. . . .

The immediate enactments which both sections of the Opposition are pledged to put into effect inevitably mean the abandonment of the protective system. . . .

The United States protective tariff, much reduced in 1913, was last March restored to the most prohibitive level in force for many years. . . .

Against the tariff proposals of the Hon. Mackenzie King and all whom in this contest he represents, against the tariff proposals of Mr. Wood and Mr. Crerar, and all whom they represent, I ask the people of Canada to pronounce.

Already there is unsettlement of business conditions resulting in unemployment and loss to all classes. A persistent anti-protection campaign, resulting in uncertainty and lack of confidence, has so disturbed and curtailed production as to account for many thousands being out of work today. A decisive verdict by the Canadian people will be the signal for returning confidence for renewed productive activities and for better times. . . .

There are other subjects of importance and these I have on several platforms discussed and shall again discuss. . . . On the shoulders of the people themselves the responsibility now is placed. They must decide, and I pray that the gravity of that decision every man and every woman will fully comprehend. They must decide between sure and ordered progress and perilous experiment; they must decide between the certain fruits of a strong and stable Government and that sterility and despair which can be the only product of class alliances and the balancing of groups; they must decide between a tariff policy which, in Canada's position, is the very root of her prosperity, and the progressive absorption of Canadian industries and with them Canadian manhood and womanhood in the ever-expanding system of the United States.

To the women of Canada I make especial appeal. The Government now in office, supported by the party which I have the honor to lead, extended to you three years ago the federal franchise. Your rights of suffrage are now in every respect the same as the suffrage rights of men. This was done voluntarily as an act of justice. The services of women in the war had been such that, in the judgment of the Government and the party that supported it, their qualifications for franchise had been demonstrated and their right of franchise had been earned. Nevertheless there were those opposed to us who resisted the Government's action in this regard and who still insist that such action was wrong. . . . Through the long struggle of the war, the women of our country proved themselves equal with men in stern unselfish patriotism and fervent devotion to duty. I confidently hope that in the execution of the trust reposed in them now, they will prove to be a steadying and enlightening force in our public life, that they will show forth an example of public conduct dictated by love of country alone, and will thus vindicate to all the world, their right to share with men responsibilities for public affairs.

(Signed)

ARTHUR MEIGHEN.

29. Mackenzie King's Election Statement, 4 December 1921

(*Gazette*, Montreal, 5 December 1921)

The beginning of the end of a time-honoured tradition appears in Mackenzie King's failure to issue an election "manifesto" at the beginning of the 1921 campaign. He did however issue this statement immediately before the voting took place. Whereas Meighen's manifesto avoided virtually all issues except the tariff, King's statement evades concrete issues altogether.

To the Electors of Canada:

The political campaign, now drawing to a close, has demonstrated clearly that, in the exercise of your franchise on December the sixth, you will be called upon to decide, as respects the next five years:

(1) — Whether the affairs of our country are to continue to be administered by an autocratic executive, indifferent alike to the will of the people and the rights of Parliament, as the Meighen administration has been ever since its usurpation of power nearly a year and a half ago; or

(2) — Whether, at this critical time in our country's affairs and the unsettled condition of other countries, we in Canada, are to experiment, in our federal politics, with government by class primarily in the interests of a class; or

(3) — Whether we are to have a return to representative and responsible government, in the fullest meaning of the words, with a due

recognition of the character of the House of Commons as a deliberate assembly, and of the supremacy of Parliament in all that pertains to our domestic, inter-imperial, and international affairs.

As matters stand:

A vote for the so-called National Liberal and Conservative party is a vote in favor of autocratic government;

A vote for the so-called Progressive party is a vote in favor of government by class;

A vote for the Liberal party is a vote in favor of a return to government of the people, by the people, for the people, irrespective of any privilege or special favor.

What Canada needs today is, not Meighen, as the Premier's publicity bureau asserts; nor any experimenting with group government, or further attempts at coalitions; but a government of the country's ablest men, broadly representative of all classes and parts of our Dominion, and with a mind and purpose of its own. Only by an administration which in all its policies is prepared to avoid the extremes of reaction and radicalism, and which in itself is broadly representative of all the constituent elements of our population— farmers and labor, the business and professional classes, the returned men and others—can we hope to secure, in matters of government, that co-operation between citizens of all occupations and callings which is necessary not less to a due consideration of particular needs than to the advancing of interests held in common, and which, moreover, is an absolute essential of national unity.

If, in virtue of the confidence which I believe is about to be expressed by the people of Canada in the Liberal party through its candidates in the several constituencies, I should be called upon, as leader of the Liberal party, to form a new government, it will be my supreme aim to see that the administration of the nation's affairs is entrusted to a government of the character described; that a spirit of moderation and toleration is evidenced in the furtherance of all its policies; and that, in the expenditure of public moneys, publicity is substituted for secrecy, as the only effective means of ensuring honesty, economy and efficiency in matters of national concern.

(Signed)
W. L. MACKENZIE KING.

3. *The General Election of 1925*

In the general election held on 29 October 1925 the Conservatives under Arthur Meighen won the largest group of seats in the House of Commons, and Mackenzie King's government was left dependent on the support of the diminished group of Progressives. The Conservatives took 116 seats, the Liberals 101, the Progressives 24, and Labour and Independents 4. See Graham, *Arthur Meighen*, II.

30. Mackenzie King States the Issues, 5 September 1925

(*Gazette*, Montreal, 7 September 1925)

The Prime Minister opened his campaign at Richmond Hill, Ontario, in his own riding of North York, with the speech from which extracts are given here.

. . . What are some of the national problems pressing for solution?

First and foremost is the problem of taxation. The reduction of taxation lies at the root of all else. . . . We must continue our policy of economy and retrenchment. There are limits, however, to what economy and retrenchment in the public service can effect. They need to be supplemented by important policies in other directions.

That brings me to a consideration of three outstanding national problems of the greatest importance — the transportation problem, the problem of immigration, and the fiscal problem. To these I should add a fourth, the constitution and powers of the Senate. . . .

It is one of the fundamental principles of the Liberal party to ensure that the control and management of the national railways is divorced completely from political influence and control. . . .

In the actual operation of the Canadian National Railways there is marked improvement. As was the case with the public accounts of the regular Government services, operating deficits have been changed into surpluses during the period of the present administration. . . .

The railway problem, to my mind, is the most important of all problems pressing for immediate solution. Can taxation be substantially reduced till we have overcome the deficits on our national railways? Can the National Railways or the Canadian Pacific Railway reduce rates so long as there are deficits in the case of the one and reductions in earnings in the case of the other? Can either of our great railway systems prosper as it should until some measure of restricted competition is substituted for the present unrestricted competition between the two?

There seem to be two possible solutions of the railway problem in Canada:

1. The amalgamation of the Canadian Pacific and Canadian National railways under some equitable scheme which would reasonably protect the proprietors of both systems. 2. The continuance of the two systems as separate entities, but with the introduction, either voluntarily or compulsory, of a sufficient degree of control over both systems to eliminate waste. Of those who advocate amalgamation, the believers in private ownership of railways would absorb the Canadian National Railways in the Canadian Pacific Railway. The believers in Government ownership of railways would absorb the Canadian Pacific Railway in the Canadian National Railways. Each designates the process of absorption by the word amalgamation. In either case the result would be the creation of a monopoly, and that, I venture to say, the most powerful monopoly in the world. It would mean a complete monopoly of the railway transportation industry in Canada, and the centralization of enormous power in the hands of a few individuals.

For my own part, I am unalterably opposed to monopolies of any kind, and above all others to railroad and banking monopolies, whether they be government or private owned. Surely, however, between the extreme of unrestricted competition on the one hand and the extreme of complete monopoly on the other, there are many measures that might be adopted under authority of Parliament which would be to advantage alike of the Canadian National Railways and the Canadian Pacific Railway Company, and of benefit also to the general public. It is not for me, at this time, to say in any final way what those measures should be. Finality in this, as in all matters of legislative enactment, belongs to Parliament.

I have always contended, as you know, that Government ownership of railways should be given a fair trial. That has been the policy of the present administration with respect to the vast railway system which we found in a disorganized and decentralized condition when we took office in December, 1921. We searched this continent and Great Britain for the man to undertake the work of co-ordination, consolidation and administration. When we had satisfied ourselves that we had found the right person, we appointed Sir Henry Thornton and gave him a three years contract with an undertaking that if in that period of time he demonstrated his capacity to administer the system to the satisfaction of the public, the contract would be renewed with due recognition of his services. That obligation has been fulfilled, and Sir Henry's services retained for a further period. I think it will be generally conceded that we have the right man in the right place. . . .

I said a moment ago that I did not believe in monopoly. . . . Competition is better than monopoly. Whether it be of public or privately-owned roads of which we speak, it must never be forgotten that the railways are made for the people and not the people for the railways. . . .

How closely allied the problems of transportation and immigration are will be apparent in a moment's reflection. The one without the other is incapable of satisfactory solution. We require a vigorous immigration policy, a policy which will recognize the interrelation and interdependence of transportation and immigration, a policy moreover, which will have regard for quality in the class of immigrants to be brought to Canada, and regard as well for our own industrial standards and conditions. . . .

Within the past few days an arrangement has been come to between the department of immigration and the railway companies whereby their agencies overseas will be brought into more effective co-operation with each other, and with the Government, thus effecting a measure of the kind of enlightened co-operation to which I alluded a moment ago. Another all-important step has been taken in the appointment of a minister of immigration who will be in a position to give his entire time to the important work of that department. As the country knows, the Hon. Mr. Robb, in addition to being minister of immigration, has for two years past been acting minister of finance, owing to the impaired health of Right Hon. Mr. Fielding. After having held the important post of minister of finance in the Government of Canada for a period in all of some nineteen years, Mr. Fielding has asked to be relieved of its responsible duties. . . . The country will be pleased to know that the Hon. Mr. Robb has agreed to take the portfolio of finance, and to give his undivided time and attention to the affairs of a department he has administered so admirably and efficiently during the past two years. . . .

I come now to the Government's fiscal policy. The policy of the Conservative party as advocated by the present leader of the Opposition is, as respects the tariff, one primarily for all-round and higher protection. The policy of the Liberal party is a tariff primarily for revenue. We recognize that a tariff is a tax, and we believe that taxation should be made to bear as lightly as possible upon the people. Especially do we believe that the instruments of production essential to the development of our basic industries and the necessaries of life should be taxed as lightly as possible.

We have already given substantial evidence of our resolve to carry out our policy of reduction of duties on the instruments of production, and of our ability so to do in a manner which, whilst of immediate benefit to consumers and producers at large, is calculated to prove of benefit also and not of injury to the industries most concerned. The Robb budget of 1923 was comparable to the Fielding budget of 1897 in what it effected by way of tariff reductions with unmistakable advantages to the great basic industries of agriculture, lumbering, fishing and mining, and consequent benefit to all industry deriving its raw material and its markets from these sources.

Our fiscal reforms have not stopped there. Another feature of our policy has been the encouragement of export trade by treaties and the encouragement in particular of inter-Imperial preferential trading in a manner which will help our ports and railways. By giving a discount of 10 per cent. off the preferential rate of duty on goods entitled to the British preference, and the conditions we have attached to other preferential treaties, we have diverted practically the entire trade with the Mother Country and sister Dominions to our own ports, much to their benefit and to the benefit of our railways as well.

We have removed the sales tax in whole or in part from a large list of commodities in the nature of the necessities of life, and on all implements of production, and we have made not a few other tariff reductions. Whilst being careful to have regard for existing conditions and the well-being of established industry and trade, we have moved steadily in the direction of freeing industry and the consuming public from a burden of taxation they would otherwise have had to bear. . . .

Let me say a word about the national policy, the N.P. so-called, of the days of Sir John A. Macdonald, and the National Policy of today. . . .

A National Policy of today is not a policy which will give Canada a place in her own eyes. It is a policy which will give Canada a place in the eyes of the world. It is a policy not of home markets, but of world markets.

I shall go a step further and say that Mr. Meighen's tariff policy, far from being a National Policy, is the reverse of national. The old N.P. aimed at binding Canada together. If a higher tariff is applied now, it will split Canada into fragments. It will set the East against the West; it would break Confederation. We cannot have either high tariff or absolutely free trade in Canada, as I shall hope presently to show. Our tariff must have regard for all parts of the country in its present state of development.

It may not be an easy matter to bring about the tariff best suited to our national needs. Such a tariff will certainly not be brought about by a ministry acting blindly or action upon insufficient or unreliably information. It can, I believe, be brought about as the result of careful investigation, accurate knowledge and expert opinion, applied to the tariff as a means of revenue, and which will have regard for the safeguarding of our established industries against conditions elsewhere that may be prejudicial to their well-being and development. A tariff so framed and fashioned should inspire trust and confidence.

An advisory board of taxation would have all the advantages of a tariff commission without any of its obvious limitations or disadvantages. It would have many additional advantages, among them the fact that it would function more efficiently and at a minimum of cost to the country. Were a tariff commission, such as is suggested by the leader of the Opposition, to be formed, it would mean, to begin with, the creation of a new department of Government or what is equivalent, and in the end information would have to be obtained in most part from Government departments by calling in or corresponding with the very officials who under the proposed arrangement will compose the permanent members of the board. . . .

I come now to the fourth of the reasons I have mentioned why an appeal should not be delayed. I have spoken of the difficulties with which the present Government has had to contend through not having a majority in the House of Commons. Our difficulties unfortunately have not been confined to the Commons. We have, in fact, been face to face with a Senate chamber politically hostile to our own, and one that has not hesitated to make its hostility known and felt on innumerable occasions. I need not enumerate the many measures that have passed the Commons, only to be thrown out or emasculated by the Senate — measures of social and moral reform, of restriction of gambling, of railway aid, of relief to Home Bank depositors,* of extension of rural credits, measures of special concern to returned soldiers, to labor and to others.

---

*The Home Bank closed its doors in August 1923, the first Canadian bank to fail since 1911, and the last to the time of writing. The House of Commons accepted the Senate amendments reducing the amount of relief, and the resulting Act (15-16 George V, Chap. 45, 27 June 1925) made available a sum not exceeding $3 million to pay persons found to be in special need not more than 35% of their claims against the bank.

To amend the constitution and the powers of the Senate, two steps are necessary. The Senate itself must be a party to the reform recommended, and the Imperial Parliament must act. It is reasonable, I think, to assume that before the Imperial Parliament would enact the necessary legislation by way of amendment to the British North America Act, it would expect on a matter of this kind an address of both Houses of the Canadian Parliament. . . . There are two ways of bringing about accord between the two Houses in the matter of an address to the Imperial Parliament: One, the indirect method of summoning a conference of representatives of all the provinces of the Dominion and seeking at such a gathering to obtain unanimity of view with respect to the amendments of the constitution and powers of the Senate; the other, the appointment of senators prepared to support Senate reform. An agreement reached at such a conference, if introduced in the form of a resolution, would scarcely fail to pass both Houses.

As is known, the Government has declared its intention of calling a conference of the provinces to deal with the question of Senate reform. Mr. Meighen is asking why the conference has not yet been called. I shall give him the answer. It is that the conference should be preceded by a general election, at which the reform of the Senate is a principal issue, in order that its deliberations may be influenced by the known will of the people. . . .

The conference method at its best is reform from without. There still remains need for action endorsing the conference proposals on the part of the Senate itself. That, with respect to some who are at present members of the Upper Chamber, is none too certain. What is required is to reform the Senate from within, not from without. Reform from within can be effected only by making certain of the presence in the Senate of a sufficient number of members who can be relied upon to support and carry through that chamber whatever measure of Senate reform may be sent from the Commons as a part of Government policy. . . . I shall undertake to say that no further appointments will be made by the present Government to the Senate except upon the distinct understanding that the appointee will give whole-hearted advocacy and support to any measure of senate reform the Government, as a part of Government policy, may ask both Houses of Parliament to adopt. . . .

31. Arthur Meighen Opens his Campaign, 9 September 1925

(*Gazette*, Montreal, 10 September 1925)

The Leader of the Opposition sounded the keynote of his campaign in this speech at Wingham, Ontario. It illustrates the extent to which the tariff issue had possession of Meighen's mind; but it also suggests why Mackenzie King feared him more than any other antagonist.

. . . You will not expect me to occupy any considerable time in making reply to the speech delivered by the Prime Minister on Saturday last. The speech of a Government leader opening a campaign if it is to be of any value should review the actual accomplishments of his Government and constitute as well a clear declaration of principles which his party proposes to submit for public approval. From the first word to the last that speech can be read without finding reference to one single achievement, and for the very good reason that the page of achievements of the Mackenzie King Government is a blank. Within the four corners of the speech there is not a single sentence which declares a principle that any practical man can understand. The whole is an opaque mass of ill-founded and contradictory excuses. . . .

For many years I have sought earnestly to impress upon the people of Canada that the great subject of policy in this Dominion was tariff policy. In 1921 I took my stand definitely and firmly on this issue and challenged the official programme of both the Liberal party and the new Progressive party. Mr. King flinched this issue. He flinched it in the Maritime Provinces under one pretext and in Quebec under another. In fact, in Quebec, there was only one Liberal candidate who stood four-square to the tariff pledges of their party.

They flinched it in industrial Ontario and they were true to it in one section of Canada and one only, and that the western plains. For the four years since that contest they have feebly fumbled and floundered; they have stepped this way and they have stepped that way, and they have always threatened that with each succeeding year they would reduce protection and still more reduce it until in the words of one of their members the "death-knell of protection" would be rung. Throughout these four years of Mr. King's government I have continued to the utmost of my energy in every part of Canada to drive home the biggest fact in the whole political being of our country, that a sound and strong and definite protective policy is the only means by which we can live and prosper. Mr. King now says, as if by way of complaint, that I have the same programme today which was defeated in 1921. There are many who doubt whether this policy really was defeated in 1921. He and his party flinched the issue and confused the electors of Canada under a tornado of misrepresentation. But whether it was defeated in 1921 or not the principle I preached then is a sound principle and true. I preach it now just as I preached it then and this time the people of Canada are not going to be befuddled by the twisting and shifting practices of Mr. King. This time the people of Canada know his record and on the 29th of October they are going to give their verdict on its record.

But already the same old methods are at work. There are four things, Mr. King says, which must be decided: Transportation, immigration, tariff policy and Senate reform. Anything at all to mix the issue up. Anything at all to obscure the record of these barren years. Anything at all to confuse the public. Four issues, said Mr. King, transportation, immigration, tariff policy and Senate reform. I put this question to each one of you; I put it to the people of Canada.

Is there any person in this Dominion, either man or woman, who knows today what the Government wants done on this transportation question, what the Government wants done on immigration, or what the Government wants done on Senate reform? Can any human being define now what the Government's policy is on any one of the three? Mr. King says he wants a mandate on these three. What does he want a mandate to do? He has not told us and he is not going to tell us. . . .

We talk about this thing and we talk about that; we want more immigrants, we want more products to sell, we want more goods to transport, more traffic for our railways, more work for our people; these objects cannot be reached by mere talk, there must be a basic, underlying policy upon which the retrogression of these years can be stopped and a greater expansion begun. That basic, underlying policy is clearly and concretely expressed in a resolution moved in Parliament last session, to which the Conservative party in that House unanimously committed its faith and upon which we appeal to the judgment of the Canadian people. Within the terms of that resolution are embraced the lines of action upon which, we believe, the parliament of the future must proceed if Canada is to get on her feet and go on. This resolution Mr. King and the whole Government of Mr. King opposed and there the issue is joined. The document itself I shall read and my greatest desire is that it shall find its way into every home in Canada, that every worker, every farmer, every tradesman, every man without money and every man with money, and, as well, all the women of this Dominion, will study its every line carefully, judge its value and express their opinion by their votes.

That, in the opinion of this House, to meet the situation which has resulted from a strengthening in late years of the protective system the world over, particularly in the United States; to give new life to industry and productive enterprise; to preserve and enlarge the Canadian market for Canadian farm products; to stimulate the development of Canadian resources by the Canadian people and thus create employment for our workers; to increase the traffic of our railways by which alone an all-round reduction of freight rates can be secured; and, as well, to provide added revenue and thus bring about a reduction of internal taxation, this Dominion requires an immediate revision of the Canadian tariff on a definitely and consistently protective basis.

That such revision should apply to natural products such as farm products, fish and coal with no less thoroughness than to manufactured goods.

That to the same ends steps should be taken to conserve for Canadian development our essential and irreplaceable resources in material and power.

That while every effort should be directed toward the establishment of a system of preference within the Empire no preference should be given at the expense of the Canadian worker and all preference should be conditional on the use of Canadian ports.

That a tariff commission should be appointed representative of the three great classes of Canadian industry, agriculture, manufacturing and labor and be entrusted with the duty of studying Canadian tariff problems in their every bearing and of making from time to time such recommendations to the Government as it deems in the general public interest with the reasons therefor, and with power also, where it finds unfair advantage is being taken of protective duties, of making recommendations to be given effect by the Government for removing or reducing tariff schedules or imposing special excise taxes upon products in respect of which such advantage is taken, and that its reports, findings, recommendations and reasons therefor be given to the public.

That to enable the products of the western and maritime provinces to reach more readily the markets so developed the special transportation burdens borne by these provinces should be shared by the whole Dominion either by contribution to long haul freight or by assistance in some other form.

If this resolution is not the right policy for Canada the Conservative party should not be in power. If it is the right policy for Canada there is one party and one party alone which can give it effect, and that is the party of Macdonald, the party of Cartier, the party of Thompson. We have trifled for years with theories and fads. While sixty-five other countries of the world have been raising their tariff, Canada under Mr. King, has been reducing; while the United States of America multiplied its tariff nearly 50 per cent., Mr. King in Canada nibbled piece by piece from ours and discouraged every industry in the country by threatening to nibble more....

In the old days Mr. King used to boast of what he would do for the farmers of Canada. But his Australian treaty has dealt a cruel blow to Canadian agriculture. He has allowed Australia to keep in effect an utterly prohibitive tariff against Canadian farm products. . . . We are told the West is against protection and Mr. King lays this fact before you as the reason why he cannot do anything else than he is doing. If the West is against protection, who is responsible? Mr. King and those like him are responsible, for in order to get votes they have preached for decades to our western population that our farmers were oppressed by a protective system. I know something of western Canada.

For many years I have sought to convince the people there that this Dominion as a Dominion could live and make its way by a protective system and no other system, and I believe today the farmers realize they have accepted at far too high a value all this propaganda of Liberal-Progressive orators on the subject of the tariff. The West does feel that the larger industrial portions of our country have much more to gain by a protection policy than they and I believe the West is right in asking that some special concession be made in order that they may receive a more equitable distribution of the advantages of the general policy of the country. The maritime provinces ask for special concessions too and the maritime provinces in my judgment are absolutely right in their demand that their peculiar position in this confederation be recognized.

It is the proposal of the Conservative party that we pin our faith to a self-reliant and unmistakable protective policy on behalf of the whole country, put into effect a Canada-first policy in every sphere of our agricultural and commercial life and we propose as well that the entire Dominion shall bear a share of the transport of eastern and western productions over the long distances which divide us now. We propose in that way to bring the Maritimes closer industrially to Ontario and Quebec and we intend to bring the western provinces closer to the east. With industry stimulated, production revived, commerce restored, railway revenues improved, the Dominion will be well able, and the Dominion will be ready, to help the provinces further removed and make all feel that the burden of one is the burden of the whole, that the success of one is the success of the whole, that the Dominion is not and should never be a series of disconnected and rival sections, but a great united nation.

On these principles, and these alone, can the prosperity or even the integrity of this Dominion be ensured. Before the first quarter of this century is through, the inefficient and helpless group of men who are known still as the Government of our country will receive their farewell at the hands of the electors, and Canada will again be launched on the path which leads to unity, to concord and to progress.

32. Robert Forke's Election Statement, 16 September 1925

(*Gazette*, Montreal, 17 September 1925)

This statement issued at Winnipeg is notable for its lack of assurance; it suggests the voice of a movement past its prime.

. . . As the leader of the Progressive group in the House of Commons I am in accord with the Prime Minister in thinking that the people should be consulted as to their wishes in regard to the problems of transportation, immigration, taxation and trade, and reform of the Senate.

The policy of the Progressives upon these questions has been clearly formulated. We desire that public ownership of the railways comprising the Canadian National System shall be fully and fairly tried. This involves the reduction of the capitalization of the national roads to a figure representing their reasonable value as an investment, the most economical and efficient management attainable and the elimination of duplicate services by fair adjustments as between the Canadian National and Canadian Pacific systems. To avoid political interference with the National Railways the functions of the Department of Railways and Canals ought to be clearly defined and its duties discharged impartially as between all the railways of the country. . . .

The Progressive group is in favor of increasing the population of the Dominion as rapidly as possible both by immigration and by retention of the people already here. These ends are to be attained by making agriculture and the primary industries profitable and prosperous, rather than by spending public owned money on propaganda abroad and subsidies to immigration and shipping agencies. The successful and contented settler is the natural and the best immigration agent. Improvement of the conditions of life and industry within the country is the soundest immigration policy.

Trade and taxation policies are intimately associated. The Progressive group in Parliament and its supporters in the country regard the removal of protective duties upon all necessaries of life and instruments of production as indispensable to the growth of our population and the development of our national resources. Protection confers special privileges upon some industries at the expense of the people generally and bears with peculiar severity upon the primary producers. As a method of taxation the tariff is inequitable, placing the heaviest burden upon those consumers who have the least ability to pay.

So far as possible taxes should be direct and should be proportioned to ability. Since the war the revenue from the tariff has declined in proportion to the total revenues collected. It can no longer be argued that it is virtually the only source of revenue or that alternatives cannot be employed. The further reduction of import duties, accompanied eventually by the abolition of all duties of a protective character, is essential to the prosperity of the people and the establishment of equity in taxation. The retention of the income tax, without reduction until the proposed fiscal reforms have been established, and the revenue requirements have been reduced to the lowest figure possible, is imperative.

The Progressive policy in regard to the Senate contemplates the placing of the membership of that body upon an elective basis in order to make it responsible to the will of the people and to bring it into line with democratic principles. It is recognized that the problem is not a simple one in view of the nature of the Canadian Confederation and the necessity for safeguarding the rights of minorities. The application of the elective method in place of appointment of members for life commends itself as more likely to produce a Senate acceptable to the people.

. . . I desire to urge upon the electors the necessity for returning to Parliament every candidate pledged to support Progressive policies. . . . The measures desired by the West would be equally efficacious for the removal of the economic disabilities of the primary producers and consumers in the East. The Progressive policy is a national policy and strikes at the fundamental errors in the past administration of public affairs.

It is sometimes alleged that the Progressives have failed during the last Parliament to bring about these reforms or to induce a clearer understanding of national requirements among the masses of the people owing to the "class" character of the Progressive movement. It is true that the basis of the movement was, and is, agrarian; the Progressive movement finds its greatest strength among those who suffer most from present injustice. But it is also true that it has done much to modify legislation and Government policy, and to ameliorate the conditions of which complaint is rife. The lack of unanimity, which is found in every Progressive movement, and the political inexperience of the representatives, have been heavy handicaps. Up to the present the Progressive influence has not succeeded in bringing about that realignment of political forces into "Progressive" and "reactionary" which must precede genuine reform and the re-birth of real Liberalism in Canada. The opportunity for achieving this realignment has not yet passed.

A strong Progressive group in the next Parliament, consisting of members fearless and outspoken in the advocacy of Progressive principles and careless of moribund political parties, and of the maintenance in office of particular ministers, would exercise a salutary influence upon Canadian public life; and that is the immediate need of the country. The absorption of the Progressives by the Liberal party, whether in or out of office and under whatever guise effected, would postpone for a generation the attainment of necessary reforms, the re-shaping of our national policies and the infusion into Canadian public life of that moral courage and idealism which slavish partisanship has well-nigh destroyed.

The alleged "failure" of the Progressive movement to fulfil its mission within the life of a single parliament should not be made the occasion for retreat or the excuse for its abandonment. Progressivism is not less virile now than it was in 1921. The triumph of the ideals which have inspired the Progressive movement is ultimately certain. Let us go into the fight with confidence and courage, unhampered by vain regrets for the past or by unfounded fears for the future.

4. *The General Election of 1926*

The general election held on 14 September 1926 centred largely on the "constitutional question," which originated in the Governor General's refusing Mr. King a dissolution of Parliament at a time when what amounted to a motion of censure against the government, resulting from the Customs scandal, was before the House of Commons.* Though the Liberals did not obtain a formal clear majority, their 116 seats plus the 10 Liberal-Progressives and one Independent Liberal made them secure; Robert Forke, now the Liberal-Progressive leader, entered the new King cabinet (see above, **32**). The Conservatives won 91 seats, the Progressives 12, the United Farmers of Alberta 11, while there were 3 Labour seats and 1 Independent. See Graham, *Meighen*, II, and Neatby, *William Lyon Mackenzie King*, II.

33. Arthur Meighen's Opening Statement, 20 July 1926

(*Gazette*, Montreal, 21 July 1926)

Mr. Meighen opened his campaign in Ottawa with the long speech of which extracts are given here, emphasizing the Customs scandal, denying the existence of a constitutional issue, and again dwelling on the tariff question.

. . . Into the revelations of the past session I intend now to inquire. . . .

What then is the story of this session? It has been constituted in the main of the work of what is known as the Stevens' committee. This committee was established early in the session on the demand of the Hon. H. H. Stevens, member for Vancouver Centre, after an attack on the administration of the Customs and Excise Department, which in the severity of its terms and the confidence with which it was launched, startled the entire Dominion. . . .

The evidence is now in the hands of the people of Canada. It covers only a fraction of the operations of the Customs and Excise Department, but within that fraction it has discovered and absolutely established such a profundity of incompetence, inefficiency, and

*See also above,**1-7**.

neglect, such a mass of malfeasance on the part of officials high and low and of the minister himself, indeed such a welter of wickedness as has never been paralleled before in the revelations of any Canadian parliament. . . .

But now I am going to come to the verdict of the House of Commons. Again I emphasize the fact that the House of Commons was not a prejudiced jury — counting the Conservative members prejudiced if you like. Certainly the Progressive members were not prejudiced against the Government. It is only the truth which I think all of them would agree to in the way I put it, that their leaning was in favor of the Government. Some of them were, indeed, about as strong supporters of the Government as any Liberal elected. A series of amendments were proposed. The Government fought desperately to avoid a direct decision; they struggled for days to lure their Progressive friends into blind alleys, and to get them to vote for something which would have wiped completely out the Stevens' amendment censuring the Government. In all these arts they failed. . . . a House of Commons in which Liberals, Progressives and Independents together numbered twelve more than the Conservatives, this House of Commons censured the administration by a majority of 10. . . .*

I ask you, the people of Ottawa, and through you I ask the people of Canada, do you think that a Government with those hundreds of pages of evidence staring them in the face, do you think a Government buried under the revelations which that evidence contains, do you think a Government censured by a Parliament where the majority were its friends, do you think such a Government should be exonerated by the people of Canada? . . .

Everybody knows the people will give no such verdict. No one understands better than Mr. Mackenzie King himself; that is why he seeks desperately for some other issue to engage the people's minds. It is only natural that he would come to the conclusion that any issue in the world would be better for him than the issue raised by the Customs Committee. Not unnaturally he likes a constitutional issue and today he struggles to convince his Liberal followers that some great constitutional issue has arisen, and that the people do not need to think about the customs scandal any more. The name of His Majesty's representative is dragged into the arena — something never done before in the history of elections in Canada. The conduct of His

*On the vote on the Stevens amendment on 29 June, after the Meighen government had replaced King's.

Majesty's representative was challenged flatly by Mr. Mackenzie King on the floor of Parliament. From this challenge his party now seeks to escape, and from that challenge I think Mr. Mackenzie King himself would now like to escape. Nothing could be worse for Canada than to impeach the conduct of the representative of the Throne and bring the great and revered link of Empire into the turmoil of political strife. Nothing could be more indefensible, nothing indeed more censurable than that such a step should be taken in the presence of the admitted truth that the representative of His Majesty acted with scrupulous honesty. This fact everybody admits. As a matter of truth, there is no constitutional issue. Are there any people in Canada really of opinion that the late government or any government at any time was entitled to dissolve a parliament while a vote of censure was under review? . . . It can be definitely stated that never within a century, never in the history of parliamentary government as we have it today, has any prime minister ever demeaned himself to ever ask for dissolution while a vote of censure on his own government was under debate. In the present case that happened. . . .

I will tell you now what the present Government considers its duty to the people of Canada. . . .

Already we have taken steps to eradicate the cancer in the Customs Department. . . .

We ask for a mandate from the Canadian people to end the weary years of fickleness and instability in financial and fiscal affairs; to restore definitely and clearly the principle of protection in the tariff of Canada, a principle and practice upon which all can rely, upon which industry can depend, upon which workers can depend, but a principle and practice which none will be permitted to abuse. We propose that stability and tranquillity will take the place of disturbance and unrest, and that the great resources of this country will be conserved for the development of our own nation and not of another, and for the multiplication of the people and the retention of our own sons and daughters at home.

We propose to lay the basis of a practical, vigorous and fruitful immigration policy, and that basis shall be first of all, employment for the people of Canada. . . .

We propose to take practical steps along the lines of our resolution of June, 1925, to extend to producers of the Maritime Provinces and the Western Provinces, the markets of central Canada, and especially to extend the use of Canadian coal by Canadian consumers and the employment by Canadian shippers of our own Maritime ports. . . .

Our appeal now to the people of Canada can be put in a few words and with these words I close. We ask them to study the policy embodied in the resolution by which the Conservative party stands, moved in the House of Commons on the 2nd of June, 1925. We believe the great articles of policy there laid down are sound for this Dominion and when given effect will make for unity, prosperity and expansion. We lay before them the administrative record of the late government as revealed by the files of its own committee and from the mouths of its own witnesses, and we ask you to condemn with your votes inefficiency and gross infidelity to public trust. We appeal to our fellow-citizens in every section of this country, of every class and occupation, to rise to the height of true Canadians and think in terms of the whole country, and to call for the sane, consistent application of the only principle of fiscal policy by which this Dominion can live, hold its children, gather its immigrants and grow to a great nation. Finally we appeal for the union of all workers, employers, farmers, everybody in sympathetic and practical co-operation to press forward the great movement through which the basic industrialists of our country, the producers from our soil, will at last come into their own.

34. Mackenzie King's Opening Statement, 23 July 1926

(*Gazette*, Montreal, 24 July 1926)

In this speech in Ottawa Mr. King opened his campaign, indicating that he had chosen the constitutional issue as his battleground.

. . . Is there a man or woman in this Dominion who has not direct-ly benefitted by the reduction in taxation effected under the Robb budget? . . .

Add to all this a reduction in the national public debt and a balanc-ing of the national budget over a series of years, together with an expansion of trade and a favorable balance of exports over imports unparalleled in the peacetime history of the Dominion, and you have a record which has not been equalled by any government in Canada.

This is a part of the record on which we make our appeal for the support of the electors of Canada. We need not promise reductions in taxation—we have already given reductions; we need not promise prosperity—everyone knows that prosperity has returned and that, with a continuation of Liberal policies, prosperity has come to stay. . . .

I come now to the concluding days of the session and to the dissolution of Parliament.

Mr. Meighen and the members of his party would have the public believe that the reason I sought dissolution at the time I did was in order to avoid "a vote of censure" being passed upon the administration because of certain facts disclosed before a special committee of the House of Commons with respect to the administration of the Department of Customs, which committee was appointed in the opening days of the session and brought in its report as the session was drawing its proceedings to a close. To this I give the most emphatic denial.

First of all may I be permitted to point out that the word "censure" or its equivalent in Parliamentary terminology neither appears in the Stevens amendment or the report of the special committee which it sought to amend, nor in any amendment or in any report. The Stevens amendment uses the words "wholly indefensible" in reference to the alleged failure of myself and the Government "to take prompt and effective remedial action" with respect to certain matters in the customs, and the words "utterly unjustifiable" in reference to one particular act of Mr. Boivin. These words have become enlarged upon and their meaning exaggerated in party controversy and public discussion into a "censure of the Government," "a censure of the entire administration," involving its resignation. . . .

Mr. Meighen says there is no constitutional issue. Let me tell the present Prime Minister that he will find before the present campaign is over that there is a constitutional issue greater than any that has been raised in Canada since the founding of this Dominion. It is a constitutional issue not raised by His Excellency the Governor-General, but by Mr. Meighen himself, and Mr. Meighen has only himself to thank that the issue has been raised and that it overshadows everything else.

If the customs matter were the all-important matter which Mr. Meighen would like the people to believe it is, and he desired to make it the issue in a campaign, why, when sent for, did he not advise His Excellency the Governor-General that he was unable to form a government, and, therefore, for His Excellency to send again for me and let me have a dissolution? That was all he needed to do; that was the constitutional course for him to pursue, and if he had been half as chivalrous with His Excellency as His Excellency sought to be with him, that is the advice he would have tendered and not made the Crown a party to a series of unconstitutional acts such as have not been paralleled, I believe, in the history of British parliamentary institutions.

Serious as is the issue which has been raised with respect to the relations of Prime Minister to Governor-General, it pales into relative insignificance when compared with the issue of Prime Minister to Parliament raised by the actions of Mr. Meighen himself. To have become Prime Minister by accepting full responsibility for His Excellency's refusal to grant dissolution, knowing at the time, as Mr. Meighen full well did, that he could not hope constitutionally to carry on, and that, as he himself later admitted, dissolution was necessary and inevitable, was bad enough. It is as nothing, however, in comparison with his unconstitutional behaviour as a prime minister, from the moment he assumed office under the Crown and proceeded to advise His Excellency, in daring, as he did, to ignore, defy and insult the entire membership of both Houses of Parliament, when Parliament itself was actually in session. . . .

Having ignored Parliament by assuming office without being in the least entitled to its confidence, having defied Parliament by seeking to impose upon its members the subterfuge of a phantom ministry, and continuing to govern with a ministry declared by the Commons to be infringing the privileges of its members, having insulted Parliament by summarily closing its doors in the face of honorable members of both Houses, having made the representative of the Crown in Canada a party to all these illegal, invalid and unconstitutional acts, the self-appointed prime minister then proceeds to enlarge the cabinet which Parliament had put out of existence before its untimely birth. I know of nothing in British history comparable to this, since the days of Charles I. It may be all very dramatic, very daring, but there is not a vestige of constitutional right or power which it does not undermine.

For a period of two weeks; including three days during which Parliament was in session, Mr. Meighen did not hesitate to advise His Excellency with respect to all Canada's domestic, inter-Imperial and international affairs and to administer all the departments of the Government of Canada without a single minister sworn in office, save himself. He alone was the Government of Canada over that period of time. If that is not anarchy or absolutism in government I would like to know to what category political philosophy would assign government carried on under such conditions. Surely it will not be termed responsible self-government under the British parliamentary system? . . .

It is the principles of liberty and freedom embedded in the British Constitution, and secured to those who live within its guarantee, that have made men of many races and many climes a great brotherhood in name and in heart. In the community of British nations which comprise the Dominions beyond the seas it is the anchor which holds all true to the little isles in the northern sea. In Canada, in Australia, in New Zealand, in South Africa, in Newfoundland, in Ireland, it is the sustaining and enduring element of loyalty alike to the Crown and to the flag. It is the counter-magnet to all tendencies of separation from Britain or to annexation to other lands. That is the Constitution by which the Liberal Party in Canada stands, for which it is prepared to fight today, it is in the name of all of freedom, liberty and loyalty which the British Constitution serves to inspire that I now ask my fellow Canadians in the name alike of King and Country to vindicate its might and majesty at the polls.

35. Ernest Lapointe Defines the Constitutional Issue, 23 July 1926

(*Gazette*, Montreal, 24 July 1926)

Hon. Ernest Lapointe, former Minister of Justice, speaking tonight from the same platform as Mr. Mackenzie King, joined with his leader in thrusting to the forefront of the Liberal party campaign the constitutional issues rising out of the formation of the Conservative Government and the dissolution of the fifteenth Parliament. Practically all of Mr. Lapointe's speech dealt with this matter. . . .

Mr. Lapointe denied that the Liberal party was "dragging the crown into the political arena." Mr. Meighen was doing it. "He is ingloriously sheltering behind the Crown. It is Mr. Meighen we are attacking and nobody else. Mr. Meighen and his friends need not worry," added Mr. Lapointe, "we are loyal to the Crown."

The former Minister of Justice enumerated at some length "seven grave errors, which have been made and which we, Canadians, are bound to repudiate at the polls."

1. The refusal to accept the advice of the Prime Minister to dissolve Parliament on June 28.

2. The summoning of Mr. Meighen and his being given the task of forming a government.

3. The creation of a "shadow cabinet" of acting ministers, none of whom had taken the oath of office.

4. The administration of departments by acting ministers contrary to law.

5. The interview between Mr. Forke and His Excellency on June 28. For this Mr. Meighen was responsible.

6. The granting of dissolution to a non-existing government.

7. The dissolution of Parliament in contempt of the rights of the people.

It was said that the campaign was to be one of flag waving. "It is behind the British flag and under its glorious protection that we will wage this fight for Canadian autonomy and self-government," said Mr. Lapointe. . . .

5. The General Election of 1930

The general election of 28 July 1930 was dominated in very large measure by economic conditions. The New York stock market crash of October 1929 heralded the Great Depression. By the following summer the vulnerable Canadian economy had suffered severely and unemployment was widespread. Radio broadcasting was used extensively for the first time in a general election campaign. Mr. King's Liberal government was heavily defeated, getting only 87 seats against 138 for the Conservatives led by Mr. R. B. Bennett. The United Farmers of Alberta got 9, the United Farmers of Ontario 1, the Liberal-Progressives 3, Labour 3, the Progressives 2 and Independents 2. See Neatby, *William Lyon Mackenzie King*, II.

36. Mackenzie King's "Five-Cent-Piece Speech"

(*Debates, House of Commons*, 3 April 1930)

This famous and uncharacteristically impolitic outburst by the Prime Minister was repeatedly quoted against him during the subsequent campaign.

Right Hon. W. L. MACKENZIE KING (Prime Minister): . . . Every winter in this country, ever since there was a winter or a Canada, there has been unemployment and there always will be. . . . But in the absence of any representations whatever from any provincial government to the federal government for aid . . . , or representations indicating that there is an unemployment situation which the provinces cannot cope with, we have no right to say that there is any national unemployment problem in this country. . . .

. . . A Liberal government was returned to power in this country in 1921 on certain policies which we believe have made for prosperity, which we believe have made for economy, which we believe and which the country knows have made for a reduction of public debt and a reduction of taxation. We, as a Liberal government, are standing by our policies and are seeking to maintain our position. But hon. gentlemen opposite say to us: Now that you have got the country into this favourable position, we ask you to take part of the moneys that you may raise in taxes from the people of this Dominion as a whole, and give it to other administrations to spend, and to whom, if you please? To a Tory government in the province of British Columbia; to a Progressive government in the province of Alberta; to a Tory government in the province of Saskatchewan; to a Progressive government in the province of Manitoba; to a Tory government in the province of Ontario; to a Tory government in the province of New Brunswick; to a Tory government in the province of Nova Scotia. No request has come from or has been made on behalf of either Quebec or Prince Edward Island, where there are Liberal governments attending to the affairs of the province. If you wish to play politics, that is the way to play it. Give to these Tory governments and to those Progressive governments at the present or all times money raised by taxation of the people of Canada as a whole to spend in their respective provinces and thereby save them raising taxes for their own purposes.

Mr. IRVINE:* Who asked them to spend money?

Mr. MACKENZIE KING: They are not getting the money to hoard it.

Mr. IRVINE: What money?

Mr. MACKENZIE KING: The money my hon. friends are asking to be paid out for unemployment relief to these provinces.

Mr. IRVINE: Did the Prime Minister read the resolution?

Mr. MACKENZIE KING: May I conclude what I have to say? So far as giving money from this federal treasury to provincial governments is concerned, in relation to this question of unemployment as it exists to-day, I might be prepared to go a certain length possibly in meeting one or two of the western provinces that have Progressive premiers at the head of their governments —

Some hon. MEMBERS: Oh!

Mr. MACKENZIE KING: — but I would not give a single cent to any Tory government.

Mr. BENNETT: Shame!

Mr. STEVENS: Shame!

Mr. MACKENZIE KING: Do my hon. friends say "shame"?

Mr. BENNETT: Yes, shame!

*William Irvine, United Farmers of Alberta, M.P. for Wetaskiwin.

Mr. Mackenzie King: What is there to be ashamed of?

Mr. Stevens: You ought to be ashamed of that.

Mr. Mackenzie King: My hon. friend is getting very indignant. Something evidently has got under his skin. May I repeat what I have said? With respect to giving moneys out of the federal treasury to any Tory government in this country for these alleged unemployment purposes, with these governments situated as they are to-day, with policies diametrically opposed to those of this government, I would not give them a five-cent piece.

Mr. Cahan:* Why give it to a Progressive government?

Mr. Speaker: Order.

Mr. Mackenzie King: My Tory friends do not like it. They think that they are the only ones who are entitled to the administration of affairs. . . .

37. R. B. Bennett Presents his Program, 9 June 1930

(*Gazette*, Montreal, 10 June 1930)

These are extracts from a Canadian Press report of Mr. Bennett's opening address at Winnipeg.

. . . The Conservative leader . . . summarized as follows his platform for the coming election:

"(1) – We pledge ourselves to a policy of protection for Canadians in the development of our national resources, our agricultural and industrial life, and our consumers from exploitation.

"(2) – We pledge ourselves to foster and develop agriculture and the livestock and dairy industries now so sadly neglected.

"(3) – We pledge ourselves to the stabilization of economic conditions, and to continuity of trade and freedom from the manipulation of home and foreign tariffs.

"(4) – We pledge ourselves to the development of interprovincial trade, and of a Canadian fuel policy, and development of a foreign market.

"(5) – We pledge ourselves to the improvement of the whole scheme of Canadian transportation northward by the completion of

---

*C. H. Cahan, Conservative, M.P. for St. Lawrence–St. George (Montreal).

the Hudson Bay route,* and the construction of such branches as may be necessary to render it most readily available to every part of Canada; to the Pacific slope by a Peace River outlet, and east and west by the development of the St. Lawrence waterways, and we pledge ourselves to aid existing traffic channels and to increase port facilities on the Great Lakes, Hudson Bay and the Atlantic and Pacific oceans, and to the establishment of a national highway system.

"(6) – We pledge ourselves to foster and support a plan for greater Empire trade to be based on mutual advantage.

"(7) – We pledge ourselves to a national old age pension scheme.

"(8) – We pledge ourselves to such compensation adjustment as will ensure the benefit of the above policies to every part of Canada."

In emphatic terms, Mr. Bennett denied a report that the identity of the Canadian National Railways might not be preserved if the Conservative party were returned to power. Unequivocally, the Opposition chieftain pledged his party to the preservation of the Canadian National Railways. . . .

"Amalgamation, never; competition, ever; that is the policy I shall follow," the Conservative Leader asserted. . . .

"I need hardly say to you," Mr. Bennett said in opening his remarks, "how grateful I am to you for coming here in such large numbers this summer evening while we discuss together some of the problems of our country. . . . I think I must pay some tribute to the men of science who have made possible my speaking to men and women of the Dominion and in every part of Canada tonight.

"That great invention which we are utilizing and which will enable me to speak to every province of Canada is one of the marvels of scientific achievement. . . .

"When the dread spectre of industrial instability stalks before you, when men walk the streets hungry, when our products grow old in storehouses, when the whole machinery of trade is smashed by an alien hand, what does the Liberal Government do? It tells you not to complain, not to whisper of your sorrows to your wife or children, above all to say nothing that may provoke the United States. For any protest, any sign of vexation carried over the border, would distress the gentle nature of our cousins and cause them to look askance at this confident northern race. . . .

"And after this pitiful gesture of propitiation rightly and sternly rejected, what does the Leader of the Government do to make you forget this, after his long time solicitude for a country which can very

*See below, **134.**

well look after itself? He and his Government begin again to rock the boat by introducing measures under the pious cloak of Empire trade. What do they mean by that?

"If you look at the tariff schedules they make strange reading. . . . If it means we should admit free into our markets Empire goods in competition with our own, without securing a real benefit to ourselves, and without obtaining a preferred place in their markets for our own products, then I oppose it, as did Sir John A. Macdonald.

"For it is not good for Canada. I give place to no man in my love for our Empire, but there is a greater love in my life and that is my love for Canada. Judge me by that. . . .

"The United States learned a long time ago that to become a great nation it must first look to itself. It, therefore, began to build up its home market by keeping out of it the goods of other nations. There was a time when if foreign countries had had their way they could have smashed its youthful industries, dried up its revenue, and wrecked its transportation systems and left it a country of idle workmen, of futile manufacturers, of starving agriculturists. Look at it now, marching to the slogan of 'America First.' It developed its industries, its natural resources, encouraged and protected its agriculture, so that out of a slow beginning it has grown to these gigantic proportions, where, if the countries affected do not take definite action, its strength will prevail and its purposes [be] imposed on the other countries its pledged purpose it is industrially to subdue. That is the story of the United States. It had the start of us. Today it is more powerful than we.

"Unless you are content to become its economic vassal you must do as it did. You must fight for your own, and there is no place for Canada but at the top. (Applause). . . .

"Listen, you agriculturist from the West, and all the other parts of Canada. You have been taught to applaud free trade. Tell me where did free trade ever fight for you? You say our tariffs are only for the manufacturers. I will make them fight for you as well. I will use them to blast a way into the markets that have been closed to you."

Mr. Bennett spoke of the vastness of Canada's resources and closed with a ringing appeal for a pro-Canada policy.

38. Mackenzie King Defends the Government's Record, 16 June 1930

(*Gazette*, Montreal, 17 June 1930)

These passages are from a Canadian Press report of King's "keynote" campaign speech, delivered at Brantford, Ontario, and heard over "an all-Canadian radio hook-up." He made virtually no reference to unemployment.

. . . "There are three outstanding issues in the present campaign," the Prime Minister said. "The first is the record of the government in the discharge of its public duties since it first assumed office. The second is the budget of 1930, representing as it does the views of the present administration on important questions of fiscal and trade policy. The third, is the direct issue of a choice between the Liberal and Conservative parties as the representatives of Canadian opinion at the Imperial and economic conferences which are to be held in London in September of the present year. . . .

"Were there no other issue before the people, I should ask for nothing more than that we should be judged fairly and squarely on the manner in which, having regard for all circumstances, we have administered the affairs of Canada during the past eight and a half years," asserted Mr. King in dealing with the record of the government. "For in that time the country has been lifted out of a veritable slough of despond, and out of years of depression it has been brought into years of prosperity which have not been equalled in its history. . . .

"Standing on a record of sound progressive accomplishment we approach the problems of the future with the same faith, courage and optimism which have made possible the achievements of the past years. The 'whispers of death,' the fear of returning depression, the complaints of an exodus which has ceased, the misgivings for the future, I shall leave to Mr. Bennett and other leaders of the Conservative party whose last tenure of office was indelibly associated with acute economic depression, and whose minds apparently are still shackled to the gloomy memories of other days. . . .

"Let me invite you to look beyond the Empire to the world at large. When did Canada ever hold a place in world affairs such as she holds today? Far be it from me to say that this place has been gained by any single path. Broadly speaking, there has been the sudden steep ascent of war, in which there were common heroism and common sacrifices, and there has been the long, gradual, constitutional endeavor for representative and responsible government, in which at every stage the Liberal party has been the pathfinder and pioneer."

The Conservative party had opposed every step of the way toward the responsible self-government in Canadian external affairs, the Prime Minister charged.

"When we sought and won the right to negotiate our own treaties we were told that we were seeking separation because, forsooth, we asked His Majesty in regard to an international negotiation on a matter of Canadian concern to give full powers to a Canadian Minister of the Crown instead of to the British ambassador at Washington. When a little later we opened a legation at Washington and subsequently at Paris and Tokio we were again told that we were pursuing the path of separation. Mr. Bennett is saying a great deal about Canada first. Just what does his Canada first mean? Perhaps he will tell us where he stands on the right to make our own treaties, and on the establishment of Canadian legations in other lands, and on Canada's status of co-equality with the motherland. I am not sure where he stands today, but I know where he stood in the session of Parliament just closed."

Then Mr. King turned to the budget of 1930, which he termed the second great issue of the campaign. Policies must be framed to meet existing conditions, he said. The National Policy of 1878 would not suit the Canada of 1930. What was more, he declared, the old national policy advocated by the Conservatives had not always served to meet conditions in the past.

"It is apparent . . . that both a high tariff and free trade are sectional policies when applied to the existing conditions in Canada. What then is the answer? The answer given by the Liberal party to a conflict of interests arising out of the tariff is the same as it is with respect to a conflict of interests in all other directions. To the greatest possible extent sectional interests must be reconciled in the light of the larger interests of the whole. This can be effected only by moderation and compromise. Face the facts of our situation. Take Canada as it is, with its changing needs and its conflicting interests. Acknowledge the facts of geography and of divergent industrial development in East, and Centre, and West. And having examined the realities of the situation, and having considered the demands of different sections for policies suited to their needs, so mould our social, transportation and fiscal policies as to hold the scales evenly between class and creed and section. Thus weld a far flung country into a united Canadian nation. . . .

"The budget of 1930 was . . . influenced also and in a special degree by our relations with two countries with which we are most closely associated in matters of commerce. The one is Great Britain. The other is the United States.

"When Mr. Hoover assumed office as president of the United States on March 11, 1929, the United States congress began carrying out a far-reaching revision of the tariff in conformity with the pledges given by the Republican party during the presidential campaign of the previous year. As that revision proceeded, it became increasingly apparent that the duties against Canadian agricultural products would be raised to such an extent as to cut off a considerable proportion of the existing Canadian exports to that country. . . . Subsequently, a condition developed in Great Britain which led to a marked curtailment of purchases of Canadian wheat. . . . It became apparent that if Canada was to maintain a British market for Canadian wheat it was desirable that measures should be taken by diverting to Great Britain, many of the purchases being made at present in the United States and in other ways, to increase British imports to Canada and thus create an economic and psychological condition in Great Britain more favorable to the importation of Canadian wheat. . . .

". . . The purpose kept in mind by the government . . . in bringing about a revision of the iron and steel schedules, was the double one of promoting a greater efficiency and productivity in the Canadian iron and steel industry, and at the same time of diverting a large proportion of our necessary imports of iron and steel products from the United States to Great Britain. This in turn was in conformity with the announced intention of the government to facilitate trade with those countries which are willing to trade with Canada on equal terms. . . .

". . . In past years, moreover, a large proportion of our early fruits and vegetables have been purchased from the United States. We believe that the British West Indies are capable of supplying us with an increasing share of this business. Under the existing trade agreement those islands have assured us of a preference in their market. In accordance, therefore, with our declared policy of trading with those who are willing to trade with us, we have made provision for the free entry into Canada of fruits and vegetables under the British preference. . . .

". . . Great Britain purchases far more from Canada than we buy from her. If we are to maintain in Great Britain an assured market for Canadian wheat and other articles of export, we must be prepared to increase our imports from that country. This, as I have already explained, can be done without necessarily increasing our total importations, but merely by diverting to Britain, who gives us a free entry into her markets and who is of our own household, purchases which have formerly been made in other countries, but which countries today do not give to us equal or like opportunities of trade. . . . We have studied the situation with the utmost care and have revised the tariff schedules with the definite aim of diverting a considerable portion of trade from the United States and other countries to Great Britain. We firmly believe that this policy will receive the whole-hearted approval of the Canadian people. . . ."

There appeared, said Mr. King, to be a fundamental difference between the Liberal party and the Conservatives as to the nature of trade. In the House of Commons, he said, Hon. R. J. Manion had declared that trade was war. In the opinion of the Prime Minister trade was exchange. Hon. R. B. Bennett, Conservative leader, had taken a somewhat similar stand to Dr. Manion in his recent Winnipeg speech. . . .

". . . There are business men, salesmen and commercial travellers in this audience. Let me ask you this question: Did you ever secure an order by force? Did you ever gain trade by ill-will against your customer? . . .

"I come now to the third of the issues. . . . You are being called upon to decide which party — the Liberal or Conservative — is to represent Canadian opinion at the Imperial and economic conferences to be held in London this year. . . .

"I do . . . say, what in very truth I believe to be the fact, that so far as intra-Empire trade is concerned, 'we are, at last, at the meeting of the ways,' and that the acceptance of this budget by the people on July 28th will do more than all else to ensure for Canada's representatives at the economic conference in London that favorable response to our attitude and action which we believe will be given by the government of Great Britain and by the governments of all the sister dominions of the Empire. It may not be going too far to say that the acceptance or rejection of our budget may help to determine whether the highways of Empire are to become, as we hope they may increasingly become, the avenues of a British commerce expanding ever so widely, o'er land and sea, or, whether in so far as the component parts of the Empire are concerned, its highways are to remain indistinguishable from the other trade routes of the world."

6. The General Election of 1935

In the general election of 14 October 1935 the Depression, which had been largely responsible for defeating Mackenzie King in 1930, made a similar contribution to the shattering defeat of R. B. Bennett, whose "New Deal" legislation (below, **132-133**) failed to rescue his government from the pit of unpopularity into which it had fallen. The Conservatives got only 39 seats against the Liberals' 171. Social Credit, now appearing on the national political scene, got 17 (above, **24**); the Co-operative Commonwealth Federation (above, **23**) got 7. There were 5 Independent Liberals, 1 Independent Conservative, 2 Liberal-Progressives, 1 Independent and 1 United Farmers of Ontario-Labour member elected. The Reconstruction Party, led by H. H. Stevens who had resigned from the Bennett cabinet, elected only its leader. The party leaders' references to the long-threatened Italian war of aggression against Ethiopia which finally broke out early in October were uniformly isolationist in tone.

39. Mackenzie King on the Political Situation, 31 July 1935

(*Gazette*, Montreal, 1 August 1935)

Radio played an even larger part in this campaign than in the previous one. Mackenzie King began his campaign with a series of three broadcasts; extracts from the first one follow.

Ottawa, July 31.– Turning his back upon any "so-called National Government," declaring that "we have been living too much under a reign of terror," warning the people against any continuance of a "Tory dictatorship," disposing of the Stevens party as the outgrowth of a party quarrel, and of the C.C.F. group as a result of the continued depression, and appealing to the electorate for an overwhelming mandate to ensure liberating measures getting past a "Tory Senate," the Liberal leader, Rt. Hon. W. L. Mackenzie King, in his first radio broadcast this evening, sounded the first note in the battle cry of his party. . . .

Third parties in Canada invariably originated when Conservatives were in power, Mr. King said, and disappeared when Liberals took over the administration and prosperity returned. He referred to Canadian history to prove the point, the rise and fall of the patrons of industry, the Equal Rights Party, the Progressives.

"Today, history is once more repeating itself. We have in the field as third parties seeking nation-wide recognition, not the Progressive Party, or other of the third parties of previous general elections, but the C.C.F. and the Reconstruction Party. Each of these parties has come into being under Tory administration since Mr. Bennett assumed office. Each is a product of the depression and discontent, which Tory policies have served to aggravate and prolong. My hope and expectation is that history will continue to reveal the sequence with which we are already familiar....

"It was not until someone began to preach the doctrine that parliamentary methods were not suited to these times; that the constitution was an obstacle to progress; that shorter and swifter methods were necessary to obtain results, even if they involved sweeping aside parliamentary restraints, and overriding the constitution, that in Europe, parliaments and democracies alike began to disappear. Have we not all heard this very sort of language from Mr. Bennett, Mr. Woodsworth and Mr. Stevens?

"And what has come in the stead of parliamentary methods? Hitlerism in Germany, Fascism in Italy, Communism in Russia, and in all, the death of democracy. Is that what we wish to see happen in Canada?...

"For my part, I propose to stand or fall upholding, in all things, the parliamentary method of government....

"That is why, amongst other changes which are being advocated today, I am opposed to the movement in favor of a so-called national government, either as desirable at the moment or as something to be effected in the course of the next Parliament. Rightly understood, I believe national government to be but another form of dictatorship, the most subtle of all, perhaps, because its name and its pretensions are so plausible....

"Traced to its source—the source that is financing the present movement—it will, I believe, be found that the demand for national government is a last desperate effort on the part of certain persons, enjoying privileges denied to others, to deal with the railways, the tariffs, and taxation, in a manner which will serve to further their own special interests....

"In plain English, national government, if established at this time, would sacrifice democracy to serve the end of plutocracy....'"

40. Mackenzie King on Unemployment, 5 August 1935

(*Gazette*, Montreal, 6 August 1935)

In his second broadcast, on 2 August, Mackenzie King devoted himself to the Liberal party program which he had presented in Parliament in February 1933.* The third, of which extracts are given here, dealt with the paramount issue of unemployment.

. . . In 1930, the Liberal leader continued, Premier Bennett estimated there were 117,000 unemployed in Canada. The census of 1931 placed the number at 393,000. The most conservative estimate today placed it at 400,000 — "it is at least well within the mark to say that the number of unemployed in Canada today is four times what it was when the Bennett Government assumed office."

Those figures dealt only with the unemployed. In May, 1935, there were 1,272,000 Canadians on relief, unemployed persons and their dependents. This reflected "something of the extent of Mr. Bennett's failure to redeem his promises to end unemployment and to abolish the dole.". . .

"To cope with this nation-wide situation, the Liberal party proposes, if returned to power, to adopt the policies which it has consistently advocated, and which are set forth in the paragraph that appears as the first item in the statement of the party's position, which I read to you on Friday evening last. . . . The paragraph is as follows:

" 'Unemployment of first concern.' "

" 'The Liberal party believes unemployment is Canada's most urgent national problem. It would deal with the present emergency conditions through a representative national commission, which would co-operate with the provinces and municipalities in the administration of unemployment relief and in an endeavor to provide work for the unemployed.

" 'As permanent measures, the Liberal party is pledged to introduce policies which will serve to provide employment by reviving industry and trade; and to introduce a national system of unemployment insurance.'. . .

**Debates, House of Commons*, 27 February 1933.

"There will necessarily be two main divisions in the commission's work," explained Mr. King. "The one will have to do with the administration of unemployment relief. The other will have to do with the endeavor to provide work for the unemployed. . . . A guarantee of provincial co-operation is to be found in the fact that, save in one province, out of nine, Liberal Governments are already in office. . . .

"The Commission would be especially requested to consider the early transfer of the relief camps from the control of the Department of National Defence, and to enlist the co-operation of every possible agency likely to be of service in the permanent establishment of young unemployed men in the normal economic life of the country."

Mr. King referred to his own lifelong interest in labor and social problems. . . .

41. R. B. Bennett on the Danger of War, 6 September 1935

(*Gazette*, Montreal, 7 September 1935)

The opening of Mr. Bennett's campaign was delayed by an illness and his visit to England for the celebration of King George V's Silver Jubilee. It began with a series of four broadcasts. This is an extract from the first.

. . . "Now, in world politics, Canada should be secure. For she has no ambitions which peace cannot gratify. If trouble comes it will be somebody else's fault, not ours. And I conceive it to be the solemn duty of government, by all just and honorable means, to see that Canada is kept out of trouble. We have bought and paid for security and for peace, and we mean to have them.

"Mr. King has told you that should the question of Canada's participation in a European war arise, that question would be determined only by Parliament.

"But, as Mr. King must know, under the law that question can only be determined by Parliament. So that his statement adds nothing new to the discussion.

"In peace, the Conservative party stands for Canadian rights, and stands against the economic aggression of any foreign country. So also in war. We will not be embroiled in any foreign quarrel where the rights of Canadians are not involved. . . ."

42. Messrs. King and Lapointe on the Danger of War, 7 September 1935

(*Gazette*, Montreal, 9 September 1935)

Mackenzie King and his chief Quebec lieutenant dealt with external problems at a meeting in Quebec City; extracts from a report of it follow.

. . . Mr. King was not alone in referring to the place of Canada as regards war, for Hon. Mr. Lapointe had something to say, which he felt to be so important that he issued his remarks to the Press in writing. They constitute the best summary, reading:

"Newspapers are requesting public men to define their stand on the grave conflict which actually threatens the peace of the world. I desire that my words on this subject be published as I utter them. I do not want to allow unscrupulous opponents to again falsely charge the Liberals of this province with using the war as an election weapon. I now repudiate any such malicious representation. I will even say that I sincerely believe that Mr. Bennett and the other political leaders do not differ with me as to the stand Canada should take.

"This being said, I state that in my opinion no interest in Ethiopia, of any nature whatever, is worth the life of a single Canadian citizen. No consideration could justify Canada's participation in such a war, and I am unalterably opposed to it. . . .

"The duty of the Canadian Government in the circumstances is to co-operate with the League of Nations to prevent or to stop such war. I still believe that common sense will prevail, and that the catastrophe will be avoided. . . ."

. . . Mr. King said: "I ask myself, if word comes from Europe at any moment, from British channels or otherwise that war is commencing in the Near East, and the Empire is involved, what will be the answer of Mr. Bennett? I want him to be very positive in regard to what he will say in reply to any demand. I read what he said last night. He said we should not be drawn into any war where our interests were not affected. Who is going to determine? Those who have Imperial ideas, who have different ideas from us, who do not see quite on the same world-scale as they do? What I want to say to the Prime Minister is that, there being no Parliament, and this being a period when he has run beyond the time of the life of Parliament, he has no right to commit this country, directly or indirectly, in any shape or form, as to what should be done before Parliament meets. Until a Parliament comes into being, I care not what the situation may be, Mr. Bennett has no right to commit this country by any word or action which may involve the people of Canada in any war. For my part, I believe the people of Canada would strongly oppose our country going to war in regard to any situation that related to economic interests in the Near East. I do not believe that the people of Canada would say that interests of that kind come within the category of things which affect Canada. What I want to make very clear, as far as a Liberal administration, as far as the Liberal party is concerned, we believe in the supremacy of Parliament, as representing the people, and when no Parliament is in session then we say that if any action as to peace or war is to be taken there should be a mandate from the people themselves, even in the form of a plebiscite, before we take any action.

"Action speaks louder than words. I have told you of a situation which arose, which was as critical as what may happen.* You can trust the Liberal party to see to it that, as regards the great questions which involve the lives of men and women, any Liberal Government will see to it that not a single life is unnecessarily sacrificed in regard to any matter beyond what affects the safeguarding and rights of our own country."

43. R. B. Bennett Proposes a Remedy for Unemployment, 9 September 1935

(*Gazette*, Montreal, 10 September 1935)

This is an extract from the Prime Minister's second broadcast of the campaign.

. . . Solution of the unemployment problem would be the greatest possible step in the direction of improving the standard of living, said Mr. Bennett. Political opponents had said much about his pledge to end unemployment and he had no objection.

"I did say that I would end unemployment. I would not have you in any doubt upon that point. I made that statement at the city of Moncton during the campaign of 1930. I repeat that statement here tonight. I make it as sincerely now as I did then.

*King had described what he had done at the time of the Chanak incident of 1922 (below, **163-167**), emphasizing that he had taken the attitude that "no action would be taken in Canada in regard to war without Parliament being consulted." This was the only point where the *Gazette* recorded the audience as applauding.

"After five years of experience of the right and wrong way in which to deal with the problems of the depression, I have finally, in a sense reluctantly, but quite irrevocably, determined on what we conceive to be the only practical solution of the problem in its present form. . . ."

Though his Government had not ended unemployment, it had reason to be proud of its record. It had reduced unemployed in numbers from 738,000 in 1933 to less than 500,000 now. It had provided relief and set in motion extensive public works. Experience showed public works were a help but not a solution. . . .

"Therefore I come to my proposal. In my opinion and in the opinion of my colleagues, the first step to be taken by way of a permanent solution of this problem is to remove from the labor market all those workers who have reached the age where, especially under conditions of today, the worker's social interest, the state's economic interest, equally suggest the wisdom of retirement.

"It is, of course, clear to all of us that the old rules governing hours of labor and years of labor can no longer apply, because we live in changed economic conditions. . . .

"This new economic trend has already influenced the retirement schemes of certain private enterprises. And these enterprises, after careful estimate of all the factors involved, have met the new conditions by determining upon a retirement age of 60 years.

"The Government recognizes this principle. And, in conformity with it, will introduce into Parliament legislation to make it effective. . . .

"The application of this principle will mean, in the first year of its operation, the withdrawal from the labor market of 120,000 people, and provide that number of jobs for younger workers.". . .

44. R. B. Bennett as Economic Reformer, 14 September 1935

(*Gazette*, Montreal, 16 September 1935)

This is from the final section of Mr. Bennett's fourth broadcast.

. . . "There is something very fine about Liberalism and something very fine about the academic way in which Mr. King expounds the doctrines of Liberalism. Before the days of monopolies, before the days of concentrations of business, when there was a controlling market-place, when there was a balancing competition, before the days of economic nationalism, before the days when modern industrial conditions, when modern ways of life, necessarily and basically changed our whole economic scheme of things — before those days Liberalism was real and vital. In this modern world it is but a ghost.

"In the old days its economic doctrine — which was to leave things alone and let business run itself — was a good doctrine. Its political doctrine — which was to leave things alone and let the country run itself — was not a bad doctrine. Cherish the memory of it, if you will, but realize that in these practical and trying and fast-changing conditions it can be but a memory. Raise this Liberal ghost and it will haunt you upon that backward trail which you must travel if laissez faire is to be your guide."

Canadians should regard the record of the Government only as evidence of what it was capable of doing in the future and as proof of the effectiveness of Conservative policy.

"Just let me read this partial list so you may have it in mind: Central Bank, the Marketing Act, Farm Loans, Farmers' Creditors' Arrangement Act, unemployment insurance, minimum wages, eight-hour day, day of rest, the economic council, the Housing Act, an act creating a board of commerce and industry, amendments to the Companies Act, amendments to the Criminal Code protecting investors and abolishing unfair practices, the Wheat Board Act.*

"It is an impressive legislative record, don't you think? and it is beginning to work wonderfully well. We are ahead of the results which we expected up to date. How far have we got to go, how long it will take to get the results necessary to your well-being, I do not know. But the main thing is that we will keep on going until we do. And another important thing for you to remember is that we know where we are going."...

7. The General Election of 1940

Mackenzie King was rarely wrong on a question of pure politics, and the result of his sudden decision to call an election (announced in the Speech from the Throne during the one-day session of Parliament on 25 January 1940), justified his judgment. The occasion was the resolution condemning the federal government for lack of vigour in the war

*On Bennett's reform measures, see below, pp. 313-14.

effort, which Premier Mitchell Hepburn of Ontario, supported by the
opposition leader, George Drew, had obtained from the provincial
legislature on 18 January. In the voting on 26 March the Liberals
gained the greatest majority ever given to a Canadian government up
to that time, winning 178 seats (in addition to 3 Liberal-Progressives
and 3 Independent Liberals) as against 39 for the National Government (Conservative) party led by Dr. R. J. Manion. There were 10 "New
Democracy" (Social Credit) seats, all in Alberta; 8 went to the C.C.F.,
and 1 Independent Conservative, 1 Independent, 1 "United Reform"
and 1 "Unity" candidate were elected. The Liberals retained a large
majority of the Ontario seats. See Pickersgill, *The Mackenzie King
Record*, I, and Granatstein, *The Politics of Survival*.

45. Dr. R. J. Manion Defines "National Government," 31 January 1940

(*Gazette*, Montreal, 1 February 1940)

This is part of a press release.

Regarding my proposal published last Friday — the day after Mr.
King impulsively and unfairly dissolved Parliament — that if elected I
would form a national government, I am being flooded with letters,
telegrams and telephone messages of approval. But accompanying
some of these messages, and also in some of the press, is the suggestion that I elaborate my plan. Therefore I gladly do so in this brief
press release.

My idea is that at this time of world crisis and national danger our
people do not want petty bickerings of party continuously sounding
in their ears. They do want, when this election is over, a government
of the best men available, irrespective of politics, to handle our war
effort so that such evils as patronage, favoritism and extravagance
will be wholly eliminated....

When I form this government, I intend, so far as possible, that
both the old parties, and, if practicable, all important parties in the
House of Commons, shall be represented in it — at any rate, no out-
standingly able man would be kept out of such government because
of his political affiliations.

Leaders in business and industry would necessarily be included.
Incidentally, it is time that the Labor Department, for example,
should have at its head some outstanding labor man who under-

stands the problems of this large body of our citizens, just as the great industry of agriculture is usually, and should always be, represented by a practical agriculturist. These departments are merely mentioned as illustrations, for the purpose of clarifying my intention. . . .

46. Manion Repudiates Conscription, 8 February 1940

(*Gazette*, Montreal, 9 February 1940)

In March 1939 Dr. Manion had been the first to proclaim the formula of no conscription for overseas service (see below, **189**). This is an extract from a Canadian Press report of a speech at Brockville, Ontario.

. . . Dr. Manion claimed that "in every section of Canada where conscription is unpopular" it was being rumored that national government meant conscription as the Union Government did in 1917.

"I note that even Mr. King in his broadcast last night made an implied reference to the same thing," he said.

"No one knows better than Mr. King my position against conscription because he was present in the House on March 30 last when I made my position quite clear. In that speech I very frankly opposed conscription, as I do now, on the grounds among others that it is unnecessary under present-day conditions of warfare (it has proved true since this war began); that in the last war its chief result was national disunity and misunderstanding while it raised very few men for our armies; and, finally, that the first duty of a public man is to hold this country together, to maintain national unity and understanding, not to disrupt the country and to cause serious disharmony and disunity, resulting in the impairment of our war effort at this very critical time in the life of our nation, when an enthusiastic war effort is so essential.

"While opposing conscription then, as I do now, I advocated complete co-operation, short of conscription, beside Britain in case of war.". . .

47. Mackenzie King on National Government, 23 February 1940

(*Gazette*, Montreal, 24 February 1940)

An extract from a Canadian Press report of one of the Prime Minister's election broadcasts.

. . . The Prime Minister asked Dr. Manion to whom he would turn for those who would form his union government in the event of his success at the polls. "Who are the men inside or outside of his own party who will be asked to join him?" he queried.

If the Liberal Ministry were defeated it would be condemnation of its war effort. The Prime Minister wondered if any members of a discredited ministry would be asked to join him.

"I think you should ask him what Liberals he has in mind. Has he any hope of getting the consent of the outstanding members of the party to join him?". . .

"An opposition is our strongest protection against violent and revolutionary change. That is one of the reasons why Parliament itself, by statute, has made the Leader of the Opposition a salaried officer. His position in Parliament, in many respects, is second only to that of the Prime Minister. . . .

"In order that there may be no misunderstanding about the position of the members of the present Government, I should like to make that position very clearly known. In saying what I do, I speak with the authority and support of every member of the Cabinet.

"If, after an appeal has been made to the country on our war effort and our policies, we are not returned to power, those of us who are elected, together with our following, will not betray our parliamentary duty, but will constitute His Majesty's Loyal Opposition. I make that simple, straightforward statement, so that there will be no mistake in the minds either of the people, or of Dr. Manion concerning our position; and no recriminations later on because anyone was left in doubt.". . .

"We face a future unknown and unpredictable. We cannot tell what calamities may strike us before the present year is ended, or what perils may be upon us in 1941 or 1942. Failure to view the situation as a whole, and to take account of all conceivable possibilities, might be fraught with the gravest dangers. There must be no surrender to the insistent clamor of those who refuse to look beyond the problems of the moment.

"The great co-operative war effort which this government has planned is gaining every day in momentum. Our hope lies in the gathering of our strength to meet the gathering of the storm.

"No one can doubt the courage, the will, the endurance of the people of Canada. But the possession of these qualities is not alone sufficient to ensure victory. They must be marshalled and guided by a government that is strong, steady, vigorous, patient, provident and experienced."

48. Manion Changes His Party's Name, 28 February 1940

(*Gazette*, Montreal, 29 February 1940)

Sault Ste. Marie, Ont., February 28. — (CP) — Hon. R. J. Manion, National Conservative leader, today outlined his views on party designations in the following statement:

"All candidates to whom I shall give recognition will be supporters of national government. All candidates who belong to the National Conservative Party are supporters of the national government movement, but it is anticipated that there will be national government candidates who do not belong to the National Conservative Party.

"I personally prefer to use the term national government in describing our candidates but I have no objection to any candidate describing himself in any other way, provided he makes it clear that he is a supporter of the proposal to establish a national government."

8. *The General Election of 1945*

The general election of 11 June 1945 took place between the defeat of Germany and the surrender of Japan. John Bracken, the Progressive Conservative leader (above, **25**), who now sought a seat in the House of Commons for the first time, had not declared firmly for conscription until June 1944. He fought the election, however, largely on a platform of full compulsory service for the war with Japan. On 4 April 1945 Mackenzie King announced that service in the Pacific would be limited to those who volunteered for it. With the end of the German war conscription had lost most of its interest for the public. King's government was returned with a reduced majority, getting 126 seats

(Liberal and Independent Liberal) against 66 (including 1 Independent) for the Progressive Conservatives, 29 (including 1 Independent) for the C.C.F., 13 (all from Alberta) for Social Credit, 2 for the anti-war Bloc Populaire, 8 unattached Independents and 1 Labour Progressive (i.e. Communist) (*Gazette*, Montreal, 20 June 1945).

49. John Bracken's Declaration of Policy, 15 May 1945

(*Gazette*, Montreal, 16 May 1945)

These are leading points from among a great number stated in John Bracken's "charter" as presented in a speech in Ottawa.

. . . This party stands for the most effective utilization of our total resources of manpower as well as wealth for the winning of the war. It has advocated compulsory selective service on a national basis as the only fair and democratic way to secure vitally needed reinforcements. It has steadily championed the cause of active service men and their next of kin.

One fundamental principle underlies our manpower policy—in war and in peace—equality of service and sacrifice for all Canadians. Only on the basis of this policy can lasting bonds of national unity be forged. . . .

International trade is a two-way street. We must sell more and buy more. . . .

The objective is full employment—jobs for all. . . .

In our economy up to now the farmer, his family and farm workers have been in the class of the forgotten man. . . . What we propose is a complete and scientific program for the farmer. . . .

We believe fishermen, like farmers, are entitled to their fair share of the national income. . . .

Our objective is to guarantee to business men, large and small, the right to trade under conditions favorable to individual enterprise, new industries and venture capital. . . .

Canada's future as a free nation is best assured as a member of the British Commonwealth. . . .

British and American peoples must work together in close harmony.

In any international organization for maintaining world security

Canada must be prepared to make firm commitments and to provide the means and accept the responsibility to discharge these commitments to the full.

This party believes that Canada's international and commonwealth relations are and have been for some years of such importance that the appointment of a full time minister responsible for the Department of External Affairs is long overdue. It will be our policy to make this change.

Our objective is the earliest possible defeat of Japan. To accomplish this we will:

Take such steps as are necessary to carry out Canada's fair share of responsibility for the victorious ending of the war in the Pacific.

See to it that none of the Canadian armed forces who have already served in an active theatre of war need fight Japan, except as they choose to volunteer without coercion of any kind whatsoever.

Insofar as Canadian troops have been promised or are required, send to the Pacific theatre of war physically fit N.R.M.A. troops, thereby giving practical application to our policy of equality of service and sacrifice.

. . . We propose Dominion-provincial conferences at frequent intervals, regardless of the political stripe of the various provincial governments.

The nation has outlived its constitution of seventy-eight years ago. This is a fact which must be faced. Amendments to the British North America Act are needed, particularly in the fields of labor, social security, taxation and financial relationship.

This party is opposed to the principle of concentration of power in Ottawa. It supports the guaranteed rights of racial and religious minorities. Nevertheless, it believes that men of goodwill with the nation's interest at heart can be brought into agreement on such constitutional amendments as may be necessary. It proposes moving in this direction and promptly.

We will at the first session of Parliament after the election abolish the fee payable for radio licenses which we regard as an unnecessary and unwarranted nuisance tax.

Our objective is that all Canadians shall have decent, healthful housing conditions. . . .

50. Mackenzie King's Opening Address, 16 May 1945

(*Gazette,* Montreal, 17 May 1945)

A short extract from a speech made at Vancouver.

. . . The responsibility of leadership for nearly six years of war was preceded by years of responsibility for leading our country through a dark period of growing international tension and external danger. Going back only to the days of Munich, it is a responsibility which I have borne, without a day's freedom from anxiety, for seven years. . . .

Let me draw to your attention a very significant fact. . . . Over the years of war, associations — intimate and far-reaching associations — have been formed not only between nations, but between the men who have been directing the nations. We have been working together, meeting most critical situations as they have arisen, month by month, day by day — yes, in many cases, hour by hour.

The men who have been directing the governments of the Allied Nations have come to know each other, to share each other's confidences and to trust one another. In our relations with our closest Allies, particularly with the United Kingdom and the United States, this has been specially true of the men who had been administering Canada's affairs throughout the war. At this of all times, when Canada's future so largely depends on our relations with other countries, are you going to sever relationships between these governments and between the past and the future? Are you going to substitute for the present administration whose members and policies you know, an entirely new administration, whose members are unknown, and whose policies are untried? . . .

No greater mistake could be made than to decide the elections on any single issue. The new Parliament will have many problems to face. Among the number will be that of continuing Canada's war effort against Japan. Until Japanese militarism has been defeated and destroyed, this will remain our first objective. . . .

It will be well to remember that the prosecution of the war against Japan will be only one of the pressing problems which have immediately to be faced. Any attempt to make an issue of the war effort against Japan, or any other single question would but serve to blind the country to the real issues which have to be faced in the post-war era.

A main task of the Canadian Government from now on will be to maintain full employment and to provide social security for the people of our country. . . .

It is as the leader of a government pledged to the promotion of world security and world prosperity in the international arena and to policies of full employment and social security in our country that I am seeking once more an expression of the confidence of the people of Canada.

51. Mr. King Strikes a Personal Note, 2 June 1945

(*Gazette*, Montreal, 4 June 1945)

The personal appeal to Quebec, from which extracts are given here, was delivered in Montreal.

. . . Out of the many contacts, personal and official, established through the Department of External Affairs over the past 25 years, there has been brought into being a powerful influence for good in the adjustment of international difficulties and the establishment of permanent peace. I wonder if the people of Canada, on June the 11th, are going to cast aside one like myself who has wrestled with these problems on Canada's behalf for more than a quarter of a century. I wonder if, at this of all times, they are going to entrust the direction of Canada's international affairs to a leader who has never been inside the Canadian House of Commons, or to one who, however interested he may be in matters of foreign policy, has yet to find a place in the international arena.

Ladies and gentlemen, it is just 36 years ago today that I was invited by Sir Wilfrid Laurier to become a member of his cabinet. I was, on that day, the youngest minister of the Crown in Canada. I have since inherited Sir Wilfrid Laurier's mantle as leader of the party of which he will ever remain the foremost figure. I have had, in the office of Prime Minister, to go through most of the experiences and many of the trials which Sir Wilfrid Laurier encountered in the years he was in office.

I am proud, indeed, to say that in the course of my association with him I never failed him once, so far as I can recall, but was close to his side in every conflict. I went down to defeat, fighting for better trade relations with the United States in the great reciprocity campaign of 1911. . . .

I saw Sir Wilfrid defeated by an unholy alliance between the Nationalists of this province and the Tories of the other provinces of Canada. I saw all that grew out of that ignoble and treacherous plot. I need not give you the record. It will be for all time a blot of shame on the pages of our country's history.

But the question I wish to put to you tonight, to you who know the truth of what I am saying, is whether you, the people of the province of Quebec, intend to allow the tactics of 1911 to be repeated successfully in 1945, and to have Mackenzie King in 1945, suffer the fate of Sir Wilfrid Laurier in 1911? Please don't forget that in 1911 it was the men who called themselves Nationalists, the men who spoke of themselves as Independents, but whose campaigns were being financed by the Tory party, were the men who contributed in largest measure to the defeat of Laurier. I hope history is not going to repeat itself in any success of the alliance between Mr. Bracken and a new generation of so-called independents.

Let me make this perfectly clear. This is the last general election which I intend to contest. But, as I said in my opening address in Vancouver some weeks ago, I am heart and soul in this fight. I should welcome another term of office, not, I can assure you, for the added burdens and anxieties it cannot fail to bring. I would welcome it because it will enable me to carry through the social reforms which will bring lasting benefits to generations to come. I would like to write one more chapter to my life devoted to national unity and the well-being of all. I would like to see established among the nations of the world a permanent peace and social justice. This can only be accomplished on our part by a party sufficiently strong to be independent of all other parties. If Canada's voice is to count in the councils of nations, the government must not have to rely upon the men of other parties or no party at all. . . .

. . . No greater service was ever rendered to Canada than the service rendered by my French speaking colleagues in the cabinet. . . .

I wish to publicly acknowledge the debt I owe to their cooperation in helping me steady the ship of state that weathered the gale. Their presence in the ministry speaks more emphatically than words. I wish to mention particularly the Minister of Justice, Hon. Louis St. Laurent. No man could possess a more able counsellor, a truer friend. When I asked Mr. St. Laurent to join the government following the loss it had sustained in the death of Hon. Ernest Lapointe, I was in serious need of a man of outstanding ability to replace him.

Mr. Lapointe was a man with whom I differed in race and religion but never for what we thought was for the good of the country. If Mr.

St. Laurent had not come into the cabinet on that occasion, I doubt whether I would be speaking to you at the present time. Someday you may know what all this has meant to me and to you.

The Liberal party is undivided nationally and not ashamed to use the party name and proclaim liberal principles and policies. . . . It is the only one that can be elected with an overall majority. If we are to maintain our unity and fulfill our destiny, a substantial majority is essential.

At this time we are in a better position to serve the interests of the people than any other party in the whole country.

III.
Law, Justice and Police

A.
Criminal Justice

52. The Criminal Code: "Section 98"

(9-10 George V, Chap. 46)

"Section 98" of the Criminal Code (as it became in the Revised Statutes, 1927) was a product of the postwar "Red scare" and specifically of the Winnipeg Strike of May 1919. This highly conservative legislation, permitting the police to act on mere suspicion, became a target of defenders of civil rights and particularly of J. S. Woodsworth. It was maintained and used by the Bennett government during the Depression years, and was finally repealed (with the blessing of Mackenzie King's Minister of Justice, Ernest Lapointe) only in 1936, by 1 Edward VIII, Chap. 29. See McNaught, *A Prophet in Politics.*

(Assented to 7th July, 1919)

1. The following sections are inserted immediately after section ninety-seven of the *Criminal Code*, chapter one hundred and forty-six of the Revised Statutes of Canada: —

"97A. (1) Any association, organization, society or corporation, whose professed purpose or one of whose purposes is to bring about any governmental, industrial or economic change within Canada by use of force, violence or physical injury to person or property, or by threats of such injury, or which teaches, advocates, advises or defends the use of force, violence, terrorism, or physical injury to person or property, or threats of such injury, in order to accomplish such change, or for any other purpose, or which shall by any means prosecute or pursue such purpose or professed purpose, or shall so teach, advocate, advise or defend, shall be an unlawful association.

"(2) Any property, real or personal, belonging or suspected to belong to an unlawful association, or held or suspected to be held by any person for or on behalf thereof may, without warrant, be seized or taken possession of by any person thereunto authorized by the Chief Commissioner of Dominion Police or by the Commissioner of the Royal Northwest Mounted Police, and may thereupon be forfeited to His Majesty.

126

"(3) Any person who acts or professes to act as an officer of any such unlawful association, and who shall sell, speak, write or publish anything as the representative or professed representative of any such unlawful association, or become and continue to be a member thereof, or wear, carry or cause to be displayed upon or about his person or elsewhere, any badge, insignia, emblem, banner, motto, pennant, card, button or other device whatsoever, indicating or intended to show or suggest that he is a member of or in anywise associated with any such unlawful association, or who shall contribute anything as dues or otherwise, to it or to any one for it, or who shall solicit subscriptions or contributions for it, shall be guilty of an offence and liable to imprisonment for not more than twenty years.

"(4) In any prosecution under this section, if it be proved that the person charged has, —

(a) attended meetings of an unlawful association; or,

(b) spoken publicly in advocacy of an unlawful association; or,

(c) distributed literature of an unlawful association by circulation through the Post Office mails of Canada, or otherwise;

it shall be presumed, in the absence of proof to the contrary, that he is a member of such unlawful association.

"(5) Any owner, lessee, agent or superintendent of any building, room, premises or place, who knowingly permits therein any meeting of an unlawful association or any subsidiary association or branch or committee thereof, or any assemblage of persons who teach, advocate, advise or defend the use, without authority of the law, of force, violence or physical injury to person or property, or threats of such injury, shall be guilty of an offence under this section and shall be liable to a fine of not more than five thousand dollars or to imprisonment for not more than five years, or to both fine and imprisonment.

"(6) If any judge of any superior or county court, police or stipendiary magistrate, or any justice of the peace, is satisfied by information on oath that there is reasonable ground for suspecting that any contravention of this section has been or is about to be committed, he may issue a search warrant under his hand, authorizing any peace officer, police officer, or constable, with such assistance as he may require, to enter at any time any premises or place mentioned in the warrant, and to search such premises or place, and every person found therein, and to seize and carry away any books, periodicals, pamphlets, pictures, papers, circulars, cards, letters, writings, prints, handbills, posters, publications or documents which are found on or in such premises or place, or in the possession of any person therein at the time of such search, and the same, when so seized may be carried away and may be forfeited to His Majesty.

"(7) Where, by this section, it is provided that any property may be forfeited to His Majesty, the forfeiture may be adjudged or declared by any judge of any superior or county court, or by any police or stipendiary magistrate, or by any justice of the peace, in a summary manner, and by the procedure provided by Part XV of this Act, in so far as applicable, or subject to such adaptations as may be necessary to meet the circumstances of the case.

"97B. (1) Any person who prints, publishes, edits, issues, circulates, sells, or offers for sale or distribution any book, newspaper, periodical, pamphlet, picture, paper, circular, card, letter, writing, print, publication or document of any kind, in which is taught, advocated, advised or defended, or who shall in any manner teach, advocate, or advise or defend the use, without authority of law, of force, violence, terrorism, or physical injury to person or property, or threats of such injury, as a means of accomplishing any governmental, industrial or economic change, or otherwise, shall be guilty of an offence and liable to imprisonment for not more than twenty years.

"(2) Any person who circulates or attempts to circulate or distribute any book, newspaper, periodical, pamphlet, picture, paper, circular, card, letter, writing, print, publication, or document of any kind, as described in this section by mailing the same or causing the same to be mailed or posted in any Post Office, letter box, or other mail receptacle in Canada, shall be guilty of an offence, and shall be liable to imprisonment for not more than twenty years.

"(3) Any person who imports into Canada from any other country, or attempts to import by or through any means whatsoever, any book, newspaper, periodical, pamphlet, picture, paper, circular, card, letter, writing, print, publication or document of any kind as described in this section, shall be guilty of an offence and shall be liable to imprisonment for not more than twenty years.

"(4) It shall be the duty of every person in the employment of His Majesty in respect of His Government of Canada, either in the Post Office Department, or in any other Department to seize and take possession of any book, newspaper, periodical, pamphlet, picture, paper, circular, card, letter, writing, print, publication or document, as mentioned in the last preceding section, upon discovery of the same in the Post Office mails of Canada or in or upon any station, wharf, yard, car, truck, motor or other vehicle, steamboat or other vessel upon which the same may be found and when so seized and taken, without delay to transmit the same, together with the envelopes, coverings and wrappings attached thereto, to the Chief Commissioner of Dominion Police, or to the Commissioner of the Royal Northwest Mounted Police."

53. The Quebec "Padlock Law," 1937

(Quebec Statute, 1 Geo. VI, Chap. 11)

After the federal Parliament repealed section 98 of the Criminal Code (above, **52**), the Union Nationale government of Premier Duplessis in Quebec passed this "Act to protect the Province against communistic propaganda." Civil rights organizations pressed the government at Ottawa to disallow it, but this was not done.

(Assented to, the 24th of March, 1937)

. . .

3. It shall be illegal for any person, who possesses or occupies a house within the Province, to use it or allow any person to make use of it to propagate communism or bolshevism by any means whatsoever.

4. The Attorney-General, upon satisfactory proof that an infringement of section 3 has been committed, may order the closing of the house against its use for any purpose whatsoever for a period of not more than one year; the closing order shall be registered at the registry office of the registration division wherein is situated such house, upon production of a copy of such order certified by the Attorney-General. . . .

12. It shall be unlawful to print, to publish in any manner whatsoever or to distribute in the Province any newspaper, periodical, pamphlet, circular, document or writing whatsoever propagating or tending to propagate communism or bolshevism.

13. Any person infringing or participating in the infringement of section 12 shall be liable to an imprisonment of not less than three months nor more than twelve months, in addition to the costs of prosecution, and, in default of payment of such costs, to an additional imprisonment of one month. . . .

14. Any constable or peace officer, upon instructions of the Attorney-General, of his substitute or of a person specially authorized by him for the purpose, may seize and confiscate any newspaper, peri-

odical, pamphlet, circular, document or writing whatsoever, printed, published or distributed in contravention of section 12, and the Attorney-General may order the destroying thereof. . . .

54. Extracts from the Report of the Archambault Commission, 1938

(Report of the Royal Commission to Investigate the Penal System of Canada, Ottawa, 1938)

A commission, presided over by Mr. Justice Joseph Archambault of the Quebec Superior Court, was appointed in 1936 to report upon Canada's much-criticized penal system. Its report raised a standard of reform and has served as the basis for a gradual improvement of the system. A new Penitentiary Act passed in 1939 (3 George VI, Chap. 6) embodied its recommendation of substituting for the former Superintendent of Penitentiaries a three-man Penitentiary Commission under the Minister of Justice. This Act was to come into effect when proclaimed, but it was not proclaimed because of the outbreak of war (see the statement of Mr. St. Laurent, House of Commons, 9 November 1945). It came into effect after the passage in 1945 of an amending act (9-10 George VI, Chap. 28). A basic recommendation of the Archambault Commission, the centralization of the penal system under federal control, has never been carried out.

. . .

SUMMARY OF RECOMMENDATIONS

. . . The *underlying principle* to be followed in interpreting the recommendations contained in this report is to evolve a penal system with the primary purpose of protecting society. It is of the greatest importance that this system should be characterized by that firm dignity that is traditional in the British administration of justice. There is no place in it for weak sentimentality or for cruel severity.

Centralized Control

1. The Canadian penal system should be centralized under the control of the Government of Canada, with the federal authorities taking charge of all the prisons in Canada, the provinces retaining only a sufficient number to provide for offenders against provincial statutes, prisoners on remand, and those serving short sentences.

2. An immediate conference between the federal and provincial authorities should be held with a view to obtaining the full co-operation of the provincial authorities in putting the recommendations of the Commission into effect.

Reorganization of Administration

3. There should be a complete reorganization of the headquarters administration of Canadian penitentiaries to include giving effect to the recommendations in this report as to the retirement of certain officers.

4. A Prison Commission, composed of three members removable only for cause, should be appointed with full authority over the management of penitentiaries, empowered to appoint staff, and to act as a central parole board. The Commission should be responsible directly to the Minister of Justice and to Parliament. . . .

6. A planned reconstruction of the personnel of the penitentiary staffs throughout Canada should be effected in order that officers who have special training will be enlisted in the service. . . .

8. A training school for penitentiary officers should be established on the lines of the courses at Wakefield, England. . . .

10. After careful study of the penitentiary staffs by the Prison Commission, all hopelessly incapable officers should be retired.

11. New officers to fill vacancies in the penitentiary service should be selected on a merit basis only and no consideration should be given to political influence.

12. The pay of officers should be brought up to a reasonable standard, having regard to the type of service performed. . . .

14. There should be a thorough and complete revision of the penitentiary rules and regulations based on the principles contained in this report, with special regard to:

(*a*) the protection of society;

(*b*) the safe custody of inmates;

(*c*) strict but humane discipline;

(*d*) reformation and rehabilitation of prisoners.

15. An official Board of Visitors should be appointed in connection with each penitentiary. This board should be composed of a county court judge (in Quebec, a judge of the Court of Sessions), a representative of an officially recognized social welfare association, and a medical doctor. It should be under the control of the Prison Commission, and its duties should be similar to those of the boards of visitors appointed in connection with the convict prisons in England.

Classification

16. A complete revision of the methods of classification of prisoners should be made, with provision for a thorough medical and psychiatric examination of prisoners.

17. The necessary legislation should be enacted to provide for sentencing habitual offenders to preventive detention in a separate institution to be provided for that purpose.

18. All incorrigible and intractable prisoners in the penitentiaries should be segregated in one institution.

19. Separate institutions, based on the principles of the English Borstal system, should be established to permit of special treatment being given to young offenders between sixteen and twenty-one years of age. . . .

20. All insane prisoners should be entirely removed from the prison population and treated in hospitals for the insane.

21. The mentally deficient should be segregated in the ordinary institutions under the direction of a trained psychiatrist. . . .

Prison Discipline

25. Prison offences should be tried before a prison court composed of three officers and there should be a right of appeal to the Board of Visitors. The rules governing prison offences should be simplified.

26. Corporal punishment should be abolished except for the offences of assaulting an officer, mutiny, and incitement to mutiny. . . .

Use of Firearms

29. The principle contained in the International Standard Minimum Rules in regard to the use of firearms should be strictly adhered to, namely, — "Officials should never use their firearms nor force against a prisoner except in self-defence, or in cases of attempted escape when this cannot be prevented in any other way. The use of force should always be restricted to what is necessary.". . .

32. Gun cages in the shops and chapels should be abolished from all institutions except those for incorrigible or habitual offenders.

Recreation

33. Provision should be made for more outdoor physical exercise . . . with recreational games permitted according to the age and classification of prisoners. Further provision should be made . . . for more indoor recreation. . . .

34. Visiting and writing privileges should be extended. . . .

Education

37. A complete reorganization of the educational system should be made . . . with special consideration for the young offenders, more frequent library privileges, and a simplified system of book distribution.

Medical service

38. The medical service should be reorganized. . . .

39. After a careful survey of their respective requirements by the Prison Commission, provision should be made for psychiatric services at all penitentiaries. . . .

Prison Employment

42. A complete reorganization of prison industries should be made in all Canadian penal institutions.

43. A thorough survey should be made to discover the requirements of the various government departments and institutions that can be supplied by properly equipped prison industries. . . .

Women Prisoners

55. Arrangements should be made with the provincial authorities for the confinement of women prisoners, such as are now incarcerated in the Women's Prison at Kingston, in provincial jails and reformatories for women. . . .

Amendments to the Criminal Code

57. A complete revision of the Criminal Code should be undertaken at once. . . .

Prevention of Crime

60. The appointment and discharge of police officers, whether federal, provincial, or municipal, and the administration of police departments should be entirely removed from the suspicion of political influence.

61. A definite system of training police officers along the lines now followed in Great Britain should be adopted in all provinces of Canada.

62. The interest of the public should be enlisted in an organized manner, having regard to the vital importance of the prevention of crime by reducing juvenile delinquency, and the assistance of social service agencies and churches and schools in co-operation with the home should be organized to this end.

63. The responsibility of the state for the financial support of community clubs, boys' and girls' clubs, and leisure time programs should be recognized. They are a means of preventing or, at least, reducing, juvenile and adolescent delinquency. . . .

B.
Police Organization

55. The Royal Canadian Mounted Police, 1919

(10 George V, Chap. 28)

By this amendment to the Royal Northwest Mounted Police Act Canada acquired for the first time a fully effective national police force. Unlike the R.N.W.M.P. which it replaced, which had operated only in the western provinces and the Territories, the Royal Canadian Mounted Police worked in all parts of the country. The Dominion Police, which had had its earliest origin in measures taken for border security during the American Civil War, ceased to exist. The word "Mounted" was retained for sentimental reasons connected with the popular reputation of the R.N.W.M.P.

(Assented to 10th November, 1919)

1. The Royal Northwest Mounted Police shall hereafter be called and known as The Royal Canadian Mounted Police, and wherever the words "Royal Northwest Mounted Police" occur in the Royal Northwest Mounted Police Act, chapter ninety-one of the Revised Statutes of Canada, 1906, and in the Acts in amendment thereof, the words "Royal Canadian Mounted Police" are substituted therefor.

2. . . . (2) Subsection one of section seven of the said Act is repealed and the following is substituted therefor: —

"7. (1) The headquarters of the Force shall be at such place as the Governor in Council from time to time appoints."*. . . .

(4) Subsection one of section fourteen of the said Act is amended by striking out the words "able to ride" in the second line thereof. . . .

3. (1) Notwithstanding the provisions of section fourteen of the said Act with respect to age, constables appointed under the provisions of the *Dominion Police Act*, chapter ninety-two of the Revised Statutes of Canada, 1906, and the Acts in amendment

*When the new Act came into effect on 1 February 1920, the headquarters was moved from Regina to Ottawa, where it has since remained.

thereof, shall be eligible for appointment as constables in the Royal Canadian Mounted Police. . . .

(3) No appointments shall hereafter be made of any Chief Commissioner of Police, Commissioner of Police or constable under the provisions of the said *Dominion Police Act.* . . .

IV.
Social Life and Institutions

A.
Population and the Growth of Cities

The statistics that follow demonstrate the comparatively slow growth of the population of Canada during the period, and the steadily increasing urbanization of the country.

56. Estimated Population of Canada, 1914-1945
(at 1 June) (in thousands)

(M. C. Urquhart and K. A. H. Buckley, eds., *Historical Statistics of Canada*, Cambridge and Toronto, 1965)

1914..........7,879	1925...........9,294	1936..........10,950
1915..........7,981	1926...........9,451	1937..........11,045
1916..........8,001	1927...........9,637	1938..........11,152
1917..........8,060	1928...........9,835	1939..........11,267
1918..........8,148	1929..........10,029	1940..........11,381
1919..........8,311	1930..........10,208	1941..........11,507
1920..........8,556	1931..........10,376	1942..........11,654
1921..........8,788	1932..........10,510	1943..........11,795
1922..........8,919	1933..........10,633	1944..........11,946
1923..........9,010	1934..........10,741	1945..........12,072
1924..........9,143	1935..........10,845	

57. Population, Rural and Urban, Census Years

(Urquhart and Buckley, *Historical Statistics of Canada*)

These figures are based on the 1956 census definition, which considerably extended the official definition of "urban"; see Urquhart and Buckley, p. 5.

Year	Urban	Rural	Total
1921	4,257,443	4,530,506	8,787,949
1931	5,574,005	4,802,781	10,376,786
1941	6,548,326	4,958,329	11,506,655

58. Population of Major Cities, Census Years

(*Canada Year Book*, 1946)

Figures for "greater cities," i.e. built-up areas centring on major municipalities, are available only beginning in 1931. The 1941 figures in general reflect the retardation of growth by the Depression.

	1921	1931	1941	"Greater cities" 1931	"Greater cities" 1941
Montreal	618,506	818,577	903,007	1,023,158	1,139,921
Toronto	521,893	631,207	667,457	810,467	900,491
Vancouver	163,220	246,593	275,353	308,340	351,491
Winnipeg	179,087	218,785	221,960	284,295	290,540
Hamilton	114,151	155,547	166,337	163,710	176,110
Ottawa	107,843	126,872	154,951	175,988	215,022
Quebec	95,193	130,594	150,757	172,517	200,814
Windsor	55,935	98,179	105,311	110,385	121,112
Edmonton	58,821	79,127	93,817		
Calgary	63,305	83,761	88,904		

B.
Trade Unionism and Labour Policy

59. Statistics of Trade Union Membership in Canada, 1914-1945

(Urquhart and Buckley, *Historical Statistics of Canada*)

Two points that emerge from this table are (a) the relative smallness of union membership throughout the period, and (b) the importance of the two world wars and the resultant industrialization of the country (see below, **98**) in expanding it. Specific factors making for expansion in the Second World War period were the aggressive organizing campaigns of the labour congresses and the encouragement given by government policy (below, **63**, **64**).

Year	Total union membership	(thousands) Membership in unions with international affiliation
1914	166.2	140.5
1915	143.3	114.7
1916	160.4	129.1
1917	204.6	164.9
1918	248.9	201.4
1919	378.0	260.2
1920	373.8	267.2
1921	313.3	222.9
1922	276.6	206.2
1923	278.1	203.8
1924	260.6	202.0
1925	271.1	199.8
1926	274.6	202.5
1927	290.3	204.4
1928	300.6	211.3

	Total	International
1929	319.5	230.4
1930	322.4	230.9
1931	310.5	215.9
1932	283.1	176.1
1933	285.7	167.7
1934	281.3	161.4
1935	280.6	143.6
1936	322.7	174.8
1937	383.5	217.5
1938	381.6	230.5
1939	359.0	216.7
1940	362.2	227.0
1941	461.7	288.0
1942	578.4	379.0
1943	664.5	425.4
1944	724.2	468.0
1945	711.1	471.0

60. Judgment of Judicial Committee of the Privy Council in *Toronto Electric Commissioners* v. *Snider*, 1925

(Richard A. Olmsted, ed., *Decisions of the Judicial Committee of the Privy Council relating to the British North America Act, 1867 and the Canadian Constitution, 1867-1954*, II, Ottawa, 1954)

This decision invalidated the Industrial Disputes Investigation Act of 1907 (6-7 Edward VII, Chap. 20), which was commonly called the Lemieux Act, though in fact it was largely the work of W. L. Mackenzie King, Lemieux's Deputy as Minister of Labour. The conciliation procedure which it provided had in general worked satisfactorily (see Volume IV of this series, and Dawson, *William Lyon Mackenzie King*, I). The decision, apart from its particular effect, is one of the landmarks in the Judicial Committee's progressive destruction of the Dominion government's general "peace, order and good government" powers under the British North America Act. Of Lord Haldane's retrospective comment on the judgment in *Russell* v. *The Queen* (the closest the Judicial Committee ever came to mere flippancy in a Canadian decision) Mr. Justice Bora Laskin has said that "it has been well heaped with the ridicule it deserves" ("Peace, Order and Good Government Re-examined," *Canadian Bar Review*, 1947, reprinted in W. R. Lederman, ed., *The Courts and the Canadian Constitution*,

Toronto, 1964). Unfortunately the ridicule did not reduce the decision's legal effect. The Industrial Disputes Investigation Act was finally repealed by the Industrial Relations and Disputes Investigation Act (11-12 George VI, Chap. 54, assented to 30 June 1948), which was generally similar in its principles but applied only to disputes in enterprises "within the legislative authority of the Parliament of Canada" or lying within the scope of agreements with provincial governments.

. . .

VISCOUNT HALDANE. It is always with reluctance that their Lordships come to a conclusion adverse to the constitutional validity of any Canadian statute that has been before the public for years as having been validly enacted; but the duty incumbent on the Judicial Committee, now as always, is simply to interpret the British North America Act and to decide whether the statute in question has been within the competence of the Dominion Parliament under the terms of s. 91 of that Act. In this case the Judicial Committee have come to the conclusion that it was not. To that conclusion they find themselves compelled, alike by the structure of s. 91 and by the interpretation of its terms that has now been established by a series of authorities. They have had the advantage not only of hearing full arguments on the question, but of having before them judgments in the Courts of Ontario, from which this appeal to the Sovereign in Council came directly. . . .

The particular exercise of legislative power with which their Lordships are concerned is contained in a well-known Act, passed by the Dominion Parliament in 1907, and known as the Industrial Disputes Investigation Act. . . .

. . . It is, in their Lordships' opinion, now clear that, excepting so far as the power can be invoked in aid of capacity conferred independently under other words in s. 91, the power to regulate trade and commerce cannot be relied on as enabling the Dominion Parliament to regulate civil rights in the Provinces.

A more difficult question arises with reference to the initial words of s. 91, which enable the Parliament of Canada to make laws for the peace, order and good government of Canada in matters falling outside the Provincial powers specifically conferred by s. 92. For *Russell* v. *The Queen* was a decision in which the Judicial Committee said that it was within the competency of the Dominion Parliament to establish a uniform system for prohibiting the liquor traffic throughout Canada excepting under restrictive conditions. It has been observed subsequently by this Committee that it is now clear that it was on the ground that the subject matter lay outside Provincial powers, and not on the ground that it was authorized as legislation for the regulation of trade and commerce, that the Canada Temperance Act was sustained: see *Attorney-General for Canada* v. *Attorney-General for Alberta*. But even on this footing it is not easy to reconcile the decision in *Russell* v. *The Queen* with the subsequent decision in *Hodge* v. *The Queen* that the Ontario Liquor Licence Act, with the powers of regulation which it entrusted to local authorities in the Province, was intra vires of the Ontario Legislature. Still more difficult is it to reconcile *Russell* v. *The Queen* with the decision given later by the Judicial Committee that the Dominion licensing statute, known as the McCarthy Act, which sought to establish a local licensing system throughout the Dominion, was ultra vires of the Dominion Parliament. . . .

It appears to their Lordships that it is not now open to them to treat *Russell* v. *The Queen* as having established the general principle that the mere fact that Dominion legislation is for the general advantage of Canada, or is such that it will meet a mere want which is felt throughout the Dominion, renders it competent if it cannot be brought within the heads enumerated specifically in s. 91. Unless this is so, if the subject matter falls within any of the enumerated heads in s. 92, such legislation belongs exclusively to Provincial competency. No doubt there may be cases arising out of some extraordinary peril to the national life of Canada, as a whole, such as the cases arising out of a war, where legislation is required of an order that passes beyond the heads of exclusive Provincial competency. Such cases may be dealt with under the words at the commencement of s. 91, conferring general powers in relation to peace, order and good government, simply because such cases are not otherwise provided for. . . . Their Lordships think that the decision in *Russell* v. *The Queen* can only be supported to-day, not on the footing of having laid down an interpretation, such as has sometimes been invoked of the general words at the beginning of s. 91, but on the assumption of the Board, apparently made at the time of deciding the case of *Russell* v. *The Queen*, that the evil of intemperance at that time amounted in Canada to one so great and so general that at least for the period it was a menace to the national life of Canada so serious and pressing that the National Parliament was called on to intervene to protect the nation from disaster. An epidemic of pestilence might conceivably have been regarded as analogous. . . .

61. The Fair Wages and Eight Hour Day Act, 1930

(20-21 George V, Chap. 20)

This Act passed shortly before the dissolution of Parliament in 1930 may be interpreted as one of those moves in the direction of a liberal social policy which Mackenzie King tended to make at moments when they were likely to be politically advantageous.

(Assented to 30th May, 1930)

. . .

3. (1) Every contract made hereafter with the Government of Canada for construction, remodelling, repair or demolition of any work shall be subject to the following conditions respecting wages and hours:—

   (*a*) All persons in the employ of the contractor, sub-contractor, or of any other person doing or contracting to do the whole or any part of the work contemplated in the contract shall be paid such wages as are generally accepted as current from time to time for competent workmen in the district in which the work is being performed for the character or class of work in which they are respectively engaged; provided that wages shall in all cases be such as are fair and reasonable;

   (*b*) The working hours of persons while so employed shall not exceed eight hours per day except in such special cases as the Governor in Council may otherwise provide, or except in cases of emergency, as may be approved by the Minister [of Labour]. . . .

4. The wages and hours of all workmen employed by the Government of Canada on such works as are described in section three, and who are excluded from the operation of the *Civil Service Act,* shall be those set forth in paragraphs (*a*) and (*b*) of section three.

5. (1) The Governor in Council, on the recommendation of the Minister, may make regulations with regard to wages and hours herein provided for and without limiting the generality of the foregoing may provide by regulation for,—

   (*a*) the method of determining what are current or fair and reasonable wages and the preparation and use of schedules of rates relating thereto;

   (*b*) rates of wages for overtime;

   (*c*) classifications of employment or work;

   (*d*) the publication and posting of wage schedules;

   (*e*) payment of wages to employees in case of default by the contractor or other party charged with such payment and recovery thereof from such contractor or other party;

(f) the keeping of proper books and records and the examination of the same by Government officers;

(g) persons who may be employed on works referred to in this Act;

(h) the subletting of contracts;

(i) the penalties to be imposed for breaches of the provisions of this Act or regulations made hereunder;

(j) generally for the due enforcement of the provisions of the Act and regulations....

62. Premier Hepburn Defies the C.I.O., 1937

(Statement by Premier Hepburn, *Globe and Mail*, Toronto, 9 April 1937)

Probably the most important development in trade unionism during the period covered by this volume was the rise of industrial unionism as distinguished from the older organizations based on crafts. In 1935 the Committee for Industrial Organization (later Congress of Industrial Organizations) (C.I.O.) was formed in the United States under the aggressive leadership of John L. Lewis. Its Canadian affiliates came into prominence as a result of the attack by Premier Mitchell F. Hepburn of Ontario arising out of a United Automobile Workers' strike at Oshawa. Hepburn dismissed two members of his cabinet, J. A. Roebuck and David Croll, who disagreed with his attitude. The affair recalls the apprehensions aroused by the "One Big Union" movement in 1919 (below, **68**). Whatever may be thought of Hepburn's performance in retrospect, it received much contemporary support and undoubtedly won him the Ontario election of October 1937. See Neil McKenty, *Mitch Hepburn* (Toronto, 1967).

The Government regrets very much that the employees of General Motors have seen fit to follow the suggestions of the C.I.O. paid propagandists from the United States, and to desert their posts at a time when both the employees and the industry itself were in a position to enjoy a prosperity not known since 1929....

This is the first open attempt on the part of [John L.] Lewis and his C.I.O. to assume the position of dominating and dictating to Canadian industry. The Government completely concurs in the attitude of the company that it is going to remain clear of the domination of professional labor profiteers of the C.I.O., who are making an effort to exact their monthly toll from the pay envelopes of the Oshawa workers. . . .

After reviewing the activities of these foreign agitators, and the chaos created by them in the United States, I am satisfied that the policy as dictated by them will be one of ever-increasing and impossible demands, culminating in the course of time in the entire loss of the tremendous and increasing export trade now being enjoyed by the automobile industry of Ontario. There is no reason why Ontario companies should be placed in the position of having to submit to foreign jurisdiction. . . .

This morning the company's executives were refused admission to the plant. This in itself constitutes the first illegal act, and I hope it will be the last.

However, the Government is taking every precaution and has already enlisted the support of the Ottawa Government, and there will be available sufficient police to maintain law and order. . . .*

63. The Canadian Congress of Labour, 1940

(*Labour Gazette*, October 1940)

In 1936 in the United States the unions participating in the C.I.O. (above, **62**) were expelled from the American Federation of Labor. This was paralleled in Canada in 1939, when the Canadian unions adhering to the C.I.O. were expelled from the Canada Trades and Labour Congress. The following year, as noted here, the All-Canadian Congress of Labour (established in 1927) formed with the C.I.O. unions the Canadian Congress of Labour. Not until 1956 did the T.L.C. and C.C.L. come together as the Canadian Labour Congress. See H. A. Logan, *Trade Unions in Canada: Their Development and Functioning* (Toronto, 1948).

The tenth regular convention of the All-Canadian Congress of Labour was held at Toronto, Ont., on September 9-12. . . .

In opening his address the president [A. R. Mosher] referred briefly to the establishment of the All-Canadian Congress of Labour and to the Congress of Industrial Organizations. Mention was made

*The federal government sent a force of Royal Canadian Mounted Police to Toronto, where they were held in readiness. Hepburn himself enrolled a body of special constables. But there was no disorder whatever during the strike.

of the expulsion by the Trades and Labour Congress of Canada of the membership of Canadian locals affiliated with the C.I.O., and it was President Mosher's contention that in the normal course of events these locals would have established, for legislative purposes, a central body in Canada somewhat similar to the Trades and Labour Congress. The delegates were informed that to facilitate the Canadian locals taking whatever action they deemed best, the international industrial unions granted them complete autonomy in so far as legislative matters were concerned. The president reviewed the steps leading up to the affiliation of these bodies with the Congress necessitating the changing of the constitution to provide for the establishment of a new Congress.

In reviewing the progress of the war, President Mosher stated that "as Canadian workers and Canadian citizens, we believe that the primary consideration which should be in our minds at this time is the winning of the war." The speaker contended "that the greatest service which we can render to Canada is to organize the largest possible number of workers in the shortest possible time, and to obtain for them adequate representation in the councils of the nation, both in peace and war.". . .

The report of the executive . . . reviewed the steps leading up to formation of a provisional committee of six members, three from the Congress and three from the Canadian Committee of Industrial Organizations, to complete negotiations and draw up a new draft constitution. . . .

The aims and objects of the new Congress, as outlined in the preamble to the constitution, are as follows:

Whereas the workers of Canada are entitled to freedom of organization, full rights of collective bargaining, and economic security for themselves and their dependents;

And whereas, for the attainment of these objectives, effective organization of the workers is essential in both the economic and legislative fields;

And whereas division of the forces of the workers and ineffective forms of organization retard their efforts to accomplish their purposes;

And whereas all Canadian workers, organized into unions of their own choice, Local, National or International, should be afforded the fullest opportunity to unite for their common benefit, so that by their full participation and co-operation in one central body the economic and social welfare of the workers of Canada may be secured and protected:

Be it therefore resolved that we, in convention assembled, establish for the benefit of all Canadian workers a central labour body to be known as The Canadian Congress of Labour.

The purposes of the Congress are set forth in the following sections of the constitution:

Section 1. — The purposes of the Congress shall be to promote the interests of its affiliates and generally to advance the economic and social welfare of the workers of Canada.

Section 2. — It shall seek to accomplish this in the economic field by developing the widest and the most effective organization of the workers, establishing wherever necessary, Organizing Committees for this purpose, and assisting existing unions to organize the unorganized workers in their respective industries. It shall, at all times, promote the principle of organization within an industry. It shall, co-operating with its affiliates, establish special funds and furnish other assistance for the purpose of carrying out the organizing objectives of the Congress....

Membership in the organization was established on the following basis:

Section 1. — Any bona-fide organization of Canadian workers, whether Local, National or International in character, shall be eligible for membership in the Congress.

Section 2. — Any body of ten or more workers, not a part of any National or International union, may be chartered directly by the Congress as a Local union.

Section 3. — Any National union or Locals thereof, the Canadian Locals of any International union, and any union temporarily functioning as an Organizing Committee, or Local branches thereof, may affiliate with the Congress, either directly or through the appropriate executive or other Canadian central body of such National or International union or Organizing Committee....

64. Summary of the Wartime Labour Relations Order, 1944

(*Labour Gazette*, February 1944)

From the outbreak of war in 1939 the King government followed a labour policy designed to avoid industrial strife, a policy which was embodied in a series of orders in council (see Logan, *Trade Unions in Canada*, pp. 15-17). This policy may be said to have been codified in order P.C. 1003 of 17 February 1944. The order itself is printed in the same issue of the *Labour Gazette* as the summary reproduced here, which is given for the sake of brevity.

A Dominion-wide measure to provide for compulsory collective bargaining between employers and employees in war industry and procedure for the settlement of industrial disputes was tabled in the House of Commons recently by the Honourable Humphrey Mitchell, Minister of Labour. The measure is in the form of an order in council, to be known as the Wartime Labour Relations Order (P.C. 1003, Feb. 17, 1944, passed under the authority of the War Measures Act).

Recommendations for a measure of this kind were made by the National War Labour Board. . . . Following receipt of these recommendations, copies of the report were forwarded to the provincial governments and a three-day conference between the Dominion and Provincial Ministers of Labour and their officers was held in Ottawa in November last at which these recommendations and the further proposals submitted by the Dominion Department of Labour arising therefrom were discussed.

Subsequently, and in accordance with the arrangements arrived at at the conference, a draft of the proposed Labour Relations Regulations was sent out to the provinces, and the national trade union organizations and the major employers' organizations with a request for a full expression of the views and suggestions of such parties in reference to the same.

The present regulations represent the final result following from the various steps so taken. . . .

SUMMARY OF REGULATIONS

The regulations will be administered by a Board to be known as the Wartime Labour Relations Board to consist of a Chairman, a Vice-Chairman and not more than eight other members.

The regulations apply to the following classes of employers and their employees:

Firstly, employers in industries of a National or interprovincial character which are ordinarily within Dominion jurisdiction and including crown companies engaged in the handling or manufacture of war supplies;

Secondly, employers in war industries as such industries are described in the regulations or subsequently added to by the Governor-in-Council as the result of later experience or changed wartime conditions;

Thirdly, all other industry within a province where such province by appropriate legislative action brings the same within the scope of the regulations.

In other words the Dominion Government has under these regulations extended its jurisdiction over employer-employee relations which are normally exclusively within the provincial field, to the extent considered necessary to adequately cover employer and employees in war industry but without attempting to include other industry which has not a direct bearing on war production.

In so far as these latter industries are concerned, each province may make its own decision as to whether or not they shall be brought under the regulations.

Provision is made for an agreement between the Dominion and any province to set up suitable provincial administrative agencies to deal locally and promptly with matters of a local nature. The Dominion Board established under the regulations will, however, be responsible for the formulation of general policy and regulations to ensure necessary uniformity in the application of the regulations whether administered through the Board itself or through provincial agencies.

Provision for Compulsory Collective Bargaining

The provisions for compulsory collective bargaining and settlement of disputes include the following:

(i) A procedure is established for the election of bargaining representatives by a majority vote of employees and for the certification of such representatives by the Board;

(ii) Compulsory collective bargaining may then be initiated by either the employer or the bargaining representatives of the employees on notice to the other party and the parties are thereupon required to negotiate with each other in good faith to complete a collective agreement;

(iii) In event an agreement cannot be reached without outside assistance, conciliation services are provided initially by the use of a Conciliation Officer and subsequently, by the appointment of a Conciliation Board. Until bargaining representatives have been appointed and during the prescribed process of negotiation for collective agreement, strikes by employees are prohibited and, in like manner, lockouts by employers are prohibited during the period of negotiation. No provision has been provided for the imposition of a compulsory agreement by the Board binding upon the parties in event that no agreement is arrived at between them.

(iv) Negotiations for the renewal of an agreement may be initiated by notice by either party within the sixty-day period prior to the expiry thereof, and following upon such notice the parties must negotiate in good faith with each other for the renewal of the agreement.

(v) Where a collective agreement has been entered into, new bargaining representatives may not be elected until after ten months have elapsed.

Grievance Procedure and Settlement of Disputes

The provision made for the settlement of grievances and disputes is designed to place upon the employers and employees concerned the joint responsibility for the settlement thereof by their own action rather than by the imposition of a settlement by an outside agency.

In the first place the parties must provide in every collective agreement entered into hereafter for a procedure for the final settlement of grievances arising out of the application or violation of the terms of the agreement without stoppage of work, and in any instance where this is not so provided the Board is required to establish an appropriate procedure for this purpose. Resort to strikes or lockouts is accordingly unnecessary and is forbidden during the term of a collective agreement.

Where there is no collective agreement in effect and a dispute arises in respect of any change in existing conditions of employment proposed by an employer, a sixty-day delay is provided to enable the employees to elect bargaining representatives and for the initiation of collective bargaining proceedings.

Unfair Practices

Unfair practices on the part of employers and employees and trade unions or employees' organizations are defined and prohibited and penalties provided for failure to observe such prohibitions.

The prohibitions against employers include a prohibition against employers seeking to dominate or interfere with trade unions or employees' organizations or contributing financial support to them; against refusing to employ or discriminating against members of trade unions or employees' organizations; and against the dismissal of an employee for belonging to a trade union or employees' organization or exercising his rights as a member or officer thereof.

The prohibitions against trade unions and employees' organizations include a prohibition against the use of coercion or intimidation to join a trade union or employees' organization; against activities in working hours at the place of employment to persuade an employee to join a trade union or employees' organization, except with the consent of the employer; and from supporting, encouraging or engaging in a slowdown or other activities designed to restrict or limit production.

The Industrial Disputes Investigation Act* is to be of no effect while the Wartime Labour Relations Order is in force, except as to matters pending. Certain orders in council relating to matters covered by the new order are revoked or suspended.

*See above, p. 141.

C.
The Aftermath of the First World War

The tremendous upheaval of the war and Canada's deep involvement in it were certain to have consequences for society that would be felt for many years. Here two immediate phenomena are illustrated: the war's impact upon the social philosophy of the Canadian Methodist Church, and the troubles of 1919 in Winnipeg. On the remarkable explosion of radicalism within Canadian Methodism during the war, see J. M. Bliss, "The Methodist Church and World War I," *Canadian Historical Review*, September 1968.

The Winnipeg General Strike (15 May–25 June 1919) was the most extreme example of the outburst of social and industrial discontent, fanned by postwar disruptions, which affected many Canadian cities in 1919. Frightened politicians and citizens, with the Bolshevik success in Russia before their eyes, feared that the country was threatened with social revolution; these apprehensions are reflected in amendments to the Criminal Code and the Immigration Act (**52** and **82**). Whether the strike was really inspired to any considerable extent by revolutionary socialism, or whether it was mainly the product merely of local economic grievances and explosive temporary circumstances, is still discussed. See D. C. Masters, *The Winnipeg General Strike* (Toronto, 1950), and McNaught, *A Prophet in Politics*.

The social tempest of 1919 produced reform programs from various sources, including two royal commissions whose recommendations are quoted here. But the storm passed without eliciting much in the way of practical social reform; and some of the measures recommended were not taken until many years had passed. See the succeeding section, pp. 169-78.

65. The Methodist "Social Gospel," 1918

*(Journal of Proceedings of the Tenth General Conference of the Methodist Church . . .
October 2nd to 17th, 1918* (Toronto, 1918)

What follows is an extract from the approved report of the Tenth General Conference's committee on "The Church, The War and Patriotism." A statement of similar effect was produced by the committee on Evangelism and Social Service under the heading "The Lost Opportunity of Methodism."

. . .

II. — CHURCH LEADERSHIP IN THE NATION

. . . Without seeking at this time to commit the Church to a definite programme of economic policy, we would present for the consideration of our people the following statement which reflects our point of view:

1. The present economic system stands revealed as one of the roots of the war. The insane pride of Germany, her passion for world-domination found an occasion in the demand for colonies as markets and sources of raw materials — the imperative need of competing groups of industries carried on for profits.

2. The war has made more clearly manifest the moral perils inherent in the system of production for profits. Condemnation of special individuals seems often unjust and always futile. The system rather than the individual calls for change.

3. The war is the coronation of democracy. . . . The last century democratized politics; the 20th century has found that political democracy means little without economic democracy. The democratic control of industry is just and inevitable.

4. Under the shock and strain of this tremendous struggle, accepted commercial and industrial methods based on individualism and competition have gone down like mud walls in a flood. National organization, national control, extraordinary approximations of national equality have been found essential to efficiency. . . .

The conclusion seems irresistible. The war is a sterner teacher than Jesus and uses far other methods, but it teaches the same lesson. The social development which it has so unexpectedly accelerated has the same goal as Christianity, that common goal is a nation of comrade workers, as now at the trenches, fights so gloriously — a nation of comrade fighters [*sic*].

With the earthquake shocks of the war thundering so tremendous a reaffirmation to the principles of Jesus, it would be the most inexcusable dereliction of duty on the part of the Church not to re-state her programme in modern terms and redefine her divinely-appointed goal.

The triumph of democracy, the demand of the educated workers for human conditions of life, the deep condemnation this war has passed on the competitive struggle, the revelation of the superior efficiency of rational organization and co-operation, combine with the unfulfilled, the often forgotten, but the undying ethics of Jesus, to demand nothing less than a transference of the whole economic life from a basis of competition and profits to one of co-operation and service.

We recognize the magnificent effort of many great employers to make their industrial organization a means of uplift and betterment to all who participate, but the human spirit instinctively resents even the most benevolent forms of government, while self-government is denied. The noblest humanitarian aims of employers, too, are often thwarted by the very conditions under which their business must be carried on.

That another system is practicable is shown by the recent statement of the British Prime Minister....

The British Government Commission has outlined a policy which, while accepting as a present fact the separation of capital and labor, definitely denies the right of sole control to the former and insisting on the full organization of workers and employers, vests the government of every industry in a joint board of employers and workers, which board shall determine the working conditions of that industry.

This policy has been officially adopted by the British Government and nothing less can be regarded as tolerable even now in Canada.

But we do not believe this separation of labor and capital can be permanent. Its transcendence, whether through co-operation or public ownership, seems to be the only constructive and radical reform.

This is the policy set forth by the great labor organizations and must not be rejected because it presupposes, as Jesus did, that the normal human spirit will respond more readily to the call to service than to the lure of private gain.

The acceptance of this report, it cannot be too clearly recognized, commits this Church, as far as this representative body can commit it, to nothing less than a complete social reconstruction. When it shall be fully accomplished, and through what measures and processes, depend on the thinking and the goodwill of men and, above all, on the guiding hand of God. But we think it is clear that nothing less than the goal we have outlined will satisfy the aroused moral consciousness of the Church or retain for the Church any leadership in the testing period that is upon them. And in such an heroic task as this our citizen armies will find it possible to preserve, under the conditions of peace, the high idealism with which they have fought for democracy in France. . . .

66. Winnipeg's Bloodiest Day

(*Manitoba Free Press*, 23 June 1919)

The disorders on 21 June which precipitated the intervention of federal forces and in fact led to the end of the strike were not the work of the Strike Committee but of "returned soldiers" supporting the strike. Some ex-soldiers were for it, others against it. In these extracts, some obvious misprints have been corrected.

One rioter shot dead — Mike Sokolowski, 552 Henry Avenue.
Between 60 and 70 persons injured; 30 treated in hospitals and scores in drug stores.
Upwards of 100 arrests, and many more pending.
These three brief sentences give the effect of the rioting in Winnipeg on Saturday afternoon, when Main street, opposite the City Hall, was the scene of the culmination of the disturbances which have disfigured the history of the city since the general sympathetic strike began over five weeks ago. . . .

Mayor's Statement

On Saturday night Mayor [Charles F.] Gray gave out the following statement covering the day's riots:
. . . At about half-past ten a.m. [on the 21st] I was called to the rooms at the Royal Alexandra hotel of the minister of labor, Senator [Gideon] Robertson, and there met Commissioner [A. Bowen] Perry of the Royal Northwest Mounted Police; A. J. Andrews, K.C., local deputy minister of justice, and a committee of returned soldier strikers. . . .
This committee again* asked me for permission to parade, but I absolutely refused. They then asked me to pull the street cars off the

*Newspapers of 21 June carried a proclamation by Mayor Gray reiterating a former proclamation "that there shall be no parades until the end of the strike."

street. This I also refused. They then stated they would have a parade anyway, and I remarked that I would have to stop it peacefully if possible — if not, other measures would have to be taken.

I was there until about a quarter to two in the afternoon when the chief of police rang me up and told me large crowds were gathering. I immediately repaired to the city hall and so advised the chief. A few minutes later we communicated again over the telephone, when it developed that it was not likely that with the special police at his disposal he could control the crowd, now swelled to many thousands. I, therefore, suggested that the R.N.W.M.P. should parade the streets, in which he concurred. I at once drove to R.N.W.M.P. headquarters and in presence of the provincial attorney-general asked Commissioner Perry to aid the civil police in the prevention and, if need be, the quelling of riot.

I returned to the city hall and some little time later witnessed the arrival of the Mounted Police, who in open formation advanced north up Main street. They endeavored to disperse the crowds, but were booed and jeered, and when after proceeding north a couple of blocks, they returned, they were pelted with stones and bottles by the mob. When at about twenty-five minutes to three I noticed that the Mounted Police were being hard pressed by a rabble of aliens, I read from the parapet of the city hall the riot act in the prescribed manner.

Before re-entering the building — that is to say two or three minutes later — I heard a few scattered shots, and as the R.N.W.M.P. at this time had not received the order to draw their revolvers, I presume these came from the mob.

As conditions were rapidly approaching a serious tumult, I immediately drove to Fort Osborne barracks, asked for Brigadier-General [H. D. B.] Ketchen, General Officer Commanding Military District No. 10, signed in the prescribed manner my papers for calling out the military in aid of the civil authority to quell riots, and handed same to General Ketchen. . . .

While in barracks, I received a report from the Officer Commanding the R.N.W.M.P. that his force had been so hard pressed that he had deemed it advisable to fire a volley into the crowd,* and that this resulted in a temporary check of close hostilities.

General Ketchen at once turned out a military force which I accom-

---

*A high proportion of the individuals mentioned in the casualty list in the *Free Press* of 23 June as wounded by bullets are shown as hit in the leg or foot, suggesting that the fire was pretty carefully controlled. Most of the names are Anglo-Saxon.

panied as Chief Magistrate. On arriving at the corner of Portage avenue and Main street this force supported in column of route the R.N.W.M.P. who proceeded to clear Main street as far as St. John's avenue in the north end. . . .

67. Extract from the Report of the Mathers Commission, 1919

(Report of Commission appointed...to enquire into Industrial Relations in Canada..., supplement to *Labour Gazette,* July 1919)

While the Winnipeg Strike was in progress a Dominion royal commission appointed in April 1919 and headed by Chief Justice T. G. Mathers of Manitoba was urgently investigating the state of industrial relations in the country at large; its report was signed three days after the strike ended. It deserves to be called a prescient document; but apart from the fact that some of its recommendations (e.g., proportional representation) have never found acceptance, others (e.g., unemployment insurance) waited until another war to be realized.

. . .

16. . . . That serious unrest does exist is abundantly established by witnesses representing different shades of opinion and by the number of labour disputes which have taken place during the last few months, some of which are still pending and others threatening.

17. The unrest is most pronounced in western Canada. There it assumes a distinctly different character from that which prevails in eastern Canada. In several western cities labour was represented by many holding extreme radical views. Undoubtedly a portion of the labour unrest at present prevailing is to be ascribed to the upheavals in Europe and the disturbed state of the public mind generally owing to the war. This has given rise to a desire on the part of workers generally to secure a position for themselves in a comparatively short period of time, which otherwise might have been the result of evolution during a long period of years. This desire varies in degree amongst different groups of workers. One group lays down as a principle the complete possession by themselves of the machinery of production and the full product of their toil, whilst the group at the

other extreme would be satisfied with merely a larger purchasing power of the wages they receive. In between these groups lie the more moderate, and we believe the majority, who would welcome co-operation and industrial peace until by a gradual process of evolution a system may be ushered in by which the workers will receive a more adequate share of what their labour produces.

18. Many employers are in agreement with the workers as to the need for an ultimate change in the basis of industry, but are not in agreement as to how to achieve this object.

19. All changes should be made step by step, because we can only see a little way ahead, and each successive step should be based on the experience gained by the steps already made. At the same time we should determine the general direction in which we want to go, which should be towards the health, happiness and prosperity of the workers and the service of the community.

20. The workers of this country are devoting a great deal of thought to the study of economic questions. This educational process is apparently going on amongst them to a greater extent than amongst the employers of labour. Some of the literature read may not be sound, and the mental training of some of the workers may not be of a nature to enable them to thoroughly understand it, yet we are convinced that the good sense and sound judgment of the workers enable them to discriminate between what is sound and what is unsound. For this reason, extreme doctrines have not been accepted by any but a minority of the working people. Though the advocacy of extreme views both by speech and by the distribution of literature may be a contributing cause to occasional outbursts, the real causes of unrest are of a more fundamental nature.

21. The chief causes of unrest may be enumerated as follows:
   1. Unemployment and the fear of unemployment.
   2. High cost of living in relation to wages and the desire of the worker for a larger share of the product of his labour.
   3. Desire for shorter hours of labour.
   4. Denial of the right to organize and refusal to recognize Unions.
   5. Denial of collective bargaining.
   6. Lack of confidence in constituted government.
   7. Insufficient and poor housing.
   8. Restrictions upon the freedom of speech and press.
   9. Ostentatious display of wealth.
   10. Lack of equal educational opportunities. . . .

SUMMARY

For convenient reference we list below our conclusions: —

We recommend that legislation be enacted to provide for:

(a) Fixing of a minimum wage, specially for women, girls, and unskilled labour. (Par. 46.)

(b) Maximum work day of 8 hours and weekly rest of not less than 24 hours. (Par. 52.)

We recommend immediate enquiry by expert boards into the following subjects, with a view to early legislation:

(a) State insurance against unemployment, sickness, invalidity and old age. (Par. 36.)

(b) Proportional representation. (Par. 68.)

We recommend that suitable action be taken by the Government to:

(a) Regulate public works to relieve unemployment. (Par. 31.)

(b) Help the building of workers' homes. (Par. 69.)

(c) Establish a bureau for promoting Industrial Councils. (Par. 99.)

(d) Restore fullest liberty of freedom of speech and press. (Par. 70.)

Other general recommendations are:

(a) Right to organize. Recognition of Unions. (Par. 59.)

(b) Payment of a living wage. (Par. 44.)

(c) Collective bargaining. (Par. 65.)

(d) Extension of equal opportunities in education. (Par. 72.)

(e) Steps towards establishment of Joint Plant and Industrial Councils. (Pars. 85 and 98.)

(f) That the findings of the Commission be put into effect in all work controlled by the Government where the principles of democratic management can be applied....

In conclusion, your Commissioners desire to say that they have had a unique opportunity of observing the manufacturing, mining and agricultural resources of this country. They were impressed by the variety, magnitude and character of many of the manufacturing and industrial plants visited, and by the enterprise displayed in their operation. What is required to make the Dominion great and prosperous and its population contented and happy is a spirit of co-operation on fair and equitable lines amongst all classes. We have suggested a means by which co-operation may be promoted; but the worker is looking forward to a changed condition of life and a new status in industry, and we must be prepared to meet the changing conditions as they arise, in the same spirit of co-operation and good will.

The nations of the world by the Peace Treaty have adopted principles which until now were but ideals. As Canada is just entering the stage of greatest development we have an opportunity unique among the nations for growth in harmony with those new principles. . . .

(Signed),

T. G. MATHERS, Chairman.
CARL RIORDON,
CHAS. R. HARRISON,
TOM MOORE,
JOHN W. BRUCE.

THOS. BENGOUGH,
        Secretary.

68. Extracts from the Robson Commission's Report, 1919

(*Royal Commission to Enquire into and Report upon the Causes and Effects of the General Strike which recently existed in the City of Winnipeg ... Report of H. A. Robson, K.C., Commissioner* [Winnipeg, 1919])

The government of Manitoba appointed H. A. Robson to investigate the strike. When he wrote his report the trials of eight strike leaders for seditious conspiracy were pending, and this doubtless led him to write in more general terms than he might otherwise have done. (Seven of the eight were convicted, one of them on only one of seven counts.) The conclusions are in many ways similar to those of the Mathers report (above, **67**).

. . .

The specific and immediate cause of the general strike was the refusal by the employers in the Iron Contract shops to recognize the demands of the workers for agreement by those employers on the method of collective bargaining indicated by the Metal Trades Council on behalf of the employees. The general concurrence of labour therein and the determination upon a general strike was due to the mood in which workers of all classes were at that particular time. Labour considered the refusal of the demand for collective bargaining as claimed by the Metal Trades Council to be a blow struck at Labour organization. . . .

The general discontent among Labour has been very acute in and about Winnipeg. It has been fomented by the Socialist leaders hereafter referred to....

The conditions of certain branches of Labour in Winnipeg at the time of the Strike and to which he attributed the Strike was described by Mr. James Winning, who was, at the time of the Strike, President of the [Winnipeg] Trades and Labour Council. Mr. Winning made a concise but comprehensive statement at one of the hearings.... I have no doubt it gives a true and unexaggerated delineation of the mind of Labour in Winnipeg immediately prior to the Strike.... Mr. Winning said:

> A. "Labour was very much dissatisfied—dissatisfied with conditions as they existed. The cause of the dissatis-faction was, in my opinion—or at least one of the causes—was unemployment. Another cause was the high cost of liv-ing; lack of the Government to give adequate relief; long hours of employment, inadequate wages, undesirable work-ing conditions, profiteering, the growing intelligence on the part of the working class of economic inequalities in mod-ern society; the refusal on the part of some of the employers to recognize the right of the employee to organize labour; the refusal on the part of the employers to recognize the right of collective bargaining, and probably a great many other causes; those are some of the causes that I feel were directly the cause of the unrest which was prevalent before the strike took place in May.
>
> Now, if I may be permitted to say so, unemployment or the insecurity of a man's job is the greatest nightmare of the working class. When a man is out of a job he gets into debt....
>
> The cost of living, as everybody knows, has been reaching the sky-lights this last four or five years, and the wages which the workers have been receiving from time to time have not been adequate to cope with this high cost of living, the result is, that when a man does get a job he is in debt and he has got to strain himself with those inadequate wages which he receives when he gets the job, to clear off that debt. . . ."

There has for a long time past existed in Winnipeg an element which strongly advocated socialistic views. The group of men who have forced themselves to the front in that way directed their energies towards the conversion of [sic] their ideas of the working classes of Winnipeg. They were particularly successful with the foreign element and, since the revolutions in Europe gave point to socialistic propaganda, Europeans of the Russian and Austrian type in this country were most willing disciples of these leaders.... The Socialistic leaders were not in the true sense labour leaders. It was unfortunate that, from different causes, genuine labour was given the appearance of being linked up with the movements of these men.... These leaders made the utmost use of the Strike to advance their plans. They attempted to convert the Strike into a practical socialistic movement and to thrust themselves into its leadership. It is not hard to understand how the foreign element in the workers followed this leadership immediately when the Strike was declared, but it is impossible to believe that the great mass of workers, intelligent and loyal to British institutions, and who accepted the existing order of things, no matter how discontented they were, acquiesced in all that was said and done....

The official publication of the Winnipeg Trades and Labour Council, known as the "Western Labour News," a weekly newspaper, had in August, 1918, succeeded a paper known as "The Voice," formerly published by a private company in the interests of labour.

The new paper almost from its inception up to the date of the General Strike bears the ear-marks of a frankly socialistic publication rather than that of an advocate of Trade Unionism and its principles...

A perusal of the files of this paper from the date of its first issue until the day upon which the General Strike was called, leads the undersigned to conclude that it played a large part in fanning the discontent of the working class, and bringing this discontent to such a pitch, that as a class, the working people of Winnipeg were in an extremely receptive mood when the proposal of the General Strike was brought before them.

Mention must here be made of the part this publication played in the advocacy of the organization known as the "One Big Union.".....

The proceedings of the Calgary [Labour] Convention [of March 1919] were lengthy and a long report was published in the issue of the paper on March 21st.... It was at this Convention that the decision was reached to take a vote of Union Labour in Western Canada upon the question of severing the affiliation of the various craft unions from their Internationals and forming all classes of workers into one big union, that is, craft unionism was to be displaced by industrial unionism....

The aim of the One Big Union movement as stated in the editorial column of the "Western Labour News" in its issue of May 16th . . . was stated as follows: "The aim of this movement is the securing of the control of industry by all who work through industrial organization. Nothing short of the ultimate elimination of the profit system will satisfy Labour."

It may be stated generally as a result of a perusal of the columns of the "Western Labour News" from its inception in August, 1918, to May 16, 1919, that its character throughout was toward radical social-ism rather than craft unionism. . . . The circulation of this newspaper undoubtedly had a large part in stirring up discontent and bringing it to a head. . . .

The direction of the Strike was in the hands of a Central Strike Committee of fifteen elected by a larger General Strike Committee consisting of three delegates from each affiliated union, which latter body exercised supervision over the activities of the smaller body. . . .

It should be said that the leaders who had brought about the Gen-eral Strike were not responsible for the parades or riots which took place, and, in fact, tried to prevent them. The leaders' policy was peaceful idleness, but turbulent persons affected by this extraordi-nary condition broke loose and were responsible for the street dem-onstrations and violence that took place during the Strike. . . .

Mr. Winning states as one of the causes of the discontent which brought about the Strike, the growing intelligence on the part of the working class of economic inequalities in modern society. This may mean that Labour does not get its due compensation out of the results of its efforts. . . . To Labour the picture presented is this:

The other elements of the community never seem to be in want, neither in the matter of food, clothing, suitable residence, education, medical and other professional attention, or even recreation, yet Labour is not only never assured but is very often deprived of the essentials of these things. The matter could be elaborated in detail. Winnipeg unfortunately presents a prominent example of these extremes. There has been, and there is now, an increasing display of carefree, idle luxury and extravagance on the one hand, while on the other is intensified deprivation. . . .

It must be apparent to all that a system of capital and labour should continue to exist. There must be something to provide the necessary incentive to effort or progress will cease. It would be as bad for Labour as for Capital if the incentive to capital to press forward were withdrawn, but it is the office of Government to see that these two important factors maintain proper regard for each other. If Capital does not provide enough to assure Labour a contented existence with a full enjoyment of the opportunities of the times for human improvement, then the Government might find it necessary to step in and let the state do these things at the expense of Capital. . . .

The undersigned respectfully submits that it is only by application in concrete form of the good intentions of Government and of the employer that Labour will develop a contented spirit. Volumes are written, and there are conferences innumerable, with the object of removing what are called Labour troubles. Unless these are followed by immediate application of something that Labour can see and realize, and that has its immediate and direct benefit upon the individual at his work and in his home they will be fruitless.

There should be no difficulty in deriving the means for the carrying out of the specific objects above mentioned. It is submitted that there should be a scheme of taxation of those who can afford it and application of wealth to the reasonable needs of the others in the community whose lot in life has not been favored.

The undersigned finds that to a great mass of steady Labour the strike was at its commencement, or very soon afterward, a regrettable occurrence, but they found themselves unable to retrace their steps. There is still grave dissatisfaction. It is necessary that steady Labour should see that it has the consideration from the Government and other elements of the population, and that such consideration takes practical form. Otherwise it is not likely to remain silent. . . .

Nov. 6th, 1919.   H.A. ROBSON.

D.
Social Security and Welfare

69. A Conservative Elder Statesman Opposes Old Age Pensions, 1927

(*Debates of the Senate*, 24 March 1927)

Sir George Foster had not held office since 1921, when he was appointed to the Senate. His views on the Old Age Pensions Bill which became law in 1927 (below, **70**) typify the traditional conservative position on welfare legislation.

Right Hon. Sir GEORGE E. FOSTER:

Shortly, my ideas run along this line, and I have formed those ideas largely out of experience and observation during my lifetime. Contemporaries of my own time, are in my mind now, many of them, who considered it not only a duty but a privilege, after having passed through the sustaining years of parental care and provision — a duty which they cheerfully assumed, and a privilege of which they gladly availed themselves — to take care of those who had been the source of their nourishment and care through many years of youth.

I have noticed that in those cases this conduct had a double effect: it made for personal self-reliance and responsibility, and for the strengthening of family ties, that a boy should think of himself not only as fulfilling a duty but exercising a privilege, in the old age of his parents, when they needed his effort and his aid, by helping them. I am sure such convictions aid and strengthen that invisible but very important family tie that binds youth and old age together and makes a solid and durable unit and thus adds stability to the nationhood which is made up by those units.

On the other hand, I have observed that under the old age pension system there is a certain amount of influence taken away from the thought, which should be in every man's mind through his business and working days, that by frugality and economy, by methods of life insurance or otherwise, he should prepare in days of health, strength and labour capability, for rainy days, as we sometimes call them, which are sure to come to all of us some time in our lives. My fear is that if we give the youth the idea that when the rainy days come the Government will step in and do what formerly was within his own power to do, there will be a weakening of the bond of which I have spoken and consequently an injury to the character and stability of family life and nationhood. . . .

Now, with reference to this measure, I do not believe in the principle on which it is founded. I do not believe it has the elements of justice or fairness in it. I do not believe it is possible in its present state to be carried out. But it has been placed before the Senate for the second time, after the popular body has been changed. Therefore my position to-day is this: I let it go back with all its imperfections on its head, with all its inconsistency and practical impossibility, with the idea that when it comes down to the point of application . . . it will be found to be such an amalgam of impossibilities, impracticabilities and unfairnesses, that there will be an attempt to produce a measure which may come again before the popular assembly and before the Senate, having as its principal features those factors which I believe are essential to the proper working out of a successful pension insurance scheme for old age.

Taking that view, I do not propose to vote against the second reading of this Bill. . . .

70. The Old Age Pensions Act, 1927

(17 George V, Chap. 35)

This limited act, probably the best possible within the existing constitutional circumstances, was passed by the Mackenzie King government under pressure from the Co-operative Commonwealth Federation and after obstruction in the Senate. The question had been considered by a Special Committee of the House of Commons appointed in 1924 and 1925. Following passage in 1951 of an amendment to the British North America Act giving the Dominion Parliament power in the matter, the more effective Old Age Security Act became law later in the same year.

(Assented to 31st March, 1927)

. . .

3. The Governor in Council may make an agreement with the Lieutenant-Governor in Council of any province for the payment to such province quarterly of an amount equal to one-half of the net sum paid out during the preceding quarter by such province for pensions pursuant to a provincial statute authorizing and providing for the payment of such pensions to the persons and under the conditions specified in this Act and the regulations made thereunder. . . .

5. Before any agreement made pursuant to this Act comes into operation the Governor in Council shall approve the scheme for the administration of pensions proposed to be adopted by the province, and no change in such scheme shall be made by the province without the consent of the Governor in Council. . . .

8. (1) Provision shall be made for the payment of a pension to every person who, at the date of the proposed commencement of the pension: —

(*a*) is a British subject, or, being a widow, who is not a British subject, was such before her marriage;

(*b*) has attained the age of seventy years;

(*c*) has resided in Canada for the twenty years immediately preceding the date aforesaid;

(*d*) has resided in the province in which the application for pension is made for the five years immediately preceding the said date;

(*e*) is not an Indian as defined by the *Indian Act*;

(*f*) is not in receipt of an income of as much as three hundred and sixty-five dollars ($365) a year, and

(*g*) has not made any voluntary assignment or transfer of property for the purpose of qualifying for a pension. . . .

9. (1) The maximum pension payable shall be two hundred and forty dollars yearly, which shall be subject to reduction by the amount of the income of the pensioner in excess of one hundred and twenty-five dollars a year. . . .

71. J. S. Woodsworth Calls for Unemployment Insurance, 1930

(Debates, House of Commons, 1 April 1930)

As the Depression came on and unemployment increased, demands for social legislation were more and more loudly heard, especially from the Co-operative Commonwealth Federation group in Parliament, and there was increasing impatience with constitutional limitations. On the government attitude at this time, see also Mackenzie King's notorious "five-cent-piece speech" (above, **36**). On the later history of unemployment insurance, see below, **72**.

Mr. J. S. WOODSWORTH (Winnipeg North Centre): Mr. Speaker, year after year, we in this corner, have tried to bring the question of unemployment to the attention of the house. . . .

Anyone who has been engaged in social work cannot help but be impressed by the hopelessness of the condition in which the ordinary worker finds himself when out of a job. I have been more or less closely associated with the unemployed of my own city for the past twenty-five years. Sometimes we have had more and sometimes less unemployment, but every year in the winter time we have people who are praying that the spring may come in order that they may earn enough to buy something to eat for themselves and their families. . . .

We have to-day men in the building trades employed for only six, seven or at most eight months in the year. What are they to do during the other months? . . . Consider the coal miners in Alberta, from whom I am getting heartbreaking letters almost daily, asking that something be done. If these companies cannot market their coal what is the poor miner to do? He cannot move anywhere else; he has to stay there and suffer, and naturally he looks to some authority to do something for him. . . .

We have been told again and again that unemployment is primarily a municipal or provincial responsibility. I quite admit that sixty years ago when a man was out of a job in a little rural area in Ontario or Quebec, this was clearly a local responsibility. . . .

But the situation is entirely changed to-day, and when the Dominion government throws out of equilibrium our population by introducing hundreds of thousands, yes millions of people into this country, the responsibility ceases to be merely local in character and becomes Dominion-wide. Further, as long as the Dominion government so largely controls the country's fiscal policies which may make or unmake an industry, the Dominion government cannot avoid responsibility for ensuing unemployment....

I for one am getting a little bit tired of being told by the government that almost any proposal is ultra vires. We are informed in case after case that this has been the declaration of some mysterious people — I do not know just who they are — called the law officers of the crown....

Reference has been made by previous speakers to what the Minister of Labour said at London. I would be glad if by his speech he has given the public generally the idea that unemployment insurance in this country is needed. I suppose that would be a gain.... I want to get this situation cleared up. I should like the public to know whether the government does or does not intend to do anything along the line of unemployment insurance. If it does not, I think the people of this country will turn to somebody who will. On the other hand, if the government intends to go ahead with a scheme, some of us here are prepared to back them up to the limit. But we should like to know, and the public has a right to know, what the government proposes to do.

I do not want to go into the details of unemployment insurance. May I say simply that it is generally recognized the world over that under the existing system, with the evils and maladjustments that have arisen, it has become essential that until some better system is brought in, some sort of unemployment insurance should be provided. Here let me give credit to the Prime Minister; he agrees with that position. Well then, I ask, what action may we expect the government to take at this time?...

Hon. PETER HEENAN (Minister of Labour): ...I desire to take this opportunity of making my position clear, if it is not clear already. First let me say to hon. members who are advocating unemployment insurance that their appeal is no stronger than the appeals I made on the floor of the Ontario legislature when I was a member of that house. I thought at that time, and still think, that that was the proper place to advocate a contributory unemployment insurance plan....

Unemployment insurance will be adopted in Canada only after public opinion has been educated to the necessity for such legislation....

In this case public opinion certainly must include the working men.... I know a number of working men — and I have known more since I made my remarks at London — who oppose a contributory system of unemployment insurance. Many claim that the employer should stand the whole cost....

72. The Unemployment Insurance Act, 1940

(4 George VI, Chap. 44)

For the background of this Act, whose validity depended on the British North America Act, 1940, see the note on that Act, above, **12**.

(Assented to 7th August, 1940)

. . .

4. (1) This Act shall be administered by a Commission to be called "The Unemployment Insurance Commission", which shall consist of three Commissioners, who shall be appointed by the Governor in Council and of whom one shall be a Chief Commissioner. . . .

13. (1) Subject to the provisions of this Act, all persons who are employed in any of the employments specified in Part I of the First Schedule to this Act, not being employments specified as excepted employments in Part II of that Schedule* shall be insured against unemployment in manner provided by this Act. . . .

17. (1) The funds required for providing insurance benefit and for making any other payments which under this Act are to be made out of the Unemployment Insurance Fund, established under this Part of the Act, shall be derived partly from moneys provided by Parliament, partly from contributions by employed persons and partly from contributions by the employers of those persons.

(2) Subject to the provisions of this Act and to any regulations made thereunder, a contribution at the weekly rate provided in the Second Schedule to this Act shall be payable for each calendar week during the whole of which an employed person is employed by an employer. . . .

27. Every person who being insured under this Act is unemployed and in whose case the conditions laid down by this Act (in this Act referred to as "statutory conditions") are fulfilled, shall, subject to the provisions of this Act, be entitled to receive payments (in this Act referred to as "insurance benefit" or "benefit") at weekly or other prescribed intervals at such rates as are authorized by or under the Third Schedule to this Act, so long as the statutory conditions continue to be fulfilled and so long as he is not disqualified under this Act for the receipt of benefit: Provided that the Commission may make regulations providing that in the case of a juvenile under eighteen years of age benefit may be paid to a person by whom such juvenile is mainly or wholly maintained.

---

*There was a long list of excepted employments, including agriculture, fishing, nursing, teaching and the public service.

28. The receipt of insurance benefit by an insured person shall be subject to the following statutory conditions, namely, —

   (i) that contributions have been paid in respect of him while employed in ensurable employment for not less than one hundred and eighty days during the two years immediately preceding the date on which a claim for benefit is made;

  (ii) that he has made application for insurance benefit in the prescribed manner, and proves that he was unemployed on each day on which he claims to have been unemployed;

 (iii) that he is capable of and available for work but unable to obtain suitable employment; and

 (iv) that he proves either that he duly attended, or that he had good cause for not attending, any course of instruction or training approved by the Commission for the purpose of becoming or keeping fit for entry into or return to employment. . . .

SECOND SCHEDULE
Rates of Contribution
(Sec. 17)

Reference Number for Class	Class of Employed Persons	Weekly Rate	
		Employer	Employed Person
0	While earning less than 90 cents a day. . . . or While under 16 years of age . . .	18 cents	9 cents (paid on his behalf by the employer)
1	Earning $5.40 but less than $7.50 in a week	21 cents	12 cents
2	Earning $7.50 but less than $9.60 in a week	25 cents	15 cents
3	Earning $9.60 but less than $12.00 in a week	25 cents	18 cents
4	Earning $12.00 but less than $15.00 in a week	25 cents	21 cents
5	Earning $15.00 but less than $20.00 in a week	27 cents	24 cents
6	Earning $20.00 but less than $26.00 in a week	27 cents	30 cents
7	Earning $26.00 but less than $38.50 in a week or $2,000 a year . . .	27 cents	36 cents

. . .

THIRD SCHEDULE

. . .

3. Where the contributions paid in respect of an employed person during the two years immediately preceding the claim for benefit are in only one class, the rates of benefit shall be—

Weekly Rate of Benefit

Class	Single Person	A Person with Dependent
1	$ 4 08	$ 4 80
2	5 10	6 00
3	6 12	7 20
4	7 14	8 40
5	8 16	9 60
6	10 20	12 00
7	12 24	14 40

73. Extracts from the Debate on the Family Allowances Bill in the House of Commons, 1944

(*Debates, House of Commons,* 25 July 1944)

This measure, a landmark in Canadian social policy, was recommended by the National War Labour Board and by the Department of Finance, as a step to relieve hardships caused by wartime wage stabilization. But the "baby bonus" also had political overtones. Mackenzie King felt that it would counter the appeal to the electorate of the Co-operative Commonwealth Federation's social policies, which appeared to be powerful. The 1942 platform of the Progressive Conservative party had committed it also to a social security program (above, **24**); it nevertheless criticized the Liberal measure on a variety of grounds, including the argument that it amounted to a special favour to Quebec. The bill aroused considerable opposition within King's own party and cabinet, but it went far to cut the ground from under the feet of the other parties. See Pickersgill, *The Mackenzie King Record,* I and II, and Granatstein, *The Politics of Survival.*

Right Hon. W. L. Mackenzie King (Prime Minister) moved the

second reading of bill No. 161, to provide for family allowances.

He said....

It has always been a part of the policy of the party to which I belong to do as much as possible to further equality of opportunity....

The figures that I have just given to the house will surely make it apparent that, among the working population of our country having large families, there is not, so far as the parents are concerned or so far as the children are concerned, anything approaching equality of opportunity in the battle of life.... As I have pointed out, 84 per cent of the children in Canada under sixteen are dependent upon only 19 per cent of the gainfully employed!

What opportunity have the children of families in humble circumstances with the whole of the battle of life ahead of them where you have differences of this kind existing? It is part of the business of the state to seek to help remove those differences and to bring about as close an approach as possible to equality of opportunity....

The government, at different times, has set out its post-war policy. I should like to give this measure its true place by pointing out that it is a part of the government's post-war policy of reconstruction in the large sense of the word.... we have as a part of the government's reconstruction policy three broad divisions: one relating to demobilization and reestablishment; another to reconstruction, dealing with the economic aspects thereof, particularly employment; and a third dealing with human well-being and health....

...That there is a changing order emerging in the world as a consequence of the war, is more or less obvious; but when we talk about demanding a new order of things either we mean what we say or we do not. If we mean what we say we will see that the new order places its emphasis on life rather than upon wealth....

The new order seeks to shift the emphasis from the sacredness of possession to the sacredness of life; to weigh against each other the relative values of personality and its rights, and property and its rights; to compare standards of living with standards of trade; and to contrast human resources with material resources....

This brings me to the question of the cost. Some hon. members will say that this measure is going to cost a lot of money. I might ask the house how much this war is costing, how much we are actually spending each day for the war. I doubt very much if the cost of this measure will bear comparison with expenditure on the war as it is being incurred, and so largely met, by this country to-day. It is about two week's [sic] expenditure, in fact. If it is going to help to carry the country safely through the period of readjustment and for years to come serve to avoid a large measure of unrest that otherwise will be inevitable, if in its place it is going to bring contentment and at the same time help to develop a strong and vigorous nation, I think we will be able to count the cost as not being in any way excessive. . . .

In conclusion I wish to say a word about one charge that has been brought against the government arising out of the introduction of this measure. It has been described as being "legal bribery". . . . I wish the leader who made that statement in the name of his party* were on the floor of this house at the moment. . . .

I resent that charge very strongly, and in a personal way. . . .

When I gave up the idea of an academic career and came to Ottawa in 1900 to start a Department of Labour in Canada, I was not seeking to bribe the Canadian people. I was seeking to establish an agency of government which through the years would tell more and more for the betterment of the conditions of the people of Canada. . . .

When I was defeated in 1911 and out of parliament for a time, did I give up my interest in social questions and in the well-being of the people? I have in my hand a book of which I am proud, *Industry and Humanity*. The book is a study in the principles underlying industrial reconstruction. The book was written at intervals in that period when I was not in parliament. . . . If hon. members would read a chapter entitled "Principles Underlying Health" they will find the advocacy of a national minimum standard of life, the advocacy of social security, the advocacy of the very measure we are introducing in parliament at this time. . . .

. . . I have fought for measures of social security and national well-being in season and out of season, in parliament and out of parliament, in this country and in other countries. I have fought for them wherever the opportunity presented itself, and win or lose in the future, I intend to fight for them to the end of my days. When that moment comes there will not be any thought of bribery associated with my name in this country, if I can leave nothing else to my fellow men, I will at least leave to my party and to my country an honourable name.

Mr. GORDON GRAYDON (Leader of the Opposition):† . . . We support the purpose and principle of elevating the standard of family life among the masses of our people, but we do not believe that this bill will adequately and effectively carry that out. Some of the reasons for such a stand I shall now enumerate:

*John Bracken.
†In the absence of John Bracken, who had not yet sought a seat in the Commons.

1. It is unconstitutional and invades the jurisdiction of the provinces. . . .

2. It seriously endangers the setting up of minimum wage standards in Canada, and may be accepted in many instances as a substitute for better wage levels. . . .

3. It adds a further strain on our national unity. There is but one province which has maintained the high birth rate and large family which was so characteristic of Canada's pioneer strains. That province's contributions to the general revenue will be out of proportion to the heavier deflection of payments that will have to come from other provinces to pay that province's heavier share of these subsidies. . . .

5. It foreshadows the building of a giant peace-time bureaucracy with its inevitable controls, offices, inspectors and machinery. . . .

9. It denies the basic principles of social justice. Such justice calls not for the mass treatment of all people as the same, such as marked unemployment relief, but for treating life as it is, individually and the needs of families differently as they are different. . . .*

Mr. M. J. COLDWELL (Rosetown-Biggar):† Mr. Speaker, . . . I want to say immediately that we of this party welcome heartily the introduction of this measure. However, I wish it were part of a wide social security programme much more comprehensive than any of the measures that have been placed before this house up to the present time, or perhaps I should say, up to this stage of the session.

This afternoon as I discuss this measure I am thinking of the years that have gone by. I think of 1921 when the late Mr. J. S. Woodsworth appeared as the member for Winnipeg North Centre. I think of the many years he spent endeavouring to popularize social security measures in this house as he succeeded to a large degree in popularizing them across the country. I have no doubt whatever that it is not only because of the new order, of which the Prime Minister . . . speaks, but because of the long process of education carried on in this country by pioneers for social security that this important bill has reached its second reading to-day. As one of the party which has consistently urged the adoption in this country of comprehensive social security measures, I welcome this proposal.

*Graydon proceeded to move that the bill be referred to the Special Committee on Social Security and redrafted in co-operation with the provinces. The Speaker ruled this amendment out of order; Graydon appealed the ruling and the House sustained the Speaker. The Conservatives did not vote against the bill, which passed without opposition.
†Leader of the Co-operative Commonwealth Federation party.

I regret that the constitutional argument has been introduced at this time by the official opposition. I think that was a move to shelve this important matter, and I am glad, Mr. Speaker, that your ruling has been sustained. . . .

. . . to-day we have had the satisfaction of hearing the Prime Minister on the floor of this chamber echo in other words the slogan of the party for which I speak. We ask, however, why is it that such measures were not introduced years ago?

. . . But to-day we have this measure, and in spite of the fact that it is belated, in spite of the fact that we regard it as only one short step, we welcome it because it is a recognition that human rights must come before property rights in our land. . . .

Here I wish to interject my opinion that the financial commitment which the government is making — and this bill definitely commits the government to certain payments — ought to have been part of the budget. I agree that, instead of coming into effect on July 1, 1945, it should have come into effect, if brought in earlier this session, on July 1, 1944, or now at the latest, January 1, 1945, and the government ought to have carried out its constitutional obligation — I think there is one — when it provides for an expenditure, to make at least some provision therefor in the budget. . . .

74. The Family Allowances Act, 1944

(8 George VI, Chap. 40)

(Assented to 15 August, 1944)

. . .

3. Subject as provided in this Act and in regulations, there may be paid out of unappropriated moneys in the Consolidated Revenue Fund from and after the first day of July, one thousand nine hundred and forty-five, in respect of each child resident in Canada maintained by a parent, the following monthly allowance: —

(a) in the case of a child less than six years of age, five dollars per month;

(b) in the case of a child six or more years of age but less than ten years of age, six dollars per month;

(c) in the case of a child ten or more years of age but less than thirteen years of age, seven dollars per month;

(d) in the case of a child thirteen or more years of age but less than sixteen years of age, eight dollars per month:

Provided that the allowance payable shall, in respect of a fifth child maintained by the parent, be reduced by one dollar and in respect of a sixth child and a seventh child respectively so maintained, by two dollars and in respect of an eighth child and each additional child respectively so maintained, by three dollars.

4. . . . (2) The allowance shall cease to be payable with the payment for the month when the child attains his sixteenth birthday or when, being above the age of six years and physically fit to attend school, he fails to attend school or to receive equivalent training as prescribed in the regulations or when he dies or ceases to reside in Canada or, in the case of a female child, when she marries. . . .

E.
Prohibition:
Ontario as an Example

Canada has always been a relatively hard-drinking country, and the social problems thus caused ensured in turn the existence of a formidable prohibition movement. The latter found its great opportunity during the First World War, when prohibition could be justified as a war measure. Beginning in the prairie provinces, provincial legislation against the public sale of alcoholic beverages was enacted from 1915 onwards. Only Quebec escaped the fullest force of the movement. There a referendum in April 1919 approved the continued sale of beer and light wines in the province. In the country at large prohibition brought serious troubles in its train. The laws were widely defied; bootlegging became rampant; it was alleged that respect for law generally was being undermined; and there was endless trouble on the border, where "rum runners" conducted a profitable illicit trade in Canadian spirits with the United States, which in 1918 had taken the decision to go "dry" nationally. A contemporary historian wrote, "The 'hundred years of peace' on the border came to an end with prohibition" (Carl Wittke, *A History of Canada,* rev. ed., New York, 1933). Within a decade of prohibition's triumphs a powerful reaction set in, beginning, like the original movement, in the West. The provincial prohibitory laws tended to be replaced by measures providing for "government control" of the sale of liquor. It was generally declared that the "open bar" would never be allowed to return, but the tendency as years passed was for the laws to become increasingly permissive. It is out of the question to deal with the problem as it presented itself in every province, so Ontario is taken here as an example. It is amply apparent that prohibition became a dominant provincial political issue in the 1920s.

75. The Plan for Prohibition in Ontario, 1916

(*Globe*, Toronto, 23 March 1916)

The influence of Manitoba's legislation on that of Ontario is made clear in this excerpt.

Ontario will go "dry" within a few months, probably in September, and may remain in that position for two or three years before the people vote on prohibition. A declaration to this effect was made in the Legislature yesterday by Hon. W. J. Hanna, who, in introducing the eagerly-awaited prohibition measure, explained that the Government had decided it would not be advisable to take a referendum until the soldiers returned from the war. The Provincial Secretary pointed out that the war might last another year and that it might be at least six months after hostilities ceased before the soldiers reached Canada. It would take further time to get their names on the voters' lists, and the vote in any case could not take place in less than two or three years at best. . . .

Hon. Mr. Hanna, in opening, said the bill was on somewhat similar lines to the act known as the Macdonald act in Manitoba, which had been upheld by the Privy Council as being within the powers of the Province. They had followed that bill particularly as to the prohibiting sections. . . .

"Then you ask, 'What about the trade?' Is the trade being wiped out entirely? Will there be no opportunity in this Province to buy liquor for those who may need it in their business or in their profession? In that connection we have followed the Macdonald act. The House will recall — those of you who have read the Macdonald act — that the provision is for licensing druggists. It has not been without some consideration, it has not been entirely without difficulty, that we came to the adoption of the Macdonald act in toto in this connection. . . .

"I may say to the House the druggists are not anxious to have the trade. . . . We propose to ask the druggists to co-operate with us in the administration of these sections. . . ."

76. Premier William Hearst Explains the Ontario Temperance Act, 1916

(*Globe*, Toronto, 5 April 1916)

The atmosphere which produced prohibition is well exemplified in this excerpt. The most striking feature is the absence of opposition. The Liberal leader, N. W. Rowell, supported the Conservative government on this issue. It is perhaps relevant that both he and Premier Hearst were Methodists. The Methodist Church had no monopoly of the prohibition movement, but it provided the spearhead of it.

Not the faintest rumbling of the threatened opposition was heard in the Legislature yesterday when the prohibition bill was given a second reading without division and amid a demonstration of applause from both sides of the House. Any murmurings that might have existed prior to the debate among Conservatives who could not altogether see eye to eye with the Government must have been largely dissipated by the exceptionally fine speech of Premier Hearst, who rose nobly to a big occasion. Those who had not been converted to the advanced character of the temperance legislation either kept quiet or remained away from the Chamber, and nothing stood in the way of what was a great temperance victory....

The Premier said that Ontario's annual drink bill was estimated at from $30,000,000 to $40,000,000, but worse still, between ten and twelve million dollars was paid for imported liquors, spirits, malt liquors and wines, which was equal to the annual revenue of the Province.

Speaking of the example of England, where the traffic had become so entrenched that the Government had been able to take only partial measures by reason of the anti-prohibition habits and sentiments of the people, Mr. Hearst said: "Surely we, as a young country in the making, must so shape our legislation and educate our people that no Government of this country will have to make the admission the Government of Great Britain has had to make, and be like that Government — impotent to remove the evil...."

"The situation in the old land to-day speaks to us in this new land in tones of thunder to avoid the path that land has taken and to shake off that which hampers progress in times of peace and may destroy entirely in times of war."

Every effort they could put forth would be necessary to win the war. "The soil of France and Flanders is red to-day with the blood of

Canada's best and bravest," continued the Premier.... "Is this the time to talk of personal liberty, to think of our pleasures, our appetites, our enjoyments, when the civilization of the world is hanging in the balance . . .?"

Premier Hearst was sure a prohibitory law enacted by the consent of the people could be enforced and would be enforced. In a democratic country like Canada they must bow to the sovereign will of the people. He pointed out that several of the Provinces of Canada had already gone "dry" and that the prospect was that other Provinces would soon vote in favor of wiping out the bars. He thought the call in Ontario was just as insistent as elsewhere. In the United States a few months ago over six thousand barrooms were closed and seven States went "dry". In Russia the sale of vodka had been stopped. It had strengthened the nation and enabled the Russians to play a heroic part.

77. Extracts from the Ontario Temperance Act, 1916

(Ontario statute, 6 George V, Chap. 50)

These are short extracts from a very long and complicated Act. Whereas the 18th Amendment to the United States Constitution (1918) forbade "the manufacture, sale or transportation of intoxicating liquors," the Ontario legislators were content with prohibiting sale; even that was permitted within very narrow limits.

(Assented to 27th April, 1916)

. . .

40. No person shall by himself, his clerk, servant or agent, expose or keep for sale or directly or indirectly or upon any pretence or upon any device sell or barter or, in consideration of the purchase or transfer of any property or thing, or at the time of the transfer of any property or thing, give to any other person any liquor without having first obtained a license under this Act authorizing him so to do, and then only as authorized by such license.

41.—(1) Except as provided by this Act, no person by himself, his clerk, servant or agent shall have or keep or give liquor in any place wheresoever, other than in the private dwelling house in which he resides, without having first obtained a license under this Act authorizing him so to do, and then only as authorized by such license. . . .

(3) This section shall not prevent any person engaged in mechanical business or in scientific pursuits from having in his possession alcohol for mechanical or scientific purposes... or prevent any minister of the gospel from having in his possession wine for sacramental purposes. . . .

(4) Nothing in this section shall prevent the keeping in any public hospital or in any private hospital, sanatorium for consumptives, or private sanitarium, liquor for the use of patients, but no such liquor shall be consumed by any person other than a patient, and then only when prescribed or administered by a physician as provided by section 51 of this Act. . . .

51.–(1) Any physician who is lawfully and regularly engaged in the practice of his profession, and who shall deem any intoxicating liquors necessary for the health of his patients, may give such patient or patients a written or printed prescription therefor, addressed to a druggist and not exceeding six ounces, except in the case of alcohol for bathing a patient or other necessary purpose, or liquor mixed with any other drug is required [sic] when a quantity not exceeding one pint may be prescribed, but no such prescription shall be given except in cases of actual need, and when in the judgment of such physician the use of liquor is necessary, or such physician may administer the liquor himself, and for that purpose may have one quart in his possession when visiting his patients. . . .

(a) Upon the prescription of a duly qualified medical practitioner a vendor under this Act may sell and supply for strictly medicinal purposes –

   (1) Ale, beer, and porter in quantities not exceeding one dozen bottles, containing not more than three half pints each at any one time;

   (2) Wines and distilled liquor not exceeding one quart at any one time. . . .

147.–(1) On the first Monday in the month of June, 1919, there shall be submitted to the vote of the electors of the Province of Ontario qualified to vote at the election of members to the Legislative Assembly the question:

"Are you in favour of the repeal of *The Ontario Temperance Act.*". . .

78. The Strange Case of the Rev. Mr. Spracklin

(*Globe*, Toronto, 9 November 1920)

One of the most bizarre incidents of the prohibition era in Ontario concerned the Rev. J. O. L. Spracklin, who combined the vocation of a Methodist minister in Sandwich, Ontario, with that of a prohibition enforcement officer. He was appointed an inspector after he had publicly complained of conditions in Sandwich and particularly at the Chappell House. He killed the proprietor of the Chappell House during a raid on the hotel which he led. Spracklin was tried for manslaughter and acquitted (*Globe*, 25 February 1921). See R. Greenaway, *The News Game* (Toronto, 1966).

(Staff Correspondence of the Globe.)

Windsor, Nov. 8. — Rev. J. O. L. Spracklin, special License Inspector of Essex county, was justified in the shooting of Beverly Trumble of the Chappell House here last Saturday evening.

A Coroner's jury this morning after brief deliberation, and following pointed addresses from Coroner J. S. Labelle and Crown Attorney J. H. Rodd, found that Rev. Mr. Spracklin had shot in self-defense.

The verdict reads:

"We, your Coroner's jury, find that Beverly Trumble came to his death from a bullet wound from an automatic pistol fired by J. O. L. Spracklin, Inspector, in self-defense, at about 3.30 a.m., November 6, 1920, at the Chappell House in the town of Sandwich." . . .

79. Extracts from Premier Ferguson's Election Statement, October 1926

(*Globe*, Toronto, 19 October 1926)

This statement summarizes the development of events which led Premier G. Howard Ferguson to believe that public opinion would support his Conservative government in its decision to repeal the Ontario Temperance Act. His calculations proved sound; in the general election on 1 December the Conservatives took 75 seats as against 37 for all other parties. The Liberals, led by W. E. N. Sinclair, opposed the Ferguson policy and still stood for prohibition; they got only 17 seats, in addition to three taken by Independent Liberals.

... All the laws of the Province have been rigidly enforced and the Attorney-General* has faced the difficult task of enforcing the Ontario Temperance Act with courage and rectitude.

It is universally recognized that the administration of this act is one of the most difficult features that falls to the responsibility of any Government. This task has been rendered the more difficult because of the undoubted division of opinion existing in the Province with respect to it, and the apparent lack of support which the enforcement of the act received in many sections of the Province. The whole problem of temperance legislation and temperance advance has been occupying the serious attention of the Government for a considerable period.

In reaching a conclusion, as to what is best to be done in the interests of temperance and the moral welfare of the Province there are many factors that must be taken into account. . . .

1. It is admitted that to ensure general observance and a satisfactory administration of any law it must command the support of a strong public opinion.

2. The Ontario Temperance Act, passed as a war measure in 1916, admittedly in advance of normal public sentiment, has during the ten years of its existence been supported and vigorously enforced by three different Governments, all of which were in sympathy with the principle of the act.

3. The repeated votes upon the question of temperance indicate a marked falling off in the sentiment in support of the Ontario Temperance Act. Within a period of five years two plebiscites were submitted and approximately the same number of votes cast in each case. In 1919 68 per cent. of the votes cast were in support of the act and 32 per cent. against the act; while in 1924 51 per cent. voted for the act and 49 per cent. against it.

4. Ontario is surrounded east, west and south by sources of illicit traffic which it is physically impossible to effectually combat. . . .

5. The wide divergence of attitude between urban and rural communities toward the Ontario Temperance Act.

6. The numerous deaths from poison alcohol over a considerable period, culminating last summer in the death of about 60 people in various parts of the Province, have filled the public, as well as the Government, with horror and alarm.

7. Despite the vigilance and best efforts of the law enforcement

---

*The Attorney General, W. F. Nickle (cf. below, p. 196) resigned at this point rather than support the Ferguson policy.

officers, bootlegging flourishes and those engaged in supplying the
demand for liquor are growing rich in the traffic. . . . Would it not be
better that this demand should be supplied through properly controlled channels and the profits, instead of enriching the few, be
available for the extension and improvement of hospitals, education,
highways and other public services?

8. Although the maximum number of prescriptions that may be
issued by each doctor has been successively reduced from 100 to 50,
and later to 30, per month, yet the aggregate annual number, with
slight variation, has, over a period of years, increased. And the total
sales from the Government Dispensaries are greater today than ever.

9. The former active campaign to formulate public opinion upon
the subject of temperance has, during recent years, been practically
abandoned by the organized temperance forces.

With all these considerations before us, the question naturally
arises:

Are we reducing the consumption of liquor in Ontario?

Are we controlling in the best possible manner its distribution and
eliminating the evils which follow from its abuse?

Should we continue to dispense liquor through Government agencies without official sanction or control?

If the Government is to be held responsible for the law and its
enforcement, should the Government not have the right to say by
whom and under what conditions liquor may be purchased? . . . I
am convinced that from the standpoint of the moral well-being of the
people our methods can be improved.

With this object in view the Government proposes to amend the
Ontario Temperance Act and substitute for the doctor an independent Commission, who will have the authority to issue to all citizens
over 21 years of age, who desire to purchase spirituous or malt
liquors for their own use, an annual permit upon which shall be
entered each purchase, and which may be suspended or cancelled at
any time for abuse or misconduct.

When the present law came into operation a large portion of the
Province had banished the sale of liquor under local option. The
views so expressed will be scrupulously observed and no sale of
spirituous and malt liquors will be allowed in these areas. The Commission may, however, establish at such places as it may select in
other portions of the Province dispensaries for the sale of spirituous
and malt liquors in sealed packages to persons holding official permits.

The Commission may, also, upon the request by petition of a reasonable number of resident ratepayers of any municipality in such

latter portion of the Province, requesting the sale of beer by the glass at tables in standard hotels, notify such municipality of its intentions to permit such sale, and unless, within a reasonable time, from the date of such notice the municipality passes a by-law under the terms of the well-established local option law against such sale, such permission may be granted. . . .

80. Extracts from the Liquor Control Act (Ontario), 1927

(Ontario statute, 17 George V, Chap. 70)

This Act substituted for prohibition a system of government sale of liquor carried on under very close restrictions. It was, however, the beginning of a process of liberalization, extending over many years, which seemed to be generally supported by public opinion.

. . .   *(Assented to 5th April, 1927)*

4. There shall be a Board known as "The Liquor Control Board of Ontario" consisting of one, two or three members as may be determined from time to time by the Lieutenant-Governor in Council, with the powers and duties herein specified, and the administration of this Act, including the general control, management and supervision of all Government liquor stores shall be vested in the Board. . . .

10. It shall be the duty of the Board and it shall have power,—

(a) to buy, import and have in its possession for sale, and to sell liquor in the manner set forth in this Act;

(b) to control the possession, sale, transportation and delivery of liquor in accordance with the provisions of this Act;

(c) to determine the municipalities within which Government liquor stores shall be established, throughout the Province, and the situation of the stores in any municipality;

(d) to make provision for the maintenance of warehouses for beer or liquor and to control the keeping in and delivery of or from [sic] any such warehouses;

(e) to grant, refuse or cancel permits for the purchase of liquor. . . .

30. Stores to be known as Government stores may be established by the Board at such places in the Province as are considered advisable for the sale of liquor in accordance with the provisions of this Act and the regulations made thereunder, and the Board may from

time to time fix the prices at which the various classes, varieties and brands of liquor shall be sold and such prices shall be the same at all such Government stores.

31. The sale of liquor at each Government store shall be conducted by a person appointed under this Act to be known as a "vendor" who shall, under the directions of the Board, be responsible for the carrying out of this Act and the regulations made thereunder, so far as they relate to the conduct of such store and the sale of liquor thereat.

32.–(1) A vendor may sell to any person who is the holder of a subsisting permit, such liquor as that person is entitled to purchase under such permit....

(2) Except as provided by the regulations no liquor sold under this section shall be delivered until, —

    (a) the purchaser has given a written order to the vendor, dated and signed by such purchaser and stating the number of his permit, and the kind and quantity of the liquor ordered; and

    (b) the purchaser has produced his permit for inspection and endorsement by the vendor; and

    (c) the purchaser has paid for the liquor in cash; and

    (d) the vendor has endorsed or caused to be endorsed on the permit the kind and quantity of the liquor sold and the date of the sale.

33. No liquor shall be sold to any purchaser except in a package sealed with the official seal as prescribed by this Act and such package shall not be opened on the premises of a Government store....

68. Nothing contained in this Act shall be construed as interfering with the operation of *The Canada Temperance Act** applicable to any part of Ontario, and no Government store shall be established in a municipality in which *The Canada Temperance Act* has been brought into force and is still in force.

69.–(1) Except as provided by the regulations, no store shall be established by the Board for the sale of liquor in any municipality or portion of a municipality in which at the time of the coming into force of *The Ontario Temperance Act*, a by-law passed under *The Liquor License Act* [of Ontario] or under any other Act, was in force

---

*41 Victoria, Chap. 16, 10 May 1878 (see Volume IV of this series).

prohibiting the sale of liquor by retail unless and until a vote has been taken to establish government stores in the manner hereinafter provided. . . .

145. The Acts and parts of Acts set out in Schedule "A"* hereby are repealed. . . .

*Schedule "A" lists the Ontario Temperance Act, 1916 (above, **77**), the numerous Acts amending that Act, and (in whole or in part) several related statutes.

F.
Immigration

81. Statistics of Immigrant Arrivals in Canada, 1914-1945

(Urquhart and Buckley, *Historical Statistics of Canada*)

The largest number of immigrants ever recorded as entering Canada in a single year was in 1913, when over 400,000 persons were admitted. The number showed signs of declining even before the outbreak of the First World War the following year. Since that time the statistics have reflected the fact that immigrants, welcomed in times of prosperity, are widely regarded with suspicion in times of social unrest and depression; while in periods of warfare immigration inevitably falls very low.

1914.........150,484	1925......... 84,907	1936..........11,643
1915......... 36,665	1926.........135,982	1937..........15,101
1916......... 55,914	1927.........158,886	1938..........17,244
1917......... 72,910	1928.........166,783	1939..........16,994
1918......... 41,845	1929.........164,993	1940..........11,324
1919.........107,698	1930.........104,806	1941.......... 9,329
1920.........138,824	1931......... 27,530	1942.......... 7,576
1921......... 91,728	1932......... 20,591	1943.......... 8,504
1922......... 64,224	1933......... 14,382	1944..........12,801
1923.........133,729	1934......... 12,476	1945..........22,722
1924.........124,164	1935......... 11,277	

82. Extracts from the Amendments to the Immigration Act, 1919

(9-10 George V, Chaps. 25 and 26)

These extracts should be read with the contemporary amendments to the Criminal Code which became Section 98 (above, **52**). They reflect the current fear of Bolshevism and specifically the alarm aroused by the Winnipeg Strike. It will be noted that the amendments of 1919 authorized the deportation of British subjects (other than Canadians by birth or naturalization) for, among other things, being members of organizations teaching "disbelief in or opposition to organized government." Attempts to modify these portions of the Act were long unsuccessful; in 1926 the House of Commons passed an amendment providing that persons accused of sedition could not be deported without a jury trial, but it was defeated in the Senate. The reference to organizations teaching opposition to organized government was removed in 1928 (by 18-19 George V, Chap. 29), but in general the 1919 amendments remained in the Immigration Act until it was revised in 1952, and even then much of their substance was incorporated in the new Act (see Revised Statutes of Canada, 1952, Chaps. 145 and 325).

(Assented to 6th June, 1919)

. . .

2. (1) . . .

    (ii) Canadian domicile is lost, for the purposes of this Act, by a person voluntarily residing out of Canada not for a mere special or temporary purpose but with the present intention of making his permanent home out of Canada, or by any person belonging to the prohibited or undesirable classes within the meaning of section forty-one of this Act;

    (iii) Notwithstanding anything contained in the preceding subparagraph (ii), when any citizen of Canada who is a British subject by naturalization, or any British subject not born in Canada having Canadian domicile, shall have resided for one year outside Canada, he shall be presumed to have lost Canadian domicile and shall cease to be a Canadian citizen for the purposes of this Act, and his usual place of residence shall be deemed to be his place of domicile during said year. . . .

3. . . . (6) Section three of the said Act [concerning prohibited classes] is further amended by adding the following paragraphs thereto: —

    "(j) Persons who in the opinion of the Board of Inquiry or the officer in charge at any port of entry are likely to become a public charge;

    "(k) Persons of constitutional psychopathic inferiority;

    "(l) Persons with chronic alcoholism;

    "(m) Persons not included within any of the foregoing prohibited classes, who upon examination by a medical officer are certified as being mentally or physically defective to such a degree as to affect their ability to earn a living;

"(n) Persons who believe in or advocate the overthrow by force or violence of the Government of Canada or of constituted law and authority, or who disbelieve in or are opposed to organized government, or who advocate the assassination of public officials, or who advocate or teach the unlawful destruction of property;

"(o) Persons who are members of or affiliated with any organization entertaining or teaching disbelief in or opposition to organized government, or advocating or teaching the duty, necessity, or propriety of the unlawful assaulting or killing of any officer or officers, either of specific individuals or of officers generally, of the Government of Canada or of any other organized government, because of his or their official character, or advocating or teaching the unlawful destruction of property;

"(p) Enemy aliens or persons who have been alien enemies and who were or may be interned on or after the eleventh day of November, one thousand nine hundred and eighteen, in any part of His Majesty's dominions or by any of His Majesty's allies;

"(q) Persons guilty of espionage with respect to His Majesty or any of His Majesty's allies;

"(r) Persons who have been found guilty of high treason or treason for an offence in connection with the war, or of conspiring against His Majesty, or of assisting His Majesty's enemies during the war, or of any similar offence against any of His Majesty's allies;

"(s) Persons who at any time within a period of ten years from the first day of August, one thousand nine hundred and fourteen, were or may be deported from any part of His Majesty's dominions or from any allied country on account of treason or of conspiring against His Majesty, or of any similar offence in connection with the war against any of the allies of His Majesty, or because such persons were or may be regarded as hostile or dangerous to the allied cause during the war;

"(t) On and after the first day of July, one thousand nine hundred and nineteen, in addition to the foregoing 'prohibited classes,' the following persons shall also be prohibited from entering or landing in Canada: — Persons over fifteen years of age, physically capable of reading, who cannot read the English or the French language or some other language or dialect: Provided that any admissible person or any person heretofore or hereafter legally admitted, or any citizen of Canada, may bring in or send for his father or grandfather, over fifty-five years of age, his wife, his mother, his grandmother or his unmarried or widowed daughter, if otherwise admissible, whether such relative can read or not and such relative shall be permitted to enter. . . .

14. Section forty of the said Act, as enacted by chapter twelve of the statutes of 1911, is repealed and the following is substituted therefor: —

"40. Whenever any person, other than a Canadian citizen or person having Canadian domicile, shall be found an inmate of or connected with the management of a house of prostitution or practising prostitution, or who shall receive, share in or derive benefit from any part of the earnings of any prostitute or who manages or is employed by, in, or in connection with any house of prostitution or music or dance hall or other place of amusement or resort habitually frequented by prostitutes, or where prostitutes gather, or who in any way assists any prostitute or protects or promises to protect from arrest any prostitute or who shall import or attempt to import any person for the purpose of prostitution or for any other immoral purpose, or who has been convicted of a criminal offence in Canada or who admits the commission prior to landing or entry to Canada, of a crime involving moral turpitude, or has become a professional beggar or a public charge or practices polygamy, or has become an inmate of a penitentiary, gaol, reformatory, prison, asylum or hospital for the insane or the mentally deficient, or an inmate of a public charitable institution, or enters or remains in Canada contrary to any provision of this Act, it shall be the duty of any officer cognizant thereof, and the duty of the clerk, secretary or other official of any municipality in Canada wherein such person may be, to forthwith send a written complaint thereof to the Minister [of Immigration and Colonization], giving full particulars."

15.* Section forty-one of the said Act is repealed and the following is substituted therefor: —

"41. (1) Every person who by word or act in Canada seeks to overthrow by force or violence the government of or constituted law and authority in the United Kingdom of Great Britain and Ireland, or Canada, or any of the provinces of Canada, or the government of any other of His Majesty's dominions, colonies, possessions or depen-

---

* The text here given is that of the *second* amendment to the Immigration Act passed in the session of 1919 (Chap. 26), which passed through all its stages in a single day (6 June). Though generally similar to the section it replaced, the new section 41 was rather more stringent. Sub-section (2) was not in the first amendment.

dencies, or advocates the assassination of any official of any of the said governments or of any foreign government, or who in Canada defends or suggests the unlawful destruction of property or by word or act creates or attempts to create any riot or public disorder in Canada, or who without lawful authority assumes any powers of government in Canada or in any part thereof, or who by common repute belongs to or is suspected of belonging to any secret society or organization which extorts money from or in any way attempts to control any resident of Canada by force or by threat of bodily harm, or by blackmail, or who is a member of or affiliated with any organization entertaining or teaching disbelief in or opposition to organized government shall, for the purposes of this Act, be deemed to belong to the prohibited or undesirable classes, and shall be liable to deportation in the manner provided by this Act, and it shall be the duty of any officer becoming cognizant thereof and of the clerk, secretary or other official of any municipality in Canada wherein any such person may be, forthwith to send a written complaint to the Minister, giving full particulars: Provided, that this section shall not apply to any person who is a British subject, either by reason of birth in Canada, or by reason of naturalization in Canada.

(2) Proof that any person belonged to or was within the description of any of the prohibited or undesirable classes within the meaning of this section at any time since the fourth day of May, one thousand nine hundred and ten, shall, for all the purposes of this Act, be deemed to establish *prima facie* that he still belongs to such prohibited or undesirable class or classes.''. . .

83. French-Canadian Nationalist Pressure against Jewish Immigration, 1933

(*L'Action nationale*, Montreal, September 1933)

Various pressure-groups made representations on the subject of immigration. Here French-Canadian ultra-nationalists during the Depression oppose all immigration, but particularly that of Jews. Adolf Hitler had come to power in the previous January, and Jews who could do so were fleeing Germany. On the *Ligue d'Action nationale* see below, **122**.

(Translation)

Montreal, 5 June 1933

Sir George Perley,
Acting Prime Minister,
Ottawa.
Sir,

The *Ligue d'Action Nationale* brings to your attention that M. Aisenbud, secretary general of the Zionist Federation of Belgium, has just made among others the three following declarations, according to the Belgian newspapers of 21 May last:

a) Judaism is ruined in Germany and 700,000 Jews are being forced to leave German territory.

b) A worldwide committee is being formed at Paris with a view to collecting in the first instance a sum (ten million pounds) which would make it possible to transport the Jews to South America and Canada.

c) There will stay in Belgium only those German Jews who can make by their inventions, their private industrial processes, an important contribution to the country's prosperity.

The directors of the *Ligue d'Action Nationale,* concerned for the higher interests of Canada, met in assembly last Saturday and voted the following resolution: That the frontier of Canada should be completely closed *sine die* in this time of general unemployment which weighs so heavily on the national budget; that the government of Canada should remain completely inflexible in the face of whatever Jewish pressure, national or worldwide, may be brought to bear, to ensure that no consideration be shown to a group which is accused by Germany of Marxism and communism, and which in itself moreover could not be a useful element for Canada, being on account of its faith, its customs and its unassimilable character a source of division and dispute, and hence of weakness for the Canadian people.

Yours sincerely and devotedly,
LA LIGUE D'ACTION NATIONALE,
Per A. Vanier.

G.
Abandonment
of Titles

84. Report of a Special Committee of the House of Commons, 1919

(House of Commons Journals, 1919, pp. 251-2)

One consequence of the First World War was the abandonment of the conferring of titles of honour on Canadians. A good many knighthoods and one or two baronetcies were awarded in recognition of various wartime services, and it is evident that there was considerable adverse public reaction. This committee report was approved by a resolution of the House of Commons on 22 May 1919, after an amendment that would have referred it back to the committee had been negatived by 96 to 43 in a non-party vote. No further titles were conferred on Canadians until 1933 (below, **85**). See *Canadian Annual Review, 1919*, pages 157-71, and *Robert Laird Borden, His Memoirs*, II.

Mr. Nickle,* from the Special Committee appointed to consider and report upon the propriety of presenting an address to His Most Excellent Majesty the King, praying that His Majesty may be graciously pleased to refrain hereafter from conferring any titles upon such of his subjects as are domiciled or living in Canada, except such titles as have reference to professional or vocational appellations conferred in respect to commissions issued by His Majesty to persons in the Military or Naval Services of Canada, or to persons engaged in the administration of justice in the Dominion; and that

* W. F. Nickle, Conservative member for Kingston, who had made himself the spearhead of the movement against titles. In 1918 an attempt by Nickle and others to put a resolution against titles through the House had been frustrated by Sir Robert Borden, but the discussion of 1919 took place while Sir Robert was absent from the House on account of the Paris Peace Conference. Borden attributed Nickle's attitude to the fact that the President of the University of Toronto and the Principal of McGill had received knighthoods, but the Principal of Queen's University, Kingston (who was Nickle's father-in-law) was passed over.

His Majesty may also be pleased to consider the question of taking measures to ensure the extinction at the death of the present possessors of the hereditary titles at present in existence in the Dominion; and further that His Majesty may also be pleased to take into consideration the question of in future conferring honours, titular distinctions and decorations upon subjects of His Majesty ordinarily resident in Canada, including those who have performed overseas, in Canada, or elsewhere, naval, military and civilian services in connection with the war, presented the following as their Report:—

Your Committee are of the opinion and recommend that an address be presented to His Most Excellent Majesty the King, in the following words:—

"TO THE KING'S MOST EXCELLENT MAJESTY.

Most Gracious Sovereign.

We, Your Majesty's most dutiful and loyal subjects, the House of Commons of Canada in Parliament assembled, humbly approach Your Majesty, praying that Your Majesty may be graciously pleased:—

(a) To refrain hereafter from conferring any title of honour or titular distinction upon any of your subjects domiciled or ordinarily resident in Canada, save such appellations as are of a professional or vocational character or which appertain to an office.

(b) To provide that appropriate action be taken by legislation or otherwise to ensure the extinction of an hereditary title of honour or titular distinction, dignity or title as a peer of the realm, on the death of a person domiciled or ordinarily resident in Canada at present in enjoyment of an hereditary title of honour or titular distinction, dignity or title as a peer of the realm,* and that thereafter no such title of honour, titular distinction, dignity or title as a peer of the realm, shall be accepted, enjoyed or used by any person or be recognized.

All of which we humbly pray Your Majesty to take into your favourable and gracious consideration."

A suggestion was made that the titles of "Right Honourable" and "Honourable" be discontinued, but the suggestion did not meet with the approval of the Committee.

Your Committee, however, do not recommend the discontinuance of the practice of awarding military or naval decorations, such as the Victoria Cross, Military Medal, Military Cross, Conspicuous Service Cross, and similar decorations to persons in military or naval services of Canada for exceptional valour and devotion to duty.

---

* This was doubtless primarily directed at the few baronetcies held in Canada. No such action as recommended was ever taken.

Your Committee further recommends that appropriate action be taken by legislation or otherwise to provide that hereafter no person domiciled or ordinarily resident in Canada shall accept, enjoy or use any title of honour or titular distinction hereafter conferred by a foreign ruler or government.

85. Question and Answer on Titles, 1933

(*Debates, House of Commons,* 17 May 1933)

This and the following item illuminate the policy of R. B. Bennett's government of 1930-35 on titles. It is evident that Bennett believed in them, and believed too that the Commons resolution of 1919 (above, **84**) was no bar to recommending appointments. During 1933-35 a number of distinguished Canadians received knighthoods; but since Bennett's defeat in the election of 1935 no further titles have been conferred on Canadians domiciled in Canada. During the Second World War, however, many Canadians' services were recognized by appointments to orders of chivalry in classes below those involving titles (e.g., C.B. or O.B.E.), and many received decorations for gallantry. Mr. Bennett himself moved to England after his retirement from politics, and in 1941 received a viscountcy. When the Order of Canada was set up in 1967, it provided for no class carrying a title.

CONFERRING OF TITLES

Mr. MERCIER (Laurier-Outremont):

Do the recent decorations granted in the Order of St. Michael and St. George, and in the Order of St. Gregory the Great, mean that Canadians holding titles in any order may now accept promotions in the same order as long as such promotions do not carry any rank or title?

Mr. BENNETT:

1. The promotion of the Right Honourable Sir George Halsey Perley, K.C.M.G., to be an ordinary member of the first class or Knights Grand Cross of the Most Distinguished Order of St. Michael and St. George, was made in conformity with established constitutional practice, it being the considered view of His Majesty's government in Canada that the motion, with respect to honours, adopted on the 22nd day of May, 1919, by a majority vote of the members of the Commons House only of the thirteenth parliament (which was dis-

solved on the 4th day of October, 1921) is not binding upon His Majesty or His Majesty's government in Canada or the seventeenth parliament of Canada.

2. The government has no official knowledge of promotions in or appointments to the Order of St. Gregory the Great. *

86. A Further Statement by R. B. Bennett on Titles

(*Debates, House of Commons*, 23 May 1933)

CONFERRING OF TITLES

Right Hon. R. B. BENNETT (Prime Minister): In reply to the question asked yesterday by the right hon. the leader of the opposition [Mackenzie King], I have to inform him that section 17 of the British North America Act, 1867, provides that there shall be one parliament of Canada, consisting of the Queen (King), an upper house, styled the Senate, and the House of Commons, and it is the considered view of His Majesty's government in Canada that a resolution passed by one house of parliament is legally effective only as an expression of the opinion of those who support such resolution in that house, and this is particularly true with respect to the prerogatives of the crown.

The sovereign can only be deprived of a prerogative right by statute of parliament, in very special form, which the government does not propose to introduce†. . . .

---

*This is a Papal order.

†It may be worth noting that on 14 March 1934 the House of Commons defeated by 113 to 94 a private member's resolution against titles moved by Humphrey Mitchell, then Labour member for East Hamilton and later Mackenzie King's Minister of Labour.

H.
The Status of Women

87. The Judicial Committee Decides that Women Are Persons, 1929

(Henrietta Muir Edwards and others v. Attorney-General for Canada, Olmsted, Decisions of the Judicial Committee of the Privy Council relating to the British North America Act, 1867, II)

This decision, making a material change in the position of women under the Canadian constitution, was the result of a petition by five western women led by Mrs. Emily Ferguson Murphy of Edmonton, the first Canadian woman to be appointed a magistrate. The first woman senator appointed was Mrs. Cairine Wilson of Ottawa, 1930. On the admission of women to the House of Commons, see above, 16.

Appeal . . . by special leave from a judgment of the Supreme Court of Canada, dated April 24, 1928, in answer to a question referred to that Court by the Governor General under s. 60 of the Supreme Court Act.

The question referred was "Does the word 'persons' in s. 24 of the British North America Act, 1867, include female persons?"

By s. 24: "The Governor General shall from time to time, in the Queen's name, by instrument under the Great Seal of Canada, summon qualified persons to the Senate; and, subject to the provisions of this Act, every person so summoned shall become and be a member of the senate and a senator.". . .

The Supreme Court of Canada unanimously answered the question referred in the negative. . . .

Oct. 18. The judgment of their Lordships was delivered by
LORD SANKEY L.C.*. . .

Their Lordships are of opinion that the word "persons" in s. 24 does include women, and that women are eligible to be summoned to and become members of the Senate of Canada. . . .

* Lord Chancellor.

The exclusion of women from all public offices is a relic of days more barbarous than ours, but it must be remembered that the necessity of the times often forced on man customs which in later years were not necessary. . . .

No doubt in any code where women were expressly excluded from public office the problem would present no difficulty, but where instead of such exclusion those entitled to be summoned to or placed in public office are described under the word "person" different considerations arise.

The word is ambiguous, and in its original meaning would undoubtedly embrace members of either sex. . . .

Customs are apt to develop into traditions which are stronger than law and remain unchallenged long after the reason for them has disappeared.

The appeal to history therefore in this particular matter is not conclusive. . . .

. . . their Lordships do not think it right to apply rigidly to Canada of to-day the decisions and the reasons therefor which commended themselves, probably rightly, to those who had to apply the law in different circumstances, in different centuries, to countries in different stages of development. Referring therefore to the judgment of the Chief Justice [of Canada] and those who agreed with him, their Lordships think that the appeal to Roman law and to early English decisions is not of itself a secure foundation on which to build the interpretation of the British North America Act of 1867. . . .

The British North America Act planted in Canada a living tree capable of growth and expansion within its natural limits. The object of the Act was to grant a Constitution to Canada. "Like all written constitutions it has been subject to development through usage and convention": Canadian Constitutional Studies, Sir Robert Borden (1922), p. 55.

Their Lordships do not conceive it to be the duty of this Board — it is certainly not their desire — to cut down the provisions of the Act by a narrow and technical construction, but rather to give it a large and liberal interpretation so that the Dominion to a great extent, but within certain fixed limits, may be mistress in her own house, as the Provinces to a great extent, but within certain fixed limits, are mistresses in theirs. . . .

If Parliament had intended to limit the word "persons" in s. 24 to male persons it would surely have manifested such intention by an express limitation, as it has done in ss. 41 and 84. . . .

A heavy burden lies on an appellant who seeks to set aside a unanimous judgment of the Supreme Court, and this Board will only set aside such a decision after convincing argument and anxious consideration, but having regard: (1.) To the object of the Act—namely, to provide a constitution for Canada, a responsible and developing state; (2.) that the word "person" is ambiguous, and may include members of either sex; (3.) that there are sections in the Act above referred to which show that in some case the word "person" must include females; (4.) that in some sections the words "male persons" are expressly used when it is desired to confine the matter in issue to males; and (5.) to the provisions of the Interpretation Act; their Lordships have come to the conclusion that the word "persons" in s. 24 includes members both of the male and female sex, and that, therefore, the question propounded by the Governor General should be answered in the affirmative, and that women are eligible to be summoned to and become members of the Senate of Canada, and they will humbly advise His Majesty accordingly.

V.
Economic Life
and Policy

A.
Trade and Commerce

1. The Bennett Tariff Policy, 1930-1931

88. Amendment of the Customs Tariff, 1930

(21 George V, Chap. 3)

The pronouncements and platforms of the major political parties on the tariff issue during our period are to be found in Part II above. R. B. Bennett in 1930 proclaimed his intention of using the tariff to "blast a way" into world markets (see p. 102). After his triumph in that year's election he lost no time. A special session of Parliament in September authorized a large increase in tariff rates on a considerable range of commodities. In 1931 another revision (by 21-22 George V, Chap. 30) extended the increases over many more. See Orville John McDiarmid, *Commercial Policy and the Canadian Economy* (Cambridge, Mass., 1946).

(Assented to 22nd September, 1930)

1. Section six of the *Customs Tariff*, chapter forty-four of the Revised Statutes of Canada, 1927, as amended by chapter thirteen of the Statutes of 1930, is repealed, and the following is substituted therefor: —

"6. (1) In the case of articles exported to Canada of a class or kind made or produced in Canada, if the export or actual selling price to an importer in Canada is less than the fair market value of the same article when sold for home consumption in the usual and ordinary course in the country whence exported to Canada at the time of its exportation to Canada, or is less than the fair market value or value for duty thereof as determined under the provisions of section thirty-seven of the *Customs Act*, or is less than the fair market value thereof as fixed by the Governor in Council under the provisions of section thirty-seven of the *Customs Act*, or is less than the value for duty thereof as determined by the Minister under the provisions of paragraphs (*a*) and (*e*) of section forty-one of the *Customs Act*, or is less than the fair market value thereof as fixed by the Minister under the provisions of section forty-three of the *Customs Act*, there shall, in addition to the duties otherwise established, be levied, collected and paid on such article, on its importation into Canada, a special or dumping duty, equal to the difference between the said selling price of the article for export and the said fair market value thereof or value for duty thereof; and such special or dumping duty shall be levied, collected and paid on such article although it is not otherwise dutiable. . . .

(6) If at any time it appears to the satisfaction of the Minister that any person owning or controlling or interested in a business in Canada and also in any other country, or any person carrying on a business in any other country and owning or controlling or interested in a business operating in Canada, and by reason thereof is enabled to import goods for further manufacture or assembling or for resale, and while complying with the legal requirements on importation disposes of such imported goods, whether in the form as imported or as further processed, assembled or manufactured, at prices below the duty paid value thereof as entered at Customs plus, if any, the cost of processing, assembling or further manufacturing in Canada, the Minister may declare that goods of such class or kind were and are on importation subject to an additional special or dumping duty not exceeding fifty per cent and authorize such action as is deemed necessary for the collection thereof. . . .

2. The said *Customs Tariff*, as amended by chapter thirteen of the Statutes of 1930, is further amended by adding thereto the following sections: —

"17. The Governor in Council may, from time to time, prohibit the importation into Canada of any goods exported directly or indirectly from any country not a contracting party to the Treaty of Versailles, executed at Paris, France, on the 28th day of June, 1919.*. . .

"18. In the event of the producers of goods other than agricultural products increasing prices in consequence of the imposition of any duty under the provisions of this Act, the Governor in Council may reduce or remove such duty.". . .

NOTE. The Act concludes with a detailed list of amendments to the tariff rates (Schedule A) which it is not practicable to reproduce here. The range of goods covered included iron and steel and many

*This was presumably directed at Soviet Russia.

machines, and a variety of textiles. Comparing the new schedule with those formerly in effect (see particularly *Revised Statutes of Canada*, 1927, Chap. 44, and 20-21 George V, Chap. 13, 30 May 1930), we find for instance that woollen fabrics and clothing, previously paying 27½% under the British preference, 35% under the Intermediate tariff and 35% under the General tariff, now paid 30%, 40% and 40% respectively. (Goods from the United States were subject to the General tariff at this period, in the absence of any Canadian-U.S. trade agreement.) Knitted garments, formerly paying 20%, 30% and 35%, were now to pay respectively 25%, 25% and 45%. Electric motors and parts, formerly paying under the three tariffs 15%, 25% and 27½%, would now pay 25%, 33⅓% and 37½%. The 1930 Act did not cover automobiles. That of 1931 raised the general tariff on passenger cars worth between $1200 and $2100 from 20% to 30%; on other motor vehicles it was raised from 27½% to 40%. A wide range of parts and accessories to be used in the manufacture of cars in Canada remained free under all three tariffs, as they had been before.

89. Extracts from the Tariff Board Act, 1931

(21-22 George V, Chap. 55)

The Tariff Board was set up by the Bennett government, partly perhaps to provide expert advice in connection with an increasingly complex subject, partly to meet criticism of the Bennett tariff policies voiced at home and abroad. See, e.g., A. W. Currie, *Canadian Economic Development* (Toronto, 1942).

(Assented to 3rd August, 1931)

. . .

3. (1) There shall be a Board to be called the Tariff Board, consisting of three members appointed by the Governor in Council. . . .

(7) No member shall be eligible to be a candidate for election to the House of Commons of Canada until after the expiration of two years from the date when he ceased to be a member of the Board.

4. (1) In respect of goods produced in or imported into Canada the Board shall, at the request of the Minister [of Finance], make inquiry as to —

(*a*) the price and cost of raw materials in Canada and elsewhere, and the cost of transportation thereof from the place of production to the place of use or consumption;

(b) the cost of efficient production in Canada and elsewhere, and what increases or decreases in rates of duty are required to equalize differences in the cost of efficient production;

(c) the cost, efficiency and conditions of labour, including health of employees, in Canada and elsewhere;

(d) the prices received by producers, manufacturers, wholesale dealers, retailers and other distributors in Canada and elsewhere;

(e) All conditions and factors which affect or enter into the cost of production and the price to the consumers in Canada;

(f) generally, all the conditions affecting production, manufacture, cost and price in Canada as compared with other countries;
and report to the Minister.

(2) The Board shall make inquiry into any other matter, upon which the Minister desires information, in relation to any goods which, if brought into Canada or produced in Canada, are subject to or exempt from duties of customs or excise, and shall report to the Minister, and the inquiry into any such matter may include inquiry as to the effect which an increase or decrease of the existing rate of duty upon a given commodity might have upon industry or trade, and the extent to which the consumer is protected from exploitation.

(3) The Board may be empowered by the Governor in Council to hold an inquiry under section fifteen of the *Customs Tariff*, in the same manner as the judge of the Exchequer Court or any other judge therein referred to may be so empowered. . . .

(4) The Governor in Council may empower the Board to make any investigation or hold any inquiry authorized by the provisions of the *Combines Investigation Act*, or of a relative nature. . . .

(5) It shall also be the duty of the Board to inquire into any other matter or thing in relation to the trade or commerce of Canada which the Governor in Council sees fit to refer to the Board for inquiry and report.

(6) Inquiries under this section shall be conducted in a summary manner in public, except as otherwise expressly provided in this or any other Act of the Parliament of Canada, and the respective reports to be made pursuant to its provisions shall succinctly state the facts so ascertained; and each report shall be accompanied by a copy of the evidence, if any, taken, and by a copy of all information obtained in connection with the inquiry.

5. (1) The Board shall have the power of summoning before them any witnesses, and of requiring them to give evidence on oath, or on

solemn affirmation if they are persons entitled to affirm in civil matters, and to produce such documents and things as the Board deem requisite.

(2) The Board shall give reasonable opportunity to persons who may not have been summoned, to appear before them and give evidence upon oath or solemn affirmation as aforesaid, on any matter relevant to an inquiry then being held by the Board. . . .

(5) The Board shall have the same power to enforce the attendance of witnesses, and to compel them to give evidence, as is vested in any court of record in civil cases. . . .

6. Whenever a report has been made under this Act, a copy thereof and a copy of the evidence, if any, taken, and of the information obtained (except such evidence and information as was of a confidential character under sub-section ten of section five hereof)* in connection therewith shall be laid before Parliament by the Minister within fifteen days after the opening of the next session thereafter, or within fifteen days after the making of the report if Parliament is then in session. . . .

11. (1) From and after a date to be fixed by the Governor in Council, all the powers, functions and duties of the Board of Customs shall be assigned to and be transacted by the Tariff Board constituted by this Act. . . .

2. The Pattern of Trade Agreements, 1932-1938

The Ottawa Agreements of 1932 (below, **90**) are an episode in the history rather of protection than of the freeing of trade. Franklin D. Roosevelt became President of the United States in 1933, and in 1934 obtained from Congress a statute enabling him to make reciprocal trade agreements with foreign states without further congressional approval. R. B. Bennett, his views changing as the Depression went on, had already approached Washington with a proposal for such an agreement. The U.S. administration—perhaps unwilling to afford Bennett what might be an advantage in the approaching Canadian election—nevertheless hung back until the vote had taken place which returned Mackenzie King and the Liberals to power. An agreement (the first general trade treaty to come into effect between the two countries since the old Reciprocity Treaty lapsed in 1866) was then made within a few weeks (15 November 1935). In 1937 the King

* Omitted.

government made a new agreement with Britain, replacing that of 1932 and more liberal in its terms (the agreement forms a schedule to the United Kingdom Trade Agreement Act, 1937, 1 George VI, Chap. 17). Finally, on 17 November 1938, Canada signed a new trade agreement with the U.S. by which both sides obtained concessions, and Britain made an agreement with the U.S. the same day. (The Canadian agreement is a schedule to the Canada-United States of America Trade Agreement Act, 1939, 3 George VI, Chap. 29.) The high-tariff period associated with Bennett's name and with the Depression was over, and a degree of triangular reciprocity had come into being. See *Canadian Annual Review, 1937 and 1938*, 25, 49-50; *The Memoirs of Cordell Hull* (2 vols., New York, 1948); R. Wilbur, *The Bennett Administration, 1930-1935* (Canadian Historical Association Historical Booklet No. 24, 1969); *Dana Wilgress Memoirs* (Toronto, 1967); Richard N. Kottman, *Reciprocity and the North Atlantic Triangle, 1932-1938* (Ithaca, N.Y., 1968).

90. Extracts from the Ottawa Trade Agreement between Canada and the United Kingdom, 1932

(Schedule to 23-24 George V, Chap. 2, 25 November 1932)

The origins of the Imperial Economic Conference held at Ottawa in July and August 1932 are to be found in R. B. Bennett's invitation extended during the Imperial Conference of 1930 (below, **184**). Though widely advertised as likely to provide a cure for the existing depression, it was an uncomfortable meeting, particularly as between Britain and Canada. The British delegation was repelled by Bennett's aggressiveness and his unaccommodating economic nationalism. There probably would have been no agreement had not the hopes that had been built upon the conference made agreement politically important to both sides, but particularly to the British. See Keith Feiling, *The Life of Neville Chamberlain* (London, 1946), and *Dana Wilgress Memoirs*. Trade agreements between Canada and South Africa, the Irish Free State and Southern Rhodesia were also made at Ottawa.

We, the representatives of His Majesty's Government in the United Kingdom and of His Majesty's Government in Canada hereby agree with one another, on behalf of our respective Governments, as follows: —

ARTICLE 1.—His Majesty's Government in the United Kingdom undertake that Orders shall be made in accordance with the provisions of Section 4 of the Import Duties Act, 1932, which will ensure the continuance after the 15th November, 1932, of entry free of duty into the United Kingdom of goods consigned from any part of the British Empire and grown, produced or manufactured in Canada which by virtue of that Act are now free of duty subject, however, to the reservations set forth in Schedule A appended hereto.

ARTICLE 2.—His Majesty's Government in the United Kingdom will invite Parliament to pass the legislation necessary to impose on the foreign goods specified in Schedule B appended hereto, the duties of customs shown in that Schedule in place of the duties (if any) now leviable.

ARTICLE 3.—His Majesty's Government in the United Kingdom undertake that the general ad valorem duty of 10% imposed by Section 1 of the Import Duties Act, 1932, on the foreign goods specified in Schedule C shall not be reduced except with the consent of His Majesty's Government in Canada.

ARTICLE 4.—It is agreed that the duty on either wheat in grain, copper, zinc or lead as provided in this Agreement may be removed if at any time Empire producers of wheat in grain, copper, zinc and lead respectively are unable or unwilling to offer these commodities on first sale in the United Kingdom at prices not exceeding the world prices and in quantities sufficient to supply the requirements of the United Kingdom consumers. . . .

ARTICLE 9.—His Majesty's Government in Canada will invite Parliament to pass the legislation necessary to substitute for the duties of customs now leviable on the goods specified in Schedule E the duties shown in that Schedule, provided that nothing in this Article shall preclude His Majesty's Government in Canada from reducing the duties specified in the said Schedule so long as the margin of British preference shown in that Schedule is preserved or from increasing the rates under the intermediate or general tariff set out in the said Schedule.

ARTICLE 10.—His Majesty's Government in Canada undertake that protection by tariffs shall be afforded against United Kingdom products only to those industries which are reasonably assured of sound opportunities for success.

ARTICLE 11.—His Majesty's Government in Canada undertake that during the currency of this Agreement the tariff shall be based on the principle that protective duties shall not exceed such a level as will give United Kingdom producers full opportunity of reasonable competition on the basis of the relative cost of economical and efficient production, provided that in the application of such principle special consideration may be given to the case of industries not fully established.

ARTICLE 12. — His Majesty's Government in Canada undertake forthwith to constitute the Tariff Board for which provision is made in the Tariff Board Act 1931.*

ARTICLE 13. — His Majesty's Government in Canada undertake that on the request of His Majesty's Government in the United Kingdom they will cause a review to be made by the Tariff Board as soon as practicable of the duties charged on any commodities specified in such request in accordance with the principles laid down in Article 11 hereof and that after the receipt of the Report of the Tariff Board thereon such report shall be laid before Parliament and Parliament shall be invited to vary wherever necessary the Tariff on such commodities of United Kingdom origin in such manner as to give effect to such principles.

ARTICLE 14. — His Majesty's Government in Canada undertake that no existing duty shall be increased on United Kingdom goods except after an inquiry and the receipt of a report from the Tariff Board, and in accordance with the facts as found by that body.

ARTICLE 15. — His Majesty's Government in Canada undertake that United Kingdom producers shall be entitled to full rights of audience before the Tariff Board when it has under consideration matters arising under Articles 13 and 14 hereof. . . .

ARTICLE 22. — This Agreement between His Majesty's Government in the United Kingdom and His Majesty's Government in Canada is to be regarded as coming into effect as from the date hereof (subject to the necessary legislative or other action being taken as soon as may be practicable hereafter). It shall remain in force for a period of five years, and if not denounced six months before the end of that period shall continue in force thereafter until a date six months after notice of denunciation has been given by either party. . . .

Signed on behalf of His Majesty's Government in the United Kingdom: —

NEVILLE CHAMBERLAIN.

Signed on behalf of His Majesty's Government in Canada: —

R. B. BENNETT.

20th August, 1932.

*Above, **89**.

NOTE. The attached detailed schedule of changes in the Canadian tariff on goods from the United Kingdom is too long to print, but some examples can be given. On the whole the range of the 200-odd items is rather limited and the concessions small, reflecting the hard bargaining that took place and the narrow approach of the protectionist Canadian administration. "Common and colourless window glass", which under the British Preferential tariff as fixed in 1930 had paid from 1¼ to 3¼ cents per pound, now came in free. There were concessions on iron, steel and textiles, but they were frequently limited to types of goods not made in Canada, or types intended for further manufacture in Canada. Motor vehicles, which under the preferential rate had paid 15% in 1931, were now admitted free, as were motorcycles. Motor buses were not included in the concession.

91. An English Comment on the Results of the Ottawa Agreements

(*The Economist*, London, "Dominion of Canada Special Review," 18 January 1936)

This is a commentary on the trade figures for the years 1931-32 to 1934-35. These showed a great increase in Canadian exports to the United Kingdom, from $174 million in 1931-32 to $274 million in 1934-35; the corresponding figures for exports to the United States were $235 million and $224 million respectively. Canadian imports from the U.K. amounted to $106 million in 1931-32, sank to $86 million in 1932-33 and rose only to $111 million in 1934-35. The corresponding figures for imports from the U.S. were $351 million, $232 million and $303 million.

These figures show that, as compared with 1931-32, Canada has made a small increase in her purchases from the United Kingdom, roughly 4 per cent., but has cut her purchases from the United States by $48 millions, or 13 per cent. On the other hand, Canada has increased her sales in the United Kingdom by $100 millions, or nearly 60 per cent., and has seen her sales to the United States decrease by $11 millions, or about 5 per cent. It is also made plain that whereas in 1931-32 Canada's imports from the United Kingdom bore a ratio of 60 per cent. to her exports to the United Kingdom, by 1934-35 the ratio had fallen to 41 per cent., and the actual balance of trade in favour of Canada had increased from $68 millions to $163 millions. Clearly, therefore, the British-Canadian tariff agreement has operated greatly to the benefit of Canada, and in a much smaller degree to the benefit of Great Britain.

92. Order in Council Giving Effect to Canada-U.S. Trade Agreement of 1935

(Order in Council P.C. 3946, 23 December 1935, Prefix to Statutes of Canada, 1936)

This order in council placed the agreement in effect pending the passage of a statute. See above, p. 208.

Whereas there has been laid before His Excellency the Governor General in Council a report from the Secretary of State for External Affairs,* dated 20th December, 1935, representing, — with the concurrence of the Ministers of Finance and National Revenue.

That, under the authority of Section 4, subsection (g) of the Customs Tariff, the Governor in Council may, by Order in Council extend the benefit of the Intermediate Tariff to any foreign country the produce or manufactures of which have previously been subject to the rates of customs duties set forth in the General Tariff, and

That, under the authority of Section 11 of the Customs Tariff, the Governor in Council may, by Order in Council, make such reductions of duties on goods imported into Canada from any other country as may be deemed reasonable by way of compensation for concessions on Canadian products granted by any such country, and

That in Article I of the Trade Agreement between Canada and the United States of America, signed at Washington on the 15th November, 1935, the United States of America undertook to grant to Canadian goods unconditional and unrestricted most-favoured-nation treatment in all matters concerning customs duties, and in Article IV of that Agreement undertook to exempt articles, the growth, produce or manufacture of Canada, enumerated and described in Schedule II annexed to the Agreement, on their importation into the United States of America, from ordinary customs duties in excess of those set forth and provided for in the said Schedule, and

That in Article XV of the Trade Agreement it was agreed that the provisions of Article I and of Articles III and IV, respectively, should,

* Who was also Prime Minister.

subject to the reservations and exceptions elsewhere provided for in the Agreement, be applied by Canada and the United States of America on and after January 1st, 1936, pending ratification of the Agreement in respect of Canada, and

That by a proclamation of the 7th December, 1935, the President of the United States of America has taken the requisite and appropriate steps to apply the provisions of these Articles to goods imported into the United States of America from Canada on and after the 1st January, 1936.

NOW THEREFORE, in order to give effect to the provisions of Article I and Article III of the said Trade Agreement, His Excellency the Governor General in Council ... is pleased, under the powers granted by Section 4, sub-section (g) and Section 11 of the Customs Tariff, to order and it is hereby ordered:

1. That natural or manufactured products originating in and coming from the United States of America, shall, on and after January 1st, 1936, when conveyed without trans-shipment from a port of the United States of America or from a port of a country enjoying the benefit of the British Preferential or Intermediate Tariff into a customs port of Canada, enjoy the tariff treatment hereunder indicated: —

(a) The benefit of the Intermediate Tariff;

(b) The benefit of the tariff treatment authorized by Orders in Council 1103 of the 6th day of June, 1933, 1560 of the 1st day of August, 1933, 615 of the 11th day of March, 1935, and 1164 of the 30th day of April, 1935;

(c) The benefit of the rates of duty set forth in Schedule I annexed to the Trade Agreement and applicable to goods, the growth, produce or manufacture of the United States of America, as enumerated and described therein.

2. That tariff treatment provided for in the immediately preceding paragraph shall apply to goods imported, or taken out of warehouse for consumption, on and after January 1st, 1936, and to goods previously imported for which no entry for consumption has been made before that date.

3. Restraint of Trade: Anti-Combines Legislation

Anti-combines legislation in Canada is too complicated a subject to be illustrated at full length here. The history of it is outlined in some

detail in V. W. Bladen, *An Introduction to Political Economy* (rev. ed.,
Toronto, 1956) and in L. A. Skeoch (ed.), *Restrictive Trade Practices in
Canada* (Toronto, 1966). It begins with statutes of 1889 (later incorporated in the Criminal Code, where it remains) and 1910 (see Volume IV
of this series); these proved ineffective. A new phase, under two statutes of 1919, the Board of Commerce Act and the Combines and Fair
Prices Act (9-10 George V, Chaps. 37 and 45 respectively) ended when
the Judicial Committee of the Privy Council declared these acts
unconstitutional in 1922. The new Combines Investigation Act, 1923,
forms the basis of the modern legislation. In 1935 the Bennett government (by 25-26 George V, Chap. 54), transferred the administration of
the Act to a Dominion Trade and Industry Commission set up as a
result of the Price Spreads investigation (below, **131**); but part of the
Dominion Trade and Industry Commission Act was found invalid by
the courts, and the incoming King government restored the previous
system (by 1 George VI, Chap. 23, 10 April 1937). The new Act substituted a Commissioner for the Registrar of the 1923 Act. Inadequate
staff, however, limited investigations under the Act until after the
Second World War.

93. Extracts from the Combines Investigation Act, 1923

(13-14 George V, Chap. 9)

(Assented to 13th June, 1923)

. . .

2.   In this Act, unless the context otherwise requires, —

(*a*) The expression "Combine" in this Act shall be deemed to have
reference to such combines immediately hereinafter defined as
have operated or are likely to operate to the detriment of or
against the interest of the public, whether consumers, producers or others; and limited as aforesaid, the expression as used in
this Act shall be deemed to include (1) Mergers, Trusts and
Monopolies so called, and (2) the relation resulting from the
purchase, lease, or other acquisition by any person of any control over or interest in the whole or part of the business of any
other person, and (3) any actual or tacit contract, agreement,
arrangement, or combination which has or is designed to have
the effect of (i) limiting facilities for transporting, producing,
manufacturing, supplying, storing or dealing; or (ii) preventing, limiting or lessening manufacture or production; or (iii)
fixing a common price or a resale price, or a common rental, or a

common cost of storage or transportation; or (iv) enhancing the price, rental or cost of article, rental storage or transportation; or (v) preventing or lessening competition in, or substantially controlling within any particular area or district or generally, production, manufacture, purchase, barter, sale, storage, transportation, insurance or supply; or (vi) otherwise restraining or injuring trade or commerce. . . .

3. The Governor in Council may by order in council name a Minister of the Crown to be charged with the general administration of this Act, and the Minister so named shall be so charged accordingly.

4. (1) The Governor in Council shall appoint a Registrar to be known as the "Registrar of the Combines Investigation Act."

(2) The office of Registrar may be held either separately or in conjunction with any other office in the public service. . . .

(3) It shall be the duty of the Registrar (a) to receive and register, and subject to the provisions of this Act, to deal with applications for investigation of alleged combines; (b) to bring at once to the Minister's attention every such application; (c) to conduct such correspondence with the applicant and all other persons as may be necessary; (d) to call for such returns and to make such inquiries as the Registrar may consider to be necessary in order that he may thoroughly examine into the matter brought to his attention by any application for an investigation; (e) to make reports from time to time to the Minister; (f) to conduct such correspondence with Commissioners as may be necessary, and to receive and file all reports and recommendations of Commissioners; (g) to keep a register in which shall be entered the particulars of all applications, inquiries, reports and recommendations, and safely to keep all applications, records of inquiries, correspondence, returns, reports, recommendations, evidence and documents relating to applications and proceedings conducted by the Registrar or any Commissioner, and when so required transmit all or any of such to the Minister; (h) to supply to any parties on request information as to this Act or any regulations thereunder; (i) generally to do all such things and take all such proceedings as may be required in the performance of his duties under this Act or under any regulations made thereunder.

5. Any six persons, British subjects, resident in Canada, of the full age of twenty-one years, who are of the opinion that a combine exists, or is being formed, may apply in writing to the Registrar for an investigation of such alleged combine, and shall place before the Registrar the evidence on which such opinion is based. . . .

6. Whenever such application shall be made to the Registrar, or

whenever the Registrar shall have reason to believe that a combine exists or is being formed, or whenever so directed by the Minister, the Registrar shall cause an inquiry to be made into all such matters whether of fact or of law with respect to the said alleged combine as he shall consider necessary to enquire into with the view of determining whether a combine exists or is being formed which operates or is likely to operate to the detriment of or against the interest of the public, whether consumers, producers or others.

7. If, after such inquiry as he deems the circumstances warrant, the Registrar is of the opinion that the application is frivolous or vexatious, or does not justify further inquiry, he shall make a report in writing to the Minister setting out the application, the statement or statements, the inquiry made and the information obtained, and his conclusions. The Minister shall thereupon decide whether further inquiry shall or shall not be made, and shall give instructions accordingly. In case the Minister decides that further inquiry shall not be made, he shall notify the applicant of his decision, giving the ground thereof. The decision of the Minister shall be final and conclusive, and shall not be subject to appeal or review.

8. The Registrar may at any time as part of such inquiry by notice in writing, require any person, and in the case of a corporation any officer of such corporation, to make and render unto the Registrar, within a time stated in such notice, or from time to time, a written return under oath or affirmation showing in detail such information with respect to the business of the person named in the notice as is therein specified. . . .

9. If, after the receipt by the Registrar of any return made in purported compliance with this Act, the Registrar or the Minister shall consider that circumstances so justify, or if after a return under this Act has been required, none is made, or none is made within a time set in the notice requiring such return, or within such further time as the Registrar or the Minister may upon special application allow, the Registrar shall have power (a) to investigate the business, and (b) to enter and examine the premises, books, papers and records of and in the possession of the person making or failing to make such return.

10. The Governor in Council may from time to time appoint one or more persons to be Commissioners under this Act. Every Commissioner shall have authority to investigate the business, or any part thereof, of any person who is or is believed to be a member of any combine or a party or privy thereto, and who is named in the order in council appointing the Commissioner; every Commissioner shall have authority to enter and examine the premises, books, papers and

records of such person. The exercise of any of the powers herein conferred on Commissioners shall not be held to limit or qualify the powers by this Act conferred upon the Registrar. . . .

25. Whenever, in the opinion of the Minister an offence has been committed against any of the provisions of this Act, the Minister may remit to the Attorney General of any province within which such alleged offence shall have been committed, for such action as such Attorney General may be pleased to institute because of the conditions appearing, (1) any return or returns which may have been made or rendered pursuant to this Act and are in the possession of the Minister and relevant to such alleged offence; and (2) the evidence taken on any investigation by the Registrar or a Commissioner, and the report of the Registrar or Commissioner. If within three months after remission aforesaid, or within such shorter period as the Governor in Council shall decide, no action shall have been taken by or at the instance of the Attorney General of the Province as to the Governor in Council the case seems in the public interest to warrant, the Solicitor General may on the relation of any person who is resident in Canada and of the full age of twenty-one years permit an information to be laid against such person or persons as in the opinion of the Solicitor General shall have been guilty of an offence against any of the provisions of this Act; and the Solicitor General may apply to the Minister of Justice to instruct counsel to attend on behalf of the Minister at all proceedings consequent on the information so laid, and upon such application the Minister of Justice may instruct counsel accordingly. . . .

34. Nothing in this Act shall be construed to apply to combinations of workmen or employees for their own reasonable protection as such workmen or employees. . . .

B.
Agriculture

1. *The Marketing of Wheat*

94. The Canadian Wheat Board Act, 1935

(25-26 George V, Chap. 53)

The problems of wheat marketing during the First World War led the Canadian government to appoint a Board of Grain Supervisors to regulate prices and control the trade. In 1919 this was replaced by the Canadian Wheat Board, appointed by order in council on 31 July 1919; its powers were continued for eighteen months by 10 George V, Chap. 9 (10 November 1919) but it ceased to exist in 1920. The gap was filled in some degree by the co-operative "Wheat Pool," which during the Depression was supported by the Dominion government. Despite pressure from western farmers, the government refused to reinstitute the Wheat Board until 1935, when this Act was passed as part of R. B. Bennett's reform program. See D. A. MacGibbon, *The Canadian Grain Trade* (Toronto, 1932) and *The Canadian Grain Trade, 1931-1951* (Toronto, 1952); Currie, *Canadian Economic Development;* and Herbert Heaton, *The Story of Trade and Commerce with Special Reference to Canada* (rev. ed., Toronto, 1952).

(Assented to 5th July, 1935)

. . .

3. (1) There shall be a board to be known as The Canadian Wheat Board which shall consist of three members appointed by the Governor in Council. . . .

7. The Board shall undertake the marketing of wheat in interprovincial and export trade and for such purposes shall have all the powers of a corporation and without limitation upon such powers the following: —

(*a*) to receive and take delivery of wheat for marketing as offered by the producers therefor;

(*b*) to buy and sell wheat: Provided that no wheat shall be

219

purchased by the Board except from the producers thereof;

(c) to store and transport wheat;

(d) to operate elevators, either directly or by means of agents. . . ;

(e) to pay to producers delivering wheat at the time of delivery or at any time thereafter as may be agreed upon such fixed price per bushel, according to grade or quality or place of delivery, as may be determined by the Board with the approval of the Governor in Council; and to issue to such producers when such wheat is purchased certificates indicating the number of bushels purchased, the grade, quality and the price, which certificates shall entitle producers named therein to share in the equitable distribution of the surplus, if any, of the operations of the Board during the crop year, it being the true intent and meaning of this section that each producer shall receive for the same grade and quality of wheat the same price on the Fort William basis. . . .

8. It shall be the duty of the Board: —

(a) to fix a price to be paid to the producers for wheat delivered to the Board as by this Act provided, subject to the approval of the Governor in Council;

(b) to sell and dispose of from time to time all wheat which the Board may acquire, for such price as it may consider reasonable, with the object of promoting the sale and use of Canadian wheat in world markets;

(c) to sell and dispose of stocks of wheat and contracts for the delivery of wheat acquired from Canadian Co-operative Wheat Producers Limited* and the wheat represented by such contracts as may be reasonably possible, having regard to economic and other conditions. . . ;

(j) to offer continuously wheat for sale in the markets of the world through the established channels: Provided that the Board may, if in its opinion any existing agencies are not operating satisfactorily, take such steps as it deems expedient to establish, utilize and employ its own or other marketing agencies or channels. . . .

13. (1) As soon as the Board receives payment in full for all wheat delivered during any crop year, there shall be deducted from the receipts all moneys, disbursed by or on behalf of the Board for expenses, including all payments connected with or incident to the operations of the Board, including the remuneration, allowances, travelling and living expenses of the Commissioners, the members of

*The "Wheat Pool."

the Advisory Committee and the officers, clerks and employees of the Board.

(2) After deducting the aforesaid expenses, the balance shall be distributed *pro rata* amongst the producers holding certificates issued pursuant to paragraph (*e*) of section seven of this Act, in accordance with the regulations of the Board approved by the Governor in Council....

95. The Wheat Board Acquires Monopoly Powers, 1943

(Report of the Canadian Wheat Board, Crop Year 1943-1944)

The wartime developments here described are perhaps more effectively characterized in the Wheat Board's *Report* for the crop year 1945-1946: "In September, 1943, the status of the Canadian Wheat Board was changed from that of a voluntary board to that of a monopoly...." In 1947 these wartime emergency powers were placed on a statutory basis by an amendment to the Canadian Wheat Board Act (11 George VI, Chap. 15, 14 May 1947).

The crop year commenced with a fixed initial wheat price of 90¢ per bushel basis No. 1 Northern in store at Fort William/Port Arthur or Vancouver, as provided by The Canadian Wheat Board Act.

On September 27th [1943] the Dominion Government announced an important change in wheat policy. The new policy involved the following actions:

(1) The discontinuance of trading in wheat futures on the Winnipeg Grain Exchange;

(2) The acquisition by the Board, on behalf of the Dominion Government, of all stocks of unsold cash wheat in Canada on the basis of the closing prices on September 27th, 1943;

(3) The raising of the fixed initial price from 90¢ per bushel to $1.25 per bushel for No. 1 Northern wheat basis in store Fort William/Port Arthur or Vancouver;

(4) The closing out of the 1940-41, 1941-42 and 1942-43 Wheat Board Crop Accounts on the basis of closing market prices on September 27th, 1943;

(5) The use of Government-owned wheat (Items 2 and 4 above) to meet requirements under Mutual Aid and to provide wheat for subsidized domestic purchasers.

The foregoing were the main features of the revised wheat programme announced by the Dominion Government on September 27th, 1943; a programme which was made effective until July 31st, 1945. The new wheat policy was set forth in detail under Order in Council P.C. 7942 dated October 12th, 1943.

2. The Mechanization of Agriculture

96. Massey-Harris Makes the Machines

(Annual Reports, Massey-Harris Company, Limited)

The revolution in agriculture—particularly prairie agriculture—after the First World War was marked by two especially striking developments: the replacement of the horse by the tractor (see also below, **110**), and the appearance of the "combine" (the combined reaper and thresher, at first horse- or tractor-drawn, later self-propelled). These extracts from reports of Canada's largest manufacturer of farm implements give glimpses of the development. See E. P. Neufeld, *A Global Corporation: A History of the International Development of Massey-Ferguson Limited* (Toronto, 1969).

1926

The reputation which the Company has always enjoyed in Canada and other countries is being fully maintained by the high quality of the workmanship and sturdy construction of the implements now being produced. It may not be inappropriate to state that at no time in its history has there been built such a complete line of agricultural implements suitable for practically all field conditions. It is gratifying to record that the sale of the Company's "Reaper-Thresher"—the greatest labour-saving harvesting machine yet introduced—is steadily increasing. In view of the fact that experience has demonstrated that it reduces the cost of harvesting by more than one-half, it is believed that its more general use in those areas for which it is suitable will have a marked influence in lowering the production cost of all cereal crops.

1927

The aim has been not merely to maintain the recognized quality of the Company's line of implements, but, by a continuous and extensive program of experiment and research, to improve their efficiency and durability. To meet the demands caused by the rapidly increasing movement towards power farming, it has been necessary not only to maintain the regular line of horse-drawn implements, but to adapt the larger machines for tractor use. During the year notable advances have been made in the further development of the Company's reaper-thresher. To complete the line of power machinery a well-known tractor and stationary thresher have been added.

1929

The war and the economic depression which followed in its wake have speeded up the mechanization of agriculture by accelerating the swing of the pendulum from animal to mechanical power. This change, which normally would have taken half a century, is being accomplished in a brief decade. New power has imposed entirely new conditions and requirements, which manufacturers of farm machinery are endeavouring to meet. So drastic are these changes that almost a complete redesigning of farm machinery has been necessary, and yet the new machines must, in many cases, be capable of operation by either form of power. The predominant thought in agriculture is lower cost of production. Therefore, new machines at every point of comparison with preceding equipment must show lower labour costs, lower power costs, higher speeds of operation, higher efficiency, and longer life.

1939

The year's operations were again marked by continued progress in engineering and design of machinery demanded by the rapid expansion of "Power Farming" in all agricultural territories. This machinery included the new self-propelled Combine, "101" Junior Tractor, semi-mounted Tractor Mower, Power Swather, Cultivator, Drill, new line of Grain Grinders, several new types of Plows, and in addition further modification of many of our other machines.

1940

Substantial progress in the engineering and development of new machines has again been made. A Self-Propelled Combine, smaller than the one introduced last year, is now available and the Tractor line has been appreciably enlarged with the introduction of the small "81" Tractor and the large "201" and "202" models.

3. Reclaiming the Drought Areas

97. The Prairie Farm Rehabilitation Act, 1935

(25-26 George V, Chap. 23)

This Act passed in the last days of the Bennett government was an attempt to deal with the desperate problem of the "drought and soil drifting areas" of the Prairies (cf. below, **123**). It seems to be generally agreed that the organization thus modestly set up had very satisfactory results. See Currie, *Canadian Economic Development*, and J. R. H. Wilbur, "R. B. Bennett as a Reformer," Canadian Historical Association *Historical Papers*, 1969.

(Assented to 17th April, 1935)

. . .
3. (1) The Governor in Council may establish a committee to be known as the Prairie Farm Rehabilitation Advisory Committee, hereinafter called "the Committee," the members of which shall hold office during pleasure.

(2) One of the members of the Committee shall be appointed Chairman by the Governor in Council.

(3) The Committee shall consist of the following: —

(a) one representative of the Manitoba Grain Growing Farmers from the drought and soil drifting areas;

(b) one representative of the Saskatchewan Grain Growing Farmers from the drought and soil drifting areas;

(c) one representative of the Alberta Grain Growing Farmers from the drought and soil drifting areas;

(d) one representative of Saskatchewan Live Stock Farmers from the drought areas;

(e) one representative of Alberta Range Farmers from the drought areas;

(f) one representative of Mortgage Companies of Canada;

(g) one representative of the Canadian Bankers' Association;

(*h*) one representative each from the Canadian Pacific Railway Company and the Canadian National Railways;

(*i*) two representatives from the Dominion Department of Agriculture; and

(*j*) one representative of the Government in each of the Provinces of Manitoba, Saskatchewan and Alberta.

4. The Committee shall consider and advise the Minister [of Agriculture] as to the best methods to be adopted to secure the rehabilitation of the drought and soil drifting areas in the Provinces of Manitoba, Saskatchewan and Alberta and to develop and promote within those areas systems of farm practice, tree culture and water supply that will afford greater economic security and to make such representations thereon to the Minister as the Committee may deem expedient. . . .

6. The Minister may appoint such temporary technical, professional and other officers and employees as he may deem necessary and expedient for carrying out the provisions of this Act and the salaries and expenses of such officers shall be fixed by the Governor in Council. . . .

8. For the purposes of this Act the sum of seven hundred and fifty thousand dollars shall be appropriated and paid out of the Consolidated Revenue fund of Canada during the fiscal year 1935-36 and for each fiscal year for a further period of four years a sum not exceeding one million dollars per annum as may be necessary to continue and extend the work undertaken under this Act. . . .

C.
Industry (Statistics)

98. Statistics on the Growth of Manufacturing

(Urquhart and Buckley, *Historical Statistics of Canada*)

This table illustrates, graphically if a trifle crudely, the growth of manufacturing industry in Canada. Figures for the census year 1910 are included for purposes of comparison. There appear to be no comparable figures for the years between 1910 and 1917. The table reflects the great expansion of manufacturing during the First World War, the fact that the ground then gained was never wholly lost, the collapse during the Depression after 1929, and the second great wartime expansion in 1940-45. It is worth noting that the steady expansion continued after 1945 with only a slight temporary setback in the year 1946.

Gross Value of Production, 1910-1945

(thousands of dollars)

1910.......1,151,722	1926.......3,090,179	1936.......3,000,721
1917.......2,768,046	1927.......3,223,012	1937.......3,623,426
1918.......3,165,139	1928.......3,543,551	1938.......3,335,985
1919.......3,152,237	1929.......3,840,871	1939.......3,472,828
1920.......3,667,579	1930.......3,236,606	1940.......4,526,618
1921.......2,491,280	1931.......2,516,057	1941.......6,072,067
1922.......2,389,216	1932.......1,979,012	1942.......7,548,215
1923.......2,690,344	1933.......1,952,904	1943.......8,725,350
1924.......2,606,650	1934.......2,392,388	1944.......9,066,846
1925.......2,808,485	1935.......2,652,520	1945.......8,245,186

99. British and Foreign Investment in Canada

(F. A. Knox, "Excursus: Canadian Capital Movements and the Canadian Balance of International Payments, 1900-1934," in Herbert Marshall, Frank A. Southard, Jr., and Kenneth W. Taylor, *Canadian-American Industry* (New Haven, 1936); *Canada Year Book*, various years 1939-50)

With the growth of industry came the problems presented by the "foreign" ownership of Canadian enterprises. This table is incomplete; official estimates were made beginning in 1926, but none appears to have been published for 1938 or for the five war years between 1939 and 1945. The available figures show the transition from a situation in which Britain was the greatest external investor in Canada to one in which her share was far exceeded by that of the United States, and U.S. domination of the Canadian economy was beginning to cause alarm. The year 1922 was the first in which the U.S. drew ahead. The process was accelerated by British financial difficulties in the two world wars, and by Canadian tariff policies, which encouraged U.S. firms to open branch plants in Canada. See Heaton, *The Story of Trade and Commerce*; Currie, *Canadian Economic Development*; W. T. Easterbrook and Hugh G. J. Aitken, *Canadian Economic History* (Toronto, 1958); and A. E. Safarian, *Foreign Ownership of Canadian Industry* (Toronto, 1966).

British and Foreign
Estimated/Capital Investment in Canada, 1914-1945

(31 December) *(millions of dollars)*

	United Kingdom	United States	Other	Total
1914	2,778.5	880.7	177.7	3,836.9
1915	2,772.2	1,069.6	175.2	4,017.0
1916	2,840.3	1,306.9	175.5	4,322.7
1917	2,738.7	1,577.3	176.6	4,492.6
1918	2,729.0	1,630.0	176.6	4,535.6
1919	2,645.2	1,818.1	173.5	4,636.8
1920	2,577.3	2,128.2	164.6	4,870.1
1921	2,493.5	2,260.3	152.2	4,906.0
1922	2,463.8	2,593.0	150.2	5,207.0
1923	2,470.7	2,794.4	149.2	5,414.3
1924	2,371.6	3,094.0	150.0	5,615.6
1925	2,345.7	3,219.2	149.2	5,714.1

	United Kingdom	United States	Other	Total
1926*	2,591.5	3,108.8	63.3	5,763.6
1927	2,637.8	3,338.5	63.9	6,040.2
1928	2,698.7	3,551.7	71.8	6,322.2
1929	2,773.9	3,794.4	77.3	6,645.6
1930	2,792.3	4,098.5	88.2	6,979.0
1931	2,729.4	4,056.4	84.4	6,870.2
1932	2,687.2	4,045.2	83.5	6,815.9
1933	2,682.8	4,491.7	190.0	7,364.5
1934	2,729.5	4,112.1	123.5	6,965.1
1935	2,729.3	4,044.6	123.6	6,897.5
1936	2,718.9	3,974.0	129.7	6,822.6
1937	2,684.8	3,932.4	147.8	6,765.0
1939	2,475.9	4,151.4	286.0	6,913.3
1945	1,750.0	4,990.0	352.0	7,092.0

*Figures for 1926 and later are official estimates of the Dominion Bureau of Statistics.

D.
Transport and Communications

1. Railway Nationalization

The consequence of railway overbuilding in the Laurier era, when two new transcontinental lines were constructed (see Volume IV of this series), was a large degree of railway nationalization under Borden, and the creation of the Canadian National Railways. The adoption of the policy of public ownership under a Conservative government was certainly not the result of socialist theory; the near-bankruptcy of the corporations concerned, and their national importance, seemed to leave little real alternative. See G.P. deT. Glazebrook, *A History of Transportation in Canada* (Toronto, 1938); Easterbrook and Aitken, *Canadian Economic History;* and G. R. Stevens, *Canadian National Railways,* II: *Towards the Inevitable, 1896-1922* (Toronto, 1962).

100. Extracts from the Drayton-Acworth and Smith Reports, 1917

(*Report of the Royal Commission to Inquire into Railways and Transportation in Canada,* Ottawa, 1917)

On 13 July 1916 the Canadian government appointed by order in council a royal commission to consider transportation, and specifically the status of the three existing transcontinental railway systems, including "The reorganization of any of the said railway systems, or the acquisition thereof by the State; and in the latter case the most effective system of operation, whether in connection with the Intercolonial Railway or otherwise." The Chairman of the Commission was Alfred H. Smith, President of the New York Central Railroad; the members were Mr. (later Sir) W. M. Acworth, an English railway expert (who replaced Sir George Paish, the original appointee), and

Sir Henry Drayton, Chairman of the Canadian Board of Railway Commissioners. Drayton and Acworth submitted a report favouring a form of public ownership; Smith, perhaps predictably, a minority report recommending persistence with a policy relying upon private enterprise.

Drayton-Acworth Report

. . .

SUMMARY OF CONCLUSIONS AND RECOMMENDATIONS

We summarize our conclusions and recommendations as follows:–

1. The mileage of Canadian railways is very great in proportion to the population of the country. It has increased out of proportion to the increase of population. . . .

3. The net return is so low as to prove that more railways have been built than can be justified on commercial grounds under present conditions.

4. The public investment in railways is very large. The total amount of public capital involved in direct construction of Government lines, and cash aid, land grants and guarantees to private companies, is $968,451,000, not counting the value of lands still unsold.

5. Public aid to the principal companies, including subsidies, land grants, and guarantees, amounts to over $680,000,000. In the case of the Grand Trunk Pacific it amounts to nearly two-thirds of the total investment; in the case of the Canadian Northern to over three-quarters. . . .

7. The development of Canada justified two transcontinental lines. It did not justify three. The Grand Trunk and Canadian Northern should have been amalgamated.

8. The Grand Trunk Pacific system has cost nearly $200,000,000. The interest charges amount to over $8,800,000 per annum. The net income last year was $826,653. The liability of the Grand Trunk Company for interest amounts to over $5,000,000 per annum at present, and will rise to over $7,000,000 in 1923.

9. *We cannot recommend* that the Grand Trunk Company be unconditionally released from their liability. The responsibility for the National Transcontinental line rests mainly with the Government, but that for the Grand Trunk Pacific proper belongs primarily to the Grand Trunk. . . .

10. The Grand Trunk Company proper has made unjustifiable charges to capital. Its lines have not been adequately maintained. . . . The country is suffering from the company's inability to give ade-

quate service. The Grand Trunk railway ought to be managed in Canada, and not from London.

11. *We recommend* that the control both of the Grand Trunk Pacific and of the Grand Trunk be assumed by the people of Canada on terms hereafter set out.

12. The Canadian Northern has been financed mainly by the issue of guaranteed securities. Till 1914 it met the interest from its own resources. Since that date the Government has assumed very heavy obligations on behalf of the company. There is little prospect that the company would be able in the near future to relieve the Government of these obligations. . . .

14. *We estimate* that as a separate undertaking it would require fully $70,000,000 of new capital within the next five years.

15. *We do not recommend* that further public aid be given to the Canadian Northern as at present constituted.

16. The Canadian Northern common stock represents no cash investment, and has no present value, either on the basis of the cost of reproduction of the property, or on the basis of its earning power.

17. *We recommend* that the public take control of the Canadian Northern Company on terms hereafter set out.

18. On the assumption that the people of Canada take control of the Grand Trunk, Grand Trunk Pacific, and Canadian Northern, we consider possible methods of management and operation.

19. *We do not consider that operation by a Minister directly responsible to Parliament would be in the public interest.* It would not secure better service or lower rates.

20. If the Government operated these three railways, it would be bound in fairness to the Canadian Pacific shareholders to take over their railway also. The Canadian Pacific gives good service and should not be interfered with.

21. Special objections to direct Government ownership and operation are: —

　(1) That Canadian railways operate more than seven thousand miles of line subject to the foreign jurisdiction of the United States;

　(2) That the Canadian Government resources are required for war purposes.

22. *We therefore reject* the idea of direct Government ownership and operation.

23. *We do not recommend* that the Grand Trunk, Grand Trunk Pacific and Canadian Northern Companies be allowed to go into the hands of a receiver. . . .

25. We have discussed and rejected the following suggestions:–

Transfer of all three railways to the Canadian Pacific.

Transfer of the Canadian Northern or a portion of it to the Canadian Pacific.

26. There is no possibility of forming a new commercial company to take over the three railways. . . .

27. Having come to the conclusion that direct ownership and operation by the Government is to be avoided, and that ownership and operation by a commercial company is not possible, *we recommend that a new public authority, a Board of Trustees be incorporated by Act of Parliament as the "Dominion Railway Company"; and that the Canadian Northern, Grand Trunk and Grand Trunk Pacific be transferred to this body.*

28. *We recommend* that the Government assume responsibility to the Dominion Railway Company for the interest on the existing securities of the transferred companies.

29. *We recommend* that the Intercolonial and National Transcontinental be also transferred to the Dominion Railway Company. . . .

30. *We recommend that the whole of the Dominion Railways be operated by the Trustees as one united system, on a commercial basis, under their own politically undisturbed management, on account of, and for the benefit of, the people of Canada.*

31. *We recommend* that there be five Trustees, three railway members, one member selected on the ground of business and financial experience, and one as specially possessing the confidence of railway employees; that the original Trustees be named in the Act constituting the Board; and that their tenure of office be substantially the same as that of judges of the Supreme Court.

32. *We recommend* that the original Trustees retire after 3, 4, 5, 6, 7 years, respectively, according to a prescribed scheme; that they be eligible for reappointment; and that all appointments subsequent to the original statutory appointments be by the Governor General in Council on the nomination of the Trustees themselves.

33. We lay stress on the importance of the Board being non-political, permanent, and self-perpetuating. . . .

34. We give reasons for concluding that railways are not a proper subject for direct Parliamentary control. We point to a general tendency in modern democracies to withdraw certain subjects from this control. And we show that under Parliamentary control the general interest of the whole community tends to be subordinated to the particular local and individual interests.

35. *We recommend* that the authority of the Railway Commission be extended to include the Dominion Railway Company's system. . . .

47. We deal with the legal position of the Trustees; and point out that the Canadian Northern, Grand Trunk and Grand Trunk Pacific Companies will continue to exist; and that consequently the rights of their security holders will remain undisturbed. . . .

Smith (Minority) Report

. . .

Consideration of all phases of the problem leads me to recommend the following remedies for the existing situation:–

Let the Canadian Pacific alone; let the Grand Trunk operate the eastern lines now held by that company and the Canadian Northern; let the Canadian Northern operate the western lines, now held by that company and the Grand Trunk Pacific system; let the Government operate the connections or procure their operation by private companies; all of which should be done under arrangements that are equitable and yet look to the not distant day when the country will have survived the war and resumed its prosperous growth. . . .

Facing the urgency of the need, considering the part which the Government has taken and the responsibility which it shares, and keenly alive to the magnitude and the importance of the tasks now placed upon the railroads and the greater tasks which they will face, I see no safe alternative but that the Government shall continue, with discrimination and resort to all available safeguards, and under a policy of proper regulation and co-ordination of effort, to aid the necessitous railroads of the Dominion until such time, which I hope and believe will not be far distant, when these will become self-sup- porting and the problem will be solved.

101. Extracts from the Act Providing for Purchase of the Stock of the Canadian Northern, 1917

(7-8 George V, Chap. 24)

The most urgent aspect of the railway problem was the financial straits of the Canadian Northern, with its only lately completed main line running from Quebec City to Vancouver. The Borden government could not bring itself to accept either the letter of the Drayton-Acworth proposals, which would have handed the embarrassed railways over to a self-perpetuating Board divorced from parliamentary control, while allowing them to retain their formal separate legal existence, or the Smith report, which would have continued doles from the public treasury to privately owned lines. It decided to take ownership of the Canadian Northern and operate it through a Board appointed by the government and responsible to Parliament (see the statement by Sir Thomas White, Minister of Finance, in the House of Commons on 1 August 1917). There was a severe parliamentary battle, involving the use of closure, before this Act was passed. See Roger Graham, *Arthur Meighen*, I: *The Door of Opportunity* (Toronto, 1960).

(Assented to 20th September, 1917)

. . .

1. His Majesty may acquire the six hundred thousand shares of capital stock of the Canadian Northern Railway Company (par value sixty million dollars), not now held by the Minister of Finance in trust for His Majesty, on such terms and conditions satisfactory to the Governor in Council as may be set out in an Agreement to be made between His Majesty and the owners and pledgees of not less than five-sixths thereof, and for a price to be determined by arbitration as hereinafter provided. . . .*

3. (1) So soon as the said five-sixths of the said shares have been transferred as aforesaid, the Governor in Council may assist the Canadian Northern Railway Company, or any Company included in the Canadian Northern Railway System, in paying and settling any indebtedness of such Company or postponing the payment thereof on such terms as may be agreed upon, and for such purposes may make advances out of the Consolidated Revenue Fund: Provided, however, that until authorized by Parliament, the total of such advances shall not exceed the sum of twenty-five million dollars. . . .

102. Arthur Meighen on Public Ownership

(Debates, House of Commons, 28 April 1919)

In 1919 the government brought down legislation providing for the organization of the Canadian National Railways (below, **103**). In the debate on it Arthur Meighen, then Minister of the Interior, played a large part.

Mr. MEIGHEN: . . . Government ownership is wise when properly applied, when the circumstances are such that it is sound principle to

*The arbitrators, after hearing prolonged arguments in 1918, decided that the value of the 600,000 shares was $10,800,000.

apply it, and it gets to be a sound principle proportionately as the competitive element is eliminated and the element of monopoly takes its place—in proportion as the industry is evolved into that stage of maturity in which it becomes a monopoly, and essentially for its best operation must be operated by the State. Here we have this case, the Government of Canada owning to-day approximately one-half the railway mileage of this country. We propose to operate that mileage aside from politics in a separate organization responsible to the Government of this country, responsible to Parliament; operating it, I repeat, aside from political influence wholly and entirely. That is what we propose. We have all the conditions here for Government operation. We have first the condition of necessity; we have every condition that can obtain. . . .

Now, I say, we are going to compete with the Canadian Pacific. The Canadian Pacific has great charter powers and a tremendous organization, and in that competition we shall require the loyal support of every representative of the people of this country. We shall have to hold the balance in our legislative jurisdiction even, between the Canadian Pacific and our own road.

103. An Act to Incorporate Canadian National Railway Company and Respecting Canadian National Railways, 1919

(9-10 George V, Chap. 13)

This Act represents the government's attempt to produce a non-political organization for the control of railways in the spirit of the Drayton-Acworth Report. It did not actually come into effect until 1923, when an order in council unified the government's railway holdings, bringing the Grand Trunk under what was already called the Canadian National Railways. The King government had by then appointed Sir Henry Thornton as President and Chairman of the Company.* The Act still forms the basis of the national railway system. See Glazebrook, *History of Transportation*.

(*Assented to 6th June, 1919*)

WHEREAS His Majesty on behalf of the Dominion of Canada has acquired control of the Canadian Northern Railway Company and of the various Constituent and Subsidiary Companies comprising the

*See King's statement of 1925 on Thornton, above, pp. 79-80.

Canadian Northern System . . . , and it is expedient to provide for the incorporation of a Company under which the railways, works and undertakings of the Companies comprised in the Canadian Northern System may be consolidated, and together with the Canadian Government Railways operated as a national railway system: Therefore His Majesty, by and with the advice and consent of the Senate and House of Commons of Canada, enacts as follows: —

1. The Governor in Council may nominate such persons as may be deemed expedient, not less than five, nor more than fifteen, to be Directors of the Company hereby incorporated, and upon such nomination being made the persons so nominated, and their successors, and such other persons as may from time to time be nominated by the Governor in Council as Directors, shall be and are hereby incorporated as a Company, under the name of "Canadian National Railway Company," hereinafter called "the Company". No stock ownership shall be necessary to qualify a Director.

2. The Directors shall hold office from one annual meeting to another or until their successors are appointed, unless removed by the Governor in Council for cause. Upon any vacancy occurring the Governor in Council may fill the vacancy by the appointment of a successor. The continuance of a vacancy or vacancies shall not impair the powers of the Board of Directors. . . .

3. The Governor in Council may declare that the Company shall have a capital stock, with or without shares, to such amount as may from time to time be deemed expedient. All such stock shall, until otherwise ordered by the Governor in Council, be vested in the Minister of Finance on behalf of His Majesty. . . .

9. Whenever under the provisions of the *Railway Act*, or any other statute or law, the approval, sanction or confirmation by shareholders is required, such approval, sanction or confirmation may be given by the Governor in Council. . . .

11. The Governor in Council may from time to time by Order in Council entrust to the Company the management and operation of any lines of railway or parts thereof, and any property or works of whatever description, or interests therein, and any powers, rights or privileges over or with respect to any railways, properties or works, or interests therein, which may be from time to time vested in or owned, controlled or occupied by His Majesty, or such part or parts thereof, or rights or interests therein, as may be designated in any Order in Council, upon such terms and subject to such regulations and conditions as the Governor in Council may from time to time decide. . . .

26. The Company may, with the approval of the Governor in Council, issue bonds, debentures, debenture stock, perpetual or terminable, or other securities . . . in respect of the mileage of the lines of railway which it, from time to time, constructs, acquires, owns or controls, — not including the Canadian Government Railways nor exceeding, with outstanding securities, in the aggregate seventy-five thousand dollars ($75,000) per mile. . . .

104. The Grand Trunk Railway Acquisition Act, 1919

(10 George V, Chap. 17)

The final and perhaps most difficult stage of nationalization was the acquisition of the Grand Trunk Railway, including its subsidiary the Grand Trunk Pacific, with its main line terminating at Prince Rupert, B.C.* The Grand Trunk dated from 1853, was largely owned in Britain, and had been in financial difficulties from the beginning. See Leslie T. Fournier, *Railway Nationalization in Canada: The Problem of the Canadian National Railways* (Toronto, 1935) and A. W. Currie, *The Grand Trunk Railway of Canada* (Toronto, 1957).

(Assented to 10th November, 1919)

WHEREAS the present capital stock of the Grand Trunk Railway Company of Canada consists of the following: —

Four per cent (4%) guaranteed stock	£12,500,000
First preference five per cent (5%) stock	3,420,000
Second preference five per cent (5%) stock	2,530,000
Third preference four per cent (4%) stock	7,168,055
Common stock	23,955,437
	£49,573,492

And whereas the present outstanding debenture stocks of the Grand Trunk Railway Company of Canada consisting of —

Five per cent (5%) Grand Trunk debenture stock	£ 4,270,375

*The Grand Trunk owned 100 per cent of the stock of the G.T.P. See First Schedule of Agreement between the King and the Grand Trunk Railway Co., attached to 10-11 George V, Chap. 13, 11 May 1920.

Five per cent (5%) Great Western
debenture stock 2,723,080
Four per cent (4%) Grand Trunk debenture
stock 24,624,455
Four per cent (4%) Northern
debenture stock 308,215

£31,926,125

(hereinafter called the "present debenture stocks"), are entitled to certain voting powers at meetings of shareholders of the Grand Trunk Railway Company of Canada;

And whereas it is expedient that His Majesty should acquire the whole of the capital stock of the Grand Trunk Railway Company of Canada except the four per cent (4%) guaranteed stock above referred to and should have power to acquire the said four per cent (4%) guaranteed stock:

Therefore His Majesty, by and with the advice and consent of the Senate and House of Commons of Canada, enacts as follows: —
. . .

2. Subject to the provisions of this Act, His Majesty the King, represented by the Minister of Railways and Canals of Canada, acting under the authority of the Governor in Council (hereinafter called the "Government") may enter into an agreement (hereinafter called the "said agreement") with the Grand Trunk Railway Company of Canada (hereinafter called the "Grand Trunk") and with such other companies and interests as the Government may think necessary, for the acquisition by the Government of the entire capital stock of the Grand Trunk, except the four per cent (4%) guaranteed stock of the Grand Trunk, amounting to £12,500,000 the latter being hereinafter called the "present guaranteed stock.". . .

4. As part of the consideration for such acquisition, the Government may agree to guarantee the payment of: —

(a) Dividends payable half yearly, at four per cent per annum, upon the present guaranteed stock;

(b) The interest upon the present debenture stocks as and when payable, in accordance with the terms thereof.

These guarantees to take effect upon the date of the appointment of the Committee of Management hereinafter mentioned. . . .

Provided that concurrently with such guarantee of dividends and interest upon the present guaranteed stock and the present debenture stocks, respectively, the voting powers at meetings of shareholders of the Grand Trunk now vested in or exercisable by the holders of the said stocks respectively shall cease and determine absolutely. . . .

6. The value, if any, of the first, second and third preference stocks and the common or ordinary stock of the Grand Trunk now issued and outstanding to the face values above mentioned . . . shall be determined by a Board of three Arbitrators, one to be appointed by the Government, one by the Grand Trunk, and the third shall be Sir Walter Cassels, Judge of the Exchequer Court of Canada. . . .

7. As soon as said agreement has been ratified by a majority in voting power of the holders of the stocks enumerated in the preamble to this Act, present in person or by proxy and voting at a special general meeting of such stockholders duly called for the purpose of considering such agreement;

(a) A Committee of Management shall be formed consisting of five persons, two to be appointed by the Grand Trunk, two by the Government, and the fifth by the four so appointed, to insure the operation of the Grand Trunk System (in so far as it is possible so to do) in harmony with the Canadian National Railways, the two systems being treated in the public interest as nearly as possible as one system. The Committee shall continue to act until the preference and common stocks are transferred to or vested in the Government, when it shall be discharged. . . .

8. The said agreement shall provide for: —

. . .

(d) The entrusting to the said Committee of Management by the Minister of Railways and Canals as Receiver of the Grand Trunk Pacific Railway System,* on terms to be approved by the Governor in Council, of the exercise of such of his powers as Receiver as the Governor in Council may deem requisite in order that the operation and management of the said Grand Trunk Pacific Railway System may be conducted in harmony with the operation of other railways and properties under the control of the said Committee. . . .

11. Upon the transfer to or vesting in the Government of the preference and common stock as herein provided for, the Governor in Council may provide for the discharge of the receivership of the Grand Trunk Pacific Railway System and the termination and withdrawal of the proceedings in the Exchequer Court of Canada relating thereto. . . .

*After being informed that the government would give no more aid to the Grand Trunk Pacific under existing conditions, the Grand Trunk informed the government that the G.T.P. would have to cease operations. The government then placed the G.T.P. in receivership (9 March 1919).

NOTE: In contrast with the result of the Canadian Northern arbitration, in the Grand Trunk case the arbitrators decided in September 1921 by a vote of two to one that the preference and common shares were valueless. (It may be noted that the common stock had never paid a dividend, the preference stock "only intermittently".) The English holders of these stocks were thus deprived of their property without compensation. Whether this was justified or not, Canada as a field for British investment received a bad black eye; and this may have reinforced the contemporary trend against British capital coming to the Dominion (above, **99**).

105. Extracts from the Canadian National-Canadian Pacific Act, 1933

(23-24 George V, Chap. 33)

In 1931 the Bennett government, spurred by the manner in which the Depression was accentuating the problems of the railways, appointed a new Royal Commission on Transportation with Mr. Justice L. P. Duff as chairman. The commission reported in the following year, recommending measures to divorce further the Canadian National Railways from politics, criticizing excessive competition between the C.N.R. and the Canadian Pacific, calling attention to what it considered C.N.R. extravagance, and urging a policy of economical co-operation between the two railways. The report became the basis of this Act of 1933. One result was the co-operative "pool trains" in central Canada, jointly operated by the two systems until long after the Second World War. See Fournier, *Railway Nationalization in Canada.*

(Assented to 23rd May, 1933)

. . .

4. (1) The Governor in Council may vacate all nominations heretofore made to the Board of Directors of the National Company pursuant to section three of the National Act, and may appoint in the place and stead of and in succession to the incorporators of that Company three Trustees. . . .

(2) One of such Trustees shall be their Chairman. He shall devote his whole time to performance of the duties of his office. . . .

7. No Trustee shall be removed from office, nor suffer any reduction in salary, during the term for which he is appointed, unless for assigned cause and on address of the Senate and House of Commons of Canada. . . .

10. (1) The Trustees shall appoint, on terms to be fixed by them, and with the titular rank of President, a person other than one of themselves to execute and perform, under and in consultation with them, the powers, authorities and duties of chief operating office of National Railways, as such powers, authorities and duties shall be

from time to time defined by by-law or resolution of the Trustees and committed for execution and performance. The President shall report and be responsible to the Trustees and to them alone....*

16. (1) The National Company ... and the Pacific Company ... are, for the purposes of effecting economies and providing for more remunerative operation, directed to attempt forthwith to agree and continuously to endeavour to agree, and they respectively are, ... authorized to agree, upon such co-operative measures, plans and arrangements as are fair and reasonable and best adapted (with due regard to equitable distribution of burden and advantage as between them) to effect such purposes. They are further directed that whenever they shall so agree they shall endeavour to provide through negotiations with the representatives of the employees affected, as part of such measure, plan or arrangement or otherwise, for a fair and reasonable apportionment as between the employees of National Railways and Pacific Railways, respectively, for such employment as may be incident to the operation of such measure, plan or arrangement....

27. Nothing in this Act shall be deemed to authorize the amalgamation of any railway company which is comprised in National Railways with any railway company which is comprised in Pacific Railways nor to authorize the unified management and control of the railway system which forms part of National Railways with the railway system which forms part of Pacific Railways....†

106. The *Winnipeg Free Press* on Railway Amalgamation, 1933

(Editorial, *Winnipeg Free Press*, 4 September 1933)

Before the Royal Commission of 1931, and on other occasions, the President of the Canadian Pacific, Mr. (later Sir) E. W. Beatty, advocated amalgamation of the Canadian National and Canadian Pacific systems to the extent of unified management by the C.P.R. Here the *Free Press* characteristically pays its respects to a renewal of this campaign.

*Sir Henry Thornton (above, p. 235) had resigned under criticism in 1932.
†The system by which the C.N.R. was controlled by a Board of Trustees (above, 105) was short-lived. In 1936 the new King government put through Parliament an Act (1 Edward VIII, Chap. 25, 23 June 1936) which restored control by a board of directors appointed by the Governor in Council.

RETURNING TO THE ATTACK

Viewing the great attempt of President Roosevelt to lift the United States out of its difficulties, the Montreal Star says that the effect on Canadians will be to lead to a demand that their own government also take extraordinary steps to improve the situation in this country. This is by way of introduction to the declaration that our greatest problem is that of our railways and the difficulties with which the two railway systems are now struggling. The Star's method of solving the problem, of course, is to get rid of the government railway system by allowing the Canadian Pacific railway to take it over. The Montreal newspaper is apparently beginning a new campaign along these lines.

As long as both the railways continue to suffer severely from the depression, a renewal of the attack on the Canadian National was to be expected, in spite of the legislation passed at the last session of Parliament* which provided for the continuance of the two railways as separate corporations co-operating as far as possible under the present emergency conditions.

Whatever might be done about the difficult position of the Canadian National, the solution that will never be adopted is to allow the private company to absorb the Canadian National, thus creating a colossal railway corporation towering above the government and wielding an immense influence. Those who look to a great private railway monopoly in Canada, may just as well forget about it. The Canadian people will never accept that plan, nor any other plan which they think will likely lead to the same result. . . .

2. *The Internal-Combustion Engine Works a Revolution*

The revolution produced by the internal-combustion engine was well under way before 1914, and it reached its greatest height after 1945; but between those years this invention made an extraordinary change in the world, replacing horse-power with mechanical power on the ground (cf. above, **96**) and making practicable the large-scale transportation of people and goods by air. In the First World War motor transport and aerial warfare were important novelties; in the Second they were universal and dominant.

*Above, **105**.

One middle-class Canadian family's experience may demonstrate what was happening. The editor's father graduated from medical school in 1885, and for some years he practised in small Ontario towns, making his rounds with a horse and buggy. Before the turn of the century he moved to Toronto, and thereafter he abandoned the horse and turned to the bicycle, then having its short heyday. On 4 August 1914, the day the British Empire went to war with Germany, he bought his first automobile, a Model T Ford.

107. Statistics of Production and Registration of Motor Vehicles in Canada, 1914-1945

(Urquhart and Buckley, *Historical Statistics of Canada*)

This table reflects the vast increase in the number of motor vehicles in use in Canada during the period, and the parallel increase in production. Note the collapse of manufacture during the Depression after 1929, and the great production of military vehicles (classified under "Commercial") during the Second World War. No production figures are available before 1918.

| | Production | | Motor Vehicles |
| | Passenger Cars | Commercial Vehicles | Registered in Canada |
	(number)		*(thousands)*
1914			74.2
1915			95.3
1916			128.3
1917			203.5
1918	69,801	7,319	276.9
1919	68,408	7,899	342.4
1920	79,369	10,174	408.8
1921	57,401	5,148	464.8
1922	79,094	8,169	509.4
1923	106,226	19,226	576.0
1924	98,365	18,043	645.3
1925	120,205	26,397	724.0
1926	154,061	30,440	832.3
1927	137,290	29,603	939.7
1928	176,096	17,527	1,069.3

	Passenger Cars	Commercial Vehicles	Registered in Canada
1929	188,721	50,293	1,187.3
1930	115,535	16,742	1,232.5
1931	64,629	17,487	1,200.7
1932	48,332	10,095	1,113.5
1933	47,510	12,003	1,083.2
1934	80,118	24,205	1,129.5
1935	111,782	37,315	1,176.1
1936	108,340	33,790	1,240.1
1937	132,835	54,417	1,319.7
1938	105,392	42,325	1,394.9
1939	90,148	47,057	1,439.2
1940	102,664	113,102	1,500.8
1941	91,331	173,588	1,572.8
1942	11,966	216,057	1,524.2
1943	Nil	178,064	1,511.8
1944	Nil	158,038	1,502.6
1945	1,866	130,777	1,497.1

108. General Motors Quietly Takes Over

(*Financial Post*, Toronto, 23 November 1918)

The McLaughlin family, formerly manufacturers of horse-drawn vehicles, had been making cars at Oshawa, Ontario, since 1908. For some years before 1918 General Motors, the American corporation, had owned just short of a majority of the shares of the McLaughlin Motor Car Co. Ltd., the rest being owned by the McLaughlin Carriage Co. In November-December 1918 the McLaughlin companies were reorganized into General Motors of Canada, Limited, and the U.S. corporation bought out the McLaughlin interest. It is interesting that the *Financial Post* thought Colonel McLaughlin's appointment to the American board the only aspect worthy of comment. The incident illustrates two processes which were already under way: the concentration of motor car manufacture in the United States in the hands of a few great corporations, and the acquisition of total control of the Canadian motor industry by those corporations. See Arthur Pound, *The Turning Wheel: The Story of General Motors through Twenty-Five Years, 1908-1933* (New York, 1934).

Following the recently-arranged reorganization of the General Motors Corporation's Canadian interests, it is announced that R. S.

McLaughlin, president of the McLaughlin Motor Car Co., Limited, of Oshawa, has been elected a director and member of the executive of the big United States Corporation.

109. Glimpses of the Coming Air Age, 1930

(*Report of the Department of National Defence, Canada, for the fiscal year ending March 31, 1931 (Militia and Air Services)*)

By 1930 civil aviation in Canada was beginning to develop on a considerable scale, but this document shows that it was still in a pioneer stage. There was still no effective commercial air service between cities (below, **111**).

CIVIL GOVERNMENT AIR OPERATIONS

The Director of Civil Government Air Operations is responsible to the deputy minister for the administration and control of all civil air operations required by any department of the Government.

During the year 1930 the Departments of the Interior, Agriculture, Indian Affairs, Mines, Public Works, Marine and Fisheries, and National Defence availed themselves of [R.C.A.F.] aircraft for a variety of purposes. . . .

Forest fire protection operations for the Department of the Interior, Forestry Branch, covered approximately 92,005,466 acres of forest land in Manitoba, Saskatchewan, and Alberta.

Eleven mobile photographic detachments were engaged in air photography.

The total flying time for all units during the year was 13,640 hours 14 minutes. . . .

CIVIL AVIATION DIVISION

The Controller of Civil Aviation is responsible to the Deputy Minister of National Defence for the administration of Air Regulations and the control of commercial and private flying in Canada, the location and equipment of airways, construction of airship bases and the oversight of flying clubs. . . .

STATISTICS

There were in Canada 100 commercial aircraft operators, 527 licensed civil aircraft, 402 licensed commercial air pilots, 309 private air pilots, 370 licensed air engineers, and 77 aerodromes.

Comparative figures showing flying activities are given below for 1929 and 1930, including the Ontario Provincial Air Service, whose pilots flew 875,735 miles, and light aeroplane clubs, which totalled approximately 1,120,000 miles; in fact all flying done in Canada except that of the air services of the Department of National Defence and privately owned aircraft.

	1929	*1930*
Number of flights	144,143	156,574
Number of hours	79,786	92,993
Number of passengers	124,751	124,875
Number of passenger-miles	6,114,997	5,408,676
Pounds of freight	3,903,908	1,759,259*
Pounds of mail (contract)	430,636	474,199

Commercial flying comprised the following: —

(*a*) Transportation services: Scheduled mail, passenger flights, and express routes.

(*b*) Commercial services; including flying instruction, air photography, timber cruising, forest and fishery patrols, passenger and express services, taxi, sight-seeing tours, exhibition flying, etc.

(*c*) Mining companies: Mining, exploration and prospecting.

(*d*) Ontario Provincial Air Service: Forest fire protection, timber cruising, air photography, and transportation.

(*e*) Light Aeroplane Clubs: Instruction and exhibition flying.

The greatest volume of flying was done in Canada by the fixed-base and itinerant operator, comprising flying instruction, air photography, timber cruising, forest and fishery patrols, passenger and express services, taxi, and sight-seeing tours, etc. One hundred operators were engaged, of which fourteen conducted schools of flying. The distance flown by these operators was 4,143,857 miles.

Four mining companies employed aircraft as an aid to exploration and prospecting in various parts of Canada; their pilots flew a distance of 594,856 miles, as far north as Herschel Island and Coronation Gulf. . . .

*These figures presumably reflect the onset of the Depression.

AIR MAIL

During 1930, 19 regular air mail routes were operated under Post Office contracts with commercial firms. . . . The following services were operated: —

Yearly* Services. — Montreal-Detroit, Montreal-Albany, Sioux Lookout-Red Lake Area, Toronto-Buffalo, Winnipeg-Calgary, Regina-Moose Jaw-Edmonton, Fort McMurray-Aklavik, Peace River-North Vermilion, Osklaneo-Chibougamau (superseded in September by the service Amos-Chibougamau), Amos-Sisco, Montreal-Moncton-Saint John. . . .

In addition to the regular mail contracts a special service authorized by the Post Office is operated between Whitehorse and Dawson, Y.T. . . .

. . . Surveys made for the extension of the prairie airways west to Vancouver indicated that the southern route via the Crowsnest pass and Grand Forks was the shortest and safest. It was therefore decided to include the city of Lethbridge on the transprairie schedule and to make this point the junction for the north-south and east-west mails. . . .

DEVELOPMENT OF AIRWAYS

. . . The following shows the ground facilities provided for airways throughout Canada in 1930.

Lighted Government airports	1
Partially lighted Government airports	1
Lighted public airports	9
Lighted intermediate aerodromes	38
Rotating electric beacons	39
Stationary electric beacons	1
Acetylene range lanterns	56
Radio beacon stations	5

Total distance lighted: —

Eastern Airways	190 miles
Western Airways	1,125 miles
Total distance lighted	1,315 miles

. . .

*That is, all-year-round as distinct from seasonal.

ST. HUBERT AIRPORT AND AIRSHIP BASE

During 1930 the mooring tower was completed and additional construction work undertaken on the aerodrome. . . .*

The British Airship R. 100 made its first transatlantic flight to Canada on July 29, and arrived in Montreal [St. Hubert] on the morning of August 1. The mooring of the airship was carried out successfully and the facilities prepared for her reception [were] entirely satisfactory. A flight was made by R. 100 to Ottawa, Toronto and Niagara Falls, and return to Montreal on August 9. The airship was refuelled, gassed, and reballasted and started on her return journey to England on August 13.

110. The Horse Still Has His Day, 1932

(*Globe*, Toronto, 2 July 1932)

For many years the Toronto Open Air Horse Show offered a free spectacle for the citizens on Dominion Day. This account is evidence that the horse was still important in commercial life in 1932. But the show was held for the last time in 1935. The internal-combustion engine had won a final victory.

The rain descended on the judged and the unjudged alike. Also on the judges. It was not regarded. No Dominion Day cloudburst can quench the ardor [of] the horse lovers and the horses that take part in Toronto's annual open air Horse Show.

"Parade Takes Place, Rain or Shine." It said so on the official entry list. Accordingly the thirtieth anniversary parade of the Toronto Open Air Horse Show took place yesterday morning in the thickest of the downpour.

The working horses of Toronto were the pride of the parade. Pampered beauties of the show horse classes came out to be judged, but not all of them stayed the parade's course, as every working horse did. Police mounts and army horses, Street Commission, milk

*During the Imperial Conference of 1926 even Mackenzie King's imagination was touched by the exposition of the British plans for using dirigibles for communication between Commonwealth countries, and he pledged co-operation on the spot; the St. Hubert mooring tower and the flight of the R. 100 were the result. But the whole dream crumbled with the disastrous crash of the sister airship R. 101 in France in October 1930, and the St. Hubert tower was never used again. The future of trans-oceanic air navigation lay with heavier-than-air machines.

wagon, bread wagon and coal wagon horses, express horses and car-
tage horses, heavy-draught, light-draught, and delivery, five
hundred of the pick of the city's working horses took the rain in their
stride, let the color run where it would from their ribbons and
paraded through the wet, wet streets.

The parade started from Queen's Park, Inspector Crosbie's
mackintosh-covered cohorts leading the van. At half-past eleven it
came around to Queen's Park again. The sun shone then. The band
played airs from light operas that were in their prime when the horse
had no gasoline-propelled rival. Applause rippled ahead of the
prancing procession. Cups shone and ribbons fluttered. It was a
moment to make any horse forget his wetting and step high.

Unquestionably "Sandy" found it so. Sandy is 26 years old, and
knows all there is to know about horse shows and delivering milk.
He added another first to his string of prizes yesterday....*

Mayor [William J.] Stewart, assisted by President T. A. Crow,
presented the cups to the winners. Miss Ruth Stewart, 13-year-old
daughter of the Mayor, took three of them....

111. The Trans-Canada Air Lines Act, 1937

(1 George VI, Chap. 43)

This Act established a national air line on principles similar to those
governing the Canadian National Railways and organized through the
agency of that corporation. Mackenzie King's Minister of Transport,
C. D. Howe, explaining the measure to the House of Commons on 25
March 1937, made it evident that the task of providing air service
between urban centres was so large, urgent and expensive that only
the resources of the government were equal to carrying it out. He said,
"I think we are getting the best features of government ownership
without the obligation of direct government operation which in the
past has been troublesome." The Act was amended in 1938 to make it
more directly applicable to overseas as well as domestic operations.
The amendments are included here.

(Assented to 10th April, 1937)

...

3. The following persons, namely, Valentine Irving Smart, Robert
Knowlton Smith, Charles Peter Edwards, Edward Burton Jost and

*Sandy worked for the City Dairy Co. He placed first in the "old horse class,"
single horse and outfit.

Findlay Malcolm Maclennan together with such persons as become shareholders of the Corporation are hereby incorporated under the name of "Trans-Canada Air Lines."*

4. The persons named in the next preceding section shall be the provisional directors of the Corporation. . . .

6. (1) The Corporation shall be under the management of a Board of Directors composed of seven persons, elected and appointed as hereinafter provided.

(2) It shall not be necessary that a director be a shareholder of the Corporation, but no person shall be elected or appointed as a director or shall continue to hold office as such who is not a British subject who has been continuously resident in Canada for not less than five years prior to the date of his election or appointment.

(3) Four directors shall be elected by the shareholders of the Corporation and three directors shall be appointed by the Governor in Council. . . .

7. (1) The authorized capital of the Corporation shall be five million dollars divided into shares of one hundred dollars each, represented by share certificates.

(2) The shares of the capital stock of the Corporation shall be offered for subscription to the Canadian National Railway Company at par.

(3) The Canadian National Railway Company is hereby authorized to subscribe for, underwrite, purchase, hold, and, subject to the provisions of this Act, sell and dispose of the shares of the capital stock of the Corporation.

Provided however that the Canadian National Railway Company shall not sell or dispose of more than twenty-four thousand nine hundred shares except with the approval of Parliament. . . .

9. Shares of capital stock shall not be transferable except to such persons engaged or interested in aviation as are approved by the Minister.

10. No shares shall be held by any person other than a British subject resident in Canada or a corporation incorporated under the laws of Canada or of any province and controlled by British subjects ordinarily resident in Canada, and if any shares are held by any person or corporation not authorized by this section to hold shares the same may be forfeited to His Majesty by order of the Exchequer Court of Canada on the application of the Minister.

11. (1) The Minister shall, with the approval of the Governor in Council, be entitled at any time to acquire from the shareholders all

*The name was changed to Air Canada in 1964.

of the shares of the capital stock of the Corporation on payment to the shareholders of the book value thereof, and the Governor in Council may by order vest the said shares in the Minister. . . .

12. (1) Subject to the provisions of this Act, The Canadian National Railway Company may issue notes, obligations, bonds and other securities (hereinafter in this section called "securities") not exceeding the sum of five million dollars for the purpose of acquiring the capital stock of the Corporation, and the Governor in Council may authorize the guarantee of the principle and interest of such securities on behalf of His Majesty. . . .

14. The Corporation is authorized, —

(a) to establish, operate and maintain air lines or regular services of aircraft of all kinds, to carry on the business of transporting mails, passengers and goods by any means, and either by the Corporation's own aircraft and conveyances or by means of the aircraft and conveyances of others, and to enter into contracts with any person or company for the interchange of traffic. . . .

(d) to carry on its business throughout Canada and outside of Canada.

14A.* The Corporation may, with the approval of the Governor in Council, purchase or otherwise acquire, hold, pledge and dispose of shares in the capital stock of a company to be incorporated under the laws of England upon application by the following companies, acting in co-operation, namely, Imperial Airways Limited or such other company as may be nominated by the Government of the United Kingdom, Aer-Rianta, Teoranta, or such other company as may be nominated by the Government of Eire, and the Corporation, for the purposes, *inter alia*, of establishing and carrying on the business of an aerial transport company operating a trans-Atlantic service between Europe and North America.

15. (1)† The Governor in Council may authorize the Minister [of Transport] to enter into a contract with the Corporation (to be known as the Trans-Canada contract) for the organization, operation and maintenance by the Corporation of lines of aircraft (to be known as the Trans-Canada Lines) for the speedy and efficient transport of passengers, and goods across Canada and between and within the several provinces thereof, and between points in Canada and points outside of Canada, over routes wholly within or partly within and partly outside of Canada.

*Added by the amending Act, 2 George VI, Chap. 15 (7 April 1938).
†Substituted by the amending Act of 1938 for a section under which the Trans-Canada contract referred only to operations within Canada.

(2) The Trans-Canada contract shall provide, —...

(c) for the payment to the Corporation, at the end of each calendar year of the initial period [ending 31 December 1939], of a subsidy equal to the deficit, if any, resulting from operations during such calendar year, which subsidy shall be payable out of moneys to be appropriated by Parliament for that purpose;

(d) for the transport of passengers and goods by the Corporation at tariff charges on a competitive basis with other similar transportation services in North America. ...

E.
Public Finance and Taxation

112. Extract from the Income War Tax Act, 1917

(7-8 George V, Chap. 28)

One consequence of the First World War was a great increase in direct taxation. Until 1914 the Dominion drew its revenue largely from customs and excise duties. But during the conflict and in the postwar years various "war" taxes were imposed to meet the enormous new expenditures the war involved. Some of these became permanent features of the taxation system. This was notably the case with the income tax, first introduced in 1917, and the sales tax, introduced in 1920. In 1921, for the first time, revenue from the new direct taxes exceeded that from customs duties. See *Canada Year Book, 1938*, pp. 834-52.

(Assented to 20th September, 1917)
. . .

4. (1) There shall be assessed, levied and paid, upon the income during the preceding year of every person residing or ordinarily resident in Canada or carrying on any business in Canada, the following taxes: —

(*a*) four per centum upon all income exceeding fifteen hundred dollars in the case of unmarried persons and widows or widowers without dependent children, and exceeding three thousand dollars in the case of all other persons;

and in addition thereto,

(*b*) two per centum upon the amount by which the income exceeds six thousand dollars and does not exceed ten thousand dollars; and,

(*c*) five per centum upon the amount by which the income exceeds ten thousand dollars and does not exceed twenty thousand dollars; and,

(*d*) eight per centum of the amount by which the income exceeds twenty thousand dollars and does not exceed thirty thousand dollars; and, (*e*) ten per centum of the amount by which the income exceeds thirty thousand dollars and does not exceed fifty thousand dollars; and,

(*f*) fifteen per centum of the amount by which the income exceeds fifty thousand dollars and does not exceed one hundred thousand dollars; and,

(*g*) twenty-five per centum of the amount by which the income exceeds one hundred thousand dollars.

(2) Corporations and joint stock companies, no matter how created or organized, shall pay the normal tax upon income exceeding three thousand dollars, but shall not be liable to pay the supertax*....

113. Paying for the First World War

(*Debates, House of Commons*, 5 June 1919)

This extract from the 1919 budget speech of Sir Thomas White, Sir Robert Borden's Minister of Finance, in the nature of things presents only a preliminary and incomplete accounting of the colossal cost of the war; but the general pattern emerges clearly. A feature of war finance which to contemporaries was very novel and remarkable was the extent to which the government's needs were met by borrowing inside Canada. Sir Thomas gave statistics indicating that, to the time of his speech, a total of $1,405,416,400 had been raised by five war loans.

Hon. Sir THOMAS WHITE (Minister of Finance) ...

The war is over and all nations are engaged in counting the cost, estimating the condition in which their finance and trade have been left after the fiery tempest which has passed over the world, and devising ways and means to repair the ruin which has been wrought.

It seems to me that what the House and the people of Canada will first desire to learn from the Budget speech will be what has been the cost of the war to Canada, what is our present financial position, what it will be when demobilization has taken place and our war expenditure is completely at an end, and what are the additional annual charges which must be met as the result of the war.

*This Act defines supertax as that authorized by "paragraphs (*b*) to (*g*), both inclusive, of section four of this Act." Businesses were already subject to special taxation under the Business Profits War Tax Act, 1916, and were permitted to deduct from income tax for 1917 the amounts paid under that Act.

To these topics I shall first address myself. The fiscal year of the Dominion closes on March 31. According to our system some time is required for the completion of the services and bringing into account of all items attributable to the year closed on that date, but a fairly accurate forecast may be given of what the completed accounts will reveal.

With regard to the cost of the war to the Dominion, the books of the Finance Department show as of March 31 last a total principal war expenditure of $1,327,273,848. The portions incurred in respect of the several years during the continuance of the war are as follows:

$ 60,750,476 for 1914-15
$166,197,755 for 1915-16
$306,488,814 for 1916-17
$343,836,801 for 1917-18
$450,000,000 for 1918-19

Over the same fiscal period, namely from April 1, 1914 to March 31, 1919, the total expenditure upon ordinary account, that is to say, the current outlays of the Dominion in respect of its various services aggregated $832,757,589. The expenditure upon capital and other accounts for which by the practice of all our Governments provision might properly be made by borrowing, and for which assets of equivalent value were created for the permanent benefit of the people of Canada, amounted during the five years in question to $180,277,873.

Leaving capital expenditure aside and applying the surplus available from our revenues over and above the amount required to meet current outlays it will appear that we have met the principal cost of the war from taxation to a total aggregate amount of $275,943,977. If we take into account the amount contributed during the five year period for interest upon war debt and for pension charges the total paid from revenue on account of the war to March 31, 1919, is $438,293,248.

Now let us approach the subject from another angle. Aside from the cost of the war and how that cost was met, the vital question before us to-day is what is the amount of the total net national debt of Canada and how does it compare with the net debt at the end of the fiscal year immediately preceding the war.

On March 31, 1914, the net national debt was $335,996,850. On March 31, 1919, the net national debt was $1,584,000,000.

There remains to be considered what further increase in the national debt will be made during the present fiscal year which will end on March 31, 1920.

The war, so far as actual fighting is concerned, was terminated by the armistice of November 11 last; but . . . the present year is, so far as expenditure is concerned, a war year. It is impossible to estimate accurately what our demobilization expenditure for 1919-20 will be, but we may be sure that it will not be materially less than $300,000,000.

Assuming that we shall not be able, in view of the magnitude of our reconstruction programme, to pay any substantial part of our demobilization expenditure from revenue, we may calculate that when demobilization is complete and no further outlays are necessary on what I may call the principal of our war expenditure the total net debt of Canada will stand at not less than $1,950,000,000, or in round figures $2,000,000,000. . . . The increase during the five year war period is thus shown in round figures at $1,614,000,000. . . .

Mr. Speaker, I do not in the least desire to minimize the gravity of so great a debt as now confronts us on the threshold of the new era upon which we are entering. It will constitute a burden upon the people of Canada for generations to come. Fighting for the principles for which we stood we could not and did not count the money cost which is really the least part of our sacrifices in the war. The realization that at the greatest crisis in all history when the fate of world freedom was trembling in the scale of destiny, this gallant country of eight million people put its all to the hazard in the mightiest of conflicts for the cause of truth and justice, will be the lofty inspiration to greater effort which will enable Canada to carry and ultimately extinguish the heavy obligations entailed by the war. . . .

In considering the subject of our national debt an important aspect from the viewpoint of its bearing upon our financial standing and credit is whether it is owed to our own people or abroad. . . . From the national standpoint a public debt owed to a nation's own people is not nearly so serious an obligation as if owed abroad. The interest paid upon it is disbursed at home and remains part of the national resources. . . . In this respect and bearing especially in mind the fact that before the war Canada's borrowing for federal, provincial, municipal and business purposes was principally in Britain and the United States and not in Canada, the situation as to our national debt may be regarded with satisfaction.

In round figures the total outstanding securities of the Dominion Government are held as follows: in Great Britain, $326,700,000; in the United States, $150,873,000; in Canada, $1,510,000,000.

Some hon. MEMBERS: Hear, hear. . . .

Sir THOMAS WHITE: . . . On account of this being, as respects expenditure, a war year, we shall have to float at least one further loan in Canada for purposes connected with the war and demobilization.... *

114. The Bank of Canada Act, 1934

(24-25 George V, Chap. 43)

One of R. B. Bennett's innovations in the latter part of his administration was the creation for the first time of a national central bank. Though the bank was subject to strong government influence and in fact functioned largely as an arm of the government, under Bennett's legislation it was not publicly owned.

(Assented to 3rd July, 1934)

WHEREAS it is desirable to establish a central bank in Canada to regulate credit and currency in the best interests of the economic life of the nation, to control and protect the external value of the national monetary unit and to mitigate by its influence fluctuations in the general level of production, trade, prices and employment, so far as may be possible within the scope of monetary action, and generally to promote the economic and financial welfare of the Dominion: Therefore, His Majesty, by and with the advice and consent of the Senate and House of Commons of Canada, enacts as follows: —

. . .

3. (1) There shall be established a bank to be called the Bank of Canada....

5. (1) The Bank shall be under the management of a Board of Directors composed of a Governor, a Deputy Governor and seven directors....

(2) In addition to the Members of the Board as constituted by subsection one of this section, the Deputy Minister of Finance or, in case of his absence or incapacity at any time, such other officer of the Department of Finance as the Minister may nominate for the time being, shall be, by virtue of his office or of such nomination, as the case may be, a member of the Board, but shall not have the right to vote.

6. (1) The Governor and Deputy Governor shall be men of proven

---

*The sixth and final war loan (November 1919) realized $678,000,000 (*Canada Year Book, 1920*, p. 10).

financial experience and each shall devote the whole of his time to the duties of his office.

(2) No person shall hold office as Governor or Deputy Governor or Assistant Deputy Governor, who, —

(a) is not a British subject; or

(b) is a member of either House of Parliament or of a Provincial Legislature; or

(c) is employed in any capacity in the public service of Canada or of any Province of Canada or holds any office or position for which any salary or other remuneration is payable out of public moneys; or

(d) is a director, officer or employee of any other bank or financial institution or has an interest as a shareholder in any bank or other financial institution. . . .

8. (1) The Governor, Deputy Governor and Assistant Deputy Governor shall each be appointed as hereinafter provided for a term of seven years or, in the case of the first Governor, Deputy Governor and Assistant Deputy Governor, for such shorter period as the Governor in Council may determine.

(2) The first Governor, Deputy Governor and Assistant Deputy Governor shall be appointed and their salaries shall be fixed by the Governor in Council and thereafter appointments shall be made by the directors with the approval of the Governor in Council. . . .

9. (1) Notwithstanding anything contained in section ten of this Act,* the first, or provisional directors of the Bank shall be the following members of the Civil Service of Canada, namely, The Deputy Minister of Finance; The Counsellor of the Department of External Affairs; The Comptroller, Government Guarantee Branch; The Comptroller of the Treasury; The Comptroller of Currency; The Director of Estimates and Assistant Secretary to the Treasury Board, and The Solicitor to the Treasury, who shall remain in office until replaced by directors duly elected in their stead at the first general meeting of shareholders. The said first or provisional directors shall serve without remuneration. . . .

17. (1) The capital of the Bank shall be five million dollars but may be increased from time to time pursuant to a resolution passed by the Board and ratified at a meeting of shareholders and approved by the Parliament of Canada.

(2) The capital shall be divided into shares of fifty dollars each, represented by share certificates, which shall be offered by the Minister at not less than par for public subscription in Canada and shall

*Concerned with the qualification of directors.

be allotted by him to persons eligible to hold shares in such manner as he may in his discretion determine.

(3) In the event of any of the shares (whether of the original or any subsequent issue) not being subscribed for by the public within a reasonable period the Minister [of Finance] shall subscribe for such shares, and notwithstanding any other provision of this Act, payment for the same shall be made out of the Consolidated Revenue Fund....

(8) Shares may be held only by or for the beneficial ownership of British subjects ordinarily resident in Canada, or corporations organized under the laws of the Dominion of Canada or of any province and controlled by British subjects ordinarily resident in Canada but not more than fifty shares shall be held by or for the benefit of any one person other than the Minister. . . .

18. (1) No shares of the capital stock of the Bank shall be held by or for the benefit of any chartered bank or any director, officer, clerk or employee of any such bank. . . .

21. (1) The Bank may

(a) buy and sell gold, silver, nickel and bronze coin and gold and silver bullion;

(b) effect transfers of funds by telegram, letter or other method of communication . . . ;

(c) buy and sell or rediscount short term securities issued or guaranteed by the Dominion of Canada or any province, having a maturity not exceeding two years from the date of acquisition by the Bank. . . .*

23. (1) The Bank shall act as fiscal agent of the Government of Canada without charge and, subject to the provisions of this Act, by agreement, may also act as banker or fiscal agent of the government of any province.

(2) The Bank, if and when required by the Minister so to do, shall act as agent for the Government of Canada in the payment of interest and principal and generally in respect of the management of the public debt of Canada. . . .

24. (1) On and after the day on which the Bank is authorized to commence business the Bank shall, except as provided in the *Bank Act*, have the sole right to issue notes payable to bearer on demand and intended for circulation in Canada and may, subject to the provisions of section twenty-six of this Act, issue such notes to any

*The balance of this section, a long technical statement of the bank's powers to buy and sell, to make loans or advances, etc., is omitted.

amount. Such notes shall be legal tender, and shall be the first charge upon the assets of the Bank. . . .*

(4) The form and material of the notes shall be subject to approval by the Minister: Provided that notes in either the English or the French language shall be available as required. . . .

115. The Bank of Canada Act Amendment Act, 1938

(2 George VI, Chap. 42)

> After defeating Bennett in the election of 1935, the Liberals proceeded to amend the Bank of Canada Act (by 1 Edward VIII, Chap. 22, 23 June 1936). This Act strengthened the government's control of the bank, providing for two classes of stock, one to be held by the public and one by the Minister of Finance, who would appoint a majority of the directors. This amendment also gave the Governor a veto over actions of the board, subject to appeal to the Minister; and whereas the Act of 1934 had provided that banknotes should be available in either English or French, it was enacted in 1936 that each note should be "printed in both the English and the French languages." This further amendment of 1938 brought the bank completely under government ownership.

(Assented to 1st July, 1938)

. . .

5. Section nine of the said Act, as enacted by section six of the said amending Act [of 1936], is repealed and the following substituted therefor: —

"9. (1) The Minister with the approval of the Governor in Council shall as of the first day of March in each year appoint for terms of three years each a sufficient number of directors to provide that there shall be eleven directors: Provided, however, that every director holding office at the date of the coming into force of this subsection shall continue as a director up to and including the last day of February in the year of the expiration of the term of office for which he was elected or appointed. . . ."

7. Section seventeen of the said Act, as enacted by section ten of the said amending Act, is repealed and the following substituted therefor: —

*Until this time paper money had been issued partly by the Dominion government and partly by the chartered banks.

"17. (1) The capital of the Bank shall be five million dollars but may be increased from time to time pursuant to a resolution passed by the Board of Directors and approved by the Governor in Council and by the Parliament of Canada.

(2) The capital shall be divided into one hundred thousand shares of the par value of fifty dollars each, which shall be issued to the Minister to be held by him on behalf of the Dominion of Canada...."

F.
Dominion-Provincial Economic Relations

116. Order in Council Appointing the Royal Commission on Dominion-Provincial Relations, 1937

(P.C. 1908, 14 August 1937, printed in the Commission's *Report*)

The Depression after 1929 emphasized the economic problems of the Canadian federal system, and it was evident that there was a case for some redistribution of fiscal powers as between the federal government and the provinces. The King government appointed what came to be known as the Rowell-Sirois Commission to investigate and report on these matters. The order in council making the appointment is a succinct statement of the problem. See Currie, *Canadian Economic Development.*

The Committee of the Privy Council have had before them a report, dated August 5th, 1937, from the Right Honourable W. L. Mackenzie King, the Prime Minister, submitting — with the concurrence of the Minister of Finance and the Minister of Justice: —

1. That, as a result of economic and social developments since 1867, the Dominion and the provincial governments have found it necessary in the public interest to accept responsibilities of a character, and to extend governmental services to a degree, not foreseen at the time of Confederation;
2. That the discharge of these responsibilities involves expenditures of such a magnitude as to demand not only the most efficient administrative organization on the part of all governments but also the wisest possible division of powers and functions between governments. That particularly is this the case if the burden of public expenditures is to be kept to a minimum, and if the revenue-raising powers of the various governing bodies are to

possess the adequacy and the elasticity required to meet the respective demands upon them;

3. That governmental expenditures are increased by overlapping and duplication of services as between the Dominion and provincial governments in certain fields of activity. That in other respects the public interest may be adversely affected by the lack of a clear delimitation of governmental powers and responsibilities;

4. That representations have been made on behalf of several provincial governments and by various public organizations that the revenue sources available to provincial governments are not in general adequate to enable them to discharge their constitutional responsibilities, including the cost of unemployment relief and other social services and the payment of fixed charges on their outstanding debt; that, consequently, if they are to discharge their responsibilities, either new revenue sources must be allotted to them or their constitutional responsibilities and governmental burdens must be reduced or adjustment must be made by both methods;

5. That representations have been made by provincial governments that municipal governments which have been created by, and derive their powers and responsibilities from, the provinces, are confronted with similar problems; that, in particular, necessary municipal expenditures have placed an undue burden on real estate and are thereby retarding economic recovery; also that the relations between provinces and municipalities are an essential part of the problem of provincial finances;

6. That, finally, it has been represented that unless appropriate action is taken the set-up of governmental powers and responsibilities devised at the time of Confederation will not be adequate to meet the economic and social changes and the shifts in economic power which are in progress without subjecting Canada's governmental structure to undue strains and stresses.

The Prime Minister, therefore, with the concurrence of the Minister of Finance and the Minister of Justice, recommends: —

1. That it is expedient to provide for a re-examination of the economic and financial basis of Confederation and of the distribution of legislative powers in the light of the economic and social developments of the last seventy years;

2. That for this purpose the following be appointed Commissioners under Part I of the Inquiries Act: —

The Honourable Newton W. Rowell, LL.D., Chief Justice of
Ontario;

The Honourable Thibaudeau Rinfret,* Justice of the Supreme
Court of Canada;

John W. Dafoe, Esquire, LL.D., of the City of Winnipeg, Man.;

Robert Alexander MacKay, Esquire, Ph.D., Professor of Government, Dalhousie University, Halifax, N.S.; and

Henry Forbes Angus, Esquire, M.A., B.C.L., Professor of Eco-
nomics, University of British Columbia, Vancouver, B.C.

3. That, without limiting the general scope of their inquiry, the
Commissioners be instructed in particular: —

(a) to examine the constitutional allocation of revenue sources
and governmental burdens to the Dominion and provincial
governments, the past results of such allocation and its suit-
ability to present conditions and the conditions that are likely to prevail in the future;

(b) to investigate the character and amount of taxes collected from
the people of Canada, to consider these in the light of legal
and constitutional limitations, and of financial and economic conditions, and to determine whether taxation as at present
allocated and imposed is as equitable and as efficient as can
be devised;

(c) to examine public expenditures and public debts in general,
in order to determine whether the present division of the
burden of government is equitable, and conducive to efficient administration, and to determine the ability of the
Dominion and provincial governments to discharge their
governmental responsibilities within the framework of the
present allocation of public functions and powers, or on the
basis of some form of reallocation thereof;

(d) to investigate Dominion subsidies and grants to provincial
governments.

4. That the Commissioners be instructed to consider and report
upon the facts disclosed by their investigations; and to express
what in their opinion, subject to the retention of the distribution of legislative powers essential to a proper carrying out of the
federal system in harmony with national needs and the promotion of national unity, will best effect a balanced relationship
between the financial powers and the obligations and functions

*Mr. Justice Rinfret resigned very shortly on account of ill health. He was
replaced by Professor Joseph Sirois of Laval University, who was himself
appointed in 1938 to replace Chief Justice Rowell as chairman when Rowell's
health broke down.

of each governing body, and conduce to a more efficient, independent and economical discharge of governmental responsibilities in Canada.

The Prime Minister, with the concurrence of the Minister of Finance and the Minister of Justice, further recommends that the Honourable Newton W. Rowell, LL.D., Chief Justice of Ontario, be Chairman of the said Commission....

117. "Abstract of the Leading Recommendations" of the Rowell-Sirois Commission, 1940

(Report of the Royal Commission on Dominion-Provincial Relations, Ottawa, 1940, Section G)

The Rowell-Sirois Commission did its work thoroughly, employing a highly competent research staff to assist it. Its voluminous report, quite apart from the merits of its recommendations, which many good judges approved, is a great source of information on economic relations between the Dominion and the provinces, and an important contribution to Canadian economic history.

The Report which the Commission has prepared is the outcome of two-and-a-half years of carefully planned study. In the course of this period the Commission has held sessions in the capital of every province of Canada and at Ottawa. It has had the benefit of the collaboration of many of the provincial governments, of the evidence of federal and provincial civil servants, of representations made by a large number of organizations in every province of Canada. The Commission has given careful consideration to the requests and suggestions presented to it and has also, with the assistance of a very able research staff, instituted inquiries of its own into the financial, economic and social problems which came within the scope of its terms of reference.

The conclusions which the Commission has reached are, therefore, not sudden inspirations but the result of careful deliberation. The Commissioners consider it both remarkable and significant that, on questions on which the most divergent views are widely and tenaciously held both by public men and by private citizens, they should have arrived at complete agreement. This agreement is not the result of compromise or of give and take but reflects a sincere unanimity of judgment on the great issues which confront the nation. Its significance is enhanced by the fact that the four Commissioners are men from different regions of Canada, men who differ widely in background and in training, as well as in general outlook; and it is also significant that the conclusions which they have reached are far from being the views which any one of them held at the outset of the inquiry. Whether or not the Report will be successful in presenting clearly and forcefully to others the considerations which have carried weight with the Commission, and in convincing others of the validity of the conclusions which the Commissioners have formed, the future alone can show. But in drawing attention to the changes which have taken place in their own views, in the light of the studies which have been made, the Commissioners hope that they may predispose others to peruse both the Report and the research studies which accompany it before arriving at their final opinion as to the merits of the recommendations which the Commission has made.

In the present summary the aim is to set out the principal recommendations embodied in the Report and to indicate briefly the reasons for them. At the heart of the problem lie the needs of Canadian citizens. These needs, whether material or cultural, can be satisfied only if all the provincial governments in Canada are in a position to supply those services which the citizen of today demands of them. The ability of provincial governments to meet the demands of their citizens depends in part on the constitutional powers which they enjoy, in part on their financial capacity to perform their recognized functions. The striking fact in the Commission's study of Canadian conditions is that many provinces, whose financial position is not the result of emergency conditions, are unable to find the money to enable them to meet the needs of their citizens. The basic problem before the Commission lies, therefore, in finding a way in which the financial position of the provinces could be improved and assured, without disastrous financial consequences to the Federal Government on whose efficient functioning all provinces are dependent. National unity and provincial autonomy must not be thought of as competitors for the citizen's allegiance for, in Canada at least, they are but two facets of the same thing—a sane federal system. National unity must be based on provincial autonomy, and provincial autonomy cannot be assured unless a strong feeling of national unity exists throughout Canada.

Some provincial governments explained to the Commission that they could pay their way, and perform their functions to their own complete satisfaction, if the Dominion were to assume this or that onerous service, or were to withdraw from this or that field of taxation, or were to increase their subsidies. But, on examination, it was found that a solution on these lines could not be generalized and that, while it might meet the needs of one or more of the provinces, it would do so at the cost of impairing the Dominion's finances, or of prejudicing the position of other provinces. The Commissioners were, therefore, compelled to dismiss any such solution as inadequate.

The Commission did, however, find one onerous function of government which cannot, under modern conditions, be equitably or efficiently performed on a regional or provincial basis. This function is the maintenance of those unemployed who are employable and of their dependents. In reaching this conclusion (which is amply supported by the Evidence and the research studies) the Commission merely confirmed conclusions which had been reached by earlier Commissions.[1] So firmly is the Commission convinced of the validity of this conclusion that, even when it comes to consider the situation which will arise if its main recommendations are not implemented, it proceeds on the assumption that the relief of the unemployed who are able and willing to work will become a federal function.

Another function closely analogous to that of relief for employables is that of assistance to a primary industry (e.g., agriculture) in the form of operating cost advances. When relief is on a small scale the responsibility can be borne without difficulty by the province. But in the event of widespread disaster with which a province is unable to cope without assistance from the Dominion, or in the event that the Dominion by such means as an exclusive marketing organization has already established effective control of the industry concerned, the Commission recommends that the Dominion should assume direct administrative and financial responsibility rather than render indirect assistance by way of advances to the provinces affected.

The Commission's treatment of these expensive functions of government may be contrasted with its treatment of another expensive function, namely the payment of non-contributory old age pensions. As the Federal Government is already paying as high a proportion of their cost as it can reasonably pay without assuming control of the administration of the pensions, and as the Commission was convinced that it is more satisfactory that the provinces should continue

[1] The National Employment Commission and La Commission des Assurances Sociales de Québec.

to administer non-contributory old age pensions, it could not recommend any further financial help to the provinces in this connection. But the Commission is of the opinion that if non-contributory old age pensions were to be superseded or supplemented by a contributory system the latter should, for various reasons, be under the control of the Dominion.

There is, however, an important financial burden of which provincial governments can be relieved without any sacrifice of autonomy. This is the deadweight cost of their debt service. The burden taken up by the Dominion, if it were to assume this deadweight cost, would be less than the burden of which the provinces were relieved because, as maturities occurred, the debts could be refunded more advantageously by the Dominion than by the provinces. To this extent a saving would accrue to Canadian taxpayers. The Commission has, therefore, recommended that the Dominion should assume all provincial debts (both direct debts and debts guaranteed by the provinces) and that each province should pay over to the Dominion an annual sum equal to the interest which it now receives from its investments. The reason for this proviso is that it would not be expedient that the Dominion should take over liability for a debt which represented a self-liquidating investment retained by a province. Conditions governing future provincial borrowing are outlined in detail in the Report.

In the case of one province this recommendation as to debt requires an important modification. The provincial debt of the Province of Quebec is low in comparison with the per capita debt of other provinces, and is an unusually low fraction of the combined municipal and provincial debt of the Province. To meet this situation, which has arisen through the policy of this Province in imposing on municipalities onerous functions which are performed elsewhere by provincial governments, the Commission has recommended that the Dominion should take over 40 per cent of the combined provincial and municipal net debt service in Quebec.

If the provinces are relieved, in accordance with this recommendation, of the deadweight burden of their debt, it is not unreasonable that they should surrender to the Dominion the subsidies, whatever their character, which they now receive. Prince Edward Island alone would give up subsidies more than equivalent to the deadweight cost of its debt, and, as will be seen, this apparent loss will be more than made up in other ways. The abolition of the provincial subsidies will be in itself no inconsiderable reform, for their history (which is fully examined in the Commission's research studies) is long and tortuous. The subsidies have been based on no clear principles and it has been impossible to say whether or not different provinces have received equal treatment. Specious reasons have often been advanced, and not infrequently accepted, in support of readjustments in order to avoid the full implications of genuine reasons, and negotiations between the Dominion and the provinces have lacked the candour which is desirable in a democracy.

Up to this point the Commission's proposals, enormously beneficial as they would be to the provinces, would be very onerous to the Dominion. The Commission had, therefore, to consider how to provide the Dominion with sources of revenue which would enable it to carry its new burdens. This inquiry (as will be seen) was combined with the consideration of efficiency and equity in taxation specifically entrusted to the Commission. There could be no question of increasing the legal taxing powers of the Dominion since these are already unlimited. But the provinces, in return for the benefits which they would receive, and for further payments which the Commission finds it necessary to recommend, should be prepared to renounce some of the taxes which they employ (or are entitled to employ) at present. The Dominion, for its part, should be able and willing to refrain from competing with the provinces in respect of sources of revenue left to them and should leave the provinces free to collect these revenues in whatever way appears to them most efficient even if the method of indirect taxation should be involved.

Just as the assumption of provincial debts by the Dominion will lead to savings in interest from which taxpayers will benefit, so there are several taxes from which, if they are under unified control, as great a revenue can be obtained as at present with less hardship to the taxpayer. What is more important, a reorganization of these taxes, of a character which is possible only if they are under unified control, can remove many hindrances which in the recent past have been detrimental to the expansion of the national income (i.e., to the sum total of the incomes of all citizens of Canada). As this income expands, as the result of what may be fairly termed greater efficiency in taxation, the same revenue as at present can be obtained by taxes imposed at lower rates than those of today.

The first of the taxes which the Commission recommends that the provinces should renounce is the tax on personal incomes. Not all provinces impose this tax. Those which get most revenue from it are often taxing incomes which other provinces think that they should have a share in taxing, because they are in part at least earned in them although they are received in those provinces in which investors live, or in which large corporations have their head offices. Nor is this all. The general equity of the whole Canadian tax system — and the Commission has been instructed to concern itself with equity as well as with efficiency in taxation — requires that the tax on personal incomes, which is one of the very few taxes capable of any desired graduation, should be used to supplement other taxes and should be uniform throughout Canada.

The second form of taxation which the Commission recommends that the provinces should forgo includes those taxes imposed on corporations which individuals or partnerships, carrying on the same business as the corporation, would not be required to pay, and taxes on those businesses which only corporations engage in. They include, therefore, the tax on the net income of corporations and a multitude of taxes devised to raise revenue from particular classes of corporations which a province cannot conveniently subject to a tax on net income. They do not include bona fide licence fees, the power to impose which would remain with the province. These provincial corporation taxes are peculiarly vexatious to those who pay them and particularly detrimental to the expansion of the national income. The cost of tax compliance is high. The tax is often payable by a corporation which has no net income. The tax is very likely to be a tax on costs rather than on profits. These taxes are also a frequent source of interprovincial jealousy. Great benefits may be expected if they are swept away and the equivalent revenue raised by federal taxes chiefly on corporate net income.

To ask the provinces to give up the entire revenue which they now derive from taxing corporations would, however, intensify a grievance of which the Commission received complaint in more than one province; for the Dominion would receive a tax on income which was in part derived from the depletion of irreplaceable natural wealth. It is clearly desirable that revenue of this character should be used for developmental work which will compensate for the damage which has been done to the resources of a province. The Commission has, therefore, recommended that the Dominion should pay over to the province concerned 10 per cent of the corporate income derived from the exploitation of the mineral wealth of the province. When what is required is the conservation of natural resources by maintaining their productivity, rather than compensation for depletion by new investment, the provinces are in a position to use their own taxing power.

The third tax which the Commission recommends that the provinces should forgo consists of various forms of succession duty. These differ from the income taxes in that they have not hitherto been used by the Dominion: but they are taxes to which the Dominion might at any time be compelled to resort. The use made of them by the provinces has given rise to bitter complaint because the provinces have not made equitable arrangements with one another so as to tax each item in an estate in one province only. The differences in rates between provinces, and the dangers of double taxation, seriously distort investment in Canada. The potential competition between provinces desirous of attracting wealthy residents has made it impossible to use these delicate instruments of taxation as a means for giving effect to social policies. Many provinces feel aggrieved because estates which have been built up by investment throughout the whole of Canada are taxed, not for national purposes, but for the benefit of strategically situated provinces.

If the Commission's recommendations stopped at this point, they would, instead of being enormously beneficial to the provinces, leave some of them in a parlous financial position. After the provinces had, on the one hand, been relieved of the cost of unemployment relief and of the deadweight burden of their debt, and had, on the other hand, given up their right to impose personal income taxes, corporation taxes and succession duties, they would find themselves with far less variable expenditures than in the past and with less variable revenues. It is, therefore, possible to form an idea of the size of the probable surplus or deficit of each province. There is a purpose in making this calculation for, if a province were left with a prospective annual deficit, it would not be able to provide for the reasonable needs of its citizens unless it were able, without causing hardship, to increase the revenue which it derived from the sources remaining at its disposal, or to reduce its expenditures while still providing services equivalent to those provided by other provinces.

At this point there must be a refinement in the calculations. What is significant for the purposes of the Commission is the size of the surplus or deficit which would exist in a province if it were to provide the normal Canadian standard of services and impose taxation of normal severity. It is not the services which each province is at present providing, but the average Canadian standard of services, that a province must be put in a position to finance. It is not the revenue which its taxes yield at their present level which matters, but the revenue which it would derive from them if its people were as heavily taxed as Canadians in general. Just as in the case of debt it is necessary to take account of the fact that some provinces are more accustomed than others to provide services for their people through municipalities or other agencies instead of directly. The Commission has, therefore, attempted to compute, province by province, what the cost would be if the province and its municipalities taken together were to provide services on the Canadian standard. Adjustments have been made for the cost of the developmental services appropriate to the province, and for the weight of taxation in the province. The result has been that the Commission has been able to make a recommendation as to the amount, if any, which each individual province should receive from the Dominion annually to enable it to provide normal Canadian services with no more than normal Canadian taxation. The calculations involved were not easy and presented peculiar difficulties in Quebec because of the extent to which educational and social services in that Province are provided, not out of taxation, but by the Church. But the calculations have been made and the Commission recommends that each province found to be in need of such a payment should receive it by way of an annual National Adjustment Grant from the Dominion. This grant as originally fixed would be irreducible. The Commission recommends, however, that National Adjustment Grants should be re-appraised every five years. For special emergencies, which might arise in respect of any province (and which exist in one province today), special provision should be made, as it would be undesirable either to fix an annual grant in perpetuity on the basis of conditions that are transitory, or to fail to provide for serious emergencies. The Commission believes that these provisions will permit of the necessary elasticity in the financial relations between the provinces and the Dominion which has been lacking in the old subsidy system.

In order to assure all provinces of fair and equal treatment in the matter of grants, and in order to assure the general taxpayer that any new or increased grant is justified on the basis of the comparative need of the province concerned, it will be essential that all requests from the provinces with respect to grants should be examined as scientifically and objectively as possible. The Commission, therefore, recommends the establishment of a small permanent commission (which may be called the Finance Commission), assisted by an adequate technical staff, to advise upon all requests for new or increased grants, and to re-appraise the system of grants every five years.

The recommendations which have been described would, if implemented, safeguard the autonomy of every province by ensuring to it the revenue necessary to provide services in accordance with the Canadian standard. Every provincial government (including those whose position will be so good as to make adjustment grants unnecessary) would be placed in a better financial position than it is in today. And the financial position of every province would be immeasurably more secure than it is today. The Commission looks on this as its primary achievement. It is convinced that this fundamental problem must be faced and it has not been able to discover any alternative way in which it could be solved. The recommendations which the Commission has made must be judged as a whole. They cannot with fairness either to the provinces or to the Dominion be considered in isolation for any one of them taken alone might produce grotesque results.

At what cost, it may be asked, will the provinces have secured these advantages? There will be a certain cost to the Dominion and, therefore, to the Dominion's taxpayers. The taxes forgone by the provinces, if replaced by Dominion taxes of equal yield, would not provide all the money which the Dominion will probably be called on to pay under the Plan. It is necessary to say "probably" because the Dominion, unlike the provinces, will be left with highly variable expenditures (e.g., those on unemployment relief) and variable revenues. The long-run effects of the proposed arrangements should, as has been explained, be to increase employment and to increase the national income and, therefore, the national revenue. But the expectation of the Commission is that the Dominion, in the first instance, will have to increase taxes somewhat. Even without increasing tax rates it will obviously increase the taxes payable by citizens of those provinces which have no personal income tax today. It is hardly necessary to add that, in view of the end to be attained, the price seems low.

There will, of course, be adjustments. At every stage of the Commission's inquiry it has endeavoured to frame recommendations which, if implemented, will avoid the minor hardships or inequities that might result if the measures which have, perforce, been somewhat crudely described in this summary, were crudely applied. One or two examples will be given here. Others will be found in the Report itself. But the whole spirit of the Report would suggest that analogous adjustments should be made, even if the Commission has not thought of them and, therefore, has not mentioned them.

If the administration of a service or the collection of a tax is transferred from one government to another it is desirable that those who have administered the service or collected the tax in the past should continue to do so in the future and that their skill and experience should not be lost to the nation nor their personal expectation of continuous employment disappointed. The Commission has, therefore, recommended that the Dominion, if it takes over a provincial function, should continue the employment of those previously employed by the provincial government concerned. This recommendation is particularly important when questions of language are involved.

If a tax now levied by one government is to be replaced by a tax levied by another the new tax should be adjusted to the circumstances of the people on whom it is to be imposed, and advantage should be taken of the opportunity to design the new tax as equitably as possible. Thus, if the Dominion collects succession duties, it is important that the administration for their collection should be decentralized and that small estates should be rapidly cleared without correspondence having to go through Ottawa. And the taxation scales should be arranged so as to tax an estate more lightly when it is divided among many children.

If legislative powers (e.g., in relation to unemployment insurance) are to be conferred on the Dominion in addition to those which it now enjoys, it is important that they should be strictly defined so as to avoid the danger of their being extended by interpretation in unexpected ways which might interfere with the civil code in Quebec, or with the corresponding interests of other provinces.

This brief summary would lose its way among details were it to attempt to enumerate the recommendations — some of them important recommendations — which the Commission has felt bound to make in its Report. What has been said should indicate the structure of the Dominion-provincial financial relations which would, in the opinion of the Commission, characterize a healthy federal system in Canada. Before passing on to mention a few of the subsidiary recommendations, it may be worth while to point out that the Commission's financial proposals are, in terms of the economic life of 1939, very similar to what the provisions of the British North America Act were in terms of the economic life of 1867.

In the first place the Dominion assumed provincial debts in 1867, as it would do today were effect to be given to the Commission's recommendations. In the second place the Dominion was expected to exercise in 1867 the chief taxing power of that time (customs and excise) as, under the Commission's proposals, it is expected to exercise other chief taxing powers of today (the personal income tax, corporation taxes and succession duties). In the third place the Dominion was to pay subsidies in 1867 to enable the provinces to perform the functions entrusted to them without having to resort to oppressive taxation. Under the Commission's proposals the Dominion would pay National Adjustment Grants for precisely the same purpose. It is true that a different measure of the amount to be paid to each province would be adopted now than that which was then considered appropriate. But this difference is more apparent than real, for it arises from the inequalities of wealth which have developed as between the provinces. Equal per capita subsidies did conform in some rough approximation to the fiscal needs of 1867. They would not do so today. The Commission hopes that the methods which it has employed for calculating the appropriate adjustment grants will be able to accomplish what the per capita formula was intended to achieve in 1867, for, though the means have changed, the end remains the same, namely the maintenance of provincial governments which can provide the necessary services for their people.

It will be noted that, in the recommendations which have been summarized, nothing has been said of one of the major problems of Canadian governmental finance — the problem of municipal finance and of the burdens which have been placed on real estate. On this subject the Commission received numerous representations and was made fully aware of the seriousness of the situation. But the Commission was in a peculiar position, in so far as the municipalities were concerned, for they are the creatures of the provinces in which they are situated and their financial powers and duties are such as the province chooses to confer on them. The financial plan which has been described has taken account of municipal expenditures and taxation as part of the provincial picture and it will, if it is implemented, have very important indirect effects on municipal finance. It will relieve the municipalities of their share in providing relief for employables and their dependents. It will put every provincial government in a better position than it is in today for extending such aid as it may think fit to its municipalities, whether by relieving them of the cost of services which they now perform, or by contributing financially to the cost of these services. In the case of the Province of Quebec, as has been explained, the Dominion would assume a portion of the municipal debt. In every province the way would be cleared for dealing (if the province so desires) with municipal debts generally in the same sort of way that the Commission has recommended should be adopted for provincial debts. Such a step would, in turn, facilitate much needed reforms in the structure of municipalities, particularly in the great metropolitan areas. But the future of the municipalities lies in the hands of the provinces.

One or two illustrations must suffice to show that other matters have come under consideration which are not closely related to the main financial questions. The Commission did not consider that it lay within its terms of reference to deal with the desirability, or undesirability, of the Dominion having power to implement its treaty obligations (otherwise than under section 132 of the British North America Act), if implementation would require legislation on topics within the exclusive jurisdiction of the provinces. But the Commission did consider that it could recommend that the Dominion should have power to implement conventions of the International Labour Organization. These partake of the character of international legislation. Many of the parties to them are countries with civil codes not dissimilar to that of Quebec; others are countries with English common law. Some are Catholic: others Protestant. In these circumstances it seemed that the rights of particular provinces were adequately protected against any encroachment of the federal power. And if international normative legislation of this character is desirable it is through the Dominion Government that Canada must become a party to it.

In respect to marketing legislation great difficulty has been experienced in framing Dominion and provincial legislation which will cover the whole field, even when the wishes of Dominion and provinces are identical. The Commission has sought to remedy this situation by recommending that the Dominion and the provinces should have concurrent legislative powers to deal with the marketing of a named list of natural products to which additions may be made from time to time by common consent.

Nor is this the only instance in which it has seemed appropriate that a power of delegation should form part of Canadian federal relations. The Commission has recommended that this power should be quite general and that the Dominion should be able to delegate any of its legislative powers to a province, and that a province should be able to delegate any of its legislative powers to the Dominion. Delegation should provide a convenient means of dealing with specific questions as they may arise from time to time without limiting in advance the power of either the Dominion or the provinces. In some instances one or more of the provinces might be prepared to delegate powers to the Dominion while other provinces were unwilling, and in such cases the advantages of a power of delegation over constitutional amendment would lie in flexibility.

The Commission has come to consider the transportation problem of Canada one of the problems which cannot be solved without close collaboration between the Dominion and the provinces. It realizes, however, that its own technical competence is slight in this field and has, therefore, confined itself to discussing the issues which will have to be faced, in the hope of doing something to clarify the problem of jurisdiction. It points out, however, the great advantage which might be derived from a Transport Planning Commission which would be concerned both with planning transportation developments in a broad way, and with facilitating the co-operation between the Dominion and the provinces in transportation matters which is necessary for the taxpayer.

While the Commission believes that new governmental machinery should be a kept at a minimum, it nevertheless considers that special provision should be made to facilitate co-operation between the Dominion and the provinces. In an earlier day, when the functions of government were relatively few and administrative organization relatively simple, it may have been possible for Dominion and provincial governments to operate largely in watertight compartments. But with the great expansion of governmental functions, and the growing complexity of administration, it is no longer possible to do this without serious loss of efficiency and economy in government. Co-operation between the autonomous governments of the federal system has today become imperative. The Commission recommends as the principal means to this end that Dominion-Provincial Conferences, which have hitherto met at infrequent intervals, should now be regularized, and provision made for frequent meetings, say every year. It urges further that the Conference should be provided with an adequate and permanent secretariat for the purpose of serving the Conference directly, and of facilitating co-operation between the Dominion and the provinces in general.

The special claims advanced by certain governments have been considered in detail in the body of the Report. Although these claims will have little financial importance if the Commission's main financial proposals are implemented, it was deemed advisable to examine them on their merits and to report upon them in view of the desirability of clearing up old grievances in any general settlement between the provinces and the Dominion.

Many complaints about the working of the federal system were also presented to the Commission by private organizations. The Commission viewed such complaints as important evidence, but in many cases their subject matter fell outside its terms of reference.

*   *   *

In conclusion of this summary it remains to add that the decisions underlying the recommendations contained in the Report were reached before the outbreak of War. The Commission decided, after deliberation, to complete the Report exactly as it would have been completed had War not been declared. Although it it true that the War is certain to produce great changes in the structure of the Canadian economy, it is equally true that the nature and extent of these changes, dependent as they are on the length and intensity of the struggle, cannot be predicted at the present time. The basic recommendations of the Commission concerning the re-allocation of the functions of government and the financial relations of the Dominion and the provinces were framed with the possibility of emergencies in mind and are, it is hoped, sufficiently flexible to be adjusted to any situation which the War may produce.

Of the subsidiary recommendations many are concerned with matters not in the least likely to be affected by the strains and stresses of War, while some may require modification in the light of events. The need for some action designed to enable the people of Canada to throw their whole weight into any great national effort, such as the struggle to which they have committed themselves, and at the same time to ensure the smooth working of the social and educational services on which the welfare of the mass of the people depends, is far greater and far more urgent in time of War and of post-War reorganization than it is in time of peace. And it is precisely to these two main objectives that the chief recommendations of the Commission have been directed.

It has been the aim of the Commission to frame proposals which will, if implemented, place jurisdiction over the social services in the hands of the governments most likely to design and administer them, not merely with the greatest economy and the greatest technical efficiency, but with the regard for the social, cultural and religious outlook of the various regions of Canada, which is essential to genuine human welfare. The financial proposals have been designed to enable every province of Canada to rely on having sufficient revenue at its command in war-time as in peace-time, in years of adversity as in years of prosperity, to carry out the important functions entrusted to it. They are also designed to produce this result while leaving the fiscal powers of the Dominion as wide in fact as they have always been in law, so that it may direct the wealth of the nation as the national interest may require. If some such adjustment of Canadian economic life appeared sufficiently urgent to lead to the appointment of the Commission in time of peace, how much more urgent is it in time of war? How much more urgent will it be in the critical transition from war to peace again?

The Report must face the verdict of public opinion and opinion is not the same in war as in peace. The Report was prepared with peace-time opinion in mind. But it is the hope of the Commission that the gravity of the hour will dispose people in all regions of

Canada to take serious thought of their country's welfare and to look at the broad lines of the recommendations, keeping matters of detail in rational perspective. For the Report, while taking account of possibility of war as of any other emergency, was framed with a view to a future which will, it is hoped, be in the main one of peace, and it is on its merits with respect to this supposedly peaceful future that the Report must stand or fall. The Commission does not consider that its proposals are either centralizing or decentralizing in their combined effect but believes that they will conduce to the sane balance between these two tendencies which is the essence of a genuine federal system and, therefore, the basis on which Canadian national unity can most securely rest.

> JOS. SIROIS
> Chairman,
>
> JOHN W. DAFOE
>
> R. A. MacKAY
>
> H. F. ANGUS

Alex. Skelton,
    Secretary.

Adjutor Savard,
    French Secretary.

118. The Dominion-Provincial Taxation Agreement Act, 1942

(6 George VI, Chap. 13)

The Dominion-Provincial Conference assembled in Ottawa to deal with the Rowell-Sirois Report (14-15 January 1941) was a total failure; three wealthy provinces, Ontario, Alberta and British Columbia, whose premiers respectively were Mitchell Hepburn, William Aberhart and T. D. Pattullo, refused to have anything to do with the scheme. But the provincial premiers generally acknowledged that in wartime the needs of the federal government must have priority, and this cleared the way for temporary arrangements as provided by the Act here printed. See Pickersgill, *The Mackenzie King Record*, I, chapter 7.

(Assented to 28th May, 1942)

WHEREAS the Dominion and the provinces and certain municipalities have been levying taxes upon incomes and upon corporations, and it is expedient during the continuation of the present war and for a certain re-adjustment period thereafter that the Dominion only should levy such taxes: Therefore, His Majesty, by and with the advice and consent of the Senate and House of Commons of Canada, enacts as follows: — ...

2. The Minister of Finance, with the approval of the Governor in Council, may enter into an agreement with the government of any of the provinces of Canada to provide, in accordance with and subject to such terms and conditions as may be set out therein, that the province and its municipalities shall cease to levy personal income and corporation taxes as defined in such agreement and subject to such exceptions as may be set out in such agreement, for the duration of the war and for a certain re-adjustment period thereafter, and to provide for the payment of compensation by the Dominion to the province therefor.

3. The annual amount of such compensation shall be,

(a) in the case of the provinces of British Columbia, Alberta, Manitoba, Ontario and Quebec, respectively as follows:

British Columbia $12,048,367.51
Alberta 4,080,860.64
Manitoba 5,054,740.92
Ontario 28,964,039.54
Quebec 20,586,074.56

being an amount in each case calculated as equivalent to the total revenue obtained by the said provinces from personal income and corporation taxes during the fiscal year of each of said provinces and of municipalities therein ending nearest to the thirty-first day of December, 1940, which by the terms of the agreement will cease to be levied; and

(b) in the case of the provinces of Nova Scotia, New Brunswick, Prince Edward Island and Saskatchewan, respectively as follows:

Nova Scotia $2,585,308.72
New Brunswick 3,278,574.15
Prince Edward Island 264,769.94
Saskatchewan 4,330,471.29

being an amount in each case calculated as equivalent to the net debt service paid by the province during its fiscal year ending nearest to December 31, 1940 (not including contributions to sinking funds) less the revenues obtained by the province from succession duties during the said fiscal year. . . .

4. The agreement may also provide that in the case of the Provinces of Nova Scotia, New Brunswick, Prince Edward Island, Manitoba and Saskatchewan, the Dominion shall pay by way of additional subsidy during each year of the term of the agreement the respective amounts hereinafter set forth:

Nova Scotia	$ 325,769.31
New Brunswick	371,493.30
Prince Edward Island	437,174.02
Manitoba	600,000.00
Saskatchewan	1,500,000.00

5. The agreement may also provide, in accordance with and subject to such terms and conditions as may be set out therein, that the Dominion shall pay with respect to each year of the term of the agreement to the province the amount by which the net receipts during the said year from the tax imposed by the province on the sale of gasoline are less in each case than the following amounts:

Nova Scotia	$ 2,853,363.82
New Brunswick	2,101,072.01
Prince Edward Island	307,901.72
Quebec	11,803,248.13
Ontario	26,608,290.59
Manitoba	2,678,148.64
Saskatchewan	3,397,279.42
Alberta	3,221,975.68
British Columbia	3,763,625.95

being an amount in each case calculated as equivalent to the net receipts of the province from the tax imposed by the province on the sale of gasoline during the fiscal year of the province ending nearest to December 31, 1940. . . .

G.
Return of Natural Resources to the Prairie Provinces

When the province of Manitoba was created in 1870, and the provinces of Saskatchewan and Alberta in 1905, control of public lands and other natural resources was retained by the Dominion for national purposes, particularly to enable the Dominion government to pursue active and consistent settlement policies. By 1930 prairie settlement was virtually complete, and after agreement with the provinces a series of Dominion statutes passed in 1930 transferred the resources to provincial control. In the case of Manitoba the basis of the settlement was a royal commission report rendered in 1929, following a preliminary agreement made between the Dominion and the province in 1928. In the cases of Saskatchewan and Alberta, there was provision in the 1930 arrangements for royal commissions to report whether the provinces should be paid compensation for losses incurred as a result of the Dominion control of resources since 1905. Both commissions reported in 1935; each recommended payment of a lump sum of $5,000,000, plus interest since 1930.

119. Order in Council Setting up the Royal Commission on the Transfer of the Natural Resources of Manitoba

(P.C. 1258, 1 August 1928, printed in the *Report* of the Commission, Ottawa, 1929)

The Committee of the Privy Council have had before them a report dated 14th July, 1928, from the Right Hon. W. L. Mackenzie King, Prime Minister and President of the Privy Council, submitting that following a conference held at Ottawa on the 3rd and 4th days of July, 1928, between representatives of the Government of Canada and of the Government of Manitoba, an agreement was concluded as to the method and basis of settlement of the question of the administration and control of the natural resources of the said Province of Manitoba, as follows: —

1. The Province of Manitoba to be placed in a position of equality with the other provinces of Confederation with respect to the administration and control of its natural resources, as from its entrance into Confederation in 1870.

2. The Government of Canada, with the concurrence of the Government of Manitoba, to appoint a commission of three persons to inquire and report as to what financial readjustments should be made to effect this end.

3. The Commission to be empowered to decide what financial or other considerations are relevant to its inquiry.

4. The findings of the Commission to be submitted to the Parliament of Canada and to the Legislature of Manitoba.

5. Upon agreement on the financial terms following consideration of the report of the commission, the respective Governments to introduce the necessary legislation to give effect to the financial terms as agreed upon, and to effect the transfer to the province of the unalienated natural resources within its boundaries, subject to any trust existing in respect thereof, and without prejudice to any interest other than that of the Crown in the same.

6. Pending this transfer, the policy of the Government of Canada in the administration of the natural resources of Manitoba to be in accord with the wishes of the Government of the Province.

The Committee, therefore, on the recommendation of the Right Hon. the Prime Minister and President of the Privy Council, advise that...

The Hon. W. F. A. Turgeon, a Judge of the Court of Appeal of Saskatchewan,

The Hon. T. A. Crerar, of the City of Winnipeg, Province of Manitoba, and

Charles M. Bowman, of the Town of Waterloo, in the Province of Ontario, Esquire, Chairman of the Board of Directors of the Mutual Life Assurance Company of Canada,

(the Commissioners agreed upon by both Governments), be appointed Commissioners to conduct such inquiry....

120. Extracts from Agreement between the Governments of Canada and Manitoba, 14 December 1929

(Schedule to the Manitoba Natural Resources Act passed by the Dominion Parliament, 20-21 George V, Chap. 29, 30 May 1930)

Following the report of the Turgeon Commission, and its acceptance by the governments of Canada and Manitoba, this agreement was made and became the basis of the Manitoba Natural Resources Act. The Alberta Natural Resources Act (20-21 George V, Chap. 3) and the Saskatchewan Natural Resources Act (20-21 George V, Chap. 41) also received the royal assent on 30 May 1930.

. . .

1. In order that the Province may be in the same position as the original Provinces of Confederation are in virtue of section one hundred and nine of the *British North America Act, 1867*, the interest of the Crown in all Crown lands, mines, minerals (precious and base) and royalties derived therefrom within the Province, and all sums due or payable for such lands, mines, minerals or royalties, shall, from and after the coming into force of this agreement, and subject as therein otherwise provided, belong to the Province, subject to any trusts existing in respect thereof, and to any interest other than that of the Crown in the same, and the said lands, mines, minerals and royalties shall be administered by the Province for the purposes thereof, subject, until the Legislature of the Province otherwise provides, to the provisions of any Act of the Parliament of Canada relating to such administration; any payment received by Canada in respect of any such lands, mines, minerals or royalties before the coming into force of this agreement shall continue to belong to Canada whether paid in advance or otherwise, it being the intention that, except as herein otherwise specially provided, Canada shall not be liable to account to the Province for any payment made in respect of any of the said lands, mines, minerals or royalties before the coming into force of this agreement, and that the Province shall not be liable to account to Canada for any such payment made thereafter. . . .

20. In lieu of the provision made by section five of the statute two George the Fifth chapter thirty-two*. . . , Canada will, from and after the date of the coming into force of this agreement, pay to the Province by half-yearly payments in advance, on the first days of January

*The Manitoba Boundaries Extension Act, 1 April 1912.

and July in each year, an annual sum based upon the population of the Province as from time to time ascertained by the quinquennial census thereof, as follows: —

The sum payable until the population of the said Province reaches eight hundred thousand shall be five hundred and sixty-two thousand five hundred dollars;

Thereafter, until such population reaches one million two hundred thousand, the sum payable shall be seven hundred and fifty thousand dollars;

And thereafter the sum payable shall be one million one hundred and twenty-five thousand dollars. . . .

22. In order to provide an adequate financial readjustment in favour of the Province for the period intervening between its entrance into Confederation in 1870 and the first day of July, 1908, before which date it received either no subsidy in lieu of public lands or a smaller subsidy than it should have received in order to put it on an equality with the other Provinces, Canada, forthwith after the coming into force of this agreement, will, in accordance with the report of the hereinbefore recited Commission, pay to the said Province the sum of four million, five hundred and eighty-four thousand two hundred and twelve dollars and forty-nine cents with interest thereon at the rate of five per cent per annum from the first day of July, 1929. . . .

H.
The Depression
After 1929

These documents do something to illustrate general social and economic conditions during the "Dirty Thirties," while dealing also with some specific aspects and incidents. For some suggestions on cultural aspects of life during the Depression, see **143** below, in connection with the Dominion Drama Festival.

121. A Cape Breton Fisherman Complains

(Letter from Geo. W. Sweet, Neil's Harbour, N.S., *Halifax Chronicle,* 17 May 1933)

... while looking over the Highway Report for 1931 I noticed that the District Superintendent for Victoria County received for the year salary $1,350, car maintenance and expense allowance, $1,321.45, total, $2,671.45, which is money enough to support six of the average families in this district for a year in good condition.

Now compare this with what the fishermen of the Northern Coast of Victoria receive for their labours. So far as can be determined at the present time we are to receive two dollars per hundred lbs. for our lobsters, which, for the average catch of three thousand lbs., will be $60.00, out of which the fisherman has to feed his family for three months. He has to buy nails, laths, twine and rope for his traps. He has to buy rubber clothes and boots. If he uses his motor boat he has to buy gasoline. He will be expected to pay a road tax, a municipal tax and a relief tax. Then he has to pay his school tax, his sugar tax and his money order tax and many other taxes that he doesn't know anything about. He has to get up at two o'clock in the morning to haul his traps, as it is usually calm in the early morning, and oftentimes has to eat bread and molasses for his breakfast before he sets out.

... It is hard to collect taxes now and if we don't soon get some changes in affairs in this county it is going to be a mighty lot harder.

122. French-Canadian Nationalist Reaction to the Depression

(Dominique Beaudin, "Capitalisme étranger et vie nationale," *L'Action nationale*, June 1933)

In January 1933, at the nadir of the Depression, a group called the Ligue d'Action Nationale began publishing in Montreal a little monthly magazine, *L'Action nationale*. It was a revival of an earlier one called successively *L'Action française* and *L'Action canadienne-française*. The Ligue's president was Esdras Minville, and among its directors were the Abbé Lionel Groulx and René Chaloult. The mark of the times is evident in the magazine's constant emphasis on economic problems, and particularly on the domination of the Quebec economy by "foreign" capitalists.

(Translation)

A European economist — a cousin from France, let us say — is travelling through the province of Quebec. He has little time to spare; but from his rapid journey across the Laurentian countryside he hopes to carry away a general picture. He goes from Hull to Gaspé, from Chicoutimi to Saint-Jean. He goes through our great cities, our centres of a certain importance, several of our villages. He looks with astonishment at the great river, its many tributaries, their powerful falls, our vast forests, our fertile fields. . . . And here, briefly summarized, is his conversation with his guide:

"Who till these fields?"

"The descendants of French pioneers."

"Who are these settlers?"

"The same."

"Who exploit these forests?"

"American financiers."

"And who are these wood-cutters?"

"French Canadians."

"Who own these hydro-electric plants?"

"Anglo-Canadians."

"And these enormous factories?"

"The same people."

"And those mines?"

"English or American companies."

"Who are those workers?"

"French Canadians."

"Who are the proprietors of those stores?"

"Jews."

"And the customers?"

"French Canadians."

"But you told me that your people dominate the government of the province?"

"Quite true."

The economist, a careful traveller, takes note of this information. One can already see his conclusion: "After many struggles, this French race has won freedom to govern itself in a corner of Canada; it nevertheless remains in economic servitude to foreign interests. That is a serious matter for its future. And nevertheless its leaders don't appear to be worried about it."

Everyone who has made a "tour of Laurentia" will recognize the force of this easy observation; he will remember that the actual face of Quebec proclaims it. There where our explorers raised the coat of arms with the fleur de lys, there where the Indian bathed with French blood a soil that had never known cultivation, rises a factory owned by the American or the Anglo-Canadian. The rivers that carried our missionaries are harnessed for the profit of capitalists who are foreign to our race; the forest where so many Louis Héberts have laboured belongs to them likewise. On the economic field of action one no longer recognizes the descendants of the pioneers. M. Edouard Montpetit wrote in 1921, "Along with the old political struggles, always still with us, there is also the menace of a domination which wears a peaceful appearance, undertaken by powerful interests, and heavy with consequences." To say that this menace still exists would be an understatement. For after twelve years our positions do not seem to have been strengthened nor our forces of resistance increased.

Foreign capitalism, undoubted master of the great enterprises, surrounds the province and binds it fast. If it is not in order to give way wholly to alarm, we should at least take note of the situation, and admit frankly that our economic future is seriously compromised and that this state of things means unpleasant consequences for our national life.

Nobody dreams of denying that our farmers own the soil of this province, that some of our people live by being small traders, that certain ones even have a position in industry. But we form the great majority of the population, and in the economic field we are payers of tribute to the minority. . . .

123. A Cry from the Dust Bowl

(Letter in *Winnipeg Free Press*, 2 September 1933)

All wheat farmers suffered by the fact that during the Depression the price of wheat fell to the lowest point in several centuries. Many in the West, particularly in south Saskatchewan, were victimized simultaneously by an unprecedented period of drought. See James H. Gray, *The Winter Years: The Depression on the Prairies* (Toronto, 1966).

To the Editor — At a well attended representative meeting of the ratepayers of Glen Bain and Pinto Creek municipalities, held at Obthorpe school, Monday evening, Aug. 28, the following action was unanimously taken.

The district has experienced its fifth total crop failure and the people are in immediate need of food, clothing, bed clothing and fuel (the amount provided by the relief commission is inadequate for the needs of the people). We have received one grocery order in three months, averaging approximately $1.00 per person, and the total amount for clothing for the last year was $7 for adults, $5 for a boy and $4 for a girl under 17, which is inadequate to supply the needs of the people who have had no income.

Children are going to school underfed and without adequate clothing.

It was therefore resolved that the commission be requested to supply food, clothing and feed immediately, and be respectfully asked to increase the amount allowed and also to make all orders open.

Also it was requested that the provincial government be asked if they have the money to pay for relief requested, and if they have not the money that they make it known.

STEWART YOUNG,
Secretary of the meeting.

Kincaid [Saskatchewan], Aug. 28, 1933.

124. Getting By on the Prairies

(One of a series of articles by Frank H. Williams, *Winnipeg Free Press*, 2 September 1933)

How families in stricken prairie areas have managed to live during these trying times.

Those too proud to accept relief have exhibited considerable ingenuity in devising ways and means of augmenting the family income.

For one thing the old spinning wheel has come back into use again. In a small Manitoba town a blacksmith took advantage of this sudden demand for spinning wheels to revamp his shop into a spinning wheel factory and business boomed so quickly he had to take on additional help.

In the Edenwold district, east of Regina, one family with butter and eggs to sell debated whether it was worth while to spend the money for gasoline to take their produce to Regina. They solved the problem by filling the old Model T Ford with cut firewood and the sale value of the wood paid the expenses of the trip.

Another farmer near Rouleau, Sask., despaired of selling his hogs in the ordinary way for the price was at rock bottom. He conceived the idea of manufacturing the entire hog into sausage and the word spread that his sausage was good, so he was forced to go out and buy the hogs of his neighbors.

The spinning industry was revived because the price of wool was so low as to make it unprofitable to sell. The government instructors quickly adapted their training to the changed conditions and showed the farm women how to make blankets out of the raw wool.

Unable to buy new cars and by the same token unable to buy gasoline for the old car, or even to buy a buggy, the farmers have taken the engines out of their old Model T Fords, hitched a tongue and whiffle-trees to the front axle and called it a "Bennett" buggy. Others have put a seat on the front wheels of a Model T and have christened this an "Anderson" cart. Probably Premiers Bennett and Anderson* will not feel flattered at the use of their names in this connection, but it is a reflection of the spirit of the times. . . .

One item of expense the farmer has eliminated is that of flour. With thousands of bushels in his granaries that the market price doomed to remain there, the farmer took five or ten bushels to the small grist mill for his own flour. If he had no money to pay for the

*J. T. M. Anderson, Premier of Saskatchewan, 1929-34. His "Co-operative" (Conservative) government was badly defeated by the Liberals led by James G. Gardiner in the 1934 election.

milling he left the bran and shorts with the miller in payment.

The average farm family has limited its purchases to sugar and tea, for which no substitutes can be found on the land. A few dozen eggs or a few pounds of butter can take care of these requirements. Some enterprising businessmen, such as local theatre and skating rink managers offered to take wheat and barley as payment for admission prices.

They tell the story of a Manitoba farmer who met two acquaintances outside a beer parlor.

"Let's go in for a beer," he suggested.

The three quaffed their bottles of beer and when the host arose to go he turned to the hotel-keeper.

"I'll bring you ten bushels of barley to pay for that," he said.

Until organized relief measures came to the aid of the farmer the fuel problem was his greatest worry. You can drive a day at a time in some parts of Saskatchewan and never see a tree or a bush. Those farmers burned coal in the good days, but in their necessity they had no money with which to buy coal. So they burned barley.

But they have caught a vision of better times, with the upward trend of the wheat market. Those courageous enough to hold their crop over from last year have sold it this summer, mostly in small lots, for a carload shipment would excite comment and perhaps invoke a seizure order from the bank, the implement agent or the mortgage company. So they have sold a lot of their grain a hundred bushels at a time and they are paying their small debts, preferably their store bills. They feel the banks, the implement companies and the mortgage companies can wait a bit longer for their money....

There will be money to spend in western Canada this year if the market price of grain keeps up. The farmer is starved for everything that contributes to the comfort and well-being of his family and as soon as he gets some surplus cash he will turn it loose into the avenues of trade....

125. The Soldiers Go to Stratford

(Canadian Press dispatch, *Winnipeg Free Press*, 28 September 1933)

This occasion at Stratford, Ontario, was one of very few when troops were called in to meet a Depression emergency. In general the Royal Canadian Mounted Police or other police forces dealt with instances of disorder. The troops were brought to Stratford at the request of the local police commission. There was no trouble after their arrival.

Stratford, 27 September.

... 120 soldiers of the Royal Canadian regiment, brought here during the day as a precautionary measure in connection with strikes of furniture factories and the plant of the Swift Canadian company, a meat packing concern, remained quartered in the armouries. They were armed, equipped with steel helmets and had four small tanks.*

Presence of the soldiers who came from London and Toronto, aroused some indignation . . . among Great War veterans who held importation of extra Ontario provincial police had been instrumental in causing disorders Tuesday [26th] at the Swift plant, during which six persons were injured.

126. Bennett Confronts the Relief Camp Strikers

(*Globe*, Toronto, 24 June 1935)

The concentrations of unemployed men in the relief camps were natural foci of discontent and targets for agitators, some of whom no doubt came from Canada's small but active Communist Party. This episode in Ottawa arose from a strike in West Coast camps. The strikers "marched" on Ottawa (by freight train); they were stopped at Regina but allowed to send representatives to the national capital to meet the government.

Ottawa, June 23.
(*Special and C.P.*)

Bitter, angry words, prompted by frayed tempers, flew on Parliament Hill about noon on Saturday [22nd] when unemployed delegations interviewed Prime Minister Bennett. The interview, lasting nearly two hours, ended with the Premier refusing the six demands made by the jobless trekkers.

The meeting reached a tense anti-climax [*sic*] when one of the spokesmen for the workless shouted at the Prime Minister: "You're a liar!"

Mr. Bennett had told the men there could be no compliance with the first demand, for work and wages on a five-day week, six-hour day, and at 50 cents an hour.

"I ask you," the Premier said, "if you think you are playing the

*These were actually universal carriers. There were no tanks in Canada in 1933.

part of good citizens when you work against a country that is doing the best it can for you."

"We want work and wages," interjected Arthur Evans, of Vancouver, spokesman for the Regina camp of the on-to-Ottawa army. "You give us work and wages and see how we will take advantage of it."

"I come from Alberta," Mr. Bennett replied, "where you were arrested for stealing the funds of your union."

"You're a liar," Evans cried. "It was for fraudulent conversion."

"Well, call it that if you like."

"It was for fraudulently converting the money to feed the starving miners — instead of sending it down to the pot-bellied international officers in Indianapolis," Evans rejoined.

The hearing broke up in some disorder, with Evans declaring the Government would have to take the responsibility for whatever might eventuate and accusing Mr. Bennett of raising the "Red bogey."

A second delegation of jobless, who said they had been sent by the unemployed of Ontario and Quebec, interviewed the Prime Minister and his Cabinet aides.

Mr. Bennett was quiet-spoken throughout the interview. He refused all of the demands and told the delegation that they could go back to the camps and await, as others were doing, the opportunity of securing employment.

He gave a blunt warning that communism would not be tolerated, and declared that the jobless had been victims of professional agitators. . . .

127. The Dominion Day Riot in Regina, 1935

(*Globe*, Toronto, 2 July 1935)

This was perhaps the most violent and tragic incident of the Depression in Canada. Assistant Commissioner S. T. Wood of the Royal Canadian Mounted Police stated afterwards (*Globe*, 3 July 1935) that he had given the orders for the police action, which was justified under Section 98 of the Criminal Code (above, **52**). He was reported as saying that the police did not intend to disperse the meeting at the market square, but went there to arrest the strike leaders.

Regina, July 1 (*CP*).

Gun-fire* blazed out in riot-torn Regina tonight leaving one police-man dead and a striker dying as steel-helmeted Royal Canadian Mounted Police and city constables clashed with 3,000 relief-camp deserters and sympathizers.

City Detective [Charles] Miller was seized by the strikers and beaten to death, eyewitnesses said. Sticks were battered over his head as a group of men seized him at the Market Square behind the police station....

Scores were injured by flying rocks and any other missiles the milling strikers could lay hands on. Tear-gas sent men, women and children fleeing from the Market Place where a meeting, called for the purpose of raising funds for the stranded strikers, was broken up.

Arthur Evans, one of the leaders of the on-to-Ottawa trek of 2,000 relief-camp workers, was arrested along with at least 26 others....

First outbreak occurred when the helmeted mounted police swooped down upon the strikers and supporters meeting in the market square. They appeared as a spokesman began a plea for funds to aid the strikers, ordered by authorities to remain in Regina. They have camped here since June 14, when they were first halted on their "on-to-Ottawa" trek from Western relief camps....

128. The End of Relief Camps

(Editorial, *Globe*, Toronto, 2 July 1936)

On the relief camps for single unemployed men set up under Army direction, see James Eayrs, *In Defence of Canada*, I (Toronto, 1964), and John Swettenham, *McNaughton*, I (Toronto, 1968).

With the closing of relief camps Dominion Day marked the end of one visible manifestation of the depression. No one will be sorry to see them out of business, if more satisfactory provision is made for the men accommodated there over a period of three years. Whether or not camp concentration was advisable depends, like many another thing, on the point of view. To a large number of the men thus cared for it was a sort of rounding up to be resented. The trouble in Vancouver and the attempted trek to Ottawa, which brought a Royal

*"In the course of the attacks on the police shots were fired by the city police although the R.C.M.P. did not use guns." (*Canadian Annual Review, 1935 and 1936*, p. 312).

Commission of investigation, are easily recalled. Complaints in other parts of the country have been numerous. Yet the camps provided housing and food for thousands of foot-loose men unable to get sustaining employment, and in this respect served a purpose which could not well have been met otherwise. They may have bred ill will toward authority, but no one can say how far the rebellious spirit would have gone if the same men had been left to shift for themselves.

"As an emergency measure," Hon Norman Rogers* told the House of Commons, "these camps may have been justified, but as a permanent feature of social organization in Canada they cannot be supported on grounds either of social utility or of Governmental economy." To continue them on their present basis, he said, would be to institutionalize them and to encourage an attitude of hopelessness on the part of those for whom they were designed to make provision in a period of economic extremity.

The question received prompt consideration from the present Government, with admirable results. Although July 1 was set as the ultimate date of closing, steps were taken to reduce the number of campers as quickly as possible. Those remaining on May 1 totalled 14,276, following a voluntary exodus of some 6,100. Arrangements were made with the railways to absorb 10,000 on deferred maintenance work, while a large number have been provided for on farms and elsewhere. The exodus of the final days, it is reported, involved only 1,500, so the camps have been closed in a progressive and orderly manner.

On Dominion Day of last year the camp strikers began a riot at Regina which brought death to one policeman and injuries to others. This year most of them, possibly, are too busy to think about riots.

Unfortunately, the work being given through Government intervention cannot be permanent, and it is not to be assumed that the whole problem is solved. . . .

*Minister of Labour in the Mackenzie King Cabinet, 1935-39.

I.
The Depression Robs Newfoundland of Responsible Government, 1933

One result of the Depression was a change in Newfoundland's form of government. By 1932 the island, which had enjoyed responsible government since 1855 and had full Dominion status, found itself in such straits that it was obliged to ask Britain and Canada for help to enable it to pay the interest on its debt. A joint loan was made on condition of a royal commission being appointed to report on Newfoundland's affairs. The commission was composed of Lord Amulree (United Kingdom), C. A. Magrath (Canada) and Sir William Stavert (Newfoundland). The events that followed, leading to the temporary establishment of government by a commission responsible to the United Kingdom government, are described in the documents below.

129. Newfoundland Asks for the Temporary Suspension of Self-Government

(First Schedule to the Newfoundland Act, 1933, 24 Geo. 5, Ch. 2, 21 December 1933) (British statute)

ADDRESS PRESENTED TO HIS MAJESTY BY
THE LEGISLATIVE COUNCIL AND HOUSE OF
ASSEMBLY OF NEWFOUNDLAND.

TO THE KING'S MOST EXCELLENT MAJESTY:
Most Gracious Sovereign:
We, Your Majesty's most dutiful and loyal subjects, the Legislative Council and Assembly of Newfoundland, humbly approach Your Majesty praying that—

Whereas in the present emergency Your Majesty's Island of New-foundland is unable from its own resources to defray the interest charges on the public debt:

And whereas the Royal Commission appointed by Your Majesty's Warrant bearing the date the seventeenth day of February, 1933, to examine into the future of Newfoundland has recommended that for the time being, until such time as the Island may become self-sup-porting again, the administration of the Island should be vested in His Excellency the Governor acting on the advice of a specially created Commission of Government and that during such period Your Majesty's Government in the United Kingdom should assume general responsibility for the finances of Newfoundland and should, in particular, make such arrangements as may be deemed just and practicable with a view to securing to Newfoundland a reduction in the present burden of public debt:

And whereas Your Majesty's Government in the United Kingdom have signified their readiness subject to the approval of Parliament to accept the recommendations of the Royal Commission and have made detailed proposals for carrying those recommendations into effect:

Now, therefore, Your Majesty may be graciously pleased to sus-pend the Letters Patent under the Great Seal bearing the date at Westminster the Twenty-eighth day of March, 1876, and Letters Pat-ent under the Great Seal bearing the date at Westminster the Seven-teenth day of July, 1905,* and to issue new Letters Patent which would provide for the administration of the Island, until such time as it may become self-supporting again, on the basis of the recommen-dations which are contained in the Report of the Royal Commission and of which a summary is set out in the Annex hereto:

And further that Your Majesty may be graciously pleased to cause to be laid before the Parliament of the United Kingdom at its present Session such a measure as may enable them to be given immediate effect.

---

*These Letters Patent related to the office of Governor of Newfoundland.

ANNEX.

EXTRACT FROM REPORT OF ROYAL COMMISSION APPOINTED BY HIS MAJESTY'S WARRANT BEARING DATE THE SEVENTEENTH DAY OF FEBRUARY, NINETEEN HUNDRED AND THIRTY-THREE.

We therefore recommend that the Newfoundland Government, recognising that it is impossible for the Island to surmount unaided the unprecedented difficulties that now confront it, should make an immediate appeal for the sympathetic co-operation of Your Majesty's Government in the United Kingdom in the adoption and execution of a joint plan of reconstruction, of which the following would be the main features: —

(a) The existing form of government would be suspended until such time as the Island may become self-supporting again.

(b) A special Commission of Government would be created which would be presided over by His Excellency the Governor, would be vested with full legislative and executive authority, and would take the place of the existing Legislature and Executive Council.

(c) The Commission of Government would be composed of six members, exclusive of the Governor, three of whom would be drawn from Newfoundland and three from the United Kingdom.

(d) The Government Departments in the Island would be divided into six groups. Each group would be placed in the charge of a Member of the Commission of Government, who would be responsible for the efficient working of the Departments in the group, and the Commission would be collectively responsible for the several Departments.

(e) The proceedings of the Commission of Government would be subject to supervisory control by Your Majesty's Government in the United Kingdom, and the Governor-in-Commission would be responsible to the Secretary of State for Dominion Affairs in the United Kingdom for the good government of the Island.

(f) Your Majesty's Government in the United Kingdom would, for their part, assume general responsibility for the finances of the Island until such time as it may become self-supporting again, and would, in particular, make such arrangements as may be deemed just and practicable with a view to securing to Newfoundland a reduction in the present burden of the public debt.

(g) It would be understood that, as soon as the Island's difficulties are overcome and the country is again self-supporting, responsible government, on request from the people of Newfoundland, would be restored.

130. The Under-Secretary of State for the Dominions Discusses the Newfoundland Bill

(*Parliamentary Debates, House of Commons*, United Kingdom, Fifth Series, Volume 284, 12 December 1933)

These are extracts from the speech closing the debate on the second reading of what became the Newfoundland Act (see above, **129**), which gave effect to the recommendations of the Amulree Commission.

The UNDER-SECRETARY of STATE for DOMINION AFFAIRS (*Mr. Malcolm MacDonald*): I have listened to every word which has been spoken in the two Debates we have had upon this subject, and I think that the series of interesting speeches which have been delivered is the best tribute that could have been paid to the Report of the Royal Commission....

...I do not think that anyone has sought to dispute the terrible state of affairs in Newfoundland described in the pages of the Report. The people of the country are, for the most part, wretchedly poor, the economic position of the country is at this moment precarious, and, in fact, an exceedingly dangerous state of affairs has been brought to a head by the inability of the Newfoundland Government to meet the services of the public debt out of Newfoundland's resources. These desperate conditions are features of the problem on which we are all agreed. . . . If that desperate state of affairs is true, there are two possible alternative policies between which the Government had to choose. The first was simply to allow things to slide and to allow the Newfoundland Government to default....

...If the bondholders were the only people interested in our saving Newfoundland from default at this moment, the Government would not be going into the intricate and comprehensive policy which is contemplated at the present time. The fact is, as is written on every page of the report, that there are other people concerned, other people interested in our avoiding default by Newfoundland besides the bondholders, and those people are the whole population of Newfoundland. The poor fishermen, the poor agriculturists and the small number of industrial workers would all have heaped upon them even worse distresses than they are experiencing to-day if we were to stand by and allow things to slide and allow Newfoundland to default....

... The Royal Commission's Report indicates the processes that would follow upon default. It lays it down that default would shatter the credit of the Island, that that would lead to the impairment of confidence, and that that in turn would lead to the limitation of the trade of an Island which depends very largely on imports for giving the people the necessities of life. That reduction of trade would result in more unemployment and in a general lowering of the standard of life of the people....The report...indicates that a large proportion of the population even now are depending upon public relief, and one realises that that proportion would be enormously increased if the disaster of default were allowed to take place....

There is only one other alternative to avoiding default [sic], and that is to devise means to enable the Government of Newfoundland to meet the services of the public debt....

... Hon. Members have referred to the truck system* and have asked why the people of Newfoundland continue to be exploited by that system. The government would very much like to see that system go. It is a system which we have not tolerated in this country for the last century; we abolished it in this country 100 years ago. But the Royal Commission themselves say that this habit, the truck system, is

"now so deeply ingrained both among the merchants and the fishermen that an alteration can only be effected gradually."

It is in order that that alteration can be effected at all that we are seeking to preserve the safe foundations upon which our constructive policy must be built. ... The report will be very carefully considered by the new Government, and the first purpose of the new Government will be to push ahead with the policy of development in the interest of the whole population of the Island....

The Government's policy is a policy which bristles with difficulties. It is not going to be a policy which is easily run or easy to achieve success by, but at any rate it is a policy which should command the good will of every Member of this House, and it is a policy which the Governor and the commissioners and the whole of the people of Newfoundland should be determined to work successfully.

*The "practice of paying workmen in goods instead of money or in money on the understanding that they will buy provisions &c. of their employers" (*Concise Oxford Dictionary*).

So far as this House is concerned — this House on which so many responsibilities already lie — in asking hon. Members to give this Bill a Second Reading I would only remind them that the great imperial reputation of this country will not suffer through her coming generously to the aid of the oldest British Colony.

J.
Stevens, Bennett and Economic Reform, 1934-1935

On R. B. Bennett's reform program as presented in the election campaign of 1935, see above, **44**. It has been pointed out that Bennett's mind was apparently turning to reform long before his "New Deal" speeches of 1935 and before H. H. Stevens' Price Spreads investigation made the public aware of radicalism within the Conservative party; in particular, the drafting of his unemployment insurance law was under way as early as 1933 (see Wilbur, "R. B. Bennett as a Reformer"). Several of Bennett's reforming statutes have been dealt with above: the Bank of Canada Act **(114)**, the Canadian Wheat Board Act **(94)**, and the Prairie Farm Rehabilitation Act **(97)**. The most important documents relating to the whole rather complicated episode are reproduced in J. R. H. Wilbur, ed., *The Bennett New Deal: Fraud or Portent?* (Toronto, 1968).

131. Extracts from the Stevens Commission Report, 1935

(Report of the Royal Commission on Price Spreads, Ottawa, 1935)

By the beginning of 1934 H. H. Stevens, Bennett's Minister of Trade and Commerce, had become convinced that the practices of big business were harming the country and had turned to radical solutions for Canada's economic problems. As chairman of a Special Select Committee of the House of Commons appointed to investigate the spread between prices received by producers and those paid by consumers, which was subsequently converted into a royal commission (see below, p. 314, he incurred the hostility of many businessmen and became a problem for the Prime Minister. Before the commission reported he had resigned from the government. The report is very long and the recommendations very detailed; only brief representative extracts can be given here. One of the most interesting aspects of the report is its acceptance of the idea of regulated monopoly.

SUMMARY OF RECOMMENDATIONS

Chapter III: Concentration and the Corporate System of Business

1. Amendments to the Dominion Companies Act. . . .*
2. Provisions to Prevent "Stock-Watering". . . .
5. The whole trend of law should be towards putting the managers and directors in a trustee capacity, with respect to all security holders. . . .

Chapter V: Labour and Wages

The major recommendations of this chapter are better administration of the labour laws now on both provincial and Dominion statute books, miscellaneous improvements in this legislation, a few types of new legislation, and more continuous study of, investigation into and publicity for the whole range of problems covered by the title of this chapter. In detail they are as follows: —

1. More complete organization of industry into employers' and trade association. . . .
2. More complete organization of workers into trade unions. More adequate recognition of trade unions by governments and employers.
3. More adequate appropriations, larger and better staffs for labour law administration, both Dominion and provincial.
4. Improved provincial minimum wage laws. . . .
5. Hours of labour laws. . . .
8. Amendment to the Criminal Code to make certain undesirable industrial relations practices indictable offences.†
9. Amendment of the Fair Wages and Eight Hour Day Act, 1930. . . .‡
12. Division of Research, Standards and Services. The creation in the federal Department of Labour of an entirely new division. . . .
13. National regulation of employment conditions preferably by Dominion legislation, if feasible, or, alternatively by inter-provincial co-operation.

---

*Done by 25-26 George V, Chap. 55, 5 July 1935.

†Done by 25-26 George V, Chap. 56, 5 July 1935, dealing with penalties for discrimination in trade, breaking minimum wage laws, or false advertising. Not interfered with by the Judicial Committee.

‡Above, **61**. This was done by 25-26 George V, Chap. 39, 28 June 1935.

1. Thorough exploration of the constitutional possibility of the enactment of Dominion labour legislation.
2. If such legislation is now precluded by insuperable constitutional obstacles, the necessary amendment of the B.N.A. Act. . . .

Chapter VIII: The Consumer

1. Consumer Standards: Marking, Labelling, etc.
    1. Extension of the functions of the National Research Council to include the preparation of consumer standards and specifications and the analysis and testing of consumer products.
    2. Creation of a Consumer Commodity Standards Board, as a section of the Federal Trade and Industry Commission, with the following duties: —
        a. The establishment of consumer standards. . . .
        b. Enforcement of such standards as might be established.
        c. Publication of findings of non-conformity to standards set up, of harmful or injurious substances, or of excessive price spreads. . . .
    6. A term "Canada Standard" should be adopted exclusively for products conforming to official standards as established. . . .

Chapter IX: The Problem of State Control

GENERAL RECOMMENDATIONS

1. Federal Trade and Industry Commission.
    1. Structure:
        a. To consist of five members appointed by the Governor in Council, as a semi-autonomous Board under the President of the Privy Council.
        b. Its status both in its authority and in its relation to the responsible Minister and Parliament, to be similar to that of the Board of Railway Commissioners.
    2. Functions:
        a. Administrative
            (1) Rigorous administration of an amended Combines Investigation Act, for the purpose of retaining and restoring competition whenever possible.
            (2) On instruction from the Governor in Council, to regulate monopoly, when competition cannot or should not be restored or enforced.
            (3) On instruction from the Governor in Council, to sanction

and supervise agreements for industrial self-government.

(4) To prohibit unfair competitive practices

    (*a*) Such practices should not be set out in detail in the Act setting up the Commission, but a general definition of unfairness should be included....

    (*c*) Certain practices such as discriminatory discounts, rebates and allowances, territorial price discrimination and predatory price-cutting, should be included within this definition.

    (*d*) The Commission should act by inquiry, hearings and where necessary, prohibitory orders.

    (*e*) An appeal from these orders to the Exchequer Court of Canada, should be permitted....

    (*g*) In more serious cases, the Commission might prosecute directly under the Act for the offence of competing unfairly.

    (*h*) The results of its major findings should be published.

(5) To supervise generally, or co-operate in the administration of existing laws relating to merchandising and business practices for which no other agency exists.

(6) To administer new laws for the protection of the consumer.

(7) To administer the regulation of new security issues for protection of the investor.

(8) To co-operate with Chambers of Commerce and Boards of Trade in the development of commercial arbitration or the refereeing of business disputes.

(9) To co-operate with other Government agencies, whether federal, provincial or municipal, in the solution of trade and industrial problems.

b. Advisory

(1) To Government

    (*a*) To recommend to the Governor in Council the recognition and regulation of monopoly in special situations where competition cannot be restored.

    (*b*) If so requested by an industry, and after investigation, to recommend to the Governor in Council the granting of powers of "self-government" in special situations where competition seems undesirable....

(2) To Industry

    In co-operative trade practice conferences to advise

industry and secure its advice about the elimination of unfair trade practices.

c. Investigation and Publicity
   (1) Full power to inquire into the organization and practices of any industry.
   (2) General economic investigation.
   (3) Full publicity to the results of any investigation.
   (4) Authority to require that firms or industries publish such information about prices or other matters as may be in the public interest.

2. Amendments to the Combines Investigation Act. . . .*
3. Proposals for the Extension of the General Statistical Work of the Dominion Bureau of Statistics.

[EXTRACTS FROM TEXT OF THE REPORT]

Concentration and the Corporate System of Business

. . .

Many of the remedies which we suggest for the evils disclosed involve amendments or additions to existing legislation. This brings up at once the question of jurisdiction. It is obvious that the existence of ten jurisdictions, each having the right to make its own laws for the incorporation and regulation of limited liability companies — and each in fact exercising this right — greatly complicates the problem of control through such legislation. It is not part of this report to discuss fully the problems arising from multiple jurisdictions, but the question is so important that it cannot be ignored.

One possible solution for this problem would be to amend the constitution so that the Dominion Parliament would obtain exclusive jurisdiction over companies by the provinces surrendering such jurisdiction over property and civil rights as would be needed to secure effective control. Difficult as this solution may appear, it would in practice be the most satisfactory one.

A more realizable alternative would be to obtain uniformity in the essential features of the Dominion Companies Act, and the provincial Acts through the co-operation of the legislatures concerned. Though two Dominion-Provincial Conferences have not succeeded in securing uniformity by this method, we think that the difficulties in the way of such an achievement can be overcome.

But whatever may be the solution of this constitutional problem, it

*Done by 25-26 George V, Chap. 54, 5 July 1935.

is clear that growing public resentment necessitates further social control of the financial operations of companies. Accordingly, it is urged here that, within its legal competence, the Dominion should to the very limit give leadership with a strict Act. We feel that the prestige of a Dominion incorporation is such that the provinces will follow such a lead. If they do not, then the question of securing uniformity by constitutional amendment would have to be considered. . . .

Labour and Wages

. . .

The evidence before the Commission proves that, in certain industries, the sweat shop still survives in Canada and that, more generally, unemployment and low wages have reduced many workers to a state of abject poverty. It is difficult, however, accurately to measure the influence of mass buying on this situation. . . . In this discussion of labour and wages, we feel warranted in stating the conclusion that mass-buyers — by their own cut-price sales, by their patronage of cut-price manufacturers, in some instances by the maintenance of oppressive working conditions in their own factories, and by their purchasing systems which force their own buyers to drive very hard bargains and to seek out distress sellers — have tended to intensify the inevitable effect of the depression on wage rates and working conditions. It is necessary to qualify this conclusion by stating also that inadequate managerial experience, ignorance of costs and unethical practices on the part of the manufacturers themselves, and the tolerance of inadequate labour legislation and administration by the community as a whole, must also share a large part of the responsibility for present deplorable conditions. . . .

Distribution

. . .

A large number of examples of price spreads in different departments were submitted to us by our investigators and the variation in initial mark-up . . . is illustrated by the following brief extracts from these tables:

	Total Laid down Cost	Initial Selling Price	Initial Mark-up Amount	Per cent to Cost of Sales
Description	$	$	$	
Men's pyjamas	1.50	2.98	1.39	87.42
Men's negligee shirts	0.45	0.75	0.30	66.67
Cambray shirts	0.69	0.95	0.26	37.68
Boy's suits	3.60	9.95	6.35	176.39
Boy's britches	0.81	1.15	0.34	41.97
Women's coats	7.08	10.74	3.66	51.69
Women's dresses	7.95	29.50	21.55	271.07
Shoulder of pork	0.11	0.10	0.01*	9.09*
Beef hearts	0.04	0.08	0.04	100.00
Men's top coats	13.60	25.00	11.40	83.8
Blue waist overalls	1.19	1.49	0.30	25.2
Solid walnut end-tables	1.03	0.95	0.08*	7.8*
Mercurochrome	0.10½	0.25	0.14½	138.1
Lysol	0.22	0.27	0.05	22.00

. . .

Large-scale distribution in its earlier development did undoubtedly make a contribution to the economic progress of this country by helping to narrow the spread between producer and consumer, and by the introduction of new and efficient methods of merchandising. In recent years, however, as we have seen, steady and conservative growth was succeeded by a period of unwarranted expansion which nullified many of the benefits of the earlier developments and has resulted in charges that the mass merchandiser has become an obstacle to sound business progress.

This recent expansion has concentrated retail business in fewer and fewer hands. Although Canada has approximately 125,000 retail outlets, three of these accounted for 10.5 per cent of total sales; one alone for more than 7 per cent. In view of this, we think it is fair to say that these three stores occupy a dominating position in the retail field. . . .

The concentration in retail distribution already achieved has had certain undesirable effects. Socially, it has meant that in approximately one-third of the retail business of this country, the personal factor has largely disappeared with the inevitable weakening of the ideals of service to the community, so long and honourably

*Loss.

associated with the local independent store. That such a development has occurred in other phases of economic life, makes it none the less to be regretted in the field of distribution.

Economically, the unwarranted expansion in recent years in distributive, as in industrial organizations, has not contributed to the general welfare. As long as conditions were prosperous, the consequences of such expansion did not make themselves apparent, but since the advent of the depression, it has become clear that the existence of unwieldy merchandising concerns with an enormous burden of fixed charges and rigid expenses, has resulted not so much in lowering the cost of distribution as in a bitter fight to maintain the position achieved by various methods, among which might be mentioned the exercise of mass buying pressure to force down the cost of purchases.

One result of this mass buying pressure and the unfair competitive practices we have already indicated, has been to demoralize business generally and to provide a means of exploiting the weaker manufacturer, the worker, and the primary producer. Certain of these practices, such as price discrimination, excessive discounts, secret and discriminatory rebates, unearned advertising allowances, discriminatory free deals, loss leaders as commonly used, are unfair in the economic sense. Others, such as deceptive packaging, misleading advertising, short weighting, are unfair in the ethical sense. All of them we unreservedly condemn.

We believe that the abuses of large-scale distribution can be prevented without interfering with its legitimate development. At the same time, we feel that this development is not legitimate if it is made possible only by unfair competitive advantages at the expense of the smaller and less favoured distributor. We are not condemning mass merchandising as such. It has in the past played and in the future, if certain reforms are brought about, may continue to play an important part in our developing economy. We are condemning, however, certain practices which we have discovered in our inquiries into this form of distribution. . . .

The Problem of State Control

. . .

The strongest case for individualism rested in its promise of "the greatest good of the greatest number" and in its real achievement of increased production, with a relatively small outlay of effort to control a largely self-regulating economic machine. We have cited much evidence which indicates that the growth of imperfect competition profoundly modifies the terms in which this argument can now be realistically phrased. We are convinced that certain forms of inter-vention are likely to be less expensive than the wastes of goods and of life that the collapse of the economic system, even if it still retains recuperative power, periodically occasions. We believe, however, that the loss of political freedom and individual liberty would be too high a price to pay for the autocratically planned economy of state capitalism, fascism, or communism (even if they should achieve their avowed economic goals), and we are confident that it is still within the capacity of Anglo-Saxon nations to work out a system of social control in which freedom can be preserved without economic paralysis, and in which, without dictatorship, production can be made less unstable and the distribution of wealth and income less unequal and less inequitable. . . .

132. "The Premier Speaks to the People": Extracts from Bennett's "New Deal" Broadcasts, 1935

(*The Premier Speaks to the People: The Prime Minister's January Radio Broadcasts issued in book form*, Dominion Conservative Headquarters, Ottawa [1935])

In spite of his break with Stevens, Bennett himself, under the impul-sion of the economic crisis and the Price Spreads inquiry and the strong encouragement of his brother-in-law, W. D. Herridge, the Canadian Minister in Washington, was moving left. Before the Price Spreads report was finally published (April 1935) the millionaire Prime Minister, in five broadcasts on 2-11 January, proclaimed what was generally regarded as his version of President Roosevelt's "New Deal" and declared himself in favour of using the power of the state to improve the lot of the worker. These speeches astonished the country and shook many Conservatives.

FIRST ADDRESS, 2 JANUARY

. . . In the last five years, great changes have taken place in the world. The old order is gone. It will not return. We are living amidst condi-tions which are new and strange to us. Your prosperity demands cor-rections in the old system, so that, in these new conditions, that old system may adequately serve you. The right time to bring about these changes has come. Further progress without them is improbable. . . .

Canadians are not those from whom unpleasant facts should be concealed. The people of this country were born optimists, but they were born realists as well. They demand the truth, however disturbing it may be. And *the truth IS disturbing. The world is in tragic circumstances. The signs of recovery are few and doubtful. The signs of trouble are many, and they do not lessen. The world is searching pathetically for safety and prosperity. It will find them only when each nation, resolute to effect its own regeneration, will come to a meeting place with all the others, in the spirit which declares that even the most powerful among them has no real economic independence of the rest.*

That time has not yet come. Meanwhile, dangers abound....

...I shall...show you that the time has come for a radical change in the policy of the Government. You will, I know, agree upon its necessity and approve its timeliness. I shall exactly explain what this policy is and develop my plans for its execution. After you are fully acquainted with what has taken place and with the conditions of today, I am confident that this policy will receive your enthusiastic support. Without your support, I am unable to carry it out. Therefore, when you have had an opportunity to thoroughly examine the whole condition of affairs, I will ask you for a decision. You will not be hurried. You will have ample time to test this programme of reform and to decide upon its value. I will then invite your considered opinion as to whether reform is in fact necessary, and as to whether my programme of reform is wise. If you say yes, then I will not rest until I have put it into operation. But if you say no — if you are satisfied with conditions as they now are, if you think that there is not need for reform, if you feel that the Government is not required to do anything more — then I am not willing to continue in this office. *For if you believe that things should be left as they are, you and I hold contrary and irreconcilable views. I am for reform.*

And, in my mind, reform means Government intervention. It means Government control and regulation. It means the end of *laissez faire*. Reform heralds certain recovery. There can be no permanent recovery without reform. Reform or no reform! I raise that issue squarely. I nail the flag of progress to the masthead. I summon the power of the State to its support.

Who will oppose our plan of progress? It will be interesting and instructive to see....

SECOND ADDRESS, 4 JANUARY

...Now, as to the industrial worker, whether in city or country parts: there are two or three particular things I wish tonight to say about this great labour group. *The first is that I believe there should be a uniform minimum wage and a uniform maximum working week.* I hold the view that if we are to have equality of social and political conditions throughout this land, we must have equality in economic conditions as well. Labour in one part of Canada must not be at a disadvantage with labour in another part. That is wrong socially and it is foolish in a business sense, for clearly it creates a disequilibrium in the nation's industrial life. *There must be an end to child labour. There must be an end to sweat shop conditions. There must be an end to the reckless exploitation of human resources and the trafficking in the health and happiness of Canadian citizens. There must be an end to the idea that a workman should be held to his labour throughout the daylight hours of every day.* I for one, believe that our workers must have more leisure. If all our scientific improvements, our intensive organization, our inventions, all our mechanical triumphs, all the devices which make for increased production and simplification of production, — if all these things do not help the worker to greater happiness and to a better and healthier life, what is the use of them? . . .

Then there is another phase of the worker's life upon which we must have a more definite agreement and arrangement. When, because of fluctuations in industrial conditions, the worker is thrown out of employment, he should not be punished when the fault is that of the machine. For whatever is the cause of these depressions, whoever is to blame for them (if anyone is to blame), assuredly it is not the workman. *If he is able and willing to work, but can get no work, provision must be made for his security in a decent way.* By this I do not mean the dole. The dole is a rotten thing. It is alike an insult to the worker and to those who profess to have control of our industrial system. . . .

However few or many unemployed we normally may have, no man must be left to the uncertainties of private charity or to the humiliation of government gratuity. He must not be unemployed in the old, hateful sense of the word. As a member of our economic society, he should have security, — provided always that he is willing to work. That is a condition precedent. . . . This security will be provided by means of unemployment insurance. For this reason, I believe in unemployment insurance, not as a means of bolstering up a faulty system, but as an element in establishing a sound modern one.

I believe the more in it after my experience in these trying times with various forms of government relief. None of them are satisfactory. In the circumstances, they were the very best that could be devised. But they were essentially emergency measures to meet an emergency condition. *Now that we have achieved some measure of control over economic conditions and can operate without fear of imminent disaster, we are going to do away, as quickly as possible, with emergency relief measures and put in a permanent system of sound and scientific insurance against unemployment.*

There is another time in the worker's life which must not be forgotten; that time is when, because of old age, he is no longer able to work. As a citizen, he should have security. It should be a normal and essential function of the State to see that its people, who have contributed to the productivity of the state, who have given their best to the support of the industrial machine, who have spent their vigorous manhood in labour, are not in want, when their working days are over. This system of insurance should be on the same social and economic principle as that of Unemployment Insurance, involving the recognition of thrift on the part of those who will provide for their old age. *The present Old Age Pensions Act is unscientific and obsolete and must give way to something which will serve you better.*

Likewise, health insurance and accident and sickness insurance must be developed in the same way....

133. The Dominion Trade and Industry Commission Act, 1935

(25-26 George V, Chap. 59)

The statute book of 1935 contains a series of reform laws enacted under Bennett, several of which were declared *ultra vires* by the Judicial Committee of the Privy Council in 1937 (the Judicial Committee's action in this matter was fully discussed in a series of articles in the *Canadian Bar Review*, notably in the number for June 1937). Among these victims were three Acts whose validity had been held to derive from the fact that they were intended to carry out international obligations of Canada undertaken through the International Labour Office. They were the Weekly Rest in Industrial Undertakings Act, 25-26 George V, Chap. 14, 4 April 1935; the Limitation of Hours of Work Act, Chap. 63, 5 July 1935; and the Minimum Wages Act, Chap. 44, 28 June 1935. The Judicial Committee also shot down the Unemployment and Social Insurance Act, Chap. 38, 28 June 1935 (see above, p. 16). The Dominion Trade and Industry Commission Act, here printed in part, was considered to embody the chief recommendations of the Price Spreads Commission. Most of it escaped the Judicial Committee's shotgun (though section 14 was declared *ultra vires*); but after the 1935 change of government it remained largely a dead letter. The King ministry restored the old machinery of combines investigation (above, p. 215). The Dominion Trade and Industry Commission Act was finally repealed by the National Trade Mark and True Labelling Act, 13 George VI, Chap. 31, 10 December 1949.

(Assented to 5th July, 1935)

Whereas on the second day of February, 1934, the House of Commons passed a Resolution that a Select Special Committee of that House be appointed to inquire into and investigate the causes of the large spread between the prices received for commodities by the producer thereof and the prices paid by the consumers therefor, and the system of distribution in Canada of natural and manufactured products; and whereas a Select Special Committee was accordingly appointed and proceeded with the investigation and on the twenty-ninth day of June, 1934, reported that the investigation could not be completed before Parliament prorogued and recommended that the members of the Select Special Committee be appointed commissioners under Part I of the *Inquiries Act* to continue and complete the investigation and report to the Minister of Trade and Commerce; and whereas the members of the Select Special Committee were accordingly appointed commissioners under the *Inquiries Act* and continued and completed the investigation and reported on the ninth day of April, 1935; and whereas the majority of the commissioners recommended that a Federal Trade and Industry Commission be established with powers to regulate commerce and industry; and whereas it is expedient and in the public interest that effect be given to the aforesaid recommendations in so far as it is within the competence of Parliament so to do: Therefore His Majesty, by and with the advice and consent of the Senate and House of Commons of Canada, enacts as follows: — ...

3. (1) There shall be a Commission to be known as the Dominion Trade and Industry Commission consisting of three Commissioners, of whom one shall be the Chief Commissioner and another the Assistant Chief Commissioner.

(2) The members for the time being of the Tariff Board shall, by virtue of holding office as members of the said Board and by virtue of

this Act, be the Commissioners,* and the Chairman and the Vice-Chairman of the said Board shall be the Chief Commissioner and Assistant Chief Commissioner respectively.

(3) Each Commissioner shall hold office only during such time as he continues to hold office as a member of the Tariff Board....

13. The Commission shall be charged with the administration of the *Combines Investigation Act* and shall exercise all the powers and jurisdiction and perform all the duties conferred on the Commission under the said *Combines Investigation Act.*

14. (1) In any case where the Commission, after full investigation under the *Combines Investigation Act,* is unanimously of opinion that wasteful or demoralizing competition exists in any specific industry, and that agreements between the persons engaged in the industry to modify such competition by controlling and regulating prices or production would not result in injury to or undue restraint of trade or be detrimental to or against the interest of the public, or where such agreements exist and in the unanimous opinion of the Commission but for their existence wasteful or demoralizing competition would exist in any specific industry, the Commission may so advise the Governor in Council and recommend that certain agreements be approved.

(2) The Governor in Council may, if of opinion that the conclusions of the Commission are well founded, approve of any such agreement, and shall make regulations requiring the Commission to determine from time to time whether the agreement is resulting in injury to or undue restraint of trade or is detrimental to the public interest.

(3) The Commission shall require persons engaged in the industry to furnish full information relating to operations within the industry under the agreement and may at any time, of its own motion and in its absolute discretion, advise the Governor in Council to rescind the approval of the agreement and the Governor in Council may rescind the approval accordingly.

(4) In any case where the Governor in Council has approved an agreement under this section, no prosecution of a party to such agreement shall be instituted under the *Combines Investigation Act* or

*This is contrary to the letter and the spirit of the Stevens report. V. W. Bladen (*Introduction to Political Economy*, ed. 1956, p. 233) remarks, "This may have been merely a temporary expedient till the constitutionality of the Commission was established; otherwise it would have to be considered deliberate sabotage." However, in the discussion in the Commons (6 and 17 June 1935) R. B. Hanson, Stevens' successor as Minister of Trade and Commerce, showed himself well satisfied with the Tariff Board expedient, and defended it largely on grounds of economy. The government's attitude seems equivocal.

under sections four hundred and ninety-eight and four hundred and ninety-eight A or any other relevant section of the *Criminal Code* for an offence arising in the performance of such agreement, except with the consent of the Commission.

15. (1) The Commission shall be charged with responsibility to recommend the prosecution of offences against acts of the Parliament of Canada and regulations thereunder, relating to commodity standards and the Attorney General of Canada may require the Director of Public Prosecutions to institute criminal proceedings for the punishment of any such offence.

(2) The Commission may,—

(a) study, investigate, report and advise upon any question relating to commodity standards, the grading of commodities and the protection of consumers generally;

(b) inquire and hear representatives of industry and trade and of consumers as to the desirability of establishing commodity standards and grades for any commodity and report thereon to the Minister [the President of the Council].

16. In addition to its powers and duties under any other statute or law, the National Research Council shall, on the request of the Commission, from time to time,—

(a) study, investigate, report and advise upon all matters relating to commodity standards. . . .

18. (1) Notwithstanding anything contained in *The Unfair Competition Act, 1932,* or any other statute or law, the words "Canada Standard" or initials "C.S." shall be a national trademark and the exclusive property in and the right to the use of such trademark is hereby declared to be vested in His Majesty in the right of the Dominion of Canada, subject to the provisions of this Act.

(2) Such national trademark, as applied to any commodity pursuant to the provisions of this Act or any other Act of the Parliament of Canada, shall constitute a representation that such commodity conforms to the requirements of a specification of a commodity standard for such commodity or class of commodity established under the provisions of any Act of the Parliament of Canada. . . .

20. The Commission shall receive complaints respecting unfair trade practices and may investigate the same and, either before or after an investigation, if of opinion that the practice complained of constitutes an offence against any Dominion law prohibiting unfair trade practices, may communicate the complaint and such evidence, if any, in support thereof as is in the possession of the Commission to

the Attorney General of Canada with a recommendation that all persons who are parties or privies to such offence be prosecuted for violation of the applicable Act. The Attorney General of Canada, if he concurs in such recommendation, may refer it with such complaint and such evidence, if any, either to the Director of Public Prosecutions or to the Attorney General of the province within which the offence is alleged to have been committed for such action as may seem to be appropriate in the circumstances.

21. (1) The Governor in Council may appoint an officer to be called the Director of Public Prosecutions with a salary not exceeding twelve thousand dollars per annum. . . .

22. It shall be the duty of the Director of Public Prosecutions under the superintendence of the Minister of Justice

(a) to institute, at the instance of the Attorney General of Canada criminal proceedings for violation of any of the laws prohibiting unfair trade practices in cases which appear to be of importance or difficulty or in which special circumstances or the refusal or failure of any other person to institute, such proceedings appear to render the action of such Director necessary to secure the due prosecution of an offender;

(b) to give such advice or assistance to the Attorney General of any province in connection with the prosecution of offenders against laws prohibiting unfair trade practices as appears necessary to secure the prosecution of such offenders;

(c) to assist the Commission in the conduct of any investigation where it is alleged or complained that an offence against any of the laws prohibiting unfair trade practices has been or appears to be about to be committed. . . .

VI.

Northern Development and the Mining Frontier

Northern Development and the Mining Frontier

The early part of the twentieth century witnessed important discoveries of both precious and base metals in the Laurentian Shield (see Volume IV of this series), and in the 1920s there was much expansion of mining activity, notably in Northern Ontario and Quebec. The period covered in this volume was further marked, however, by discovery and development in the West and the North, influenced and facilitated by advances in science and technology. The events dealt with here are representative of a series which did something to diversify the Canadian economy, enrich the country, and make Canada rather less of a narrow ribbon of settlement along the American border.

134. "On to the Bay": The Hudson Bay Railway

(Western Canada's Short Outlet to the Markets of the World: The Hudson Bay Route. Issued by "On-to-the-Bay" Association of Canada, Winnipeg, n.d.)

The Hudson Bay Railway was begun under Laurier in 1910 and continued under Borden, but construction was stopped in 1918 before it was completed. The "On-to-the-Bay" Association was formed at Winnipeg in 1924 to advocate finishing the line. Its propaganda was apparently effective; the King government, then in a very weak position after the 1925 election (above, p. 78), announced in the Speech from the Throne on 8 January 1926 that the railway would be completed. The terminus was changed from Nelson to Churchill, and the first cargoes sailed from that port in 1931. But not a great deal of wheat has moved by the Bay; a major difficulty has been the high insurance rates prevailing on the risky sea route through Hudson Strait, which has been usable for only a little more than two months in the year. See Glazebrook, *History of Transportation in Canada.* The pamphlet quoted here is undated, but internal evidence suggests a date of 1927, by which year the essential victory was won. The On-to-the-Bay Association however was still producing pamphlets at least as late as 1929, the year the steel reached Churchill.

320

. . .

No matter how important a discovery may be its great potentialities become practically useless unless they be linked up with world
traffic. The importance of the Hudson Bay route lies in the fact that
not only does it give signal advantage in local conditions but it also
opens up new avenues for trade with foreign countries.

For trade between the Maritime provinces and Western Canada,
and as an international highway permitting the free flow of traffic
from Europe to the Orient or from the Northern States to Europe, the
Hudson Bay Route stands pre-eminent.

For saving in time and distance no other route can compare with it.
Between England and Eastern Asia via Suez is about 16,000 miles and
via New York and San Francisco about 11,000 miles, and via Port Nelson and Prince Rupert less than 8,000 miles. From Port Nelson to Vancouver is over eleven hundred miles shorter than from Montreal to
Vancouver, equivalent to more than two days saving in time across
Canada.

The completion of the Hudson Bay Railway is essential if we
would place Canada in a strategic position to engage in a greater development of our resources and to achieve a dominant position among
nations.

Montreal is the foremost grain shipping port in Canada, shipping
less than one half of Canada's exportable surplus of wheat. . . .

Montreal Harbour is closed five months in the year.

Evidence supports the claim that Port Nelson being a tidewater
port can be made an all year port.

The distance from the centre of production in Canada to seaboard
is greater than the distance from production centres to seaboard in
countries which compete with Canada.

Montreal is seventeen hundred miles from centre of production in
Canada.

Port Nelson not only holds a central position in Canada, it is also
practically the centre of the North American continent. . . .

Port Nelson is only seven hundred miles from the centre of
production, a saving of one thousand miles over Montreal and is the
same ocean distance as Montreal to Liverpool. . . .

"ON-TO-THE-BAY"
(By Geo. Duncan, Swift Current)

Since this prairie began to be furrowed by man
    And return him the fruits of his labours,
He has struggled in vain to dispose of his grain
    To his profit, as well as his neighbours'.

For the long railway route as the only way out
  Is at best very slow and expensive;
But a road to the "Bay" would our efforts repay,
  And our commerce become more extensive.

Other interests may rave, present outlets to save,
  Which to them are but gold-flowing fountains;
But when linked to the "Bay" all will honor the day
  From the "Red" to the great Rocky Mountains.

Then our slogan today, shall be "On-to-the-Bay,"
  And our sympathy ever grow warmer,
Till we clear party mist, and compel all to list
  To the needs of our great prairie farmer.

135. Aircraft in the North

(Report of the Department of National Defence, Canada, for the fiscal year ending March 31, 1929 (Militia and Air Services))

On this topic, see also **110**, above. The Royal Canadian Air Force did a great deal of essentially civil developmental work in the North between the two world wars, and the expedition connected with the Hudson Bay route was one of the most considerable projects.

Hudson Strait Expedition, 1927-28

In January, 1927, a decision was reached by the Government to complete the Hudson Bay railway and terminals,* and to send an expedition to Hudson strait. The expedition was under the direction of the Department of Marine. . . . The object of the expedition to Hudson strait was to obtain by air photography and reconnaissance accurate information in regard to ice conditions and to study requirements necessary to ensure safe navigation. The expedition left Halifax on July 17, 1927, arriving at Port Burwell on July 27, 1927, where Base "A" was established. Base "B" was established at Nottingham Island, and Base "C" at Wakeham Bay. The general equipment of the three bases was practically the same and comprised the following: Two Fokker aircraft complete with floats, skis and wheels for landing and all necessary accessories including spare engines. One 30-foot motor launch, one Fordson tractor, radio apparatus consisting of two gasolene engines to generate power, with two 150-foot

*As we have seen (above, p. 320) it was actually a year earlier.

steel masts, gasolene, oil, coal, stoves, bedding, one skiff, guns, rifles and ammunition. Seven buildings, comprising officers' and mens' dwellings, radio house, storehouse, blubber house, and two hangars, were erected at each base. The expedition consisted of 44 all ranks. The Department of Marine and Fisheries provided for personnel comprising doctors, wireless engineers and operators (for ground communications only) storekeepers and cooks. The Royal Canadian Corps of Signals was responsible for wireless communication and equipment, and provided one officer and three other ranks for this purpose. The Royal Canadian Air Force received the major portion of responsibilities in the organization, and provided 6 officers and 12 airmen. The Royal Canadian Mounted Police detailed one member for duty at each base.

A system of routine and special patrols, for all three bases, was drawn up and approved. The patrols commenced from Port Burwell, October 23, 1927; Nottingham Island, October 11, 1927; and Wakeham Bay, September 9, 1927. Flying was done on pontoons until the first ice appeared in the strait. Flying was carried out whenever the weather was favourable. Fog and storms hampered operations and on three occasions aircraft were lost or forced down by bad weather.* Operations continued until August 3, 1928, when navigation conditions rendered further air operations unnecessary. The expedition returned to Halifax, arriving there in October, 1928. The results of the air patrols observing ice conditions has [sic] been compiled by the Department of National Defence, together with maps, tables, figures, etc., and the whole transferred to the Department of Marine. . . . Two hundred and twenty-seven patrols were carried out during the period, the total flying time being 369 hours 44 minutes. Two thousand two hundred and eighty-five photographs were taken.

136. Oil in Alberta

(*The Financial Post Survey of Mines, Canada and Newfoundland, 1929 . . . Special Section on Alberta Oils*, Toronto, 1929)

The prospect of future wealth for the province of Alberta opened up with the discovery of the Turner Valley oilfield in the southwestern part of the province in 1914. Oil was already beginning to replace coal as fuel, and the tremendous development of the internal combustion

*The reference is apparently to forced landings; the aircraft did not become total losses.

engine (above, p. 242) would shortly make it still more important. This account reflects the expansion of Alberta production (and promotion) during the boom years of the late twenties. But the great days of Alberta oil prosperity came only after the Leduc field south of Edmonton was discovered in 1947.

Alberta oil companies have attracted much attention in the last year. Values have risen enormously. And undoubtedly there will be further profits in this industry. Several hundred new companies have been formed. Many of these have good prospects. Turner Valley is the principal field so far, but there is a strong belief, based on geological opinion formed after as careful investigation as is possible, that other fields, perhaps even more important than Turner Valley, will be developed.

The Wainwright area, 125 miles southeast of Edmonton, has, after Turner Valley, attracted the most attention. . . . Considerable interest also is shown in the Waite Valley. . . .

Production of crude petroleum, including naphtha, in Alberta, grew from 216,050 barrels in 1926, to 318,741 barrels in 1927 and to 488,268 barrels in 1928. Thus in two years the production has doubled. There is every indication, from the figures so far obtained, that there will be a great increase in 1929 over 1928. There are (June, 1929) about 28 wells in Alberta producing crude or naphtha, of which 24 are in Turner Valley and four in the Wainwright field. . . .

137. Gilbert LaBine Finds a Mine, 1930

(Account by Mr. LaBine, 1936, in *Uranium in Canada*, published by Eldorado Mining and Refining Limited, Ottawa, 1964. Reprinted by permission of Information Canada.)

The pitchblende deposit on the remote shores of Great Bear Lake, referred to here, was to become famous and strategically important as a source of uranium. Note the importance of the aeroplane to the prospector. Air transport also provided the means of developing the mine on the site.

I went in by airplane and took in a sectional canoe, and I was fully prepared to remain all that Summer. I would say that in the area we had in mind for prospecting, the shoreline would probably cover 500 miles (800 km.). We had about 1,600 pounds (700 kg.) of supplies, including this sectional canoe, and we took in two pieces of iron so that we could make a sled.

After landing at the Camsell River we started in to do reconnaissance work across sections of the country in order to get a picture of the geology. We landed at Point 56, which is just the western entrance of Echo Bay, on the night of the 14th of May. On the 15th of May we relayed our supplies over by sled in water up to our knees, across Echo Bay, and finally found a place to land where there was timber. We made our headquarters there for some time and went back to get our second load of supplies, and after we brought up the balance of our supplies my associate, or assistant, Charles St. Paul, went snow-blind.

So he remained in camp for a few days, until he recovered, and I started in doing some prospecting in that vicinity. On the morning of the 16th of May, about half a mile from where we were camped, I was following around the shore of an island and I discovered what I considered a beautiful looking vein. I started out and followed it up, and felt sure investigation would prove it to be silver.

As I looked over to the shore, a distance of about 300 (90 m.) or possibly 400 feet (120 m.) I noticed a great wall there that was stained with cobalt bloom and copper green. I walked over to this place and investigated it thoroughly, and found all of the associated ores of cobalt, including silver.

Following along, I found a tiny piece of dark ore, probably the size of a large plum. Looking more closely, I found the vein. I chipped it off with my hammer, and there it was — pitchblende!

138. Eldorado on the Eve of Atomic Energy

(*The Financial Post Survey of Mines, 1940-41*, Montreal, 1940)

This describes the company built upon Gilbert LaBine's find of 1930 (above, **137**) as it was ten years later. Already it was known in some quarters that uranium could be used for purposes much more formidable than colouring pottery. In 1942 the Canadian government, aware now of the Allied atomic bomb projects, began to acquire the stock of Eldorado and arranged for resumption of mining at Great Bear Lake; and in 1944 the company, by then known as Eldorado Mining and Refining Limited, was expropriated and became a Crown corporation. See C.P. Stacey, *Arms, Men and Governments: The War Policies of Canada* (Ottawa, 1970).

Eldorado Gold Mines Ltd.

(Ont. Incorp., Feb. 10, 1926)

. . .

Company — Owns pitchblende-silver property at Great Bear Lake, N.W.T., and a refinery at Port Hope, Ont. Due to a heavy accumulation of mine concentrates ahead of the refinery, active mining operations were discontinued at the Great Bear property in June, 1940, until the refinery should catch up with the mine. Concentrates were estimated to be sufficient for 3 to 4 years operations in June, 1940. Uranium, used in coloring pottery, approaches in importance radium, the co.'s most important product.

Property — Approx. 4,000 acres at LaBine Point, Echo Bay, Great Bear Lake, N.W.T. . . .

Equipment — Diesel mining plant and 100-ton concentrator installed at LaBine Point, N.W.T.   Port Hope, Ont., refinery, for production of radium, uranium and small quantities of silver, copper, cobalt and nickel, is capable of treating 90-100 tons of concentrates monthly and of producing 9 grammes of radium per month. . . .

Dividends — None yet paid. . . .

VII.
Religious
and Cultural
Development

A.
Religious Organization: Church Union

The most important occurrence in church organization in Canada during the period covered by this volume was the union of the Methodist, Presbyterian and Congregational churches to form the United Church of Canada, the country's largest Protestant communion, with over two million members at the census of 1931. Discussion of this project began as early as 1902, and the "Basis of Union" was completed in essentials in 1908. Although there was provision for individual congregations to "opt out" of the union (below, sec. 10), no Methodist congregation and only eight Congregational ones did so. But 784 out of 4,512 Presbyterian congregations refused to concur, and as a result a separate but smaller Presbyterian church continued to exist. There was considerable bitterness, and the question "literally divided families as well as congregations." See Claris Edwin Silcox, *Church Union in Canada, Its Causes and Consequences* (New York, 1933).

139. The United Church of Canada Act, 1924

(14-15 George V, Chap. 100)

The passing of the Dominion enabling act here printed in part was only one aspect of the complex legal process of bringing church union about; for with special reference to the question of church property, in the light of provincial jurisdiction over "property and civil rights" under the British North America Act, it was necessary also to obtain parallel legislation from the various provincial legislatures.

(Assented to 19th July, 1924)

Whereas The Presbyterian Church in Canada, The Methodist Church and The Congregational Churches of Canada have by their petition represented that, believing the promotion of Christian unity to be in accordance with the Divine Will, they recognize the obligation to seek and promote union with other churches adhering to the same fundamental principles of the Christian faith, and that, having the right to unite with one another without loss of their identity upon terms which they find to be consistent with such principles, they have adopted a Basis of Union which is set forth in Schedule A to this Act and have agreed to unite and form one body or denomination of Christians under the name of "The United Church of Canada;" and have prayed that it may be enacted as hereinafter set forth; and whereas it is expedient to grant the prayer of the said petition: Therefore His Majesty, by and with the advice and consent of the Senate and House of Commons of Canada, enacts as follows: — . . .

2. This Act shall come into force on the tenth day of June, 1925, except the provisions required to permit the vote provided for in section ten being taken, which shall come into force on the tenth day of December, 1924. . . .

4. (a) The union of the said Churches, The Presbyterian Church in Canada, The Methodist Church and The Congregational Churches, shall become effective upon the day upon which this Act comes into force and the said Churches as so united are hereby constituted a body corporate and politic under the name of "The United Church of Canada," hereinafter called "The United Church;" . . .

(c) Notwithstanding anything in this Act contained, members of any non-concurring congregation hereinafter mentioned shall be deemed not to have become, by virtue of the said union or of this Act, members of The United Church. . . .

5. Save as hereinafter provided, all property, real and personal, belonging to or held in trust for or to the use of The Presbyterian Church in Canada, The Methodist Church and The Congregational Churches, or belonging to or held in trust for or to the use of any Corporation, Board Committee or other body, whether incorporated or un-incorporated, created by or under the government or control of, or in connection with, any of the said churches, shall from and after the coming into force of this Act be vested in The United Church, to be held, used and administered, subject to the provisions of this Act, in accordance with the terms and provisions of the Basis of Union.

6. Subject to the provisions of section eight hereof,* all property, real or personal, belonging to or held by or in trust for or to the use of any congregation of any of the negotiating churches, shall, from and after the coming into force of this Act be held, used and administered

*Section 8, not printed, deals with special property of certain congregations.

for the benefit of the same congregation as a part of The United Church. . . .

10. (a) If any congregation in connection or communion with any of the negotiating churches shall, at a meeting of the congregation regularly called and held at any time within six months before the coming into force of this Act, or within the time limited by any statute respecting The United Church of Canada passed by the legislature of the Province in which the property of the congregation is situate, before such coming into force, decide by a majority of votes of the persons present at such meeting and entitled to vote thereat not to enter the said Union of the said Churches, then and in such case the property, real and personal, belonging to or held in trust for or to the use of such non-concurring congregation shall remain unaffected by this Act, except that any church formed by non-concurring congregations of the respective negotiating Churches into which such congregation enters shall stand in the place of the respective negotiating Churches in respect of any trusts relating to such property. . . . The vote herein provided for shall be taken by ballot in such form and manner and at such time within the limit prescribed by this subsection as the congregation may decide: Provided that not less than two weeks shall be allowed for the taking of said vote by ballot as aforesaid. . . .

11. (a) Notwithstanding anything in this Act contained, such non-concurring congregations or any one or more of them as may be determined, shall be entitled to whatever the Commission hereinafter mentioned shall determine to be a fair and equitable share of the property, real and personal, rights, powers, authorities and privileges of or in connection with the respective parent church or churches, that is to say, The Presbyterian Church in Canada, The Methodist Church or The Congregational Churches, as the case may be, vested in The United Church by this Act.

(b) All the equities (if any) of the non-concurring congregations, or any of them, under this section, shall be determined exclusively by a Commission to consist of nine members, of whom three shall be appointed by the non-concurring congregations at a conference of representatives thereof, three by The United Church from its members, and the remaining three by the six members so appointed. The names of such persons shall be submitted to the Chief Justice of Canada, and if he is satisfied after making such inquiry as he deems proper or desirable that they fairly represent the parties so appointing them, their names shall be approved by

him in writing and they shall thereupon be deemed for all purposes to be duly appointed. . . .

29. Inasmuch as questions have arisen and may arise as to the
powers of the Parliament of Canada under the *British North America
Act* to give legislative effect to the provisions of this Act, it is hereby
declared that it is intended by this Act to sanction the provisions
therein contained in so far and in so far only as it is competent to the
Parliament so to do.*

SCHEDULE A.

THE BASIS OF UNION

as prepared by the Joint Committee of the Presbyterian, Methodist
and Congregational Churches, and approved by the Supreme Courts
of these Churches.

GENERAL

1. The name of the Church formed by the union of the Presbyterian, Methodist, and Congregational Churches in Canada, shall be
"The United Church of Canada."

2. It shall be the policy of The United Church to foster the spirit of
unity in the hope that this sentiment of unity may in due time, so far
as Canada is concerned, take shape in a Church which may fittingly
be described as national. . . .†

---

*The matter was never directly submitted to the Judicial Committee of the
Privy Council, but its decision in the Saltsprings case of 1931 concerning a
congregation in Nova Scotia has been regarded as indirect acceptance of the
Dominion legislation.

†The document proceeds to define the doctrine and polity of the new church
at length.

B.
Education and
Cultural Conflict

The question of the status of the French language in schools, which had once caused serious trouble in Manitoba (see Volume IV of this series) was making similar difficulty in Ontario, and between Ontario and Quebec, when the First World War broke out. For Ontario's so-called "Regulation 17" (actually "Circular of Instructions No. 17," June 1912) see Volume IV. It imposed severe limitations on French both as a language of instruction and a subject of study. The "Franco-Ontarian" cause was taken up loudly in Quebec and particularly by Henri Bourassa in *Le Devoir.* The issue added heat to the bad feeling which the war almost immediately began to cause between English and French Canada. In 1918, when the general atmosphere was already beginning to improve somewhat, Pope Benedict XV issued an encyclical enjoining calm and moderation, which had considerable effect. But only in 1927, when the tumult and shouting had died in Quebec and the war was long over, was a formal change of policy made in Ontario. See Mason Wade, *The French Canadians* (Toronto, 1955) and Robert Rumilly, *Histoire de la province de Québec,* Vols. XIX-XXI (Montreal, n.d.). There are interesting letters in R. C. Brown and M. E. Prang, eds., *Canadian Historical Documents Series,* III, *Confederation to 1949* (Toronto, 1965).

140. Henri Bourassa on "The Prussians of Ontario," 1914

(*Le Devoir*, Montreal, 21 December 1914)

Henri Bourassa, beginning with a limited and grudging support of the war (below, **209**), rapidly grew more and more hostile to it and more and more frequently coupled references to it with mentions of the "persecution" of the French-speaking people of Ontario. In the light of this editorial, it is not hard to understand why he became, in Mason Wade's phrase, "the most hated man in Canada," or why Ontario politicians felt that while the agitation in Quebec was carried on in such terms it was politically impossible to withdraw from the policy of Circular 17.

(Translation)

All men of feeling, all serious-minded men, conscious of their duties and their dignity as Canadian citizens, will make it a point of honour to be at the Monument National this evening.

They owe it to themselves to support the effort initiated by the Catholic Youth Association to come to the assistance of the French minority in Ontario.

For two years the French Canadians of the neighbouring province have undergone, for defending their language, a more violent persecution than the French-speaking people of Alsace and Lorraine have ever suffered under the Prussian heel.

The regime of harassment imposed on them in the name of "British civilization" touches them in their national and civil liberty and constitutes a flagrant violation of the constitution. In the last analysis, it is attacking the source of their religious life. On this point, those who sponsor this persecution make less and less mystery.

In the name of religion, of freedom, of loyalty to the British flag, the French Canadians are being called upon to go and fight the Prussians of Europe. Are we to allow the Prussians of Ontario to impose as masters their domination in the very heart of the Canadian Confederation, under the shelter of the British flag and British institutions?...

141. Ontario Relaxes Its Language Policy, 1927

(Report of the Minister of Education [of Ontario] *for the Year 1927)*

The Minister making this report, G. Howard Ferguson, was also Premier (1923-30). Dr. F.W. Merchant, whose name is attached to the report that effected the liberalizing of policy here described, had likewise made in 1912 the report on which Circular 17 was based.

Language Instruction in Schools

In 1927, the committee of enquiry, consisting of Dr. F.W. Merchant, Chief Director of Education, His Honour Judge [J.H.] Scott, and Mr. Louis Coté, appointed to deal with the question of the language instruction in schools attended by French-speaking pupils, concluded their labours. Their unanimous report, based upon an exhaustive study of the whole situation, was widely circulated and met with general approval. This is an old problem in educational administration, since for more than forty years various and different methods have been tried with the design of finding a satisfactory solution. The committee's investigation convinced them that previous methods to train the children in these schools as they have a right to be trained, and as the interests of the Province demand, had not met with success. The conclusion they reached was that in future more reliance must be placed upon sympathetic and helpful advice and supervision and efficient teaching rather than upon some general rules which do not, and cannot, provide for the great variety of conditions that exist. It was, therefore, resolved to restore the old classification of elementary schools which had been in force in the Province for generations, that is, Public Schools and Separate Schools, and to cease regarding a certain number of them as entitled to a classification by themselves based on language distinction.* After the opening of the schools in the autumn, therefore, the new plan went into force and the Inspectors were instructed, without the adoption of some fresh uniform regulations that would not adequately apply to individual schools, to make a study of each case, as circumstances required, and to consult with a departmental committee to determine the course that ought to be followed. This committee consists of a Director of English Instruction and a Director of French Instruction who were appointed to maintain a constant personal contact with the schools, making a continuous study of the conditions and the requirements of each school, so that they will at all times be fully qualified to aid and advise pupils, teachers and school boards in carrying on their work. These two Directors, along with the Chief Inspector of the Province and the local inspector, constitute a common authority, subject in all respects to the Minister, for dealing with all important matters bearing upon schools, and more particularly with peculiar cases and unusual conditions. It is my intention to keep in close touch with the inspection and supervision of these schools, so as to make sure that the proper policy is being pursued in each case, and that with the willing co-operation of both English and French-speaking people, the official language of the Province will be properly taught.

*These were the "English-French schools" defined in Circular 17.

C.
The Arts

The tone of Canadian society in the period covered by this volume was strongly materialistic. In the days before 1929 Canadians in general were chiefly interested in making as much money as they could; after 1929 many of them were mainly concerned with getting enough to eat. And yet the period deserves to be remembered as one in which some breaches were made in the ramparts of philistinism — breaches that would be enlarged with the passing of time. Here advances are noted in two fields — painting and community drama. It is surely a matter of interest that the rather remarkable little theatre movement which crystallized in the Dominion Drama Festival was a product of the Depression years. On the important question of radio broadcasting, see below, **147-150**.

142. *The Times* of London Comments on Canadian Painting, 1924

(*The Times*, 6 May 1924)

The British Empire Exhibition held at Wembley, England, in 1924, was probably the first occasion when Canadian painting attracted much attention abroad. Of the artists mentioned in this notice, four — Harris, MacDonald, Casson and Lismer — were members then or later of the now-famous "Group of Seven" (which had had its first exhibition in 1920, in Toronto). Tom Thomson had been closely associated with members of the Group and powerfully influenced the movement it represented. Some conservative Canadians, disliking the Group's stark portrayal of the landscape of the Canadian Shield, disliked also this acceptance of it in Britain. On the Group, see Lawren Harris, "The Group of Seven in Canadian History," Canadian Historical Association *Report,* 1948, and F. B. Housser, *A Canadian Art Movement: The Story of the Group of Seven* (Toronto, 1926). A more recent book, lavishly illustrated, is Peter Mellen, *The Group of Seven* (Toronto, 1970).

335

In view of what the Prince of Wales said at the Academy Banquet about the art section of the British Empire Exhibition at Wembley, a few words may be said about the general scope of the collections in the Palace of Arts. Detailed description must wait for catalogues,* but all the pictures are hung, and all the works of sculpture are in their places, and so "the first show of British art of a truly Imperial nature," as the Prince described it, is already prepared for visitors.

British "home" art is represented by a retrospective section ranging from Hogarth down to the end of the 19th century, followed by a modern section covering all schools and tendencies of the present day. . . .

From these "home productions" we pass to the special rooms devoted to Australia, Canada and India, with all sorts of interesting changes in the art represented. The Australian section is remarkable for breadth of treatment. . . . Australian painters are getting to work upon native subjects. An interesting feature in the Indian room is the group of works by members of the Tagore school. . . .

Emphatic design and bold brushwork are the characteristics of the Canadian section; and it is here in particular that the art of the Empire is taking a new turn. The influence suggested is that of Russia — as exemplified by such painters as Roerich — but it is likely that the effect is due chiefly to a certain similarity in the landscape of the two countries. At any rate, there can be no question that Canada is developing a school of landscape painters who are strongly racy of the soil. The most striking work at Wembley is "The Jack Pine," by the late Tom Thomson (1877-1917), but similar qualities — of bold simplification and emphatic statement with a full brush in strong colour — are to be seen in the works by Mr. Lawren Harris, Mr. Albert H. Robinson, Mr. James E. H. MacDonald — whose "Beaver Dam" is one of the best pictures in the room — Mr. Alfred J. Casson, and Mr. Arthur Lismer. If it were only as introducing us to the painters of Canada — practically unknown here before — a visit to the Palace of Arts at Wembley would be worth while. . . .

*The newspaper's later comments (28 May) are less pungent than those printed here, and incidentally some of the Canadian artists' names are misspelled.

143. Lord Bessborough on the Dominion Drama Festival, 1935

(The Curtain Call, Toronto, Vol. 7, No. 3, December 1935; reprinted from *Morning Post,* London)

The Earl of Bessborough, Governor General from 1931 to 1935, deserves much of the credit for initiating the Dominion Drama Festival. The Festival in turn did much to keep "live theatre" in existence in Canada during the period after touring companies had been killed by the talking film and the Depression, and before the rise of a Canadian professional theatre after the Second World War. This latter development Bessborough does not seem to have foreseen; but his Festival probably did a good deal to encourage it. At the same time the Festival had some national importance as an institution which brought together in friendly rivalry groups from English and French Canada and people from every section of the country.

Just before I went to Canada as Governor-General, at the beginning of 1931, I remember being entertained at a farewell luncheon at the Savoy by friends who had, for a number of years, taken part in theatrical performances at my home in the country.

In the course of after-luncheon speeches, the hope was expressed that I should find interesting theatrical enterprise going on in Canada. One of my hosts, who had just returned from a tour in Canada, however, said: "Abandon any such hope, the theatre in Canada is dead." I remember thinking at the time that when I returned home from Canada I hoped to be able to prove that my friend was wrong. I think I can show that if what he said was true at the time he said it, it is far from true today.

There is not, of course, nor has there ever been, a professional theatre in Canada. Canadian-born artists who have made the stage a career have always had to go to New York, London, or Paris to carry out their ambition. Mr. Raymond Massey is a notable example. But in the past, for many years, companies, including leading English, French, and United States artists, regularly visited Canada. Sir Henry Irving, Madame Sarah Bernhardt—to mention only two famous names—and their successors were all regularly seen in their best-known plays in different parts of Canada. Companies from New York, Paris, and London followed one another in succession. . . .

When I arrived in Canada in 1931 I found that all this activity had come to an end. The film had ousted the living drama. The theatre habit had died. Theatres taken over by film companies left few places available for companies to rent. In addition to this, the world depression had practically killed touring by professional companies, either from England or from France.

It was during the height of the economic gale that I learnt that a certain library in Canada was doing better business than it had done for years. People who had previously no time left to spare from dashing about in motor-cars to cocktail parties, or dances, or camps, had begun to turn to reading, and their appetite quickly grew in the feeding. It was at about the same time that the head of a musical organization — which helps people who wish to learn music to get in touch with teachers — told me that he could hardly now put his hand on enough teachers to meet the increased demand created by the number of potential pupils all over the country.

Literature and music both began to obtain a sway upon the minds of the people. Was the drama not to find its place, too, in this cultural development? The answer came quickly. Almost overnight drama leagues sprang into being in towns large and small, even quite small, all over Canada. This development did not escape notice in London, for an English actor exclaimed publicly and somewhat derisively Canada has gone amateur!

Let us examine what had actually happened. . . . Canada was left practically without any drama. What did the people do? Quite instinctively, and without any prompting or previous consultation, in centres thousands of miles removed from one another, they laid the foundations of a people's theatre. They did, in fact, what our ancestors in England did in the Middle Ages — they started community drama. In the autumn of 1932 I learnt that literally hundreds of drama leagues were in active operation all over Canada, some already possessing their own little theatres.

Having for some years watched with interest the growth of the British Drama League at home, I ventured a suggestion. I said: "Why not harness and consolidate this national movement by holding a Dominion Drama Festival?" This was in October, 1932. Six months later, in April, 1933, an extremely successful festival took place in Ottawa. A hundred groups had meantime competed in local Festivals in the Provinces, and as a result of elimination, twenty-four English and French speaking groups came to Ottawa. They represented all Provinces, and included groups from both Halifax and Vancouver....

In 1934, the extent of the enthusiasm of those concerned and of the

public interest aroused were proved...by the fact that the competi-
tions were attended by over 50,000 members of the public. Several of
the plays entered that year were by Canadian authors. One lady was
represented by two plays, one written in French and one in English....

At the final festival at Ottawa in April, 1935, a group from Vancouver, who had not sufficient funds at their disposal to come by
train, travelled 3,500 miles by motor omnibus. Several nights they
slept in the omnibus in order to keep down hotel expenses. Thus
they travelled, there and back, 7,000 miles in order to appear for
thirty minutes on the Ottawa stage in the trial scene from "St. Joan".
This most exhausting journey did not prevent the lady who played
"Joan" from winning the trophy for the best woman's performance
of the week....

Having said so much, I think I can now meet my friend to whose
remarks at the luncheon at the Savoy, in 1931, I have already referred,
and assure him that the theatre is far from dead in Canada. But if he
should say: That is all very well, but what of the prospects of the professional theatre? I would reply: Have you not in this great field wonderful potential audiences? There are now in Canada many
thousands, first of all, of active performers only too ready to study
and learn from trained exponents of the dramatic art. Then there are
tens of thousands of supporters of the Drama Leagues taking an
active and intelligent interest in the drama, and many more who
have begun to regain the theatre habit.

If professional companies from England should once again make
up their minds to invade this great field of operations, might I with
great deference make this suggestion? Send only the best....

D.
The Sciences

It would be absurd to argue that the history of the National Research Council of Canada is the history of natural science in Canada since 1916, when the Council was founded; but the Council's activity has to a considerable extent reflected the advance of science in the country, and the fellowships of various sorts which it granted from the beginning to finance study and research have had a great influence on the development of science in the universities. See M. Thistle, *The Inner Ring: The Early History of the National Research Council of Canada* (Toronto, 1966). H. M. Tory, ed., *A History of Science in Canada* (Toronto, 1939) is unfortunately slight.

144. Extracts from the First Report of the National Research Council of Canada, 1916-1918

(Report of the Administrative Chairman of the Honorary Advisory Council for Scientific and Industrial Research of Canada for the Year ending March 31, 1918)

The National Research Council of Canada was founded as a result of the impulse of the First World War, and largely in imitation of a British example; as the founding order in council recites, the British government set up in 1915 a cabinet committee and an advisory council designed to provide a permanent organization for promoting scientific and industrial research. The notable emphasis on the industrial and commercial motive, and the attention given to the subsidization of scientific research, are points of interest. In the absence of parallel economic motivation, activity in the arts remained without similar public support until after the creation of the Canada Council in 1957.

On June 1, 1916, there was constituted by Order in Council a Sub-Committee of the Privy Council, consisting of the Right Honourable Sir George E. Foster, K.C.M.G., Minister of Trade and Commerce (Chairman), the Honourable the Ministers of the Interior, Agriculture, Mines, Inland Revenue, and Labour, with the object of having charge of all measures to foster the scientific development of the industries of Canada, in order that during and after the present war these may be in a position to supply all Canadian needs and extend Canadian trade abroad.

Under this Sub-Committee of the Privy Council, and by its direction,* an Honorary Advisory Council for Scientific and Industrial Research was constituted on the 29th of November of the same year, composed of eleven representatives of the scientific, technical, and industrial interests of Canada.

This Research Council, by the direction of the Chairman of the Sub-Committee of the Privy Council, was charged with the following duties: —

(a) To ascertain and tabulate the various agencies in Canada, which are now carrying on scientific and industrial research in the universities and colleges, in the various laboratories of the Government, in business organizations and industries, in scientific associations, or by private or associated investigators.

(b) To note and schedule the lines of research or investigation that are being pursued by each such agency, their facilities and equipment therefor, the possibilities of extension, and, particularly, to ascertain the scientific manpower available for research and the necessity of adding thereto.

(c) To co-ordinate these agencies so as to prevent overlapping of effort, to induce co-operation and team work, and to bring up a community of interest, knowledge, and mutual helpfulness between each other.

(d) To make themselves acquainted with the problems of a technical and scientific nature that are met with by our productive and industrial interests, and to bring them into contact with the proper research agencies for solving these problems, and thus link up the resources of science with the labour and capital employed in production so as to bring about the best possible economic results.

(e) To make a scientific study of our common unused resources, the waste and by-products of our farms, forests, fisheries and industries, with a view to their utilization in new or subsidiary processes of manufacture and thus contributing to the wealth and employment of our people.

(f) To study the ways and means by which the present small number of competent and trained research men can be added to

*In fact, the appointment of an "Honorary Advisory Committee" (of nine, not eleven members) was authorized by the order in council (published as Appendix E of the report here printed, and there dated 6 June 1916) which set up the Committee of Council on Research.

from the the students and graduates of science in our universities and colleges, and to bring about in the common interest a more complete co-operation between the industrial and producing interests of the country and the teaching centres and forces of science and research.

(g) To inform and stimulate the public mind in regard to the importance and utility of applying the results of scientific and industrial research to the process of production by means of addresses to business and industrial bodies, by the publication of bulletins and monographs, and such other methods as may seem advisable. . . .

Research Council Act. — The interest which the members of the Council have manifested in the service they are enthusiastically rendering has been given an enduring character through the establishment of the Council as a permanent organization by the Act which received vice-regal assent on August 29, 1917,* and which gives to the Council, under the supervision of the Sub-Committee of the Privy Council powers and responsibilities, the wise exercise of which must greatly enhance its usefulness. . . .

Studentships and Fellowships. — To increase the number of investigators in science who may be induced to follow a career as such in connection with the Canadian industries, the Council established twenty-five studentships and fellowships to be awarded to young graduates of our Universities and Technical Colleges, who have given evidence of the possession of the special knowledge and capacity required for the conduct on their part of independent research in some department of Science, which bears on industrial processes. Owing to the depletion of the student ranks in our Universities, which has been going on for the last three years, the number of such graduates has been very small, and, in consequence, only seven were found qualified for appointment, three to fellowships and four to studentships, all of whom are now engaged in research, each on a different problem, under the supervision of the professor or director of a laboratory in one of four different Universities. . . . The Council hopes to increase the number of appointees for the year now commencing. . . .

Associate Committees. — In order that the Council may have the assistance of the best expert advice along a number of technical lines, it appointed several committees, composed of a number of leading specialists, to whom may be referred, as the occasion may require,

*7-8 George V, Chap. 20. This was repealed and replaced by 14-15 George V, Chap. 64, 19 July 1924, under which the Council remained an unpaid honorary body, but a salaried president was provided as chief executive officer.

questions and problems in the solution of which the wide experience and technical knowledge of each such committee may be of very great service. Three of these are permanent organizations: the Associate Chemical Committee, the Associate Committee on Mining and Metallurgy, and the Associate Committee on Forestry. It has been arranged that the chairman of each shall be a member of the Council. . . .

145. Canada's First Nobel Prize in Science: Insulin, 1923

(*Globe*, Toronto, October-November 1923)

In view of the considerable reputation of Canadian medical schools, it is not surprising that the first scientific Nobel Prize awarded to Canadians was in the field of medicine—to Drs. F. G. Banting and J. J. R. Macleod for discovering the insulin treatment of diabetes. The *Globe*, announcing the awards on 26 October 1923, said, "It is understood that the prize was awarded jointly, in view of the fact that Professor MacLeod [*sic*], as head of the Department of Physiology at the University of Toronto, directed the work in the laboratories where Dr. Banting conducted the investigations which led up to the discovery of insulin." Banting was one of the eminent Canadians who received knighthoods under the Bennett regime (above, **86**). See Andrew Hunter, "Sir Frederick Grant Banting," *Proceedings, Royal Society of Canada*, 1941. For Dr. Best's recollections, *Selected Papers of Charles H. Best* (Toronto, 1963).

29 October

Dr. F. G. Banting, discoverer of insulin, on Saturday expressed his gratification with the coming of a Nobel Prize to Canada, and stated that the award that has been made to Prof. J. J. R. McLeod [*sic*] and himself will be devoted to medical research in the University of Toronto. Dr. Banting also declared that he would share his portion of the award with Charles H. Best, who so ably assisted him in his long search for insulin.

"I am extremely gratified that the Nobel award should come to Canada and to the university," he said. "I desire to share my portion of the award with Mr. Best, with whom I have been so intimately associated and who has contributed so much toward insulin, in order that he may have the recognition that is due. The award will be devoted to scientific research to be carried on in the University of Toronto."

8 November

The sum of $10,000, half Dr. J. J. R. Macleod's share of the Nobel Peace Prize [sic] for the discovery of insulin, is to go to Dr. J. B. Collip, professor of the University of Alberta, in recognition of the invaluable part played by Prof. Collip in the ultimate perfection of insulin to the point where its human application was possible. The gift is being made by Dr. Macleod as an appreciation of the contribution to the work made by Dr. Collip....Though Dr. Collip has occupied a professorial position with the University of Alberta for some years, the greatest part of his research work was conducted while he was on an extended leave at the University of Toronto....

It is difficult to outline the manner in which each of the men contributed toward the joint development, a member of the medical profession prominently connected with the research work of the University told The Globe last night. The work was "team-work" in its best sense....

Dr. Collip's particular contribution was in the purification of Banting's and Best's new pancreatic extract....

146. Extracts from the Report of the National Research Council for 1945-1946

(Twenty-Ninth Annual Report of the National Research Council of Canada, 1945-1946)

This report covers the fiscal year during which the Second World War ended. Detail concerning the innumerable war projects on which the Council was engaged is omitted. The First World War had brought it into existence; the Second greatly expanded its work and facilities. See Wilfrid Eggleston, *Scientists at War* (Toronto, 1950). While the war lasted, inevitably military projects had priority; but it is worth noting that by 1946 the Council, which in its early days had felt obliged to concentrate exclusively on work of direct industrial or commercial importance (above, **144**), was devoting some attention to "pure science." Nevertheless it still thought it politic to emphasize that even this pursuit would produce ultimate material advantages.

The National Research Council of Canada met the impact of war in 1939 with one central laboratory* and a small but efficient and very keen laboratory staff. Growth throughout the war years was substantial and during this first year of peace, the attention of Council has been directed chiefly towards the orderly conversion to peacetime applications of the new and enlarged facilities developed to meet war needs.

In addition to its central laboratory, the Council established 21 other laboratories during the war, each for a specific requirement in connection with the war effort. Some of these were small and temporary, others larger and of a permanent nature. These laboratories were located all across Canada from Halifax to Vancouver. . . .

The Associate Committee structure, a distinctly Canadian mechanism of proven effectiveness, has been extended and strengthened. Grants in aid of postgraduate research, and the award of scholarships were continued during the war and are now being augmented.† Provision of trained personnel is sound insurance for commercial progress and industrial development. . . .

Outstanding developments were reported by the National Research Council of Canada in 1945-46. Among these were the investigations relating to atomic energy,‡ the release of information on radar research, the design and construction of a plywood tailless aircraft which was ready for flight trials at the end of the year, and the development to the pilot-plant stage of a process for the production of butylene glycol from wheat. . . .

In the laboratories at Ottawa the work of reconversion to peacetime applications of war research and the initiation of new problems are being pushed forward rapidly. Staff now number about 1,400 persons of whom one-half are of professional grade. This represents considerable growth during the war, and is commensurate with the record of industrial progress in Canada. Research activities must be maintained on a steadily increasing scale if Canada is to go forward and hold the place she has gained during the war, as an industrial nation. . . .

*In Ottawa; opened in 1932.
†The report of the Council for 1944-45 stated that since 1916 the Council had made "approximately 1,200 awards, at an overall cost of about $830,000 . . . to about 700 different individuals."
‡See below, 263.

While a large part of the work in the Division of Chemistry has been of direct application to industry — paints, rubber, textiles, petroleum, explosives, etc. — about one-third of the research work in the division is of fundamental significance. Progress in the industrial application of science depends on the advancement of basic scientific knowledge. . . .

E.
Control of
Radio Broadcasting

Radio broadcasting began soon after the First World War. As we have seen, it first became an important political instrument in Canada in the general election campaign of 1930 (above, p. 98). By that time it was clear that its control presented a national problem of the greatest importance, culturally and as a matter of national identity. As with the railways (above, **100-106**) it came to be a question of public ownership versus private enterprise. The parties were clearly defined. On the side of private ownership were the people who saw broadcasting primarily as a business to make money out of; they were organized in the Canadian Association of Broadcasters, and incidentally, as in the railway controversy, the Canadian Pacific Railway was active on behalf of private enterprise. The cause of public control was upheld by a group of what would be called today "concerned" citizens who formed the Canadian Radio League; the moving spirits were Alan Plaunt and Graham Spry. Their financial resources were limited but their spirit of dedication was formidable. The result was a compromise, but strongly biased towards public ownership; private broadcasting was not completely abolished, but the Canadian airwaves were solidly placed under national and public control. See Margaret Prang, "The Origins of Public Broadcasting in Canada," *Canadian Historical Review,* March 1965, and Frank W. Peers, *The Politics of Canadian Broadcasting, 1920-1951* (Toronto, 1969).

147. Extracts from the Report of the Aird Commission, 1929

(*Report of the Royal Commission on Radio Broadcasting,* Ottawa, 1929)

The Dominion government exercised control over broadcasting under the old Radiotelegraph Act of 1913 (3-4 George V, Chap. 43) and from 1922 collected from owners of receiving sets an annual licence fee of $1.00. In 1928 controversy over religious broadcasting

347

led to the appointment of a Royal Commission with Sir John Aird as chairman. As in the case of the railways in 1917 (above, **100**), pragmatism rather than theory led the commission to recommend public ownership. Aird, who was president of the Canadian Bank of Commerce, was no socialist; but he and his colleagues unanimously advised that broadcasting in Canada should be handed over to what would now be termed a Crown corporation.

In our survey of conditions in Canada, we have heard the present radio situation discussed from many angles with considerable diversity of opinion. There has, however, been unanimity on one fundamental question — Canadian radio listeners want Canadian broadcasting. This service is at present provided by stations owned by private enterprise and with the exception of two, owned by the Government of the province of Manitoba, are operated by the licensees for purposes of gain or for publicity in connection with the licensees' business. We believe that private enterprise is to be commended for its effort to provide entertainment for the benefit of the public with no direct return of revenue. This lack of revenue has, however, tended more and more to force too much advertising upon the listener. It also would appear to result in the crowding of stations into urban centres and the consequent duplication of services in such places, leaving other large populated areas ineffectively served.

The potentialities of broadcasting as an instrument of education have been impressed upon us; education in the broad sense, not only as it is conducted in the schools and colleges, but in providing entertainment and of informing [sic] the public on questions of national interest. Many persons appearing before us have expressed the view that they would like to have an exchange of programs with the different parts of the country.

At present the majority of programs heard are from sources outside of Canada. It has been emphasized to us that the continued reception of these has a tendency to mould the minds of the young people in the home to ideals and opinions that are not Canadian. In a country of the vast geographical dimensions of Canada, broadcasting will undoubtedly become a great force in fostering a national spirit and interpreting national citizenship.

At the conclusion of our inquiries, it is our task, [of] the importance of which we are deeply conscious, to suggest the means as to how broadcasting can be carried on in the interests of Canadian listeners and in the national interests of Canada. The Order in Council appointing us to undertake this work contains the suggestion that the desired end might be achieved in several ways provided funds are available, viz: —

(a) the establishment of one or more groups of stations operated by private enterprise in receipt of a subsidy from the Government;

(b) the establishment and operation of stations by a Government-owned and financed company;

(c) the establishment and operation of stations by Provincial Governments.

We have examined and considered the facts and circumstances as they have come before us. As our foremost duty, we have concentrated our attention on the broader consideration of the interests of the listening public and of the nation. From what we have learned in our investigations and studies, we are impelled to the conclusion that these interests can be adequately served only by some form of public ownership, operation and control behind which is the national power and prestige of the whole public of the Dominion of Canada.

PROPOSED ORGANIZATION

The system which we propose does not fall within the exact category of any of those suggested in the Order in Council, but is one which might be regarded as a modification of (b), i.e., "the establishment and operation of stations by a Government-owned and financed company." As a fundamental principle, we believe that any broadcasting organization must be operated on a basis of public service. The stations providing a service of this kind should be owned and operated by one national company. . . .

SUMMARY OF RECOMMENDATIONS

The following is a summary of our principal recommendations, viz: —

(a) That broadcasting should be placed on a basis of public service and that the stations providing a service of this kind should be owned and operated by one national company; that provincial authorities should have full control over the programs of the station or stations in their respective areas;

(b) That the company should be known as the Canadian Radio Broadcasting Company; that it should be vested with all the powers of private enterprise and that its status and duties should correspond to those of a public utility;

(c) That a Provincial Radio Broadcasting Director should be appointed for each province to have full control of the programs broadcast by the station or stations located within the boundaries of the province for which he is responsible;

(d) That a Provincial Advisory Council on radio broadcasting should be appointed for each province, to act in an advisory capacity through the provincial authority;

(e) That the Board of the company should be composed of twelve members, three more particularly representing the Dominion and one representing each of the provinces;

(f) That high-power stations should be erected across Canada to give good reception over the entire settled area of the country during daylight; that the nucleus of the system should possibly be seven 50,000 watt stations; that supplementary stations of lower power should be erected in local areas, not effectively covered by the main stations, if found necessary and as experience indicates;

(g) That pending the inauguration and completion of the proposed system, a provisional service should be provided through certain of the existing stations which should be continued in operation by the Canadian Radio Broadcasting Company; that the stations chosen for this provisional service should be those which will give the maximum coverage without duplication; that all remaining stations not so needed should be closed down;

(h) That compensation should be allowed owners of existing stations for apparatus in use as may be decided by the Minister of Marine and Fisheries;* that such apparatus should become the property of the Canadian Radio Broadcasting Company; that the more modern and efficient of these sets of apparatus should be held available for re-erection in local areas not effectively served by the high-power stations; that the cost of compensation should be met out of an appropriation made by Parliament;

(i) That expenditure necessary for the operation and maintenance of the proposed broadcasting service should be met out of revenue produced by license fees, rental of time on stations for programs employing indirect advertising, and a subsidy from the Dominion Government;

(j) That all facilities should be made to permit of chain broadcasting by all the stations or in groups; that while the primary purpose should be to produce programs of high standard from Canadian

---

*The minister charged with administering the existing Radiotelegraph Act.

sources, programs of similar order should also be sought from other sources;

(k) That time should be made available for firms or others desiring to put on programs employing indirect advertising; that no direct advertising should be allowed; that specified time should be made available for educational work; that where religious broadcasting is allowed, there should be regulations prohibiting statements of a controversial nature or one religion making an attack upon the leaders or doctrine of another; that the broadcasting of political matters should be carefully restricted under arrangements mutually agreed upon by all political parties concerned; that competent and cultured announcers only should be employed.

(l) That consideration should be given to the question of introducing legislation which would compel users of electrical apparatus causing interference with broadcast reception to suppress or eliminate the same at their own expense;

(m) That the licensing of stations and such other matters prescribed in the Radiotelegraph Act and Regulations issued thereunder for the control of radio stations in general should remain within the jurisdiction of the Minister of Marine and Fisheries; that that authority should continue to be responsible for the collection of license fees and the suppression of inductive interference causing difficulties with radio reception.

. . .

> JOHN AIRD (Chairman).
> CHARLES A. BOWMAN.
> AUGUSTIN FRIGON.

DONALD MANSON (Secretary).
September 11, 1929.

148. *Le Devoir* on Quebec's Claim to Control Broadcasting

(Editorial by Emile Benoist, *Le Devoir*, Montreal, 2 February 1931)

Georges Pelletier of *Le Devoir* was a member of the executive committee of the Canadian Radio League, and the newspaper supported the League's stand. On the disposal of the provincial claims, see below, p. 352.

(Translation)

M. Taschereau* wants to control radio within the boundaries of the province of Quebec, and in a letter to M. Alfred Duranleau, Minister of Marine, he warns the federal government that the province of Quebec will put forth a law for the administration of the licences of broadcasting stations and the control of radio.

And he adds that eminent lawyers agree in recognizing the province's legal jurisdiction over radio.

We have great respect for the eminent lawyers who are advising the prime minister, but we think all the same that there is nothing like knowing what you're talking about to help you talk sensibly. . . .

The United States has left Canada six complete wavelengths and a share of some others. If Canada broadcast on the American wavelengths, it would scramble all radio reception among our neighbours, and if the United States broadcast on our wavelengths we would hear nothing but frightful confusion. Similarly it is clear that if Quebec broadcasts on wavelengths allotted to the other provinces, there will again be fine confusion.

That is the situation, then. Quebec broadcasts do not just invade Ontario territory, but American territory also, just as Ontario and American broadcasts invade our territory. And one must insist on this point. Neither Quebec nor Ontario nor the United States can prevent things from being this way. In other words, the radio waves and the air of heaven are not at our government's service. . . .

How then can the prime minister, in face of these facts, pretend seriously that radio is exclusively in the provincial domain?. . .

149. The Canadian Radio Broadcasting Act, 1932

(22-23 George V, Chap. 51)

Nearly three years elapsed after the Aird Commission reported before legislation was passed. The change of government in 1930 and the onset of the Depression contributed; there was much public controversy; and there was also legal uncertainty. But in 1931 the Supreme Court of Canada ruled that the Canadian Parliament had jurisdiction to regulate and control radio communication; and when Quebec carried an appeal to the Judicial Committee of the Privy Council, that tribunal, contrary to the trend of many of its Canadian decisions, fully supported the Supreme Court (9 February 1932; see Richard A.

*Louis-Alexandre Taschereau, Liberal Premier of Quebec, 1920-36.

Olmsted, ed., *Decisions of the Judicial Committee of the Privy Council relating to the British North America Act, 1867* . . . , III [Ottawa, 1954], 18-30). The Bennett government then arranged for the appointment of a special committee of the House of Commons on broadcasting. The Canadian Radio League, which had been fighting since 1930 for the principles of the Aird report, presented a brief arguing that private broadcasting inevitably meant American control: "The question is the State or the United States?" (Prang, "Origins of Public Broadcasting"). The committee recommended public ownership. The result was the Act here printed, incorporating the Aird recommendations in great part though by no means entirely.

(Assented to 26th May, 1932)

. . .

3. (1) A commission to be known as the Canadian Radio Broadcasting Commission is hereby constituted and shall consist of a chairman, a vice-chairman and a third commissioner who shall be appointed by the Governor in Council and who shall hold office for periods of ten, nine and eight years respectively. (2) The Chief Commissioner shall be paid an annual salary of ten thousand dollars, and each of the other commissioners an annual salary of eight thousand dollars. . . .

4. The Commission may employ such technical, professional and other officers, and clerks and employees as may be necessary. Such officers, clerks and employees shall be appointed pursuant to the *Civil Service Act.* . . .

6. (1) The Governor in Council may appoint not more than nine Assistant Commissioners who shall hold office during pleasure, and who shall not receive any salary but may be paid an annual amount by way of honorarium, to be fixed by the Governor in Council. There shall not be more than one Assistant Commissioner appointed in any province and the appointment shall be made after consultation with the Government of the Province in which the Assistant Commissioner resides.

(2) It shall be the duty of the Assistant Commissioner to organize and to act as chairman of provincial or local advisory committees, and, at the request of any private station, to organize an Advisory Committee or Sub-Committee, for the purpose of co-operation with such station. . . .

7. (1) The Commission shall from time to time convene meetings of a General Council which shall consist of the Commissioners and the Assistant Commissioners, and which may include representatives of the local advisory committees and of private stations.

(2) The functions of the General Council shall be to advise with regard to the general policy of the Commission, including the general composition, character and co-ordination of national and local programmes, the apportionment of time and any other matters which the Commission or the Minister [of Marine] may refer to the General Council.

8. The Commission shall, notwithstanding anything contained in the *Radiotelegraph Act*. . . and in the regulations made thereunder, but subject to the power of the Minister to license stations, have power to regulate and control broadcasting in Canada carried on by any person whatever, including His Majesty in the right of the province or of the Dominion, and without restricting the generality of the foregoing, these powers shall extend to the following matters:

- *(a)* The Commission shall determine the number, location and power of stations required in Canada;
- *(b)* the Commission shall determine the proportion of time that is to be devoted by any station to national and local programmes respectively and the proportion of advertising that is to be authorized, which shall not unless by permission of the Commission, exceed five per cent of any programme period, and may prescribe the character of such advertising;
- *(c)* the Commission may make recommendations to the Minister with regard to the issue, suspension or cancellation of private broadcasting licences, and notwithstanding anything contained in the *Radiotelegraph Act* or regulations, the Minister may issue, suspend or cancel such licences;
- *(d)* notwithstanding anything contained in the *Radiotelegraph Act* or regulations, or in any licence heretofore issued thereunder, the Commission shall have power to allot channels to be used by stations in Canada and may cancel any allotment and substitute any other therefor;
- *(e)* the Commission may prescribe the periods to be reserved periodically by any station for national programmes;
- *(f)* the Commission may prohibit the organization or operation of chains of privately operated stations in Canada;
- *(g)* the Commission may, subject to the approval of the Minister, assist and encourage the construction of small private stations.

9. The Commission shall have power to carry on the business of broadcasting in Canada and, without restricting the generality of the foregoing, may:

(a) make operating agreements with private stations for the broadcasting of national programmes;

(b) acquire existing private stations either by lease or, subject to the approval of Parliament, by purchase;

(c) subject to the approval of Parliament, construct such new stations as may be required;

(d) operate any station constructed or acquired under the provisions of paragraphs (b) and (c) of this section; provided that the time allotted to local programmes by the Commission in respect to any such station shall be subject to the management of the station director, or other officer in charge of such station, who shall, in respect to the local programmes, act in consultation with and in accordance with the policy formulated by the local Advisory Committee, or Sub-Committee thereof assigned to such station;

(e) originate programmes and secure programmes from within or outside Canada, by purchase or exchange, and make the arrangements necessary for their transmission;

(f) make contracts with any person (or persons) in Canada or outside for the purpose of securing artists to perform in connection with programmes originated by the Commission;

(g) subject to the approval of Parliament, take over all broadcasting in Canada;

(h) do any other thing reasonably necessary for the performance of its functions and powers hereunder. . . .*

14. (1) The Commission may expend for the purposes of this Act the moneys appropriated by Parliament for such purposes.

(2) The moneys appropriated for such purposes shall not exceed the estimated revenue from receiving licences, private commercial broadcasting licences and amateur broadcasting licences and from the business of the Commission under this Act. . . .

150. The Canadian Broadcasting Act, 1936

(1 Edward VIII, Chap. 24)

The Act of 1932 (above, 149) did not work well. The financial support provided for the Canadian Radio Broadcasting Commission was

*The Act proceeds to give the Commission powers of expropriation and specifies that there shall be no compensation for termination of a private station's licence or cancellation of allotment of a channel.

inadequate (the government did not even make over to it the whole sum collected in licence fees) and private broadcasters remained active and hostile. R. B. Bennett however steadily defended the principle of public broadcasting. After the 1935 change of government the new Act here printed was passed. It incorporated features which various critics, including the Canadian Radio League, had advocated, notably the appointment of a general manager. (See Peers, *Politics of Canadian Broadcasting*.) It remained unchanged in essentials until after the Second World War and the advent of television. During this period the Canadian Broadcasting Corporation, always criticized and no doubt deserving criticism, nevertheless was certainly a force strengthening national feeling and encouraging native literary, musical and dramatic talent.

(Assented to 23rd June, 1936)

. . .

3. (1) There shall be a Corporation to be known as the Canadian Broadcasting Corporation which shall consist of a board of nine governors appointed by the Governor in Council and chosen to give representation to the principal geographical divisions of Canada.

(2) The Governor in Council shall designate one of the Governors to be the Chairman and one to be the Vice-Chairman of the Corporation.

(3) The Governors shall hold office for three years, provided that of those first appointed one third shall be appointed to retire in one year, one third in two years and one third in three years. . . .

(7) The Chairman shall receive an honorarium of one thousand five hundred dollars per annum and if an executive council is established by bylaw, each of the other Governors on such executive committee shall receive an honorarium of one thousand dollars per annum; other Governors of the Corporation shall each receive fifty dollars for each meeting they attend, but shall not receive more than five hundred dollars in any one year. . . .

6. There shall be a general manager who shall be chief executive of the Corporation and who shall be appointed by the Governor in Council on the recommendation of the Corporation. . . .

8. The Corporation shall carry on a national broadcasting service within the Dominion of Canada and for that purpose may:—

    (a) maintain and operate broadcasting stations;

    (b) establish, subject to approval of the Governor in Council, such stations as the Corporation may from time to time consider necessary to give effect to the provisions of this Act. . . .

(d) make operating agreements with private stations for the broadcasting of programmes;

(e) originate programmes and secure programmes, from within or outside Canada, by purchase or exchange and make arrangements necessary for their transmission. . . .

(h) publish and distribute, whether gratis or otherwise, such papers, periodicals, and other literary matter as may seem conducive to any of the objects of the Corporation;

(i) collect news relating to current events in any part of the world and in any manner that may be thought fit and to establish and subscribe to news agencies;

(j) acquire copyrights in any literary, musical or artistic works, plays, songs, gramophone records, news and other matter....

(n) acquire private stations either by lease or, subject to the approval of the Governor in Council, by purchase....

10. Notwithstanding anything contained in this Act, the Corporation shall not, unless the approval of the Governor in Council has first been obtained: —

(a) enter into any agreement involving any expenditure in excess of ten thousand dollars;

(b) enter into any agreement or lease for a period exceeding three years;

(c) acquire any personal property, the cost of acquisition of which exceeds the sum of ten thousand dollars, or in any manner dispose of any personal property having an original or book value exceeding the sum of ten thousand dollars. . . .

14. (1) The Minister of Finance shall deposit from time to time in the Bank of Canada or in a chartered bank to be designated by him to the credit of the Corporation: —

(a) the moneys received from licence fees in respect of private receiving licences and private station broadcasting licences, after deducting from the gross receipts the cost of collection and administration, such costs being determined by the Minister from time to time;

(b) any appropriation granted by Parliament for the purposes of the Corporation; and

(c) any advances or grants to the Corporation which are authorized to be made from Consolidated Revenue Fund.

(2) The Corporation shall retain for the purposes of this Act all moneys received by it arising out of its business. . . .

16. The Governor in Council, on the recommendation of the Mini-

ster [of Transport], may authorize the Minister of Finance to place to the credit of the Corporation working capital advances from any unappropriated moneys in the Consolidated Revenue Fund, but the aggregate amount of such advances outstanding at any one time shall not exceed one hundred thousand dollars, and such advances shall be repayable to the Minister of Finance on demand.

17. (1) The Governor in Council may authorize the construction, extension or improvement of capital works of the broadcasting facilities of the Corporation in Canada and, on the recommendation of the Minister, may authorize the Minister of Finance to place to the credit of the Corporation from any unappropriated moneys in the Consolidated Revenue Fund such sum or sums as may be necessary to carry out such construction, extension or improvement of capital works: provided that the total amount which may be so authorized for the said purposes shall not exceed five hundred thousand dollars.

(2) Such moneys so advanced shall bear such rate of interest and shall be amortized on such terms and conditions as may be fixed by the Governor in Council. . . .

21. No private station shall operate in Canada as a part of a chain or network of stations except with the permission of, and in accordance with the regulations made by, the Corporation.

22. (1) The Corporation may make regulations: —

- (a) to control the establishment and operation of chains or networks of stations in Canada;
- (b) to prescribe the periods to be reserved periodically by any private station for the broadcasting of programmes of the Corporation;
- (c) to control the character of any and all programmes broadcast by Corporation or private stations;
- (d) to determine the proportion of time which may be devoted to advertising in any programmes broadcast by the stations of the Corporation or by private stations, and to control the character of such advertising;
- (e) to prescribe the proportion of time which may be devoted to political broadcasts by the stations of the Corporation and by private stations, and to assign such time on an equitable basis to all parties and rival candidates. . . .

(3) Dramatized political broadcasts are prohibited.*

(4) The names of the sponsor or sponsors and the political party, if

*Clearly a result of Liberal indignation over the "Mr. Sage" broadcasts of the Conservatives in the 1935 campaign.

any, upon whose behalf any political speech or address is broadcast shall be announced immediately preceding and immediately after such broadcast.

(5) Political broadcasts on any dominion, provincial or municipal election day and on the two days immediately preceding any such election day are prohibited.
. . .

24. (1) The Minister shall, before dealing with any application for licence to establish a new private station or for increase in power, change of channel, or change of location of any existing private station, or making any regulations or changes in regulations governing the activities of private stations, refer such application or regulation to the Corporation, and the Corporation shall make such recommendations to the Minister as it may deem fit. The approval of the Governor in Council shall be obtained before any licence for any new private station is issued....

25. The Corporation shall, from the date of the coming into force of this Act, take possession of all property and assets and assume all the obligations and liabilities of the Canadian Radio Broadcasting Commission. . . .

27. *The Canadian Radio Broadcasting Act,* 1932, chapter fifty-one of the statutes of 1932, is repealed. . . .

VIII.
External Affairs
and Defence

A.
The Commonwealth and National Independence

1. The First World War, 1914-1918: Constitutional Developments

In some respects the First World War was the most important event in Canadian history — notably in its ultimate influence upon the constitutional position and status of Canada in the Empire (as it was still called in 1914) and in the world at large. These developments began while the war was still in progress.

151. Sir Robert Borden's "Toy Automata" Letter, 4 January 1916

(*Documents on Canadian External Relations, Volume I, 1909-1918*, Department of External Affairs, Ottawa, 1967)

The significance of this much-published letter to Sir George Perley, Canadian High Commissioner in London, is considerably diminished by the fact that Borden followed it up with a cable directing Perley to take no action upon it. Nevertheless it is presumably a valuable reflection of Borden's thinking. On one series of events that had nettled him see Gaddis Smith, *Britain's Clandestine Submarines, 1914-1915* (London and New Haven, 1964). It is worth while to recall that only a few days earlier Borden had announced a planned increase in the size of Canada's forces from 250,000 to 500,000 men. See Robert Craig Brown, "Sir Robert Borden, the Great War and Anglo-Canadian Relations" in John S. Moir, ed., *Character and Circumstance: Essays in Honour of Donald Grant Creighton* (Toronto, 1970).

. . . During the past four months since my return from Great Britain, the Canadian Government (except for an occasional telegram from

362

you or Sir Max Aitken)* have had just what information could be gleaned from the daily Press and no more. As to consultation, plans of campaign have been made and unmade, measures adopted and apparently abandoned and generally speaking steps of the most important and even vital character have been taken, postponed or rejected without the slightest consultation with the authorities of this Dominion.

It can hardly be expected that we shall put 400,000 or 500,000 men in the field and willingly accept the position of having no more voice and receiving no more consideration than if we were toy automata. Any person cherishing such an expectation harbours an unfortunate and even dangerous delusion. Is this war being waged by the United Kingdom alone, or is it a war waged by the whole Empire? If I am correct in supposing that the second hypothesis must be accepted then why do the statesmen of the British Isles arrogate to themselves solely the methods by which it shall be carried on in the various spheres of warlike activity and the steps which shall be taken to assure victory and a lasting peace?

It is for them to suggest the method and not for us. If there is no available method and if we are expected to continue in the role of automata the whole situation must be reconsidered. . . .

152. Imperial War Cabinet and Imperial War Conference, 1917

(*The War Cabinet, Report for the Year 1917*. British Parliamentary Papers, Cd. 9005, 1918)

David Lloyd George, on becoming Prime Minister of the United Kingdom (December 1916), took a more imaginative attitude towards the question of consultation with the Dominions than that of his predecessor, H. H. Asquith. The result was the meetings of the Imperial War Cabinet and Imperial War Conference in the spring of 1917. See *War Memoirs of David Lloyd George* (6 vols., London, 1933-36), IV, and the Borden *Memoirs*, II.

*"General representative for Canada at the front"; afterwards Lord Beaverbrook.

Imperial Affairs

A. THE IMPERIAL WAR CABINET

The outstanding event of the year in the sphere of Imperial affairs has been the inauguration of the Imperial War Cabinet. This has been the direct outcome of the manner in which all parts of the Empire had thrown themselves into the war during the preceding years. Impalpable as was the bond which bound this great group of peoples together, there was never any doubt about their loyalty to the Commonwealth to which they belonged and to the cause to which it was committed by the declaration of war. Without counting the cost to themselves, they offered their men and their treasure in defence of freedom and public right. From the largest and most prosperous Dominion to the smallest island the individual and national effort has been one of continuous and unreserved generosity. It is not within the province of a Record, which is essentially concerned with the history of the administration of the United Kingdom, to describe in detail the achievements of the individual Dominions. Such an account, to do full justice, would require a separate record from each Oversea Government of its own internal administration. Surveying the position as a whole, however, great progress has been made during 1917 in the organisation both of the man-power and other resources of the Empire for the prosecution of the war. The British Army is now a truly Imperial Army, containing units from almost every part of the Empire, including not only all the Dominions and India, but the West Indies, East and West Africa, and a large number of volunteers from the Malay States, the Straits Settlements, Ceylon, Hongkong and other places within and without the Empire. The total contribution of the British Commonwealth to the armies fighting for freedom now is 7,500,000 men. . . .

The real development, however, of 1917 has been in the political sphere, and it has been the result of the intense activity of all parts of the Empire in prosecuting the war since August, 1914.

It had been felt for some time that, in view of the ever-increasing part played by the Dominions in the war, that it was necessary that their Governments should not only be informed as fully as was possible of the situation, but that, as far as was practicable, they should participate, on a basis of complete equality, in the deliberations which determined the main outlines of Imperial policy. Accordingly, one of the first acts of the new Government was to send a telegram on December 14th inviting the Dominion Prime Ministers, not to an ordinary Imperial Conference but to a Special War Conference of the

Empire, in the following terms: "They therefore invite your Prime Minister to attend a series of special and continuous meetings of the War Cabinet in order to consider urgent questions affecting the prosecution of the war, the possible conditions on which, in agreement with our Allies, we could assent to its termination, and the problems which will then immediately arise. For the purpose of these meetings, your Prime Minister will be a member of the War Cabinet."

It was also felt, in view of the keen enthusiasm which had manifested itself in India for the cause for which the Empire had entered the war, and of the invaluable services which the Indian troops and others had rendered to the common cause, that it was right that India should also be represented at the Conference. A telegram was therefore also sent to the Viceroy of India to send representatives to assist the Secretary of State for India in representing the views and needs of India at the Conference, thus giving India for the first time representation in the councils of the Empire.

These invitations were accepted by all the Dominions as well as by India. In some cases the Prime Ministers were able to come, and brought some of their colleagues as assessors on matters in which they had special experience. Canada was represented by the Right Hon. Sir Robert Borden, Prime Minister, and Sir George Perley, Minister of the Overseas Military Forces, who were accompanied by the Hon. Robert Rogers, Minister of Public Works, and the Hon. J. D. Hazen, Minister of Marine Fisheries and Naval Service. Australia was unfortunately prevented at the last minute, owing to a general election, from sending any representatives. New Zealand was represented by the Right Hon. W. F. Massey, Prime Minister, and the Right Hon. Sir J. G. Ward, Minister of Finance and Posts. South Africa was represented by Lieut.-General the Right Hon. J. C. Smuts, Minister of Defence; Newfoundland by the Right Hon. Sir E. P. Morris, Prime Minister. India was represented by the Secretary of State for India, the Right Hon. Austen Chamberlain, M.P., accompanied by three assessors, namely, the Hon. Sir J. S. Meston, K.C.S.I., Lieutenant-Governor of the United Provinces; Colonel His Highness the Maharajah Sir Ganga Singh, Bahadur, G.C.S.I., G.C.I.E., Maharajah of Bikaner; Sir S. P. Sinha, Member Designate of the Executive Council of the Governor of Bengal. The Secretary of State for the Colonies, the Right Hon. Walter H. Long, M.P., was *ex officio* a member of the Imperial War Cabinet and spoke on behalf of the Crown Colonies and Protectorates.

Practical convenience determined that the War Conference should be divided into two parts. On the one side were meetings of what came to be known as the Imperial War Cabinet, which consisted of the Oversea Representatives and the Members of the British War Cabinet sitting together as an Imperial War Cabinet for deliberation about the conduct of the war and for the discussion of the larger issues of imperial policy connected with the war. On the other side was the Imperial War Conference presided over by the Secretary of State for the Colonies, which consisted of the Oversea Representatives and a number of other Ministers, which discussed non-war problems or questions connected with the war but of lesser importance.

The proceedings of the Imperial War Cabinet which held fourteen meetings between March 20th and May 2nd, 1917, were secret. On the 17th May, however, the Prime Minister gave to the House of Commons a short appreciation of the work of the Imperial War Cabinet, from which the following is an extract: —

"The Imperial War Cabinet was unanimous that the new procedure had been of such service not only to all its members but to the Empire that it ought not to be allowed to fall into disuetude. Accordingly, at the last session I proposed formally, on behalf of the British Government, that meetings of an Imperial Cabinet should be held annually, or at any intermediate time when matters of urgent Imperial concern require to be settled, and that the Imperial Cabinet should consist of the Prime Minister of the United Kingdom and such of his colleagues as deal specially with Imperial affairs, of the Prime Minister of each of the Dominions, or some specially accredited alternate possessed of equal authority, and of a representative of the Indian people to be appointed by the Government of India. This proposal met with the cordial approval of the Overseas Representatives, and we hope that the holding of an annual Imperial Cabinet to discuss foreign affairs and other aspects of Imperial policy will become an accepted convention of the British Constitution.

"I ought to add that the institution in its present form is extremely elastic. It grew, not by design, but out of the necessities of the war. The essence of it is that the responsible heads of the Governments of the Empire, with those Ministers who are specially entrusted with the conduct of Imperial Policy should meet together at regular intervals to confer about foreign policy and matters connected therewith, and come to decisions in regard to them which, subject to the control of their own Parliaments, they will then severally execute. By this means they will be able to obtain full information about all aspects of Imperial affairs, and to determine by consultation together the policy of the Empire in its most vital aspects, without infringing in any degree the autonomy which its parts at present enjoy. To what constitutional developments this may lead we did not attempt to settle. The whole question of perfecting the mechanism for 'continuous consultation' about Imperial and foreign affairs between the 'autonomous nations of an Imperial Commonwealth' will be reserved for the consideration of that special Conference which will be summoned as soon as possible after the war to readjust the constitutional relations of the Empire. We felt, however, that the experiment of constituting an Imperial Cabinet in which India was represented had been so fruitful in better understanding and in unity of purpose and action that it ought to be perpetuated, and we believe that this proposal will commend itself to the judgment of all the nations of the Empire."

In addition, it may perhaps be useful to quote the opinion of one of its Oversea Members, Sir Robert Borden, as to the significance of the meetings of the Imperial Cabinet. Speaking on April 3rd to the Empire Parliamentary Association, he said: —

"It may be that in the shadow of the war we do not clearly realise the measure of recent constitutional development . . . the constitutional position which has arisen from the summoning of an Imperial War Cabinet. The British Constitution is the most flexible instrument of government ever devised. It is surrounded by certain statutory limitations, but they are not of a character to prevent the remarkable development to which I shall allude. The office of Prime Minister, thoroughly recognised by the gradually developed conventions of the Constitution, although entirely unknown to the formal enactments of the law, is invested with a power and authority which, under new conditions demanding progress and development, are of inestimable advantage. The recent exercise of that great authority has brought about an advance which may contain the germ and define the method of constitutional development in the immediate future. It is only within the past few days that the full measure of that advance has been consummated.

"For the first time in the Empire's history there are sitting in London two Cabinets, both properly constituted and both exercising well-defined powers. Over each of them the Prime Minister of the United Kingdom presides. One of them is designated as the 'War Cabinet,' which chiefly devotes itself to such questions touching the prosecution of the war as primarily concern the United Kingdom. The other is designated as the 'Imperial War Cabinet,' which has a wider purpose, jurisdiction and personnel. To its deliberations have been summoned representatives of all the Empire's self-governing Dominions. We meet there on terms of equality under the presidency of the First Minister of the United Kingdom; we meet there as equals, he is *primus inter pares*. Ministers from six nations sit around the Council Board, all of them responsible to their respective Parliaments and to the people of the countries which they represent. Each nation has its voice upon questions of common concern and highest importance as the deliberations proceed; each preserves unimpaired its perfect autonomy, its self-government, and the responsibility of its Ministers to their own electorate. For many years the thought of statesmen and students in every part of the Empire has centred around the question of future constitutional relations; it may be that now, as in the past, the necessity imposed by great events has given the answer.

"The Imperial War Cabinet as constituted to-day has been summoned for definite and specific purposes, publicly stated, which involve questions of the most vital concern to the whole Empire. With the constitution of that Cabinet, a new era has dawned and a new page of history has been written. It is not for me to prophesy as to the future significance of these pregnant events; but those who have given thought and energy to every effort for full constitutional development of the oversea nations may be pardoned for believing that they discern therein the birth of a new and greater Imperial Commonwealth."

B. THE IMPERIAL WAR CONFERENCE

The discussions and decisions of the Imperial War Conference, which met in the Colonial Office, have already been partly published in a Blue Book. The most important resolution passed by the Conference dealt with the future constitutional organisation of the Empire and was moved by Sir Robert Borden in the following terms: —

"The Imperial War Conference are of opinion that the readjustment of the constitutional relations of the component parts of the Empire is too important and intricate a subject to be dealt with during the war, and that it should form the subject of a special Imperial Conference to be summoned as soon as possible after the cessation of hostilities.

"They deem it their duty, however, to place on record their view that any such readjustment, while thoroughly preserving all existing powers of self-government and complete control of domestic affairs, should be based on a full recognition of the Dominions as autonomous nations of an Imperial Commonwealth, and of India as an important portion of the same, should recognise the right of the Dominions and India to an adequate voice in foreign policy and in foreign relations, and should provide effective arrangements for continuous consultation in all important matters of common Imperial concern and for such necessary concerted action, founded on consultation, as the several Governments may determine."*....

153. Imperial War Cabinet and Imperial War Conference, 1918

(*The War Cabinet, Report for the Year 1918*. British Parliamentary Papers, Cmd. 325, 1919)

In 1918 the Imperial War Cabinet had to deal not only with the final stages of the war but also with the arrangements for the part to be played by the Empire (for which, it will be noted, the word "Commonwealth" was now beginning to be used) in the making of peace. For a striking example of the part played by Sir Robert Borden in the I.W.C. in 1918, see below, **213**.

Imperial Affairs

A. THE IMPERIAL WAR CABINET

With every year that has passed the participation of the Empire as a whole in the war has become more complete and more intimate. In every sphere of war effort and sacrifice — in the raising and equipping of troops, in the furnishing and control of food-stuffs and raw materials, in the financing of their efforts by loan or taxation, in the cheerful acceptance of inevitable restrictions on the economic life of the individual and the community — the various units which compose the British Commonwealth showed, in the past year, that their loyalty to the common cause and their determination to ensure its victory were only strengthened by the prolongation and the increas-

---

*This was Resolution IX of the Conference, passed on 16 April 1917. It was seconded by W. F. Massey of New Zealand (not by Lieut.-General J. C. Smuts of South Africa, as stated in the Borden *Memoirs*, II, 668, though Smuts powerfully supported it). For the discussion, see Ollivier, *The Colonial and Imperial Conferences from 1887 to 1937* (3 vols., Ottawa, 1954), II, 194-216. It has been widely assumed, on the basis of slight investigation, that Smuts was primarily responsible for the resolution. In fact, it seems to have originated with Borden, who worked closely with other members of the conference, particularly Smuts, in developing it into its final form.

ing cost of the struggle. Those efforts and sacrifices were crowned by the amazing series of victories won by British arms in the closing half of a year which deserves to rank with 1759 as *annus mirabilis*, a year of wonders. And in those victories the troops of every portion of the Empire played a conspicuous part. In the West, the forces of every British Dominion shared equally with the troops of the old Homeland and with our gallant Allies the glory of finally breaking down the resistance of the German Armies. In the East, General Allenby, with an army composed almost exclusively of the forces of the British Commonwealth, and, in very large measure, of Indian troops, achieved a success, more complete in the purely military sense than any other single victory in this war. Particulars of the military and economic effort of the different portions of the Empire, and of the part played by their forces in the various theatres of war will be found in the appropriate sections of this Report. It is enough here to note the truly Imperial character of the war as an external phenomenon in order to appreciate its inevitable effect upon the internal constitutional relations of the component parts of the British Commonwealth.

The common effort and sacrifice in the war have inevitably led to the recognition of an equality of status between the responsible Governments of the Empire. This equality has long been acknowledged in principle, and found its adequate expression in 1917 in the creation, or rather the natural coming into being, of the Imperial War Cabinet as an instrument for evolving a common Imperial policy in the conduct of the war. The nature of the constitutional development involved in the establishment, as a permanent institution, of the Imperial Cabinet system, was clearly explained by Sir Robert Borden in a speech to the Empire Parliamentary Association on the 21st June, 1918: —

> "A very great step in the constitutional development of the Empire was taken last year by the Prime Minister when he summoned the Prime Ministers of the Overseas Dominions to the Imperial War Cabinet. We meet there on terms of perfect equality. We meet as Prime Ministers of self-governing nations. We meet there under the leadership and the presidency of the Prime Minister of the United Kingdom. After all, my Lord Chancellor and Gentlemen, the British Empire, as it is at present constituted, is a very modern organisation. It is perfectly true that it is built up on the development of centuries, but, as it is constituted to-day, both in territory and in organisation, it is a relatively modern affair. Why, it is only 75 years since responsible govern-

ment was granted to Canada. It is only a little more than fifty years since the first experiment in Federal Government,—in a Federal Constitution,—was undertaken in this Empire. And from that we went on, in 1871, to representation in negotiating our Commercial Treaties, in 1878, to complete fiscal autonomy, and after that to complete fiscal control and the negotiation of our own treaties. But we have always lacked the full status of nationhood, because you exercised here a so-called trusteeship, under which you undertook to deal with foreign relations on our behalf, and sometimes without consulting us very much. Well, that day has gone by. We come here, as we came last year, to deal with all these matters, upon terms of perfect equality with the Prime Minister of the United Kingdom and his colleagues. It has been said that the term 'Imperial War Cabinet' is a misnomer. The word 'Cabinet' is unknown to the law. The meaning of 'Cabinet' has developed from time to time. For my part I see no incongruity whatever in applying the term 'Cabinet' to the association of Prime Ministers and other Ministers who meet around a common council board to debate and to determine the various needs of the Empire. If I should attempt to describe it, I should say it is a Cabinet of Governments. Every Prime Minister who sits around that board is responsible to his own Parliament and to his own people; the conclusions of the War Cabinet can only be carried out by the Parliaments of the different nations of our Imperial Commonwealth. Thus, each Dominion, each nation, retains its perfect autonomy. I venture to believe, and I thus expressed myself last year, that in this may be found the genesis of a development in the constitutional relations of the Empire, which will form the basis of its unity in the years to come."

The second session of the Imperial War Cabinet opened on June 11th. The United Kingdom was represented by the Right Hon. D. Lloyd George, Prime Minister (in the Chair), by the members of the British War Cabinet, and by the Right Hon. A. J. Balfour, the Secretary of State for Foreign Affairs, the Right Hon. W. Long, the Secretary of State for the Colonies, the Right Hon. Viscount Milner, the Secretary of State for War, the Right Hon. Sir E. Geddes, the First Lord of the Admiralty, and the Right Hon. Lord Weir, the Secretary of State for the Royal Air Force. Canada was represented at the meetings by the Right Hon. Sir Robert Borden, Prime Minister, and by the Hon. N. W. Rowell, President of the Privy Council of Canada. Australia, which, owing to a general election, had been unable to send any representatives in 1917, was represented by the Right Hon. W. M. Hughes, Prime Minister, and by the Right Hon. Sir J. Cook,

Minister of the Navy. New Zealand was again represented by the Right Hon. W. F. Massey, Prime Minister, and by the Right Hon. Sir J. G. Ward, Minister of Finance. South Africa was represented by Lieutenant-General the Right Hon. J. C. Smuts, Minister of Defence, and by the Hon. H. Burton, Minister of Railways and Harbours. Newfoundland by the Right Hon. W. F. Lloyd, Prime Minister. In the representation of India an important and significant change was introduced. Whereas at the previous session India had been represented by the Secretary of State for India, accompanied by three assessors, she was on this occasion represented by the Secretary of State for India, the Right Hon. E. S. Montagu, and the Hon. S. P. Sinha, Member of the Executive Council of the Governor of Bengal, who, in accordance with the statement of the Prime Minister in the House of Commons on May 17th, 1917, was deputed to this country as the representative of the people of India. The Maharaja of Patiala also attended the meetings as the spokesman of the Princes of India.

The second session of the Imperial War Cabinet coincided with the most critical phase of the military operations in the Western Theatre. When it opened the German offensive had just attained what was to prove its climax by the advance from the Chemin des Dames to the Marne. Everything depended on whether another German offensive succeeded in achieving a military decision during the two or three months before the emergency measures for bringing over the American Army and reinforcing the depleted British divisions could take effect. The offensive failed, and before the full session of the Imperial War Cabinet closed the great Allied counter-offensive was already in full progress. The deliberations of the Imperial War Cabinet are necessarily secret, but it is well-known that they were not confined to the all-absorbing military problems, but covered the whole field of Imperial policy, including many aspects of foreign policy and the war aims for which the British Commonwealth was fighting. It is worth noting, in this connection, that the Oversea members of the Imperial War Cabinet not only helped to settle the policy to be adopted by the British Government at the session of the Allied Supreme War Council at Versailles in July, but also attended one of the meetings of the Supreme War Council in person.

During this second session certain improvements were also introduced in the actual machinery of the Imperial War Cabinet system. It was felt that the Dominion Prime Ministers should, as his colleagues on the Imperial War Cabinet, correspond directly with the Prime Minister of the United Kingdom whenever they wished to do so. The experience of the past year had also shown the practical inconvenience resulting from the fact that, while the Prime Ministers of the Dominions could only attend the Imperial War Cabinet for a few weeks in the year, matters of the greatest importance, from the point of view of the common interest, inevitably arose and had to be decided in the interval between the sessions. The natural remedy for this defect lay in giving the Imperial War Cabinet continuity by the presence in London of Oversea Cabinet Ministers definitely nominated to represent the Prime Ministers in their absence. The Imperial War Cabinet, consequently, on July 30th, accepted the following Resolution: —

I. (1) The Prime Ministers of the Dominions, as members of The Imperial War Cabinet, have the right of direct communication with the Prime Minister of the United Kingdom, and *vice versa*.

(2) Such communications should be confined to questions of Cabinet importance. The Prime Ministers themselves are the judges of such questions.

(3) Telegraphic communications between the Prime Ministers should, as a rule, be conducted through the Colonial Office machinery, but this will not exclude the adoption of more direct means of communication in exceptional circumstances.

II. In order to secure continuity in the work of the Imperial War Cabinet and a permanent means of consultation during the war on the more important questions of common interest, the Prime Minister of each Dominion has the right to nominate a Cabinet Minister either as a resident or visitor in London to represent him at meetings of the Imperial War Cabinet to be held regularly between the plenary sessions.

It was decided that arrangements should be made for the representation of India at those meetings.

After the close of the second session several meetings of the British War Cabinet were attended by such representatives of the Dominions as still remained in the United Kingdom, but before the arrangements contemplated in the second of the above Resolutions could take effect the rapid collapse of the Central Powers precipitated the whole question of the discussion of terms of peace. The moment this was realised the Dominion Prime Ministers were warned to be in readiness to come over in order to be in close touch, as members of the Imperial War Cabinet, with the whole situation, and to take part in the discussions between the Allies as to the peace settlement itself.

The Viceroy of India was also invited to send representatives to London for the same purpose.

By November 20th, 1918, the third Session of the Imperial War Cabinet had commenced the consideration of the many questions relating to the Peace Settlement. Before the end of the year not less than twelve meetings had been held, although it was not until December 18th that the numbers of the Imperial War Cabinet were completed, except for the representatives of New Zealand, by the arrival of General Botha, representing South Africa, and the Maharaja of Bikaner and Sir S. P. Sinha. Two of the most interesting of these meetings were held on the morning and afternoon of December 3rd, when the Imperial War Cabinet met M. Clemenceau and Marshal Foch, Representatives of France, and Signor Orlando and Baron Sonnino, Representatives of Italy, who had arrived in London for an important Conference. Important meetings were also held before and after Christmas, at the time of President Wilson's visit. Thus the year 1918, which had confronted the Imperial War Cabinet with so many anxious and critical war problems, left them at its close engaged on the scarcely less difficult, but certainly less anxious, questions of the Peace Settlement.

B. IMPERIAL WAR CONFERENCE

In 1918, as in 1917, an Imperial War Conference was held in London concurrently with the meetings of the Imperial War Cabinet, under the Chairmanship of the Secretary of State for the Colonies. This Conference was, for the first time, fully representative of all parts of the Empire, since members from Australia, who had been unavoidably absent in 1917, were present as well as Ministers from all the other self-governing Dominions and India.

A great part of the deliberations of the Conference was of a confidential nature and entirely unsuitable for publication—at any rate during the war, but it was found possible to publish (Cd. 9177) a certain part of the discussions, and the great majority of the Resolutions passed. . . .

2. The Paris Peace Conference, 1919

The institution of the Imperial War Cabinet represented an advance in the status of the Dominions within the Empire. At the subsequent Peace Conference they achieved something rather more difficult:

recognition by foreign nations that they possessed "a sovereign status of some sort." So far as Canada was concerned it is clear that the conference was mainly an opportunity for asserting this status. The Canadian representatives had, and could have had, comparatively little influence upon the European settlement; the five great Allied powers (the United States, Britain, France, Italy and Japan), and primarily the first four, kept the essential decisions in their own hands. See G. P. deT. Glazebrook, *Canada at the Paris Peace Conference* (Toronto, 1942); and the documents in R. A. MacKay, ed., *Documents on Canadian External Relations*, Volume 2, *The Paris Peace Conference of 1919* (Department of External Affairs, Ottawa, 1969).

154. Telegrams between Sir Robert Borden in London and the Acting Prime Minister (Sir Thomas White) in Ottawa on Representation at the Conference

(Canada, Sessional Papers, No. 41j, Special Session 1919)

The mood of the Canadian government at the end of the war is powerfully reflected in these cables.

Telegram, dated December 4, 1918, from the Acting Prime Minister, Ottawa, to Sir Robert Borden, London

Council to-day further considered Canadian representation at Peace Conference and is even more strongly of opinion than when you left, that Canada should be represented. Council is of opinion that in view of war efforts of Dominion other nations entitled to representation at Conference should recognize unique character of British Commonwealth composed of group of free nations under one sovereign and that provision should be made for special representation of these nations at Conference, even though it may be necessary that in any final decisions reached they should speak with one voice; that if this is not possible then you should form one of whatever delegation represents British Commonwealth. It surely is not contemplated that each nation at war should have exactly same numerical representation as Great Britain and France. Should not representation be to some extent commensurate with war efforts? Would you like Order in Council passed or any other official action taken declaring attitude of Government on question of Canadian representation at Conference? If so, please cable.

Telegram, dated London, January 2, 1919, from Sir Robert Borden to the Acting Prime Minister, Ottawa

In [Imperial War] Cabinet to-day I took up question of represent-ation of the Dominion and spoke very frankly and firmly as to Canada's attitude. My proposal which I consider the most satisfac-tory solution that is practicable and which was accepted by the Cabi-net is as follows: —

First, Canada and the other Dominions shall each have the same representation as Belgium and other small allied nations at the Peace Conference.

Second, as it is proposed to admit representatives of Belgium and other small allied nations only when their special interests are under consideration, I urged that some of the representatives of British Empire should be drawn from a panel on which each Dominion Prime Minister shall have a place.

I pointed out that Canada has no special interest such as South Africa, Australia and New Zealand, in respect of additional territory and that the basis of representation accorded to small allied nations would, therefore, be unsatisfactory from Canadian point of view. I emphasized the insistence of Canada on this recognition and I urged that the British Empire has the right to define the constitutional rela-tions between the nations which compose it and their consequent right to distinctive representation. It is anticipated that British Empire will have five representatives entitled to be present at all meetings of Conference. I expressed my strong opinion that it would be most unfortunate if these were all selected from the British Islands. Probably three will be named and two others selected from the panel for each meeting. The panel will comprise both British and Dominion Ministers. No public announcement can be made until these proposals have been communicated to Allied Governments and accepted. I shall be glad to have views of Council. My proposal really gives to Dominions fuller representation than that accorded to small allied nations such as Belgium.

Telegram, dated Ottawa, January 4, 1919, from the Acting Prime Minister to Sir Robert Borden

If Peace Conference in its composition is to express spirit of democracy for which we have been fighting, as Council thinks it should, small allied nations like Belgium which have fought with us throughout war should be entitled to representation throughout whole Conference, even if limited to one member, and if this were agreed proposal that Canada should have same representation as

Belgium, and other small allied nations, would be satisfactory, but not otherwise. Canada has had as many casualties as the United States and probably more actual deaths. Canadian people would not appreciate five American delegates throughout the whole Conference and no Canadian entitled to sit throughout Conference, nor would they appreciate several representatives from Great Britain and Canada none. There will be great disappointment here if you are not full member of Conference. We fully appreciate that you are doing everything in your power to secure suitable representation for Canada.

Telegram, dated Ottawa, January 16, 1919, from Acting Prime Minister to Sir Robert Borden (in Paris)

Announcement as to Canadian representation at Peace Conference most favourably received. Hearty congratulations on success of your efforts in this regard.

155. Memorandum concerning the Dominions as Parties and Signatories to the Peace Treaties

(Canada, Sessional Papers, No. 41j, Special Session 1919)

This is the Memorandum referred to in paragraph 7 of Loring Christie's Notes (below, **156**).

Memorandum circulated by Sir Robert Borden on behalf of the Dominion Prime Ministers

(1) The Dominion Prime Ministers, after careful consideration, have reached the conclusion that all the treaties and conventions resulting from the Peace Conference should be so drafted as to enable the Dominions to become Parties and Signatories thereto. This procedure will give suitable recognition to the part played at the Peace Table by the British Commonwealth as a whole and will at the same time record the status attained there by the Dominions.

(2) The procedure is in consonance with the principles of constitutional government that obtain throughout the Empire. The Crown is the supreme executive in the United Kingdom and in all the Dominions, but it acts on the advice of different Ministries within different constitutional units; and under Resolution IX of the Imperial War Conference, 1917, the organization of the Empire is to be based upon equality of nationhood.

(3) Having regard to the high objects of the Peace Conference, it is also desirable that the settlements reached should be presented at once to the world in the character of universally accepted agreements, so far as this is consistent with the constitution of each State represented. This object would not be achieved if the practice heretofore followed of merely inserting in the body of the convention an express reservation providing for the adhesion of the Dominions were adopted in these treaties; and the Dominions would not wish to give even the appearance of weakening this character of the peace.

(4) On the constitutional point, it is assumed that each treaty or convention will include clauses providing for ratification similar to those in the Hague Convention of 1907. Such clauses will, under the procedure proposed, have the effect of reserving to the Dominion Governments and legislatures the same power of review as is provided in the case of other contracting parties.

(5) It is conceived that this proposal can be carried out with but slight alterations of previous treaty forms. Thus: —

(a) The usual recital of Heads of State in the Preamble needs no alteration whatever, since the Dominions are adequately included in the present formal description of the King, namely, "His Majesty the King of the United Kingdom of Great Britain and Ireland and of the British Dominions beyond the Seas, Emperor of India."

(b) The recital in the Preamble of the names of the Plenipotentiaries appointed by the High Contracting Parties for the purpose of concluding the treaty would include the names of the Dominion Plenipotentiaries immediately after the names of the Plenipotentiaries appointed by the United Kingdom. Under the general heading "The British Empire" the sub-headings "the United Kingdom," "The Dominion of Canada," "The Commonwealth of Australia," "the Union of South Africa," etc., would be used as headings to distinguish the various plenipotentiaries.

(c) It would then follow that the Dominion Plenipotentiaries would sign according to the same scheme.

(6) The Dominion Prime Ministers consider, therefore, that it should be made an instruction to the British member of the Drafting Commission of the Peace Conference that all treaties should be drawn according to the above proposal.

Hotel la Perouse,
    Paris.
12th March, 1919.

156. Loring Christie's Notes on the Conference, July 1919

(*External Affairs*, April 1964)

Loring C. Christie, one of the small staff of the Department of External Affairs, was a member of the Canadian delegation to Paris and a confidential assistant of Sir Robert Borden. After a dozen years away from the Department he rejoined it in 1935 and when he died in 1941 was Canadian Minister to the United States. The references to Annexes have been deleted from these contemporary notes as printed here.

1. The object of these notes is to outline the development at the Paris Peace Conference of the status of Canada as an international person or entity. The main points in the sketch will be the character of the representation secured by Canada at the Conference, her position as a Signatory of the Treaties concluded there, and her status as a Member of the League of Nations and of the International Labour Organization.

2. In the early stages of the war it had been announced in the various Parliaments of the Empire that the Dominions would be fully consulted concerning the terms of peace. (*See* United Kingdom Parliament, April 14, 1915, 71 H.C.Deb., 5s., col. 16-18; Canadian Parliament, January 31, 1917, Debates, House of Commons, Official Report, Session of 1917, vol. 1, page 300). The sessions of the Imperial War Cabinet, held in the spring of 1917 and the summer of 1918, afforded so far as they went the means for carrying out this understanding. During the negotiations leading up to the armistice there naturally presented itself the specific question of Dominion representation at the Conference of belligerent Powers which it was certain would be held to conclude the terms of peace. This question was first officially raised from Ottawa by telegraphic correspondence between the Prime Minister of Canada and the Prime Minister of the United Kingdom; thereafter it was taken up immediately on the arrival of the Canadian Ministers in London in November, 1918, and the discussion continued there until their departure for Paris early in January, 1919.

(a) The discussion took place in the Imperial War Cabinet and in less formal meetings between English and Dominion Ministers. At the outset the assumption was that only five places could be secured for the British Empire at the peace table. On this assumption various methods of meeting the case of the Dominions were canvassed, consisting mostly of variations on what was known as the panel system, under which the representation of the British Empire in the Peace Conference discussions would be selected from day to day, according to the subject, from a panel made up of representatives of the United Kingdom and the Dominions. But on consideration it became apparent that this method would not of itself be sufficient in practice to take care of the various political elements in Great Britain that were entitled to or had been promised representation and at the same time to meet the legitimate claims and aspirations of the Dominions in view of the decisive force they had exerted in the actual determination of the issues of the war. Accordingly in the end the Prime Minister of Canada proposed that we should press, not only for a British Empire representation of five involving the panel system, but also for distinctive representation for each Dominion similar to that accorded to the smaller Allied Powers; and this proposal was accepted by the Imperial War Cabinet. . . .

3. The Preliminary Peace Conference began at Paris on January 12, 1919, and the question of procedure, including that of representation, was taken up at the outset in the Council of First Delegates or Prime Ministers and Foreign Secretaries of the Principal Allied and Associated Powers, commonly known as the Council of Ten. The United States delegates at once objected to the proposal for distinctive representation for the British Dominions, President Wilson saying that it would not be understood by his people. Mr. Lansing, United States Secretary of State, proposed that there might be five technical delegates of the Dominions, and questioned the title of the Dominions to take part in the discussion of European arrangements. But after full discussion in the British Empire Delegation, and a strong protest from the Prime Minister of Canada, the United States delegates receded at the next meeting of the Council of Ten and the proposal was carried; so that the larger Dominions were each of them accorded a representation equal to that of the more important small Powers.

4. The Council of Ten, after reaching this agreement as to Dominion representation, gave additional representation to Belgium and Serbia. The Canadian Ministers immediately submitted a Memorandum protesting against this decision; though it was recognized that it was too late to change it.

5. Accordingly the Rules of the Conference as adopted at the Plenary Session of January 18, 1919, provided for a British Empire representation of five Plenipotentiary Delegates (including Dominion representatives under the panel system), and in addition for two Plenipotentiary Delegates each for Canada, Australia, South Africa

and India, and one for New Zealand. Their status was made the same as that of the smaller Powers, or "belligerent Powers with special interests," as the more important of these were officially described. In addition they were entitled to bring Technical Delegates.

As explained elsewhere, the form which the organization and proceedings of the Peace Conference actually took did not entirely accord with the scheme of the Rules adopted at this Plenary Session.

6. In the result, through this combination of the panel system for the British Empire Delegation with their own distinctive representation, the Dominions secured a peculiarly effective position.

(a) At the Plenary Sessions there were sometimes three Canadian Plenipotentiary Delegates — two representing Canada and one representing the British Empire.

(b) At all times throughout the Conference, the Dominion Delegates were at the heart of the machine and had access to all the papers recording the proceedings of the Conference. This enabled them effectively to watch and check the proceedings in the interest of their respective Dominions, and placed them in a position distinctly more advantageous than that of the small Powers, who did not receive the confidential papers of the Conference such as the minutes of the Council of Ten and the Council of Five.

(c) Dominion Ministers were nominated to and acted for the British Empire on the principal Inter-Allied Commissions of the Peace Conference, which were appointed by the Conference from time to time to consider and report upon special aspects of the conditions of peace. . . .

(d) All the Dominion Prime Ministers took part in the Council of Ten when the disposition of the German Colonies was being discussed and decided.

(e) The Prime Minister of Canada on several occasions attended as the British Empire representative on the Council of Five. He also attended the Council of Four on several occasions to put forward the British Empire case in respect of the clauses on economic questions, on the international control of ports, waterways and railways, and on submarine cables.

(f) It is especially significant of the new status that during his last month in Paris, the Prime Minister of Canada regularly acted as chairman of the meetings of the British Empire Delegation (which was but the Imperial War Cabinet under another name), whenever the Prime Minister of the United Kingdom was unable to attend.

7. A further development concerns the signature of the various treaties concluded at the Conference. Hitherto the practice in respect

of a political treaty has been to insert an article or reservation providing for the adhesion of the Dominions sometime after its signature and ratification by the Government of the United Kingdom. It was thought that this method would be inappropriate on this occasion in view of the new position that had been secured and of the part played by Dominion representatives at the peace table. Accordingly the Prime Minister of Canada proposed that the assent of the King as High Contracting Party to the various treaties should in respect of the Dominions be signified by the signature of Dominion plenipotentiaries, and that the preamble and other formal parts of the treaties should be drafted accordingly. This proposal was adopted, in the form of a Memorandum, by all the Dominion Prime Ministers at a meeting summoned by the Prime Minister of Canada, and was put forward on their behalf. The proposal was accepted by the British Empire Delegation and the Conference substantially as made; and the various treaties have been drawn up accordingly; so that the Dominions appear as Signatories, and their concurrence in the treaties, subject to ratification, is thus given in the same manner as that of all the other Powers.

8. This development involved the issuance by the King, as High Contracting Party, of Full Powers to the various Dominion Plenipotentiary Delegates; and in order that the Full Powers issued to the Canadian Plenipotentiaries might be based upon formal action of the Canadian Government an Order in Council was passed on April 10, 1919 (P.C. 800), granting the necessary authority. At the same time the Prime Minister of Canada addressed a communication to the Prime Minister of the United Kingdom requesting that some appropriate step should be taken to establish the connection between this Order in Council and the issuance of the Full Powers, so that it might formally appear of record that they were issued on the responsibility of the Government of Canada. It happens that under British practice the Letters Patent constituting a Full Power are signed by the King as Head of the State without any counter-signature; so that the formal connection between the action of the Canadian Government and the issuance of these full powers by the King can be established without anomaly.

9. The new status of the Dominions is manifested again in the constitution of the League of Nations. Having enjoyed a status at the Peace Conference like that of the "Powers with special interests," the Dominions took the ground that they should be similarly accepted in the future international relationship contemplated by the League. The League of Nations Commission, while inclined to accept this position in principle, did not at the outset accept all its implications.

The first draft of the Covenant of the League made provision for Dominion membership, but it was obscure as to the character of Dominion representation. But the document was professedly tentative; the Dominion case was pressed; and in its final form as amended and incorporated in the Treaty of Peace with Germany, the status of the Dominions as to membership and representation in the Assembly and Council was recognized as being in all respects the same as that of other Members of the League. They are to become Members as Signatories of the Treaty; and the words of the document make no distinction between them and other Signatory Members. With especial reference to Article 4, the Prime Minister of Canada obtained from President Wilson and Messrs Clemenceau and Lloyd George a signed declaration "that upon the true construction of the first and second paragraphs of that Article, representatives of the self-governing Dominions of the British Empire may be selected or named as members of the Council."

10. The constitution of the International Labour Organization affords a still further manifestation of the development. Questions arose here similar to those involved in the constitution of the League of Nations; for the Labour Organization is analogous to that of the League. Corresponding to the Council of the League there is a Labour Governing Body, consisting of Delegates nominated by a limited number of governments, in addition to employers' and employees' Delegates; while corresponding to the Assembly of the League there is the General Labour Conference. The draft Convention presented by the Commission on International Labour Legislation to the Plenary Session of April 11, 1919, while contemplating that Dominion Government Delegates might be sent to the General Conference, definitely excluded them from the Governing Body; for in defining that body it declared that "No High Contracting Party, together with its Dominions and Colonies, whether self-governing or not, shall be entitled to nominate more than one member." A resolution having been moved in the same Plenary Session that the Peace Conference approve this draft Convention, the Prime Minister of Canada immediately moved that the resolution be amended by adding the following:

"The Conference authorizes the Drafting Committee to make such amendments as may be necessary to have the Convention conform to the Covenant of the League of Nations in the character of its membership and in the method of adherence."

This amendment carried, and as a consequence the Labour Convention was finally amended so that the Dominions were placed on the same footing as other Members of the International Labour Organization, becoming eligible for selection like others to nominate Government Delegates to the Governing Body; though it was only at the last minute, and after the Prime Minister of Canada had carried the matter up to the Council of Four, that the Drafting Committee struck out the objectionable clause quoted above.

11. The Treaty of Peace was largely drafted in the first instance by Commissions of the Peace Conference; though many Articles were drafted by the Drafting Committee on instructions from the Council of Ten, the Council of Five or the Council of Four. In the case of the League of Nations Covenant and the Labour Convention and General Principles there were special Plenary Sessions to consider and adopt the proposals. For the rest, however, the participation of the Powers other than the five Principal Powers was more formal than substantial, except of course in respect of the Articles affecting them specially. It is true that the Conditions of Peace were submitted to and adopted by the secret Plenary Session of May 6th before their presentation to the Germans; but it was a highly formal proceeding.

The Dominions, however, were much better placed. As already seen the Dominions were prominently represented on the various Commissions of the Peace Conference, and at times the Prime Ministers attended the Council of Ten, while in addition the Prime Minister of Canada on a number of occasions took part in the work of the Council of Four and the Council of Five. More than that, every Commission Report, every aspect, every section of the Conditions of Peace was first considered in meetings of the British Empire Delegation (whose personnel was the same as that of the Imperial War Cabinet) before the assent of the British Empire was given. The Dominions' participation in the making of peace has been substantial indeed.

12. In recalling the successive stages of the advance in status attained by the Dominions at the Peace Conference it is to be noted that in every instance the initiative was taken by Canada; and whether or not the other Dominions at all times joined in pressing these steps, nevertheless each one in the final result received the full benefit of the advance.

13. For a good many years Canada has been in a position, should the occasion warrant it or should she so desire, to affirm herself definitely as an international person or entity. The occasion arose at Paris. We had not in fact been entirely lacking in direct international relationships, but they were of an economic character and their political or constitutional implications had not been expressly defined.

The settlement of the results of the war provided the first occasion on which Canada became conscious that she was directly and vitally concerned in a world political conference. The occasion was met and Canada through her representatives has definitely declared herself as in some degree an international person. Representatives of the Canadian Government sat at the peace table with those of other countries; they presented their Full Powers and they signed in the same way; Canada becomes a member of the League of Nations and the International Labour Organization on the same footing as others. In all this the Dominion has appeared directly, in person, not through another; in everything that met the eye, in the method in which they appeared and entered into relationships, contractual or otherwise, in fact in all their functioning, the Canadian representatives were practically indistinguishable from the other national representatives present. All this is unmistakable evidence of a new position in the world definitely assumed.

What this will ultimately mean in its relation to the British Commonwealth lies in the realm of speculation. But as it stands at present the British Commonwealth has clearly become before the world something different from what it was. For our own purposes we had regarded ourselves as made up of distinct political units; but we had not made that clear in our relations with others. Now we have done so; the Dominions have asserted a sovereign status of some sort and have for some purposes entered the Family of Nations. There were at Paris, and will be, anomalies; but the history of international law and custom is itself full of anomalies; it is also not without material for guidance in considering what may be done with such an International Person, or combination of International Persons, however unprecedented, as the British Commonwealth has now definitely resolved itself into. The development has proceeded in the direction contemplated by the Resolution on the Constitution of the Empire agreed to by the Imperial War Conference, 1917;* it remains for the special Imperial Conference contemplated therein to deal with whatever further readjustments of the constitutional relationships of the Empire are necessary, and to suggest "effective arrangements for continuous consultation in all important matters of common Imperial concern, and for such necessary concerted action, founded on consultation, as the several Governments may determine."

*Above, 152.

157. Ratification of the German Treaty by Canada

(Canada, Sessional Papers, No. 41j, Special Session 1919)

Although the British government attempted to argue that separate ratification of the treaties by the Dominions was unnecessary, Sir Robert Borden firmly insisted that the King should not be advised to ratify the German treaty before it had been considered by the Canadian Parliament. See Borden, *Memoirs*, II, Chap. XXXVII.

Telegram from the Governor General to the Secretary of State for the Colonies

OTTAWA, 12th September, 1919.

Most urgent.

Following Order in Council approved to-day. Begins: —

At the GOVERNMENT HOUSE AT OTTAWA,

12th September, 1919.

PRESENT:

THE GOVERNOR GENERAL IN COUNCIL.

WHEREAS, at Versailles, on the twenty-eighth day of June, nineteen hundred and nineteen, a Treaty of Peace (including a protocol annexed thereto between the Allied and Associated Powers and Germany) was concluded and signed on behalf of His Majesty, for and in respect of the Dominion of Canada, by plenipotentiaries duly authorized for that purpose by His Majesty on the advice and recommendation of the Government of the Dominion of Canada.

AND WHEREAS the Senate and House of Commons of the Dominion of Canada have by resolution approved of the said Treaty of Peace;

AND WHEREAS it is expedient that the said Treaty of Peace be ratified by His Majesty for and in respect of the Dominion of Canada;

Now, therefore, the Governor General in Council, on the recommendation of the Secretary of State for External Affairs, is pleased to order and doth hereby order that His Majesty the King be humbly moved to approve, accept, confirm and ratify the said Treaty of Peace, for and in respect of the Dominion of Canada. Ends.

(Sgd.) DEVONSHIRE

3. The Imperial Conference of 1921 and Imperial Foreign Policy

The Imperial Conference of 1921 is notable (a) for its refusal to proceed with the plan for a conference to discuss changes in the constitution of the Commonwealth as proposed by Resolution IX of 1917 (above, **152**), and (b) as a landmark in the development of Dominion influence on imperial foreign policy and the concept — which proved to be short-lived — of a common foreign policy arrived at after consultation between the countries of the Commonwealth. There appears to be little doubt that in this conference the Prime Minister of Canada, Mr. Meighen, prevented the renewal in some form of the Anglo-Japanese Alliance. See Graham, *Meighen*, II; J. B. Brebner, "Canada, the Anglo-Japanese Alliance and the Washington Conference," *Political Science Quarterly*, March 1935; and (a much more recent and better-documented account), M. G. Fry, "The North Atlantic Triangle and the Abrogation of the Anglo-Japanese Alliance," *Journal of Modern History*, March 1967. There are many papers on this and other episodes of this period in Lovell C. Clark, ed., *Documents on Canadian External Relations*, III (Ottawa, 1970).

158. Extracts from Proceedings of the Conference

(*Summary of Proceedings and Documents*, British Parliamentary Papers, Cmd. 1474-1921)

The conclusion on foreign policy (not a formal resolution) was the closest an Imperial Conference ever came to firm approval for a unified foreign policy. The resolution on constitutional relations displeased Sir Robert Borden, then retired. It amounts to a declaration that the interests of the Commonwealth are adequately served by existing arrangements, and that no further definition of Commonwealth relationships is required.

. . .

III. FOREIGN POLICY

The Conference ... addressed itself to a detailed consideration of the Foreign Policy of the British Empire. ... The discussions, which covered the whole area of foreign policy, and extended over many days, proved most fruitful. ... They revealed a unanimous opinion as to the main lines to be followed by British policy, and a deep conviction that the whole weight of the Empire should be concentrated behind a united understanding and common action in foreign affairs. In this context, very careful consideration was given to the means of circulating information to the Dominion Governments and keeping them in continuous touch with the conduct of foreign relations by the British Government. . . .

XIV.   THE PROPOSED CONFERENCE ON CONSTITUTIONAL RELATIONS

Several plenary meetings and several meetings of the Prime Ministers were devoted to a consideration of the question of the proposed Conference on the Constitutional relations of the component parts of the Empire, and the following resolution was adopted: —

"The Prime Ministers of the United Kingdom and the Dominions, having carefully considered the recommendation of the Imperial War Conference of 1917 that a special Imperial Conference should be summoned as soon as possible after the War to consider the constitutional relations of the component parts of the Empire, have reached the following conclusions: —

"(a) Continuous consultation, to which the Prime Ministers attach no less importance than the Imperial War Conference of 1917, can only be secured by a substantial improvement in the communications between the component parts of the Empire. Having regard to the constitutional developments since 1917, no advantage is to be gained by holding a constitutional Conference.

"(b) The Prime Ministers of the United Kingdom and the Dominions and the Representatives of India should aim at meeting annually, or at such longer intervals as may prove feasible.

"(c) The existing practice of direct communication between the Prime Ministers of the United Kingdom and the Dominions, as well as the right of the latter to nominate Cabinet Ministers to represent them in consultation with the Prime Minister of the United Kingdom, are maintained."

159. Foreign Policy: Meighen's Three "Conclusions"

("Stenographic Notes of a Meeting of Representatives of the United Kingdom, the Dominions and India." 6th Meeting, 24 June 1921, King Papers, P.A.C.)

These propositions were advanced by Mr. Meighen as his contribution in a series of "general statements on foreign policy" made early in the Conference.

. . . The Dominions, while enjoying full control of their own affairs, inclusive, in many essential phases of their affairs with other countries, are nevertheless nations within the British Empire. While it is quite true that should Great Britain become embroiled in war every considerable country in the world would be affected, the British Dominions would obviously be affected more immediately and vitally than would countries without the Empire. Whatever course any Dominion might decide to take, its liability to attack would be unquestioned, and its whole existence might become at once in jeopardy. The degree of this special peril might vary with the character or location of Britain's enemy, but that it would always exist is beyond argument. Upon the soundness, therefore, of British Foreign Policy, upon the wisdom of the broad principles governing that policy, very important consequences, as respects the Dominions, depend.

Associated with the above consideration is the further fact that there exists no council or body responsible to the Dominions, or to any Dominion, which can advise our common Sovereign in relation to foreign affairs.

One other truth of paramount importance to Canada is that, incident to our very position on the map of the world, our distinctively Canadian relations with the United States, as respects all phases of mutual concern, are in their very nature so vast and so vital to us that the control of those relations has become and must remain a matter incident to our autonomy. The conduct of affairs as between the entire Empire and that Republic is also of far-reaching concern to Canada. . . .

Out of these postulates it might seem the following might be concluded: —

1. There should be regular, and so far as possible, continuous conferences between the responsible representatives of Britain and the self-governing Dominions and India with a view, among other things, of determining and clarifying the govern-

ing principles of our relations with foreign countries, and of seeking common counsel and advancing common interests thereupon.

2. That while in general final responsibility rests with the Ministry advising the King, such Ministry should, in formulating the principles upon which such advice is founded and in the application of those principles, have regard to the views of His Majesty's Privy Council in other Dominions and of the Representatives of India.

3. That as respects the determination of the Empire's foreign policy in spheres in which any Dominion is peculiarly concerned the view of that Dominion must be given a weight commensurate with the importance of the decision to that Dominion. Speaking for Canada, I make this observation with particular reference to our relations with the United States.

I may be permitted to say that, added to the above specific conclusions, there is another that it seems to me must be constantly brought forward. The British Empire is now, as it has been for centuries, a union of people under varying forms of connection, spread throughout the world. It has become, of more recent times, a Commonwealth of free nations living under widely diverse conditions. Clearly, any principles underlying the conduct of external relations of such a Commonwealth of Nations must be, more and more, of such simple and understandable character that they will be generally acceptable to the various and widely scattered peoples that comprise the Empire.

With particular reference to this last, and what I might describe as an overriding conclusion, a few further remarks may be ventured. The erection of a League of Nations was, in some degree, the outcome of a longing among the world's democracies for the bringing about of such diplomatic relations among the nations as would remove the complexities and perplexities of the system of balancing friendships and animosities which had prevailed. In so describing diplomatic proceedings it is needless to add that I do not do so by way of attributing special blame, or any blame, to Great Britain. A nation must define its course in the world as it is. But we have a League of Nations now. What effective part it is to play in the new order, or in bringing improvement to the past order, no one can foretell, and well-informed opinion is naturally divided. But, speaking my own mind and speaking for Canada, the overwhelming determination is that every energy should be devoted, and every caution and restraint exercised, to make possible the success of the League, to help and advance its cause. It seems to me logically to follow that we should now seek to avoid inviting the return of any conditions that would be regarded as anomalous to, or out of harmony with, the general scheme and purpose of the League of Nations, or that could fairly be considered as evidencing distrust in the effectiveness of its organisation. I do not carry the argument further at the present time, but only say that, to my mind, sub-alliances or groupings of Powers, under whatever name, are not easily reconcilable with confidence in, or even fidelity to, the fundamental purposes of the League. . . .

Coming to Conclusion 2, it will be noted that the statement of our present position, as regards the determination of such matters of foreign policy as affect the entire Empire, has reference to conditions as they actually exist. . . . Nor is it overstating the present position to say that the right of a Dominion in respect of important engagements to have its consent obtained before being bound, and in cases where the interest of a Dominion is paramount to have its voice accepted, has grown into an indefeasible constitutional recognition. Time and good sense and mutual trust will doubtless clarify the difficulties of the position and establish an effective working practice. But there has been and is no body authorised as such to advise His Majesty in relation to foreign affairs except the United Kingdom Government. I make no conjecture as to the durability of the conditions I have described; I merely say they do exist. While they exist, the importance of His Majesty's Government taking into account, and at times indeed depending upon, the special interest of the Dominion concerned, giving effect to the views of such Dominion, can scarcely be overstated. On the care and fidelity with which the views of the Dominions are regarded depend, it seems to me, in large degree not only the continuance of the relations I have described, but the success with which we discharge our mission as a Commonwealth of Nations. I add, and add with emphasis, my conviction that, whatever evolution of these relations time and circumstances may bring about, the unity of our peoples will remain undisturbed.

In commenting upon Conclusion 3. . . I desire to refer, by way of illustration, to the position of Canada as respects the United States. . . . The course of the United States' policy in every field affects Canada. Their numbers are many times the numbers of the Dominion in population; their decisions, their lines of policy, consequently affect us in profound degree. We live in constant and vital touch with this problem from day to day. The maintenance, and if it is by any means possible, the betterment, of relations between the British Empire and the United States of America should be, as the Foreign Secretary has well said "the pivot of Britain's world policy." To no country does this truth appeal with such tremendous force as it does to Canada.

The heart of the Dominion beats true to-day, as it has always done, to British institutions and to British connection. We believe that there is one thing of first importance to Britain and the other Dominions, and of not only first but vital importance to Canada, and therefore having wrapt within it, in a peculiar way, our future, and that is the continuance and improvement of our relations with the American people. . . .

160. The Anglo-Japanese Alliance

("Stenographic Notes of a Meeting of Representatives of the United Kingdom, the Dominions and India," King Papers, P.A.C.)

These are excerpts from the record of a very long discussion, which was given a completely new turn by the opinion of the Lord Chancellor (Lord Birkenhead) given on 30 June that the notice sent to the League of Nations concerning the Alliance had not constituted denunciation of it.

2ND MEETING, 21 JUNE 1921: OPENING SPEECH BY MR. W. M. HUGHES, PRIME MINISTER OF AUSTRALIA

. . . The world wants peace. Which policy is most likely to promote, to ensure, the world's peace? As I see it, the renewal of the Treaty with the Japanese Empire. . . . As it is vital in the interest of civilisation that a good understanding should exist between America and ourselves, we should endeavour to do everything in our power to ascertain exactly what it is to which America takes exception in this Treaty. We ought not to give her room for criticism which the world could support. We must make it perfectly clear that the Treaty is not aimed against her, and that it could never be used against her. War with America is unthinkable. . . .

8TH MEETING, 28 JUNE 1921: SPEECH BY LORD CURZON, FOREIGN SECRETARY

. . . When the Covenant of the League of Nations was passed, it was clear to us that if the Treaty were renewed in its present form it would be incompatible in many respects with the provisions laid down in the Covenant, and accordingly in July last year Japan and ourselves made an intimation to the League of Nations that in the event of renewal after July of this year it would have to be done — and we should be glad to do it — in a form compatible with the conditions laid down in the Covenant of the League. . . . The question of this agreement would be one of the main subjects that we would consider here, and as this meeting was not to take place until the present month of June, and it was clear that we should be running rather near to the date of expiration in July, it was obviously necessary to make some provision for the temporary prolongation of the Treaty. . . . It was eventually decided to suggest a prolongation of three months. That was agreed to, I think, by all the Dominions, but as a matter of fact, Japan has not agreed to it at this moment, and as things stand, within a fortnight from now that Treaty wholly disappears. . . . I think in the next day or two the extension of the Treaty for three months, that is to say until October 13th of the present year, will be agreed to. . . . The view of our lawyers is that, unless steps are taken to annul it [the notice given] in the course of a few days, the agreement automatically expires on the 13th July, 1921. . . .

. . . There is no doubt whatever that Japan warmly hopes that the agreement will be renewed in some form or other. . . . From the wider point of view I must confess myself that I should feel some anxiety at the position in which you had an Ally for something like twenty years, against whom you have to bring so little in the way of charge, as in the case of Japan, who on the whole has done you so well, who has been faithful to the Alliance, and is anxious that it should be renewed, and for the renewal of which such a good case can be made out, but where I had to be the minister who wiped it off the slate and said: "No, America is so important to us that we really cannot have anything more to do with you at all." I do not think that would be a very strong or a very defensible position to take up. . . .

. . . The Papers you have had circulated to you will have shown you that the Admiralty here are in favour of the renewal of the Agreement with Japan, not necessarily in the same form as now, but in a manner that will safeguard the suspicions of America. . . .

In conclusion, the Conference may ask me what are the alternatives before us. . . . Of course, we can cancel the Agreement altogether, although I have said that from some points of view there are formidable objections to this, and the Conference will have realised that it is not the course I would, personally, recommend.

Secondly, we can continue it: we might renew it in its present form, but with the modifications required to bring it into harmony with the Covenant of the League. . . . That I do not recommend. . . . The military clauses would excite very great suspicion and alarm in America, and we have gone beyond the stage at which renewal either in its present form or something like it is practicable.

The third alternative is one which was proposed in one of Sir Auckland Geddes's telegrams,* namely, to expand the present agreement into a tripartite agreement. In theory this has many attractions, but it seems to be doubtful whether the Senate would pass it, or if American public opinion is prepared for it. . . .

The fourth alternative is one which, I think, on the whole, the Foreign Office is rather disposed to recommend, always subject to what may be said here, namely, that the Agreement, if renewed, should be renewed in a different form, and after consultation with the United States on the one hand and with China on the other, and with the League of Nations; its renewal being accompanied by an expression of willingness on our part to join the United States Government in an examination by Conference between interested parties of the Pacific problem [as] suggested by Mr. Meighen. . . . I think the practical choice lies between the two — between a temporary renewal with a view to a large discussion and a more complete solution, or the renewal in a different form for a term of years, let us say four, capable of being either extended or dissolved at the end of that time. . . .

Mr. Hughes: Which alternative does the British Government prefer?

Lord Curzon: When we considered it here, the Cabinet was inclined to favour renewal for a term of years.

Mr. Churchill [Colonial Secretary]: The situation has been altered by the telegrams from the United States, which were not before us when we considered this. They have since arrived from Sir Auckland Geddes, who reported originally that it would do no harm in America if the renewal took place. . . .

Mr. Meighen: . . . Article VI provides for the running on of the Alliance unless the contracting parties should have notified twelve months before the expiration of the ten years an intention to terminate that Treaty. I am not able to understand how it can be read to bring about absolute termination next month.

Lord Curzon: It arose in this way. The letter, which was written by both parties in combination to the League of Nations in July of last year, is regarded by the competent lawyers as equivalent to an announcement of denunciation. . . .

Mr. Balfour [Lord President of the Council, United Kingdom]: I have to speak in a double capacity, for . . . it so happens that I am the Chairman of the Sub-Committee or the Standing Committee, I think it is called, of the Committee of Imperial Defence, which has been

*Sir Auckland Geddes was British Ambassador in Washington.

entrusted with the work of considering this very important problem. We were clear that, from a strategic point of view, there could be no doubt whatever that it is to the advantage of this country to renew the Alliance. . . .

. . . until Singapore is rendered the place which we think it ought to be made, a place of concentration, a place of refitting and refuelling, until this is done, we are at a relative disadvantage undoubtedly in the Pacific, and that is a very strong strategical reason, putting all wider considerations apart, why we should remain on the most friendly terms with Japan and why we should continue a policy we have hitherto pursued with such success, which is that of joint action with Japan in the Far East. . . .

9TH MEETING, 29 JUNE 1921: SPEECH BY MR. MEIGHEN

Prime Minister, we have now come to what is undoubtedly the most important subject of discussion at this Conference. . . .

Perhaps it will contribute to rapidity if I say at the outset that I feel compelled to oppose the renewal of the Alliance. I would regret to see the Treaty continued in any form at all. . . .

. . . The Treaty . . . had certain ends to serve from our point of view. It was framed admittedly to meet first of all a Russian menace, and secondly, on its renewal in 1911, a German menace. . . . As we find ourselves now, both those menaces are removed. . . .

Speaking generally as to Alliances, I am quite sure I am speaking the opinion of the Dominion of Canada when I say it naturally is averse to any Alliances at the present time. We do regard the formation of groups and Alliances, even though they are not counter to the Covenant of the League of Nations, as likely to subvert its purpose. . . .

I come now to the subject of British-American relations. Canada does not claim that in the general question of the renewal or the non-renewal of this Treaty her voice must be specially heard. Not at all. The Empire is concerned as an Empire, and so is every part. But as regards this aspect, its effect on British-American relations, we do feel that we have a special right to be heard. We say that because we know, or ought to know, the United States best, and because in the continuance and improvement of our relationship with them we have a vital concern. If from any cause, or from the initiation of any disastrous policy, we should become involved in worse relationships than we are now, Canada will suffer most of all. And if, in the last awful event — God forbid it should ever come! — we reach the penalty of war, Canada will be the Belgium. Consequently, in the preservation and improvement of that relationship we are eagerly, critically concerned. But we view this question not from the standpoint of the

United States, we view it from this standpoint, that if, as I believe, the Foreign Secretary is sincere when he says that British-American friendship is the pivot of our world policy, it follows that in determining the wisdom from our own point of view of any engagement a major consideration must be its probable effect on that friendship.

From the beginning of the discussion I know that the Foreign Secretary has stated that any renewal should be in a form satisfactory to the United States, and that we must carry that country with us in any course that we take. Well, I am going to say this. I do not believe that it is possible to have an agreement in any form at all, however negative, that will be really satisfactory to the United States. . . . that any agreement for an exclusive confidential relationship that this country enters into with Japan will not injure our relations with the United States is to my mind impossible, no matter what are its terms. It will be used by every fomentor of strife against Great Britain. The existing engagement has been so used all these years. It had a definite clause in 1911 that it should not involve us in war with the United States, but the very existence of that Treaty has undoubtedly injured British-American relations. Its continuance will do so even more, and for this reason, that the just objects, which were patent to American statesmen before, are not patent to American statesmen now. . . .

. . .When the old Treaties were made there were five, perhaps six, Great Powers — you might say more; now there are three Great Powers, powers of the first order and strength, and those are Japan, Great Britain and the United States. Does it stand to reason that two of these can group themselves together in a special relationship in a sphere in which all three have great interests and the third be unaffected, the third look with favour upon it? It does not appeal to my reason, I do not think it is possible. . . . I think . . . [Japanese statesmen] believe that, in the event of a conflict with the United States, they will have us benevolently by their side. Then it is, from their point of view, a contemplatable contest; otherwise it is not. They look undoubtedly for this country to assume a position of benevolent neutrality, if not better. . . . The American public understand these things. . . .

That country has behaved with scrupulous correctness, at least its Government has, up to now. I think the best people are looking to this Conference to take up a position that will enable them to bring about a better state of affairs. The passing of a recent resolution by the American Senate so indicates. . . . I do think we cannot ignore the passing of that remarkable resolution by their Senate on the very eve of this Conference. It is the resolution asking for a Conference with Japan and Great Britain looking to a reduction of armaments. . . .

If this renewal is intended to create a combination against an American menace which is to succeed the German menace, which in turn succeeded the Russian menace of 1902, then there can be no hope of ever carrying Canada into the plan.

The claim is sometimes made, sometimes left to be implied, that this Alliance with Japan is to be the pivot of a new world alignment. That only needs to be stated to excite despair in the minds of the people of our country. The future is dark if we have to start now on that path. I can only add that there is no possibility of convincing Canada or making any appeal to her at all with those words in our mouth — none at all. I am not saying that other reasons for renewal may not be adduced, but this implication of providing against a possible menace in America cannot carry conviction. We ourselves have got along with the United States for 100 years, and have overcome many difficulties, and we meet there a spirit which convinces us that we can still get along.

I addressed a cablegram to the Prime Minister of the United Kingdom in February last, outlining the position that we felt then this matter was in and the course it should take. I stated that the success of the Alliance, so far as China was concerned, had not been impressive, that the objects for which it was created and continued no longer existed, and that, on the other hand, the objections that had some force at the time of the conclusion of the three Treaties, had now far greater force. I took the stand that it would be wise to seek some other expedient rather than the renewing of the Alliance. I suggested at that time that it would be useful for us in Canada, in a purely informal way, to ascertain whether or not the United States would sit down with the British Empire and with the other Powers having special interests in the Pacific and Far East and seek to come to some understanding as to the preservation of those interests, and as to the principles which should actuate the policy of all. The four Powers mentioned were Japan, the United States, the British Empire and China.

As to the composition of the Conference we should of course be quite ready to hear discussion and suggestions as to who should be there, but those were the four proposed. My suggestion was not acceded to....

Mr. Balfour: There is one question I should like to ask Mr. Meighen. ... Have you any ground for thinking that America would like to be a third party to an agreement?

Mr. Meighen: I hoped to have that ground. That was the object of the communication I made to the Prime Minister, but in deference to his desire nothing whatever was done towards ascertaining the attitude of the United States. . . . [In terms of American public opinion] I think the prospect would be quite hopeful for some kind of participation on their part in a broad, inclusive arrangement that need not take the shape of a formal or rigid Treaty; but I cannot say definitely.

Mr. Hughes: Mr. Prime Minister . . . we are asked by Mr. Meighen to disregard the views expressed by the American Ambassador on a matter on which he is surely entitled to be heard, and to listen to what Mr. Meighen calls the "Voice of America." . . . But is the position as Mr. Meighen put it? I do not think it is. I listened, as well as I was able, to Mr. Meighen's argument. It is quite obvious that his views, as the views of all men, are coloured, like the dyer's hands, by what they work in. We all naturally reflect our environment. Mr. Meighen's most certainly reflect his. The policy he thinks right is one which the "Voice of America" would acclaim. But what we have to ask ourselves is this: Is this Empire of ours to have a policy of its own, dictated by due regard to its own interests, compatible with its declared ideals, of which it has no reason to be ashamed, and from which it has deviated as little as any nation, or is to have a policy dictated by some other Power? That is what we must decide. . . .

Well, what will happen if we do not make this Alliance with Japan? Does Mr. Meighen suggest for one moment that America will be more ready to discuss disarmament with us? Does he suggest that she will abandon that naval programme of hers? Does he suggest that our refusal to renew the Treaty that has existed now for nearly twenty years, that has never been responsible for a breach of the world's peace during the whole of that period, which, indeed, has done something to preserve it, and which excited little or no attention and no objection in America until the moment when she resolved to be a Great Naval Power, will ensure the cordial co-operation of America in a policy of disarmament? I do not believe so for one moment. . . .

. . . What does he offer us? Something we can grasp? What is the substantial alternative to the renewal of the Treaty? The answer is, that there is none. If Australia was asked whether she would prefer America or Japan as an Ally, her choice would be America. But that choice is not offered her. As against the substance she is offered the shadow. She calls to America saying "Here are we with a coast-line of 13,000 miles, with a great continent to defend, within three weeks of a thousand millions of Asiatics; will you come to us if we call?" But to the call of our young democracy in its remote isolation, there is no answer. Now let me speak plainly to Mr. Meighen on behalf of Australia. I, for one, will vote against any renewal of the Anglo-Japanese Alliance upon one condition and one only, and that is that America gives us that assurance of safety which our circumstances absolutely demand. . . . Mr. Meighen has not touched upon two facts which stand out; one, that America's real objection to this Treaty in any form is the fear of Japan; and the other, the hatred of Britain by certain sections in America. . . .

10TH MEETING, 29 JUNE 1921 (AFTERNOON)

Mr. Hughes: . . . Who will defend Australia? How is its safety to be assured? Mr. Meighen, perhaps, does not quite appreciate just how Australia stands in this respect, but when I tell him that we devoted to naval and military purposes, including our obligations arising out of the war 70 millions sterling, he will perhaps understand we cannot shoulder any greater burden. If he will look at his own budget and ours he will see what it means to have a great nation like America as his neighbour, under whose wing the Dominion of Canada can nestle in safety. . . .

I do not wish to prolong the debate. I must regard Mr. Meighen's presentation of the case as not the case for the Empire, but as the case for the United States of America. . . . I am for the renewal of this Treaty, and I am against delay. . . .

Mr. Massey [New Zealand]: . . . Mr. Hughes has put the point of view of Australia, and put it forcibly and well, and everything he has said applies to the other British countries south of the line just as much as to Australia itself. . . .

. . . My country will not look to any other country than Britain for protection so long as the British Empire exists. We are part of the British Empire and we look to the British Empire to protect us. We are not going to look to any other country, and we are not going to accept protection from any other country except the Government of the British Empire itself. . . .

11TH MEETING, 30 JUNE 1921

Mr. Massey: . . . I hope I have made my position clear. It is simply this. I think the Treaty should be renewed, but at the same time I think we should do everything we possibly can to promote a friendly understanding with the Government and people of the United States. . . .

Mr. Lloyd George: We have had a very remarkable discussion. . . .

. . . I think it would be even a more serious decision than that with which we are confronted, if we had to decide between an Alliance with Japan and friendship with America. I do not think that is necessary, and I will give my reasons later on, or rather emphasise certain suggestions which have been put forward. Friendship with America is fundamental. It is a dominant principle in all British policy, and it is inconceivable that we should embark upon any policy that would involve a breach with the United States of America. That, I think, is accepted as an axiom by all those who sit around this table. Let me put the effect of a non-renewal of this Treaty upon our relations with Japan. I do not accept the statement that a renewal would involve a quarrel with America, but I have absolutely no doubt that the refusal to renew would involve a breach with Japan. . . .

. . . Somebody comes and helps you in your business relations when in a very tight corner, when you could not have done without him, and then somebody else comes along who has quarrelled with somebody else, who is a still more powerful person, and you say: "Well, I am very sorry I have to cut you in future, because otherwise this very powerful gentleman will not take any notice of me and might scowl." I venture to say that there is not one of us sitting at this table who would behave like that. Why should we like the British Empire to do something that we should not dream of doing in our own personal relations with each other?

Now that is my view. We must not insult Japan. She stood by her compact to the very last letter. She has never been at a Peace Conference where she has not stood by us right through and through. In the war she stood by us and she stood by us in peace, and now to drop her is something, I think, which, so far from winning the friendship of America, would win the contempt of America.

Mr. Hughes: Hear, hear.

Mr. Lloyd George: That is my view. The American is not that type of man. If we were beginning from the start, I do not know what we should do, but two years after the war, when this gallant little people in the East backed us through thick and thin, now to drop them — we cannot do it. I think the British Empire must behave like a gentleman. That is one plea I put in for the renewal of the Treaty with Japan. . . .

. . . It has been suggested that we should renew the alliance for a year, in order to give time for that Conference. I do not believe that is necessary. . . . something was done last year which was [considered] tantamount to a denunciation. That has not been the Foreign Secretary's view, and it is not the view of Japan. This morning we decided to submit the question to the Lord Chancellor, who would confer with the Solicitor-General. . . .

The Lord Chancellor: The Cabinet asked me this morning to give my attention to this matter. . . .

. . . Prime Minister, I make no observations on the policy in the matter, but upon the technical matter on which you have asked my opinion for the purpose of this Conference I have no hesitation whatever in saying that we should adhere to the view that no denunciation has taken place....

Mr. Meighen: The situation is this, as I understand it. . . . the Treaty . . . does not expire on the 13th or until a year's notice of denunciation has been given. . . . I should certainly have reconsidered my remarks had I known it. I took pains to find out what the situation was. . . .

12TH MEETING, 1 JULY 1921

Mr. Meighen:...We find ourselves confronted with a new and material circumstance. . . . The position that Canada took was fairly completely disclosed in the correspondence of last February between myself and the Prime Minister of Great Britain. It was fully understood, I can well see, by the Foreign Secretary, and it was very fairly stated by him in his address before this Conference. I did, however, listen to a rather forceful attack, not on the position that Canada really took, but on a caricature of that position stated by the Prime Minister of Australia, and, I am afraid I must say, apparently acquiesced in by the Prime Minister of Great Britain. Judging from their speeches I am afraid I failed in the address I made here to improve upon the communications of February. I must indeed have destroyed the entire effect of those communications in my remarks. It has been assumed that we are called upon here to discuss an alternative which involved the waiving aside of Japan, the cutting of that nation, the refusal even to speak to her, and the giving of the hand of fellowship instead to the United States of America. . . . Indeed, it was assumed that we had urged upon the Conference a policy which would mean the taking of a course in international affairs, which, if the parallel were taken in private affairs, would be ungentlemanly....

. . . The description given of my argument was wrong in another respect. I was even charged with espousing the cause of the United States of America, and with having argued the whole matter from their standpoint, instead of from the standpoint of the British Empire. That charge has at least the element of novelty as applied to me. . . . I assumed that the necessity of friendship with America was, in fact, part of our world policy. It was so stated by the Foreign Secretary. I took his words to mean what they said. That being so, I sought to argue, and, to reinforce my argument, pointed out two things: first, the propinquity of Canada to the United States of America, and secondly, the resulting effect that Canada is able to understand their attitude. I gave my opinion that a renewal in any form under the conditions that presented themselves there would be unfavourable to those relations. I did not say that there would be a breach or quarrel — not at all. I did not even intimate that. I meant just what I said, that it would prejudice our relations, that it would not conduce to improvement. . . .

We are now at this point. The agreement, as just revealed, goes on, if nothing is done, indefinitely, subject to the right of either side to denounce on a year's notice. . . . I think we should agree that it should proceed for a year, and in that respect I would give my concurrence to the suggestion of the Foreign Secretary. . . : —

> "B." "Temporary renewal of the existing agreement (brought into harmony with the Covenant of the League of Nations, and with mention of India possibly omitted) for a space of, say, one year from October 1921, so as to provide for the holding of an International Pacific Conference in the interval.". . .

. . . I therefore would urge this, that the Foreign Secretary does, what I feel sure he is disposed to do, meet the representatives of Japan, China and of the United States, and being frank with them ask them to be just as frank with him. He should seek to find out precisely what each of them wants, what each of them expects. He should make known the position of this country, its friendship for Japan, its friendship for America, its friendship for China, and he should endeavour to get the assent of them all to what he described as the Pacific Conference. . . .

Mr. Lloyd George: Although I am not in agreement with Mr. Meighen's preliminary criticism . . . I feel sure the Conference will agree with the conclusion of Mr. Meighen that the Foreign Secretary should explore the grounds and by communicating with the representatives of America, Japan and China, find out exactly what the position is. There is only one part of Mr. Meighen's proposals which I think it would be difficult or impossible for us in that form to comply with. . . . In order to carry out the Foreign Secretary's proposals now on the present basis we should give notice to Japan that twelve months hence the agreement would come to an end. That would be very undesirable before we enter into a Conference. . . .

13TH MEETING, 1 JULY 1921 (AFTERNOON)

. . .

Mr. Meighen: I want to say a word or two so that my position be not misconstrued. I am very sorry the discussion proceeded at all past the first statement of the Foreign Secretary. . . . I do not want, by inference or specific statement, anything to go to Japan which intimates that this Treaty in its present form, or even after making it subordinate to the Covenant of the League of Nations, is the policy of this Empire. . . .

APPENDIX (B) (AGREEMENT BY THE MEETING)

1. The Secretary of State for Foreign Affairs will notify the Japanese Government that the position is changed and that the British Government are advised that no notification to denounce the Treaty has been given. Consequently, the Anglo-Japanese Treaty of the 13th July, 1911, remains in operation.

2. The British Government will inform the League of Nations that we are dealing with the whole Eastern and Pacific question in a larger spirit; that any new arrangement will be in harmony with the Covenant; and that in the meanwhile we are prepared to state that wherever the Covenant is in conflict with the Treaty the Covenant prevails.

3. The Secretary of State for Foreign Affairs will approach the representatives in London of the United States of America, China and Japan in order to find out whether, the Anglo-Japanese Alliance, as modified by paragraph (2), being still in existence, they will enter into a Conference on the matter.

4. The Secretary of State for Foreign Affairs will report to the present meeting later on.

5. The British Government will not notify its intention to denounce until a settlement has been arrived at by the new Conference or a new Treaty has been drawn up by common agreement to replace the present one. (Should the Conference fail, the existing agreement as adapted to meet the requirements of the Covenant of the League goes on.)

20TH MEETING, 8 JULY 1921

This meeting began with a protest by Mr. Hughes against the manner in which Lord Curzon had conducted his interviews with the foreign representatives, which, he suggested, was not in accord with the Conference's agreement.

. . .

Mr. Hughes: I have no objection to the [Pacific] Conference so long as it is agreed to renew the Alliance. . . .

Mr. Meighen: I think what has been done most faithfully carries out the instructions of the Conference. At the time, I protested and said I wanted somewhat different circumstances. I wanted a new and modified Treaty for a year and that was not accepted, the majority prevailed, and its instructions have been carried out faithfully.

Mr. Massey: That is to say that the Treaty stands?

Mr. Lloyd George: Yes, and on that basis Lord Curzon was to negotiate a Conference in the Pacific.

21ST MEETING, 11 JULY 1921

. . .

Mr. Lloyd George: . . . Now, this is the suggested statement which I am to make in the House of Commons: — *

". . . The broad lines of Imperial policy in the Pacific and the Far East were the very first subject to which we addressed ourselves at the meetings of the Imperial Cabinet, having a special regard to the Anglo-Japanese Agreement, the future of China and the bearing of both those questions on the relations of the British Empire with the United States. We were guided in our deliberations by three main considerations. In Japan we have an old and proved ally; the agreement of twenty years' standing between us has been of very great benefit, not only to ourselves and her, but to the peace of the Far East. In China there is a very numerous people with great potentialities who esteem our friendship highly, and whose interests we, on our side, desire to assist and advance. In the United States we see to-day, as we have always seen, the people closest to our own aims and ideals with whom it is for us not merely a desire and an interest, but a deeply-rooted instinct to consult and co-operate. Those were the main considerations in our meetings, and upon them we were unanimous. . . .

". . . All the representatives of the Empire agreed that our standpoint on these questions should be communicated with complete frankness to the United States, Japan and China with the object of securing an exchange of views which might lead to more formal discussion and conference. Lord Curzon accordingly held conversations last week. . . . He expressed at these conversations a very strong hope that this exchange of views might, if their Governments shared our desire in that respect, pave the way for a Conference on the problems of the Pacific and the Far East. The reply of the President of the United States was made public by the American Government this morning. It is known to the House. Mr. Harding has taken the momentous step of inviting the Powers to a Conference on the limitation of armaments to be held in Washington in the near future, and he also suggests a preliminary meeting on Pacific and Far Eastern questions between the Powers most directly interested in the peace

---

*This statement was made to the House later the same day, with only very minor verbal alterations. The phrase "Imperial Cabinet" used in this draft was changed in one case (but not in others) to "Imperial Conference." No objection had been made to it.

and welfare of that great region, which is assuming the first importance in international affairs. I need not say that we welcome with
the utmost pleasure President Harding's wise and courteous initiative. In saying this, I know that I speak for the Empire as a whole. . . ."

Mr. Lloyd George: Take the general draft of the statement. Is it the
line that the Conference would like taken?

Mr. Massey: Yes.

Mr. Hughes: Yes.

Mr. Meighen: Yes. It is very good.

Mr. Balfour: I think it is very good, I do not say that you could not
alter a word in it, but what document could you not alter a word in? . . .

161. Discussion on Constitutional Relations

("Stenographic Notes of a Meeting of Representatives of the United Kingdom,
the Dominions and India," King Papers, P.A.C.)

The discussion from which these extracts are taken arose from
Meighen's "Conclusions" (above, **159**) and from Resolution IX of
1917 (above, **152**).

22ND MEETING, 11 JULY 1921

. . .

Mr. Hughes: . . . But postulate 3 lays down "that where any
Dominion is peculiarly concerned in the Empire's foreign policy,
the view of that Dominion should be given weight commensurate
with the importance of the decision to that Dominion." And Mr.
Meighen adds that he makes this observation in regard to Canada's
relation to America. Now, if this postulate of Mr. Meighen's be
applied to all questions and to every Dominion, as he states quite
definitely it is intended, where is it going to lead us? With all
respect to Mr. Meighen, I cannot see how we can continue as a united
Empire if each one of the partners insists — as they logically may —
on exercising their autonomous rights to the extent here implied. . . .

Now these words, read along with Mr. Meighen's postulates and
general argument and his firm intention to appoint an Ambassador
at Washington, clearly indicate that in determining the foreign
policy between Britain or the Empire and the United States, Canada's
advice is to be followed. Or to put it in other words, Canada is to
determine the foreign policy of the Empire with the United States.
I do not think this would be good for the world. I am quite certain
it would not be good for the Empire. . . .

. . . I urge most strongly that we shall not lay down principles which must in effect cramp that perfect freedom which marks this Empire out from all other Empires, ancient or modern. . . . I do hope we shall attempt to do nothing that will fetter our right to discuss things on their merits; nor to reduce to writing that which will only have the effect in the end of making relations that exist between the different parts of the Empire impossible. . . .

. . . *General Smuts:* We are really discussing two different subjects, which, though related, are really different. One is the subject of the Dominions' share in foreign policy, which has been raised by Mr. Meighen, and that is really subsidiary to the other and larger question, the Constitutional Conference. . . .

. . . The Constitutional position in the Empire is . . . not a mere academic question, it is one of vital importance, and I think the time is coming, and has come, when we should do whatever we can to remove the obscurities which still cling to the situation. If we can do so by any constitutional declarations which could be made now or could be made hereafter at a Constitutional Conference, I think we should very materially assist the position in the Empire as a whole. As I say, in South Africa this separation movement has actually arisen; it has been beaten down at the recent elections, but it is by no means dead; we shall have to bear that in mind. It is also in agreement with the general trend of opinion all over the world. This movement in favour of greater national liberty and freedom is a world movement, and the British Empire will feel it too; and the more we can make it clear to the component parts of the Empire and to the world that ours is not a system of subordination . . . but that it is a system of equal States working together on principles of equality and freedom, the more we will, to my mind, stabilise the position in the British Empire and the greater power for good we shall be. . . .

Take the case now of what happened in the United States when the ratification of the Peace Treaty came forward, and objection was taken to the voting power of the Dominions in the Assembly of the League of Nations. It is quite clear that the constitutional position in the Empire was entirely misunderstood in the United States. . . . Not only from the point of view of internal public opinion in the Empire, but from the point of view of outside world opinion, I think we should clear up the situation. We can do so, I think, if half a dozen principles or declarations could be framed. . . .

Mr. Meighen: . . . I did not intend what I said to be in the nature of a resolution to which all must accede and to which a minority must submit; nor did I intend what I put forward to be regarded as of the rank of a Magna Charta or even of the Fourteen Points. . . .

Now as to the Constitutional Conference.... The fact is that in 1917 a resolution was passed calling for a special Constitutional Conference after the war.... I am not sure that if everything had been known that we know now the resolution would have been unanimous. I do not like the idea of advertising ahead that we contemplate constitutional changes. It has an unsettling effect in Canada, and it may also have in other countries.... My suggestion is this: We have to meet again. I do not see any reason for meeting arising from any necessity for constitutional changes at all. Such reasons alone are not sufficient. But I think for other reasons it will be necessary to meet again in a couple of years.... Let us if we can, determine on the name, time and place of our next meeting. I suggest that "Imperial Conference" be continued as the name. Let us decide then from a review of all the circumstances whether a change of constitutional relationships is necessitated by the experiences we shall have had. Do not let us lay anything down as agenda....

... My suggestion [with respect to co-ordinating Dominion views on foreign policy] is this, that we should have a Committee at work for the next two or three days, which would report to this meeting on that matter and we should appoint the Committee to-day. We should see if we can do something in order to make the determination of questions common to us all a real determination of us all instead of one.... *

23RD MEETING, 12 JULY 1921

Mr. Lloyd George: After the explanation Mr. Meighen gave us last night... I think he safeguarded the position of the Empire, and therefore, on that interpretation — speaking on behalf of my colleagues sitting on this side of the table — I certainly would not challenge Mr. Meighen's propositions....

Now, I should like to take another phase. There is no part of the Empire that would be as potent speaking separately as it is now when speaking as part of the British Empire.... The Dominion of Canada has the population of Roumania, Jugoslavia or Greece. It would always be a very powerful voice if it stood alone; but the influence which it would have actually exerted by itself in fashioning the world would not be comparable to that which it actually did exert as part of the British Empire Delegation. There the Dominions took part in determining the policy of the Empire, which very largely determined the peace. We consulted Roumania occasionally on Roumanian questions. We consulted Jugoslavia on Jugoslavian ques-

*This suggestion, though mentioned by Mr. Meighen again on the following day, was not acted on.

tions, and Greece on questions which affected Greece, but we never brought them into our Councils to determine what the world was going to be like for the next thousand years perhaps. But the British Empire Delegation—South Africa, Canada, Australia, New Zealand, India—they were there in our Councils. We took no line of action with regard to world policy without having constant consultations with them, and I shall never forget the great meeting when the German reply arrived, when we sat for two days to consider what answer the British Empire was going to give. It was the answer of the British Empire that prevailed; it prevailed against America; President Wilson was not in favour of some of the things which we did in the way of concession over Poland, more particularly over reparation and one or two other things. But standing alone the Dominions would not have been in that particular part of the picture; they would not have been in the very centre of things. Therefore each Dominion exercised an influence which was infinitely greater as being part of the British Empire than it would have exerted if it had stood absolutely alone. What applies to the Dominions applies equally to India and the United Kingdom. Therefore, standing together, we are each of us more powerful, and each has a greater say in the world's affairs than if each of us stood alone and pursued a policy of isolation. Therefore, I would lay down a principle, which I am sure would be accepted, that it is vital, if we are going to influence the world, that we should speak with one voice. . . .

Very well, I come now to my second proposition. It is essential we should speak with one voice, but that voice must not be the voice of Britain alone. If it is, it is not merely unfair to the rest of the Empire that we should determine policy, that we should write the cheque and expect the rest of the Empire to honour it with the blood of their sons. It is not only unfair, it is unreasonable. . . . Therefore, we must have some means of connecting and co-ordinating the voices of Empire, so that, having gathered these opinions, we can consolidate them, we can concentrate them, so that the voice as far as the outside world is concerned is one voice, but it is a voice of many chords, and what you want is to concentrate these, and how are you going to do it? . . . We have sent over to the Dominions all the essential and relevant material . . . and yet we have sought not to overburden you with material which is of no importance. . . . Most Cabinet Ministers who sit around this table confine their reading to the most vital papers that come along. Those papers are sent to the Dominions. When there is urgency, we send special cables informing the Dominions of the position of affairs. There was another suggestion which was made, I think it was at the 1917 Conference, that there should be a resident

Minister who could be summoned in cases of emergency or who could be kept informed as to what was going on here. I know the difficulty of appointing a Minister of that kind.... Still,... it has its value....

... I should very much like to have a discussion this morning upon the practical ways of arriving at conclusions on questions of Foreign Policy which will carry the whole Empire along with us in any decisions that we come to. The voice of the Empire must, of course, be communicated to the world through the British Foreign Office. I do not see any other way of doing it without breaking up the Empire, no other way of doing it, and I think it would be accepted. If we each of us indicate our separate views, the Empire as a whole will not carry the same weight. As a matter of fact, there will simply be a series of intrigues with foreign Powers. They naturally will not attach the same importance to the unity of the British Empire as we do.... I sincerely hope before we part this Conference will be able to devise some means by which the opinions of Empire can be gathered and concentrated, and be able to speak with that one voice which, spoken in 1914 without any discord, without any doubt, without any hesitation, rang throughout the world and saved it. I invite a discussion upon ways and means.

Mr. Meighen: ... I suggested a committee.... My idea was that an Imperial Conference be held two years from now, that we do not denominate it specifically a "Constitutional Conference," that we inaugurate a series of annual Conferences, or semi-annual as we may agree, at least two years from now — I do not see how you could commence earlier at the present time — that we give them all the same name, and that at the first one to be held two years from now, we give special consideration to any necessary Constitutional readjustments. In a word, that we thus execute the charge imposed upon us by the Resolution of 1917.

Now, as to the improvement of our communications, that is to say, our communications regarding foreign affairs, as to meeting the desire of the Prime Minister to enable the Empire to speak, as it must meanwhile speak, through His Majesty's Privy Council here with one voice, I was only going to say this. The right of each Dominion to have a resident representative to sit with the British Government while it is engaged in the consideration of matters that are of vital concern, was affirmed by resolution and accepted in 1918, but only for the period and for the purpose of the war. It was exercised, but not very fully or generally. I think it would be well to have that right reaffirmed, even though it may be exercised no more fully and no more generally than before, until we meet again, say, in two years' time.... Its existence, I believe, has had a good effect.... These things can be examined in detail in a committee better than here. I think that we are all anxious that some means should be found, with the least possible change and readjustment, that will enable all portions of the Empire to feel that grave steps taken and grave lines of policy followed have been taken and followed after the due deliberation and concurrence of all. Unless that is done, there is danger of the disintegration which the Prime Minister is so anxious to avoid.... I have no reason to complain myself of the fairness and care with which we have been kept informed; perhaps we get our cables more promptly than they get them in Australia or New Zealand....

Mr. Hughes: ... I am most strongly against a Constitutional Conference. There is no need for one. On the other hand, there is great danger....

Lord Curzon: ... The suggestion I made to the Prime Minister was this: That we might send out to you, to the Prime Ministers of the Dominions, once a month, or, if necessary, once a week, a selection of these extremely confidential Foreign Office papers which are now seen only by the Cabinet and circulated to our representatives in our Embassies and Legations abroad. What I would propose amounts to this: to put you on the same footing as our Embassies abroad....

Mr. Hughes: You are speaking of sending it by post.

Lord Curzon: Yes; and a great crisis leading up to war does not develop in a week or two....

24TH MEETING, 12 JULY 1921 (AFTERNOON)

Mr. Massey: ... Mr. Hughes expressed an opinion with which I agree. He referred to the resolution which we dealt with in 1917 with regard to a Constitutional Conference.... I agree with Mr. Hughes in thinking that it was a mistake at the time and that we had better drop it. I do not think a Constitutional Conference is necessary. I am not afraid of it in the very slightest, but I do not think it is at all necessary. There is no question that it stirs up a lot of discussion which certainly does not do any good....

162. Sir Robert Borden's Report on the Washington Conference of 1921-1922

(Canada, Sessional Papers, No. 47, 1922)

The Washington Conference temporarily relieved dangerous tensions in the Pacific and averted unlimited competition in naval armaments. For the British Empire, "Good political relations with the United States were substituted for the special tie with Japan" (Gwendolen M. Carter, *The British Commonwealth and International Security*, Toronto, 1947, p. 64). The United States did not choose to send separate invitations to the Conference to the Dominions; but, as at Versailles, they were represented on a British Empire delegation, while at the same time signing treaties separately in their own right. The chief achievements were a five-power treaty for the limitation of naval armament; a nine-power treaty for the protection of China, "to stabilize conditions in the Far East"; and a four-power treaty, negotiated outside the conference, "for the preservation of the general peace and the maintenance of their rights in the region of the Pacific Ocean." In each of these cases the British Empire was a signatory power, and the Canadian representative, the Ex-Prime Minister Sir Robert Borden, signed for Canada.

OTTAWA, March 15, 1922.

SIR,—I have the honour to submit the following report on the proceedings of the Conference on the Limitation of Armament, held at Washington from November 12, 1921, to February 6, 1922, which I attended as the Delegate for Canada. . . .

THE QUADRUPLE PACIFIC TREATY

Not discussed by Conference

12. Before dealing with the work of the Conference proper it will be convenient to take up a matter that was not included in the agenda and was not strictly speaking discussed by the Conference; although the result in its intimate and inseparable relation to the fundamental aims and the conclusions of the Conference itself is of the greatest significance. I allude to the Quadruple Pacific Treaty.

Anglo-Japanese Alliance

13. Before the Conference began it was recognized that disturbing questions were arising in the Pacific which might profoundly influence the future of international relations. Equally it was realized that the imminence of these questions must seriously impair the success of any proposal for the limitation of armaments unless distrust and apprehension could be removed by clearer understanding through peaceful co-operation. Among the factors that had to be taken into account was the Anglo-Japanese Alliance, which had brought into intimate relation and co-operation two great nations of the East and of the West. This Alliance was not aggressive in its purpose but rather had been intended to restrain aggressive purposes of the Gov-

ernments of Germany and Russia as formerly constituted. For the time being those Powers had ceased to exercise an important influence upon the situation. On the other hand the United States had developed a great and increasing interest, both moral and material, in all that concerned the future of the Pacific regions. In summoning the Conference the Government of that country had made apparent its desire to join whole-heartedly in international co-operation to assure the peace and welfare of those regions. . . .

14. Both parties to the Alliance had recognized that its provisions might be inconsistent with the letter and spirit of the Covenant of the League of Nations to which both were committed, and steps to cure any such inconsistency were already in the course of being taken. In the new conditions that arose after the recent war there were grave doubts as to the wisdom or expediency of military alliances of the conventional cast; many felt that such groupings might tend to inspire competitive groupings and so defeat their own avowed object of preserving the peace. For the Pacific and Far East, as for other regions, it was evident that international co-operation was more to be desired than international competition.

Negotiation of Quadruple Pacific Treaty

15. France as a great naval power possessing large interests in the Pacific region had the right to be consulted in reference to so important a question. The subject in all its aspects was discussed in the British Empire Delegation during the early weeks of the Conference. Informal conversations took place between the Heads of the four Delegations concerned. Strictly speaking these conversations were not directly concerned with the work of the Conference, although they necessarily exercised an important influence upon its results. In the end a full understanding was reached; and at the Plenary Session of December 10, 1921, it was announced by Senator Lodge of the American Delegation that the terms of a Treaty had been agreed upon between the United States of America, the British Empire, France, and Japan, "with a view to the preservation of the general peace and the maintenance of their rights in relation to their insular possessions and insular dominions in the region of the Pacific Ocean." The Treaty was signed on December 13, 1921, at the office of the Secretary of State of the United States. . . .

Effect of the Treaty

16. The Treaty is simple in structure, and the intent and effect are as plain as the instrument is simple. The Parties, it will be observed, are those chief naval powers that have island possessions in the

Pacific Ocean. Each agrees to respect the rights of the others in relation to these possessions. Should there develop in the future
between any of the Parties a controversy, arising from a Pacific question and involving these rights, that is not settled by diplomacy and
seems likely to affect their existing harmonious accord, there shall be
a joint conference of all the Parties to consider and adjust the whole
question (Article I). Or if the rights so described are threatened by
the aggressive action of any other Power, the Parties agree to consult
together fully and frankly in order to reach an understanding respecting the situation. (Article II.) The Treaty in any case is to exist for ten
years, and thereafter it is to continue in force unless any of the Parties
shall have denounced it, though in this case twelve months' notice is
necessary (Article III). Upon its ratification the Anglo-Japanese Alliance comes to an end (Article IV). Thus the Treaty does not constitute
what is known as an alliance; it imposes no military or warlike
obligations. Beyond the obligation to respect each other's rights, an
obligation which in any event is implicit in membership of the family of civilized nations, there is simply the obligation to confer when
international relations in these regions become strained or threatening; in short the Powers will not resort to war without first
endeavouring to settle their difficulties by peaceably meeting
together. The principle and device here employed are no more nor
less than what has been embodied in a very large number of conciliation and arbitration treaties of recent years, with the added advantage of a broader basis of adherence. The design and effect are to
enlist the conference method of diplomacy as a means of settling
international disputes; to give public opinion in the countries concerned and throughout the world time within which to face the
issues and consequences and so to make known its reasoned attitude; to promote international co-operation rather than to risk international rivalry in this portion of the world; and, finally, in the face of
threatened aggressive action by any other Power, to take counsel
with each other as to the particular situation. . . .

DOMINION REPRESENTATION IN THE BRITISH
EMPIRE DELEGATION

Canadian appointment
105. I ought not to conclude without some account of the general
features of Dominion representation at the Conference and of the
system and methods of the British Empire Delegation. The nature of
my appointment by the Canadian Government as the representative
of Canada may be seen from the terms of the Minute of Council

passed, of which a certified copy was handed to me before my departure for Washington. .... The Minute recites "that as the result of telegraphic communication with the Prime Minister of the United Kingdom it has been arranged that a representative of Canada should be appointed as a member of the Delegation which will represent the British Empire at the Conference on the Limitation of Armament.". ...

Form of treaties

107. The style of the treaties concluded at Washington is also of interest. .... In their formal aspects — their preamble, their preliminary statement of purpose, their recital of the names of the plenipotentiaries, and finally their signature — they were drafted according to the scheme of the Treaty of Versailles and the other treaties concluded at Paris. It is "the British Empire" in each case that is recited as one of the Powers that have resolved to conclude the treaty, and that have to that end appointed plenipotentiaries. As the appointment under our constitution proceeds from the King, the usual formal description of His Majesty, which embraces the whole British Empire, follows. Since, however, the assent of their Governments is necessary to commit the Dominions, the names of the plenipotentiaries, appointed on their advice respectively and holding Full-Powers as shown above, are set out; and they are preceded in each case by the name of the Dominion as a distinguishing heading. Finally the treaties are signed on behalf of their respective Dominions by the plenipotentaries so named. A similar formal procedure is followed for the case of India.

Ratification

108. According to custom the treaties are signed subject to ratification; but of course the method of ratification is determined for each Power by its own constitutional practice. The constitutional convention of the British Empire, under which the final act of ratification by the King of a treaty signed on behalf of a Dominion must be based on the assent of that Dominion, was fixed by the practice of recent years worked out between the members of the Empire themselves. As that practice is entirely within the control and determination of the nations of the Empire, the Washington treaties do not affect it. In like case is the question whether the treaties shall be submitted to Parliament for approval before ratification is recommended, although in this respect the practice is determined by each part of the Empire for itself; for example, it appears from the Speech of His Excellency at the opening of the present Session that with respect to the Washington Treaties the Government consider that the "approval of Parliament ought to precede their ratification on behalf of Canada.". ...

British Empire Delegation

110. These formal arrangements illustrated a recognized convention based upon a definite principle. In order to commit the British Empire Delegation as a whole to any agreement reached at the Conference, the signature of each Dominion Delegate was necessary in addition to that of the others, and any Dominion Delegate could, if convinced or instructed that his duty lay that way, reserve assent on behalf of his Government. On the other hand, in the internal economy of the body known as the British Empire Delegation the design and effect were to reconcile the principle of diplomatic unity in the Empire's international relations with the principle of co-ordinate autonomy for each self-governing nation. All the British Empire Delegates took part in the meetings of the two main Committees of the Conference, and in the Plenary Sessions; while in the Sub-Committees, whose personnel was always limited to one from each Power, a Dominion Delegate was frequently designated to represent the British Empire. Frequent meetings of the seven British Empire Delegates were held to exchange views, to discuss the Conference problems as they arose, and to reach conclusions; their technical advisers were present to furnish information and advice according to the subject at hand; while the Secretariat, including the Secretaries for the Dominions and India, also attended to assist the meeting, to record the results, and to ensure that any appropriate action should be taken afterward. The agenda of each meeting, with relevant memoranda, drafts and other necessary papers, were circulated to each Delegate in advance by the Secretariat. In the ordinary course the Chairman was Mr. Balfour; in his occasional absence the other Delegates took the Chair in rotation. These arrangements were a reproduction of the practice followed by the British Empire Delegation at Paris.

Secretariat of British Empire Delegation

111. The British Empire Delegation was served, as already indicated, by a single joint Secretariat, which included a Secretary for each Dominion and for India appointed by their respective Governments. In addition to organization and arrangements for meetings of the British Empire Delegation, the duties of this Secretariat comprised assistance to the Delegation at Conference meetings, correspondence with the Secretary General of the Conference, and, within the Delegation, the issuance of notices of Conference meetings, the summoning of experts thereto, the circulation of Conference and other documents, attendance at Delegation meetings, and many related duties of this character. The Secretary General to the British

Empire Delegation, responsible for overseeing these arrangements, was Sir Maurice Hankey (Secretary to the Cabinet of the Government of Great Britain). To those who have had close contact with these matters it is well known how greatly his unique abilities have contributed to carry out effectively the present day principle of co-operation between the Governments of the Empire, which, employed so successfully in the Imperial War Cabinets and in the British Empire Delegation at Paris, has now served equally well at Washington. It is of interest to note that on the recall of Sir Maurice Hankey to urgent duties in Great Britain shortly before the end of the Conference, Mr. Loring C. Christie, who had been acting as Secretary for Canada, was appointed Secretary General to the Delegation. In both capacities Mr. Christie discharged his duties most efficiently and acceptably. I am indebted to him for most valuable assistance in the preparation of this report.

Effect of Delegation arrangements

112. Under these various arrangements the entire Delegation kept under constant review the questions confronting the Conference and at every stage became aware of developments occurring, not only in the formal meetings of the Conference and of its Committees and Sub-Committees, but also in the course of the many informal conversations between members of Delegations. The Delegation meetings afforded the means for harmonizing the various points of view. They insured that the particular interest of any part of the Empire should be considered by the Conference. For example, the special interests of Canada, Australia and New Zealand were thus taken into account in reaching the formula in the Naval Treaty for preserving the *status quo* in respect of the fortifications of the Pacific islands (see paragraph 39 above); while the special position of India in relation to the Chinese customs tariff on goods entering by land frontiers (see paragraph 78 above) was similarly treated. Again there was the category of questions of high policy, so called; questions that by common understanding are felt by the nations to raise directly the fundamental issues of peace or the reverse; questions therefore of general concern to the whole Empire rather than of particular interest to any part; questions such as those involved in the Quadruple Pacific Treaty, in the equilibrium of power defined in the Naval Treaty, or in matters affecting the future position of the Powers in the Far East. Here too the Delegates were enabled by the meetings of the Delegation to exchange views and to reach in advance conclusions that could be put forward on behalf of the whole Empire. Throughout the Conference each Delegate was in touch with his own Government by

means of the telegraphs or the posts. Thus no Dominion could be committed without its consent, and each was enabled to state its view and exert its influence in advance of the formulation of agreement with other Powers. It should be added that in many instances the influence of the Dominions contributed very materially to the conclusions finally reached.

113. I have attempted this description and analysis of the organization of the British Empire Delegation and of its relation to the work of the Conference because this aspect is perhaps of special interest to Canada, and full information thereon is desirable. Doubtless the scheme will be susceptible of improvement as time goes on, but speaking broadly I believe the experience of this Conference has again justified it as a means whereby under our present constitutional system the Empire can effectively act at international gatherings. The formal aspects of the Treaties and of our appearance at the Conference recognize both the principle of unity and that of co-ordinate autonomy; but neither could be real without effective means whereby in advance of action the views of all would be fully and frankly exchanged and considered in common. The organization of the British Empire Delegation provided that means. Given such means and given good will, the experience of this Conference has again shown that agreement and unity may be expected to follow under no compulsion other than that imposed by the common purpose of free and equal peoples to maintain a single allegiance and to recognize their international responsibilities. Throughout the Conference, a cordial and unvarying spirit of co-operation marked the action of the British Empire Delegation; I refer not only to the relations between the principal Delegates, but also to the work of all those who in whatever capacity, whether from Great Britain or the Dominions or India, assisted in the task.

Invitation to the Conference

114. There has been some public discussion of the position of the Dominions at Washington; it has been perhaps somewhat lacking in a precise definition of the point at issue; but I understand the suggestion to be that there has been some derogation from the status of the Dominions. So far as this alludes to the method of appointment of the Dominion Delegates and their standing in the British Empire Delegation, the issuance of Full Powers, the form of the Treaties, their signature, and so on, it has been seen that the practice at Washington followed that of the Paris Peace Conference, which is the most recent outstanding precedent. The point I believe has really to do with the form of the invitation. For the Washington Conference

the invitations were issued by the United States, and so far as the Empire is concerned it was the Government of Great Britain that was formally addressed. . . . Shortly before the Conference met the suggestion became prominent that an invitation should have been addressed direct to each Dominion Government. Whether in the circumstances the suggestion was timely, whether the idea itself is expedient, what the difficulties might have been in carrying it out, it is no part of my duty to inquire; the point is one of public policy for the Government itself to consider. For the sake of clarification it may be observed however that, so far as the immediate practical aspect is concerned, the forms and practice followed at Washington were not affected by the form of the invitation; they developed independently of it, and it seems clear that in any such case they would so develop in the natural course, since it is for the British Empire to determine for itself the manner in which it will enter into obligations with other Powers. While practically the question did not affect the right of the Dominions to participate in the discussions and to signify for themselves their assent to agreements or their dissent, it does seem to involve considerations as to their status and prestige in international affairs. In that aspect it is not without importance, and it will doubtless present itself to the Governments of the Empire in the future. Whether the solution lies in the direction of separate direct invitations, or of some other alteration, notified to the other Powers, in the present methods of communication, it should leave the Powers under no misapprehension as to constitutional relationships within this Commonwealth of Nations. . . .

4. The Chanak Incident, 1922

This famous affair reflects the transition from the Borden idea of a united Commonwealth foreign policy, based on consultation, to the Mackenzie King practice under which in normal circumstances each Commonwealth country pursued independent external policies. King was told long afterwards that the decision on the night of 15 September to ask the Dominions for support against the Turks at Chanak was influenced by the fact that the British ministers chiefly concerned had been dining too well! A statement subsequently made by Winston Churchill indicates that the decision to approach the Dominions was made by the Cabinet, but that the "manifesto" concerning this and other decisions given to the press on 16 September was drafted by himself and approved by the Prime Minister (Mr. Lloyd George) after consulting "such of his colleagues as were accessible" (*Times Weekly Edition*, London, 16 November 1922). British domestic politics played a part; Stanley Baldwin — who helped to break up the Lloyd George coalition a few weeks after the incident — is reported to have said in 1923 that Lloyd George, Churchill and Lord Birkenhead had been determined to have a war with Turkey for election purposes, and Lord Beaverbrook was certain of this. However this may be, there seems to have been no effective consultation before the approach to the Dominions, and the British government wasted on a minor affair the sort of appeal that would have been more in order in a world crisis. See Lord Beaverbrook, *The Decline and Fall of Lloyd George* (London, 1963); Ramsay Cook, ed., "J. W. Dafoe at the Imperial Conference, 1923", *Canadian Historical Review*, March 1960; A. J. P. Taylor, *British History, 1914-1945* (Oxford, 1965); G. P. deT. Glazebrook, *A History of Canadian External Relations* (rev. ed., 2 vols., Toronto, 1966), Chap. 16; and David Walder, *The Chanak Affair* (London, 1969). See also the documents in *Documents on Canadian External Relations*, III.

163. The British Request, 15 September 1922

(King Papers, M.G. 26, J.1, P.A.C.)

(Cipher telegram from the Secretary of State for the Colonies to the Governor General)

SECRET

Following from Prime Minister for your Prime Minister, begins:

Cabinet to-day decided to resist Turkish aggression upon Europe and to make exertions to prevent Allies being driven out of Constantinople by Mustafa Kemal and in particular and above all to maintain freedom of Straits by securing firmly the Gallipoli Peninsula (?). The French Government have notified us that they are in agreement with us in informing Mustafa Kemal that he must not violate neutral zone by which Straits and Constantinople are protected and have so instructed their High Commissioner at Constantinople, and the Italians are also in general accord with us. We are addressing ourselves to Roumania, Serbia and Greece with a view to securing their military participation in defence of deep water line between Europe and Asia. We are notifying all the Powers aforesaid of our intention to make exertions and that we are placing a British division under orders to reinforce Sir Charles Harington, the Allied Commander-in-Chief at Constantinople. The British Navy will co-operate to the fullest extent necessary. These arrangements are intended to cover period which must elapse before a stable peace with Turkey can be secured. For this purpose a conference is being proposed, probably at Venice, possibly at Paris, and it is essential that we should be strong enough to maintain our position at Constantinople and round the Straits until this peace has been achieved. We do not think it likely that forces of Mustafa Kemal will attack if a firm front is shown by a large number of Powers acting together. His armies are estimated between sixty and seventy thousand men who have so far not had any serious resistance to encounter from the disheartened Greeks. But it is imperative we should take timely precautions. A defeat or a humiliating exodus of the Allies from Constantinople might produce very grave consequences in India and among other Mohammedan populations for which we are responsible. I should be glad to know whether Dominion Government wish to associate themselves with the action we are taking and whether they would desire to be represented by a contingent. Apart altogether from the vital Imperial and world wide interests involved in freedom of Straits for which such immense sacrifices were made in the war, we cannot forget that Gallipoli Peninsula contains over twenty thousand British and Anzac graves and that these should fall into the ruthless hands of Kemalists would be an abiding source of grief to the Empire. The announcement that all or any of the Dominions were prepared to send contingents even of moderate size would undoubtedly in itself exercise a most favourable influence on situation and might conceivably be a potent factor in preventing actual hostilities. This telegram has also been sent to the Governors-General of Commonwealth of Australia, New Zealand and Union of South Africa. Ends.

(Sd.) CHURCHILL

164. Mackenzie King Makes a Private Comment, 17 September 1922

(King Diary, quoted in Dawson, *Mackenzie King*, I)

The fact that the British ministers issued their press release so soon after the message was sent to Ottawa, plus Ottawa's slowness in deciphering the official message and informing the Prime Minister, who was away from the capital, resulted in King's hearing of the press statement before he got the message. The text of the published "manifesto" was apparently not published in Canada. It is in Winston S. Churchill, *The Aftermath* (ed. New York, 1929), pp. 452-4.

I confess it [the official message] annoyed me. It is drafted design-edly to play the imperial game, to test out centralization vs. autonomy as regards European wars. . . . I have thought out my plans. . . . No contingent will go without parliament being sum-moned in first instance. . . . I shall not commit myself one way or the other, but keep the responsibility for prlt. — the executive regarding itself as the committee of prlt. — I do not believe prlt. would sanction the sending of a contingent. The French Canadians will be opposed. I believe most if not all our members in Ont. & the maritime provinces will be opposed. I am not so sure of B.C. — I feel confident the Progressives will be opposed almost to a man. It is the time now to bring them into the Government . . . to strengthen us in our attitude of refusing to send a contingent without sanction of prlt., . . . New Zealand has offered a contingent — naturally she looks to the Br. Navy for everything. Australia will probably follow her example. I doubt if S. Africa will. I feel sure she won't. I am sure the people of Canada are against participation in this european war.

165. The Canadian Reply, 18 September 1922

(King Papers, M.G. 26, J.1, P.A.C.)

On 17 September, before this formal reply was sent, Mackenzie King had cabled Lloyd George commenting on the embarrassing situation created by the premature press release and inquiring whether the British message could be published.

(Cipher telegram from the Governor General to the Secretary of State for the Colonies)

Following from Prime Minister for your Prime Minister, begins:

The Cabinet has had under consideration the representations con-tained in your telegram of the fifteenth instant. It is the view of the Government that public opinion in Canada would demand authori-zation on the part of Parliament as a necessary preliminary to the despatch of a contingent to participate in the conflict of the Near East.

We will welcome the fullest possible information in order to decide upon the advisability of summoning Parliament.

166. Press Reports in Canada

(*Globe*, Toronto, 19 September 1922)

The *Globe* of Monday, 18 September, announcing the developments under the headline, "British Lion Calls Cubs to Face the Beast of Asia," stated that the emergency had burst upon Canada like "a bolt from the blue," without "the slightest warning." Numerous offers of service were reported. This dispatch was published the next day.

OTTAWA, Sept. 18.—At 11.30 tonight, after the night sitting of the Cabinet, the Prime Minister announced that the Dominion Government had received a reply from Premier Lloyd George to the effect that the former was not at liberty to make public the text of the British invitation, but that the substance of it might be given out. It is as follows:

"This official message is a statement of the action taken by the British Cabinet on September 15, and it asks whether the Dominion Government wishes to associate itself with the action the Imperial Government is taking, whether Canada would desire to be represented by a contingent."

Canada's reply to this message, which was drafted at tonight's Cabinet meeting and cabled immediately to London, is as follows:

"It is the view of the Dominion Government that public opinion in Canada would demand the authorization of Parliament as the necessary preliminary to the dispatching of a contingent to participate in the conflict in the Near East. We would welcome the fullest information possible, in order to decide upon the advisability of summoning Parliament."

"Such information as we have", the Prime Minister stated to the Press tonight, "is of a wholly reassuring character." Much of this has been received this evening from Hon. W. S. Fielding and Hon. Ernest Lapointe, Canada's representatives at Geneva.

The feeling of the Government, it is understood, is that the situation in the Near East does not now, and is not likely to, call for any military participation by Canada. However, if an unforeseen and large emergency should arise, the people of Canada, through their Parliament, which would be specially summoned, will have the fullest opportunity to express their desire.

167. Arthur Meighen's "Ready, Aye Ready" Speech, 22 September 1922

(*Mail and Empire*, Toronto, 23 September 1922)

Meighen made this speech, called by his biographer "the most famous utterance of his entire career," to the Conservative Business Men's Association of Toronto. It drew great applause from the audience that heard it, but was long to be used against Meighen by his opponents, particularly in French Canada. Less complete reports appeared in the Montreal *Gazette* and the Toronto *Globe*. See Graham, *Meighen*, II, and R. MacG. Dawson, *The Development of Dominion Status: 1900-1936* (Toronto, 1937).

. . . Britain is not prepared to surrender that prize of victory, because she wishes to secure that the future may belong to peace and not to war. She sends a message to the Dominions, not a mere indifferent inquiry as to what was the mind of Canada, but a message to see if the Dominions were solid behind the Motherland. The exact wording of the message we do not know, but judging from the evidence that was its purport. From Australia and New Zealand the British Government got messages of co-operation in defence of the Treaty of Sevres. Those messages have been met with an expression of gratitude from the Government, which, it is reported, intends to abide by her [*sic*] position. We were a party to the Treaty of Sevres and the trials and sacrifices that made it possible. There is no suggestion at all that we should send armed forces across the sea. Britain merely sought a declaration of solidarity on the part of the Dominions (Applause) — the existence of which the war has demonstrated once and for all. Let there be no dispute as to where I stand. When Britain's message came then Canada should have said: "Ready, aye ready; we stand by you." (Loud cheers.) I hope the time has not gone by when that declaration can yet be made. If that declaration is made, then I will be at the back of the Government. (Cheering.) By that course we do not bring the country nearer war. We take the best step in our power to ensure that war shall not come. (Applause.) . . .

5. The Halibut Treaty, 1923

There had been numerous cases before 1923 in which treaties were negotiated entirely by Canadian ministers and subsequently signed on behalf of the Crown by one or more such ministers in association with the British Ambassador accredited to the country concerned; but the Halibut Treaty made with the United States in that year is notable as the first occasion when a Canadian representative signed a treaty with a foreign state without a British representative participating. The affair was handled by the King government in an unnecessarily high-handed manner; the British government was told of the Canadian intention only two days before the signing, although the British Ambassador in Washington, Sir Auckland Geddes, had been informed a week earlier. Mackenzie King's biographer comments that King "evidently wished to postpone raising the issue so as to give the British Government very little time in which to combat the Canadian proposal if the treaty was to be signed on the appointed day" (Dawson, *Mackenzie King*, I, 434). Subsequently the United States Senate attempted to insert the provision that "none of the nationals, inhabitants, vessels or boats of any other part of Great Britain" [*sic*] should engage in the halibut fishery contrary to the convention. When Canada refused to accept the amendment it was withdrawn.

It was pointed out during the discussion of the treaty in the Canadian House of Commons that legislation to be passed by Canada and the United States for carrying it into effect would prevent nationals of any other country from obtaining the fishing bases in Canadian or U.S. territory without which halibut fishing contrary to the treaty could not be carried on.

168. Telegrams between Ottawa, London and Washington on Signing of Treaty

The Governor General (Lord Byng of Vimy) to the
Secretary of State for the Colonies (The
Duke of Devonshire), 16 January 1923

(Canada, Sessional Papers, No. 111a, 1923) (Paraphrase of cipher telegram)

SECRET

Copies of a Draft Convention between the United States and Great Britain concerning the Halibut Fishery, I understand from His

Majesty's Ambassador at Washington, were communicated by him to the Foreign Office on or about the 21st December last. With the following modifications this Draft Convention is acceptable to my Government and I have to-day telegraphed to the Ambassador at Washington:

1. Substitute the words "The Dominion of Canada" for the words "Great Britain" in the second line of the heading.

2. Substitute the word "Department" for the word "Ministry" in the second paragraph of Article 1 on page three of the Draft.

3. Add after the words "North Pacific Ocean" the words "including Behring Sea" in the second last line of the second paragraph of Article III on page five of the Draft.

To enable him to sign the Treaty so amended on behalf of the Dominion at an early date, my Government request that the Secretary of State for Foreign Affairs be informed that it is their desire that necessary full powers be given to the Honourable Ernest Lapointe, K.C., B.A, LL.B., Minister of Marine and Fisheries.

Sir Auckland Geddes to Byng, 13 February 1923

(Canada, Sessional Papers, No. 111a, 1923) (Paraphrase of cipher telegram)

SECRET

Halibut Convention. — Your telegram of February 12.* Government of the United States are equally anxious for early signature and will hasten reply as much as possible. Secretary of State and myself are laid up with influenza, which may render signature during present week difficult.

In signature of Treaty I understand the Canadian Minister of Marine will be with me and will have the full powers necessary.

---

* Omitted.

Devonshire to Byng, 13 February 1923

(Canada, Sessional Papers, No. 111a, 1923)

With reference to Your Excellency's secret despatch of the 24th January and to your telegrams of the 16th and 30th January, I have the honour to transmit to you herewith the Full Powers issued to the Honourable Ernest Lapointe, K.C., B.A., LL.B., in connection with the proposed Convention with the United States for the protection of the Pacific Halibut Fishery.*

Geddes to Byng, 14 February 1923

(Canada, Sessional Papers, No. 111a, 1923) (Paraphrase of cipher telegram)

SECRET

Enquiry made by State Department whether Mr. Lapointe will sign Treaty with me. Early reply would be much appreciated. See my telegram of February 13th.

Byng to Geddes, 21 February 1923

(Canada, Sessional Papers, No. 111a, 1923) (Paraphrase of cipher telegram)

SECRET

With reference to Your Excellency's secret telegrams of the thirteenth and fourteenth instant, relative to the signing of the Halibut Convention, the Secretary of State for the Colonies under date the fifteenth instant, has telegraphed that full powers for Mr. Lapointe were sent by mail on the thirteenth instant. On receipt of these powers, Mr. Lapointe will leave for Washington. My Ministers are of the opinion that as respects Canada, signature of the treaty by Mr. Lapointe alone will be sufficient and that it will not be necessary for you to sign as well.

---

* Full Powers issued by King George V omitted.

Geddes to Byng, 23 February 1923

(Canada, Sessional Papers, No. 111a, 1923) (Paraphrase of cipher telegram)

SECRET

Halibut Treaty. — Modifications proposed in your telegram of January 16th are still being considered by United States Government. They expect, however, to give reply to-morrow.* Until I am informed that the United States Government are ready to sign it would be preferable that Mr. Lapointe should not actually start. I have been instructed by His Majesty's Government to sign Treaty in association with Mr. Lapointe. . . .

———————

Byng to Devonshire, 28 February 1923

(Canada, Sessional Papers, No. 111a, 1923) (Paraphrase of cipher telegram)

VERY URGENT

Halibut Treaty. — The Full Powers issued to Honourable Ernest Lapointe in connection with proposed convention with United States for protection of Pacific Halibut Treaty [Fishery?] have been duly received and transmitted to Mr. Lapointe, who is at present on his way to Washington.

My Ministers are of opinion that, as respects Canada, signature of the Treaty by Mr. Lapointe alone should be sufficient. They proceeded on this assumption in asking for full powers for Mr. Lapointe. Having so notified the British Ambassador at Washington, it was with some surprise that an intimation was received from Sir Auckland Geddes to the effect that he had been instructed by His Majesty's Government to sign the Treaty in association with Mr. Lapointe. Evidently it has been assumed by His Majesty's Government that such was the wish of the Canadian Government. The view of my Ministers, however, is that the Treaty being one of concern solely to Canada and the United States, and not affecting in any particular any imperial interest, the signature of the Canadian Minister should be sufficient, and they would respectfully request that His Majesty's Ambassador at Washington be instructed accordingly.

The Government of the United States having expressed a desire

———————

* On 27 February Sir Auckland Geddes telegraphed that the United States had accepted the modifications.

that the Treaty should be signed on the afternoon of Thursday, March first, in order to obtain ratification before the Senate rises on March fourth, it is most important that word should be cabled to Washington with the least possible delay. Sir Auckland Geddes has been advised of this request. Kindly inform me, as soon after the receipt of this message as possible, of the action that may be taken by His Majesty's Government.

Devonshire to Byng, 1 March 1923

(Canada, Sessional Papers, No. 111a, 1923) (Paraphrase of cipher telegram)

SECRET

With reference to your telegram of the 28th February regarding the Halibut Treaty. The wishes of your Ministers are being telegraphed to His Majesty's Ambassador at Washington by the Secretary of State for Foreign Affairs.

169. Treaty between Canada and the United States of America for Securing the Preservation of the Halibut Fishery of the North Pacific Ocean

(Treaties and Agreements affecting Canada in Force between His Majesty and the United States of America, with subsidiary Documents, 1814-1925, Ottawa, 1927)

His Majesty the King of the United Kingdom of Great Britain and Ireland, and of the British Dominions beyond the Seas, Emperor of India, and the United States of America, being equally desirous of securing the preservation of the halibut fishery of the Northern Pacific Ocean have resolved to conclude a Convention for this purpose, and have named as their plenipotentiaries:

His Britannic Majesty: The Honourable Ernest Lapointe, K.C., B.A., LL.B., Minister of Marine and Fisheries of Canada; and

The President of the United States of America: Charles Evans Hughes, Secretary of State of the United States;

Who, after having communicated to each other their respective full powers, found in good and due form, have agreed upon the following Articles: —

ARTICLE 1

The nationals and inhabitants and the fishing vessels and boats of the Dominion of Canada and of the United States, respectively, are hereby prohibited from fishing for halibut (*Hippoglossus*) both in the territorial waters and in the high seas off the western coasts of the Dominion of Canada and of the United States, including Behring Sea, from the 16th day of November next after the date of the exchange of ratifications of this Convention to the 15th day of the following February, both days inclusive, and within the same period yearly thereafter, provided that upon the recommendation of the International Fisheries Commission hereinafter described this close season may be modified or suspended at any time after the expiration of three such seasons, by a special agreement concluded and duly ratified by the High Contracting Parties. . . .

ARTICLE 5

This Convention shall remain in force for a period of five years and thereafter until two years from the date when either of the High Contracting Parties shall give notice to the other of its desire to terminate it. It shall be ratified in accordance with the constitutional methods of the High Contracting Parties. The ratifications shall be exchanged in Washington as soon as practicable, and the Convention shall come into force on the day of the exchange of ratifications.

In faith whereof, the respective plenipotentiaries have signed the present Convention in duplicate, and have thereunto affixed their seals.

Done at the City of Washington, the second day of March, in the year of our Lord one thousand nine hundred and twenty-three.

(L.S.) ERNEST LAPOINTE
(L.S.) CHARLES EVANS HUGHES

170. Parliamentary Approval of the Treaty, June 1923

(Debates, House of Commons, 27 June 1923)

The Canadian government chose to obtain from Parliament approval of the treaty as signed (excluding the United States Senate's proposed amendment) before presenting the legislation required to make it operative.

Right Hon. W.L. MACKENZIE KING (Prime Minister) moved:
Resolved by the. . . . . House of Commons: — *

That it is expedient that Parliament do approve of the treaty between His Majesty and the United States of America providing effective measures for the preservation of the halibut fishery of the Northern Pacific ocean, which was signed at Washington on the second day of March, one thousand nine hundred and twenty-three, a copy of which has been laid before parliament, and which was signed on behalf of His Majesty, acting for Canada, by the plenipotentiary therein named, and that this House do approve of the same.

. . .

Right Hon. ARTHUR MEIGHEN (Leader of the Opposition): . . . I wonder how much better off we are. Is our autonomy in the slightest degree enlarged? Does anyone understand just how we are advantaged by the supreme glory of having the Minister of Marine and Fisheries execute this treaty alone, having, figuratively speaking, kicked the British Ambassador out of the door in the execution of a treaty with a foreign power? . . . My criticism is directed against the unnecessary and, to my mind, indelicate action by this government with relation to the historic form of executing treaties in which this country is chiefly interested. . . .

Mr. MACKENZIE KING: . . . If we are a community of free nations, is it to be said as my hon. friend, the ex-Minister of Finance (Sir Henry Drayton), has suggested with respect to the signing of a treaty affecting Canada but not affecting any imperial interest, that there is no question as to the right you have; you have the right but you must not exercise it? Mr. Speaker, we have passed that stage. We want not

* The Senate gave its approval two days later (29 June 1923), filling the blank in the resolution with the words "Senate and".

only the right, we want also to exercise our rights. We believe that in the exercise of all our rights we will gain more of strength and of influence as a nation; and, so far as the British Empire is concerned, we believe that its greatness will be proportionately greater as our strength and influence as a country increases.

Motion agreed to.

6. The Imperial Conference of 1923

The Imperial Conference of 1923 witnessed a decisive confrontation between the supporters of a common Empire foreign policy and those (led by Mackenzie King, with support from the Irish and to some extent the South Africans) who favoured decentralization. King took with him to the conference two men from outside the government service: Dean O.D. Skelton of Queen's University (who was to be appointed Under Secretary of State for External Affairs in 1925), as special adviser, and John W. Dafoe, editor of the *Manitoba Free Press*, a strong advocate of an independent policy. Encouraged by these two, the Canadian Prime Minister repudiated the policies accepted (and, to a large extent, originated) by Borden and Meighen at earlier conferences; these, King and Skelton argued, had been an aberration, a departure from Canadian tradition. Broadly speaking, King may be said to have won this battle. An Imperial Economic Conference met concurrently, without achieving large results. See Ollivier, *Colonial and Imperial Conferences*, III, and Dawson, *Mackenzie King*, I. Cf. C. P. Stacey, "From Meighen to King: The Reversal of Canadian External Policies, 1921-1923," *Transactions of the Royal Society of Canada*, 1969. On Dafoe, Ramsay Cook, *The Politics of John W. Dafoe and the Free Press* (Toronto, 1963).

171. Extracts from O.D. Skelton's Memorandum "Canada and the Control of Foreign Policy," 1923

(King Papers, P.A.C., folios C 62245-69)

This undated memorandum is the most important of a series of papers which Skelton wrote for the Prime Minister in preparation for the 1923 conference. Its principles had been forecast in an address "Canada and Foreign Policy" which Skelton—whose life of Laurier had just been published—made to the Ottawa Canadian Club on 21 January 1922 and which seems to have led King to the conclusion that the Department of External Affairs needed Skelton (*The Canadian Club Year Book, 1921-1922*, Ottawa, 1922, and Dawson, *Mackenzie King*, I, 454). This is a document of some importance in the history of Canadian foreign policy. King wrote large portions of it into his own statement on foreign policy to the Conference (see below, **173**). It is interesting that Skelton, while arguing that the developments of the last few years (the "one-voice" Empire foreign policy based on consultation) represented a reversal of traditional Canadian attitudes, chose to disregard the fact that those developments owed as much to Canadian as to British initiative and that he was himself preparing to reverse the views urged in London by Borden and Meighen. He did this in spite of the fact that he clearly had the detailed record of the 1921 Imperial Conference before him.

The fundamental question before the Imperial Conference of 1923 will be the control of foreign policy. The general question and the application of the implied or explicit general principles to specific issues will both come up for discussion. It is doubtless undesirable to discuss general questions at such a Conference except in so far as may be necessary to solve actual and practical problems. On this occasion, the discussion is inevitable. Other Dominions, particularly Australia, have announced their intention to thresh out to the full the question of Dominion share in imperial policy and of imperial control over Dominion policy. The Near East episode* and other events of the two years since the last Conference have presented practical tests of the understanding declared to have been reached in 1921. Canada's attitude in the Rush-Bagot and Halibut Treaty negotiations† has been vigorously challenged by Australia and New Zealand. Statements of the present position as to control of foreign policy have been made by a British Prime Minister (Mr. Lloyd George) and a British Foreign Secretary (Lord Curzon) which imply a direct reversal of the whole trend of Dominion development in the past half-century, and cannot be allowed to stand as an accepted and unquestioned change in imperial relations.

* The Chanak incident, above, **163-167**.

† Mr. King had proposed to bring the Rush-Bagot naval agreement up to date and had discussed the matter directly with President Harding; ultimately nothing came of this, and it was only in 1939 that the process of amending the agreement actually began. On the Halibut Treaty, see above, **168-169**.

It seems clear, then, that it will be necessary to present to the Conference Canada's view of the fundamental issues involved. It will not only be a necessity, but a distinct opportunity. There has been so much haziness and confusion on the whole subject that it will be a memorable service to reaffirm the Canadian view of the problem.

Of late years a theory of control of foreign policy of a revolutionary character has been put forward by high authorities, namely: That the British Empire can have only one foreign policy; that in the past this policy has been determined by the United Kingdom alone and that the Dominions had no share in shaping it; that now it is determined by Great Britain and the Dominions acting jointly; that the instrument of this joint policy is and must remain, the British Foreign Office; and that, with control, the Dominions have accepted a corresponding share of responsibility for the outcome of that policy; further that, conversely, in no other way can or should or has control in foreign affairs been exercised by a Dominion. These positions may be illustrated by a few quotations. . . .*

(b) *Mr. Lloyd George*, in British House of Commons, December [19]21 (Mr. Lloyd George's own more informal and more illuminating statement):

"The position of the Dominions in reference to external affairs *has been revolutionized in the course of the last four years.* The Dominions since the war have been given *equal rights with Great Britain in the control of the foreign policy of the Empire.* The machinery is the machinery of the British Government, the Foreign Office, the ambassadors. The machine must remain here. It is impossible that it could be otherwise, unless you had a Council of Empire where you had representatives elected for the purpose. . . . *The instrument of the foreign policy of the Empire is the British Foreign Office.* That has been accepted by all the Dominions as inevitable, but they claim a voice in determining the lines of our policy. . . . *The advantage to us is that joint control means joint responsibility,* and when the burden of Empire has become so vast it is well that we should have the shoulders of these young giants under the burden to help us along. . . . [At the Imperial Conference of 1921] a wide survey was taken by all the representatives of the Empire, who would honour that policy

* In addition to the statement by Lloyd George included here, Skelton quoted Lloyd George, British House of Commons, November 1921; Lord Curzon, public address, 8 November 1921; W.M. Hughes in the confidential report of the 1921 Conference and in the London *Morning Post*, 9 May 1923; and *The Round Table*, June 1923. The italics are Skelton's.

and support that policy when it was challenged. They felt that there was not one of them who was not *speaking for hundreds and thousands and millions of men who were prepared to risk their fortunes and their lives for a great Empire."*

Other utterances express the opinion that the Dominions do not now actually control the Empire's foreign policy, but that they should adopt measures to enable them to do so. . . .

As to the effect of this policy, and its complete reversal of Canadian traditions, it is sufficient to quote Sir Clifford Sifton, Ottawa, Canadian Club, April 8, 1922. . . .*

The assumption that there must be one foreign policy for the Empire in all relations is, then, not consistent with the facts and trend of past development and present practice. It is not consistent with the needs and interest of the several communities of the Empire. It does not make for the joint welfare of the whole Empire.

It is claimed that this course of action, this endeavour to change the trend of past development and to set up a common foreign policy for the whole Empire means an extension of influence and power for the Dominions. Exactly the contrary is the case. It offers a maximum of responsibility and a minimum of control. It commits a Dominion in advance to an endorsement of courses of action of which it knows little and of which it may not approve, or in which it may have little direct concern.

The real way in which the Dominions may extend their power is the way in which such extension has come in the past — by reserving for their own peoples and their own parliaments the ultimate decision as to their course of action. Only in this way can responsibility become real, can enduring friendship and co-operation between the peoples of the Empire develop. The centre of political gravity must remain in each self-governing state of the Empire. If the Dominions are committed to action by blank cheques given the Foreign Secretary by their Prime Ministers they have sham control and real responsibility. If they are committed to action only by their own parliaments and peoples, they will have real influence and responsible control. . . .

---

*See the quotation in King's statement to the conference, below, **173**.

172. Mackenzie King on the Nature of the Conference, 3 October 1923

("Imperial Conference, 1923. Stenographic Notes of the Second Meeting ... ,"
King Papers, P.A.C., folios C 62579-80)

. . .

Mr. Mackenzie King: . . . there is one other point of which I should like to make mention. Lord Curzon used the expression, and I touch on it immediately because I think this is desirable, that his conception of this gathering was that it was in the nature of a Cabinet. So far as respects the procedure to be observed and the attitude to be taken in the matters we are discussing I heartily agree, but there is a definite distinction which, I think, we should have continually in mind between a gathering which has the powers and significance of a Cabinet and one which has the powers and significance of a Conference. I look upon this gathering as a Conference of Governments. We are here as representatives of Governments, I cannot feel that I come here with any right or power to be a member of an Imperial Cabinet, using the word Cabinet in the sense in which we understand it as a body necessarily responsible to Parliament and through Parliament to the people.

Lord Curzon: I only meant what you mean, Mr. Mackenzie King. I am the strongest possible advocate of your conception of the nature of the work of this body. When I spoke of a Cabinet I only meant that we should treat each other with the confidence that Cabinet Ministers do. . . .

173. Extracts from Mackenzie King's Statement on Foreign Policy, 8 October 1923

("Imperial Conference, 1923. Stenographic Notes of the Fourth Meeting...,"
King Papers, P.A.C., folios C 62621-38)

. . .

Mr. Mackenzie King: . . . Before proceeding to make any observations on the great issues raised by the Foreign Secretary's statement, I may be expected to give a brief review of some of the external affairs of primary concern to Canada which have developed since the last meeting of this Conference. Our direct international relations are preponderatingly, though not wholly, with a single country. . . .

The United States is not, as the Foreign Secretary has very rightly implied, always easy to deal with. . . . But as far, at least, as Canada is concerned we have found the United States of late years an increasingly friendly and dependable neighbour. . . .

During Sir Robert Borden's term of office, an agreement was reached between the British, Canadian and United States Governments for the appointment of a Canadian representative at Washington. No appointment was made during Sir Robert's term of office or that of his successor, Mr. Meighen, and no appointment has thus far been made by the present Government. We shall probably suggest some revision of the original agreement, particularly in the way of omitting the provision that in the absence of the British Ambassador the Canadian Minister should take charge of the Embassy. I might add that I recently spoke with General Sir Arthur Currie about the possibility of the Government securing him for the post of Canadian Minister at Washington. He has informed me that personal and financial factors would prevent his acceptance should the position be formally offered to him. The matter stands in that way at the present time. . . .*

I mention these facts simply to illustrate what I am going to speak of, perhaps more particularly near the end of this review, why in Canada we feel very strongly that in these matters of international relations we must to some extent have a foreign policy of our own, if I may use that expression in this connexion—not a policy necessarily distinct from the policy of the British Empire—rather, I should perhaps say, we feel that we cannot confine our rights of self-government to matters of a purely domestic character, but that any questions which we have with our neighbours, or with others, which are matters of immediate and direct concern to each of us, we must have freedom in negotiating and settling. May I say at once that I do not wish to imply that we have thus far experienced any handicap of restriction from the British Government in any particular in this matter? . . .

. . . I might refer to the very true observation which Lord Curzon made on Friday as to the power of the West in United States politics. The same thing is observable and increasingly true in Canada; the prairie provinces are coming to hold the balance of power. They are largely influenced by the same factors which influence the Western States. In fact our neighbourhood to the United States is a factor which comes into nearly every equation of ours. It has a direct bearing on the question of our policy towards Europe. There is no question that, if the United States persists in its policy of isolation, and if we were to go to the other extreme of assuming daily responsibility

---

* Here Mr. King proceeded to deal with special aspects of Canadian-American relations: the Halibut Treaty (above, **168-169**), in connection with which he sought to allay any "fear that we in Canada have sought in some way to invade the rights of other parts of the British Empire," the proposed revision of the Rush-Bagot Agreement (above, **171**), the U.S. tariff, and questions of coal and pulpwood trade.

for settling the affairs of Europe, the result would be a distinct growth of Continental sentiment which would have grave danger for the Empire and afford a renewed stimulus to emigration to the United States. That is a consideration which may be overruled. If a great and clear call of duty comes, Canada will respond, whether or no the United States responds, as she did in 1914, but it is a most important consideration against intervention in lesser issues. . . .

. . . I may now pass to some general considerations as to the relations of the different parts of the Empire on questions of foreign policy. I have thought it well to bring this matter up at once, because it arises out of the remarks of the Foreign Secretary on Friday. . . . The question is involved in the Foreign Secretary's opening remark as to our coming here to assist in carrying on "the foreign policy which is not that of these islands alone, but that of the Empire," but it has been raised many times and in more specific fashion.

Public opinion in Canada was surprised some time ago by a statement of the late Prime Minister, Mr. D. Lloyd George, in the House of Commons in December 1921 to the effect that the position of the Dominions in reference to foreign affairs had been revolutionised since 1917, that the Dominions had been given equal rights with Great Britain in the control of the foreign policy of the Empire, that the instrument of this policy was, and must remain, the British Foreign Office, and that the advantage to Britain was that any such joint control involved joint responsibility.*

If any such sweeping and general agreement as Mr. Lloyd George assumes has been made, implying, if it means anything, that all the foreign affairs of the whole Empire are to be carried on through a single channel, the people of Canada have no knowledge of it. This arrangement has never been sanctioned by our Parliament. It may be sufficient to quote a comment made by Sir Clifford Sifton, who, it may be recalled, organised the campaign against the Laurier Government on Reciprocity in 1911, and the campaign for conscription in 1917: —

"This statement is rather startling after Sir John Macdonald and Sir Charles Tupper, Sir Wilfrid Laurier and Sir Robert Borden for fifty years have asserted the right of Canada to have no military or financial responsibility for a war, unless her Parliament voluntarily takes on that responsibility. We now find the Prime Minister of Great Britain making the statement that we have entered into an arrangement by which we assume responsibility for the wars of Great Britain all over the world in return for being consulted. . . . Premiers drift into London . . . no one

*Above, **171**.

very sure what is decided . . . and the Dominions become jointly responsible for everything the British Foreign Office does in every part of the world.

"I consider it an entirely impossible arrangement. I think it a complete abandonment of the theory of Dominion autonomy as it has developed for fifty years. The people of Canada have never agreed to any such arrangement, and in my judgment they never will. I think the people of Canada will demand that responsibility for engaging in any war or contributing to it shall rest exclusively with the Parliament of Canada."*

General Smuts: Who are you quoting from?

Mr. Mackenzie King: From Sir Clifford Sifton, formerly a member of the Government of Canada. Sir Clifford has been giving a number of public addresses in Canada, and these statements seem more precisely than any other I have yet read to present the point of view of our country, as I understand Canadian opinion, on the question of foreign policy.

Lord Curzon: I suppose he spoke without official authority, did he, though he is an influential and powerful person?

Mr Mackenzie King: That is quite right, Lord Curzon. I am merely quoting his speech as an illustration of a view widely held. Speaking after conference with my colleagues in the Cabinet, we would feel that those statements substantially express the Canadian Government's view. . . .†

The British Empire . . . is not a single community, homogeneous, concentrated, with uniform neighbours, problems, needs. It is a league of peoples plus an Empire; it covers all the Seven Seas. . . .

Given then these conditions — given wide scattered communities within the British Empire growing steadily in numbers, in intercourse with the world, and in the habit of self-government; given the growth of problems and difficulties especially with neighbouring countries; given the diversity of conditions and of interest and of knowledge which makes these problems in many cases distinct in each country — it is inevitable that each of these communities should

---

*Sifton's address to the Ottawa Canadian Club on 8 April 1922, entitled "The Political Status of Canada," was published in *The Canadian Club Year Book, 1921-1922* (Ottawa, 1922), pp. 112-27. King's device of putting the most unpleasant part of his message to the Conference in another man's words is worthy of note. The quotation is not absolutely accurate. On Sifton's views, see Ramsay Cook, ed., *The Dafoe-Sifton Correspondence, 1919-1927* (Manitoba Record Society Publications, II, 1966).

†The succeeding passages are direct quotations from Skelton's memorandum (above, **171**).

seek to control those foreign affairs which concern it primarily. . . .

. . . It is unnecessary to review the process by which Canada has steadily widened the range of foreign affairs with which she deals through her own Parliament and Government; trade, tariffs, immigration, boundary disputes as to power, navigation or fisheries and other questions which half a century ago were considered beyond her jurisdiction, are now unquestionably matters for her own decision, as my opening observations concretely indicated.

Clearly, then, as regards this wide and growing range of foreign affairs, the Dominions, or some of them, now possess control, and determine the policy to be followed.

It is not possible that this evolution which has proceeded steadily and with increasing acceptance for more than two generations should now be reversed, that Great Britain or Canada should decide Australia's trade policy or that South Africa should determine whether Canada shall join with the United States in the development of the proposed St. Lawrence waterway. . . .

If it is not possible or desirable that Great Britain or other Dominions should control these foreign affairs which are distinctly of primary concern to one Dominion, so it is equally impossible for the Dominions to seek to control those foreign affairs which primarily affect Great Britain. Her geographical situation, her foreign trade, the enterprise of her investors, create many relations, interests, problems which are primarily her concern and which have intimate connections with her domestic problems. As to those affairs, the Dominions have not the knowledge, the direct interest, the responsibility, which would warrant their seeking control. Great Britain also is entitled to claim self-government.

Each part of the Empire, then, has its own sphere.* But at certain points the arcs cut, the interests become common. There are issues which are of fundamental concern to all parts of the Empire; and with these all parts of the Empire must deal; the Governments of the Empire must confer; the Parliaments of the Empire, if need be, must decide.

It is true that there is no clear cut and enduring line of demarcation between these fields, between those foreign affairs which are of primary concern to one part of the Empire and those which are of joint concern. . . . In drawing the lines there will inevitably be difficulties, but goodwill and common sense and experience will settle these as they have in the past.

*The only marginal note in the copy of Skelton's memorandum in the King Papers is opposite this paragraph: "Very Good."

Again, were it considered desirable to establish a unified foreign policy on all issues, it would not be practicable.

No scheme has been worked out, no scheme, I venture to say, can be worked out, by which each part of the Empire can be not only informed but consulted as to all the relations of every other part of the Empire with foreign countries, and a really joint policy worked out. The range is too vast, the situation too kaleidoscopic, the interests too diverse, the preoccupation of each Government with its own affairs or its own existence too absorbing, to make this possible. We must face facts. It is possible to consult on matters of overwhelming and enduring common interest; it is not possible to consult on the great range of matters of individual and shifting concern.

A further questionable feature of the Empire one-foreign-policy theory is that it ignores the necessity for associating the Parliaments and peoples in the decision of foreign policy. Granted that a measure of secrecy is essential in the course of negotiations, granted that the conduct of affairs must rest largely with an experienced and specialised executive department, still it is true that it is not desirable for any Dominion or for the Empire that vital issues of foreign policy should be determined decisively in a small executive or Conference group. The problem of foreign policy is not settled when provision is made for bringing Prime Ministers together. Each Prime Minister must on important issues secure the backing of his Parliament and his people. . . .*

I must say just a word about International Conferences. . . .

At Genoa and at The Hague† we were represented. We had been invited to be present at these Conferences and, considering their nature, we felt it would perhaps be not only of interest and benefit to ourselves, but also to others if we were represented there. At Lausanne‡ we were not represented; we were not invited. We took and we take no exception to not being invited. We felt that the matters that were being discussed there were not of the same immediate and direct interest to ourselves as they were to those who were represented at the Conference and we have no exception to take to the course that was adopted.

In referring to the Lausanne Conference, perhaps I should say just a word or two about the circumstances surrounding the manner in

---

* From this point King's statement takes leave of Skelton's memorandum "Canada and the Control of Foreign Policy."
† These inconclusive conferences held in 1922 were concerned with the economic reconstruction of Central and Eastern Europe.
‡ See below, **174**

which we were asked if we would like to associate ourselves with the British Government in its policy towards the Near East, and, in particular, if we would participate by sending a contingent.* I mention this because I think it shows the great necessity for our working out, with a little more care and caution than has thus far been exercised, the means by which communications are to pass between the different Governments concerned. The first intimation I had that Canada was being asked to participate in a situation as serious as that in the Near East was when a press reporter came and showed me a despatch which he alleged had been given out by the British Government and asked what Canada was going to do in this matter. . . . This was on Saturday. . . . A communication had been received . . . by the Governor-General's Secretary. . . . It had to be deciphered, and it came to my office during the latter part of Saturday afternoon.† But in the meantime the entire press of the country, the Saturday afternoon press, had the alarmist appeal that there was likely to be war in the Near East and that New Zealand had already undertaken to send a contingent. . . . Lord Curzon spoke on Friday of the despatches and telegrams which we had been receiving from the Foreign Office. I am inclined to think that there is a doubtful value to be attached to them. They have been helpful in some particulars, but, if I may cite this case, a reference to the despatches will indicate that a couple of weeks prior to the telegram being sent, to which I have just referred, one despatch indicated that the crisis in the Near East seemed to have passed, that there was not much danger of any trouble arising of a serious character. That was the last despatch I had to place before the Cabinet before the telegram referring to possible participation in a war. These telegrams come in a bundle a week or two after the events to which they refer, and actually the information we had at that time on the Near East situation would seem to indicate that there was no crisis.

Lord Curzon: You get telegrams.

Mr. Mackenzie King: Since then, Lord Curzon, we have been receiving telegrams in regard to the Lausanne Conference and some other questions. At that time we did not; at that time we were not receiving daily telegrams. We were receiving the printed despatches which came by mail and which reached us a couple of weeks afterwards, sometimes even later.

Lord Curzon: You know, of course, Mr. Mackenzie King, that the particular manifesto to which you are referring was not a normal

---

* The Chanak incident, above, **163-167**.
† King was visiting his constituency near Toronto.

occurrence, and that it was issued without the knowledge or approval of the Cabinet. *

Mr. Mackenzie King: So I understand. . . .

I want, however, at this moment to say a word about the great care that should be exercised in respect to issuing any statements from the British Government or departments of government to the peoples of the Dominions over the heads, so to speak, of the Governments concerned. I think whatever is to be done with regard to our affairs must be done through our own Government. It will certainly create all kinds of difficulties were a practice to be adopted of having memoranda or appeals sent out from any department of the British Government to the Dominions which had not received in the first instance the authorisation of the Government of the Dominion concerned. . . .

Now just a word in conclusion about the general attitude towards Europe. . . .

The practical question. . . is whether any effective remedy for the situation is within our reach, and whether our peoples are agreed upon the value and the necessity of this remedy. . . .

. . . Lord Curzon spoke of the American point of view, and mentioned that the Americans were filled with terror at being drawn into a European situation. . . . I believe that is almost equally true of Canada. I am sure the people in the Dominion would view with great alarm the possibility of their being involved in any European situation at the present time. . . .

Our attitude is not one of unconditional isolation, nor is it one of unconditional intervention. It depends upon the specific situation in Europe and also in our own country. It would be worse than useless for the representatives of Canada here to pledge themselves to policies which have no effective backing in the country. . . .

It is sometimes asserted that Canada or the Canadian Government has latterly put forward new principles of imperial relationship, and claimed special privileges in status. That is not the case. Canada . . . still believes in responsible government, self-government, the right of each part of the Empire, as it attains a fitting degree of strength and capacity and experience, to undertake the control of its own affairs. For seventy years our most honoured leaders have done what they could to develop the basic principle of responsible government,

---

* See above, p. 419. Lord Curzon was not one of the "accessible" ministers and was not consulted. The affair caused a sharp and rather amusing exchange between him and Churchill in November 1922 (*Times Weekly Edition*, London, 16 November).

and to apply it in steadily increasing measure to the whole range of domestic and foreign affairs. . . .

. . .We believe that the decision of Great Britain on any important public issue, domestic or foreign, should be made by the people of Britain, their representatives in Parliament, and the Government responsible to that Parliament. So the decision of Canada on any important issue, domestic or foreign, we believe should be made by the people of Canada, their representatives in Parliament, and the Government responsible to that Parliament. . . .

I hope I have made it clear that in speaking for Canada . . . I have had wholly in mind only the point of view of how to help to make the relations between all parts of the Empire of a character that will tend towards permanency of relations and the successful working out of a wise development in matters pertaining to foreign policy. Also, I hope I have made it clear that, while we do feel strongly that there are some matters which more immediately affect us than they do other parts of the Empire and over which we desire an immediate and direct control, nevertheless, we are equally appreciative of the fact that there are great common interests in which all of us have an equal concern and are equally ready to share.

174. John W. Dafoe's Diary of the Conference

(Ramsay Cook, ed., "J. W. Dafoe at the Imperial Conference, 1923," *Canadian Historical Review*, March 1960)

Dafoe enjoyed the full confidence of the official Canadian delegation, and exercised some influence on King. His record is useful for areas not covered by the official transcript, from which extracts are given above, **172** and **173**.

Monday, Oct. 7 — . . . King's statement* was attacked both by Bruce [Australia] and Massey [New Zealand]. They both interpreted it as meaning that Canada did not propose to hereafter have anything to do with Empire foreign policy. King intervened on both occasions saying this interpretation was at variance with his speech. . . . King's position was supported emphatically by Irish delegation and in more general terms by Smuts of South Africa and Warren of Newfoundland. . . .

*Above, **173**.

Tuesday, November 6 — . . . Skelton . . . told me that a Prime Ministers' conference had been called for the previous afternoon. . . .*

The business before the Conference was to agree to a statement about the Conference and Empire Foreign policy which Curzon had prepared. Skelton showed me this report. It was a remarkable document. Not only did it represent the Conference as giving its general approval to the conduct of joint common affairs since the last Conference, but it announced that the Conference had laid down policies for the future which the foreign office would be authorized to carry out. It meant the acceptance in its most unqualified form of the doctrine of the joint foreign policy with joint responsibility. Its general purport is indicated by the statement in it that "The British Government is not merely anxious to proceed upon the principles of mutual co-operation and responsibility laid down at the last meeting in 1921, but it is also conscious that in all international affairs where G.B. was conducting negotiations affecting the British Empire she would speak with more powerful effect if it were known that her voice was not that of herself alone but of the entire body of states affecting [sic] the Empire. This principle does not contravene but is on the contrary in strict harmony with the practise by which individual Dominions negotiate directly with foreign governments in matters especially affecting their responsibilities." There was a Near East section in it committing all the Dominions to the Lausanne settlement† and another on Egypt which was an instruction to the Foreign Office to insist upon the four reservations which limit the sovereignty of the Kingdom and a special instruction beyond that to take any further steps that may be necessary to ensure beyond all question the control by the British of the Suez canal.

According to Skelton King rather went up into the air upon the conclusion of this statement and gave Curzon a piece of his mind. He said that he thought that he had made it quite clear that Canada did not subscribe to the theory of joint policy and joint responsibility in foreign affairs and would take no part except in matters of direct concern to her. He also insisted upon the conference being regarded as a conference between governments not having power to bind governments and commit them even to moral obligations. Yet at the close of

---

*No record of this appears in the official transcript. For King's own record, see Dawson, *Mackenzie King*, I, 474-8.

†The Dominions were not invited to the Lausanne conference which negotiated a new settlement with Turkey to replace the Treaty of Sèvres, and the Canadian government declined either to sign or to ratify the resulting treaty, though it made no objection to the British government's ratifying on behalf of the Empire.

the Conference he was asked to agree to a statement which ignored these Canadian declarations of Canadian policy and committed Canada definitely to courses [to] which she objected. He intimated that this was an illustration of tactics which made these conferences not very pleasant prospects for Canadian governments. The repeated attempts by resolutions or statements to commit them to policies to which they had expressed disagreement [sic]. He said flatly that unless there was an acceptance of the fact that these Conferences were only conferences Canada would in future decline to take part in them.

King's speech was something of a bombshell. Curzon undertook that a modification of the report should be made and submitted. . . .

Skelton said he had quite a talk with Hankey* and Hankey said they could not find out where Canada stood. Borden some years ago had asked for a share in foreign policy and last Conference Canada had agreed to uniform policy and common responsibility. Now Canada repudiated this policy.

Skelton said the position of the present Government was that the decision of two years ago was a reversal of the policy which had been developing for fifty years and its intention was to see that the effects of this aberration were removed. The futility of any system of consultation involving a measure of control was stressed by Skelton. He pointed out that Curzon while the Conference was sitting had sent a communication to the United States in the name of the Conference, and had later sent further communications, again in the name of the Conference, to France, Belgium and Italy — without the knowledge, consent or authority of the Conference — only reporting to it after the thing was done.

Hankey admitted that Curzon had taken a very improper course. . . .

175. Extracts from the Proceedings of the Conference

(Canada, Sessional Papers, No. 37, 1924)

Section VIII is the ultimate amended form of Curzon's statement to which King took such exception (above, 174). Its final paragraph was inserted on King's insistence. Section IX, on treaties, had King's full support. Section XII, on defence, is notably cautious. See Glaze-

*Sir Maurice Hankey, Secretary of the British Cabinet and senior member of the British Secretariat at the conference.

brook, *History of Canadian External Relations*, II, and Dawson, *Mackenzie King*, I.

. . .

VIII. — FOREIGN RELATIONS

The discussions on foreign relations were commenced on October 5th by the Secretary of State for Foreign Affairs, who gave to the Conference a review of the general situation in every part of the world, and the most frank exposition, first, of the main problems which have confronted the Empire during the last two years, and, secondly, of those which seem most likely to arise in the near future. . . .

Lord Curzon's review was followed by a general discussion on foreign relations, in which Lord Robert Cecil as British representative on the Council of the League of Nations, all the Dominion Prime Ministers present, the Vice-President of the Executive Council of the Irish Free State and the three members of the Indian delegation, took part.

Frequent and detailed examination was given, not only to the main features of the international situation, but to the different aspects of that situation as they developed from day to day. Nor did the Imperial Conference terminate its sittings until each subject had been carefully explored and a common understanding reached upon the main heads of foreign policy. . . .

The Conference considered the situation in the Near and Middle East and recorded its satisfaction at the conclusion of peace between the Allies and Turkey. An end had thus been brought to a period of acute political tension, of military anxiety and financial strain in the eastern parts of Europe; and more particularly had great relief been given to the sentiments of the Moslem subjects of the British throne in all parts of the world.

Another of the subjects that engaged the attention of the Conference was that of Egypt. The Conference was glad to recognize the great advance that has been made during the last two years towards a pacific settlement of this complex problem, which will safeguard important communications between several parts of the Empire.

The Conference, so much of whose time had been occupied two years ago with the question of the renewal or termination of the Anglo-Japanese Alliance and with the future regulation of the Pacific, noted with satisfaction the results of the Washington Conference, which had added immensely to the security of the world without disturbing the intimate relations that have for so long existed between the Empire and its former Ally. . . .

This Conference is a conference of representatives of the several Governments of the Empire; its views and conclusions on Foreign Policy, as recorded above, are necessarily subject to the action of the Governments and Parliaments of the various portions of the Empire, and it trusts that the results of its deliberations will meet with their approval.

IX. — NEGOTIATION, SIGNATURE AND RATIFICATION OF TREATIES

The principles governing the relations of the various parts of the Empire in connection with the negotiation, signature and ratification of Treaties seemed to the Conference to be of the greatest importance. Accordingly it was arranged that the subject should be fully examined by a Committee, of which the Secretary of State for Foreign Affairs was Chairman. The Secretary of State for the Colonies, the Prime Ministers of Canada, the Commonwealth of Australia, New Zealand, the Union of South Africa and Newfoundland, the Minister of External Affairs of the Irish Free State, and the Secretary of State for India as Head of the Indian Delegation, served on this Committee. With the assistance of the Legal Adviser to the Foreign Office, Sir C. J. B. Hurst, K.C.B., K.C., the following Resolution was drawn up and agreed to: —

"The Conference recommends for the acceptance of the governments of the Empire represented that the following procedure should be observed in the negotiation, signature and ratification of international agreements.

"The word 'treaty' is used in the sense of an agreement which, in accordance with the normal practice of diplomacy, would take the form of a treaty between Heads of States, signed by plenipotentiaries provided with Full Powers issued by the Heads of the States, and authorizing the holders to conclude a treaty."

I

The Resolution was submitted to the full Conference and unanimously approved. It was thought, however, that it would be of assistance to add a short explanatory statement in connection with part 1 (3), setting out the existing procedure in relation to the ratification of Treaties. This procedure is as follows: —

(a) The ratification of treaties imposing obligations on one part of the Empire is effected at the instance of the government of that part;

(b) The ratification of treaties imposing obligations on more than one part of the Empire is effected after consultation between the governments of those parts of the Empire concerned. It is for each government to decide whether Parliamentary approval or legislation is required before desire for, or concurrence in, ratifications is intimated by that government. . . .

XII. — DEFENCE

The Conference gave special consideration to the question of Defence, and the manner in which co-operation and mutual assistance could best be effected after taking into account the political and geographical conditions of the various parts of the Empire. . . .

After the whole field of Defence had been surveyed, the Conference decided that it would be advisable to record in the following resolutions its conclusions on the chief matters which had been discussed: —

"(1) The Conference affirms that it is necessary to provide for the adequate defence of the territories and trade of the several countries comprising the British Empire.

"(2) In this connection the Conference expressly recognizes that it is for the Parliaments of the several parts of the Empire, upon the recommendations of their respective Governments, to decide the nature and extent of any action which should be taken by them.

"(3) Subject to this provision, the Conference suggests the following as guiding principles: —

"(a) The primary responsibility of each portion of the Empire represented at the Conference for its own local defence.

"(b) Adequate provision for safeguarding the maritime communications of the several parts of the Empire and the routes and waterways along and through which their armed forces and trade pass.

"(c) The provision of Naval bases and facilities for repair and fuel so as to ensure the mobility of the fleets.

"(d) The desirability of the maintenance of a minimum standard of Naval Strength, namely, equality with the Naval Strength of any foreign power, in accordance with the provisions of the Washington Treaty on Limitation of Armament as approved by Great Britain, all the self-governing Dominions and India.

"(e) The desirability of the development of the Air Forces in the several countries of the Empire upon such lines as will make it possible, by means of the adoption, as far as practicable, of a common system of organization and training and the use of uniform manuals, patterns of arms, equipment, and stores (with the exception of the type of aircraft), for each part of the Empire as it may determine to co-operate with other parts with the least possible delay and the greatest efficiency.

"(4) In the application of these principles to the several parts of the Empire concerned the Conference takes note of: —

"(a) The deep interest of the Commonwealth of Australia, the Dominion of New Zealand, and India, in the provision of a Naval Base at Singapore, as essential for ensuring the mobility necessary to provide for the security of the territories and trade of the Empire in Eastern Waters.

"(b) The necessity for the maintenance of safe passage along the great route to the East through the Mediterranean and the Red Sea.

"(c) The necessity for the maintenance by Great Britain of a Home Defence Air Force of sufficient strength to give adequate protection against air attack by the strongest air force within striking distance of her shores.

"(5) The Conference, while deeply concerned for the paramount importance of providing for the safety and integrity of all parts of the Empire, earnestly desires, so far as is consistent with this consideration, the further limitation of armaments, and trusts that no opportunity may be lost to promote this object."...

"1. Negotiation

"(a) It is desirable that no treaty should be negotiated by any of the governments of the Empire without due consideration of its possible effect on other parts of the Empire, or, if circumstances so demand, on the Empire as a whole.

"(b) Before negotiations are opened with the intention of concluding a treaty, steps should be taken to ensure that any of the other governments of the Empire likely to be interested are informed, so that, if any such government considers that its interests would be affected, it may have an opportunity of expressing its views, or, when its interests are intimately involved, of participating in the negotiations.

"(c) In all cases where more than one of the governments of the

Empire participates in the negotiations, there should be the fullest possible exchange of views between those governments before and during the negotiations. In the case of treaties negotiated at International Conferences, where there is a British Empire Delegation, on which, in accordance with the now established practice, the Dominions and India are separately represented, such representation should also be utilized to attain this object.

"(d) Steps should be taken to ensure that those governments of the Empire whose representatives are not participating in the negotiations should, during their progress, be kept informed in regard to any points arising in which they may be interested.

"2. Signature.

"(a) Bilateral treaties imposing obligations on one part of the Empire only should be signed by a representative of the government of that part. The Full Power issued to such representative should indicate the part of the Empire in respect of which the obligations are to be undertaken, and the preamble and text of the treaty should be so worded as to make its scope clear.

"(b) Where a bilateral treaty imposes obligations on more than one part of the Empire, the treaty should be signed by one or more plenipotentiaries on behalf of all the governments concerned.

"(c) As regards treaties negotiated at International Conferences, the existing practice of signature by plenipotentiaries on behalf of all the governments of the Empire represented at the Conference should be continued, and the Full Powers should be in the form employed at Paris and Washington.

"3. Ratification

"The existing practice in connection with the ratification of treaties should be maintained.

II

"Apart from treaties made between Heads of States, it is not unusual for agreements to be made between governments. Such agreements, which are usually of a technical or administrative character, are made in the names of the signatory governments, and signed by representatives of those governments, who do not act under Full Powers issued by the Heads of the States: they are not ratified by the Heads of the States, though in some cases some form of acceptance or confirmation by the governments concerned is employed. As regards agreements of this nature the existing practice should be continued, but before entering on negotiations the governments of the Empire should consider whether the interests of any other part of the Empire may be affected, and, if so, steps should be taken to ensure that the government of such part is informed of the proposed negotiations, in order that it may have an opportunity of expressing its views."

7. Canada and the Locarno Treaties

The treaties negotiated at Locarno (and signed at London) in 1925 seemed at the time to offer a firm basis for European peace. Of special importance was the Treaty of Mutual Guarantee, by which Belgium, France and Germany agreed to accept and maintain their existing boundaries (including the demilitarized zone in the Rhineland) and Great Britain and Italy guaranteed these undertakings. Stanley Baldwin's British Conservative government did not consult the Dominions or invite them to take part in the negotiations, though it kept them informed. In the light of its own declared policies, this was not a procedure to which the Mackenzie King government could object. Article 9 of the guarantee treaty provided, "The present treaty shall impose no obligations upon any of the British Dominions or upon India, unless the government of such Dominion or of India signifies its acceptance thereof." Canada did not choose to accept. The telegram to the British government printed below is based on a long document in the King Papers (undated and unsigned, but undoubtedly by the new Under-Secretary of State for External Affairs, O. D. Skelton) which considers the pros and cons of adherence and, quite predictably, comes down strongly on the side of the avoidance of commitments. See Neatby, *Mackenzie King*, II, 179-80 and G. M. Gathorne-Hardy, *A Short History of International Affairs, 1920 to 1934* (London, 1934).

176. Byng to Amery, 8 January 1926

(King Papers, P.A.C.)

CONFIDENTIAL

Following from Prime Minister for your Prime Minister. Begins:

The questions raised by the Signing of the Treaty of Mutual Guarantee and the other Locarno agreements, and in particular the proposals as to an Imperial Conference contained in your telegrams of November 18 and December 21, have received the careful attention of the Canadian Government.

In examining the Locarno agreements and reviewing the negotiations which led to their adoption, we have been impressed by the evident reasonableness and good will and the frank facing of realities which have marked the attitude of the representatives of all the powers concerned. We have noted with particular pride the unceasing striving for peace and reconciliation in Europe and the skill and patience displayed by British statesmen in recent years. The undertaking of France and Germany to accept their present frontiers and to renounce war in favor of arbitration as a means of settling future disputes, together with the arbitration agreements between Germany and her Eastern neighbours, should ensure a new era of conciliation and co-operation among the powers of Europe. The entrance of Germany into the League will remove one of the great stumbling-blocks to its complete effectiveness.

The question whether it was advisable or necessary for Great Britain to guarantee the settlement on Germany's western borders or to decline to guarantee a settlement on her eastern borders is naturally one on which there is more room for difference of opinion. The Canadian Government recognizes the force of the considerations which led the British Government to conclude that this question, while inevitably having important consequences for other parts of the Empire, was primarily a matter of concern to Great Britain, with which its Parliament and Government were best qualified to deal. Nor would we desire to take exception to the decision of the British Government, in view of these considerations and of the urgency which was held to exist, to determine its policy without consulting the Dominions in an Imperial Conference or otherwise. The Dominions have been furnished throughout with adequate summaries of all proposals and stages of the negotiations. It is noted also that in accordance with the precedent set in 1919 in the Tripartite Treaty,* after consultation with the Dominion Prime Ministers then in Paris, and followed in the proposed Cannes Pact of three years later, Article 9 of the Treaty of Mutual Guarantee provides that no obligations shall be imposed on any of the British Dominions or upon India, unless its Government signifies acceptance—a procedure which of course implies a real freedom of choice.

* It was proposed that Britain and the United States should guarantee France against unprovoked attack by Germany. This proposal collapsed when the United States Senate rejected the Versailles settlement.

As regards Canada, the Canadian Government has not been able to conclude that it would be warranted in recommending Parliament to guarantee this European settlement. Considerations similar to those which have led the British Government to decide not to increase its obligations in the case of the eastern boundary of Germany appear to make it inadvisable for Canada to increase its obligations on either boundary. That such an increase of obligations would be involved appears from a study of specific provisions, as well as from the very fact of the negotiation of the treaty and from the provision that it is not to terminate until such time as a two-thirds majority of the Council decides that the ordinary engagements of the League afford adequate security. Such further undertakings would appear to run counter to the policy consistently advocated both by the present Canadian Government and its predecessors in endeavoring to secure a more flexible interpretation of Article 10 of the Covenant.* Instead of undertaking in advance to fight either on the side of France against Germany or on the side of Germany against France, as the case may be, in any future Rhine war, it appears advisable to leave the question of participation for determination at the time in the light both of the situation abroad and the situation at home.

The Canadian Government has considered the suggestion that an Imperial Conference should be held for discussion of this question in 1926 or 1927, and that such examination should precede any final judgment by a Dominion Government upon the matter. We agree that this question is such as may very profitably be considered in personal conference when occasion permits. It is not apparent, however, that such a conference is more essential to enable a Dominion Government to determine its policy after the signature of the treaty than it was for the British Government before signature. . . . The Canadian Government of course agrees with the view set forth in your telegram of November 18 that it would undertake no obligations under Article 9 unless the whole position had been laid before Parliament and approval of Parliament obtained. Particularly in view of the fact that it may not be possible to arrange a date for a conference convenient for all the Governments concerned earlier than in 1927, it would not seem practicable or consistent with the responsibility of the Governments and Parliaments of the Dominions, when the question is raised in Parliament, as it will inevitably be, to postpone discussion or expression of opinion until after the Conference. While considering that it will probably be necessary, therefore, to provide for a discussion in Parliament, the Canadian Government is

*See below, **191**.

quite prepared to maintain an open mind upon the question. . . .
Mackenzie King. Ends.

(sgd.) GOVERNOR GENERAL

8. The Imperial Conference of 1926

The Imperial Conference of 1926, though famous for the Balfour definition of the relationship of Britain and the Dominions (below, **178**),
was probably less important in Commonwealth development than
that of 1923 (above, 6). In spite of the recent "constitutional" controversy with Lord Byng (above, **1-7**), Canada and Mackenzie King
took a rather less active part than in the previous conference; they
were, in the words of Vincent Massey, who attended as an "adviser"
to the Canadian delegation, "conciliatory and contented" (*What's
Past Is Prologue*, Toronto, 1963, p. 112). After all, King had just won
a considerable electoral victory (above, p. 91). King played largely a
moderating and mediating role; General Hertzog of South Africa was
the radical who rocked the boat and demanded definition. See
Neatby, *Mackenzie King*, II, and Ollivier, *Colonial and Imperial
Conferences*, III.

177. A Canadian Newspaperman Comments on the Conference

(Ramsay Cook, ed., "A Canadian Account of the 1926 Imperial Conference,"
Journal of Commonwealth Political Studies, March 1965)

This is an extract from a private report to John W. Dafoe of the *Manitoba Free Press* from D. B. MacRae, who covered the conference for
that newspaper. MacRae was in the confidence of the Canadian delegation, including the chief of the Canadian secretariat, O. D. Skelton.

London, Nov. 21, 1926.

Dear Mr. Dafoe:

Enclosed is an official copy of the report of the Inter-Imperial
affairs committee which was made public yesterday. . . . The report,
unanimously agreed on, is considered the most important document
in the evolution of the empire, Skelton and Lapointe* believe it has
the basis for the most complete autonomy and that the old order has
gone. . . .

*Canadian Minister of Justice; one of the two Canadian official delegates to
the conference, the other being the Prime Minister.

The conference proceeded in a rather strange way. Hertzog jumped in early and had some backing from the Irish. Skelton told me at the beginning that the Canadians were not going to push for a declaration, as I already wrote. They were afraid they could not get anything that would not have a joker in it. After I passed on your memo.,* business seemed to pick up and then a cable from Sir C. [Clifford Sifton] seems to have bucked them up. Lapointe and Skelton seemed to be on the right track but King was side-stepping. Then he got into the battle and from that time on the Canadians and Irish worked closely together and pushed hard. Bruce [Australia] then started to come around but New Zealand and Newfoundland fought to the last. How did Newfoundland ever get in? They are hopeless. So is New Zealand. Bruce attacked old Lord Cave on the P.C. business,† holding that there was no reason why the foot of the throne should not be in Australia for the Australians. Lord Cave was the worst reactionary in the lot and finally stamped out of the conference, saying he was not going to be a party to the breaking up of the British Empire. I imagine he is the gentleman who has got the P.C. into its latest trouble. With him gone, the conference made better progress. [Sir Austen] Chamberlain and Birkenhead got on the band wagon early, having grasped the idea that it was necessary to do something, but Amery‡ fought a rear-guard action all the way. Hertzog is well pleased, according to Skelton, and the Irish are going home happy. . . .

. . . King has spent the most of the time here eating with duchesses. Skelton carried the bulk of the load and seems to have the brains. . . .

178. Extracts from the Proceedings of the Conference

(*Summary of Proceedings.* British Parliamentary Papers, Cmd. 2768, 1926)

Though the "Balfour Report" might be considered as merely registering a situation that already existed, it was by any standard an important landmark in Commonwealth development, recognizing the final attainment by the Dominions of that national status, long developing,

---

*Dafoe favoured a definition of imperial relations.
†The question of appeals from the Dominions to the Judicial Committee of the Privy Council. Viscount Cave was Lord Chancellor from 1924 until his death in 1928. Earlier he had been a Lord of Appeal. His name does not appear in the published British *Summary of Proceedings* as a participant in the conference.
‡L. S. Amery, Secretary of State for Dominion Affairs and Secretary of State for the Colonies. The two portfolios were held by the same individual until 1930, though the Dominions Office was set up as a separate organization in 1925.

which had matured much more rapidly as a result of the war of 1914-18. It looks forward to the Statute of Westminster (below, **185**).

. . .

VI. — Inter-Imperial Relations

All the questions on the Agenda affecting Inter-Imperial Relations were referred by the Conference to a Committee of Prime Ministers and Heads of Delegations, of which Lord Balfour was asked to be Chairman. The members of the Committee included the Prime Ministers of Canada, the Commonwealth of Australia, New Zealand, the Union of South Africa, and Newfoundland, the Vice-President of the Executive Council of the Irish Free State, the Secretary of State for India, as head of the Indian Delegation, the Secretary of State for Foreign Affairs, and the Secretary of State for Dominion Affairs. Other Ministers and members of the Conference attended particular meetings.

The Report of this Committee is printed *in extenso* below. It was unanimously adopted by the Conference on the 19th November and was published on the following day. In approving it, the Conference placed on record the great debt of gratitude which it owed to Lord Balfour for the services which he had rendered by presiding over the work of this Committee, and its hope that the Report would prove of permanent value and help to all parts of the British Empire.

Report of Inter-Imperial Relations Committee

I. — INTRODUCTION

We were appointed at the meeting of the Imperial Conference on the 25th October, 1926, to investigate all the questions on the Agenda affecting Inter-Imperial Relations. Our discussions on these questions have been long and intricate. We found, on examination, that they involved consideration of fundamental principles affecting the relations of the various parts of the British Empire *inter se*, as well as the relations of each part to foreign countries. For such examination the time at our disposal has been all too short. Yet we hope that we may have laid a foundation on which subsequent Conferences may build.

II. — STATUS OF GREAT BRITAIN AND THE DOMINIONS

The Committee are of opinion that nothing would be gained by attempting to lay down a Constitution for the British Empire. Its widely scattered parts have very different characteristics, very different histories; and are at very different stages of evolution; while, considered as a whole, it defies classification and bears no real resemblance to any other political organisation which now exists or has ever yet been tried.

There is, however, one most important element in it which from a strictly constitutional point of view, has now, as regards all vital matters, reached its full development — we refer to the group of self-governing communities composed of Great Britain and the Dominions. Their position and mutual relation may be readily defined. *They are autonomous Communities within the British Empire, equal in status, in no way subordinate one to another in any aspect of their domestic or external affairs, though united by a common allegiance to the Crown, and freely associated as members of the British Commonwealth of Nations.*

A foreigner endeavouring to understand the true character of the British Empire by the aid of this formula alone would be tempted to think that it was devised rather to make mutual interference impossible than to make mutual co-operation easy.

Such a criticism, however, completely ignores the historic situation. The rapid evolution of the Oversea Dominions during the last fifty years has involved many complicated adjustments of old political machinery to changing conditions. The tendency towards equality of status was both right and inevitable. Geographical and other conditions made this impossible of attainment by the way of federation. The only alternative was by the way of autonomy; and along this road it has been steadily sought. Every self-governing member of the Empire is now the master of its destiny. In fact, if not always in form, it is subject to no compulsion whatever.

But no account, however accurate, of the negative relations in which Great Britain and the Dominions stand to each other can do more than express a portion of the truth. The British Empire is not founded upon negations. It depends essentially, if not formally, on positive ideals. Free institutions are its life-blood. Free co-operation is its instrument. Peace, security, and progress are among its objects. Aspects of all these great themes have been discussed at the present Conference; excellent results have been thereby obtained. And, though every Dominion is now, and must always remain, the sole judge of the nature and extent of its co-operation, no common cause will, in our opinion, be thereby imperilled.

Equality of status, so far as Britain and the Dominions are concerned, is thus the root principle governing our Inter-Imperial Relations. But the principles of equality and similarity, appropriate to *status*, do not universally extend to function. Here we require something more than immutable dogmas. For example, to deal with questions of diplomacy and questions of defence, we require also flexible machinery — machinery which can, from time to time, be adapted to the changing circumstances of the world. This subject also has occupied our attention. The rest of this Report will show how we have endeavoured not only to state political theory, but to apply it to our common needs. . . .

IV. — RELATIONS BETWEEN THE VARIOUS PARTS OF THE BRITISH EMPIRE

Existing administrative, legislative, and judicial forms are admittedly not wholly in accord with the position as described in Section II of this Report. This is inevitable, since most of these forms date back to a time well antecedent to the present stage of constitutional development. Our first task then was to examine these forms with special reference to any cases where the want of adaptation of practice to principle caused, or might be thought to cause, inconvenience in the conduct of Inter-Imperial Relations.

(a) The Title of His Majesty the King

The title of His Majesty the King is of special importance and concern to all parts of His Majesty's Dominions. Twice within the last fifty years has the Royal Title been altered to suit changed conditions and constitutional developments.

The present title, which is that proclaimed under the Royal Titles Act of 1901, is as follows: —

"George V, by the Grace of God, of the United Kingdom of Great Britain and Ireland and of the British Dominions beyond the Seas King, Defender of the Faith, Emperor of India."

Some time before the Conference met, it had been recognised that this form of title hardly accorded with the altered state of affairs arising from the establishment of the Irish Free State as a Dominion. It had further been ascertained that it would be in accordance with His Majesty's wishes that any recommendation for change should be submitted to him as the result of discussion at the Conference.

We are unanimously of opinion that a slight change is desirable, and we recommend that, subject to His Majesty's approval, the necessary legislative action should be taken to secure that His Majesty's title should henceforward read: —

"George V, by the Grace of God, of Great Britain, Ireland and the British Dominions beyond the Seas King, Defender of the Faith, Emperor of India."

(b) Position of Governors-General

We proceeded to consider whether it was desirable formally to place on record a definition of the position held by the Governor-General* as His Majesty's representative in the Dominions. That position, though now generally well recognised, undoubtedly represents a development from an earlier stage when the Governor-General was appointed solely on the advice of His Majesty's Ministers in London and acted also as their representative.

In our opinion it is an essential consequence of the equality of status existing among the members of the British Commonwealth of Nations that the Governor-General of a Dominion is the representative of the Crown, holding in all essential respects the same position in relation to the administration of public affairs in the Dominion as is held by His Majesty the King in Great Britain, and that he is not the representative or agent of His Majesty's Government in Great Britain or of any Department of that Government.

It seemed to us to follow that the practice whereby the Governor-General of a Dominion is the formal official channel of communication between His Majesty's Government in Great Britain and His Governments in the Dominions might be regarded as no longer wholly in accordance with the constitutional position of the Governor-General. It was thought that the recognised official channel of communication should be, in future, between Government and Government direct. The representatives of Great Britain readily recognised that the existing procedure might be open to criticism and accepted the proposed change in principle in relation to any of the Dominions which desired it. Details were left for settlement as soon as possible after the Conference had completed its work, but it was recognised by the Committee, as an essential feature of any change or development in the channels of communication, that a Governor-General should be supplied with copies of all documents of importance and in general should be kept as fully informed as is His Majesty the King in Great Britain of Cabinet business and public affairs.

(c) Operation of Dominion Legislation

Our attention was also called to various points in connection with the operation of Dominion legislation, which, it was suggested, required clarification.

*The Governor of Newfoundland is in the same position as the Governor-General of a Dominion. [Note in original]

The particular points involved were: —

(a) The present practice under which Acts of the Dominion Parliaments are sent each year to London, and it is intimated, through the Secretary of State for Dominion Affairs, that "His Majesty will not be advised to exercise his powers of disallowance" with regard to them.

(b) The reservation of Dominion legislation, in certain circumstances, for the signification of His Majesty's pleasure which is signified on advice tendered by His Majesty's Government in Great Britain.

(c) The difference between the legislative competence of the Parliament at Westminster and of the Dominion Parliaments in that Acts passed by the latter operate, as a general rule, only within the territorial area of the Dominion concerned.

(d) The operation of legislation passed by the Parliament at Westminster in relation to the Dominions. In this connection special attention was called to such Statutes as the Colonial Laws Validity Act. It was suggested that in future uniformity of legislation as between Great Britain and the Dominions could best be secured by the enactment of reciprocal Statutes based upon consultation and agreement.

We gave these matters the best consideration possible in the limited time at our disposal, but came to the conclusion that the issues involved were so complex that there would be grave danger in attempting any immediate pronouncement other than a statement of certain principles which, in our opinion, underlie the whole question of the operation of Dominion legislation. We felt that, for the rest, it would be necessary to obtain expert guidance as a preliminary to further consideration by His Majesty's Governments in Great Britain and the Dominions.

On the questions raised with regard to disallowance and reservation of Dominion legislation, it was explained by the Irish Free State representatives that they desired to elucidate the constitutional practice in relation to Canada, since it is provided by Article 2 of the Articles of Agreement for a Treaty of 1921 that "the position of the Irish Free State in relation to the Imperial Parliament and Government and otherwise shall be that of the Dominion of Canada."

On this point we propose that it should be placed on record that, apart from provisions embodied in constitutions or in specific statutes expressly providing for reservation, it is recognised that it is the right of the Government of each Dominion to advise the Crown in all matters relating to its own affairs. Consequently, it would not be in accordance with constitutional practice for advice to be tendered to His Majesty by His Majesty's Government in Great Britain in any matter appertaining to the affairs of a Dominion against the views of the Government of that Dominion.

The appropriate procedure with regard to projected legislation in one of the self-governing parts of the Empire which may affect the interests of other self-governing parts is previous consultation between His Majesty's Ministers in the several parts concerned.

On the question raised with regard to the legislative competence of members of the British Commonwealth of Nations other than Great Britain, and in particular to the desirability of those members being enabled to legislate with extra-territorial effect, we think that it should similarly be placed on record that the constitutional practice is that legislation by the Parliament at Westminster applying to a Dominion would only be passed with the consent of the Dominion concerned.

As already indicated, however, we are of opinion that there are points arising out of these considerations, and in the application of these general principles, which will require detailed examination, and we accordingly recommend that steps should be taken by Great Britain and the Dominions to set up a Committee with terms of reference on the following lines: —

"To enquire into, report upon, and make recommendations concerning —

(i) Existing statutory provisions requiring reservation of Dominion legislation for the assent of His Majesty or authorising the disallowance of such legislation.

(ii) — (a) The present position as to the competence of Dominion Parliaments to give their legislation extra-territorial operation.

(b) The practicability and most convenient method of giving effect to the principle that each Dominion Parliament should have power to give extra-territorial operation to its legislation in all cases where such operation is ancillary to provision for the peace, order, and good government of the Dominion.

(iii) The principles embodied in or underlying the Colonial Laws Validity Act, 1869, and the extent to which any provisions of that Act ought to be repealed, amended, or modified in the light of the existing relations between the various members of the British Commonwealth of Nations as described in this Report."

(d) *Merchant Shipping Legislation*

Somewhat similar considerations to those set out above governed our attitude towards a similar, though a special, question raised in relation to Merchant Shipping Legislation. On this subject it was pointed out that, while uniformity of administrative practice was desirable, and indeed essential, as regards the Merchant Shipping Legislation of the various parts of the Empire, it was difficult to reconcile the application, in their present form, of certain provisions of the principal Statute relating to Merchant Shipping, viz., the Merchant Shipping Act of 1894, more particularly Clauses 735 and 736, with the constitutional status of the several members of the British Commonwealth of Nations. . . .

We came finally to the conclusion that, following a precedent which had been found useful on previous occasions, the general question of Merchant Shipping Legislation had best be remitted to a special Sub-Conference, which could meet most appropriately at the same time as the Expert Committee, to which reference is made above. We thought that this special Sub-Conference should be invited to advise on the following general lines: —

> "To consider and report on the principles which should govern, in the general interest, the practice and legislation relating to merchant shipping in the various parts of the Empire, having regard to the change in constitutional status and general relations which has occurred since existing laws were enacted."

. . .

(e) *Appeals to the Judicial Committee of the Privy Council*

Another matter which we discussed, in which a general constitutional principle was raised, concerned the conditions governing appeals from judgments in the Dominions to the Judicial Committee of the Privy Council. From these discussions it became clear that it was no part of the policy of His Majesty's Government in Great Britain that questions affecting judicial appeals should be determined otherwise than in accordance with the wishes of the part of the Empire primarily affected. It was, however, generally recognised that, where changes in the existing system were proposed which, while primarily affecting one part, raised issues in which other parts were also concerned, such changes ought only to be carried out after consultation and discussion.

So far as the work of the Committee was concerned, this general understanding expressed all that was required. The question of some immediate change in the present conditions governing appeals from the Irish Free State was not pressed in relation to the present Conference, though it was made clear that the right was reserved to bring up the matter again at the next Imperial Conference for discussion in relation to the facts of this particular case.

V. — RELATIONS WITH FOREIGN COUNTRIES

From questions specially concerning the relations of the various parts of the British Empire with one another, we naturally turned to those affecting their relations with foreign countries. In the latter sphere, a beginning had been made towards making clear those relations by the Resolution of the Imperial Conference of 1923 on the subject of the negotiation, signature, and ratification of treaties. But it seemed desirable to examine the working of that Resolution during the past three years and also to consider whether the principles laid down with regard to Treaties could not be applied with advantage in a wider sphere.

(a) *Procedure in Relation to Treaties*

We appointed a special Sub-Committee under the Chairmanship of the Minister of Justice of Canada (The Honourable E. Lapointe, K.C.) to consider the question of treaty procedure.

The Sub-Committee, on whose report the following paragraphs are based, found that the Resolution of the Conference of 1923 embodied on most points useful rules for the guidance of the Governments. As they became more thoroughly understood and established, they would prove effective in practice.

Some phases of treaty procedure were examined however in greater detail in the light of experience in order to consider to what extent the Resolution of 1923 might with advantage be supplemented....

(c) *General Conduct of Foreign Policy*

We went on to examine the possibility of applying the principles underlying the Treaty Resolution of the 1923 Conference to matters arising in the conduct of foreign affairs generally. It was frankly recognised that in this sphere, as in the sphere of defence, the major share of responsibility rests now, and must for some time continue to rest, with His Majesty's Government in Great Britain. Nevertheless, practically all the Dominions are engaged to some extent, and some to a considerable extent, in the conduct of foreign relations, particularly those with foreign countries on their borders. A particular instance of this is the growing work in connection with the relations between Canada and the United States of America which has led to the necessity for the appointment of a Minister Plenipotentiary to represent the Canadian Government in Washington. We felt that the governing consideration underlying all discussions of this problem must be that neither Great Britain nor the Dominions could be committed to the acceptance of active obligations except with the definite assent of their own Governments. In the light of this governing consideration, the Committee agreed that the general principle expressed in relation to Treaty negotiations in Section V (a) of this Report, which is indeed already to a large extent in force, might usefully be adopted as a guide by the Governments concerned in future in all negotiations affecting foreign relations falling within their respective spheres....

(e) *Channel of Communication between Dominion Governments and Foreign Governments*

We took note of a development of special interest which had occurred since the Imperial Conference last met, viz., the appointment of a Minister Plenipotentiary to represent the interests of the Irish Free State in Washington, which was now about to be followed by the appointment of a diplomatic representative of Canada. We felt that most fruitful results could be anticipated from the co-operation of His Majesty's representatives in the United States of America, already initiated, and now further to be developed. In cases other than those where Dominion Ministers were accredited to the Heads of Foreign States, it was agreed to be very desirable that the existing diplomatic channels should continue to be used, as between the Dominion Governments and foreign Governments, in matters of general and political concern.

VI. — SYSTEM OF COMMUNICATION AND CONSULTATION

Sessions of the Imperial Conference at which the Prime Ministers of Great Britain and of the Dominions are all able to be present cannot, from the nature of things, take place very frequently. The system of communication and consultation between Conferences becomes therefore of special importance. We reviewed the position now reached in this respect with special reference to the desirability of arranging that closer personal touch should be established between Great Britain and the Dominions, and the Dominions *inter se*. Such contact alone can convey an impression of the atmosphere in which official correspondence is conducted. Development, in this respect, seems particularly necessary in relation to matters of major importance in foreign affairs where expedition is often essential, and urgent decision necessary. A special aspect of the question of consultation which we considered was that concerning the representation of Great Britain in the Dominions. By reason of his constitutional position, as explained in section IV (b) of this Report, the Governor-General is no longer the representative of His Majesty's Government in Great Britain. There is no one therefore in the Dominion capitals in a position to represent with authority the views of His Majesty's Government in Great Britain.

We summed up our conclusions in the following Resolution, which is submitted for the consideration of the Conference: —

"The Governments represented at the Imperial Conference are impressed with the desirability of developing a system of personal contact, both in London and in the Dominion capitals, to supplement the present system of inter-communication and the reciprocal supply of information on affairs requiring joint consideration. The manner in which any new system is to be worked out is a matter for consideration and settlement between His Majesty's Governments in Great Britain and the Dominions, with due regard to the circumstances of each particular part of the Empire, it being understood that any new arrangements should be supplementary to, and not in replacement of, the system of direct communication from Government to Government and the special arrangements which have been in force since 1918 for communications between Prime Ministers."

VII. — PARTICULAR ASPECTS OF FOREIGN RELATIONS DISCUSSED BY COMMITTEE

It was found convenient that certain aspects of foreign relations on matters outstanding at the time of the Conference should be referred to us, since they could be considered in greater detail, and more informally, than at meetings of the full Conference....

(c) The Policy of Locarno

The Imperial Conference was fortunate in meeting at a time just after the ratifications of the Locarno Treaty of Mutual Guarantee had been exchanged on the entry of Germany into the League of Nations. It was therefore possible to envisage the results which the Locarno Policy had achieved already, and to forecast to some extent the further results which it was hoped to secure. These were explained and discussed. It then became clear that, from the standpoint of all the Dominions and of India, there was complete approval of the manner in which the negotiations had been conducted and brought to so successful a conclusion.

Our final and unanimous conclusion was to recommend to the Conference the adoption of the following Resolution: —

"The Conference has heard with satisfaction the statement of the Secretary of State for Foreign Affairs with regard to the efforts made to ensure peace in Europe, culminating in the agreements of Locarno; and congratulates His Majesty's Government in Great Britain on its share in this successful contribution towards the promotion of the peace of the world."

Signed on behalf of the Committee,
BALFOUR, *Chairman.*

November 18, 1926.

VII. — Foreign Relations

On the 20th October, the Secretary of State for Foreign Affairs made to the Conference a comprehensive statement on foreign affairs, and on the invitation of the Conference His Majesty's High Commissioner in Egypt attended and made a more detailed statement on the position and prospects in that country.

These statements were followed on the 25th October by a general discussion on foreign affairs, in which the Prime Ministers of Canada, the Commonwealth of Australia, New Zealand, the Union of South Africa, and Newfoundland, Mr. O'Higgins for the Irish Free State, Lord Winterton on behalf of the Indian Delegation, and Mr. Lapointe for Canada, took part. General appreciation was expressed of Sir Austen Chamberlain's review.

Opportunity was also taken to explain those aspects of foreign relations with which the Dominion Governments had been specially concerned during the last three years, in particular the various matters on which negotiations had been carried on between His Majesty's Government in Canada and the Government of the United States of America.

As in 1923, emphasis was laid on the vital importance to the British Empire of the maintenance of the route to the East and South Pacific via the Suez Canal, and attention was directed to the bearing of these interests on the conduct of foreign relations.

Satisfaction was expressed at the improvement in the relations of the European Powers since the Conference of 1923, and it was felt that His Majesty's Government in Great Britain were to be congratulated on their contribution towards the promotion of the peace of the world. . . .

XII. — Defence

The Conference gave much consideration to the question of defence, and to the methods by which the defence arrangements of each part of the Empire could be most effectively co-ordinated.

The Prime Minister of Great Britain initiated the discussions on the 26th October by a review of the work and organisation of the Committee of Imperial Defence, in the course of which he emphasised the purely advisory and consultative character of this body. He also outlined the chief developments which had taken place since the last Conference, notably the creation of the Chiefs of Staff Sub-Committee and the decision to establish an Imperial Defence College. . . .

The Conclusions reached by the Imperial Conference on the subject of Defence may be summarised as follows: —

1. The Resolutions on Defence adopted at the last session of the Conference are re-affirmed. . . .

5. The Conference observes that steady progress has been made in the direction of organising military formations in general on similar lines; in the adoption of similar patterns of weapons; and in the interchange of Officers between different parts of the Empire; it invites the Governments concerned to consider the possibility of extending these forms of co-operation and of promoting further consultation between the respective General Staffs on defence questions adjudged of common interest. . . .

9. The Conference takes note of the developments in the organisation of the Committee of Imperial Defence since the session of 1923. It invites the attention of the Governments represented at the Conference to the following Resolutions adopted, with a view to consultation in questions of common defence, at a meeting of the Committee of Imperial Defence held on the 30th May, 1911, in connection with the Imperial Conference of that year: —

"(1.) That one or more representatives appointed by the respective Governments of the Dominions should be invited to attend meetings of the Committee of Imperial Defence when questions of naval and military* Defence affecting the Oversea Dominions are under consideration.

(2.) The proposal that a Defence Committee should be established in each Dominion is accepted in principle. The Constitution of these Defence Committees is a matter for each Dominion to decide." . . .

*The words "and air" would be required to bring the Resolution up to date. [Note in original]

9. Representation in the United States

The development of the plan for Canadian diplomatic representation in Washington reflected that same transition from the Borden concept of imperial diplomatic unity to the idea of separate national policies which appears in the Chanak affair and the subsequent imperial conferences. Borden and, still more, the British government, felt that it was important that the Canadian minister should be part of the British embassy and should replace the ambassador when he was absent. King, as early as 1920, considered that the minister should have no responsibility whatever for British business. The long delay in implementing the plan was due in part at least to the difficulty of finding a suitable appointee who was willing to accept (above, p. 436). The Irish Free State, on the basis of the Canadian initiative, appointed a minister to Washington in 1924; the first Canadian minister did not appear there until 1927. See Dawson, *Development of Dominion Status;* H. Gordon Skilling, *Canadian Representation Abroad: From Agency to Embassy* (Toronto, 1945); and John S. Galbraith, *The Establishment of Canadian Diplomatic Status at Washington* (University of California Publications in History, Vol. 41, 1951).

179. The Governor General (The Duke of Devonshire) to the Secretary of State for the Colonies (Lord Milner), 3 October 1919

(Borden Papers, P.A.C., Memoir Notes, pp. 3900-02)

(Paraphrase of cipher telegram)

SECRET

My advisers have reached the conclusion that distinctive representation of Canada at Washington should not be longer delayed and they refer to correspondence which has taken place since 13th October 1917. Before the war the consideration of questions between Canada and the United States and the necessary action thereon constituted two-thirds or three-quarters of the work of the Embassy, if my advisers are correctly informed. The same condition will probably arise after the conclusion of peace. These questions in most cases concerned purely Canadian interests and they were often approached without the exact information which should have been available. The personnel of the Embassy has always been selected without consultation with the Canadian Government and apparently without special regard to their acquaintance with Canadian conditions or interests. Thus a strong feeling has arisen in this country that effective steps should be taken to safeguard more thoroughly Canadian interests at Washington. The two countries adjoin each other upon a boundary line of nearly four thousand miles and the social and commercial intercourse is constantly increasing. As an illustration my advisers refer to trade conditions.... It will be observed that the total trade between Canada and the United States exceeds that between the United States and all South American countries, and also exceeds by considerable margin, the total trade between Canada and the United Kingdom. Having regard to these facts my advisers have no doubt as to the necessity of distinctive representation. They are desirous of accomplishing it upon lines which will maintain and even emphasize the solidarity of the Empire but which will give to this country the distinctive representation which constitutional development in recent years both sanctions and demands. They propose therefore that such representation should be established upon the following lines which express conclusions to be embodied in an Order in Council. Begins.

(1) The Dominion of Canada shall be represented in the United States by a diplomatic agent duly accredited to the President of the United States to reside at Washington in the character of His Majesty's Envoy Extraordinary and Minister Plenipotentiary for Canada.

(2) The Canadian Minister shall be appointed by and be directly responsible to the Government of Canada. He shall receive his instructions from and shall report to the Secretary of State for External Affairs.

(3) The Canadian Diplomatic Establishment at Washington under the direction of a Canadian Minister shall, subject to an agreement to be made with the Government of the United Kingdom, constitute a part of the establishment of His Majesty's Embassy.

(4) The Canadian Minister shall conduct the negotiations and be the channel of communication at Washington in matters between the United States and His Majesty in respect of the Dominion of Canada.

(5) The Canadian Minister shall hereafter be the channel of communication in all matters between His Majesty's Embassy and the Government of Canada.

(6) With [the] object of promoting the most complete co-operation and unity of purpose, effective arrangements, to be agreed upon between the Canadian Minister and His Majesty's Ambassador, shall be made for continuous consultation in all important matters of common concern and for such necessary concerted action, founded on

consultation, as they may determine. Any matter which they may be unable to adjust by consultation between themselves shall be referred to their respective Governments for settlement.

(7) In particular such forms and modes of procedure shall be agreed upon as will prevent confusion or embarrassment on the part of the Government of the United States in respect of channels of communication.

(8) The further negotiation at Washington of matters now pending between the United States and Canada shall be conducted by and through the Canadian Minister. Ends.

As the Canadian War Mission at Washington has been practically closed down the matter is somewhat urgent, and my advisers hope that they may be favoured with the views of His Majesty's Government with as little delay as possible.

Repeated to Washington.*

180. Milner to Devonshire, 28 October 1919

(Borden Papers, P.A.C., Memoir Notes, pp. 3906-08)

(Paraphrase of cipher telegram)

SECRET

Your Ministers' proposals received in your telegram dated 3rd October have received most careful consideration by the Cabinet. Closeness of relationship between Canada and the United States and the importance of Canadian business at Washington we fully realise justifies the demand for distinctive representation of Canada in His Majesty's Embassy at Washington. At the same time we cordially reciprocate your desire that such distinctive representation should take a form which would maintain and emphasize the solidarity of the Empire and provide in the United States well balanced protection of imperial and Canadian interests.

We think, from this point of view, that it is very desirable to secure position of the Canadian representative as a part of the establishment of the Embassy and to preserve the closest connection between him and the Ambassador, so that there may be a constant interchange of views on matters of common concern. The most convenient and suitable method of carrying out this object, in our opinion, would be for the Government of Canada to recommend and

*I.e., to the British Embassy.

for The King to appoint a Minister plenipotentiary who would be next in rank in the Embassy to the Ambassador, and would have charge of Canadian affairs and conduct them with the United States Government, acting upon instructions from and reporting direct to the Canadian Government. He should take his place as Minister at the Embassy in charge of Canadian affairs, and the Government of the United States should be formally apprized by an official letter from the Secretary of State of his appointment, accrediting the Canadian Minister, and empowering him to conduct Canadian affairs direct with the United States Government. The Canadian Minister would take charge of the Embassy in the absence of the Ambassador.

In order to carry out this policy it would be essential that the Minister should reside and have his office within the precincts of the Embassy and that his Canadian Staff appointed like himself on the recommendation of the Canadian Government should have diplomatic status and be regarded as part of the diplomatic staff of His Majesty's Embassy with rank equivalent to that of their British colleagues of corresponding grades. In this way the solidarity of the Empire would be maintained and emphasized which could hardly be the case if a diplomatic agent for the Dominion of Canada were accredited independent[ly] to the President of the United States.

As the present Embassy house is not adequate for the purpose it will be necessary to find another site upon which suitable buildings can be raised.

Should experience, however, show necessity for further modifications to meet altered conditions and the new status of the Dominions, an opportunity for the full discussion of this subject will present itself at the contemplated conference on the constitution of the Empire to be held next year. In the meantime a beginning could be made at once by the establishment of a Canadian branch of the Embassy at Washington as suggested above.

We confidently hope that these proposals will meet views of the Dominion Government.

181. Comments by Mackenzie King, 1920

(*Debates, House of Commons*, May-June 1920)

17 May

Hon. W.L. MACKENZIE KING (leader of the Opposition): . . . It is not only a permanent representative that is proposed, but a Minister

Plenipotentiary is to be appointed who, to all intents and purposes, is to be the British Ambassador at Washington during the time when the British Ambassador may be away from the country or absent from duty. No one can say how long a time that will be; no one can say what questions will come up while the Canadian plenipotentiary is acting as British Ambassador at Washington. Is there any one here who believes that a step of that kind is going to be free from all kinds of possible danger? What is it that has brought about the desire to have our own representative at Washington? It is that time and again we have taken exception to what British diplomatists at Washington have done on our behalf. Is our representative likely to be so perfect that he will always satisfy British opinion? Why not let British diplomatists manage British affairs and let us manage our own affairs? . . .

There are two extreme views that may be taken in regard to a matter of this kind. One is that the affairs of Canada should be managed exclusively by the British Embassy; the other that the Canadian representative should manage the British Embassy, for part of the time as is here proposed. What seems to be the more rational course is the middle one, that in matters between Canada and other countries Canada should manage her own affairs, and that in matters between Great Britain and other countries, Great Britain should manage her own affairs, always when necessary with co-operation and conference between the two. . . .

30 June

. . . I think particularly on the question of a Canadian representative at Washington acting as Ambassador for the British Government in the British Ambassador's absence, there ought to have been on the part of the Government some effort to find out whether Parliament was likely to be united on such a project. Parliament is not united. We on this side of the House are unalterably opposed to the proposal. We believe it will lead to difficulties between the Mother Country and this Dominion, and lead to trouble between the United States and Canada. I hope my right hon. friend will construe our desire to cut down this appropriation by $30,000 as a protest primarily against having the Canadian Minister Plenipotentiary act at any time as British Ambassador in the absence of the British Ambassador.

Amendment (Mr. King) negatived; yeas 32, nays 57.

182. Commission of the First Canadian Minister to the United States, 1926

(Records of the Department of External Affairs, Ottawa)

Mr. Massey presented his letters of credence to President Coolidge on 18 February 1927. See Massey, *What's Past Is Prologue.*

George RI

GEORGE, BY THE GRACE OF GOD, OF GREAT BRITAIN, IRELAND AND THE BRITISH DOMINIONS BEYOND THE SEAS KING, DEFENDER OF THE FAITH, EMPEROR OF INDIA, ETC., ETC., ETC. TO ALL AND SINGULAR TO WHOM THESE PRESENTS SHALL COME, GREETING!

WHEREAS it appears to Us expedient to nominate some person of approved Wisdom, Loyalty, Diligence and Circumspection to represent Us in the character of Our Envoy Extraordinary and Minister Plenipotentiary at Washington with the especial object of representing in the United States of America the interests of Our Dominion of Canada;

NOW KNOW YE that We, reposing special trust and confidence in the discretion and faithfulness of Our Trusty and Well-beloved the Honourable Charles Vincent Massey, Member of Our Privy Council for Canada, have nominated, constituted and appointed, as We do by these Presents nominate, constitute and appoint him the said Charles Vincent Massey to be Our Envoy Extraordinary and Minister Plenipotentiary at Washington for the purpose aforesaid.

And We therefore request all those whom it may concern to receive and acknowledge Our said Trusty and Well-beloved Charles Vincent Massey as such Envoy Extraordinary and Minister Plenipotentiary, and freely to communicate with him upon all matters which may affect the interests in the United States of America of Our said Dominion.

Given at Our Court of Saint James, the Seventh day of December, in the Year of Our Lord One thousand Nine hundred and Twenty-six, and in the Seventeenth Year of Our Reign.

BY HIS MAJESTY'S COMMAND,
W.L. Mackenzie King
Secretary of State for External Affairs

10. Equality Within the Commonwealth

It took five years to reduce the decisions of the Imperial Conference of 1926 (above, **178**) to legislative form. The Expert Committee recommended in the Balfour Report did not meet until 1929. It took the form of a "Conference on the Operation of Dominion Legislation and Merchant Shipping Legislation," a sort of specialized Imperial Conference largely composed of lawyers. The conference produced recommendations (below, **183**) for a statute to be passed by the British parliament. These in turn were considered and approved by the Imperial Conference of 1930 (below, **184**); and after the various Dominion parliaments had passed addresses requesting such action the British Parliament enacted the Statute of Westminster, 1931. This statute firmly established the legislative equality of the Dominions with Great Britain, and is usually considered nowadays as having made the Dominions in effect independent states; though the word "independence" was nowhere used in the official records at the time.

183. Extracts from the Report of the Conference on the Operation of Dominion Legislation and Merchant Shipping Legislation, 1929

(British Parliamentary Papers, Cmd. 3479, 1930)

Canada was represented in this conference by the Minister of Justice (Mr. Lapointe), Dr. Skelton, and other civil servants, chiefly lawyers.

. . .

15. In approaching the inquiry . . . the present Conference have not considered it within the terms of their appointment to re-examine the principles upon which the relations of the members of the Commonwealth are now established. These principles of freedom, equality, and co-operation have slowly emerged from the experience of the self-governing communities now constituting that most remarkable and successful experiment in co-operation between free democracies which has ever been developed, the British Commonwealth of Nations; they have been tested under the most trying conditions and have stood that test; they have been given authoritative expression by the Governments represented at the Imperial Conference of 1926; and have been accepted throughout the British Commonwealth. The present Conference have therefore considered their task to be merely that of endeavouring to apply the principles, laid down as directing

their labours, to the special cases where law or practice is still inconsistent with those principles, and to report their recommendations as a preliminary to further consideration by His Majesty's Governments in the United Kingdom and in the Dominions.

16. The three heads of the terms of reference to the Conference, apart from the question of merchant shipping which is dealt with separately, may be classified briefly as dealing with:

(i) Disallowance and Reservation;
(ii) The extra-territorial operation of Dominion legislation;
(iii) The Colonial Laws Validity Act, 1865. . . .

PART III. — DISALLOWANCE AND RESERVATION

(1) Disallowance

18. The power of disallowance means the right of the Crown, which has hitherto been exercised (when occasion for its exercise has arisen) on the advice of Ministers in the United Kingdom, to annul an Act passed by a Dominion or Colonial Legislature.

19. The prerogative or statutory powers of His Majesty the King to disallow laws made by the Parliament of a Dominion, where such powers still subsist, have not been exercised for many years. . . .

23. The Conference agree that the present constitutional position is that the power of disallowance can no longer be exercised in relation to Dominion legislation. Accordingly, those Dominions who possess the power to amend their Constitutions in this respect can, by following the prescribed procedure, abolish the legal power of disallowance if they so desire. In the case of those Dominions who do not possess this power, it would be in accordance with constitutional practice that, if so requested by the Dominion concerned, the Government of the United Kingdom should ask Parliament to pass the necessary legislation. . . .

(2) Reservation

26. Reservation means the withholding of assent by a Governor-General or Governor to a Bill duly passed by the competent Legislature in order that His Majesty's pleasure may be taken thereon. . . .

32. Applying the principles laid down in the Imperial Conference Report of 1926, it is established first that the power of discretionary reservation if exercised at all can only be exercised in accordance with the constitutional practice in the Dominion governing the exercise of the powers of the Governor-General; secondly, that His Majesty's Government in the United Kingdom will not advise His Majesty the King to give the Governor-General any instructions to

reserve Bills presented to him for assent, and thirdly, as regards the signification of the King's pleasure concerning a reserved Bill, that it would not be in accordance with constitutional practice for advice to be tendered to His Majesty by His Majesty's Government in the United Kingdom against the views of the Government of the Dominion concerned. . . .

PART IV. — THE EXTRA-TERRITORIAL OPERATION OF DOMINION LEGISLATION

37. In the case of all Legislatures territorial limitations upon the operation of legislation are familiar in practice. They arise from the express terms of statutes or from rules of construction applied by the Courts as to the presumed intention of the Legislature, regard being had to the comity of nations and other considerations. But in the case of the legislation of Dominion Parliaments there is also an indefinite range in which the limitations may exist not merely as rules of interpretation but as constitutional limitations. So far as these constitutional limitations exist there is a radical difference between the position of Acts of the Parliament of the United Kingdom in the United Kingdom itself and Acts of a Dominion Parliament in the Dominion.

38. The subject is full of obscurity. . . .

39. It would not seem to be possible in the present state of the authorities to come to definite conclusions regarding the competence of Dominion Parliaments to give their legislation extra-territorial operation; and, in any case, uncertainty as to the existence and extent of the doctrine renders it desirable that legislation should be passed by the Parliament of the United Kingdom making it clear that this constitutional limitation does not exist.

40. We are agreed that the most suitable method of placing the matter beyond possibility of doubt would be by means of a declaratory enactment in the terms set out below passed, with the consent of all the Dominions, by the Parliament of the United Kingdom. . . .*

PART V. — COLONIAL LAWS VALIDITY ACT

49. The [Colonial Laws Validity] Act, at the time when it was passed, without doubt extended the then existing powers of Colonial legislatures. . . but it is no less true that definite restrictions of a far-reaching character upon the effective exercise of those powers were maintained and given statutory effect. . . .

* The conference proceeded to recommend the clause enacted as Section 3 of the Statute of Westminster, 1931 (below, **185**).

50. We have ... proceeded on the basis that effect can only be given to the principles laid down in the Report of 1926 by repealing the Colonial Laws Validity Act, 1865, in its application to laws made by the Parliament of a Dominion, and the discussions at the Conference were mainly concerned with the manner in which this should be done. Our recommendation is that legislation be enacted declaring in terms that the Act should no longer apply to the laws passed by any Dominion. ... *

184. The Imperial Conference of 1930

(*Summary of Proceedings*, British Parliamentary Papers, Cmd. 3717, 1930)

Canada was represented at the Imperial Conference of 1930 by the new Prime Minister, Mr. Bennett, and three members of his Cabinet. Bennett did not take O. D. Skelton with him. The conference had to take formal action to clear the way for implementing the constitutional decisions of 1926 and 1929, which it did by recommending the enactment of the Statute of Westminster. During the discussion it found itself faced with problems arising out of Canada's federal system — and specifically out of strong representations made to Bennett by the government of Ontario — which were reflected in Section 7 of the Statute as ultimately passed (below, p. 486). The conference however also had to face the growing world economic crisis, and a British government (Ramsay MacDonald's second Labour ministry) which was not yet ready to abandon free trade had to deal with the forceful tariff proposals of the Canadian Prime Minister. J. H. Thomas, Secretary of State for the Dominions, called these "humbug." Nevertheless Bennett's invitation to an Imperial Conference at Ottawa to discuss imperial trade was not rejected, and the meeting took place, though not until 1932 (above, **90**).

. . .

VI. — Inter-Imperial Relations

. . .

(a) REPORT OF THE CONFERENCE OF 1929 ON THE OPERATION OF DOMINION LEGISLATION

The Imperial Conference examined the various questions arising with regard to the Report of the Conference on the Operation of

---

* The conference went on to recommend clauses which were enacted in substance as Sections 2 and 4 of the Statute of Westminster, 1931 (below, **185**). Other recommendations, considerably amended, formed the basis of Sections 7-11 of that statute. The section of the conference report on merchant shipping legislation, here omitted, formed the basis of Sections 5 and 6 of the Statute of Westminster.

Dominion Legislation and in particular took into consideration the difficulties which were explained by the Prime Minister of Canada regarding the representations which had been received by him from the Canadian Provinces in relation to that Report.

A special question arose in respect to the application to Canada of the sections of the Statute proposed to be passed by the Parliament at Westminster, (which it was thought might conveniently be called the Statute of Westminster), relating to the Colonial Laws Validity Act and other matters. On the one hand it appeared that approval had been given to the Report of the Conference on the Operation of Dominion Legislation by resolution of the House of Commons of Canada, and accordingly, that the Canadian representatives felt themselves bound not to take any action which might properly be construed as a departure from the spirit of that resolution. On the other hand, it appeared that representations had been received from certain of the Provinces of Canada subsequent to the passing of the resolution, protesting against action on the Report until an opportunity had been given to the Provinces to determine whether their rights would be adversely affected by such action.

Accordingly, it appeared necessary to provide for two things. In the first place it was necessary to provide an opportunity for His Majesty's Government in Canada to take such action as might be appropriate to enable the Provinces to present their views. In the second place it was necessary to provide for the extension of the sections of the proposed Statute to Canada or for the exclusion of Canada from their operation after the Provinces had been consulted. To this end it seemed desirable to place on record the view that the sections of the Statute relating to the Colonial Laws Validity Act should be so drafted as not to extend to Canada unless the Statute was enacted in response to such requests as are appropriate to an amendment of the British North America Act. It also seemed desirable to place on record the view that the sections should not subsequently be extended to Canada except by an Act of the Parliament of the United Kingdom enacted in response to such requests as are appropriate to an amendment of the British North America Act.

The Conference on the Operation of Dominion Legislation in 1929, recommended a draft clause for inclusion in the Statute proposed to be passed by the Parliament at Westminster to the following effect: —

"No Act of Parliament of the United Kingdom passed after the commencement of this Act shall extend, or be deemed to extend, to a Dominion unless it is expressly declared in that Act that that Dominion has requested, and consented to, the enactment thereof."

At the present Conference the delegates of His Majesty's Government in the United Kingdom were apprehensive lest a clause in this form should have the effect of preventing an Act of the United Kingdom Parliament passed hereafter from having the operation which the legislation of one State normally has in relation to the territory of another. To obviate this, the following amendment was proposed: —

"No Act of Parliament of the United Kingdom passed after the commencement of this Act shall extend, or be deemed to extend, to a Dominion *as part of the law in force in that Dominion,* unless it is expressly declared in that Act that that Dominion has requested, and consented to, the enactment thereof."

The Delegates from some of the Dominions were apprehensive lest the acceptance of the above amendment might imply the recognition of a right of the Parliament of the United Kingdom to legislate in relation to a Dominion (otherwise than at the request and with the consent of the Dominion) in a manner which, if the legislation had been enacted in relation to a foreign state, would be inconsistent with the principles of international comity. It was agreed that the clause as amended did not imply, and was not to be construed as implying, the recognition of any such right, and, on the proposal of the United Kingdom Delegates, that a statement to this effect should be placed on record.

The Conference passed the following Resolutions: —

(i) The Conference approves the Report of the Conference on the Operation of Dominion Legislation (which is to be regarded as forming part of the Report of the present Conference), subject to the conclusions embodied in this Section.

(ii) The Conference recommends: —

(*a*) that the Statute proposed to be passed by the Parliament at Westminster should contain the provisions set out in the Schedule annexed.*

(*b*) that the 1st December, 1931, should be the date as from which the proposed Statute should become operative.

(*c*) that with a view to the realisation of this arrangement, Resolutions passed by both Houses of the Dominion Parliaments should be forwarded to the United Kingdom, if possible by 1st July, 1931, and, in any case, not later than the 1st August, 1931, with a view to the enactment by the Parliament of the United Kingdom of legislation on the lines set out in the schedule annexed.

(*d*) that the Statute should contain such further provisions as

* Not printed here.

to its application to any particular Dominion as are requested by that Dominion. . . .

(g) APPOINTMENT OF GOVERNORS-GENERAL

The Report of the Inter-Imperial Relations Committee of the Imperial Conference of 1926 declared that the Governor-General of a Dominion is now the "representative of the Crown, holding in all essential respects the same position in relation to the administration of public affairs in the Dominion as is held by His Majesty the King in Great Britain, and that he is not the representative or agent of His Majesty's Government in Great Britain or of any Department of that Government."

The Report did not, however, contain any recommendation as to the procedure to be adopted henceforward in the appointment of a Governor-General, and the Conference felt it necessary to give some consideration to this question.

Having considered the question of the procedure to be observed in the appointment of a Governor-General of a Dominion in the light of the alteration in his position resulting from the Resolutions of the Imperial Conference of 1926, the Conference came to the conclusion that the following statements in regard thereto would seem to flow naturally from the new position of the Governor-General as representative of His Majesty only.

1. The parties interested in the appointment of a Governor-General of a Dominion are His Majesty the King, whose representative he is, and the Dominion concerned.

2. The constitutional practice that His Majesty acts on the advice of responsible Ministers applies also in this instance.

3. The Ministers who tender and are responsible for such advice are His Majesty's Ministers in the Dominion concerned.

4. The Ministers concerned tender their formal advice after informal consultation with His Majesty.

5. The channel of communication between His Majesty and the Government of any Dominion is a matter solely concerning His Majesty and such Government. His Majesty's Government in the United Kingdom have expressed their willingness to continue to act in relation to any of His Majesty's Governments in any manner in which that Government may desire.

6. The manner in which the instrument containing the Governor-General's appointment should reflect the principles set forth above is a matter in regard to which His Majesty is advised by His Ministers in the Dominion concerned. . . .

XII. — *General Economic Conclusions*

It was apparent that all parts of the Commonwealth were united in a common desire that all practicable steps should be taken to promote and develop inter-Imperial trade, and at the Second Plenary Session of the Conference, held on the 8th October, a discussion of great importance took place on the methods to be used to achieve this end. The speeches made on that occasion on behalf of His Majesty's Governments in the Dominions and the Government of India are printed as an Annex to this Summary.

No statement of policy was made on behalf of His Majesty's Government in the United Kingdom during the Second Plenary Session, but at the meeting of Heads of Delegations on the 13th November, the following statement was made by their representatives: —

"1. His Majesty's Government in the United Kingdom, believing that the development of inter-Imperial markets is of the utmost importance to the Commonwealth, have declared that the interests of the United Kingdom preclude an economic policy which would injure its foreign trade or add to the burdens of the people; but that their fiscal policy does not preclude marketing propaganda and organisation which will secure valuable opportunities for the consumption of Dominion products in the United Kingdom.

2. His Majesty's Government in the United Kingdom have suggested that the Governments of the Empire should undertake to make forthwith a close examination of the various methods by which each may make the greatest possible contribution to economic co-operation within the Empire with a view to presenting reports to a Conference which, it has been suggested, should be held next year or as soon as the reports are ready.

3. In the meantime His Majesty's Government in the United Kingdom have declared that the existing preferential margins accorded by the United Kingdom to other parts of the Empire will not be reduced for a period of three years or pending the outcome of the suggested Conference, subject to the rights of the United Kingdom Parliament to fix the budget from year to year. . . .

ANNEX

STATEMENTS MADE ON BEHALF OF THE DOMINIONS AND INDIA AT THE SECOND PLENARY SESSION OF THE CONFERENCE, ON OCTOBER 8, 1930

Statement by the Prime Minister of Canada

Mr. Bennett: Before offering to this Conference the plan which, once effective, will in my opinion make for greater prosperity in all parts of the Empire, I shall briefly state the fiscal policy of the Canadian administration, of which I am the head.

FISCAL POLICY OF CANADA

The Conservative party of Canada believes in, and employs, the principle of protection of the home producer of agricultural and fabricated products from harmful interference by world competitors. But it is not part of our policy to exclude from our markets foreign goods, so long as their importation does not threaten a reduction in the high standard of living which our citizens enjoy. On the other hand, it *is* our declared policy to provide for the consumer a cheap market, by stimulating the growth of competing domestic industries to that point of development where they will be able, in fair competition with others beyond our Dominion, to offer to the Canadian public products of like quality and at prices comparable to those prevailing in the larger markets of other countries.

To achieve this result, we are obliged to consider the whole question from the point of view of both consumer and producer, and, through the employment of a flexible tariff, to ensure the proper protection of the one and safeguard from exploitation the other. This result we are on the high road to accomplish. Its accomplishment will mean vigorous industries assured of that minimum scale of production through home consumption, without which their excess products can never find a place in world markets.

In pursuance of this policy, and to meet an economic situation, brought about by world and domestic causes (it is not necessary here to determine their relative responsibility), the Parliament of Canada at a session called for the purpose in September of this year, enacted certain changes in the tariff, designed, in our view, to strengthen the position of the home producer. Certain measures were taken as part of this emergency legislation, to avoid the exploitation of the consumer; and in the good faith and good sense of the Canadian producers we have the necessary assurance of their rigid adherence to these measures.

This policy of the Conservative party has come to be known as the policy of "Canada first." In approaching the economic problems of our Empire I stand four-square behind that policy. And if this Conference is to meet these problems and provide an effective solution of them, it seems to me that my attitude towards my own country will be the attitude of you all towards yours. On no other basis can we hope to effect an enduring agreement of benefit to each one of us. I will determine what my country needs, and, if you do likewise, then we may come together and search out the means by which we can be of mutual assistance in satisfying those needs.

A POLICY OF PREFERENCE FOR EMPIRE GOODS

I rejoice that the Government of Canada finds, in the Empire scheme I have to propose, the surest promise that its duty to its own country will be fulfilled. For we believe that through the broadening of the home markets of Empire States to Empire products, in preference to the products of foreign countries, every unit of this Empire will benefit. This does not mean, of course, that an attempt should be made to exclude from Empire markets the goods of other countries. We must have — all of us — markets without the Empire, and to make those markets sure, and greater, we must place no insuperable barrier in the road of reciprocal world trade. What it does mean, however, is that we should direct the present flow of trade into more permanent Empire channels by preferring Empire goods to those of other countries. This can be done only in one way — by creating a preference in favour of Empire goods. . . .

The primary concern of Canada to-day is profitably to sell its wheat. We believe that we shall be reaching towards a solution of that problem if we can establish a better market in Great Britain. This market we want, and for it we are willing to pay, by giving in the Canadian market a preference for British goods. You may each, in your own way, apply what tests you choose to determine the value of reciprocal preferences to your own country. I am confident your conclusions will coincide with ours. . . .

DETAILS OF PROPOSED PREFERENCE

I offer to the Mother country, and to all the other parts of Empire, a preference in the Canadian market in exchange for a like preference in theirs, based upon the addition of a ten percentum increase in prevailing general tariffs, or upon tariffs yet to be created. In the universal acceptance of this offer, and in like proposals and acceptances by all the other parts of Empire, we attain to the ideal of Empire preference.

I amplify and explain this offer in the following ways: —

In the first place, the rate I have mentioned cannot be uniformly applied. The basis of the proposal is the adequate protection to industries now existent, or yet to be established. Because of this, we must ensure a certain flexibility in the preferential tariff, having regard to the fundamental need for stability in trade conditions; and must take account of such prevailing preferences as are now higher than the general one I suggest.

It follows, therefore, that this proposed preference should not be considered as a step towards Empire free trade. In our opinion, Empire free trade is neither desirable nor possible, for it would defeat the very purpose we are striving to achieve. All that is helpful in Empire free trade may be secured by Empire preferences. All that is harmful may in this way be avoided. . . .

Consistent with the fullest inquiry into the application of the principle of an Empire preference, our deliberations must be governed by the time factor. If this change in our economic relationship is to be made, it must be made without undue delay. I would, therefore, propose that this Conference, if it approve the principle, should constitute such committees as may, with the greatest expedition and thoroughness, consider the various questions incident to its operation. As we have here neither the time, nor the machinery necessary, to reach a final conclusion upon all of them, it is apparent that we must employ the technicians of our respective countries to complete the inquiry. And for that purpose I would suggest that committees be set up in each of the countries concerned; and that these committees commence immediately an exhaustive examination of the effect upon their domestic situation of the proposals I have made.

SUGGESTED CONFERENCE AT OTTAWA

I am satisfied that whatever modifications in the general plan Canada may have to suggest will be ready for submission within a period of six months. I assume that you are all capable of a like measure of expedition. And so I further propose that, when this Economic Conference has had an opportunity profitably to discuss the plan in its various aspects, it do adjourn to meet at Ottawa early next year, as the guests of the Canadian people, and that in the interval, through the instrumentalities I have suggested, full and final reports be prepared for submission to it. . . .

185. The Statute of Westminster, 1931

(22 George V, Chap. 4) (British Statute)

An Act to give effect to certain resolutions passed by Imperial Conferences held in the years 1926 and 1930.

December 11, 1931.

WHEREAS the delegates of His Majesty's Governments in the United Kingdom, the Dominion of Canada, the Commonwealth of Australia, the Dominion of New Zealand, the Union of South Africa, the Irish Free State and Newfoundland, at Imperial Conferences holden at Westminster in the years of our Lord nineteen hundred and twenty-six and nineteen hundred and thirty did concur in making the declarations and resolutions set forth in the Reports of the said Conferences:

And whereas it is meet and proper to set out by way of preamble to this Act that, inasmuch as the Crown is the symbol of the free association of the members of the British Commonwealth of Nations, and as they are united by a common allegiance to the Crown, it would be in accord with the established constitutional position of all the members of the Commonwealth in relation to one another that any alteration in the law touching the Succession to the Throne or the Royal Style and Titles shall hereafter require the assent as well of the Parliaments of all the Dominions as of the Parliament of the United Kingdom:

And whereas it is in accord with the established constitutional position that no law hereafter made by the Parliament of the United Kingdom shall extend to any of the said Dominions as part of the law of that Dominion otherwise than at the request and with the consent of that Dominion:

And whereas it is necessary for the ratifying, confirming and establishing of certain of the said declarations and resolutions of the said Conferences that a law be made and enacted in due form by authority of the Parliament of the United Kingdom:

And whereas the Dominion of Canada, the Commonwealth of Australia, the Dominion of New Zealand, the Union of South Africa, the Irish Free State and Newfoundland have severally requested and consented to the submission of a measure to the Parliament of the United Kingdom for making such provision with regard to the matters aforesaid as is hereafter in this Act contained:

Now, therefore, be it enacted by the King's most Excellent Majesty by and with the advice and consent of the Lords Spiritual and Temporal, and Commons, in this present Parliament assembled, and by the authority of the same, as follows: —

1. In this Act the expression "Dominion" means any of the following Dominions, that is to say, the Dominion of Canada, the Commonwealth of Australia, the Dominion of New Zealand, the Union of South Africa, the Irish Free State and Newfoundland.

2. — (1) The Colonial Laws Validity Act, 1865, shall not apply to any law made after the commencement of this Act by the Parliament of a Dominion.

(2) No law and no provision of any law made after the commencement of this Act by the Parliament of a Dominion shall be void or inoperative on the ground that it is repugnant to the law of England, or to the provisions of any existing or future Act of Parliament of the United Kingdom, or to any order, rule or regulation made under any such Act, and the powers of the Parliament of a Dominion shall include the power to repeal or amend any such Act, order, rule or regulation in so far as the same is part of the law of the Dominion.

3. It is hereby declared and enacted that the Parliament of a Dominion has full power to make laws having extra-territorial operation.

4. No Act of Parliament of the United Kingdom passed after the commencement of this Act shall extend, or be deemed to extend, to a Dominion as part of the law of that Dominion, unless it is expressly declared in that Act that that Dominion has requested, and consented to, the enactment thereof.

5. Without prejudice to the generality of the foregoing provisions of this Act, sections seven hundred and thirty-five and seven hundred and thirty-six of the Merchant Shipping Act, 1894, shall be construed as though reference therein to the Legislature of a British possession did not include reference to the Parliament of a Dominion.

6. Without prejudice to the generality of the foregoing provisions of this Act, section four of the Colonial Courts of Admiralty Act, 1890 (which requires certain laws to be reserved for the signification of His Majesty's pleasure or to contain a suspending clause), and so much of section seven of that Act as requires the approval of His Majesty in Council to any rules of Court for regulating the practice and procedure of a Colonial Court of Admiralty, shall cease to have effect in any Dominion as from the commencement of this Act.

7. — (1) Nothing in this Act shall be deemed to apply to the repeal, amendment or alteration of the British North America Acts, 1867 to 1930, or any order, rule or regulation made thereunder.

(2) The provisions of section two of this Act shall extend to laws made by any of the Provinces of Canada and to the powers of the legislatures of such Provinces.

(3) The powers conferred by this Act upon the Parliament of Canada or upon the legislatures of the Provinces shall be restricted to the enactment of laws in relation to matters within the competence of the Parliament of Canada or of any of the legislatures of the Provinces respectively.

8. Nothing in this Act shall be deemed to confer any power to repeal or alter the Constitution or the Constitution Act of the Commonwealth of Australia or the Constitution Act of the Dominion of New Zealand otherwise than in accordance with the law existing before the commencement of this Act.

9. — (1) Nothing in this Act shall be deemed to authorise the Parliament of the Commonwealth of Australia to make laws on any matter within the authority of the States of Australia, not being a matter within the authority of the Parliament or Government of the Commonwealth of Australia.

(2) Nothing in this Act shall be deemed to require the concurrence of the Parliament or Government of the Commonwealth of Australia in any law made by the Parliament of the United Kingdom with respect to any matter within the authority of the States of Australia, not being a matter within the authority of the Parliament or Government of the Commonwealth of Australia in any case where it would have been in accordance with the constitutional practice existing before the commencement of this Act that the Parliament of the United Kingdom should make that law without such concurrence.

(3) In the application of this Act to the Commonwealth of Australia the request and consent referred to in section four shall mean the request and consent of the Parliament and Government of the Commonwealth.

10. — (1) None of the following sections of this Act, that is to say, sections two, three, four, five and six, shall extend to a Dominion to which this section applies as part of the law of that Dominion unless that section is adopted by the Parliament of the Dominion, and any Act of that Parliament adopting any section of this Act may provide that the adoption shall have effect either from the commencement of this Act or from such later date as is specified in the adopting Act.

(2) The Parliament of any such Dominion as aforesaid may at any time revoke the adoption of any section referred to in subsection (1) of this section.

(3) The Dominions to which this section applies are the Commonwealth of Australia, the Dominion of New Zealand and Newfoundland.

11. Notwithstanding anything in the Interpretation Act, 1889, the expression "Colony" shall not, in any Act of the Parliament of the

United Kingdom passed after the commencement of this Act, include a Dominion or any Province or State forming part of a Dominion.

12. This Act may be cited as the Statute of Westminster, 1931.

11. Facing a New War, 1935-1939

From the time when Adolf Hitler came to power in Germany (1933), and still more from the Ethiopian war of 1935, Canadians found themselves facing the possibility of a new world war; and there was confused and anxious controversy as to the course their country should follow if it came. As time passed and Hitler's program of aggression developed, public opinion, in English-speaking Canada at least, gradually hardened to the point where the country, very reluctantly, faced the fact that it might have to fight again. The Munich crisis of 1938 was probably a considerable turning-point in this process. Mackenzie King's government, remembering as everyone did the threat to Canadian unity that had arisen in 1914-18, pursued a cautious policy of "no commitments" in advance of an actual outbreak. King himself, it seems, had never had any doubt that Canada would have to take part in any British war that was a war for survival (see, e.g., above, p. 437); but as late as a Cabinet meeting of 24 August 1939 he insisted on avoiding commitments until the guns were actually firing. See James Eayrs, *In Defence of Canada: II, Appeasement and Rearmament* (Toronto, 1965), and C.P. Stacey, *Arms, Men and Governments: The War Policies of Canada, 1939-1945* (Ottawa, 1970).

186. The Imperial Conference of 1937

(Imperial Conference, 1937: Minutes of the Third Meeting of Principal Delegates . . . 21st May, 1937 . . . , King Papers, P.A.C.)

The Imperial Conference of 1937 was the first since the unpleasant economic sessions at Ottawa in 1932 (above, **90**), and the last before the Second World War. Mackenzie King and four other Canadian ministers attended. There were sharp differences of opinion, notably between Canada and New Zealand (the latter advocated that the Commonwealth should be prepared to fight if necessary for collective security enforced through the League of Nations), and any declaration on military solidarity or preparedness was out of the question in the light of King's stand. The Canadian Prime Minister's statement of Canada's situation and problems as he saw them at the time is an important document. See Eayrs, *In Defence of Canada; II.*

Mr. MACKENZIE KING said. . . . Canada itself is half a continent, and covers an area larger than Europe. It has only eleven million people. Of these, over ninety per cent. are congregated in a narrow strip less than 200 miles wide adjoining the United States border, though mining development in the north is steadily giving us breadth as well as length. In this long and narrow strip, nearly 4,000 miles long by a few hundred miles wide, we have not only marked diversity of racial origins but marked diversity of economic interests, so concentrated as to establish four or five areas fairly homogeneous and united in themselves, but each differing from the other areas in preoccupation and outlook. In Europe, I may observe, the task of reconciling the divergent interests of a continent is a foreign affairs question, in which other countries are expected to take an interest. In Canada a similar, though of course a simpler continental task, is an internal affairs question, which we have to solve ourselves.

At the best of times it is not easy to work a federal system — and any other is inconceivable — in conditions of such diversity. As I have already briefly indicated in the Plenary Conference, the strains and stresses of economic depression and unemployment are to-day making the task doubly difficult. . . .

I am not asking members of governments, each of which has its own full quotas of troubles, to give consideration to ours. It is our task to find a solution, and I have no doubt that given peace and a reasonable measure of economic prosperity, we shall be able to do so. But there is one aspect of this task of maintaining national unity that is of importance beyond our borders, and that is the imperative necessity of avoiding, if at all possible, the further strain that would be involved by present controversy as to participation in overseas wars or commitments so to participate.

As to participation in League sanctions operations, there is not a sufficient difference of opinion to create any special difficulty. Such differences as exist are not sectional or racial. . . . There is no question that public and parliamentary opinion at present is emphatically against any interpretation of League policy which would involve automatic sanctions. . . .

It is when we pass from the question of League to Empire war relations that we touch a really vital issue and face the possibility of definite cleavage. It is an issue on which there has been wide and serious discussion, particularly since the intensification of European unrest and the fading of the hope that the League might solve the problem of Commonwealth war-time relations. There are many forces which would make for Canadian participation in a conflict in which Britain's interests were seriously at stake. There would be the strong pull of kinship, the pride in common traditions, the desire to save democratic institutions, the admiration for the stability, the fairness, the independence that characterize English public life, the feeling that a world in which Britain was weakened would be a more chaotic and more dangerous world to live in. The influence of trade interests, of campaigns by a part of the press, the legal anomalies of abstention, the appeal of war to adventurous spirits, would make in the same direction.

On the other hand, opposition to participation in war, any war, is growing. It is not believed that Canada itself is in any serious danger. It is felt that the burdens left by our participation in the last war are largely responsible for present financial difficulties. There is wide impatience, doubtless often based upon inadequate information, with the inability of Continental Europe to settle its own disputes. The isolationist swing in the United States, its renunciation of war profits and neutral rights in order to keep out of war, have made a strong impression on Canadian opinion. In some sections of the country opinion is virtually unanimous against any participation in either a League or a Commonwealth war. There is outspoken rejection of the theory that whenever and wherever conflict arises in Europe, Canada can be expected to send armed forces overseas to help solve the quarrels of continental countries about which Canadians know little, and which, they feel, know and care less about Canada's difficulties, and particularly so if a powerful country like the United States assumes no similar obligations. No policy in Canada is more generally accepted than that commitments of any kind, involving possible participation in war, must have prior and specific approval by parliament. The statement I made last year, that "the Canadian parliament reserves to itself the right to declare, in the light of the circumstances existing at the time, to what extent, if at all, Canada will participate in conflicts in which other members of the Commonwealth may be engaged," was not questioned by any party in parliament.

Certain it is that any attempt to reach a decision, or take steps involving a decision, in advance, would precipitate a controversy that might destroy national unity without serving any Commonwealth interest, and that the decision given on an abstract issue in advance might be quite different from the decision taken in a concrete situation if war arose. This explains why the increased defence preparations, which the Canadian government decided to recommend at the recent session of parliament, and which my colleague, the Minister of National Defence, will review at a later session, were definitely stated to be for the defence of Canada, why even so they met with wide opposition, and why no party in the House proposed preparations for operations overseas.

I shall not attempt to forecast what the decision would be in the event of other parts of the Commonwealth actually being at war. Much would depend upon the circumstances of the hour, both abroad and at home—upon the measure of conviction as to the unavoidability of the struggle and the seriousness of the outlook, and upon the measure of unity that had been attained in Canada. That is not the least of the reasons why we consider peace so vital for the preservation of the unity of the Commonwealth as much as the unity of Canada.

187. John W. Dafoe on the Debate in Canada, 17 June 1937

(Reginald G. Trotter, Albert B. Corey and Walter W. McLaren, eds., *Conference on Canadian-American Affairs held at Queen's University...June 14-18, 1937*, Boston, 1937)

John W. Dafoe, editor of the *Winnipeg Free Press*, was by 1937 the elder statesman of Canadian journalism. It is not necessary to accept in every detail his assessment of the state of opinion in that year; it is, perhaps, rather too neat in its categories. But it serves to indicate the nature of the debate that was in progress. And it proved, on the whole, to be a piece of true prophecy. It should be emphasized, with respect both to this assessment and that presented by Mackenzie King to the Imperial Conference (above, **186**) that the outbreak of war was still over two years away, and many events took place and public opinion moved on in the intervening period. The process of getting "on one side or another of a line" never did occur in the way Dafoe envisaged it in 1937.

. . .

When Canada escaped from her obligations to the League* all the other nations escaped as well, and the League, for the time being at least, disappeared as a factor in international affairs. Thereupon Canada found herself a nation with national responsibilities in an anarchic world, and Mr. King found himself faced with the problem of shaping a policy to maintain national unity in the face of greater diversities of opinion than he had ever encountered. These diversities of view might, perhaps, be roughly classified:

*After the failure of the attempt to use League sanctions to halt Italian aggression against Ethiopia, 1935 (below, **195**).

1. The isolationists, mostly pacifists, who want Canada to do nothing at all, relying upon fate, luck, providence, Great Britain and the United States.

2. The isolationists who, while determined that Canada shall take no part in war, no matter how it comes about, admit that a country might properly provide herself with means for self-defence.

3. Those who hold that Canada should avoid all commitments in advance, but should not exclude the possibility of participation in war for adequate cause; and to this end should provide herself with armaments.

4. Collectivists, who are pleased that Canada is arming in the hope that this rearmament, as well as that of Great Britain, will mean a reinforcement of the League if there should be developments bringing it again into play.

5. Imperialists, who think Canada should merge her foreign policy and her defence policy with that of Great Britain; and are in favour of rearmament on the largest possible scale.

These groups are not strictly defined. Peoples [sic] as they think about these questions pass from one to another. It is not impossible that an individual might pass through the whole category in search of a policy; and then begin again. Of this issue the whole electorate is beginning to be aware. The important thing is that they are becoming awake to the issue, and to its implications.

The policy outlined under No. 3 is that of the Government. It occupies middle ground and draws conditional support from both sides. With the exception of the pacifists there is agreement that Canada should be prepared to defend herself, though there are divergencies of opinion as to the defence policy itself.

The attitude of the Government in rejecting all commitments is disliked by the imperialists who would like to see definite engagements entered into with the other units of the Commonwealth; and it is equally objectionable to the pacifists and the 100 per cent isolationists, who demand explicit assurances that the Government will, under no circumstances, entertain the idea of war. . . .

We begin to hear quite frequently about the division of the people of Canada into two camps: North Americans and imperialists. This distinction is undoubtedly beginning to take form. . . .

With what [Salvador de] Madariaga very properly calls "the quiescent war" erupting into violence — which I cannot but think is inevitable at no distant date — the Canadian policy of preserving national unity by postponing decisions will collapse.

The classification of parties which I have submitted to you will be wiped out; and the people of Canada will begin to get on one side or another of a line which will run through every province, every township and through a good many homes as well. On one side will be the isolationists who will demand that whatever the issues and whatever the consequences to the outside world Canada shall withdraw herself from participation in the conflict. Some will support this policy from abstract principles of pacifism, some from fear, some from irrational prejudices, while many will rationalize their attitude and make out a case not without plausibility and strength.

On the other side, there will be all those who are not prepared to see Canada pull out, at the first threat of trouble, from the British Commonwealth, which, of course, would be the immediate and inevitable consequence of a formal declaration of neutrality; those who have not lost the vision of a world freed from war by the co-operation of nations of good intent who, I am very sure, are far more numerous than the politicians think; and those who hold that when Great Britain is in peril the right attitude for Canada is one of "Ready, aye ready."* The issue upon which the war might come, the form it might take, the shadow it might cast of inevitable consequences if the free nations of Europe were left to their fate, might easily weld these divergent elements into unity upon a defined programme. In spite of much that I hear to the contrary, I think they would together constitute a great multitude. . . .

188. Mackenzie King Supports Munich

Message to Neville Chamberlain (*Globe and Mail*, Toronto, 30 September 1938)

During the 1937 Imperial Conference Neville Chamberlain succeeded Stanley Baldwin as Prime Minister of Great Britain. Mackenzie King felt drawn to Chamberlain, and applauded his policy of "appeasing" Hitler by concessions. King's statement to the conference (above, 186) explains why he believed in peace at almost any price. Indeed, he abandoned his lifelong opposition to a uniform Commonwealth foreign policy to the extent of repeatedly identifying himself and Canada with appeasement. This message was sent to Chamberlain (and simultaneously published) at the moment of the Munich "settlement" made at the expense of Czechoslovakia. Written at the end of a long crisis that had seemed likely to end in war, it expresses the intense temporary relief almost universally felt at that moment. Characteristically, King at the same time sent and published an equally fulsome message to President Roosevelt praising his contribution to the settlement.

* See above, 167.

The heart of Canada is rejoicing tonight at the success which has crowned your unremitting efforts for peace. May I convey to you the warm congratulations of the Canadian people, and with them, an expression of their gratitude, which is felt from one end of the Dominion to the other.

My colleagues in the Government join with me in unbounded admiration at the service you have rendered mankind. Your achievements in the past month alone will ensure you an abiding and illustrious place among the great conciliators whom the United Kingdom, the British Commonwealth of Nations and the whole world will continue to honor.

On the very brink of chaos, with passions flaming, and armies marching, the voice of reason has found a way out of the conflict which no people in their heart desired, but none seemed able to avert.

A turning point in the world's history will be reached if, as we hope, tonight's agreement means a halt to the mad race of arms, and a new start in building the partnership of all peoples. May you have health and strength to carry your great work to its completion.

189. Dr. Manion Finds a Formula, 27 March 1939

(*Evening Telegram*, Toronto, 27 March 1939, Night edition) (Manion Papers, P.A.C.)

Appeasement fell in ruin on 15 March 1939, when Czechoslovakia came apart under Hitler's pressure, German troops occupied Prague, and the settlement so vociferously applauded in the previous September (above, **188**) collapsed. War began to seem inevitable. In Canada the leader of the Conservative opposition, Dr. R. J. Manion, who was seeking to re-establish his party in Quebec, now produced a fateful formula which had in fact been recommended to R. B. Bennett during the election campaign of 1935: no conscription for overseas service. See Stacey, *Arms, Men and Governments*, pp. 397-8.

By J. H. Fisher
Telegram Parliamentary Writer

Ottawa, March 27—"I am one of those who do not believe there is any such thing as neutrality during a war in which Britain is engaged," Dr. R. J. Manion, leader of the federal Conservative Party, told The Evening Telegram this afternoon during the course of an interview upon the position of Canada in international affairs.

His attention was drawn to the resolution which has been adopted by the Ontario Legislature in which the mobilization of Canadian manpower is urged and his answer was: "I am very strongly of the opinion, and have said so many times, that if ever we should be so unhappy as to have to take part in war again, all our people should be placed on the same basis."

"What about conscription?" Dr. Manion was asked.

"I do not believe that Canadian youth should be conscripted to fight outside the borders of Canada," was the Conservative leader's reply. "Canada can play her part in the Empire and in support of our democratic institutions by full co-operation with Britain through volunteer units, through supplying munitions, foods and other necessaries to our allies — and by fully protecting Canada's own territory."

Dr. Manion's pronouncement is of far reaching consequence as it indicates that he is in full sympathy with active co-operation with Great Britain in matters of defense even though he is not sympathetic to conscription in this country. As a matter of fact Dr. Manion questions the value of conscription.

"High military authorities have told me," he said, "that Britain would not expect Canada to send expeditionary forces as in the last war, though there would be many who would wish to go voluntarily in the air force and other services."

Then Dr. Manion continued: "Because of the danger of attack upon Canada itself and because of the necessity of maintaining Canada as a united nation I do not believe that Canadian youth should be conscripted to fight outside the borders of Canada."

"What is your view upon the resolution which was passed by the Ontario Legislature?" he was asked.

"The gist of that resolution to my mind is that in an international crisis, such as the recent one, the whole British Empire should be ready to support Britain, and secondly that the Federal Parliament pass legislation providing that in a war emergency, not only the manpower but the wealth of Canada should be mobilized to protect our free institutions.

"No one can quarrel with that attitude unless he believes that Canada should declare its independence from the Empire. For I am one of those who do not believe there is any such thing as neutrality during a war in which Britain is engaged. The enemy really makes the decision, and would attack Canada if he could. I believe I am on solid ground in that regard. And all should remember that independence would wipe out the B.N.A. [Act] and all the rights which it gives to minorities for we cannot be both in and out of the Empire at the same time."

"The Legislature referred to mobilization of manpower," Dr. Manion was reminded.

"Speaking of mobilization of our manpower and our wealth, I am very strongly of the opinion, and have said so many times, that if ever we should be so unhappy as to have to take part in war again, all our people should be placed on the same basis. In other words, no one should be permitted to enrich himself while other men are offering their lives.

"We must not forget that world conditions have remarkably changed in the last five years. Because of the great advance in military science, no part of the world is immune from attack. Hitler, through his power as a militaristic dictator, endangers the liberties of all of us; for example, Canada might be attacked on the Atlantic, or via the St. Lawrence, or on the Pacific, or through Hudson and James Bays, and I know of no adequate defenses by which we might protect ourselves against such attack. Self-preservation demands that we get our house in order."

"Will you explain what you mean by that?"

"There are two somewhat extreme views in Canada as to war.

"First there is that group who say they would send the last dollar and the last man to Britain's aid; and that other group who say we should participate in no war unless we are directly attacked. As usual, probably a moderate middle course is wisest in the interests of holding Canada together as a nation, for we would be of little service to the Empire if we smash up and either extreme course might well lead to civil war. Conscription in the last war led to violent racial antagonisms and much disharmony, and was of no real military value."

A full dress debate will take place in the House of Commons this week on Canada's foreign policy. Prime Minister King is expected to enunciate the government's attitude in detail and will also declare, it is believed, that he is opposed to conscription in Canada.

Dr. Manion's statement in favor of co-operation with Great Britain is likely to force Mr. King to go equally as far.

190. Party Leaders in Agreement, 30 March 1939

(*Debates, House of Commons*, 30 March 1939)

Three days after the Manion interview (above, **189**), Mackenzie King, in an enormously long and involved statement on foreign policy, of which only a few sentences are given here, committed himself to the principle concerning conscription which Manion had enunciated; and Manion repeated his own declaration. A basis was now in sight for national unity in case of war: no neutrality, fight alongside Britain, no conscription for overseas service. This was in fact the formula on which the country went unitedly into the Second World War some five months later.

Mr. MACKENZIE KING: . . . As I have said, it is for the government to recommend and for parliament to decide upon the course to follow. . . .

It is clear that the conditions determining the nature of participation in such a conflict have undergone a great change since the last war. . . . One strategic fact is clear: the days of great expeditionary forces of infantry crossing the oceans are not likely to recur. Two years ago, I expressed in this house the view that it was extremely doubtful if any of the British dominions would ever send another expeditionary force to Europe.

One political fact is equally clear: in a war to save the liberty of others, and thus our own, we should not sacrifice our own liberty or our own unity. . . . The present government believes that conscription of men for overseas service would not be a necessary or an effective step. Let me say that so long as this government may be in power, no such measure will be enacted. We have full faith in the readiness of Canadian men and women to rally for the defence of their country and their liberties, and to resist aggression by any country seeking to dominate the world by force. . . .

Mr. MANION: . . . In the last war the conscription of men to go to the front caused violent racial antagonisms, much disharmony, bitterness and misunderstanding—conditions from which as yet we have not wholly recovered; and on top of that I believe I am expressing the opinion of authorities when I say that it was of no real military value so far as the empire was concerned. . . .

On the other hand, neutrality, or independence, or even failure to cooperate with Great Britain, is as repugnant to a large section of Canadians as is conscription to another large section. It seems to me, therefore, that we must adopt a sane middle course in order to preserve a united Canada and, indeed, to maintain this empire. The policy that I suggest is the one which I gave three days ago in an interview: first, that there should be no conscription of Canadians to serve outside the borders of Canada; second, that we should have full cooperation with the British empire short of the conscription of men to serve outside our borders. . . . I have been told by a number of mil-

498 EXTERNAL AFFAIRS AND DEFENCE

itary authorities that expeditionary forces such as we had in the last war are not expected and probably are not wanted by Britain. . . .

Mr. J.S. Woodsworth (Winnipeg North Centre): Mr. Speaker, the speech of the Prime Minister (Mr. Mackenzie King) will, I am sure, make us all very happy. The Canadian nationalist, the imperialist, the League of Nations collectivist, the pacifist, the isolationist, the North American, the belligerent militarist — each will find some crumbs of comfort in it. I must confess that although I listened carefully throughout the two hours of his speech I really do not know, in the event of war, what action this government would take. . . . I must also congratulate the leader of the opposition (Mr. Manion) upon his new type of Toryism. His sturdy Canadianism almost puts the Liberals to shame. . . .

B.
Canada and the League of Nations

The League of Nations was set up by the Peace Conference of Paris, the Covenant of the League (below, **191**) being actually incorporated in the Treaty of Versailles. On the manner in which Canada became a member of the League and the International Labour Organization, see Loring Christie's contemporary notes (above, **156**), and more generally Glazebrook, *Canada at the Paris Peace Conference*. For a much larger collection of documents, see MacKay, ed., *Documents on Canadian External Relations*: Volume 2, *The Paris Peace Conference of 1919*.

191. Extracts from the Covenant of the League of Nations

(Canada, Sessional Papers, No. 41h, Special Session 1919)

This is from the text of the Covenant as included in the Treaty of Versailles. For an account of the casual manner in which the British Dominions came to be listed, somewhat ambiguously, under "British Empire" instead of as states in their own right, see *The Autobiography of James T. Shotwell* (Indianapolis and New York, 1961), p. 111.

The High Contracting Parties, in order to promote international co-operation and to achieve international peace and security by the acceptance of obligations not to resort to war, by the prescription of open, just and honourable relations between nations, by the firm establishment of the understandings of international law as the actual rule of conduct among Governments, and by the maintenance of justice and a scrupulous respect for all treaty obligations in the dealings of organized peoples with one another, agree to this Covenant of the League of Nations.

ARTICLE 1.

The original Members of the League of Nations shall be those of the Signatories which are named in the Annex to this Covenant and also such of those other States named in the Annex as shall accede without reservation to this Covenant. Such accession shall be effected by a Declaration deposited with the Secretariat within two months of the coming into force of the Covenant. Notice thereof shall be sent to all other Members of the League.

Any fully self-governing State, Dominion or Colony not named in the Annex may become a Member of the League if its admission is agreed to by two-thirds of the Assembly, provided that it shall give effective guarantees of its sincere intention to observe its international obligations, and shall accept such regulations as may be prescribed by the League in regard to its military, naval and air forces and armaments.

Any Member of the League may, after two years' notice of its intention so to do, withdraw from the League, provided that all its international obligations and all its obligations under this Covenant shall have been fulfilled at the time of its withdrawal.

ARTICLE 2.

The action of the League under this Covenant shall be effected through the instrumentality of an Assembly and of a Council, with a permanent Secretariat.

ARTICLE 3.

The Assembly shall consist of Representatives of the Members of the League.

The Assembly shall meet at stated intervals and from time to time as occasion may require, at the Seat of the League, or at such other place as may be decided upon.

The Assembly may deal at its meetings with any matter within the sphere of action of the League or affecting the peace of the World.

At meetings of the Assembly each Member of the League shall have one vote, and may have not more than three Representatives.

ARTICLE 4.

The Council shall consist of Representatives of the Principal Allied and Associated Powers, together with Representatives of four other Members of the League. These four Members of the League shall be selected by the Assembly from time to time in its discretion. Until the appointment of the Representatives of the four Members of the League first selected by the Assembly, Representatives of Belgium, Brazil, Spain and Greece shall be members of the Council.

With the approval of the majority of the Assembly, the Council may name additional Members of the League whose Representatives shall always be members of the Council; the Council with like approval may increase the number of Members of the League to be selected by the Assembly for representation on the Council.

The Council shall meet from time to time as occasion may require, and at least once a year, at the Seat of the League, or at such other place as may be decided upon.

The Council may deal at its meetings with any matter within the sphere of action of the League or affecting the peace of the world.

Any Member of the League not represented on the Council shall be invited to send a Representative to sit as a member at any meeting of the Council during the consideration of matters specially affecting the interests of that Member of the League.

At meetings of the Council each Member of the League represented on the Council shall have one vote, and may have not more than one Representative.

ARTICLE 5.

Except where otherwise expressly provided in this Covenant or by the terms of the present Treaty, decisions at any meeting of the Assembly or of the Council shall require the agreement of all the Members of the League represented at the meeting.

All matters of procedure at meetings of the Assembly or of the Council, including the appointment of Committees to investigate particular matters, shall be regulated by the Assembly or by the Council and may be decided by a majority of the Members of the League represented at the meeting.

The first meeting of the Assembly and the first meeting of the Council shall be summoned by the President of the United States of America. . . .

ARTICLE 10.

The Members of the League undertake to respect and preserve as against external aggression the territorial integrity and existing political independence of all Members of the League. In case of any such aggression, or in case of any threat or danger of such aggression, the Council shall advise upon the means by which this obligation shall be fulfilled.

ARTICLE 11.

Any war or threat of war, whether immediately affecting any of the Members of the League or not, is hereby declared a matter of concern to the whole League, and the League shall take any action that may be deemed wise and effectual to safeguard the peace of nations. In case any such emergency should arise the Secretary General shall on the request of any Member of the League forthwith summon a meeting of the Council.

It is also declared to be the friendly right of each Member of the League to bring to the attention of the Assembly or of the Council, any circumstance whatever affecting international relations which threatens to disturb international peace or the good understanding between nations upon which peace depends.

ARTICLE 12.

The Members of the League agree that if there should arise between them any dispute likely to lead to a rupture, they will submit the matter either to arbitration or to inquiry by the Council, and they agree in no case to resort to war until three months after the award by the arbitrators or the report by the Council.

In any case under this Article the award of the arbitrators shall be made within a reasonable time, and the report of the Council shall be made within six months after the submission of the dispute.

ARTICLE 13.

The Members of the League agree that whenever any dispute shall arise between them which they recognize to be suitable for submission to arbitration and which cannot be satisfactorily settled by diplomacy, they will submit the whole subject matter to arbitration.

Disputes as to the interpretation of a treaty, as to any question of international law, as to the existence of any fact which if established would constitute a breach of any international obligation, or as to the extent and nature of the reparation to be made for any such breach, are declared to be among those which are generally suitable for submission to arbitration.

For the consideration of any such dispute the court of arbitration to which the case is referred shall be the court agreed on by the parties to the dispute or stipulated in any convention existing between them.

The Members of the League agree that they will carry out in full good faith any award that may be rendered, and that they will not resort to war against a Member of the League which complies therewith. In the event of any failure to carry out such an award, the Council shall propose what steps should be taken to give effect thereto.

ARTICLE 14.

The Council shall formulate and submit to the Members of the League for adoption plans for the establishment of a Permanent Court of International Justice. The Court shall be competent to hear and determine any dispute of an international character which the parties thereto submit to it. The Court may also give an advisory opinion upon any dispute or question referred to it by the Council or by the Assembly.

ARTICLE 15.

If there should arise between Members of the League any dispute likely to lead to a rupture, which is not submitted to arbitration in accordance with Article 13, the Members of the League agree that they will submit the matter to the Council. Any party to the dispute may effect such submission by giving notice of the existence of the dispute to the Secretary General, who will make all necessary arrangements for a full investigation and consideration thereof.

For this purpose the parties to the dispute will communicate to the Secretary General, as promptly as possible, statements of their case with all the relevant facts and papers, and the Council may forthwith direct the publication thereof.

The Council shall endeavour to effect a settlement of the dispute, and if such efforts are successful, a statement shall be made public giving such facts and explanations regarding the dispute and the terms of settlement thereof as the Council may deem appropriate.

If the dispute is not thus settled, the Council either unanimously or by a majority vote shall make and publish a report containing a statement of the facts of the dispute and the recommendations which are deemed just and proper in regard thereto.

Any Member of the League represented on the Council may make public a statement of the facts of the dispute and of its conclusions regarding the same.

If a report by the Council is unanimously agreed to by the members thereof other than the Representatives of one or more of the parties to the dispute, the Members of the League agree that they will not go to war with any party to the dispute which complies with the recommendations of the report.

If the Council fails to reach a report which is unanimously agreed to by the members thereof, other than the representatives of one or more of the parties to the dispute, the Members of the League reserve to themselves the right to take such action as they shall consider necessary for the maintenance of right and justice.

If the dispute between the parties is claimed by one of them, and is found by the Council, to arise out of a matter which by international law is solely within the domestic jurisdiction of that party, the Council shall so report, and shall make no recommendation as to its settlement.

The Council may in any case under this Article refer the dispute to the Assembly. The dispute shall be so referred at the request of either party to the dispute, provided that such request be made within fourteen days after the submission of the dispute to the Council.

In any case referred to the Assembly, all the provisions of this Article and of Article 12 relating to the action and powers of the Council shall apply to the action and powers of the Assembly, provided that a report made by the Assembly, if concurred in by the Representatives of those Members of the League represented on the Council and of a majority of the other Members of the League, exclusive in each case of the Representatives of the parties to the dispute, shall have the same force as a report by the Council concurred in by all the members thereof other than the Representatives of one or more of the parties to the dispute.

ARTICLE 16.

Should any member of the League resort to war in disregard of its covenants under Articles 12, 13, or 15, it shall *ipso facto* be deemed to have committed an act of war against all other Members of the League, which hereby undertake immediately to subject it to the severance of all trade or financial relations, the prohibition of all intercourse between their nationals and the nationals of the covenant-breaking State, and the prevention of all financial, commercial, or personal intercourse between the nationals of the covenant-breaking State and the nationals of any other State, whether a Member of the League or not.

It shall be the duty of the Council in such case to recommend to the several Governments concerned what effective military, naval or air force the Members of the League shall severally contribute to the armed forces to be used to protect the covenants of the League.

The Members of the League agree, further, that they will mutually support one another in the financial and economic measures which are taken under this Article, in order to minimize the loss and inconvenience resulting from the above measures, and that they will mutually support one another in resisting any special measures aimed at one of their number by the covenant-breaking State, and that they will take the necessary steps to afford passage through their territory to the forces of any of the Members of the League which are co-operating to protect the covenants of the League.

Any Member of the League which has violated any covenant of the League may be declared to be no longer a Member of the League by a vote of the Council concurred in by the Representatives of all the other Members of the League represented thereon.

ARTICLE 17.

In the event of a dispute between a Member of the League and a State which is not a Member of the League, or between States not Members of the League, the State or States not Members of the League shall be invited to accept the obligations of membership in the League for the purposes of such dispute, upon such conditions as the Council may deem just. If such invitation is accepted, the provisions of Articles 12 to 16 inclusive shall be applied with such modifications as may be deemed necessary by the Council.

Upon such invitation being given, the Council shall immediately institute an inquiry into the circumstances of the dispute and recommend such action as may seem best and most effectual in the circumstances.

If a State so invited shall refuse to accept the obligations of membership in the League for the purposes of such dispute, and shall resort to war against a Member of the League, the provisions of Article 16 shall be applicable as against the State taking such action.

If both parties to the dispute when so invited refuse to accept the obligations of membership in the League for the purposes of such dispute, the Council may take such measures and make such recommendations as will prevent hostilities and will result in the settlement of the dispute.

ARTICLE 18.

Every treaty or international engagement entered into hereafter by any Member of the League shall be forthwith registered with the Secretariat and shall as soon as possible be published by it. No such treaty or international engagement shall be binding until so registered.

ARTICLE 19.

The Assembly may from time to time advise the reconsideration by Members of the League of treaties which have become inapplicable and the consideration of international conditions whose continuance might endanger the peace of the world.

ARTICLE 20.

The Members of the League severally agree that this Covenant is accepted as abrogating all obligations or understandings *inter se* which are inconsistent with the terms thereof, and solemnly undertake that they will not hereafter enter into any engagements inconsistent with the terms thereof.

In case any Member of the League shall, before becoming a Member of the League, have undertaken any obligations inconsistent with the terms of this Covenant, it shall be the duty of such Member to take immediate steps to procure its release from such obligations.

ARTICLE 21.

Nothing in this Covenant shall be deemed to affect the validity of international engagements such as treaties of arbitration or regional understandings like the Monroe Doctrine for securing the maintenance of peace. . . .

ARTICLE 23.

Subject to and in accordance with the provisions of international conventions existing or hereafter to be agreed upon, the Members of the League —

(a) will endeavor to secure and maintain fair and humane conditions of labour for men, women and children both in their own countries and in all countries to which their commercial and industrial relations extend, and for that purpose will establish and maintain the necessary international organizations;

(b) undertake to secure just treatment of the native inhabitants of territories under their control;

(c) will entrust the League with the general supervision over the execution of agreements with regard to the traffic in women and children, and the traffic in opium and other dangerous drugs;

(d) will entrust the League with general supervision of the trade in arms and ammunition with the countries in which the control of this traffic is necessary in the common interest;

(e) will make provision to secure and maintain freedom of communications and of transit and equitable treatment for the commerce of all Members of the League. In this connection, the special necessities of the regions devastated during the war of 1914-1918 shall be borne in mind;

(f) will endeavour to take steps in matters of international concern for the prevention and control of disease. . . .

ARTICLE 26.

Amendments to this Covenant will take effect when ratified by the Members of the League whose Representatives compose the Council and by a majority of the Members of the League whose Representatives compose the Assembly.

No such amendment shall bind any Member of the League which signifies its dissent therefrom, but in that case it shall cease to be a Member of the League.

ANNEX

I. ORIGINAL MEMBERS OF THE LEAGUE OF NATIONS

Signatories of the Treaty of Peace

United States of America	Cuba	Liberia
Belgium	Czecho Slovakia [sic]	Nicaragua
Bolivia	Equador	Panama
Brazil	France	Peru
British Empire	Greece	Poland
Canada	Guatemala	Portugal
Australia	Haiti	Roumania
South Africa	Hedjaz	Serbia
New Zealand	Honduras	Siam
India	Italy	Tchecko-Slovakia [sic]
China	Japan	Uruguay

States Invited to Accede to the Covenant

Argentine Republic	Norway	Sweden
Chili	Paraguay	Switzerland
Colombia	Persia	Venezuela
Denmark	Salvador	
Netherlands	Spain	

II. FIRST SECRETARY GENERAL OF THE LEAGUE OF NATIONS
The Honourable Sir James Eric Drummond, K.C.M.G., C.B.

192. Canada's First Attack on Article 10, 1919

(Minutes of 26th Meeting of British Empire Delegation, Paris, 21 April 1919, Foster Papers, P.A.C.)

The first Canadian attempt to delete or weaken Article 10 of the League Covenant was made by Sir Robert Borden and his colleagues while the text of the Covenant was still under discussion at Paris in 1919. The attack on the article was carried on in the early sessions of the League Assembly by representatives of both Conservative and Liberal Canadian governments until 1923. In that year an interpretative resolution requiring the League Council, in the event of military measures being recommended, to take account "of the geographical situation and of the special conditions of each State" (in requesting contingents) failed of the necessary unanimity by one vote, that of Persia. The meeting of the British Empire Delegation recorded below was one of those for which Sir Robert Borden was in the chair. It is worth noting that although President Wilson considered Article 10 so important, it was a powerful factor in the rejection of the Versailles Treaty by the U.S. Senate. See W. E. Armstrong, *Canada and the League of Nations* (Geneva, 1930) and Glazebrook, *History of Canadian External Relations* (1966 edition), II, Chap. 16.

. . .

Sir ROBERT BORDEN referred to the observations which he had made in his Memorandum (W.C.P. 245)* concerning Article 10 of the original draft Covenant, which was still retained as Article 10 of the present draft.

LORD ROBERT CECIL said that an effort had been made to alter this article, but no other formula could be found which was acceptable to all and the Commission [the Peace Conference's League of Nations Commission] had therefore been obliged to return to the original form. It should be remembered that Article 10 was in effect qualified to some extent by Article 19, which provided for the reconsideration by members of the League of Treaties which have become inapplicable. Most of the territorial boundaries of the world were already embodied in Treaty provisions and could therefore be reconsidered under Article 19.

Mr. DOHERTY† was opposed to Article 10. Whatever the effect of Article 19, Article 10 pledged every member of the League to preserve the territorial integrity of all the members. Article 19 contemplated careful enquiry before anything was done, but what enquiry have we made at the present time before assuming this pledge? Article 10

---

*For this long and powerful memorandum, see *Documents on Canadian External Relations*, II, Document 74 (13 March 1919).

†C. J. Doherty, Minister of Justice, Canada.

amounted to saying that whatever is, is right. It might be appropriate to guarantee the territorial integrity of the new States created by the Peace Conference, since the frontiers of these have been examined.

There was another aspect to the matter; the proposal constituted in effect a system of mutual insurance, but was it fair to cast the same liability upon all? The risks to which different members of the League were subject were by no means equal. In Canada, for instance, the risk of invasion was remote, while in France or in some Balkan States it might be great. Accordingly the element of consideration in the contract was vitiated by unfairness. Nor was it just to throw the same obligation upon young, undeveloped countries as upon long-established and wealthy States. This consideration had its practical aspect in Canada. Before the war there had been murmurings at the doctrine that when Britain was at war, Canada was at war. Now Canada was to be asked under this Covenant to accept even greater liabilities.

Sir JOSEPH COOK* said that his view was that the Dominions had not half paid for the protection and privileges which they had received from Great Britain.

Sir ROBERT BORDEN pointed out that this contention in view of the articles in the Covenant, would mean in effect that Canada should not join the League. He thought still that Article 10 should be omitted, as its purpose was covered by other Articles less open to criticism.

LORD ROBERT CECIL said that the whole Covenant rested upon the propositions that all nations were interested in the preservation of peace and that it was impossible to foretell how far a conflagration once lighted would spread. Article 10 was merely one of the safeguards. It should be emphasised that it bound the members of the League to preserve the present territorial arrangements simply against "external aggression." In other words it meant that these arrangements, whether just or unjust, should not be upset by force. Whatever other remedies should be taken, no State should be allowed to take the law into its own hands. On the other hand, everyone recognised that it would be impracticable and unwise to attempt to bind every nation to go to war on issues remote from its interests. Hence, it was left to the Council to advise upon the means by which the obligation should be fulfilled, while the Council must not only be unanimous but must include under Article 4 a representative of any member of the League interested in any question under consideration. Consequently, if there was at any time a question of asking Canada to embark upon a military expedition for the purposes of the

*Minister for the Navy, Australia.

League, a Canadian representative must be invited to attend the Council, and if he disagreed there was an end of the matter. For himself he thought it a fair and proper obligation to undertake to preserve other members of the League "against external aggression." Not only President Wilson wanted this Article, but the French were very insistent upon it, and had, indeed, pressed for a much more stringent provision.

Mr. [W. F.] MASSEY* thought that the League would be worthless without such a provision. . . .

193. Note on the Status of the Dominions in the League of Nations, 1919

(Canada, Sessional Papers, No. 41h, Special Session 1919)

This is the "signed declaration" mentioned in Loring Christie's Notes (above, **156**). In the 26th meeting of the British Empire Delegation (above, **192**) the problem of Dominion eligibility for election to the Council was discussed, and the delegation recommended (and obtained) a change in the wording of the first sentence of Article 4 from "States which are members of the League" to "Members of the League." Sir Robert Borden, however, feeling that more safeguards were necessary, obtained this declaration. See the facsimile in *Documents on Canadian External Relations*, II, frontispiece.

The following Declaration respecting the interpretation of Article 4 of the Covenant was signed by M. Clemenceau, President Wilson and Mr. Lloyd George at the Plenary Session of the Peace Conference, held on May 6th, 1919, when the draft Treaty of Peace was adopted by the Allied and Associated Powers for presentation to the German Delegation on the following day. This Declaration was incorporated in the records of the Peace Conference. The Declaration is as follows:

The question having been raised as to the meaning of Article IV of the League of Nations Covenant, we have been requested by Sir Robert Borden to state whether we concur in his view, that upon the true construction of the first and second paragraphs of that Article, representatives of the self-governing Dominions of the British Empire may be selected or named as members of the Council. We have no hesitation in expressing our entire concurrence in this view. If there were any doubt it would be entirely removed by the fact that

*Prime Minister of New Zealand.

the Articles of the Covenant are not subject to a narrow or technical construction.

Dated at the Quai d'Orsay, Paris, the sixth day of May, 1919.

(Signed)   G. CLEMENCEAU
WOODROW WILSON
D. LLOYD GEORGE

194. Canada Rejects the Geneva Protocol, 1925

(Mackenzie King to Sir Eric Drummond, Secretary General of the League, 9 March 1925) (*Debates, House of Commons*, 12 March 1925)

The Geneva Protocol was one of a succession of abortive plans for collective security produced under the auspices of the League. (Though not formally a League project, the Locarno Treaties, above, **176**, may be called the final, and temporarily successful, culmination of this sequence of effort.) The Commonwealth countries rejected the Protocol, as they had its immediate predecessor project, the Treaty of Mutual Assistance, 1924. It was during the discussion of the Protocol in the League Assembly that the Canadian representative, Raoul Dandurand, made the famous and (in the light of later events) unfortunate remark, "We live in a fire-proof house, far from inflammable materials" (2 October 1924).

In response to your communication of October twenty-seventh, nineteen twenty-four enclosing certified true copy of protocol for the pacific settlement of international disputes, and noting that it is open for signature by representatives of all members of the league, the government of Canada desires to state that after careful examination of the subject it has come to conclusions which may be summarized as follows:

First—that Canada should continue to give whole-hearted support to the League of Nations, and particularly to its work of conciliation, co-operation and publicity.

Second—that we do not consider it in the interests of Canada, of the British Empire or of the league itself to recommend to parliament adherence to the protocol and particularly to its rigid provisions for application of economic and military sanctions in practically every future war. Among the grounds for this conclusion is the consideration of the effect of the non-participation of the United States upon attempts to enforce the sanctions and particularly so in the case of a contiguous country like Canada.

Third—that as Canada believes firmly in the submission of international disputes to joint inquiry or arbitration, and has shared in certain notable undertakings in this field, we would be prepared to consider acceptance of the compulsory jurisdiction of the permanent court in justiciable disputes with certain reservations, and to consider methods of supplementing the provisions of the covenant for settlement of non-justiciable issues, including method of joint investigation, reserving ultimate decision in domestic issues and without undertaking further obligations to enforce decisions in case of other states.

Fourth—that Canada would be prepared to take part in any general conference on reduction of armaments which did not involve prior acceptance of protocol.

195. The Ethiopian Crisis, 1935: The Canadian Government Repudiates Dr. Riddell's Initiative

(Statement by Acting Prime Minister, Ernest Lapointe, 2 December 1935)
(*Documents relating to the Italo-Ethiopian Conflict*, Department of External Affairs, Ottawa, 1936)

The notably isolationist attitude taken by the contending parties in the Canadian general election campaign in the autumn of 1935 concerning the Italian aggression against Ethiopia (above, **41-42**) did not prevent Canadian representatives at Geneva from going further than either public or political opinion at home was likely to tolerate. On 2 November the Canadian advisory officer there, Dr. W. A. Riddell, suggested to the League committee dealing with economic sanctions against Italy that petroleum and its derivatives, coal, iron and steel, should be added to the list of articles already prohibited for export to the aggressor country. Riddell had sought instructions from the new King government but had not received them when he took this important initiative. He was reprimanded, and a month later the Acting Prime Minister issued the statement below, which had been approved by Mackenzie King, who was in the United States. It seems evident that the government's primary objection was to the appearance of Canada's taking a lead in the matter; King, while ready to take part in collective action by the League, was not prepared to lead or initiate. See W. A. Riddell, *World Security by Conference* (Toronto, 1947) and the documents collected in W. A. Riddell, ed., *Documents on Canadian Foreign Policy, 1917-1939* (Toronto, 1962). A recent study based on the records of the Department of External Affairs is John A. Munro, "The Riddell Affair Reconsidered," *External Affairs*, October 1969.

. . . the Government on the 31st October put into force an embargo on the export of arms and munitions to Italy and on the same date devised voluntary measures to ensure the prohibition of loans and credits. On the 15th November by an Order-in-Council coming into operation on the 18th an embargo was placed on all imports from Italy, the provisions with respect to loans and credits were validated and the export of key commodities on the list as already adopted by the League of Nations was prohibited.

With regard to the further application of the measures already adopted by the League and the possible extension of the scope of such measures, the Canadian Government has not departed in any way from the position as stated by the Prime Minister [in a press release] on the 29th October. The Government is not taking the initiative in proposing the extension of the measures with regard to the prohibition of exportation to Italy and does not propose to take the initiative in such measures. Canadian action and participation by the Canadian Government has been and will be limited to co-operation in purely financial and economic measures of a pacific character which are accepted by substantially all of the participating countries. . . .

Upon being asked for an explanation of reports as to Canadian initiative in the extension of the oil embargo, Mr. Lapointe gave the following explanation:

The suggestion which has appeared in the press from time to time that the Canadian Government has taken the initiative in the extension of the embargo upon exportation of key commodities to Italy, and particularly in the placing of a ban upon shipments of coal, oil, iron and steel, is due to a misunderstanding. The Canadian Government has not and does not propose to take the initiative in any such action; and the opinion which was expressed by the Canadian member of the Committee — and which has led to the reference to the proposal as a Canadian proposal — represented only his own personal opinion, and his views as a member of the Committee — and not the views of the Canadian Government.

C.
The Boundaries of Canada

196. The Labrador Boundary: Report of the Judicial Committee of the Privy Council, 1 March 1927

(*Times Law Reports*, vol. XLIII, 1926-1927)

In 1904 the Province of Quebec requested the Dominion government to arrange to refer the Labrador boundary dispute with Newfoundland to the Judicial Committee. Canada and Newfoundland agreed in 1907 that the reference should be made, but the actual terms were not finally settled until 1922. Canada would evidently have preferred to ask the Committee to fix a boundary, on the assumption that none existed; but Newfoundland insisted on its being asked to state where the *de facto* boundary was in the light of the records (*Documents on Canadian External Relations*, I, 1909-1918, Ottawa, 1967, Chap. IV). None of the historical documents in fact gave a precise or adequate definition. During the hearings in 1926 Premier L. A. Taschereau of Quebec visited London to watch the proceedings. When the Canadian case was lost a resolution calling for the abolition of appeals to the Judicial Committee was moved in the Quebec legislature, but was withdrawn at Taschereau's request (*Canadian Annual Review*, 1926-27, pp. 339-40). Dissatisfaction with the award has nevertheless continued to be expressed in Quebec. The record of the proceedings and the documents adduced fill 12 volumes (*In the Privy Council. In the Matter of the Boundary between the Dominion of Canada and the Colony of Newfoundland in the Labrador Peninsula* [London, 1927]), in addition to two atlases of maps produced by Newfoundland and one by Canada.

Judicial Committee of the Privy Council.

(Viscount Cave, L. C., Viscount Haldane, Viscount Finlay, Viscount Sumner, and Lord Warrington of Clyffe.)

IN RE LABRADOR BOUNDARY

. . .

Sir John Simon, K.C., Mr. Barrington-Ward, K.C., the Hon. W. J. Higgins, K.C. (Attorney-General for Newfoundland), Mr. W. T.

Monckton, and Mr. C. H. Pearson appeared for the Colony of New-foundland; Mr. H. P. Macmillan, K.C. (of the Scottish Bar), Mr. [Aimé] Geoffrion, K.C. (of the Canadian Bar), Mr. Maurice Alexander, K.C. (of the Canadian Bar), Mr. H. Stuart Moore, and Mr. C. P. Plaxton (of the Canadian Bar) for the Dominion of Canada.*

The arguments, lasting 14 days, were heard in October and November last.

The LORD CHANCELLOR, in delivering their Lordships' report, said: —

The Government of the Dominion of Canada and the Government of the Colony of Newfoundland have petitioned his Majesty to refer to the Judicial Committee of the Privy Council the following question: —

"What is the location and definition of the boundary as between Canada and Newfoundland in the Labrador Peninsula under the Statutes, Orders in Council and Proclamations?". . .

The Orders in Council and Proclamation upon which the decision must mainly depend were made in the year 1763, and it may seem strange that a question which affects (as it now appears) the jurisdiction over more than 100,000 square miles of territory has remained so long undecided. But an explanation is to be found in the fact that the region in dispute consists mainly of dense forests and bleak and inhospitable table-lands, of which the greater part is uninhabited. . . . It is only in recent years, when the growing demand for paper has attracted attention to the vast quantity of timber suitable for pulping, that a serious controversy as to its ownership has arisen. The question of boundary was first raised in or about the year 1888, and was the subject of discussion at the Halifax Conference of 1892; but no solution was then reached, and it was not until the year 1903 that the Government of Canada, having been informed that the Government of Newfoundland had issued a licence for cutting timber in the neighbourhood of the Hamilton River, raised the question in a serious form. Since that time the matter has been the subject of close and skilled investigation, and it now comes before this Board for decision. The issue so raised is, as Lord Hardwicke said in another connexion, "worthy the judicature of a Roman Senate" (*Penn v. Lord Baltimore*, 1 Ves. Sen., 444); but the duty of the Board is not to consider where the boundary in question might wisely and conveniently be drawn, but only to determine where, under the documents of title which have been brought to their notice, that boundary is actually to be found. . . .

*The day-to-day record shows Rt. Hon. C. J. Doherty, K.C., a former Minister of Justice, as an additional Canadian counsel.

. . . on March 24 [1763] — the Secretary of State wrote a letter to the Lords of Trade informing them that the King had "judged it proper that all the coasts of Labrador from the entrance of Hudson's Straits to the River of St. John's, which discharges itself into the sea nearly opposite the west end of the island of Anticosti, including that island with any other small islands on the said coast of Labrador, and also the islands of Madelaine in the gulf of St. Lawrence, should be included in the Government of Newfoundland,". . .

. . . After some discussion as to the boundaries of the proposed new government of Canada (which it was decided to call Quebec), the King agreed to the proposals of the Lords of Trade with the addition of a provision that the "interior country" to be reserved for the use of the Indians should be placed under the control of a military commander-in-chief. A draft Proclamation for giving effect to this decision . . . was approved for issue at a meeting of the Privy Council held on October 5.

By this Proclamation, which was dated October 7, 1763, the King declared that he had, with the advice of his Privy Council, granted letters patent under the Great Seal to erect within the countries and islands ceded and confirmed to him by the Treaty of Paris, four distinct and separate governments styled and called by the names of Quebec, East Florida, West Florida, and Grenada. The limits and boundaries of these governments were defined by the Proclamation, those of the government of Quebec being described as follows: —

"Firstly. — The Government of Quebec, bounded on the Labrador Coast by the river St. John, and from thence by a line drawn from the head of that river, through the Lake St. John, to the south end of the Lake Nipissim. . . ."

After defining the boundaries of the three other new governments, the Proclamation proceeded: —

"And to the end that the open and free fishery of our subjects may be extended to and carried on upon the coast of Labrador and the adjacent islands, we have thought fit, with the advice of our said Privy Council, to put all that coast, from the river St. John's to Hudson's Straights, together with the islands of Anticosti and the Madelaine and all other smaller islands lying upon the said coast, under the care and inspection of our Governor of Newfoundland.". . .

The annexation to Newfoundland of the southern coast of Labrador bordering on the gulf of St. Lawrence soon led to difficulties. . . . By the British North America (Quebec) Act, 1774, after reciting (among other things) that by the arrangement made by the Proclamation of 1763 "certain parts of the territory of Canada where sedentary fisheries had been established and carried on by the subjects of France, inhabitants of the said Province of Canada, under grants and concessions from the Government thereof were annexed to the Government of Newfoundland and thereby subjected to regulations inconsistent with the nature of such fisheries," it was enacted that the territories therein described and also "all such territories, islands and countries which have since the 10th February, 1763, been made part of the Government of Newfoundland" be annexed to and made part of the province of Quebec as created and established by the Proclamation of October 7, 1763.

. . . ultimately, by the Newfoundland Act, 1809, section 14, it was enacted: —

"That such parts of the coast of Labrador from the river St. John to Hudson's Straights, and the said Island of Anticosti and all other smaller islands so annexed to the Government of Newfoundland by the said Proclamation of the seventh day of October One thousand seven hundred and sixty-three (except the said islands of Madelaine) shall be separated from the said Government of Lower Canada and be again re-annexed to the Government of Newfoundland; any thing in the said Act passed in the Thirty-first year of His present Majesty's Reign, or any other Act, to the contrary notwithstanding."

. . . By the British North America (Seignorial Rights) Act, 1825, section 9, after reciting that under and by virtue of the Acts of 1774 and 1809 the coast of Labrador from the river St. John to Hudson's Strait and the islands above referred to were "annexed to and form part of the Government of Newfoundland," and that it was expedient that "certain parts of the said coast of Labrador should be re-annexed to and form part of the province of Lower Canada," it was enacted: —

"That so much of the said coast as lies to the westward of a line to be drawn due north and south from the bay or harbour of Ance Sablon, inclusive, as far as the fifty-second degree of north latitude, with the island of Anticosti and all other islands adjacent to such part as last aforesaid of the coast of Labrador, shall be and the same are hereby re-annexed to and made a part of the said province of Lower Canada, and shall henceforward be subject to the laws of the said province and to none other.". . .

At this point it is desirable to set out the contentions of the two parties. The contention of the Dominion is that the "coast" which by the commission and Proclamation of 1763, as modified by the subsequent statutes, was annexed to Newfoundland, is

"a strip of maritime territory, extending from Cape Chidley at the entrance to Hudson Strait, to the eastern headland of the bay or harbour of Blanc Sablon on the Strait of Belle Isle, and comprising, in its depth inland, only so much of the land immediately abutting on the sea, above low-water mark, as was accessible and useful to the British fishermen annually resorting to that coast in the ordinary conduct of their fishing operations, for the purposes of 'the open and free fishery' extended to that coast by the Royal Proclamation and carried on there and for those purposes only"; but, recognizing that it may be found impracticable to lay down such a line upon the land, Canada suggests "that the boundary be located as a line to be drawn from the eastern headland of the bay or harbour of Blanc Sablon on the south to Cape Chidley on the north at a distance from high-water mark on the seacoast of the peninsula of Labrador of one mile."

On the other hand, the contention of the colony of Newfoundland is that the boundary should be "a line drawn due north from Ance Sablon as far as the fifty-second degree of north latitude, and should be traced from thence northwards to Cape Chidley along the crest of the watershed of the rivers flowing into the Atlantic Ocean.". . .

It may be added that the colony contends that, in the event of the Dominion establishing its main contention, the littoral strip of land which would then represent the territory annexed to Newfoundland should not cross the mouth of the great Hamilton Inlet . . . but should be carried along the northern shore of that inlet and round the head of Goose Bay and so back along the southern shore of the inlet to the seacoast.

Before examining these claims in detail, their Lordships think it desirable to formulate two propositions which appear to be common to both sides, and which indeed are beyond dispute.

First, the word "coast" or "coasts" (for both are used in the documents) is a word of undefined meaning; and while it is usually to be understood in the sense which is given to it in Dr. Johnson's and other dictionaries, that is to say, as meaning "the edge or margin of the land next the sea" or "shore," there are many examples of its being used to denote a considerable tract of land bounded by and looking towards the sea. . . .

The second proposition which appears to be beyond dispute in this case is that the effect of the Orders in Council, Proclamation, and statutes which have to be construed was to give to the Government of Newfoundland not mere rights of inspection and regulation exercisable upon a line of shore, but territory which became as much a part of the colony as the island of Newfoundland itself, and which was capable of being defined by metes and bounds. . . .

In these circumstances the question to be determined is, not whether Newfoundland possesses territory upon the peninsula of Labrador, but what is the inland boundary of that territory. Is it to be defined by a line following the sinuosities of the shore at a distance of one mile or thereabouts from high-water mark, or is it to be found at the watershed of the rivers falling into the sea on that shore? No third alternative has been suggested by any person.

When the material documents are considered from this point of view, it is evident that they contain much which supports the contention that the word "coast" is to be construed as including a considerable area of land. . . .

Further, the use of the watershed or "height of land" as a boundary was undoubtedly familiar in British North America at the period in question. . . . In the Proclamation of 1763 the province of Quebec thereby constituted was defined as bounded on the south by "the high lands which divide the rivers that empty themselves into the said river St. Lawrence from those which flow into the sea." It may well be, therefore, that in allotting to Newfoundland the "coast" of Labrador the framers of the documents of 1763 had in mind as a boundary the "height of land" from which the rivers ran down to that shore — though without any accurate conception of the distance of that boundary from the sea. . . .

But perhaps the strongest argument in favour of an extended construction of the grant to Newfoundland is to be found in the terms of the Act of 1825 above quoted. By that statute, after a recital that it was expedient that "certain parts of the said coasts of Labrador should be re-annexed to and form part of the province of Lower Canada," it was enacted that "so much of the said coast as lies to the westward of a line to be drawn due north and south from the bay or harbour of Ance Sablon inclusive as far as the fifty-second degree of north latitude" should be re-annexed to and made part of that province. Now a line drawn north and south from the bay of Ance Sablon to the fifty-second degree of north latitude would penetrate the interior of the country for a distance of about 40 miles, and the land to the westward of such a line would in some of its parts cover a distance of over 100 miles from the sea; and this being so, it would seem that the language of this enactment, construed in its plain and natural meaning, points directly to the inference that the expression "coasts of Labrador" as used in 1763 and 1809 was understood by Parliament in 1825 to have comprised the interior of the country back to those limits. . . .

. . . Indeed, it may be doubted whether any person, noting upon the sketch-map the configuration of the coast as proposed by Canada to be defined, would conceive that the Crown can have intended to annex to Newfoundland an area of that shape and character, to refer to it as a "territory," and to establish a form of government there; and if, as the Colony forcibly contends, the shores of the Great Hamilton Inlet must be treated as a part of the sea coast, so that the one-mile strip would pass up the northern shore of that inlet and round the head of Goose Bay and would then return along its southern shores, the fantastic character of the boundary proposed would become even more apparent. . . .

. . . The administration of justice in Labrador has throughout been under the direction of the Government of Newfoundland. . . .

. . . No evidence was given of any exercise of a Canadian jurisdiction in any part of the territory in dispute.

It seems desirable to add some observations on the maps, of which a large number (some of great antiquity and interest) were produced by the parties. . . .

. . . Arrowsmith's map of 1857 (N 26) has some authority as having been ordered to be printed by the House of Commons for the purposes of the Hudson's Bay Committee of that year, and as having been selected as an exhibit in the Alaska Boundary case; and that map . . . assigns to that territory [Labrador] the exact boundaries now claimed for it on behalf of Newfoundland. The same observation applies . . . to a map (N 32a) compiled by Desbarats in 1873 and sent by Lord Dufferin, as Governor-General of Canada, to the British Ambassador [sic] in Washington as showing "the exact boundary on the coast and the assumed boundary in the interior." The dispatch of the Governor-General transmitting this map enclosed a copy of the report of a Committee of the Privy Council approved by the Governor-General in Council on November 12, 1874, which was in the following terms:—

"In a despatch dated 20th June, 1874, from Sir Edward Thornton to Your Excellency, inclosing a communication from the Hon. Hamilton Fish, Secretary of State at Washington, desiring to be informed whether any part of Labrador is separated from the jurisdiction of either the Dominion of Canada or that of Newfoundland.

"The Honourable the Secretary of State [of Canada] . . . reports that the boundary-line between the Dominion of Canada and Labrador is a line drawn due north and south from the Bay or Harbour of Ance au Blanc Sablon, near the Straits of Belle Isle, as far as the 52nd degree of north latitude; that Labrador extends eastward and northward from that point to Hudson's Straits.

"That the division-line in the interior separating Labrador from the Dominion of Canada has only been defined as far north as the 52nd degree of north latitude, but it has been assumed that the boundary-line in the interior would have been the direction laid down on the accompanying map, which follows the height of land. . ."

The terms of this report appear to their Lordships to be significant. . . .

Upon the whole, their Lordships, having considered the facts and arguments put before them with the care which is necessary in a matter of such grave importance, have come to the conclusion that the claim of the colony of Newfoundland is in substance made out; but there are two points of detail* to be mentioned. . . .

For the above reasons their Lordships are of opinion that, according to the true construction of the statutes, Orders in Council and Proclamations referred to in the Order of Reference, the boundary between Canada and Newfoundland in the Labrador Peninsula is a line drawn due north from the eastern boundary of the bay or harbour of Ance Sablon as far as the fifty-second degree of north latitude, and from thence westward along that parallel until it reaches the Romaine River, and then northward along the left or east bank of that river and its head waters to their source, and from thence due north to the crest of the watershed or height of land there, and from thence westward and northward along the crest of the watershed of the rivers flowing into the Atlantic Ocean until it reaches Cape Chidley; and they will humbly advise his Majesty accordingly.

*Concerning the boundary in the vicinity of the Romaine River, and Woody Island at Anse Sablon, which went to Canada.

D.
Defence Policy
Between the
Two World Wars

197. Expenditure on the Defence Departments between the Wars

(Compiled from the annual reports of the Department of National Defence)

A general view of defence policy in the years 1918-39 is best obtained from a simplified table of expenditure. The main points emerging are perhaps the following: (1) expenditures throughout the period, though varying somewhat, were always small, and therefore the forces were likewise small and ineffective; (2) though the Liberals starved the forces from 1921 on, the amounts spent were beginning to increase slightly by the advent of the Depression; (3) during the Depression the Bennett government cut the forces sharply, especially the air force; (4) the modest rearmament program undertaken by the Liberals from 1936 onward gave large priority to the air force. See Eayrs, *In Defence of Canada,* I and II; and C. P. Stacey, *The Military Problems of Canada* (Toronto, 1940) and *Six Years of War* (Official History of the Canadian Army in the Second World War, Vol. I, Ottawa, 1955).

Fiscal Year	Militia Services	Naval Services	Air Services	Miscel-laneous*	Total
		(000's)			
1918-19	380,582	13,385			393,967
1919-20	328,223	9,638	109		337,970
1920-21	26,900	1,999	2,007		30,906
1921-22	20,171	2,041	1,659		23,871
1922-23	15,248	1,378	1,004		17,630
1923-24	10,920	1,354	1,249	708	14,231
1924-25	9,951	1,399	1,377	754	13,481
1925-26	9,131	1,419	1,880	2,001	14,433
1926-27	9,158	1,597	2,197	2,052	15,006
1927-28	10,166	1,702	3,891	1,911	17,673
1928-29	11,047	1,836	5,040	1,862	19,787
1929-30	11,163	3,013	5,920	1,883	21,981
1930-31	11,026	3,597	7,147	1,960	23,732
1931-32	9,700	3,043	4,129	1,497	18,372
1932-33	8,718	2,167	1,731	1,527	14,145
1933-34	8,773	2,171	1,684	6,999	19,629
1934-35	8,888	2,226	2,258	8,932	22,305
1935-36	10,141	2,380	3,777	11,078	27,387
1936-37	11,345	4,763	5,821	4,737	26,669
1937-38	17,222	4,371	10,108	1,221	32,835
1938-39	15,768	6,589	11,216	1,224	34,799
Appropriations (pre-war):					
1939-40	21,396	8,800	29,735	4,732	64,666

*"Miscellaneous" here includes all services listed in the official reports under "General Services," "Other Services," and "Special Accounts." These were most important during the Depression; spending on unemployment relief projects, many of which had permanent military significance, rose to a peak of $10,201,000 in 1935-36. Note that there are minor discrepancies in totals, the result of the last three digits in each sum being omitted. Only from 1934-35 did the Department of National Defence include in its annual report a ten-year retrospective table of expenditure on *all* the fighting services. Before 1925-26 certain general services subsequently appearing here under "Miscellaneous" are included under "Militia Services." Figures for 1918-19 and 1919-20 are mainly on war and demobilization account. The pre-war *appropriation* figures for 1939-40 are given here because of their importance in the rearmament program, even though less than a quarter of the money was spent before war broke out.

198. The National Defence Act, 1922

(12-13 George V, Chap. 34)

This Act, later redesignated the Department of National Defence Act, placed all the Canadian defence forces under a single minister for the first time.

(Assented to 28th June, 1922)

. . .

3. There shall be a department of the Government of Canada which shall be called the Department of National Defence, over which a Minister of the Crown shall preside, who shall be the Minister of National Defence.

4. The Minister shall be charged with all matters relating to Defence, including the Militia, the Military, Naval and Air Services of Canada. . . .

7. (1) All the powers, duties and functions vested in any Minister or Deputy Minister by *The Naval Service Act*, chapter forty-three of the statutes of 1910; the *Militia Act*, chapter forty-one of the Revised Statutes of Canada, 1906; the *Militia Pension Act*, chapter forty-two of the said Revised Statutes; the *Royal Military College Act*, chapter forty-three of the said Revised Statutes, and all Acts in amendment of any of the said Acts, shall be vested in and performed and exercised by the Minister and Deputy Minister of National Defence respectively. . . .

(2) The powers, duties and functions vested in the Air Board by *The Air Board Act*, chapter eleven of the statutes of 1919, or by any order or regulation made thereunder, shall be administered, exercised and performed by or under the direction of the Minister [of National Defence]. . . .

199. The Visiting Forces (British Commonwealth) Act, 1933

(23-24 George V, Chap. 21)

This Canadian act stemming from the Statute of Westminster (above, **185**), and parallel acts passed in 1932-39 by the United Kingdom and the other Dominions, formed the legal basis for co-operation between Canadian and other Commonwealth army and air (but not naval) forces in the Second World War. Commonwealth airmen coming to

Canada for training served under them, as did Canadian airmen attached, as great numbers were, to the Royal Air Force for service abroad; under them also Canadian forces served under British higher command in the field. Note that "serving together" was interpreted as a relationship in which Canadian forces in the United Kingdom were *not* under British command; "in combination" involved placing them under such command, in Britain or abroad. See Stacey, *Six Years of War* and *Arms, Men and Governments*.

An Act to make provision with respect to Forces of His Majesty from other parts of the British Commonwealth or from a colony when visiting the Dominion of Canada; and with respect to the exercise of command and discipline when Forces of His Majesty from different parts of the Commonwealth are serving together; and with respect to the attachment of members of one such force to another such force, and with respect to deserters from such forces.

(Assented to 12th April, 1933)

. . .

3. (1) When a visiting force is present in Canada it shall be lawful for the naval, military and air force courts and authorities (in this Act referred to as the "service courts" and "service authorities") of that part of the Commonwealth to which the Force belongs, to exercise within Canada in relation to members of such force in matters concerning discipline and in matters concerning the internal administration of such Force all such powers as are conferred upon them by the law of that part of the Commonwealth. . . .*

6. (1) The forces, other than home [Canadian] forces, to which this section applies are the naval, military and air forces of His Majesty raised in the United Kingdom, the Commonwealth of Australia, the Dominion of New Zealand, the Union of South Africa, the Irish Free State, or Newfoundland.

(2) The Governor in Council,

(i) may attach temporarily to a home force any member of another force to which this section applies who is placed at his disposal for the purpose by the service authorities of that part of the Commonwealth to which the other force belongs;

(ii) subject to anything to the contrary in the conditions applicable to his service, may place any member of a home force at the disposal of the service authorities of another part of the

*The Act proceeds to go into detail concerning means of carrying out this section. Section 5 deals with the apprehension and treatment of deserters and absentees.

Commonwealth for the purpose of being attached temporarily by those authorities to a force to which this section applies belonging to that part of the Commonwealth.

(3) Whilst a member of another force is by virtue of this section attached temporarily to a home force, he shall be subject to the law relating to the Naval Service, the Militia, or the Air Force, as the case may be, in like manner as if he were a member of the home force, and shall be treated and have the like powers of command and punishment over members of the home force to which he is attached as if he were a member of that force of relative rank. . . .

(4) When a home force and another force to which this section applies are serving together, whether alone or not: —

(a) any member of the home force shall be treated and shall have over members of the home force the like powers of command as if he were a member of the home force of relative rank: and

(b) if the forces are acting in combination, any officer of the other force appointed by His Majesty, or in accordance with regulations made by or by authority of His Majesty, to command the combined force, or any part thereof, shall be treated and shall have over members of the home force the like powers of command and punishment, and may be invested with the like authority to convene, and confirm the findings and sentences of, courts martial, as if he were an officer of the home force of relative rank and holding the same command.

(5) For the purposes of this section, forces shall be deemed to be serving together or acting in combination if and only if they are declared to be so serving or so acting by order of the Governor in Council, and the relative rank of members of the home forces and of other forces shall be such as may be prescribed by regulations made by His Majesty. . . .

8. So far as regards any naval force and the members of any such force, the provisions of this Act shall be deemed to be in addition to and not in derogation of such of the provisions of any Act of the Parliament of the United Kingdom or of the Parliament of any other part of the Commonwealth as are for the time being applicable to that force and the members thereof.*

---

*Throughout the Second World War the primary basis of the legal relationship between the Royal Navy and the Royal Canadian Navy was the United Kingdom's Naval Discipline Act and King's Regulations and Admiralty Instructions, as recognized and made applicable to Canadian forces by a series of Canadian statutes and orders in council beginning with the Naval Service Act of 1910.

200. The Joint Staff Committee Makes Recommendations for Rearmament, 1936

("An Appreciation of the Defence Problems Confronting Canada . . . ," 5 September 1936, Records of Department of National Defence)

The professional heads of the three Canadian fighting services were known collectively as the Joint Staff Committee until 1939, after the Senior Air Officer, having ceased to report through the Chief of the General Staff, was redesignated "Chief of the Air Staff"; the committee then became known as the Chiefs of Staff Committee. Canadian service officers at this period commanded less respect from politicians or the public than their professional competence warranted. This paper was probably mainly the work of Colonel H. D. G. Crerar, Secretary of the Joint Staff Committee. The estimates attached to it recommended a five-year plan of expenditure totalling in all some $260,000,000, with the first year costing about $66,000,000. The government decided to spend about half this (see above, **197**). See Stacey, *Six Years of War*. The paper is printed at greater length in Eayrs, *In Defence of Canada: Appeasement and Rearmament*, Document 1.

. . .

3. AN OUTLINE OF CANADA'S DEFENCE PROBLEMS

(a) The Direct Defence of Canada

The direct defence of the national territory is, in the last analysis, the major responsibility of the armed forces of Canada. But hitherto, owing to our fortunate geographical position, this problem has not been given a high degree of priority. Canada's only neighbour is the United States and there seems to be little likelihood of a disagreement with that country which would lead to war. . . .

(b) The Defence of Canadian Neutrality in the event of a United States-Japanese War

Signs are not wanting of a growing conflict of interest between the United States and Japan in the North Pacific. . . . Should war between these countries materialize, one of the following courses would be open to Canada: —

(i) To throw in her lot with the United States independently of the rest of the British Empire.

(ii) In the event of the United Kingdom and the other Dominions deciding to act jointly with the United States, to co-operate in such action.

(iii) In the event of the United Kingdom and the other Dominions deciding to adopt a position of neutrality, to remain neutral herself.

The first is held to be an unlikely contingency. The second and third, in the view of the Joint Staff Committee, are those which this country must now anticipate and for which preliminary defence measures should now be undertaken, thus enabling Canada to secure its position in some measure, either as a co-belligerent or, alternatively, as an effective neutral.

(c) The Indirect Defence of Canada by Participation Overseas in a Major War

The possibility of a major war is becoming more apparent. Indeed, the realization is growing in many minds that the cessation of hostilities in 1918 was but an armistice.

A noteworthy feature of Canadian post-war political history has been a growing disinclination to become embroiled in European quarrels.... In spite of a sincere desire to hold herself aloof from participation in the war of 1914-18, the United States was inevitably dragged in. It is suggested that in the event of another world war the same forces would again bear the same compelling influence, possibly with even greater intensity. It seems unlikely, therefore, that in such circumstances Canada can hope to remain at peace. It follows that the despatch overseas of Canadian Forces may again be necessary....

5. A REVIEW OF RECENT DEVELOPMENTS IN THE ORGANIZATION AND EQUIPMENT OF ARMED FORCES

(a) Defence and Industry

The responsibility for national defence can no longer be held to rest solely on the Department which bears that name for it is but to repeat a truism to state that modern war imposes maximum demands on every sphere of civil activity....

(b) Developments in Naval Armaments

. . . To the necessity for secure anti-submarine defences for naval bases and shipping centres must now be added adequate air defences both for harbours and in the focal areas for trade.

Every post-war measure of development in naval warfare has tended to increased cost, increased personnel and increased technical training, and rapid rearmament is therefore more difficult and throws a heavy burden on industrial resources.

(c) Modern Requirements in Land Forces

. . . The technical advances in the design and power of weapons, developed by the experience of the last war, are now showing results in the type and capabilities of the armaments with which armies are now being equipped. . . .

It should be noted here that the Canadian Militia possesses neither armoured fighting vehicles, supplies of mechanized transport of approved design, nor modern weapons.

(d) Requirements of a Modern Air Force

Modern Air Forces are no longer merely an auxiliary to a Navy or Army. . . . While it is not contended that Canadian requirements are comparable to those of the Great Powers, it is perhaps pertinent to mention here that Canada's air force is entirely inadequate to meet her modest defence requirements; and further, that this country does not possess an aircraft industry worthy of the name. . . .

6. CANADA'S MILITARY LIABILITIES

(a) Direct Defence of Canada against Invasion

The contingency of a recourse to military action as a solution to political difficulties which might arise between the United States and Canada has been referred to above and has been dismissed on the basis of its improbability. . . .*

On the other hand, the liability of direct attack on Canada by Japanese forces has become a matter requiring urgent consideration and action in view of the menacing situation which continues to develop in the Far East. . . .

(b) The Maintenance of Neutrality

There is another aspect of local defence, the maintenance of neutrality, for which it is considered that preparations should now be made. . . .

A glance at the map will reveal that the indented and sparsely settled coast of British Columbia provides an admirable area from which Japanese submarines, and even surface craft, can develop raids against U.S. sea communications and Pacific Coast ports. . . .

It is the considered opinion of the Joint Staff Committee that Canada's existing naval, military and air forces are incapable of

---

*The paper proceeds to point out that the adverse balance of naval and air power renders the military defence of Canada against the U.S. quite impossible.

ensuring anything approaching adequate supervision of her Western coast. . . .

(c) Participation in a Major Overseas War

The two danger areas in the world today, which concern Canada no matter how reluctant that concern may be, are the Far East and Europe. Of the two, the European situation contains the most serious implications. . . .

The military problem of Canada, so far as participation in a war in Europe is concerned, is more air and land than sea. . . . There are, however, certain essential factors to bear in mind when considering the organization and composition of the forces which Canada might decide to despatch. The first is that the advent of air power and the increased mobility and protection due to mechanized and armoured vehicles have out-dated the conception of the "nation in arms." In other words, "front line" fighting will tend to absorb a smaller per-centage than hitherto of the man-power of the nation. Secondly, the speed by which these highly technical forces can be mobilized will be of the very greatest importance. Thirdly, the national arrange-ments for maintaining these forces in the field and equipping addi-tional ones, that is to say, plans and means for the organization of industry, are now in the very first category of importance.

7. THE REQUIREMENTS OF THE ARMED FORCES OF CANADA

From the above review the following appreciation emerges:

(a) The direct defence of Canada is the major responsibility of its armed forces. . . .

(b) The Indirect defence of Canada by the co-operation with other Empire forces in a war overseas is a secondary responsibility of this country, though possibly one requiring much greater ultimate effort. . . . The completion of preparations necessary to Canada for the adequate armed supervision of neutral rights and responsibilities in the event of a war in the Far East in which this country refused to participate, or those necessary in the event of circumstances compel-ling Canada to act as a co-belligerent in this contingency will, how-ever, in considerable measure, render Canada capable of taking an early part, with other Empire forces, in overseas operations.

In accordance, therefore, with the appreciation given in 7(a) above, which concerns the direct threats to the security of Canada, the Joint Staff Committee summarizes below those urgent military require-ments for which immediate, or short term, provision should now be made:

Naval Forces (Detailed Estimates annexed)*

The immediate naval requirements are to build up a fully manned and equipped naval force consisting of at least:

    6 modern torpedo boat destroyers
    4 minesweepers

with necessary base defence equipment and auxiliary vessels.† This force is the minimum required to provide reasonable security on one coast, only....

Land Forces (Detailed Estimates annexed)

(i) The modernization of the coast defences of Esquimalt, including the provision of anti-aircraft armament and equipment for the protection of the Naval base, dry dock, magazine, etc., and to provide some measure of military control over the Canadian water and air approaches to the mainland....

(ii) The seaward defences of Halifax are, in general, considered adequate in quantity.... The modernization of existing armament, defence electric lights, etc., is however necessary. No anti-aircraft defences worth the term exist at this fortress....

(iii) The reorganization of the Canadian Militia, already approved, calls for a smaller organization, but one which comprises modern formations and equipment. The necessary armament, equipment and supplies to enable one-third of this future force to mobilize without delay on a war footing, and concentrate in any part of Canada, is considered essential.

Air Forces (Detailed Estimates annexed)

(i) The immediate requirements are modern aircraft, bases, advanced and intermediate operating stations, repair and supply depots and training centres.

(ii) The aircraft requirements of Air Defence on both the West and East Coasts necessitates provision for: the reconnaissance of vast sea areas and lengthy coast lines, the attack of enemy surface craft, submarines and forces violating our territory, the defence of ports from hostile carrier or cruiser borne aircraft, co-operating with naval and military units. The mobility of air forces coupled with the fact that a main threat on both coasts at the same time is unlikely, permits great flexibility in the disposition of air units and allows ready concentration in any threatened area on either coast. For these duties, approxi-

*Omitted.

†The ten ships specified here were all obtained before war broke out. This was the only part of the whole program that was completed.

mately 300 aircraft will be required to equip 23 Squadrons and about 70 aircraft will be required for Training Schools. To minimize the cost of maintaining this force, it is proposed that 11 Squadrons should be Permanent Units and that 12 Squadrons be Non-Permanent units. . . .

201. Mackenzie King Urges the Liberal Caucus to Support His Rearmament Program, 20 January 1937

(Stacey, *Six Years of War*, p. 14)

Although the government's rearmament plan was very limited and in retrospect seems utterly inadequate to the scale of the coming emergency, it was attacked by the Co-operative Commonwealth Federation and disliked by many Liberals who considered it excessive if not unnecessary. See Eayrs, *In Defence of Canada*, II.

We are not concerned with aggression. We are concerned with the defence of Canada. . . . The possibility of conflict with the United States is eliminated from our mind. There is nothing here for an expeditionary force — only for the defence of Canada against those who might wantonly assail us or violate our neutrality. The defence of our shores and the preservation of our neutrality — these are the two cardinal principles of our policy.

You read what Meighen said in the Senate yesterday, that the amount in the estimates was not enough, that we were concerned with the defence of the Empire as a whole; that the first line of our defence was the Empire's boundaries. We cannot accept that. But we can put our own house in order [so] that we shall not be a burden on anyone else — neither a burden on the States nor a burden on England. Meighen would do so much more — at least so he says — and Woodsworth would do nothing at all. The safe policy is the middle course between these two views — the safe policy is a rational policy of domestic defence.

Let us therefore be not afraid. Too many are governed by fear in the days in which we live. Let us first of all have a complete understanding of our own policy — and then fearing neither of the extremists — let us pursue our moderate way. Let us be united on a sane policy of defence: let us explain that policy to our people and let us above all strive at all times to keep Canada *united*.

202. The Minister of National Defence Defines the Government's Priorities, 1939

(Debates, House of Commons, 26 April 1939)

Just how the priorities here stated by Mr. Ian Mackenzie were arrived at is not fully clear, but they were probably the work of Mackenzie King. Though the priorities have some relationship to the Joint Staff Committee's recommendations (above, **200**), they were certainly a political, not a military, invention; and there is little doubt that the priority given the air force stemmed from the fear of conscription in the event of war.

In 1935 and 1936, in anticipation of possible repercussions from the impending conflict in the far east it was considered the greatest risk in Canada was on the Pacific coast. Accordingly in preparing our defences the department laid down the following priorities as a guide:

1. Fortification of Pacific coast prior to Atlantic coast.

2. Development of the air force in priority to navy and, so far as possible, the navy in priority to the militia.

3. Reorganizing and re-equipping the militia as soon as our resources permit us to do so.

E.
Canada and the United Nations, 1943-1945

From the Second World War, as from the First, there emerged a world organization intended for the maintenance of peace. The official Canadian attitude to the United Nations differed materially from that towards the old League of Nations and yet had similarities. Canada did not object now to an organization to enforce peace, whereas before she had taken the view — particularly characteristic of Mackenzie King — that the League should be mainly an organ of conciliation; but she concentrated on seeking to obtain what Sir Robert Borden would have called an "adequate voice" for herself and other "middle powers," as distinct from the great powers, and on ensuring as far as possible that she would not be liable for participation in military sanctions against an aggressor without having an opportunity to be heard on the issue. See F.H. Soward, *Canada in World Affairs: From Normandy to Paris, 1944-1946* (Toronto, 1950) and F.H. Soward and Edgar McInnis, *Canada and the United Nations* (New York, 1956).

203. Mackenzie King Produces the Idea of "Functional Representation," 1943

(*Debates, House of Commons*, 9 July 1943)

The ingenious idea of "functional representation" seems to have originated in the Department of External Affairs, perhaps with Mr. H.H. Wrong. Clearly stemming from the experience of Canada with the Allied wartime organizations, it was a formula designed to ensure some significant participation in international bodies for powers below the first rank by giving them representation in proportion, not to their population or general power, but to the contribution they could make in particular economic or other areas.

534

Right Hon. W.L. MACKENZIE KING (Secretary of State for External Affairs): . . .

It is too early for me to attempt even a shadowy outline of the form of the international settlement, political and economic, which may follow the ending of hostilities. It may be useful, however, to say a word about one of its aspects. The strong bonds which have linked the united nations* into a working model of cooperation must be strengthened and developed for even greater use in the years of peace. It is perhaps an axiom of war that during actual hostilities methods must be improvised, secrecy must be observed, attention must be concentrated on victory. The time is approaching, however, when even before victory is won the concept of the united nations will have to be embodied in some form of international organization. On the one hand, authority in international affairs must not be concentrated exclusively in the largest powers. On the other, authority cannot be divided equally among all the thirty or more sovereign states that comprise the united nations, or all effective authority will disappear. A number of new international institutions are likely to be set up as a result of the war. In the view of the government, effective representations on these bodies should neither be restricted to the largest states nor necessarily extended to all states. Representation should be determined on a functional basis which will admit to full membership those countries, large or small, which have the greatest contribution to make to the particular object in question. In the world there are over sixty sovereign states. If they all have a nominally equal voice in international decisions, no effective decisions are likely to be taken. Some compromise must be found between the theoretical equality of states and the practical necessity of limiting representation on international bodies to a workable number. That compromise can be discovered, especially in economic matters, by the adoption of the functional principle of representation. That principle, in turn, is likely to find many new expressions in the gigantic task of liberation, restoration and reconstruction.

* This term, applied to the Allies during the war, was applied to the new world organization set up at the end of it.

204. Canada Comments on the Dumbarton Oaks Proposals for a World Organization, 12 January 1945

(*External Affairs*, February 1965)

In October 1944 four great powers (the United States, Britain, the Soviet Union and China) published proposals for an international organization which they had worked out at a conference at Dumbarton Oaks. These were really a draft of what became the United Nations Charter. Canada—which like all other countries except the four named had had no part in preparing the scheme—sent the four great sponsoring powers and France comments along the lines of Mackenzie King's statement of July 1943 (above, **203**).

1. The Canadian Government has welcomed the proposals for the establishment of a general international organization published by the Governments of the United States, the United Kingdom, the Soviet Union and China. Certain parts of the proposals, however, create special difficulties for Canada and probably for other states as well. The difficulties relate to the means whereby the co-operation of these states in fulfilling the obligations placed upon the Security Council can best be assured, and the authority of the Security Council thereby increased. . . .

2. The proposals recognize the primary responsibilities of the great powers for the maintenance of peace by according them permanent membership in the Security Council. It is also generally understood that, when the proposals are completed, the individual concurrence of the great powers will be required in certain important classes of decisions.* There is, however, no corresponding recognition in the proposals that the responsibilities which other members of the United Nations are asked to assume differ greatly, despite the fact that their power and their capacity to use it for the maintenance of peace range from almost zero upwards to a point not very far behind the great powers.

3. Under the proposals, a country which would be called upon to make a substantial contribution to world security has no better assurance of election to the Security Council than the smallest and weakest state. Furthermore, such a country, when not holding an elected seat on the Security Council, would be required to obligate

* A diplomatic way of referring to the veto to be accorded to the permanent members of the Security Council.

itself to accept and carry out the decisions of the Council—decisions which might entail drastic action on its part under the provisions of Paragraphs 3, 4, 5 and 6 of Chapter VIII B. Such action might even be required by the Council without any consultation with the government of the country in question. In contrast, a great power is ensured of participating fully in all the deliberations of the Security Council and is likely also to be assured of exercising a right of individual veto on many of its decisions.

4. It is open to question whether a country such as Canada could undertake to accept such an obligation or could, if the obligation were to be initially accepted, ensure effective collaboration in the indefinite future. Canada certainly makes no claim to be regarded as a great power. The Canadian record in two great wars, however, has revealed both readiness to join in concerted action against aggression and the possession of substantial military and industrial capacity. There are a number of other states the potential contribution of which to the maintenance of future security is of the same order of magnitude. The support of these states is important to the maintenance of peace, and the active collaboration of some at least of them would probably be required for the execution of major decisions of the Security Council under Chapter VIII B of the proposals.

5. The question, therefore, arises whether it is possible, within the framework of the general scheme, to devise means of associating more effectively with the work of the Security Council states of the order of international importance of Canada. This might be achieved by making some changes in the powers conferred on the Council, and by ensuring that such states were chosen to fill elected seats on the Council more frequently (or possibly for longer periods) than states with less to contribute to the maintenance of security.

6. It is suggested that decisions of the Security Council under Chapter VIII B should be made binding, in the first instance, only on states which are members of the Council. States not represented on the Council should be required to take positive action only when the decision has been endorsed by a two-thirds majority of the Assembly (when it would become binding on all members), or when the country or countries concerned have by special invitation participated on the same footing as elected members in the Council's proceedings, or when they have individually agreed with the Council to join in a particular task of enforcement. The adoption of these suggestions would make it far easier for states other than the great powers to enter into agreements making available to the organization substantial military forces, facilities and assistance, and would thus increase the effective power at the disposal of the Council. Their

adoption would also help to secure the requisite public support in countries not permanently represented on the Council.

7. By the acceptance of these suggestions, a special responsibility would be placed upon all members of the Security Council which would not be imposed on other members of the organization. Thus the changes proposed in the authority of the Council must be considered in conjunction with the suggestion for increasing the effectiveness of the elected section, since they would increase the need for ensuring that the elected section of the Council was made up of states capable of contributing to the discharge of the Council's obligations. A serious effort should, therefore, be made to devise a system of election which would provide that due regard must be paid to the international significance of the countries chosen. . . .

8. In devising methods of achieving this end, it will be generally agreed that it is important to discourage election to the Council being sought for reasons of prestige, and also to avoid the development of electoral understandings, such as those which controlled the election to the Council of the League of Nations. While it is difficult to put forward a satisfactory formula, it is believed that, given the initiative and support of the great powers, the problem can be solved.

205. Extracts from the Charter of the United Nations, Signed 26 June 1945

(*Canada, Treaty Series*, 1945, No. 7)

The Canadian memorandum of January 1945 (above, **204**) seems to have had little effect. Somewhat more was accomplished by the Canadian delegation at the San Francisco Conference (April-June 1945) at which the new world organization was set up. Neither great nor small powers were enthusiastic about the Canadian view of the composition of the Security Council, but a watered-down version of "functional representation" was written into Article 23 of the U.N. Charter. On 14 May, in an interview with Edward R. Stettinius, the American Secretary of State, Mackenzie King, who led the delegation, emphasized the probable difficulty of getting Canadian public approval for the Charter without some assurance of consultation before Canadian forces were called for (Pickersgill and Forster, *The Mackenzie King Record*, II, 386-9). This appears to have been the origin of Article 44 of the Charter. Canada, while disliking the extent to which the great powers were clearly to dominate the U.N., did not choose to be a leader of opposition on this question in the conference.

CHARTER OF THE UNITED NATIONS

WE THE PEOPLES OF THE UNITED NATIONS DETERMINED

to save succeeding generations from the scourge of war, which twice in our lifetime has brought untold sorrow to mankind, and

to reaffirm faith in fundamental human rights, in the dignity and worth of the human person, in the equal rights of men and women and of nations large and small, and

to establish conditions under which justice and respect for the obligations arising from treaties and other sources of international law can be maintained, and

to promote social progress and better standards of life in larger freedom,

AND FOR THESE ENDS

to practice toleration and live together in peace with one another as good neighbors, and

to unite our strength to maintain international peace and security, and

to ensure, by the acceptance of principles and the institution of methods, that armed force shall not be used, save in the common interest, and

to employ international machinery for the promotion of the economic and social advancement of all peoples,

HAVE RESOLVED TO COMBINE OUR EFFORTS TO ACCOMPLISH THESE AIMS.

Accordingly, our respective Governments, through representatives assembled in the city of San Francisco, who have exhibited their full powers found to be in good and due form, have agreed to the present Charter of the United Nations and do hereby establish an international organization to be known as the United Nations.

CHAPTER I

PURPOSES AND PRINCIPLES

Article 1

The Purposes of the United Nations are:

1. To maintain international peace and security, and to that end: to take effective collective measures for the prevention and removal of threats to the peace, and for the suppression of acts of aggression or other breaches of the peace, and to bring about by peaceful means, and in conformity with the principles of justice and international law, adjustment or settlement of international disputes or situations which might lead to a breach of the peace. . . .

CHAPTER II

MEMBERSHIP

Article 3

The original Members of the United Nations shall be the states which, having participated in the United Nations Conference on International Organization at San Francisco, or having previously signed the Declaration by United Nations of January 1, 1942, sign the present Charter and ratify it. . . .

Article 4

1. Membership in the United Nations is open to all other peace-loving states which accept the obligations contained in the present Charter and, in the judgment of the Organization, are able and willing to carry out these obligations.

2. The admission of any such state to membership in the United Nations will be effected by a decision of the General Assembly upon the recommendation of the Security Council. . . .

CHAPTER III

ORGANS

Article 7

1. There are established as the principal organs of the United Nations: a General Assembly, a Security Council, an Economic and

Social Council, a Trusteeship Council, an International Court of Justice, and a Secretariat. . . .

CHAPTER IV

THE GENERAL ASSEMBLY

Composition

Article 9

1. The General Assembly shall consist of all the Members of the United Nations.

2. Each Member shall have not more than five representatives in the General Assembly.

Functions and Powers

Article 10

The General Assembly may discuss any questions or any matters within the scope of the present Charter or relating to the powers and functions of any organs provided for in the present Charter, and except as provided in Article 12, may make recommendations to the Members of the United Nations or to the Security Council or to both on any such questions or matters. . . .

Article 12

1. While the Security Council is exercising in respect of any dispute or situation the functions assigned to it in the present Charter, the General Assembly shall not make any recommendation with regard to that dispute or situation unless the Security Council so requests. . . .

Voting

Article 18

1. Each member of the General Assembly shall have one vote.

2. Decisions of the General Assembly on important questions shall be made by a two-thirds majority of the members present and voting. These questions shall include: recommendations with respect to the maintenance of international peace and security, the election of the non-permanent members of the Security Council, the election of the members of the Economic and Social Council, the election of members of the Trusteeship Council in accordance with paragraph 1

(c) of Article 86, the admission of new Members to the United Nations, the suspension of the rights and privileges of membership, the expulsion of Members, questions relating to the operation of the trustee system, and budgetary questions.

3. Decisions on other questions, including the determination of additional categories of questions to be decided by a two-thirds majority, shall be made by a majority of the members present and voting. . . .

CHAPTER V

THE SECURITY COUNCIL

Composition

Article 23

1. The Security Council shall consist of eleven Members of the United Nations. The Republic of China, France, the Union of Soviet Socialist Republics, the United Kingdom of Great Britain and Northern Ireland, and the United States of America shall be permanent members of the Security Council. The General Assembly shall elect six other Members of the United Nations to be non-permanent members of the Security Council, due regard being specially paid, in the first instance to the contribution of Members of the United Nations to the maintenance of international peace and security and to the other purposes of the Organization, and also to equitable geographical distribution.

2. The non-permanent members of the Security Council shall be elected for a term of two years. In the first election of the non-permanent members, however, three shall be chosen for a term of one year. A retiring member shall not be eligible for immediate re-election.

3. Each member of the Security Council shall have one representative.

Functions and Powers

Article 24

1. In order to ensure prompt and effective action by the United Nations, its members confer on the Security Council primary responsibility for the maintenance of international peace and security, and agree that in carrying out its duties under this responsibility the Security Council acts on their behalf. . . .

Article 25

The Members of the United Nations agree to accept and carry out the decisions of the Security Council in accordance with the present Charter. . . .

Voting

Article 27

1. Each member of the Security Council shall have one vote.
2. Decisions of the Security Council on procedural matters shall be made by an affirmative vote of seven members.
3. Decisions of the Security Council on all other matters shall be made by an affirmative vote of seven members including the concurring votes of the permanent members; provided that, in decisions under Chapter VI, and under paragraph 3 of article 52, a party to a dispute shall abstain from voting. . . .

Article 32

Any Member of the United Nations which is not a member of the Security Council or any state which is not a Member of the United Nations, if it is a party to a dispute under consideration by the Security Council, shall be invited to participate, without vote, in the discussion relating to the dispute. . . .

CHAPTER VI

PACIFIC SETTLEMENT OF DISPUTES

Article 33

1. The parties to any dispute, the continuance of which is likely to endanger the maintenance of international peace and security, shall, first of all, seek a solution by negotiation, enquiry, mediation, conciliation, arbitration, judicial settlement, resort to regional agencies or arrangements, or other peaceful means of their own choice.
2. The Security Council shall, when it deems necessary, call upon the parties to settle their dispute by such means. . . .

CHAPTER VII

ACTION WITH RESPECT TO THREATS TO THE PEACE, BREACHES OF THE PEACE, AND ACTS OF AGGRESSION

Article 39

The Security Council shall determine the existence of any threat to the peace, breach of the peace, or act of aggression and shall make recommendations, or decide what measures shall be taken in accordance with Articles 41 and 42, to maintain or restore international peace and security. . . .

Article 41

The Security Council may decide what measures not involving the use of armed force are to be employed to give effect to its decisions, and it may call upon the Members of the United Nations to apply such measures. These may include complete or partial interruption of economic relations and of rail, sea, air, postal, telegraphic, radio, and other means of communication, and the severance of diplomatic relations.

Article 42

Should the Security Council consider that measures provided for in Article 41 would be inadequate or have proved to be inadequate, it may take such action by air, sea or land forces as may be necessary to maintain or restore international peace and security. Such action may include demonstrations, blockade, and other operations by air, sea, or land forces of Members of the United Nations.

Article 43

1. All Members of the United Nations, in order to contribute to the maintenance of international peace and security, undertake to make available to the Security Council, on its call and in accordance with a special agreement or agreements, armed forces, assistance, and facilities, including rights of passage, necessary for the purpose of maintaining international peace and security.

2. Such agreement or agreements shall govern the numbers and types of forces, their degree of readiness and general location, and the nature of the facilities and assistance to be provided. . . .

Article 44

When the Security Council has decided to use force it shall, before calling upon a Member not represented on it to provide armed forces in fulfillment of the obligations assumed under Article 43, invite that Member, if the Member so desires, to participate in the decisions of the Security Council concerning the employment of contingents of that Member's armed forces. . . .

CHAPTER VIII

REGIONAL ARRANGEMENTS

Article 52

1. Nothing in the present Charter precludes the existence of regional arrangements or agencies for dealing with such matters relating to the maintenance of international peace and security as are appropriate for regional action, provided that such arrangements or agencies and their activities are consistent with the Purposes and Principles of the United Nations.

2. The Members of the United Nations entering into such arrangements or constituting such agencies shall make every effort to achieve pacific settlement of local disputes through such regional arrangements or by such regional agencies before referring them to the Security Council.

3. The Security Council shall encourage the development of pacific settlement of local disputes through such regional arrangements or by such regional agencies either on the initiative of the states concerned or by reference from the Security Council. . . .

CHAPTER X

THE ECONOMIC AND SOCIAL COUNCIL

Composition

Article 61

1. The Economic and Social Council shall consist of eighteen Members of the United Nations elected by the General Assembly.

2. Subject to the provisions of paragraph 3, six members of the Economic and Social Council shall be elected each year for a term of three

years. A retiring member shall be eligible for immediate re-election.

3. At the first election, eighteen members of the Economic and Social Council shall be chosen. The term of office of six members so chosen shall expire at the end of one year, and of six other members at the end of two years, in accordance with arrangements made by the General Assembly.

4. Each member of the Economic and Social Council shall have one representative.

Functions and Powers

Article 62

1. The Economic and Social Council may make or initiate studies and reports with respect to international economic, social, cultural, educational, health, and related matters and may make recommendations with respect to any such matters to the General Assembly, to the Members of the United Nations, and to the specialized agencies concerned. . . .

CHAPTER XVIII

AMENDMENTS

Article 108

Amendments to the present Charter shall come into force for all Members of the United Nations when they have been adopted by a vote of two-thirds of the members of the General Assembly and ratified in accordance with their respective constitutional processes by two-thirds of the Members of the United Nations, including all the permanent members of the Security Council. . . .

> NOTE: The arrangement of signatures on the Charter is worthy of notice. The five "great" powers (the permanent members of the Security Council) signed first; then the rest signed in alphabetical order, Canada signing after the Byelo-Russian Soviet Socialist Republic and before Chile.

IX.
War

A.
The First World War

A few documents cannot convey to the reader the extraordinary impact upon Canada of the First World War, in which an unmilitary nation of only some eight million people sent more than 400,000 fighting men overseas and suffered more fatal casualties in action than the United States, which had a dozen times its population. There was economic effort on a scale hitherto unknown. The war was a strong force for unity in English-speaking Canada, but unfortunately its effect between English and French was divisive. Political and constitutional aspects are dealt with in Parts II and VIII, above; on war finance, see **113**; on social consequences of the war, see **65-68**. The bibliography is becoming increasingly formidable; one may mention as particularly useful G.W.L. Nicholson, *Canadian Expeditionary Force, 1914-1919* (Official History of the Canadian Army in the First World War, Ottawa, 1962); A. Fortescue Duguid, *Official History of the Canadian Forces in the Great War, 1914-1919* (only Vol. I and appendix vol. published, Ottawa, 1938); Sir W. Raleigh and H.A. Jones, *The War in the Air* (British Official History, 6 vols., Oxford, 1922-37); John Swettenham, *To Seize the Victory: The Canadian Corps in World War I* (Toronto, 1965); Gilbert Tucker, *The Naval Service of Canada, Its Official History*, Vol. I (Ottawa, 1952); D.J. Goodspeed, ed., *The Armed Forces of Canada, 1867-1967: A Century of Achievement* (Ottawa, 1967). For the effect of the war on one small community, see Leslie M. Frost, *Fighting Men* (Toronto, 1967).

1. The Outbreak of War

206. Canada's First Offer of Forces

(Governor General to Colonial Secretary, London, *Documents on Canadian External Relations*, Vol. I, 1909-1918, Department of External Affairs, Ottawa, 1967)

This telegram was sent three days before the British declaration of war on Germany.

548

TELEGRAM   Ottawa, August 1, 1914
In view of the impending danger of war involving the Empire my advisers are anxiously considering the most effective means of rendering every possible aid and they will welcome any suggestions and advice which Imperial naval and military authorities may deem it expedient to offer. They are confident that a considerable force would be available for service abroad. . . .

207. The Official Word of War

(*Canada Gazette* extra, 5 August 1914)

Canada in 1914 was still essentially a "self-governing colony," automatically involved in war by the British declaration. Not even a domestic proclamation was issued, though under the Militia Act the mobilization of units was necessarily followed by the calling of Parliament.

Ottawa, 4th August, 1914
His Royal Highness the Governor General* received a telegraphic despatch from the Secretary of State for the Colonies at 8.45 this evening announcing that war has broken out with Germany.

208. Canada's Offer Is Accepted

(Acting High Commissioner for Canada to Prime Minister, *Documents on Canadian External Relations*, I)

After a curious moment of hesitation, the Colonial Secretary gratefully accepted Canada's offer of an expeditionary force on 6 August. The new Secretary of State for War, Field-Marshal Lord Kitchener, knew that he would need all the troops he could get.

TELEGRAM   London, August 8, 1914
CONFIDENTIAL. Had interview this morning with Kitchener who

*The Duke of Connaught.

wishes personally and on behalf of War Office express his very grateful and sincere thanks for Canada's splendid offer troops. Hopes you can send him full division of twenty to twenty five thousand. Says he can use all you think best to send. His appointment as Minister War has given highest satisfaction.

[George H.] PERLEY

209. Opinions from Henri Bourassa

(*Le Devoir*, Montreal, 8 September 1914)

This ambivalent editorial by Bourassa, published in the issue of *Le Devoir* that first reported the Germans' reverse in the Battle of the Marne, foreshadows his latest violent opposition to the war and the serious difficulties that were to arise between French- and English-speaking Canada.

(Translation)

... Everyone has been talking for a month about Canada's duties to England and France. How many people have bothered about Canada's duties to herself?

If one objects that it is too late to ask this question; that the parliament and people of Canada have given the answer loudly and unanimously; that Canada's active participation in the European war is a settled thing; that it remains only to pursue this participation with all possible energy and speed—I reply that it is never too late to reflect on the consequences and the effects of one's acts. ...

To those friends of mine who ask me anxiously whether I approve today what I foresaw and condemned as early as 1899 — Canada's participation in England's wars, foreign wars for Canada—I reply without hesitation, No!

Canada, a dependency of Great Britain without responsibility, has neither moral or constitutional obligation nor immediate interest in the present conflict.

Great Britain went into it on her own account, as a result of an international situation in which she took a position purely to protect her own interests, without consulting her colonies and without regard to their circumstances or their special interests.

Canadian territory is in no way exposed to attacks from the belligerent nations. As an independent nation, Canada today would be in perfect security. ...

In law and in fact, then, Canada, a British colony, had no direct reason to intervene in the struggle. It had very serious ones for standing aside; and the future will show, perhaps only too harshly, that its military intervention, ineffective so far as the fighting nations are concerned, will have disastrous consequences for itself.

Having made these reservations, having stated these facts as markers on the road which we must travel again when the time for national readjustment comes, I hasten to examine a larger aspect of the question, on which it seems to me all Canadians should be able to agree.

Quite apart from its "obligations" as a colony, which in terms of history, the constitution and the facts amount to nothing, can Canada as a nation, an embryo nation if you will, as a human community, remain indifferent to the European conflict?

To this second question, as to the first, I reply without hesitation, No.

Canada, an Anglo-French nation, bound to England and France by a thousand racial, social, intellectual and economic ties, has a vital interest in supporting France and England, their prestige, their power, their world-wide influence.

It is her national duty, then, to contribute, within the limits of her strength and by such means of action as are suitable for her, to the victory and above all to the *endurance* of the combined efforts of France and England.

But to make this contribution effective, Canada must begin by resolutely looking her real situation in the face, must give herself an exact accounting of what she can and cannot do, and ensure her own internal security, before undertaking or prosecuting an effort which she will not, perhaps, be equal to sustaining to the end....

2. *Command and Control of the Forces and Conduct of the War*

In 1914, Canada had few if any officers possessing professional training and experience qualifying them for high command; and there were no effective precedents for the national control of considerable Canadian forces operating overseas. These matters were gradually sorted out as the war proceeded; and solutions compatible with both military efficiency and Canadian national feeling were achieved. In the last stages the Canadian Prime Minister was moved to attempt to exercise some influence on the British conduct of the war.

210. Canada's Naval Force is Placed "at Disposal," 1914

(Order in Council, *Documents on Canadian External Relations*, I)

As a result of the political controversies over naval policy that had gone on since 1910, the Canadian naval force in 1914 consisted only of two old and undermanned training cruisers purchased under the Laurier regime and neglected under Borden.

P.C. 2049   August 4, 1914

The Committee of the Privy Council have had before them a report, dated 4th August, 1914, from the Minister of the Naval Service, submitting that section 23 of the Naval Service Act ... 1910, provides that:

> 23. In case of an emergency the Governor in Council may place at the disposal of His Majesty, for general service in the Royal Navy, the Naval Service or any part thereof, any ships or vessels of the Naval Service, and the officers and seamen serving in such ships or vessels, or any officers or seamen belonging to the Naval Service.

An emergency having arisen, the Minister recommends that H.M.C.S. *Niobe* and H.M.C.S. *Rainbow*, together with the officers and seamen serving in such vessels, be placed at the disposal of His Majesty for general service in the Royal Navy.

The Committee concur in the foregoing recommendation and submit the same for approval.

211. A Canadian Takes Command of the Canadian Corps, 1917

(Minister of Overseas Military Forces to Prime Minister, *Documents on Canadian External Relations*, I)

In 1914, after discussion between the Canadian and British governments, a British regular officer, Lieut.-General E. A. H. Alderson, was appointed to command the 1st Canadian Division, and he subsequently took command of the Canadian Corps when it was formed. He was succeeded as Corps Commander in 1916 by Lieut.-General Sir Julian Byng, another British officer and an able and popular leader. When Byng was promoted to an army command the Canadian authorities exerted themselves to obtain the appointment of a Canadian; the choice fell on Sir Arthur Currie, a pre-war militia officer who since 1914 had commanded successively the 2nd Canadian Infantry Brigade and the 1st Canadian Division.

TELEGRAM   London, June 9, 1917
SECRET. Corps Commander temporarily given higher command but unlikely return to us. Matter will be definitely settled within few days. Intend insisting on appointment Canadian. Don't expect serious objection to so doing. [Major-General Sir Richard] Turner is senior but his work invaluable here don't want make change and he is of course rather out of touch with front after six months absence. Believe Currie who as senior officer at front is now temporarily in command Corps is considered most suitable for Corps by higher command and also by larger half troops although both officers have many strong friends. Think wisest course and one which would cause least friction and difficulty would be make Currie Corps Commander retain Turner here as G.O.C. [General Officer Commanding] with certain measure authority over administrative matters at front particularly on lines communication. Endeavour get War Office make them both Lieutenant Generals and so preserve Turner's seniority. Turner naturally anxious command Corps as he is by temperament fighting soldier but he will acquiesce cheerfully in our decision. Please cable your views.

PERLEY*

212. New Systems of Control

(*Report of the Ministry, Overseas Military Force of Canada, 1918*, London, n.d.)

Until the authorization of the Ministry of Overseas Military Forces of Canada, under a Canadian minister resident in London, in October 1916, Canadian overseas military administration was chaotic. Thereafter for the first time "all Canadian military control in the British Isles

*On 15 June Perley cabled further, "Have consulted military authorities unofficially. They will recommend Currie for Corps. . . ."

was concentrated in a single authority" (Nicholson, *Canadian Expeditionary Force*, p. 212). The new arrangement also facilitated clearer understandings with the British authorities concerning control in the field. The ultimate result was that while command in operations remained firmly vested in the British Commander-in-Chief, who also had the last word in disciplinary matters, in questions of organization and administration Canada controlled her own forces. There are indications that under Currie there was a degree of Canadian influence even in matters of operational command.

CANADIAN SECTION, G.H.Q.

During the progress of the War many incidents indicated that the method of control exercised by the Ministry [of Overseas Military Forces] over the Canadian Forces was capable of improvement. The desirability of a clear definition of the powers and responsibilities of the Canadian Government on the one hand, and the Imperial Government on the other, became evident. In addition to the Canadian Corps there were about 40,000 other Canadian troops in France, the supervision of whose welfare had been conducted from England. The methods of communication between the Ministry in England, the Canadian Corps, General Headquarters of the British Armies in France, and troops on the Lines of Communication, had been cumbersome and unsatisfactory. Purely Canadian matters were sometimes dealt with by those not intimately interested therein, and it was felt that in matters affecting the organisation and administration of the Canadian Forces, Canadians should manage their own affairs.

Correspondence passed between the Ministry and the War Office relative to this subject, and a conference was held with representatives of the [British] Army Council and later with the Field-Marshal Commanding-in-Chief,* at his Headquarters in France.

The outcome of these negotiations was a complete agreement between the Imperial Government and the Canadian Authorities upon the matter.

Broadly, the statement made by Canada of her position, in which the Imperial Government concurred, was that for matters of military operations the Canadian Forces in the Field had been placed by the Canadian Government under the Commander-in-Chief, British Armies in France; in matters of organisation and administration, the Canadian Government still retained full responsibility in respect to its own Forces.

It was clear that matters of organisation and administration would

*Sir Douglas Haig.

frequently have a direct bearing upon military operations and discipline, and *vice versa*, and it was agreed that in such cases these matters should be made the subject of conference between the Canadian and Imperial Authorities.

To meet this situation in France in the most effective manner, a Canadian Section of General Headquarters of the British Armies in France was formed in July, 1918, after full discussion and agreement. In forming such a Section it was not intended to interfere in any way with the responsibility of General Headquarters and the Supreme Command, in relation to matters affecting military operations or discipline, but through this Section the full control of the Canadian Government over matters of organisation and administration within its Forces was rendered capable of fruition. Important matters, such as the allotment of reinforcements in emergencies, War Establishments, the appointment of General Officers, and those other matters which from their relation to military operations should properly receive the consideration of General Headquarters, would still be made the subject of conference between the Canadian Authorities and General Headquarters. . . .

Status. — The Canadian Section at General Headquarters is a Branch of the Ministry, Overseas Military Forces of Canada, and is directly responsible to the Minister. . . .

THE GENERAL STAFF*

SCOPE AND FUNCTIONS

Up to the date of the Armistice, the chief functions of the General Staff of the Overseas Military Forces of Canada in England were the organization and direction of all branches of the Service in the British Isles, and the training of the personnel for their duties in the field.

It is of interest to record that prior to the beginning of 1917 there was no purely Canadian organization for the training of Canadian Forces in England. The training of such Canadian troops as were then in England was directed by the staffs of the Imperial Command in which the troops happened to be stationed.

It was in December, 1916, that it was pointed out to the Imperial Authorities that it would be a far more satisfactory arrangement if the Canadian Authorities in England assumed the entire responsibility for the training of their own reinforcements. To this suggestion the Imperial Authorities agreed. . . .

*The reference is to the General Staff branch at the O.M.F.C. headquarters in London.

213. Sir Robert Borden Tells the Imperial War Cabinet, 13 June 1918

Shorthand Notes of the Fifteenth Meeting of the Imperial War Cabinet . . .)

This was probably the strongest criticism of the British conduct of the war ever delivered in the Imperial War Cabinet; but it was certainly not unwelcome to David Lloyd George, the British Prime Minister, who was himself highly critical of the British army command. On the circumstances, see Borden's memorandum of 15 June 1918, *Documents on Canadian External Relations*, I, No. 341. This statement by Borden was the origin of the Committee of Prime Ministers formed by the Imperial War Cabinet to review the planning for the next stage of the war (see R.A. Preston, *Canada and "Imperial Defense,"* Durham, N.C., 1967). The extract here given is a small part of the statement, which began with an extended summary of the Canadian war effort.

. . . Now I come to some matters which were raised the day before yesterday by the Prime Minister [of the United Kingdom], and, in order to discharge my duty both to you and to my own people, I will be perfectly frank. It would be idle for me to sit here unless I was perfectly frank. I hope any observations that I make, if they are not regarded as agreeable, will be understood as having been made under a thorough sense of duty and with the most earnest desire to help, and with no other purpose whatever.

I have no special or technical knowledge of military matters. But no one could fail to be disagreeably impressed by the statement that Germany with an equal force has been able to drive us back in her recent offensive* and to inflict upon us greater losses than have been sustained by her own forces. The net result of that is that Germany now has a superiority of numbers. What is to prevent Germany with a superiority in numbers from repeating even more successfully what she did with an equality of numbers during the past three or four months? I may say that the success of the German effort during the last three months or thereabouts — since 21st March — has produced a most depressing effect upon us in Canada. I am not desirous of dwelling on matters of the past, upon which it is useless to lay undue emphasis; what I say is put forward with the desire that we may in the future avoid the terrible disasters and the unfortunate mistakes of the past. There must be a cause for our failure, and doubtless that failure depends upon more than one cause.

*Launched on 21 March 1918. Borden is here referring to the review of the war which Lloyd George gave the Imperial War Cabinet on 11 June.

It is unnecessary to say that the men of these Islands are as brave, as intelligent, and as good fighting material as can be found anywhere in the world. We have sent from Canada more than 375,000 men to the front since the commencement of this war. Of that force 175,000 men were born in the British Isles. When I speak of the good work in preparation and organisation that has been accomplished by the Canadians at the front I am speaking of a force which has been derived to the extent of two-fifths from men born in these Islands. It seems apparent, having regard to the material of which the British Army is composed, that the unfortunate results which have obtained during the past year, and especially during the past three months, are due to lack of foresight, lack of preparation, and to defects of system and organisation. Since our last meeting I sent for General Currie, the Commander of the Canadian Army Corps, and I ordered him to tell me the truth so far as he understood it with respect to the occurrences of the past few months. Before this war we [he] had no actual military experience. On the 1st August, 1914, he was an insurance and real estate agent in Vancouver,* although he had been connected with the Canadian Militia, and had studied military tactics and military affairs more or less throughout his life. Last year I heard excellent reports of the efficiency of the Canadian Army Corps. Since my arrival this year the information which has reached me, indicates beyond question that General Currie has wonderfully developed and improved its efficiency. I asked him to describe to me the incidents of the past year, the incidents of the past three months, and to tell me his own experience. I shall not go through it all, but I will give you a few incidents by way of illustration. The Canadian Army Corps were ordered to take Passchendaele. Previous attempts had been made, and I understand that they had all been unsuccessful. General Currie looked over the situation and reported that he could take Passchendaele with a loss of 15,000 men. Eventually he took it with a loss of 16,000 men. He reports to me that the gain was not worth the candle, that the result was not worth the loss, that immediately afterwards the British Army went on the defensive, and the taking of Passchendaele at so great a loss had really no result of importance. According to his report the situation, when he was called upon to attack Passchendaele, was a most indescribable confusion in all the arrangements. He gave me illustrations. . . . General Currie was informed that he would be supported by 364 guns but he found only 220. In more than one instance a battery which should have had six guns had only one or two. . . . When General Currie asked for more guns he was asked to send indents. He said he could not fight the

* Actually, in Victoria.

Germans with indents; he wanted guns, he could not get them. Incidents like this occurred all the time, not only at Passchendaele but elsewhere. There was lack of preparation and of foresight. There was also lack of proper intelligence. Three days before the offensive of the 21st March a tip was given by the British Intelligence Service to the Canadian Army Corps that there would be no offensive at all. General Currie told me that, when documents came to him signed by the Chief Intelligence Officer, he made a practice of looking at the signature, and if it was that of the Chief Intelligence Officer, he always tore up the document and threw it in the waste basket without reading it, as he was confident that it was more likely to mislead than to inform. . . .

. . . General Currie described to me the character of the barbed-wire defences which were prepared by his corps, and the co-ordination of his machine gun defences. I do not believe the Germans could possibly have got through our line had it been prepared throughout in the same manner as the defences of the Canadian Army Corps. At all events the Germans would have been stopped at a very early stage. . . .

I asked General Currie why the British Corps Commanders did not establish barbed-wire defences on the same scale as his own. He said that many of the Commanders stated that they had held the Germans in 1914 without barbed wire and that they could hold them in the same way in 1918. Apparently these officers were utterly oblivious of the remarkable changes in methods of warfare which have taken place in the meantime. . . .

I am informed that there has been conspicuous failure to remove incompetent officers. No one questions the splendid gallantry of officers, as well as men, in the British Army. Officers who make mistakes are always ready to atone by their death in fighting to the last, but mistakes, even though atoned for by death, will end in losing this war. I have reason to believe that some of these brave officers are exceedingly casual, although they are brave beyond description. This war cannot be won by casual allusion to or reliance upon what was done in 1914, and by neglect of preparation, which would have stopped the Germans.

I do not wish to be understood as suggesting that General Currie criticised all the divisions of the British army. He told me that there were many many magnificent divisions properly trained and thoroughly organised, but that there were enough not properly trained, organised or led by competent officers to give the Germans opportunity of breaking through.

THE PRIME MINISTER: Do you mean by "officers" general officers or regimental officers?

SIR ROBERT BORDEN: I think he means officers all the way through.

THE PRIME MINISTER: Including Brigadier-Generals and Corps Commanders?

SIR ROBERT BORDEN: He told me the younger members of the Staff last November or December recommended that ten Corps Commanders ought to be dispensed with and other men put in their places; but that none were removed until about the time this offensive began; perhaps shortly before; the others have not been removed. . . .

. . . Is it or is it not the case that men of great ability who have gone into the army during this war have been systematically held down to positions no higher than Brigadier-Generals? If that is the case, I say with all respect, that it amounts to scrapping the brains of the nation in the greatest struggle of history. At the outbreak of this war Canada had a small permanent army. What would have happened if we had laid down the principle, and acted upon it, that no man should fill a higher position than that of Brigadier-General unless he had been a member of our standing army? What would be the position of our Canadian Army Corps to-day if that principle had been carried out? Certainly the remarkable ability of our Commanding Officer would never have been discovered or utilised and the Canadian Army Corps would not have been in its present condition of efficiency. Doubtless the career of men who have undertaken military life as a profession must be considered; but after all the issue before us makes the career of any man of little consequence. Of what importance is the career of any man around this table, of what consequence is the career of all of us together compared with the present issue? Less than dust in the balance. If we fail to use the brains of the nation for the best purpose available we cannot have much prospect of winning this war. . . .

. . . The future of this war in more senses than one depends upon our earnestness. We came over to fight in earnest; and Canada will fight it out to the end. But earnestness must be expressed in organisation, foresight, preparation. Let the past bury its dead, but for God's sake let us get down to earnest endeavour and hold this line until the Americans can come in and help us to sustain it till the end. . . .

I venture to suggest that the Canadian Army Corps might be used with great advantage for training American troops. We live next door to these people; we understand them and they understand us. . .

there is the best possible feeling between the people of the two countries. It is singular in one way and not in another that the American people are proud of what Canada has done in this war. If the organisation can be expedited in the way I have suggested, it is desirable to attempt it. The whole issue of this war depends on the speed with which the American troops can be organised, trained, and put into the fighting line. When that is once done there cannot be much doubt as to what the result will be. If this war continues for a year or eighteen months, the United States will have a more formidable military force in the field than any of the belligerent nations. Meantime it is a question whether we shall be ignominiously defeated and driven out of France, or whether we can hold on.

I have spoken with a great deal of frankness, but I hope that what I have said will be received in the spirit in which I put it forward, and I can assure you that it is intended only to be helpful and not to discourage.

THE PRIME MINISTER: We shall consider very carefully the statement which Sir Robert Borden has just made.

3. On the Battlefield and Above It

It was, in the last analysis, the work of the Canadian fighting man that was the most important Canadian aspect of the war, and that won for the country a new imperial and international status. Here a few incidents must stand for four years of bloody conflict in which the national effort centred in the Canadian Corps on the Western Front.

214. The 1st Canadian Division in the Second Battle of Ypres, 1915

(Dispatch by Field-Marshal Sir John French, commanding British Army in France, 15 June 1915, *Naval and Military Despatches. . . November, 1914, to June, 1915*, London, 1915)

The 1st Canadian Division had its baptism of fire under dramatic and terrible circumstances: those of the first German gas attack. This desperate and costly struggle may be said to have largely made the Canadians' military reputation. The news of the battle, and later the words of Sir John French's dispatch, rang across Canada.

. . .

4. It was at the commencement of the Second Battle of Ypres on the evening of the 22nd April . . . that the enemy first made use of asphyxiating gas. . . .

Following a heavy bombardment, the enemy attacked the French Division [on the Canadians' left] at about 5 p.m., using asphyxiating gases for the first time. Aircraft reported that at about 5 p.m. thick yellow smoke had been seen issuing from the German trenches between Langemarck and Bixschoote. . . .

What follows almost defies description. The effect of these poisonous gases was so virulent as to render the whole of the line held by the French Division* mentioned above practically incapable of any action at all. It was at first impossible for anyone to realise what had actually happened. The smoke and fumes hid everything from sight, and hundreds of men were thrown into a comatose or dying condition, and within an hour the whole position had to be abandoned, together with about 50 guns.

I wish particularly to repudiate any idea of attaching the least blame to the French Division for this unfortunate incident. . . .

The left flank of the Canadian Division was thus left dangerously exposed to serious attack in flank, and there appeared to be a prospect of their being overwhelmed and of a successful attempt by the Germans to cut off the British troops occupying the salient to the East.

In spite of the danger to which they were exposed the Canadians held their ground with a magnificent display of tenacity and courage; and it is not too much to say that the bearing and conduct of these splendid troops averted a disaster which might have been attended with the most serious consequences.

They were supported with great promptitude by the reserves of the Divisions holding the salient and by a Brigade which had been resting in billets.

Throughout the night the enemy's attacks were repulsed, effective counter-attacks were delivered, and at length touch was gained with the French right, and a new line was formed. . . .

The confusion caused by the sudden retirement of the French Division, and the necessity for closing up the gap and checking the enemy's advance at all costs, led to a mixing up of units and a sudden shifting of the areas of command, which was quite unavoidable.

* In fact, the greater parts of *two* French divisions were covered by the gas cloud and overrun. The cloud did not touch the Canadians (see Map 1, Nicholson, *Canadian Expeditionary Force*); but gas was used against them later in the battle.

Fresh units, as they came up from the South, had to be pushed into the firing line in an area swept by artillery fire which, owing to the capture of the French guns, we were unable to keep down.

All this led to very heavy casualties; and I wish to place on record the deep admiration which I feel for the resource and presence of mind evinced by the leaders actually on the spot. . . .

It was only on the morning of the 25th that the enemy were able to force back the left of the Canadian Division from the point where it had originally joined the French line. . . .

215. Sir Arthur Currie on the Battle of Vimy Ridge, 1917

(Currie Diary, P.A.C.)

In the Battle of Vimy Ridge the Canadian Corps under Sir Julian Byng took from the Germans one of the most commanding positions on the Western Front. This was the first occasion when the Corps fought with its full strength of four divisions in line. When Sir Arthur Currie wrote this comment in his private diary, he was commanding the 1st Canadian Division.

Monday Apr. 9th Easter Monday. Attack launched at 5.30 A.M. For full particulars see my report, but it was a wonderful success. By 2 P.M. we had patrols on the outskirts of Farbus Wood having penetrated to a depth of 4500 yards. The Div attacked on a front of 2000 yds. Final front 750 yds. Every line was captured on time, every battalion doing equally well. Truly magnificent, grandest day the Corps has ever had, our casualties about 90 officers 2400 o.r. [other ranks]. 2nd and 3rd Divisions equally successful. 4th held up not taking all of Red Line. Loomis* slightly wounded. The sight was awful and wonderful. Men hugged the barrage. Stiff fighting, 2nd and 3rd Bdes. take over 40 machine guns, 35 t.m.'s [trench mortars], 1st Bde. 7 field guns, Div about 1500 prisoners. Hundreds and hundreds of German dead, took Bde Commander and all his Staff. Germans expected the attack but not for a week later. Had not been getting food or water, or relief for days. Wire was completely cut thanks to 106 fuze. . . .

* Commander of the 2nd Canadian Infantry Brigade in Currie's Division.

216. Recommendation for the Victoria Cross, Captain W.A. Bishop, 1917

(*Canada Gazette*, 22 September 1917)

Lt.-Col. Bishop (as he later became) was the highest-scoring British fighter pilot, credited with shooting down 72 enemy aircraft (see Arthur Bishop, *The Courage of the Early Morning*, Toronto, 1965). Note that, like many Canadian flyers, he was attached to the Royal Flying Corps from the Canadian military forces. There was no Canadian air force during the war, though a nucleus of two Canadian squadrons was being formed at the time of the Armistice.

(Extract from the fourth supplement to THE LONDON GAZETTE of the 10th August, 1917)

War Office,
11th August, 1917.

HIS Majesty the King has been graciously pleased to approve of the award of the Victoria Cross to the undermentioned Officer: —

Captain William Avery Bishop, D.S.O., M.C.,
Canadian Cavalry and Royal Flying Corps.

For most conspicuous bravery, determination and skill. Captain Bishop, who had been sent out to work independently, flew first of all to an enemy aerodrome; finding no machine about, he flew on to another aerodrome about three miles south-east, which was at least twelve miles the other side of the line. Seven machines, some with their engines running, were on the ground. He attacked these from about fifty feet, and a mechanic, who was starting one of the engines, was seen to fall. One of the machines got off the ground, but at a height of sixty feet Captain Bishop fired fifteen rounds into it at very close range, and it crashed to the ground.

A second machine got off the ground, into which he fired thirty rounds at 150 yards range, and it fell into a tree.

Two more machines then rose from the aerodrome. One of these he engaged at the height of 1,000 feet, emptying the rest of his drum of ammunition. This machine crashed 300 yards from the aerodrome, after which Captain Bishop emptied a whole drum into the fourth hostile machine, and then flew back to his station.

Four hostile scouts were about 1,000 feet above him for about a mile of his return journey, but they would not attack.

His machine was very badly shot about by machine gun fire from the ground.

217. The Record of the Hundred Days, 1918

("Interim Report on the Operations of the Canadian Corps during the Year 1918," *Report of the Ministry, Overseas Military Forces of Canada, 1918*)

In the final months of the war on the Western Front the Canadian Corps demonstrated the efficiency which Borden reported with such pride in June 1918 (above, **213**). Beginning with the great Canadian-Australian victory in front of Amiens on 8 August, there was a steady fighting advance which ended only with the Armistice on 11 November, a period which Canadian soldiers remembered as the Hundred Days. Sir Arthur Currie summarizes it here.

. . . since August 8 the Canadian Corps had fought battles of the first magnitude, having a direct bearing on the general situation, and contributing to an extent difficult to realise to the defeat of the German Armies in the field. . . .

Between August 8 and November 11 the following had been captured: —

Prisoners 31,537
Guns (Heavy and Field) 623
Machine Guns 2,842
Trench Mortars (Heavy and Light)   336

Over 500 square miles of territory and 228 cities, towns and villages had been liberated, including the cities of Cambrai, Denain, Valenciennes and Mons.

From August 8 to October 11 not less than 47 German Divisions had been engaged and defeated by the Canadian Corps, that is, nearly a quarter of the total German Forces on the Western Front.

After October 11 the disorganisation of the German Troops on our front was such that it was difficult to determine with exactitude the importance of the elements of many Divisions engaged.

In the performance of these mighty achievements all arms of the Corps have bent their purposeful energy, working one for all and all for one. The dash and magnificent bravery of our incomparable Infantry have at all times been devotedly seconded with great skill and daring by our Machine Gunners, while the Artillery lent them their powerful and never-failing support. The initiative and resourcefulness displayed by the Engineers contributed materially to the depth and rapidity of our advances. The devotion of the Medical personnel has been, as always, worthy of every praise. The Administrative Services. working at all times under very great pressure and adverse conditions, surpassed their usual efficiency. The Chaplain

Services, by their continued devotion to the spiritual welfare of the troops and their utter disregard of personal risk, have endeared themselves to the hearts of everyone. The incessant efforts of the Y.M.C.A. and their initiative in bringing comforts right up to the front line in battle were warmly appreciated by all.

I desire to record here my deep appreciation of the services of Brigadier-General N.W. Webber, B.G.G.S.,* Canadian Corps, and of the generous efforts and untiring zeal of the General Officers, Regimental Officers, the heads of all Arms, Services and Branches, and the members of the various Staffs. . . .

December 13 was set as the date on which the Allies would cross the Rhine at all points to be occupied. . . .

The 1st Canadian Division crossed by the southern bridge at Cologne, the passage being witnessed and the salute taken by General Sir Herbert Plumer, Commanding the Second British Army; and the 2nd Canadian Division crossed by the Bonn Bridge, where I took the salute. The leading troops of the respective Divisions crossed at 9.30 a.m.

The weather was bad, the day being dark, and a steady rain poured down throughout. In spite of this the spectacle was magnificent. The smart, sturdy Infantry, with bayonets fixed, marching perfectly, with colours flying and bands playing our national airs, was an impressive sight, which did not fail to bring home to the German population the great potential strength of our Army. . . .

4. The Conflict over Manpower and Conscription

No attempt is made here to illustrate every stage of the political struggle involving the formation of the Union government, the introduction of conscription, and the general election of 1917. For the statements of the party leaders in the election, see above, **26-27**. For the Military Voters Act and the War-time Elections Act, see below, **232, 233**. In addition to works cited on pp. 62, 332, and 548, see A.M. Willms, "Conscription, 1917: A Brief for the Defence," *Canadian Historical Review*, December 1956.

* Brigadier General, General Staff, Currie's senior staff officer. Like almost all senior staff officers (as distinct from commanders) in the Canadian Corps to the end of the war, Webber was a British regular.

218. The Canadian Military Commitment Is Raised

(Order in Council P.C. 36, 12 January 1916, *Documents on Canadian External Relations*, I)

After August 1914 (above, **208**) the British government from time to time informed Ottawa that additional troops would be welcome if it could provide them. In July 1915 the Canadian Cabinet fixed the number of troops authorized for overseas service, including those already raised, at not more than 150,000; later that year the 3rd Canadian Division was authorized and the total troop quota increased to 250,000 (see *Documents on Canadian External Relations*, I, Documents 141, 167, 175, 177). At the end of the year Sir Robert Borden, apparently without much consultation with his colleagues, decided to double the authorized force and made the decision public; the order in council here printed formalizes it. Borden had always thought of increasing influence for Canada in imperial councils as on a *quid pro quo* basis; displeased at this moment with the failure of the British government to inform or consult the Dominions about the war, he thought perhaps that a *beau geste* would impress it. Nicholson (p. 215) feels that the evidence indicates that the figure of 500,000 men was not a recruiting goal but the total force to be *maintained* overseas, which with replacement of casualties and other "wastage" would have been a commitment of enormous but indefinite proportions. The terms of the order in council, though somewhat vague, do not support this interpretation. See also Borden's statement in the House of Commons, 10 April 1918, concerning the force to be maintained in the coming year; it seems conclusive. Incidentally, of course, the Canadian overseas force never reached a total of anything like 500,000 men. In the summer of 1917 there were about 143,000 in France and 124,000 in England (many of the latter in hospital); total enlistments to 30 June had been 424,456, but 76,038 men had already been "discharged, etc." in Canada. (Statement of Sir Edward Kemp in House of Commons, 6 August 1917).

The Committee of the Privy Council have had before them a report by the Prime Minister dated 3rd January, 1916. . . .

The Prime Minister . . . observes that the developments in the various theatres of war during the past year unmistakably indicate the necessity of further vigorous and united effort on the part of all His Majesty's Dominions to bring to a victorious and honourable conclusion the present conflict which unquestionably involves the power, integrity and welfare of the Empire, and even constitutes a menace to its existence. The realization of the great issues thus involved in the war has elicited from the manhood of the Dominion a widespread and splendid response ever since the outbreak of hostilities. The Prime Minister is convinced that this impressive response will be continued to the further appeal which is now proposed.

He therefore recommends, with the approval of the Honourable the Minister of Militia and Defence that the last-named Minister be authorized to raise, equip and send overseas . . . officers and men not exceeding five hundred thousand, including those who have already been raised and equipped under authority of the said [earlier] Orders in Council, and including also those who have been, or may hereafter be raised for garrison and guard duty in Canada.

The Committee concur in the foregoing and submit the same for approval.

219. Sir Wilfrid Laurier Expresses a Private Opinion

(Laurier to Hon. Philippe Roy, 15 June 1916, Laurier Papers, P.A.C.)

This private letter to the Canadian Commissioner General in Paris is notable for its reference to the low rate of recruiting and the reasons for it. The crime for which France was to be punished was presumably the measure of 1905 abrogating the 1801 concordat with the Papacy and separating church and state.

(Translation)

You are quite right to be alarmed by the more and more marked division between the two elements making up our nation.

Its primary source is unquestionably to be found in the exaggerated idea of nationalist claims that is entertained from the Ottawa River to the Pacific Ocean; and these nationalists have succeeded in making the English population believe that the French race wants to impose its language as official everywhere, even in British Columbia, where the French population is not even 2%.

These exaggerations are exploited by the extremists of anglo-saxonism, and provide the regular theme of the Tory press.

This first cause of division is supplemented by another consisting in the fact that clericalism has succeeded almost completely in uniting the cause of the language to its own cause, and that is still not the whole story. The English-speaking populations are deeply irritated by the marked manner in which French Canadians have stood aside in the present conflict. On this point it must be said that they are only too right. Recruiting in the province of Quebec has not produced all the results it might have, and the primary cause is the attitude of the French-Canadian clergy who have discouraged recruiting from the beginning on the pretext that France deserved to be punished. You know this clerical mentality yourself.

That is the situation in a few words, and I doubt if any statement coming from France would have the good fortune even to be heard. The situation is perilous, but I have not yet lost hope that we can bring opinion back to sounder views.

220. Voluntary Enlistments, by Provinces and Nationalities, August 1914-31 October 1917

(*Debates, House of Commons*, 25 April 1918)

There are no reliable statistics of French-speaking (or English-speaking) enlistments, since recruits were not required to state their racial origins or mother tongues. This table* (ending with the month in which the Military Service Act came into effect) sufficiently indicates, however, that Quebec lagged seriously behind the other provinces. It also indicates that the Canadian-born lagged seriously behind the British-born. For enlistments by months, see Nicholson, *Canadian Expeditionary Force*, Appendix "C", Table 1. The peak (nearly 34,000) was reached in March 1916; thereafter recruiting fell off rapidly, and by the end of 1916 was down to about 5,000 per month.

Enlistments

Ontario	191,632
Quebec	48,934
Nova Scotia and Prince Edward I.	23,436
New Brunswick	18,022
Manitoba	52,784
Saskatchewan	26,111

* The fact that Nova Scotia and Prince Edward Island, and British Columbia and the Yukon, are bracketed together suggests that this table was based on statistics compiled by Military Districts, since these areas comprised respectively Military Districts 6 and 11. This being the case, enlistments in four relatively thinly populated western counties of Quebec, which formed part of M.D. 3 (H.Q., Kingston) would be credited to Ontario, and those in a similarly thinly populated area of Ontario forming part of M.D. 10 (H.Q., Winnipeg) would be credited to Manitoba.

Alberta.. 36,279
British Columbia and Yukon......................... 42,608
                                                                      ―――――――
                                                                        439,806

Nationalities―
    Canadian born..197,473
    British born..215,769
    Other nationalities...................................... 26,564
                                                                      ―――――――
                                                                        439,806

221. A Moderate French-Canadian Newspaper on the Military Service Bill

(Editorial, *La Presse*, Montreal, 12 July 1917)

La Presse had strongly and consistently supported recruiting from the beginning. See Mason Wade, *The French Canadians*, II.

(*Translation*)
ON A GENERAL ELECTION BEFORE IMPOSING THE LAW

... There is no doubt that if the principle of compulsory military service were approved by the majority of the Canadian electorate, the government would then resort to severe measures to put down all opposition to the law, which would then be incontestably legitimate.

We persist in hoping that Sir Robert Borden will in fact not impose conscription upon the democratic country that raised him to power for a term of five years on 21 September 1911 without first obtaining from the people a specific renewal of his mandate.

222. The French-Canadian Nationalist Position

(Editorial by Omer Héroux, *Le Devoir*, Montreal, 20 July 1917)

This and the following item from Henri Bourassa's newspaper typify the nationalist position on the Military Service Bill (below, **224**) while it was before Parliament. To a later generation, there is special interest in Bourassa's emphasis on the menace of American economic domination; though the aspect which to him seemed most menacing―the debt to U.S. bankers — turned out to be comparatively insignificant.

(*Translation*)
"The Last Man, The Last Dollar"
The phrase is the *Gazette*'s in its number of yesterday. . . .
We were thrown into the war by the act of the metropolis, we shall get out of it when the metropolis desires it. We had the right to limit our effort to putting Canadian territory in a state of defence; Mr. Bonar Law and Mr. Balfour, one after the other, have repeated to us that ancient truth, that the metropolis could not demand from us a man or a penny for its war in Europe. Even while taking part in that war, we could, like South Africa for example, have settled the extent of our own effort, decided it in accordance with the country's own condition. . . .
Mr. Borden has in fact renounced this supreme privilege of controlling the military effort of Canada. . . .
Under these conditions, if the war only lasts long enough, the one logical consequence of our attitude will be, truly enough, the sacrifice of the last man and the last dollar as the *Gazette* announces. And there was logic in Mr. Meighen's delirium when he spoke, as early as several months ago, of bankrupting the country; he was equally logical, some days back, when, supported by his chief, he gave us a glimpse beyond the present scheme of another "little bill" intended to swell the figure of a hundred thousand conscripts whom it proposes to add to the four hundred and twenty thousand volunteers.
Happily there is still time, there is still the possibility of opposing to this policy of suicide a policy of national preservation.
It is open to the supporters of limited participation, as it is to the complete opponents of participation, to say: Canada ought, like all the other countries, to take account of her resources and think of her future. The question of proportion in sacrifice, raised in the House and in the French press, should continue to be raised among us. Like Japan, which has not contributed a man to the European war, or like Italy, which has mobilized part of its men at home and has just refused the United States the right to incorporate into the American Army the enormous proportion of its nationals who are not serving in its own army, we have the right to set a limit to our effort. . . .
To the policy of suicide and bankruptcy, then, let us oppose — it is certainly time! — a policy of national preservation. Here is the natural meeting-place for all who are genuinely anxious to aid the Allies, but who also intend to bequeath a country to their sons.

223. Henri Bourassa on the Military Service Bill Debate

(Signed editorial, *Le Devoir*, Montreal, 26 July 1917)

This is the concluding section of a long editorial entitled "The End of the Debate." In another editorial "The American Conquest," published on 28 July, Bourassa developed the theme of the danger of Canada's growing debt to U.S. bankers.

(Translation)

. . . Another proof of the lack of any national concern among our parliamentarians is their criminal neglect of the economic repercussions of the war and the depopulation of the country by voluntary or compulsory recruiting. Nobody has dared to broach this serious aspect of the situation during these five weeks of discussion in which so many useless, false or hypocritical words have poured out like a continuous flow of dishwater. Not one single minister or ex-minister, not one single Liberal or Conservative member, has breathed a word about the economic enslavement of the country. None of the wordy champions of autonomy has had the patriotic courage to tell the ministers who profess so much love for the Empire that they are on the way to dismembering it far more effectively than Hindenburg's armies could ever do, and handing the country over to American finance lock, stock and barrel.

The conscriptionists have ended up by clinging to the single sentimental theme: "We must support the effort of our boys whose ranks have been thinned by the Germans." No one has had the courage to ask these cynical exploiters, "What steps have you taken to protect our soldiers against the frightful ravages of immorality around the training camps, or against the incompetence or scheming of the officers who command them at the front?" If one were to set over against the fighting men who have been killed or mutilated by German arms those have been victims of the neglect of their commanders, one would come to the opinion that there is a more urgent task than sending additional recruits as sacrifices to the god of war, of gold and of vice.

May we hope that the Senate, approaching the discussion of this serpent-bill, will show more appreciation of national problems? It is doubtful. With rare and honourable exceptions, the Senate, like the House, is made up of blind partisans whose great interest is getting ready the election platforms of their respective parties. It contains a larger proportion of war profiteers. For both groups — party men and grafters — the safety of the nation, the blood of its children, the freedom of its citizens are very secondary things by comparison with the triumph of the party and the percentage they can get out of mothers' tears and the bloody reaping of the human harvest.

Furthermore this inconceivable disregard for the supreme interests of the nation springs from a cause deeper and more general still than party spirit and greed: it arises above all from the slave mentality created by colonialism and accentuated by imperialism. It is our politicians' chief excuse.

Canadians fight for the Empire just as the Senegalese fight for France. Our statesmen, ministers, senators or members have no more idea than the chiefs of negro tribes of protecting our soldiers, defending the nation's rights or giving expression to national thinking about the practical problems of the war.

It would seem that we are supposed to be proud of this too: it is the last word in "democracy", in "human freedom", in "superior civilization".

224. The Military Service Act, 1917

(7-8 George V, Chap. 19)

This famous statute perhaps needs little comment. Politically it split both the country and the Liberal party. Its greatest weakness for its military purpose was the liberality and vagueness of the exemptions allowed; see particularly section 11(1)(d). It is worth remarking that, as strengthened by an unorthodox procedure in 1918 (below, **229**), it produced far more recruits than critics have credited it with; it actually sent some 47,500 men overseas, and there is little doubt that had the war gone on it would have produced the full 100,000 men it was intended to do (see the careful analysis in Nicholson, pp. 352-3 and Appendix "E").

(Assented to 29th August, 1917)

WHEREAS by section ten of the *Militia Act*... it is enacted as follows: —

"All the male inhabitants of Canada, of the age of eighteen years and upwards, and under sixty, not exempt or disqualified by law, and being British subjects, shall be liable to service in the Militia: Provided that the Governor General may require all the male inhabitants of Canada, capable of bearing arms, to serve in the case of a *levée en masse;*"

And whereas by section sixty-nine of the said Act it is further enacted as follows: —

"The Governor in Council may place the Militia, or any part thereof, on active service anywhere in Canada, and also beyond Canada, for the defence thereof, at any time when it appears advisable so to do by reason of emergency;"

And whereas by the said Act it is further enacted that, if at any time enough men do not volunteer to complete the quota required, the men so liable to serve shall be drafted by ballot;

And whereas to maintain and support the Canadian Expeditionary Force now engaged in active service overseas for the defence and security of Canada, the preservation of the Empire and of human liberty, it is necessary to provide reinforcements for such Expeditionary Force;

And whereas enough men do not volunteer to provide such reinforcements;

And whereas by reason of the large number of men who have already left agricultural and industrial pursuits in Canada to join such Expeditionary Force as volunteers, and of the necessity of sustaining under such conditions the productivity of the Dominion, it is expedient to secure the men still required, not by ballot as provided in the *Militia Act*, but by selective draft: Therefore His Majesty, by and with the advice and consent of the Senate and House of Commons of Canada, enacts as follows: — . . .

2. (1) Every male British subject who comes within one of the classes described in section three of this Act, and who, —

(*a*) is ordinarily resident in Canada; or,

(*b*) has been at any time since the fourth day of August, 1914, resident in Canada,

shall be liable to be called out as hereinafter provided on active service in the Canadian Expeditionary Force for the defence of Canada, either in or beyond Canada, unless he

(*a*) comes within the exceptions set out in the Schedule; or,

(*b*) reaches the age of forty-five before the class or subclass to which he belongs, as described in section three, is called out.

Such service shall be for the duration of the present war and of demobilization after the conclusion of the war. . . .

3. (1) The men who are liable to be called out shall consist of six classes described as follows: —

Class 1.—Those who have attained the age of twenty years and were born not earlier than the year 1883 and are unmarried, or are widowers but have no child.*

*This was the only class called.

Class 2. — Those who have attained the age of twenty years and were born not earlier than the year 1883 and are married, or are widowers who have a child or children.

Class 3. — Those who were born in the years 1876 to 1882, both inclusive, and are unmarried, or are widowers who have no child.

Class 4. — Those who were born in the years 1876 to 1882, both inclusive, and are married, or are widowers who have a child or children.

Class 5. — Those who were born in the years 1872 to 1875, both inclusive, and are unmarried, or are widowers who have no child.

Class 6. — Those who were born in the years 1872 to 1875, both inclusive, and are married, or are widowers who have a child or children.

(2) For the purpose of this section, any man married after the 6th day of July, 1917, shall be deemed to be unmarried....

(4) The order in which the classes are described in this section shall be the order in which they may be called out on active service, provided the Governor in Council may divide any class into subclasses, in which case the subclasses shall be called out in order of age beginning with the youngest.

4. (1) The Governor in Council may from time to time by proclamation call out on active service as aforesaid ... any class or subclass of men described in section three, and all men within the class or subclass so called out shall, from the date of such proclamation, be deemed to be soldiers enlisted in the Military Forces of Canada and subject to military law for the duration of the present war, and of demobilization thereafter, save as hereinafter provided....

(4) Any man who is called out and who, without reasonable excuse, fails to report . . . shall be guilty of an offence, and shall be liable on summary conviction to imprisonment for any term not exceeding five years, with hard labour.

5. (1) There shall be established ... the following tribunals: —

(*a*) Local Tribunals;

(*b*) Appeal Tribunals;

(*c*) A Central Appeal Judge....

10. (1) Any person aggrieved by the decision of a local tribunal, and any person authorized by the Minister of Militia and Defence, may appeal against any such decision.

(2) If the two members of a local tribunal cannot agree as to any decision to be made by them, they shall forthwith state in writing the case to be decided and cause the statement to be sent to the Registrar for the province in which the tribunal is established.

(3) (*a*) Subject to the provisions of paragraph (*b*) of this subsection there shall be an appeal from any appeal tribunal to the Central Appeal Judge.

(*b*) The Governor in Council, on the recommendation of the Central Appeal Judge, may make regulations governing the right to and fixing the conditions of appeal from an appeal tribunal to the Central Appeal Judge.

(4) The Central Appeal Judge shall be the tribunal of last resort, and the Governor in Council may, on his recommendation, appoint one or more other judges of any superior court to assist the said Central Appeal Judge in the discharge of his duties, and define their powers.

11. (1) At any time before a date to be fixed in the proclamation mentioned in section four, an application may be made, by or in respect of any man in the class or subclass called out by such proclamation, to a local tribunal established in the province in which such man ordinarily resides, for a certificate of exemption on any of the following grounds: —

(*a*) That it is expedient in the national interest that the man should, instead of being employed in military service, be engaged in other work in which he is habitually engaged;

(*b*) That it is expedient in the national interest that the man should, instead of being employed in military service, be engaged in other work in which he wishes to be engaged and for which he has special qualifications;

(*c*) That it is expedient in the national interest that, instead of being employed in military service, he should continue to be educated or trained for any work for which he is then being educated or trained;

(*d*) That serious hardship would ensue, if the man were placed on active service, owing to his exceptional financial or business obligations or domestic position;

(*e*) Ill health or infirmity;

(*f*) That he conscientiously objects to the undertaking of combatant service and is prohibited from so doing by the tenets and articles of faith, in effect on the sixth day of July, 1917, of any organized religious denomination existing and well recognized in Canada at such date, and to which he in good faith belongs;

and if any of the grounds of such application be established, a certificate of exemption shall be granted to such man....

13. .... (4) Unless further authorized by Parliament the reinforcements provided under this Act shall not exceed one hundred thousand men. ...

SCHEDULE

Exceptions

1. Men who hold a certificate granted under this Act and in force, other than a certificate of exemption from combatant service only.

2. Members of His Majesty's regular, or reserve, or auxiliary forces, as defined by the *Army Act*.

3. Members of the military forces raised by the Governments of any of His Majesty's other dominions or by the Government of India.

4. Men serving in the Royal Navy or in the Royal Marines, or in the Naval Service of Canada, and members of the Canadian Expeditionary Force.

5. Men who have since August 4th, 1914, served in the Military or Naval Forces of Great Britain or her allies in any theatre of actual war and have been honourably discharged therefrom.

6. Clergy, including members of any recognized order of an exclusively religious character, and ministers of all religious denominations existing in Canada at the date of the passing of this Act.

7. Those persons exempted from Military Service by Order in Council of August 13th, 1873, and by Order in Council of December 6th, 1898.*

225. The Halifax *Chronicle* Assails the Borden Government, October 1917

(Editorial, *Morning Chronicle*, 3 October 1917)

This was written some ten days before Borden formed his Union government. See also below, **226**.

Parliament will be dissolved and the General Elections will be held during the next few months, in accordance with the Constitution of Canada. ... To charge that the Liberal Party has forced an election, as some of the Government's hireling organs are doing, is simply a

*Respectively, Mennonites and Doukhobors.

bare-faced attempt to becloud the issue and divert public attention from the record of the Borden Government.

... The Borden Government will be tried on its administrative record. The present Government has not only been living for a year on sufferance; it has utterly lost the confidence of the people. Its partisan administration has been marked by a succession of blunders and scandals, by "inaction and indecisions" which have put Canada to shame.

It has employed the dying days of a moribund and unrepresentative Parliament to bludgeon through the House, some of the most outrageous legislative acts which ever disgraced a British country. Its Prussian "scrap of paper"* and its attack on the Electoral Lists of Nova Scotia are witnesses to its violation of the elementary principles of justice and fair play. Its Canadian Northern "deal"† and its failure to cope with the imperative question of the High Cost of Living testify that it exists for the Big Interests and not for the plain people who are the foundation of the State. Its leader has lamentably failed to rise to a great occasion and respond to a great opportunity. The country has weighed and found him unworthy of further confidence as Prime Minister.

It is the duty, then, of all good citizens to unite in electing a new Parliament that will be representative of the people and installing in office a new Government that will be worthy of Canada and of the supreme cause of freedom. It is to this high task and this imperative duty that all good citizens of Canada are now called.

226. The Halifax *Chronicle* Supports Borden's Union Government, November 1917

(Editorial, *Morning Chronicle*, 23 November 1917)

Comparison with **225**, above, suggests how disastrous the short-run effects of the conscription issue were for the Liberal party.

... the new Government is composed of the best elements of the preceding Government reformed and reinforced by leading members of the former Opposition, in whom there is every known reason to

*The War-time Elections Act, below, **233**.
†See above, **101**.

repose confidence and none to arouse suspicion. The personally untrustworthy and objectionable members of the late Administration have been got rid of. In the new Government we have men of approved ability and unquestioned personal integrity. Their policy of waging the war for Canada with all their might and by the best means available, should have universal public approval. The prospective soundness of their domestic policy is guaranteed by the bi-party composition of the Government, some of the beneficial effects of which have already been manifested.

The Opposition group is composed of divers elements. Its nucleus is "Laurier Liberalism." Outside of Quebec that signifies personal attachment to "The Old Chief," a sentiment admirable in itself, but dangerous in days such as these. Sir Wilfrid Laurier, influenced by Quebec, has announced a policy which runs counter to the ardent wishes and aims of the rest of the Dominion. The unsafe and possibly disastrous character of that policy is indicated unmistakably by the public adherence to and commendation of it by the notorious Bourassa and his traitorous Nationalists. Can any true Canadian conscientiously accept what Bourassa approves? In addition to the "Laurier Liberals" and the Bourassa Nationalists the Opposition group has the more or less close adherence of a good many men who, while denying that they are "Laurier Liberals" and declaring that they are for "winning the war," still announce themselves in opposition to the new Government which alone is pledged to wage and can wage the war successfully for Canada. It will thus be seen, and cannot be denied, that the Opposition group is composed of incompatible elements, whose only real bond of union is hostility to a Government against which nothing damaging can be alleged, whose policy is overwhelmingly approved in the Dominion, outside of Quebec Province, and which has a considerable measure of acceptance within that Province. . . .

227. An Election Riot in Sherbrooke, 1917

(*Gazette*, Montreal, 30 November 1917)

Sherbrooke is a bicultural community in the Eastern Townships of Quebec. The Unionist candidate was defeated, as were all other Unionists in Quebec except for three in Montreal. For other references to the 1917 general election, see above, **26-27**.

By a Staff Reporter

Sherbrooke, November 29.—Riotous scenes of a violence perhaps unapproached by any previous election meeting in the province were enacted tonight in connection with the meeting held in His Majesty's Theatre in the interests of the Union Government.

A crowd that was in a murderous mood sought to storm the stage from which Hon. Mr. Ballantyne, minister of marine, Hon. Mr. Doherty, minister of justice, and the Unionist candidate, Mr. W. S. Davidson, were addressing the people, and were held back only by means of a well-directed fire hose. The situation was most dangerous at the stage door, from which the hose was used with deadly precision, but it was not so spectacular as the scenes in the foyer and entrances to the theatre. Time and again, during a period of three hours, the howling mob broke through the doors, only to be repelled by the citizens who had seats on the ground floor of the theatre, and who, each time the mob broke into the theatre, rose and drove them back.

It was a series of at least twenty pitched battles. The whole front of His Majesty's Theatre, where the meeting was held, was wrecked. Not a single piece of glass was left intact, and through the broken windows stones of all sizes came hurtling into the building. . . .

228. Quebec ueber Alles

(*Mail and Empire*, Toronto, 17 December 1917)

The violence of the passions of 1917 is hard for a person who has not lived through such a crisis to understand. If *Le Devoir*'s outpourings (above, **222-223**) represent one extreme, this election-day editorial from Toronto represents the other.

WHAT IT MEANS

A vote polled in the election to-day for any candidate but the Unionist candidate is a vote against Union. It is a vote in favor of restoring the old division between English-speaking Conservatives and English-speaking Liberals, so that Quebec might be the real master of the Government of Canada. No matter what professions may be made by any candidate, if he is not the properly-endorsed candidate, if he is not the properly-endorsed candidate of the Union Government a vote for him is a vote against the Government and a vote for Laurier. A vote for a Laurier candidate is a vote for Bourassa. It is a vote against the Canadian army at the front; it is a vote against their families at home. It is a vote for smaller pensions or no pensions at all; it is a vote in favor of Canada withdrawing from the war. It is a vote against British connection, against the British Empire, a vote against the cause of the Allies. It is a vote for Germany, a vote for the Kaiser and Hindenburg and von Tirpitz and the German officer who sank the Lusitania. It is a vote against Belgium and Serbia, and a vote in favor of Austro-Hungary [sic] and Turkey. It is a vote for the Bolsheviks in Russia; a vote for an immediate and dishonorable peace.

This and much more a vote for a Laurier candidate would be; and it is so despite the fact that there are some Laurier candidates who have sons or others near and dear to them overseas. The man who has a son overseas and votes for a Laurier candidate votes to betray that son. The woman who has a husband at the front and votes for a Laurier candidate votes to her husband's hurt. A vote for a Laurier candidate is a vote for Quebec, and a vote against Canada. Those to whom the Province of Quebec is dearer than Canada ought to vote for the Laurier candidate. Mistaken as they are, they are yet logical when they vote for Laurier. He is the hope of Quebec; he is the menace to Canada. Quebec has no son more devoted to her own peculiar interests than Sir Wilfrid Laurier. He is for Quebec ueber Alles, and that is satisfactory to the Kaiser.

229. The Military Service Act Is Strengthened by Order in Council, 1918

(Order in Council P.C. 919 [20 April 1918], *Journals, House of Commons*, 19 April 1918)

The shattering though temporary success of the last great German offensive on the Western Front, beginning on 21 March 1918, had a serious impact on Canadian policy. The Military Service Act was not producing the needed men, since applications for exemption were being made and granted in great numbers. On 12 April the Minister of Overseas Military Forces (Sir Edward Kemp) cabled, "Unless 15,000 infantry reinforcements arrive before May 1st practically no trained infantry reinforcements available after July 1st" (Nicholson, p. 349). On 19 April Sir Robert Borden presented this drastic proposed order in council to the House of Commons, asking approval as a matter of urgency; he said the intention was to call out in the first instance men from 20 to 22 years old, both inclusive, and later, if needed, men of 19 and 23. The House of Commons and the Senate both approved the proposed order by resolution the same day. The cancellation of exemptions was contrary to a pledge the government had given to farmers, and there were widespread protests.

Sir Robert Borden moved, seconded by Sir George Foster, That it be resolved, — That in the opinion of this House, it is expedient that regulations respecting Military Service shall be made and enacted by the Governor in Council in manner and form and in the words and figures following, that is to say:

P.C. 919.

AT THE GOVERNMENT HOUSE AT OTTAWA

Present:

His Excellency the Governor General in Council.

Whereas there is an immediate and urgent need of reinforcements for the Canadian Expeditionary Force and the necessity for these reinforcements admits of no delay;

And Whereas it is deemed essential that notwithstanding exemptions heretofore granted a substantial number of men should be withdrawn forthwith from civil life for the purpose of serving in a military capacity;

And Whereas, having regard to the number of men immediately required and to the urgency of the demand, time does not permit of examination by exemption tribunals of the value in civil life, or the position, of the individuals called up for duty;

Therefore His Excellency the Governor General in Council, on the recommendation of the Right Honourable the Prime Minister, and under and in virtue of the powers conferred on the Governor in Council by the War Measures Act, 1914, and otherwise, is pleased to make the following regulations which shall come into force as soon as approved by resolution of both Houses of Parliament, and the same are hereby made and enacted accordingly: —

REGULATIONS

1. In these regulations, —
    (a) "Minister" shall mean the Minister of Militia and Defence.
    (b) "Act" shall mean the Military Service Act, 1917.
2. Class 1 under the Act shall, in addition to the men included

therein as in the said Act mentioned, include all men who, —

(a) Are British subjects; and

(b) Are not within the classes of persons described in the exceptions mentioned in the schedule to the Act; and

(c) Have attained the age of 19 years; but were born on or since 13th October, 1897; and

(d) Are unmarried or widowers without children; and

(e) Are resident in Canada.

3. Class 2 under the Military Service Act, 1917, shall, in addition to the men included therein as in the said Act mentioned, include all men who, —

(a) Are British subjects; and

(b) Are not within the classes of persons described in the exceptions mentioned in the schedule to the said Act; and

(c) Have attained the age of 19 years; but were born on or since 13th October, 1897; and

(d) Are married or widowers with children; and

(e) Are resident in Canada. . . .

5. The Governor in Council may direct orders to report for duty to issue to men in any class under the Act of any named age or ages or who were born in named years or any named year or part of a year and any exemption theretofore granted to any man of any such named age or year of birth shall cease from and after noon of the day upon which he is ordered so to report and no claim for exemption by or in respect of any man shall be entertained or considered after the issue to him of such order, provided, however, that the Minister may grant leave of absence without pay to any man by reason of the death, disablement or service of other members of the same family while on active service in any theatre of actual war. . . .

8. All men included in Class 1 by virtue of the provisions of these regulations shall report to the registrar or Deputy Registrar under the Act as required by Proclamation; they shall be subject to military law as in such Proclamation set out and shall, in the event of their failing to report, be liable to the penalties specified in the Act and the regulations thereunder.

9. (a) Any man now unmarried, who at any time hereafter attains the age of 19 years and is then a British subject resident in Canada and not within one of the exceptions in the Schedule to the Act, shall; and

(b) Any man who, having attained the age of 19 years, being then a British subject resident as aforesaid and not within one of the exceptions in the schedule to the Act, becomes a widower without children, shall, if the class within which he then falls has been called out on active service,

Forthwith become subject to military law and shall within ten (10) days thereafter report to the registrar or deputy registrar under the Act for the Province or the part of a Province in which he resides. He shall be placed on active service as provided by the Act, by the regulations thereunder or by these regulations, and shall, until so placed on active service be deemed to be on leave of absence without pay. . .

5. The Industrial Effort

There is a fairly general impression that Canadian munition production and its influence upon the industrialization of the country were phenomena only of the Second World War. In fact the First World War was also important in these respects. In 1914-18, however, the Canadian production effort was concentrated upon comparatively few items, and primarily upon shells.

230. The Imperial Munitions Board

(*Canada Year Book, 1920*)

This brief contemporary summary presents the essentials of an important achievement. For more detail see David Carnegie, *The History of Munitions Supply in Canada, 1914-1918* (London, 1925), which prints Sir Joseph Flavelle's final report as an appendix. Note that the Imperial Munitions Board was an arm of the British government. The Borden Cabinet doubtless favoured this arrangement partly because the earlier Shell Committee had become a political liability when its contracts were investigated by a Royal Commission.

The Munitions Industry in Canada

Iron and steel are the principal ingredients in the munitions required in modern warfare. Before the war Germany had, by bounties on production and export, so stimulated her iron and steel industry that she had far surpassed the United Kingdom in this field, producing 19 million tons of pig iron in 1913 as against Britain's 10½ million. Immediately on the outbreak of war, German armies occupied the chief iron and steel producing regions of France and Belgium, thus increasing their available resources and diminishing those of the allies. It was absolutely necessary, therefore, that Great Britain should call a new world into existence to redress the balance of the old, and enlist the assistance of the rising Canadian iron and steel industry in the struggle. As a result of overtures from the Imperial War Office, the Minister of Militia appointed a Shell Committee in September, 1914, to undertake the task of organizing the supply of shrapnel to the British Government. The first shipments were made in December, 1914, and by May 31, 1915, about 400 establishments were engaged in the manufacture of shells. In November, 1915, the work of the Shell Committee was transferred to the Imperial Munitions Board, which was directly responsible to the Imperial Ministry of Munitions. The Chairman of this Board* possessed full administrative and executive authority over the various departments, each of which was in charge of an expert. Among the departments were the Purchasing and Steel Departments, the Shipbuilding Department, the Aviation Department, the Fuse Department, the Engineering and the Inspection Departments. Industries new to Canada were established under the direction of the Board; its shipbuilding contracts amounted to some $70,000,000; more than 2,500 aeroplanes were produced in its factories, some of them for the United States Navy; the Board was also the agent of the United States Ordnance Department in arranging contracts for munitions and supplies. Its activities may be summed up in the words of the Report of the Imperial War Cabinet for 1917 as follows: —

"Canada's contribution during the last year has been very striking. Fifteen per cent of the total expenditure of the Ministry of Munitions in the last six months of the year was incurred in that country. She has manufactured nearly every type of shell from the 18-pounder to the 9·2-inch. In the case of the 18-pounder, no less than 55 per cent of the output of shrapnel shells in the last six months came from Canada, and most of these were complete rounds of ammunition which went direct to France. Canada also contributed 42 per cent of the total 4·5-inch shells, 27 per cent of the 6-inch shells, 20 per cent of the 60-pounder H.E. shells, 15 per cent of the 8-inch and 16 per cent of the 9·2-inch."

The following figures will give some idea of what Canada accomplished in the production of munitions of war: —

VALUE OF MUNITIONS AND MATERIALS EXPORTED FROM CANADA

Calendar Year	$
1914	28,164
1915	57,213,688

*Sir Joseph Flavelle

1916..	296,505,257
1917..	388,213,553
1918..	260,711,751

The effects of the establishment of the munitions industry in Canada in increasing iron and steel production is also observable in the statistics of manufactures. In 1915 the iron and steel products industry of Canada produced commodities to the value of $120,422,420, while in 1917 its products were valued at $400,385,086 and in 1918 at $443,455,779. The chemical and allied products industry was also greatly stimulated by the war. Commodities to a gross value of $45,410,486 were produced by this industry in 1915, while in 1917 the gross value increased to $133,618,658, and in 1918 the gross products were valued at $173,649,073.

To the Shipbuilding Department of the Imperial Munitions Board was due in large measure the great increase in Canadian shipbuilding which went far to defeat the most serious menace to the security of the Empire during the war—the unrestricted submarine campaign. During the calendar year 1918 there were launched the following vessels built to the order of the Imperial Munitions Board: Steel, 23 vessels with an approximate deadweight carrying capacity of 114,863 tons; wood, 45 vessels, with an approximate deadweight carrying capacity of 138,600 tons. Steel vessels to the number of 11, with an approximate carrying capacity of 48,000 tons, built to the order of the Department of Marine, as well as 11 steel vessels with a carrying capacity of 45,304 tons and 13 wooden vessels with a carrying capacity of 20,600 tons built under private contract, were launched in Canada during the same year. The total launched from Canadian shipyards during the year was thus 45 steel and 58 wooden vessels, with a carrying capacity of 208,167 and 159,200 tons respectively, a grand total of 103 vessels with a total tonnage of 367,367 tons.

6. Special and Emergency Legislation

231. The War Measures Act, 1914

(5 George V, Chap. 2)

This drastic measure, which gives the Governor in Council virtually unlimited powers in a time of emergency, is (with adjustments) still on the statute book.

(Assented to 22nd August, 1914)

. . .

3. The provisions of sections 6, 10, 11 and 13 of this Act shall only be in force during war, invasion, or insurrection, real or apprehended.

4. The issue of a proclamation by His Majesty, or under the authority of the Governor in Council shall be conclusive evidence that war, invasion, or insurrection, real or apprehended, exists and has existed for any period of time therein stated, and of its continuance, until by the issue of a further proclamation it is declared that the war, invasion or insurrection no longer exists.

5. It is hereby declared that war has continuously existed since the fourth day of August, 1914, and shall be deemed to exist until the Governor in Council by proclamation published in *The Canada Gazette* declares that it no longer exists; but any and all proceedings instituted or commenced by or under the authority of the Governor in Council before the issue of such last mentioned proclamation, the continuance of which he may authorize, may be carried on and concluded as if the said proclamation had not issued.

6. The Governor in Council shall have power to do and authorize such acts and things, and to make from time to time such orders and regulations, as he may by reason of the existence of real or apprehended war, invasion or insurrection deem necessary or advisable for the security, defence, peace, order and welfare of Canada; and for greater certainty, but not so as to restrict the generality of the foregoing terms, it is hereby declared that the powers of the Governor in Council shall extend to all matters coming within the classes of subjects hereinafter enumerated, that is to say: —

   (a) censorship and the control and suppression of publications, writings, maps, plans, photographs, communications and means of communication;

(*b*) arrest, detention, exclusion and deportation;

(*c*) control of the harbours, ports and territorial waters of Canada and the movements of vessels;

(*d*) transportation by land, air, or water and the control of the transport of persons and things;

(*e*) trading, exportation, importation, production and manufacture;

(*f*) appropriation, control, forfeiture and disposition of property and of the use thereof.

2. All orders and regulations made under this section shall have the force of law, and shall be enforced in such manner and by such courts, officers and authorities as the Governor in Council may prescribe, and may be varied, extended or revoked by any subsequent order or regulation. . . .

10. The Governor in Council may prescribe the penalties that may be imposed for violations of orders and regulations made under this Act, but no such penalty shall exceed a fine of five thousand dollars or imprisonment for any term not exceeding five years, or both fine and imprisonment, and may also prescribe whether such penalty be imposed upon summary conviction or upon indictment.

11. No person who is held for deportation under this Act or under any regulation made thereunder, or is under arrest or detention as an alien enemy, or upon suspicion that he is an alien enemy, or to prevent his departure from Canada, shall be released upon bail or otherwise discharged or tried, without the consent of the Minister of Justice. . . .

232. The Military Voters Act, 1917

(7-8 George V, Chap. 34)

While serious objection could scarcely be taken to giving the vote to all servicemen who were British subjects, whatever their age or origin, after the 1917 general election the government was accused of having manipulated the military vote under this law to ensure the return of its candidates in doubtful constituencies.

. . .

(Assented to 20th September, 1917)

1. The *Dominion Elections Act*, chapter six of the Revised Statutes of Canada, 1906, is amended by adding thereto as Part IV thereof the following provisions and forms: —

"PART IV.

"1. This Part of this Act shall apply only to a general election held during the present war or after the conclusion of peace but before demobilization.

"2. In this Part, unless by the context a contrary intention is made to appear, the expression,—...

    (c) 'Military elector' means and includes every person, male or female, who, being a British subject, whether or not ordinarily resident in Canada and whether or not an Indian, has been, while within or without Canada, appointed, enlisted, enrolled or called out for and placed on active service as one of the Canadian Expeditionary Force, the Royal Canadian Navy, the Canadian Militia on active service, or the Royal Naval Canadian Volunteer Reserve, or has been, while within Canada, appointed, enlisted or enrolled as one of the British Royal Flying Corps, Royal Naval Air Service, or Auxiliary Motor Boat Patron Service, whether as officer, soldier, sailor, dentist, nurse, aviator, mechanician or otherwise, and who remains one of any such forces or services or has been honourably discharged therefrom, or, in the case of an officer who has been permitted to resign or without fault on his part has had his services dispensed with, and every person, male or female, who, being a British subject ordinarily resident in Canada, whether or not a minor or an Indian, is on active service in Europe in any of the forces or services, military or naval, of His Majesty or of His allies.

"3. (1) Every military elector shall be qualified and entitled to vote at a general election.

(2) If he can state the electoral district wherein he last continuously resided during at least four months of the twelve months immediately preceding his appointment, enlistment, enrolment or calling out on active service, or so particularly specify a place or places within an electoral district whereat during such period of time he so resided that such electoral district can therefrom be ascertained, he shall be deemed an elector of the electoral district so stated or to be ascertained, and his vote shall be applied thereto.

(3) If he cannot state or so specify an electoral district or place wherein he has so resided for the time and within the period mentioned in subsection two but can state an electoral district or so specify a place within Canada wherein he has at any other time resided, he shall be deemed an elector of the electoral district so stated or made ascertainable and his vote shall be applied thereto.

(4) If he cannot, because of non-residence or otherwise, so state or specify, he shall be deemed an elector of, and his vote shall be applied to, such electoral district as he may indicate.

(5) No person shall be entitled, because of anything in this Part contained, to vote more than once at any election. . . . *

"12. . . .

(5) A vote for a party shall be counted as a vote for the candidate or candidates who has or have been recognized, in the manner hereinafter prescribed, as the candidate or candidates representing that party in the electoral district to which the vote has been applied. Such recognition shall be made in the case of the Government party by the Prime Minister, in the case of the Opposition party by the Leader of the Opposition, and in the case of any Independent or Labour party by the recognized leader of such party. Within five days after the day of nomination, the Prime Minister, the Leader of the Opposition, and the recognized leader of any Independent or Labour party, shall severally notify the Clerk of the Crown in Chancery of the names of the candidates recognized by them, and such notification shall forthwith be published in the *Canada Gazette* and communicated to the Assistant Clerk of the Crown in Chancery.† If a military elector votes for a party, and there is no candidate recognized as aforesaid as representing that party, his ballot shall be rejected, and the reason for the rejection shall be written and signed by the Special Returning Officer and his Clerk on the back thereof.

(6) A vote for a person by name shall be counted for such person if he is a candidate in the electoral district to which, in accordance with the endorsement or marking on the envelope, such ballot has been applied, but if otherwise, it shall be rejected, and the reason for the rejection shall be written and signed thereon as in the immediately preceding paragraph provided. Where any ballot-paper bears on its face a vote for a candidate by name and is also marked as a vote for a party other than that of which such named person is a candidate, such ballot shall be counted as a vote for the candidate named thereon.

(7) No ballot shall be rejected for uncertainty as to the party or the candidate intended to be voted for by reason only of the misplacing of any mark, or the misspelling of any name, or because of any omission of or addition to the Christian name, or the omission or addition of any prefix to any name thereon, if, notwithstanding, it is possible

---

*Details of procedure for taking the military vote are omitted.
†An official to be appointed overseas.

to ascertain by mere inspection of such ballot-paper, the party or the candidate for which or whom the voter intended to vote; nor shall any ballot be rejected as containing a possible identifying mark unless the mark is obviously intended as such. . . .

"FORM A"

BALLOT

THE VOTER, IF HE DESIRES TO VOTE FOR ANY PARTICULAR CANDIDATE OR CANDIDATES DESIGNATED BY NAME, SHALL WRITE THE NAME OF SUCH CANDIDATE OR CANDIDATES IN THE FIRST WHITE SPACE, OR IF HE DESIRES TO VOTE FOR A PARTY HE SHALL MAKE AN X WITHIN THE WHITE SPACE CONTAINING THE NAME OF THE PARTY FOR WHICH HE INTENDS TO VOTE.

LE VOTANT, S'IL DÉSIRE VOTER POUR UN OU DES CANDIDATS EN PARTICULIER DÉSIGNÉS PAR LEURS NOMS, ECRIRA LE NOM DE CE OU CES CANDIDATS DANS LE PREMIER BLANC, OU S'IL DÉSIRE VOTER POUR UN PARTI IL FERA UN X DANS LE BLANC CONTENANT LE NOM DU PARTI POUR LEQUEL IL A L'INTENTION DE VOTER.

In the electoral districts of Ottawa, of Halifax, of South Cape Breton and Richmond, of the city and counties of St. John and Albert, and of Queens, P.E.I., two candidates may be voted for.

Dans les divisions électorales d'Ottawa, de Halifax, de Cap-Breton Sud et Richmond, et de la cité et des comtés de St. John et Albert, et de Queens, I.-P.-E., on peut voter pour deux candidats.

1   I vote for }
      Je vote pour }

2   I vote for the Government }
      Je vote pour le Gouvernement }

3   I vote for the Opposition }
      Je vote pour l'Opposition }

4   I vote for the Independent Candidate }
      Je vote pour le candidat Indépendant }

5   I vote for the Labour Candidate }
      Je vote pour le candidat Ouvrier }

233. The War-time Elections Act, 1917

(7-8 George V, Chap. 39)

This is perhaps the most generally reprobated measure passed by the Borden ministry. The enfranchisement of women related to servicemen, and still more the disfranchisement of naturalized subjects and of "conscientious objectors," were obvious political expedients intended to win the approaching election for the Union government. In retrospect their moral status is more than doubtful.

. . .

(Assented to 20th September, 1917)

1. During the present war, and until demobilization after the conclusion of peace, the operation of Part I of the *Dominion Elections Act* (being sections 5 to 30 inclusive) shall be suspended, and Part II of that Act (being sections 31 to 65 inclusive) shall operate and apply as if amended, and shall be deemed to be amended, in the following respects: — . . .

(c) By striking out section 32 and inserting instead the following:–

"32. (1) The qualifications necessary to enable any male person to vote at a Dominion election in any province shall, except as by this Act otherwise provided, be those established by the laws of that province as necessary to entitle such male person to vote in the same part of the province at a provincial election.

"(2) Except in the province of Quebec, and notwithstanding anything in this Act contained, in preparing or adding to the voters' list provided for by this Act, the qualifications as to residence and domicile of electors shall, in any province where there is no relevant or applicable provision to the contrary, be residence for one year in the province and residence and domicile in the electoral district for thirty days, both of said periods to be fixed by reference to the date of the writ of election: Provided that the requirements of this section as to domicile shall apply only to such provinces as, by their law applicable to provincial elections, require domicile as one of the qualifications of an elector.

"(3) In the province of Quebec, notwithstanding anything in this Act contained, the qualifications as to domicile of female voters shall be domicile at the date of the said writ of election";

(d) By adding as section 33A, between sections 33 and 34, the following: —

"33A. (1) Every female person shall be capable of voting and qualified to vote at a Dominion election in any province or in the Yukon Territory, who, being a British subject and qualified as to age, race and residence, as required in the case of a male person in such province or in the Yukon Territory, as the case may be, is the wife, widow, mother, sister or daughter of any person, male or female, living or dead, who is serving or has served without Canada in any of the military forces, or within or without Canada in any of the naval forces, of Canada or of Great Britain in the present war: Provided that this section shall not apply to the wife, widow, mother, sister or daughter of a person no longer serving as aforesaid, unless such person has died in or has been honourably discharged from such service, or, in the case of an officer, has died in or has been permitted to resign from such service or has been dispensed by competent authority from further service, or in any case, has died after honourable discharge, resignation by permission, or dispensation from further service as aforesaid.

"(2) Such naval forces of Canada shall be deemed not to include members thereof engaged within Canada who may become members after the passing of this Act".

(e) By adding as section 33B immediately after section 33A the following: —

"33B. (1) No person possessed of the qualifications generally required by the provincial law to entitle him to vote at a provincial election shall be disqualified from voting at a Dominion election merely by reason of any provision of the provincial law disqualifying from having his name on the list or from voting, —

(i) the holder of an office; or,

(ii) any person employed in any capacity in the public service of Canada or of the province; or,

(iii) any person belonging to or engaged in any profession, calling, employment or occupation; or,

(iv) any one belonging to any other class of persons who, although possessed of the qualifications generally required by the provincial law, are, by such law, declared to be disqualified by reason of their belonging to such class.

"(2) No person whose son or grandson is serving or has served as in section 33A provided shall, by reason of the lack of any income or property qualification required by the provincial law, be deemed non-qualified to vote at a Dominion election, but all such persons, being otherwise qualified as required by this Act, shall be entitled to vote at any Dominion election;"...

2. During the present war and until demobilization after the conclusion of peace, Part III of the *Dominion Elections Act* shall operate and apply as if amended and shall be deemed to be amended in the following respects: — ...

(d) By adding as paragraphs (e), (f), (g), (h) and (i) to subsection (1) of section 67* the following:–

"(e) Any person who shall have applied pursuant to section 11, subsection (1), clause (f) of the *Act respecting Military Service* for a certificate of exemption from combatant military service on conscientious grounds, whether or not a certificate of exemption from such service shall have been granted, and unless and until it has been refused."

"(f) All persons who on the sixth day of July, 1917, were members of the religious denomination or sect called 'Mennonites' (the members of which denomination or sect were exempted from military service by Order in Council of August 13, 1873), and all persons who on said sixth day of July, 1917, were members of the religious denomination or sect called 'Doukabors' [sic] (the members of which denomination or sect were exempted from military service by Order in Council of December 6, 1898): Provided that this paragraph shall not apply to such Mennonites or Doukabors as shall have volunteered for and been placed on active service in the military or naval forces of Canada or of His Majesty in the present war."

"(g) Except as in this paragraph provided, every naturalized British subject who was born in an enemy country and naturalized subsequent to the 31st day of March, 1902. A person shall be deemed to have been born in an enemy country, within the meaning of this paragraph, if he was born in a country which forms part of the territory of any country with which His Majesty is at war: Provided that a person claiming to vote who was a natural born citizen or subject of France, Italy, or Denmark, and who arrived in Canada before the date upon which the territory in which he was born became part of Germany or Austria (as the case may be) shall not be deemed to have been born in an enemy country if he produces to the deputy returning officer an unrevoked certificate in the form W-3 in the Schedule....†

"(h) Every naturalized British subject who was born in any European country (whether or not the sovereign or government thereof is in alliance with His Majesty in the present war) whose natural language, otherwise described as "mother tongue," is a language of an enemy country, and who was naturalized subsequent to the 31st day of March, 1902.

---

*This subsection lists categories of persons disqualified from voting.
†Omitted.

Provided that nothing contained in this section shall be construed as preventing any naturalized British subject (if otherwise qualified) from having his or her name on a list of voters or from voting who — (i) is serving or has served without Canada as one of the military or within or without Canada as one of the naval forces of Canada or of His Majesty or of any of his allies in the present war, or, (ii) produces a certificate signed by the Commanding Officer of a Military District, or an officer thereto authorized by him, that that person is or has been a member of any of such forces and has been engaged in active service within or without Canada during the present war, or is a person who has applied for enlistment as a member of such forces to so serve and has been rejected only because medically unfit, or is a grandparent, parent, son or brother of a person who is or has been a member of any of such forces and has been engaged in active service, or of a person who has so applied and been so rejected; or, (iii) is or has been at any time during the present war a member of the Parliament of Canada or of a province; or, (iv) is a Christian and either a Syrian or an Armenian; or, (v) is a female voter entitled to vote under section 33A of this Act."

"(*i*) every person who has been convicted of any offence against the *Act respecting Military Service,* passed in the year 1917.;"

(*e*) By adding as section 67A, between sections 67 and 68, the following: —

"67A. Notwithstanding anything appearing in the *Act respecting Military Service,* passed in the year 1917, or in any other Act or Order in Council, —

(1) All persons who are by the terms of paragraphs (*g*) and (*h*) of section 67 of this Act disqualified from voting, with such of their sons as on polling day are not of legal age, shall be, and shall be held, exempt from combatant military and naval service; and,

(2) All persons who shall have voted at a Dominion election held subsequent to the 7th day of October, 1917, during the present war shall be held ineligible and incompetent, — (*a*) to apply for, or to be granted on the application of another, exemption from combatant military or naval service on conscientious grounds, or, (*b*) to be excepted as a Mennonite or as a Doukabor from the provisions of said *Act respecting Military Service* or exempted as such from combatant military or naval service on conscientious grounds;" ...

B.
The Second World War

Like the First World War, the Second was a tremendous episode in Canadian history and really impossible to portray within the compass of a small selection of documents. The military effort, in 1914-18 so largely concentrated upon the Canadian Corps, was in 1939-45 dispersed between three fighting services, though the army still held a wholly unofficial pride of place. The economic effort was larger and more diversified. The grim difficulty over manpower between French and English Canada recurred, but happily in a rather less violent form. On political aspects, see also Part II of this volume. As with the earlier war, books are becoming numerous. On policy aspects, see Stacey, *Arms, Men and Governments* and Eayrs, *In Defence of Canada*, II, (which carries the story through 1940). Pickersgill and Forster, *The Mackenzie King Record*, I-II, is invaluable. On the fighting forces, see Goodspeed, ed., *The Armed Forces of Canada, 1867-1967*; Tucker, *The Naval Service of Canada*, II; and the three volumes of the official army history: Stacey, *Six Years of War* and *The Victory Campaign* (Ottawa, 1960) and Nicholson, *The Canadians in Italy* (Ottawa, 1956). On the production effort there is J. de N. Kennedy, *History of the Department of Munitions and Supply* (2 vols., Ottawa, 1950) and two excellent British official books, H. Duncan Hall, *North American Supply* (London, 1955) and H. Duncan Hall and C. C. Wrigley, *Studies of Overseas Supply* (London, 1956). Some specialized works are cited at appropriate points below.

1. The Outbreak of War

234. "Form and Objectives" of Canadian War Policy, 24 August 1939

(Stacey, *Arms, Men and Governments*, p. 9)

Dr. O. D. Skelton, Under Secretary of State for External Affairs, 1925-41, was Mackenzie King's closest adviser. The paper of which the greater part is given here represents Skelton's (and King's) idea of the proper line of action for Canada in 1939; and since King recorded that it met with "general approval" in Cabinet, it may be said to represent government policy too. Note that it is a policy of limited-liability war, with army participation and action abroad kept to a minimum (and the danger of demands for conscription thereby likewise minimized).

In all the discussion in Canada about the Polish war and Canadian participation in it, there has been little consideration of the form and objectives of our participation once that participation was decided....

In framing any policy, it is assumed that there will be immediate consultation with the United Kingdom and France, and equally important, discreet consultation with Washington....

I. Military Action

The defence of Canada should be put in the foreground. . . . It should be emphasized... that we cannot in this war ignore the Pacific as we did in the last. . . . There is a big job in defending our coasts. . . .

Within the measure of our capacity, we should consider the possibility of extending aid to Newfoundland and the West Indies....

If any military action is to be taken overseas, it should, in the first instance, be in the air service rather than by military contingents. An announcement of an immediate and intensified programme of building planes and training men for air service in Canada and for a Canadian air force operating in France, would be effective from the standpoint both of military value and of consolidation of public opinion.

II. Economic Effort

While economic effort without military activity would not be a satisfying or satisfactory means of participation, it is in the economic field that we can give aid that will be most effective to our allies and most consistent with Canadian interests. . . . We should concentrate attention on the provision of munitions, raw materials and foodstuffs....

III. Closer touch with Washington

IV. Statement of War Aims

235. Ernest Lapointe Speaks to the House

(*Debates, House of Commons*, 9 September 1939)

Britain and France went to war with Germany on 3 September 1939. The Canadian government, carrying out its promise that Parliament would decide, called it into session. On 9 September, by approving the Address in reply to the Speech from the Throne, the Commons voted for war without enough opposition being manifested to divide the House. The speech of the Minister of Justice was a moving and impressive feature of the debate.

Right Hon. ERNEST LAPOINTE (Minister of Justice): Mr. Speaker, I will ask the hon. member for Beauharnois-Laprairie (Mr. [Maxime] Raymond) to forgive me if in following him I use the English language, with my usual difficulty. I do so because most of my remarks are addressed rather to the English-speaking majority in the house, and I think perhaps it is best that I should be understood by them; I know my hon. friend will understand me.

These are indeed grave and solemn circumstances, and no member can rise in his place to take part in this debate without feeling a deep sense of responsibility. The hon. member for Winnipeg North Centre (Mr. [J.S.] Woodsworth) last night, at the conclusion of his remarks, which he had made with his usual freedom of expression, thanked Providence that he could speak and have freedom to express his opinions in the Canadian parliament, under British institutions, knowing that he could not do so in other places. I believe the hon. member for Beauharnois-Laprairie may have the same feeling. But I would ask the hon. member for Winnipeg North Centre and the hon. member for Beauharnois-Laprairie whether it is not worth while for us to preserve those very institutions and that freedom of expression which we enjoy in the Canadian parliament. This session and this debate show conclusively that there are things which are worth preserving. . . .

Mr. Speaker, from the numerous documents which have been circulated and laid on the table there is one missing to which I desire to call the attention of the house, and it is an important one. I refer to the message which His Majesty the King broadcast last Sunday, the third of September. . . . His majesty said:

In this grave hour, perhaps the most fateful in our history, I send to every household of my peoples, both at home and overseas, this message, spoken with the same depth of feeling for each one of you as if I were able to cross your threshold and speak to you myself.

And further, speaking of the principle of the use of force and might against right:

Such a principle, stripped of all disguise, is surely the mere primitive doctrine that might is right. If this principle were established throughout the world, the freedom of our own country and of the whole British commonwealth of nations would be in danger.

But far more than this, the peoples of the world would be kept in the bondage of fear, and all hope of settled peace and security, of justice and liberty, among nations, would be ended.

This is the ultimate issue which confronts us. For the sake of all that we ourselves hold dear, and of the world order and peace, it is unthinkable that we should refuse to meet the challenge.

It is to this high purpose that I now call my people at home and my peoples across the seas who will make our cause their own.

Our King, Mr. Speaker, is at war, and this parliament is sitting to decide whether we shall make his cause our own. . . .

Every speech that has been made has shown that this will be a gigantic conflict—the British empire, the dominions and France against Nazi Germany, and Bolshevist Russia, who looms up on the horizon. . . .* I share largely the views and opinion of my friend the hon. member for Selkirk (Mr. [J. T.] Thorson). I know what a great friend of peace he is. Like him, I deeply regret being compelled to follow this course, but in my soul and conscience I cannot take any other.

Will you allow me, sir, to reply to a certain campaign which is being carried on in my own province by certain people? My arguments last session—and I am happy that the occasion was given to me before this conflict came to express my views on the matter—my arguments last session as to the insurmountable difficulties in the way of Canada being neutral from a real and practical point of view, and the almost insurmountable difficulties from a legal point of view, still stand. Nobody in my province—I call attention to that; newspapermen,

*The German-Soviet non-aggression pact, announced on 21 August, had cleared the way for Hitler to go to war with the West.

members of parliament or others — has answered them, has tried to answer them. Even my good friend the hon. member for Beauharnois-Laprairie, who spoke to-day for neutrality, has never said a word to show that it was possible for Canada to be neutral. . . .

I gave last session, and I will not repeat them to-day, some of the reasons why it is impossible, practically, for Canada to be neutral in a big war in which England is engaged. . . . If we had neutrality all Canadian ports would be closed to all armed vessels of Britain, and in time of war merchant ships have to arm themselves in order to travel over the ocean. As I said last year, the citizens of my city of Quebec would have to prevent the *Empress of Britain* from coming to Quebec harbour during a war, because she would have guns to protect her when travelling on the ocean. . . . We would have to intern British sailors who came to take refuge in any of Canada's ports. Does any hon. member believe that Canadians would permit British sailors to be interned anywhere in this country?

We have contracts and agreements with Britain for the use of the dry docks at Halifax and Esquimalt; we are bound by contracts. That is not neutrality. Of course we could change all that; we could cancel and break all those contracts and engagements, but does my hon. friend think that the majority of Canadians would stand for it at this time? . . .

. . . Well, some people talk of mitigated neutrality; two respectable newspapers, whose views on this question are not exactly my own, have used that expression. . . . Well, Mr. Speaker, as a constitutional student — as I think I am — as a public man and as Minister of Justice of Canada I state, with all my responsibility, that there is no such thing as mitigated or partial neutrality. A country is neutral, with all that neutrality implies in the way of rights and duties towards belligerents and other neutrals, or she is a belligerent with all that belligerency implies. . . . One respectable newspaper used the words, "neutrality sympathetic to England and Poland." Of course there again there is no such thing. . . .

Much has been said about an expeditionary force. Let me say first that I agree with what the Prime Minister said yesterday. Applications are pouring in — and they are coming from Quebec also — from people who want to enlist. Far from urging people to do so, we have so far taken the position that it is better to act in an orderly way, to avoid confusion and consult with those whom we want to help. But if the need comes, does any member of the house think any Canadian government, whether this or any other, could stop the thousands of volunteers who would like to fight for Britain and France? Does my hon. friend from Beauharnois-Laprairie believe that a government, even if he were a member of it, could resist the pressure from all parts of Canada for an expeditionary force? Unfortunately, or according to my own view fortunately, this country has to be ruled by one government, and no government could stay in office if it refused to do what the large majority of Canadians wanted it to do.....

Now I come to a rather delicate subject. . . . But, sir, I believe that at this time there are two extreme sides of opinion which we should avoid and which would make for the disunity of Canada at a time when we need the very opposite. First, there are those who close their eyes to stern realities and say that Canada can and should remain neutral. In doing so they use, towards England, towards the empire and towards France, a language which I should like to see a little more moderate, a language which I submit is not calculated to promote unity in Canada. They say — and the hon. member who preceded me said it — "for the sake of unity let us be neutral." I am telling the hon. member where I differ from him. I know, and I believe he should know, that for the sake of unity we cannot be neutral in Canada.

The other school consists of those who also close their eyes to realities and are promoting courses which would disunite Canada — because such measures will never be accepted or enforced by and in a most important section of the country. The whole province of Quebec — and I speak with all the responsibility and all the solemnity I can give to my words — will never agree to accept compulsory service or conscription outside Canada. I will go farther than that: When I say the whole province of Quebec I mean that I personally agree with them. I am authorized by my colleagues in the cabinet from the province of Quebec — the veteran leader of the senate,* my good friend and colleague, the Minister of Public Works (Mr. [P.J.A.] Cardin), my friend and fellow townsman and colleague, the Minister of Pensions and National Health (Mr. [C.G.] Power) — to say that we will never agree to conscription and will never be members or supporters of a government that will try to enforce it. Is that clear enough? . . .

May I add that if my hon. friends and myself from Quebec were forced to leave the government I question whether anyone would be able to take our place. If my hon. friends in the far corner of the house opposite:† if the Ottawa *Citizen*, which just now is waging a campaign for conscription, think they are serving Canada by splitting it at the very outset of the war, then I say they are gravely and seriously wrong.

*Senator Raoul Dandurand.
†The Social Credit group.

Provided these points are understood, we are willing to offer our services without limitation and to devote our best efforts for the success of the cause we all have at heart. And those in Quebec who say that we will have conscription, in spite of what some of us are saying, are doing the work of disunity, the work of the foe, the work of the enemy. They weaken by their conduct and their words the authority of those who represent them in the government. So far as the insults and abuses of agitators are concerned — I disdain them! They will not deter me from the path of duty, as God gives me light to see it. I will protect them against themselves. I believe the majority in my province trust me; I have never deceived them, and I will not deceive them now. I have been told that my present stand means my political death. Well, at least it would not be a dishonourable end, and I am ready to make sacrifices for the sake of being right. But let me assure you, Mr. Speaker, that if only I can keep my physical strength, fall I shall not; and my friends shall not fall, either....

I desire to conclude my remarks by referring to what was said by our gracious queen at Halifax when she was leaving Canada to return to the homeland. Her words in French went to the heart of every man, woman and child in my province. She said, "Que Dieu bénisse le Canada." God bless Canada. Yes, God bless Canada. God save Canada. God save Canada's honour, Canada's soul, Canada's dignity, Canada's conscience.

God give Canadians the light which will indicate to them where their duty lies in this hour of trial so that our children and our children's children may inherit a land where freedom and peace shall prevail, where our social, political and religious institutions may be secure and from which the tyrannical doctrines of nazism and communism are forever banished. Yes, God bless Canada. God bless our queen. God bless our king.

236. Canada Declares War

(*Canada Gazette*, extra, 10 September 1939)

Parliament having "decided," and the High Commissioner in London having obtained the King's signature, Canada declared war on Germany on 10 September. She had been formally neutral for a week after the British declaration. The comparison with 1914 (above, **206**) is interesting.

TWEEDSMUIR
(L.S.)

CANADA

GEORGE THE SIXTH, by the Grace of God of Great Britain, Ireland and the British Dominions beyond the Seas KING, Defender of the Faith, Emperor of India.

TO ALL TO WHOM these Presents shall come or whom the same may in anywise concern,

GREETING:

A PROCLAMATION

ERNEST LAPOINTE,
Attorney General,
Canada.
WHEREAS by and with the advice of Our Privy Council for Canada We have signified Our Approval of the issue of a Proclamation in the *Canada Gazette* declaring that a State of War with the German Reich exists and has existed as [of] and from the tenth day of September, 1939;

NOW THEREFORE WE do hereby Declare and Proclaim that a State of War with the German Reich exists and has existed in Our Dominion of Canada as and from the tenth day of September, 1939.

OF ALL WHICH Our Loving Subjects and all others whom these Presents may concern are hereby required to take notice and to govern themselves accordingly.

IN TESTIMONY WHEREOF We have caused these Our Letters to be made Patent and the Great Seal of Canada to be hereunto affixed. WITNESS: Our Right Trusty and Well-beloved John, Baron Tweedsmuir of Elsfield, a Member of Our Most Honourable Privy Council, Knight Grand Cross of Our Most Distinguished Order of Saint Michael and Saint George, Knight Grand Cross of Our Royal Victorian Order, Member of Our Order of the Companions of Honour, Governor General and Commander-in-Chief of Our Dominion of Canada.

AT OUR GOVERNMENT HOUSE, in Our City of Ottawa, this tenth day of September, in the year of Our Lord one thousand nine hundred and thirty-nine and in the Third year of Our Reign.

By Command,
W. L. MACKENZIE KING,
Prime Minister of Canada

2. The Quebec Election of 1939

Serious issues of national unity were raised in Quebec soon after the outbreak of war. On 24 September 1939 the provincial premier, Maurice Duplessis, called an election on the question of the threat to provincial autonomy represented by the federal government's war measures. He did not directly oppose participation in the war, though he hinted at this in a campaign speech on 4 October. The federal ministers from Quebec campaigned actively against Duplessis, stating that they would resign from the Cabinet if he was returned. In the voting on 25 October Duplessis's Union Nationale party was heavily defeated by the Liberals led by Adélard Godbout, taking only 15 seats compared with 76 in the election of 1936 which brought Duplessis to power. See [C. G. Power], *A Party Politician: The Memoirs of Chubby Power*, ed. Norman Ward (Toronto, 1966).

237. Duplessis Throws Down the Gauntlet, 24 September 1939

(*Gazette*, Montreal, 25 September 1939)

Three Rivers, Que., September 24 — (CP) — Premier Maurice Duplessis, in a statement in which he said the National Union Government wishes to consult the electors "on questions which should be brought forward in every democratic and parliamentary regime," announced tonight that Quebec provincial elections will be held October 25. . . .

A campaign has been conducted for several years and direct and indirect attempts have been made with a view to lessening considerably "and even to abolishing provincial autonomy for the purpose of forming but one Government directed by Ottawa," the statement said.

"Invoking the pretext of war, declared by the federal government, a campaign of assimilation and centralization, manifest for several years, is accentuating itself in an intolerable manner.

"Ministerial orders have been passed by Ottawa, by virtue of the War Measures Act, with the desire and the effect of centralizing at Ottawa because of the war, all the finances of individuals, municipalities, provinces and the country in general.". . .

Mr. Duplessis said Quebec's loyalty could not be doubted but "for us, to be loyal is first of all and above all to guarantee the progress and the prosperity of Canada in general and of the province in particular.''. . .

238. Lapointe Picks the Gauntlet Up, 29 September 1939

(*Gazette*, Montreal, 30 September 1939)

Portions of a statement issued in Ottawa by Ernest Lapointe, Minister of Justice.

I am being asked from many quarters whether the federal ministers from the Province of Quebec will take part in the pending provincial campaign. The following is my answer. . . .

If the controversy had remained purely provincial, we should have strictly abstained from any intervention. But Mr. Duplessis has believed it his duty not only to precipitate an election in a critical period and to sow seeds of discord at a time when national union is a sacred duty, but he has made the criticism of the federal Government an issue at that election and more particularly the criticism of the measures taken for the purpose of assuring the effectiveness and the success of the effort of Canada in the present conflict. A verdict in his favor would be a verdict against us.

Under such circumstances, we cannot remain indifferent and our duty is to take up this unprovoked challenge.

My colleagues and myself who are representing the province in the Government of the country need the confidence and the support of our fellow countrymen in order to have and to keep such authority as is necessary to the defence of their ideas and the safeguarding of their interests.

Our first duty at this time is to accomplish the intense work which the security and the interest of Canada request from us. In that work we shall not fail. But Mr. Duplessis having made us an issue in his electoral appeal, we shall ask the Province of Quebec to give us a testimony of confidence. I wonder who Mr. Duplessis would like to have in Ottawa to replace us, but the province will have the occasion to declare whether she prefers to keep us in her confidence or to give it to the friends of the Premier of Quebec. . . .

239. Lapointe on Conscription, 9 October 1939

(*Gazette*, Montreal, 10 October 1939)

Duplessis was reported as saying at Trois Rivières on 4 October that a vote for Lapointe was "a vote for participation, assimilation, centralization," and a vote for Duplessis a vote "for autonomy against conscription" (*Gazette*, Montreal, 5 October). This was Lapointe's reply.

Ottawa, October 9.—(CP)—Rt. Hon. Ernest Lapointe, federal Minister of Justice, said tonight in a radio address that victory for Premier Duplessis' National Union Government in Quebec October 25 would be his cue, and that of the other three Quebec ministers, to retire from the federal Government....

"I stated in the House of Commons that I should not be a member of any Government which imposed conscription and that I would never support such an administration. The Prime Minister has stated that the present Government would never resort to conscription."

Mr. Lapointe said that he believed he had persuaded his English-speaking fellow-citizens that Canadian unity demanded the nation refrain from compulsory overseas service.

"Mr. Duplessis says that we are standing for conscription. You know that this is not true. He knows that it is not true. We are the bulwark standing between you and conscription. We are the the wall protecting you and even those who are insulting us in the ranks of Mr. Duplessis's army."...

Attempts to break Canadian unity are "fratricidal and criminal."

"We must have tolerance and mutual respect. Such is the necessary discipline that should be maintained through the loyal will of all Canadians. This firm belief has compelled me to take up Mr. Duplessis' challenge which is fraught with danger. He is asking you for a verdict against us, a definite and clear cut vote of want of confidence.

"I have stated that I would abide by the decision of the province, and I am determined to abide by it. During the Great War, I have seen men who claimed to represent their province in the Government, while the province was unanimously opposed to them. That I will not do. I will not remain here against your will; my colleagues from Quebec will not continue in office against your will."...

3. Canada and the Higher Direction of the War

In the First World War Sir Robert Borden exerted himself to gain for Canada the right to be informed and consulted and to have some voice in decision-making. Through the Imperial War Cabinet and the British Empire Delegation at the Peace Conference something was achieved in this direction (above, Part VIII). In the Second World War there was no Imperial War Cabinet and Mackenzie King did not press hard for a part in directing the war. Had he done so, he might have had little success, for President Roosevelt and his advisers were even less anxious than Churchill to share their control with smaller powers. See Stacey, *Arms, Men and Governments*.

240. Mackenzie King Describes the Machinery for Directing the War, July 1943

(*Debates, House of Commons*, 9 July 1943)

In this speech (the same in which he produced the "functional repre-sentation" idea, above, **203**), Mackenzie King, while not emphasizing the point, made it fairly evident that Britain and the United States were in fact keeping the direction of the war almost entirely in their own hands.

. . .

Shortly after Pearl Harbor, in order to secure more rapid coopera-tion between the war efforts of the United States and the United Kingdom, a group of combined agencies was established. These agencies are:

1. The combined chiefs of staff, meeting continuously in Washing-ton, composed of the United States chiefs of staff and representatives of the British chiefs of staff;

2. The munitions assignments boards, meeting in Washington and London, to allocate finished war materials on strategic grounds as they become ready for delivery;

3. The shipping adjustment boards, also meeting in Washington and in London, to regulate the pools of shipping controlled by the United States and the United Kingdom; and

4. The combined raw materials board, meeting in Washington, charged with the duty of planning the most effective use of raw materials. There were later added two further boards, both meeting in Washington;

5. The combined food board, and

6. The combined production [and] resources board.

With one exception these bodies are composed of representatives only of the United States and the United Kingdom and their chief duty is to make recommendations to these two governments in the light of the joint study of the problems before them. They are war bodies formed for special purposes to facilitate the rapid taking of decisions on matters vital to the conduct of the war.

It is essential that the high strategy of the war should be discussed by a small group in conditions of the most absolute secrecy. To avoid giving aid to our enemies, a degree of secrecy, which would be intolerable in times of peace, must surround the taking of decisions, not only on strategy but on almost every aspect of war direction. The recommendations of the combined boards frequently concern governments other than the United States and the United Kingdom. When Canadian action is required to give effect to their recommendations, these recommendations are referred to Canada for approval. The government has sought, with a considerable measure of success, to ensure that in framing their recommendations the combined boards should give the fullest consideration to the position and resources of Canada.

A Canadian joint staff mission has offices in the building which houses the combined chiefs of staff, and it is represented at discussions of direct concern to Canada. We have developed special methods of liaison with each of the combined boards. . . .

On one board, the combined production and resources board, Canada is represented by a full member. The Minister of Munitions and Supply (Mr. Howe) is a member of this board. The board, by the way, as hon. members are aware, is meeting in Ottawa this morning.

I have outlined the chief agencies that have been established for the direction of the war effort. The government hopes that it will be found possible to have a broader basis given to some of these bodies. . . .*

---

*Canada subsequently became a member of the Combined Food Board, but in spite of protracted efforts failed to gain a seat on the Munitions Assignments Board, a much more important body.

241. Roosevelt Vetoes Canadian Participation in the First Quebec Conference, 1943

(Churchill to Mackenzie King, 25 July 1943, Stacey, *Arms, Men and Governments,* pp. 181-2)

Somewhat contrary to the impression given in his memoirs (*The Second World War: The Hinge of Fate,* Toronto, 1950), Winston Churchill suggested, when arrangements for the First Quebec Conference (of Roosevelt, Churchill and the Combined Chiefs of Staff) were under discussion, that Canada be a participant. In a message sent to Mackenzie King through the British High Commissioner in Ottawa, he proposed that King and the Canadian Chiefs of Staff might attend all *plenary* meetings at which Churchill and Roosevelt presided, and the Canadian Chiefs attend all plenary meetings of the Combined Chiefs of Staff, private Anglo-American meetings still being held when desirable. Roosevelt, as here noted, put a stop to this idea at once. King did not complain; he felt that the presence of the British and American leaders in Canada, with himself in evidence as host, would be a great political advantage to him.

. . .

2. I submitted my telegram No. —— for the High Commissioner in Canada to the President. He sees insuperable difficulties in the Canadian Chiefs of Staff attending plenary meetings of the Combined Chiefs of Staff. He points out that this will almost certainly result in an immediate demand from Brazil and China for membership of the Combined Staffs in Washington; also from Mexico as well as from the other British Dominions and Allied Nations. He tells me that McCarthy* has left for Ottawa to explain the position to you.
3. I must say I see the difficulties as of course very little business can be done when large numbers are present. It seems to me, therefore, that the Canadian and British Staffs should confer together as may be necessary but that the British alone should be represented at the combined meetings of the two principal Allies. . . .

242. "Letting England Lead"

(Mackenzie King's Diary, 17 September 1944, Pickersgill and Forster, *The Mackenzie King Record,* II, 90-91)

This is part of Mackenzie King's record of his final conversation with Winston Churchill at the time of the Second Quebec Conference.

*Leighton McCarthy, Canadian Minister to Washington.

... I repeated what I had said at the table in the evening that I had felt this war had brought the different parts of the British Empire closer together than they had been at any time, but that this was owing to the fact that we all felt a special pride in having gone into the war, voluntarily from the very beginning. Churchill had spoken eloquently of that at the table, of our not desiring an acre of land, of not wishing anything in the way of additional power, but fighting simply for the maintenance of our honour and the preservation of freedom.

As we were driving through the narrow gateway of the Citadel, between the guardrooms and the gate, I said to him that while this was true, I believed it had been due to the recognition of the complete position of each of the Dominions acting on its own; the absence of any centralization. Said that any attempts at centralization would do great harm. Churchill to my great surprise said I agree 100 percent with you, you are perfectly right. Each part of the Empire must direct completely its own affairs. The relationship must be one of co-operation not centralization. What Churchill said was not expressed just in those words but that was the meaning. What came to me as a surprise was the emphatic way in which he spoke. . . . We then spoke of the mistake it would have been to have tried to form an Empire Cabinet to run the affairs during the war. He said, you remember Menzies,* he wanted to put me out; he wanted to have the war run by himself and others. . . . I said I remembered very well what Menzies had said to me on his arrival in Canada from Britain [in May 1941]. That he wanted to speak to me very seriously about the need of having myself, himself and others control the policy of the war. I said that my last words to him at Ottawa had been that he would find when he got back to Australia that he had lost . . . the leadership of his country, also that the place of all of us as leaders of the Dominions was in our own Dominions and not in London. Churchill said you were perfectly right. He then went on to say you have been so fine about letting England lead, not making it difficult for us by insisting always on several having direction. I said it had been difficult to maintain my position at times but that as long as I knew we were being consulted and getting informed on new policies and were able to speak about them before they were settled,† I thought it was much better before the world to leave the matter of leadership in the hands of the President and himself. He said that had meant everything in the effecting of needed co-operation. . . .

*Robert Menzies, Prime Minister of Australia. He fell from power (for the moment) in August 1941.
†In fact, these things did not always happen by any means. King may have intended to remind Churchill that this was the ideal situation in his eyes.

4. Command and Control of the Forces

In 1939, unlike 1914, there were precedents concerning control of large Canadian forces abroad (see above, p. 552). In the case of the Army these were followed, and the principles were essentially the same as in 1914-18: Canadian control of organization and administration, but in operations British higher command (and in Northwest Europe in 1943-44 United States command at a still higher level). The augmented Navy was more autonomous than the tiny force of the former war; it was not placed "at disposal" of the Admiralty, but was instructed to co-operate with other Commonwealth navies to the fullest extent. In practice, Canadian ships were usually found operating under Royal Navy higher command.

With the Air Force it was rather different, thanks to the British Commonwealth Air Training Plan. In his speech of 9 September 1939 (above, **235**) Ernest Lapointe spurned the idea that Britain should be allowed to pay the cost of Canadian forces: "If Canadians go to the front line of the battle they will go voluntarily as Canadians, under the control of Canada, commanded by Canadians and maintained by the Dominion of Canada." At that time the Air Training Plan had not been proposed. The 72,000 Canadian aircrew trained under the plan were volunteers, but most of those who went overseas were not under Canadian control, commanded by Canadians or maintained by Canada, though as time passed the situation in these respects improved. The main reason for these unsatisfactory circumstances was that in December 1939, when the first Air Training Plan agreement was made, the Canadian government felt that it could not afford to pay for maintaining Canadian air units in the field in addition to paying its share of the cost of the plan. See Stacey, *Arms, Men and Governments*.

243. The Canadian Government's Directive to General Crerar, 24 May 1944

(Stacey, *The Victory Campaign*, Appendix "A")

This directive issued before the opening of the Northwest Europe campaign in 1944 represents the Canadian government's views at a late stage of the war. Note (1) the fact that the Canadian commander was given the right of appeal to his own government against an order from his British superior (the commander of the 21st Army Group) if he considered the welfare of his force required it; (2) he was also given the right in extreme cases to withdraw his force from "in combination" with British forces under the Visiting Forces Act (above, **199**) (neither of these rights was ever exercised); (3) the government was anxious that its forces should as far as possible operate united, and wished the 1st Canadian Corps to be brought back from the Mediterranean to join Crerar's army as soon as conditions allowed. Since the 1st Corps had been sent to Italy at the Canadian government's own urging, its position in this matter was weak. When the Corps finally joined Crerar the war with Germany was nearly over.

Lieut.-General H. D. G. Crerar, CB, DSO,
General Officer Commanding in Chief,
First Canadian Army.
1. You have been appointed to command the First Canadian Army with effect from the 20th day of March, 1944.*
2. The Government of Canada has approved the detailing of First Canadian Army (less 1 Cdn Corps and ancillary troops now serving in the Mediterranean theatre) and the Canadian elements of Airborne, GHQ [General Headquarters], L of C [Lines of Communication], Base or other troops now serving in the United Kingdom to act in combination with the Military Forces of His Majesty raised in the United Kingdom or any other part of the British Commonwealth now or hereafter serving under command of 21 Army Group. . . .
4. By letter dated 6 Jan 44 it has been further agreed [with the British War Office] . . . that in the event of the said [Canadian] Forces being placed in combination with 21 Army Group the Commander in Chief, 21 Army Group, may carry out certain interchanges of formations between First Canadian Army and the British component of his Force and that in anticipation of this certain appointments of the staff of Headquarters, First Canadian Army, not to exceed 50 per cent,† may be filled by Britain Officers by mutual agreement between the Commander in Chief, 21 Army Group, and the General Officer Commanding in Chief, First Canadian Army. . . .
6. The Government of Canada has further approved the participation of the said Canadian Forces in the forthcoming invasion of enemy occupied Europe as contemplated by your reports . . . dated 25 Apr 44 and 1 May 44 . . .‡

*General Crerar had replaced (after an interval) Lieut.-General A. G. L. McNaughton, who had been removed partly because of difficulties with his government over the dispatch of Canadian forces to the Mediterranean, but mainly because British military authorities considered him unsuited to commanding an army in the field.
† In practice the proportion was about 15 per cent, and the senior staff officers were Canadians.
‡ The government had insisted that Crerar go on record as approving the plans, even of operations in which he himself would not be involved.

7. It has further approved the employment of a Canadian Division and a Canadian Armoured Brigade with the necessary ancillary troops . . . in operations which while under command of 21 Army Group will not be under your direct operational command.* It will be a matter for you to issue to the officer or officers commanding such Forces appropriate instructions to enable such action to be taken as may be necessary in respect to such Forces when circumstances do not permit prior reference to you.

8. You and the Comd of any Canadian Force not operating under your command, either by reason of its being detached therefrom or otherwise, continue to enjoy the right to refer to the Government of Canada in respect to any matter in which the said Canadian Forces are, or are likely to be, involved or committed or in respect of any question of their administration. Unless you consider that the circumstances warrant otherwise, such reference will be made only when the remedial or other action deemed by you or by the Comd of such Canadian Force to be necessary has been represented to the Officer Commanding the Combined Force and he shall have failed to take appropriate action. Any such reference from any Commander in the Western European theatre will be made through you. Any such reference from G.O.C. [General Officer Commanding] 1 Cdn Corps in the Allied Armies in Italy will be made through the Chief of Staff, C.M.H.Q. [Canadian Military Headquarters, London] In the case of references made to the Chief of Staff it will be his responsibility to obtain the views of the [Canadian] Army Commander for transmission to the Government of Canada in respect of such matters as have significance to the Canadian Field Army as a whole.

9. In deciding whether to exercise the authority to withdraw the Canadian Force, or any part thereof under your command from "in combination" with which authority you are vested . . ., you will consider all the circumstances including, but not in any way to be restricted to, the following:

(a) Whether in your opinion the orders and instructions issued to you by the Commander Combined Force represent in the circumstances a task for the Canadian Forces which is a practicable operation of war;

(b) Whether in your opinion such task with the resources available is capable of being carried out with reasonable prospects of success;

*The 3rd Canadian Infantry Division and the 2nd Canadian Armoured Brigade took part in the D Day landing on the coast of Normandy, 6 June 1944, under the command of the 1st British Corps and the Second British Army.

(c) Whether in your opinion such orders, instructions or task are at variance with the policy of the Canadian Government;

(d) Your appraisal of the extent of prospective losses to the Canadian Force in relation to the importance of the results prospectively to be achieved;

(e) The effect of such withdrawal in preventing the success of the operation as a whole;

(f) All other factors which you may consider relevant. The authority to withdraw should normally be exercised by you only after reference to the Government of Canada but, where the exigencies of the moment do not permit such reference, you have, in deciding whether or not to exercise this authority, full discretion to take such action as you consider advisable after considering all the circumstances as above.

When a Canadian division or other junior formation not operating under your command is operating under the orders of the G.O.C. in C. 21 Army Group, or pursuant to orders issued under authority delegated by him will apply equally with respect to the withdrawal of such division or junior formation from "in combination". The Officer Commanding such division or other junior formation has not in himself the power to withdraw and this, if necessary, can be effected only by you on reference to you by such Officer Commanding which reference the latter has power to make under paragraph 8 of these instructions.

10. As the Forces referred to in paragraph 7 are serving in the same theatre of operations as First Canadian Army the Government of Canada considers that only the urgent requirements of military operations should justify the continuance of detachment of such forces and the resultant loss of the obvious practical advantages resulting from unified Canadian control and administration.

11. At the request of the Government of Canada certain formations of the First Canadian Army were despatched to the Mediterranean Theatre with the objects at that time of increasing the effectiveness of the Canadian participation in the war and obtaining battle experience. Now that those objects have been gained the Government of Canada regards it as highly desirable that, as soon as military considerations permit, such formations now serving in the Mediterranean theatre as well as field formations and units elsewhere, should be grouped under unified Canadian command....

13. You will keep the Minister of National Defence constantly informed as to the foregoing matters.

14. Your channel of communication on all questions including matters of general policy will be to the Chief of the General Staff [in

Ottawa] through the Chief of Staff at Canadian Military Headquarters, London.

> J. C. Murchie
> Lieut.-General,
> Chief of the General Staff

244. Extract from a Directive by General Sir Bernard Montgomery to his Forces, 20 August 1944

(Stacey, *The Victory Campaign*, pp. 267-8)

When this directive was issued General Montgomery was still commanding the whole Allied ground force in Northwest Europe, as he
had done since D Day. It relates to the final stage of the Falaise Gap
battle (below, **251**) and the next phase of operations. It should be
compared with the directive from the Canadian government, **243**
above. The Canadian authorities were concerned with the administration and the general safety and welfare of their forces; but in
operations in the field those forces got their orders from the British
Commander-in-Chief.

. . .

22. The first task of [First] Canadian Army is to keep the Normandy
    "bottle" securely corked, vide para. 7.*
23. Simultaneously with carrying out this task, the Army will develop
    a strong thrust towards Lisieux, and eastwards towards Rouen.
24. When the cork is removed from the bottle . . . then Canadian
    Army will advance to the Seine, will cross the river, and will
    operate to clear the whole Havre peninsula to the west of the
    Army boundary.

    It is important to secure the port of Havre very early; the railway
    communications from the port, eastwards and northwards, will be
    required for the maintenance of the armies and much time will be
    saved if these can be secured intact, together with all possible
    rolling stock.
25. All Scotland will be grateful if Comd. Canadian Army can arrange
    that the Highland Division should capture St. Valery.

*Paragraph 7 ran: "The bottleneck is the area Trun-Chambois. Canadian
Army will be responsible for keeping this tightly corked; the cork will not be
withdrawn without authority from me."

I have no doubt that the 2nd Canadian Division will deal very suitably with Dieppe. *

245. The "Ralston-Sinclair Agreement" on R.C.A.F. Squadrons, 7 January 1941

(Stacey, *Arms, Men and Governments*, Appendix "I")

Article 15 of the original Air Training Plan agreement, 17 December 1939, provided that Dominion graduates should be identified with their own countries either by organizing Dominion formations and units or in some other way as might be agreed on; a separate understanding between Canada and Britain specified that there should be R.C.A.F. units in the field. This arrangement was implemented by the later agreement printed here, made in London between the Canadian Minister of National Defence and the British Air Minister, Sir Archibald Sinclair. Note that Canada still insisted that the "R.C.A.F." squadrons to be formed should be paid for by Britain. All Canada paid in practice was the difference between British and Canadian rates of pay for the Canadian personnel of the squadrons. Only on 1 April 1943 did the Canadian government begin to pay the full cost of maintaining the R.C.A.F. overseas. In the meantime there had been a sometimes rather acrimonious controversy over "Canadianization," i.e. the British Air Ministry's alleged slowness in forming the R.C.A.F. units and filling them with Canadian aircrew. See Power, *A Party Politician.*

It is agreed that the arrangements referred to in Article 15 of the Air Training Agreement for identifying with Canada the Canadian pilots and air crews trained under the British Commonwealth Air Training Plan shall be on the following lines: —

1. The pilots and air crews will be incorporated into squadrons of the Royal Canadian Air Force up to the number of twenty-five, in addition to the three already serving in the United Kingdom.†

2. The exact rate of formation cannot be guaranteed since it depends on the rate at which the projected [Royal] Air Force expansion can be achieved; nevertheless the endeavour will be to form these twenty-five squadrons within the next eighteen months. . . .

* In the 1940 campaign the Highland Division had been pinned against the coast at St. Valèry and largely captured by the Germans. The 2nd Canadian Division had carried out the bloody raid against Dieppe in 1942 (below, **247**).

† These three were complete R.C.A.F. squadrons, wholly maintained by Canada.

4. All Canadian pilots and air crews from the Air Training Plan not in Royal Canadian Air Force units or formations will continue to wear Royal Canadian Air Force uniform. . . .*

6. Under the Air Training Plan and at the request of the United Kingdom Government, the Royal Canadian Air Force has concentrated on the production of pilots and air crews. This has necessitated the provision and employment in Canada of ground personnel who would otherwise have been available for service with Royal Canadian Air Force squadrons overseas. It is recognised, however, as desirable, so far as it may mutually be considered practicable, that the United Kingdom ground personnel who . . . will be required for the squadrons referred to in paragraph 2 should gradually be exchanged for Royal Canadian Air Force ground personnel employed on the Air Training Plan, with a view to achieving homogeneity of personnel in these squadrons.

7. The concentration of the Royal Canadian Air Force on the Air Training Plan may also, at the outset, result in a shortage of Royal Canadian Air Force officers with the necessary qualifications to fill posts as Squadron Commanders, Station Commanders, etc. It is recognised that, if enough Royal Canadian Air Force officers with these qualifications are not immediately available, some of these posts may require to be filled by Royal Air Force officers. The replacement of these Royal Air Force officers will be effected progressively as soon as qualified Royal Canadian Air Force officers become available for that purpose.

8. Nothing in these arrangements to implement Article 15 affects the financial responsibilities of the two Governments under the Air Training Agreement, it being understood that the cost of the twenty-five squadrons referred to in paragraph 1 above will be borne by the United Kingdom Government, except that the pay, allowances, and non-effective benefits of Royal Canadian Air Force personnel who serve in the new squadrons will be borne by the United Kingdom Government only to the extent provided for in Article 17 of the Air Training Agreement.

9. The Air Officer Commanding the Royal Canadian Air Force Overseas Headquarters, or a senior officer designated by the Canadian Government for the purpose, will at all times have access to Commanders of Stations and Groups and to Commanders-in-Chief of Commands in which Royal Canadian Air Force personnel are serving, and will be furnished by them with such information as he may desire. He will also have access to the Chief of the Air Staff. He

---

*This meant in practice merely that they wore "Canada" badges. Only a minority of Canadian graduates of the plan could be accommodated in R.C.A.F. squadrons, even when the number of squadrons was increased later.

will be furnished with advance information about any major questions which arise from time to time affecting the employment of Royal Canadian Air Force personnel and squadrons. He will be at liberty to make representations to the Air Ministry on any of the above matters.

10. The arrangements in the preceding paragraph will not affect the existing procedure for consultation between the two Governments on major questions affecting the employment of the Royal Canadian Air Force personnel and squadrons overseas.

5. The Battlefield: Land, Sea and Air

Apart from the fact that in 1939-45 three large Canadian services instead of one fought the enemy (above, p. 595), the Second World War so far as Canada was concerned differed from the First in that the army spent a long time without seeing action. The collapse of France and the British withdrawal from the Continent in 1940 condemned the growing Canadian military force in England to a garrison role there; and except for the two tragic episodes of Hong Kong and Dieppe the army did no fighting until one division took part in the invasion of Sicily in 1943. The whole overseas force — five divisions, two armoured brigades and numerous ancillary units — got into action only after the Allies invaded Northwest Europe in June 1944.

246. Extracts from the Duff Report on the Hong Kong Affair, 4 June 1942

(*Report on the Canadian Expeditionary Force to the Crown Colony of Hong Kong*, Ottawa, 1942)

The Canadian Army's first battle in the Second World War was its share in the hopeless defence of Hong Kong (8-25 December 1941). This document however may be called more a political than a military one. In the light of allegations of inefficiency that had been made, the government appointed Sir Lyman Duff, Chief Justice of Canada, a royal commissioner to investigate the organization and dispatch of the Hong Kong force. Mr. George Drew (later a Conservative premier of Ontario and leader of the federal Conservative party) served as a counsel to the commission on the nomination of the Leader of the Opposition in Parliament. He subsequently attacked the Chief Justice's report, and the affair continued to be a matter of political controversy throughout the war and even later. See Stacey, *Six*

Years of War, and Granatstein, *The Politics of Survival.*

. . .

First, of the authorization of the expedition. . . .

It was urged by Mr. Drew that the change of Government in Japan on October 16, by which a cabinet notoriously sympathetic with the Axis powers came into office, ought to have led the Canadian Government to re-examine the question of policy raised by the invitation of the United Kingdom.* I had the advantage of reading a number of despatches from the Government of the United Kingdom, which I am not at liberty to reproduce, as well as a despatch from the Canadian military authorities in England, which is reproduced in part, dealing with the probabilities concerning war with Japan, and my conclusion is that, having regard to the information of which the Government was in possession, derived from the best sources of information open to them, nothing emerged before the departure of the expeditionary force on the 27th of October which could have been considered to be a justification for the withdrawal by Canada from the responsibility she had undertaken. . . .

Second, of the selection of the units for the expeditionary force. . . .

The evidence relating to the training, equipment and personnel of the two battalions is fully examined in the Appendix.† For reasons which there appear, I am satisfied that in respect of weapon training, as in respect of other matters, this selection cannot be justly impeached as affected by any error in judgment.

Third, of the steps taken to bring the units up to strength. . . .

A period of sixteen weeks has been laid down as the standard period to be devoted to the training of an infantry recruit before sending him overseas. . . . Of the men added to the strength of the Hong Kong expedition, all but about six per cent had undergone more than sixteen weeks military training after enlistment in the active army. . . .

A considerable amount of evidence was directed to show the effect of adding to two well-trained battalions groups of lesser trained men numbering about six per cent of the strength of the two units. That evidence conclusively establishes that an efficient battalion is, and must be, capable of absorbing recruits, who have not fully completed their training, up to a much greater proportion of its strength than six

* The British government had cabled Ottawa on 19 September 1941 asking for "one or two Canadian battalions" to reinforce the garrison of Hong Kong. Two were sent.
†Omitted.

per cent, without at all detracting from the efficiency of the battalion as a whole. . . .

Five, of mechanical transport. . . .

There was a small amount of free cargo space in the ship carrying the force* and some twenty vehicles were sent to Vancouver to fill it. These, however, did not arrive before the ship sailed. Had more energy and initiative been shown by the Quartermaster General's Branch, charged with the movement of the equipment for the force, the availability of this space would have been ascertained earlier and the vehicles would have arrived in time for loading on October 24; and there is, in my opinion, no good reason for thinking that, had they arrived at that time, they would not have been taken on board. There is no evidence, however, that the troops suffered through the lack of them, or that they were not supplied at Hong Kong. . . .

After an exhaustive inquiry at the hearings and a lengthy study of the evidence . . . I am able to add a general conclusion about the Hong Kong expedition as a whole.

In October, 1941, the Canadian military authorities undertook a task of considerable difficulty. Subject only to my observation concerning twenty of the two hundred and twelve vehicles of the mechanical transport, they performed that task well. Canada sent forward, in response to the British request, an expedition that was well-trained and (subject as aforesaid, in so far as shipping facilities allowed) well provided with equipment. In spite of the disaster that overtook it soon after its arrival in Hong Kong, it was an expedition of which Canada can and should be proud.

The war came upon us when we were unprepared for it. In such circumstances, recalling military history, one would perhaps not be greatly surprised to discover that even two years after its commencement some military enterprise had been undertaken which had proved to be ill-conceived, or badly managed. The Hong Kong expedition falls under neither description.

247. Bad News by Pigeon Post: Dieppe, 19 August 1942

(Stacey, *Six Years of War*, p. 386)

The costly raid on Dieppe was, like Hong Kong, a controversial operation whose military value has continued to be discussed, but unlike

---

* The great majority of the force's vehicles had to be sent by a later ship which did not reach Hong Kong before the Japanese attack.

Hong Kong it did not become to any great extent a political question. The raiding force had of course a great variety of radio equipment; but it also took carrier pigeons along in case they might be useful. After the withdrawal from the beaches, when the ships carrying the survivors who could be brought off had turned towards England, the Military Force Commander (Major-General J. H. Roberts, commanding the 2nd Canadian Division) used a pigeon to send this grim message to Headquarters 1st Canadian Corps in Sussex.

Very heavy casualties in men and ships. Did everything possible to get men off but in order to get any home had to come to sad decision to abandon remainder. This was joint decision by [Naval and Military] Force Commanders. Obviously operation completely lacked surprise.*

248. Convoy O.N. 127 Fights Its Way Through, September 1942

(Report of Proceedings by Commanding Officer H.M.C.S. *St. Croix*, 17 September 1942, Records of Department of National Defence)

The Royal Canadian Navy expanded enormously during the war. Its main task was in the Battle of the Atlantic, fought to keep the sea-lanes to Britain open in the face of fierce attacks by German submarines. Task Unit 24.1.14, the convoy escort in this document, was a sub-unit of Task Force 24 at Newfoundland, which was commanded by a U.S. officer. The escort however consisted of five Canadian vessels and one from the Royal Navy. German records show that the 32-ship convoy was attacked by a group of no fewer than 13 submarines; in the grim four-and-a-half-day fight H.M.C. destroyer *Ottawa* was lost with 114 of her company, and seven merchant ships went down. No submarines were sunk; one was damaged on 11 September. Nevertheless it cannot be doubted that the escort's relentless attacks prevented still heavier losses to the convoy. See Joseph Schull, *The Far Distant Ships* (Ottawa, 1950); J. Rohwer and G. Hümmelchen, *Chronik des Seekrieges 1939-1945* (Oldenburg, 1968); Goodspeed, *The Armed Forces of Canada*; S.W. Roskill, *The War At Sea* ("History of the Second World War, United Kingdom Military Series"), II (London, 1956).

---

* This was a natural enough conclusion at the time, but postwar examination of German documents showed that the Germans had had no warning of the raid.

Task unit 24.1.14, consisting of H.M.C. Destroyers "St. Croix" and "Ottawa" and Corvettes "Sherbrooke", "Arvida", "Amherst" and H.M.S. "Celandine" sailed from Loch Foyle, Northern Ireland at 0730 [7:30 a.m.] the 5th September.*
2. Clyde section of convoy was sighted at 1035 and at 1135 Task unit joined main section of convoy. . . . At 1845 Loch Ewe section joined. . . .

At 1435 the 10th . . . three ships, pennants 12, 22 & 32 were torpedoed. #12 was torpedoed on the starboard side whereas #22 and #23 were torpedoed on the port side. This indicated that 2 submarines were attacking. Sherbrooke was ordered to stand by ships torpedoed; St. Croix, Celandine and Ottawa turned towards convoy and carried out sweep. At 1525 St. Croix fired a medium pattern [of depth charges] on a contact. #22 was able to continue in convoy but pennants 12 and 32 appeared to be hopeless. Sherbrooke was ordered to sink the freighter. Ottawa ordered to take up station at visibility distance astern in order to prevent submarine surfacing and following convoy.
3. . . . At 1915 Empire Oil was torpedoed on starboard quarter and about 4 minutes later was torpedoed on port bow. . . .The periscope of a submarine was observed in the convoy close to the Empire Oil after it was torpedoed and St. Croix turned and went up between 4 & 5 columns obtaining an echo range 800 yards at 1918. St. Croix fired a shallow pattern and regained contact distant 600 yards bearing 140° on which a medium pattern was fired. . . .
4. Ottawa screened St. Croix when picking up survivors from Empire Oil and herself picked up 1 boat load, being screened by St. Croix. . . .
5. At 2225 star shells and snow flakes were observed ahead and signals received from Celandine saying that a ship had been torpedoed. This was #84. At 2345 star shells were again observed and evidently, about this time, #23 was torpedoed. At 2355 an R.D.F.† contact was obtained bearing 140° at 1¼ miles. Course was altered towards it, target was closed and at 2359 wake of a submarine was observed close on the starboard beam proceeding in the opposite direction. A shallow pattern was fired but no contact regained. . . .
6. At 0125 the 11th, Arvida reported sighting a submarine on the surface 1000 yards and attacked with a 10 charge pattern believed suc-

*Various technical details are omitted, including the letter affixed to times indicating the time zone referred to. Generally speaking the times used were within an hour or two of local time, and give a fair indication of the hours of darkness and daylight.
† Radio Direction Finding=Radar. The escort's radar equipment was in fact inadequate.

cessful. About this time Amherst also attacked contact on Port bow. At 0145 Ottawa attacked contact on Port quarter but [this] was not promising and contact was not regained. . . .

15. At 0630 the 12th, Celandine who had been standing by torpedoed ships, reported having made 2 promising attacks; one in which a U-boat at 1000 yards ahead of Arvida, following convoy at 14 knots, crash dived when range 500 yards, made a good attack with shallow pattern which blew it to the surface. It submerged again at 600 yards and a second good attack was carried out after which contact disappeared. At 0445 Celandine sighted another submarine on the surface and attacked. Submarine crash dived and Celandine attacked with depth charges. . . .

22. At 0005/14 [14 September] "Witch"* reported by R. T. [radio telephone] "Believe Ottawa torpedoed". Shortly after this 2 white rockets were observed ahead and St. Croix increased to 15 knots and sighted Ottawa on port bow within 4 or 5 minutes. She was on an even keel and appeared not badly damaged. St. Croix swept up to Ottawa on her starboard side and had reached a position on her starboard bow when an explosion believed to be from a torpedo, took place at 0016. St. Croix then passed ahead of Ottawa and when sweeping down her port side, observed her to sink. Signal was made to Celandine ordering her to close at best speed and to Commodore ordering emergency turn to starboard. Flares were observed in the water where Ottawa had sunk.

23. At 0034/14th St. Croix picked up H.E.† bearing 210° and proceeded to investigate ordering Celandine to search for survivors, Arvida to screen her whilst doing so. . . . At 0058 1/2 a medium pattern was fired.

24. At 0105 Arvida reported "Tanker torpedoed on starboard side survivors in water and in boats, proceeding to Ottawa". At 0110 RDF contact was gained near where charges had been dropped and fast H.E. heard. St. Croix increased to full speed and gradually closed target until finally at 0115, wake and conning tower of submarine was sighted close under port bow. A round was fired from #3 gun and a star shell fired from #1 gun but it is not thought this was effec-

---

*H.M.S. *Witch* was senior officer's ship of the Western Local Escort from St. John's which was to relieve the *St. Croix* group. Her captain was senior to the captain of *St. Croix*, but she signalled to the latter, "Please remain senior officer until morning."
†Hydrophone Effect.

tive as the gun's crew could not see the target. The submarine crash dived when about 20 yards ahead of the bow and a pattern set to [explode at depth of] 100 feet was fired at 0117 1/2. No further contact was gained.

25. At 0135, St. Croix stopped engines when in vicinity of flares, men were observed in the water and on rafts. St. Croix ordered Arvida "Close me near torpedoed tanker so as to screen me whilst we pick up survivors". At 0140 St. Croix proceeded ahead to clear rafts as it was thought too dangerous to remain stopped when submarines were in the vicinity. At this time it was thought that the survivors were from the torpedoed tanker which was fairly close but since then it appears that they were from the Ottawa.

26. At 0157 an echo bearing 220° 1100 yards was gained but was very shortly lost. At 0221 commenced screening Celandine and Arvida who were picking up survivors. . . .

29. At 0755 the 14th, daylight, St. Croix prepared to put Doctor on board Arvida, this operation was completed at 1035 when Celandine and Arvida left at best speed for St. John's. St. Croix searched area until 1300 without sighting further survivors when course was set for St. John's.*

30. St. Croix secured alongside Harvey's #3 wharf to land survivors at 1556 the 15th. Distance travelled 2811.7 miles, fuel remaining 3 tons, Depth charges remain[ing] − 2. . . .

249. The 1st Canadian Division Takes Ortona, December 1943

("Crossing of the Moro and Capture of Ortona," report by Major-General C. Vokes, Commanding 1st Canadian Division, 14 March 1944, Records of Department of National Defence)

One of Canada's bitterest small battles of the war was the taking of Ortona, a little Adriatic seaport. The town was defended house by house by the 1st Parachute Division, considered by many the best division in the German Army. The Ortona battle followed a period of fierce fighting (4-20 December) during which the 1st Division crossed and advanced from the River Moro. The original report contains a great many military abbreviations, which here are in general expanded into the complete forms.

---

*The German account indicates that the attack on the convoy was broken off on the 14th because of the nearness of the air bases in Newfoundland.

. . .

30. On 20 Dec the attack proceeded as planned. By 0905 hrs [9:05 a.m.] Princess Patricia's Canadian Light Infantry had reached their objective and were in position to support the Loyal Edmonton Regiment by fire. By 1400 hrs, after some heavy fighting, L Edmn R and their supporting tanks were into the outskirts of Ortona and by 1800 hrs PPCLI were moved up in support. Patrols from L Edmn R reported the town strongly held.

31. During the night 20/21 Dec, large explosions were heard in Ortona and on 21 December the Loyal Edmonton Regiment and the Seaforth Highlanders of Canada commenced clearing the town. This task saw some very bloody fighting between these units and two battalions of the 1st German Parachute Division before the town was finally cleared at 1200 hrs 28 Dec. The Germans systematically destroyed houses, thus creating barriers across the streets, which they sowed liberally with Teller mines and booby traps. Our troops, in turn, systematically blew the enemy out of fortified houses by a combination of tank gun fire, anti-tank guns and hand placed charges. There was much hand to hand fighting, in which no quarter was asked or given. Ortona should long remain a proud battle honour for the units which took part.

32. During the period of the Ortona battle, which was solely an effort by the 2nd Brigade, the 12th Canadian Tank Regiment [The Three Rivers Regiment] and the 90th Anti-Tank Battery, the remainder of the Division was not idle. The 3rd Brigade, which had suffered heavy casualties, was withdrawn . . . on 22 Dec to re-organize and rest. The 1st Brigade continued active patrolling in contact with the enemy, until on 23 Dec it commenced a series of very successful operations resulting in the capture and clearing of the S. Tommaso–S. Nicola area and East towards Ortona. By 27 Dec the Brigade threatened the main coast road North of Ortona. This was not accomplished without heavy fighting against units of 1 German Para Div, in which the Brigade, especially the 48th Highlanders of Canada, distinguished itself. This effort on the part of the Brigade contributed in large measure to the loosening of enemy resistance in Ortona.

33. On 28 Dec at 1300 hrs, a patrol of PPCLI emerging from Ortona along the coast road, reached 320180.* Here contact was made with a patrol of 48 Highrs. That evening the 3rd Brigade were ordered to pass through the 1st Brigade at 0830 hrs on 29 Dec, and moving across country, to the coast road near 320180 to press on to the River Arielli.

*A map reference identifying a crossroads about two miles northwest of Ortona.

34. The 3rd Brigade commenced the advance as planned with the Royal 22e Régiment leading, followed by the Carleton and York Regiment. By nightfall the Brigade had made contact with the enemy on the line of the River Riccio and at Point 59, 311192, from which latter point the enemy was dislodged in the next day or so.

35. From this time onwards, the front began to stabilize. The winter rains had turned the ground into a morass, making free manoeuvre of tanks and infantry so difficult as to prohibit offensive operations on a large scale. . . .

36. Thus, the first period of intensive fighting by the 1st Canadian Division,* which commenced on 4 Dec and ended on 29 Dec and ended on 29 Dec 43, drew to a close. During this period the infantry battalions of the Division suffered considerable casualties, especially in Officers, NCO's [non-commissioned officers] and Riflemen.† No reinforcements were available until 23 Dec so that Battalions, towards the end, entered battle at strength greatly below an efficient fighting strength. One cannot stress too much, the great difficulties of ground caused by the continued rains, which assisted the enemy in defence, but hindered the attack, which even so, was relentlessly maintained. We smashed 90 Panzer Grenadier Division and we gave 1 German Para Division a mauling which it will long remember.

37. During this period, the field guns alone fired more than 250,000 rounds and other types, such as medium artillery, a proportionate amount. The gunners worked night and day, and the problem of feeding the guns with ammunition in the required quantities was handled in a tireless manner, under very difficult circumstances, by the Royal Canadian Army Service Corps on the Division. . . .

250. No. 6 (R.C.A.F.) Bomber Group Attacks Hamburg, Night 28-29 July 1944

(Operations Record Book, No. 6 Bomber Group, Records of Department of National Defence)

The most formidable concentration of Canadian air power in the Second World War was found in No. 6 (R.C.A.F.) Group of the R.A.F. Bomber Command. Commanded by a Canadian air vice-marshal with a predominantly Canadian staff, and composed, in the later stages, of

---

*Some would argue that the division's first period of intensive fighting was in Sicily in the previous July and August.
†That is, general-duty infantrymen in the rifle companies of the battalions.

fourteen R.C.A.F. squadrons, it was an important instrument in the policy of Canadianizing the R.C.A.F. overseas pursued by Mr. C. G. Power, the Canadian Minister of National Defence for Air. Like all formations of Bomber Command, it suffered extremely heavy casualties, losing 814 aircraft on operations. In Bomber Command as a whole almost exactly 10,000 Canadians lost their lives — nearly a quarter of the total in all three Canadian services. In the operation here described losses were particularly severe, the heaviest in fact that No. 6 Group ever suffered.

The following 239 aircraft were detailed to bomb Hamburg: . . . [aircraft from 15 squadrons listed]. 209 aircraft attacked the target, 4 failed to take off, 3 returned early, 1 crashed on take off (none of the crew injured) and 22 are missing.

Results and Weather: There was 7/10ths to 10/10ths thin cloud with tops 6000/8000 feet approaching the enemy coast, rising to 12000/15000 feet over the target area. Visibility above the cloud was good and some crews were able to visually identify the target through breaks in the cloud. P.F.F. [Pathfinder Force] was punctual though marking was somewhat scattered. Crews report bombing as dispersed among the markers. Several heavy explosions were seen including one particularly large one which gave off a yellow-orange flame accompanied by much black smoke. Many fires were visible from 40/50 miles away. The main concentration of fires appeared to be east of the aiming point in the dock area. Ground defences consisted of moderate to intense heavy flak [anti-aircraft gunfire] in barrage form. Searchlights, though numerous, were ineffective due to cloud. Enemy fighters were active in the target area and on the homeward leg to Heligoland and opposition was particularly fierce at the Danish Coast. Fighter flares were dropped from above along the route and crews report many sightings of FW.190's, ME.109's, JU.88's, and ME.110's and also two combats with unidentified 4-engined aircraft. Two JU.88's are claimed as destroyed and two unidentified as damaged. 903.3 tons of high explosive were dropped.

Casualties: The following aircraft failed to return from this operation: . . . [22 aircraft identified]. . . .

Aircraft "U" of No. 431 [Squadron] was badly shot up and four of the crew bailed out over enemy territory. The remainder were able to bring the aircraft back. It landed at Strubby. . . .

251. General Crerar Reports on the Falaise Gap Battle

(Lieut.-General H. D. G. Crerar to the Minister of National Defence, 1 September 1944, Crerar Papers)

This dispatch is the first of a series covering First Canadian Army's share in the Northwest Europe campaign. Written immediately after the events, it is an interim report rather than history. It begins with the army's "breakout" attack from the Normandy bridgehead (7 August), which was checked after an advance of several miles. It then describes the renewed attack launched on 14 August. The latter part, here printed, deals with the final crisis of the battle and the closing of the Falaise Gap.

. . .

13. It now [15 August] remained to complete the isolation of the large German forces trapped south-west of Falaise by pushing on into and beyond that town and effecting a junction with the Americans advancing from the south. This was duly accomplished within the next four days by Canadian and Polish formations, while at the same time troops of the 1st British Corps drove eastwards across the Rivers Dives and Vie.*

14. The 2nd Canadian Infantry Division was ordered to captured Falaise. This it had effected by noon of 17 Aug. At the same time the 4th Canadian and 1st Polish Armoured Divisions were directed south-eastwards towards Trun and Chambois with a view to closing the gap separating the First Canadian Army from the United States forces. Advanced elements of the 4th Canadian Armoured Division occupied Trun and the high ground to the north of it on the night of 17/18 Aug. The Polish Armoured Division occupied Chambois after considerable fighting with enemy armour.†

15. The enemy, who had been slow to realize the full extent of his danger, now made belated but desperate efforts to re-establish his eastward communications and extricate at least a part of his encircled forces. The gap between the northern and southern spearheads of the

*The 1st British Corps and the 1st Polish Armoured Division were fighting under First Canadian Army at this time, the latter being under the 2nd Canadian Corps.
†Trun was actually taken on 18 August. The Poles and the Americans seem to have entered Chambois from opposite sides at about the same time on the evening of 19 August.

Allied forces had now narrowed to the space of from one and a half to three miles separating the Trun-Chambois road from the Forest of Gouffern. Early in the afternoon of 18 Aug, our air reconnaissance reported a great mass of enemy transport attempting to move through this gap. The resources of Nos 83 and 84 Groups, RAF, were turned on to this target.* The attack was temporarily suspended on the appearance of United States armour on the edge of the target area, but was resumed after arrangements had been made for the withdrawal of the American troops. The RAF units concerned reported that during these operations 112 enemy tanks and 3057 transport vehicles were destroyed or damaged. As was almost inevitable in the case of so heavy an air attack upon a limited area closely invested by our troops, our own forces again† suffered some casualties by RAF action.

16. On the evening of 19 Aug contact was finally made between First Canadian Army and United States troops in the Chambois area. The gap was thus closed. In the course of the following day, however, the enemy made further violent attempts to break out. One of these thrusts temporarily severed communications with the Polish Armoured Division and arrangements were consequently made to supply it by air. From this time the operations of the 2nd Canadian Corps were directed chiefly towards "mopping up" the encircled enemy forces. By 21 Aug this Corps was already beginning to change front to the east.

17. In the meantime, troops of the 1st British Corps had been advancing steadily eastward. . . . Lisieux . . . was entered on 22 Aug.

18. By 23 Aug the liquidation of the enemy formations which had been encircled south of Falaise was virtually complete, the German Seventh Army had been destroyed as a fighting force, and the Fifth Panzer Army had suffered heavily and was in full retreat. The object of the operations begun on 7 Aug had thus been fully achieved. The total of enemy prisoners taken on the First Canadian Army front from 7 to 23 Aug was 18,381. Great numbers of Germans had been killed. The total casualties suffered by Canadian troops of First Canadian Army during the period, including killed, died of wounds, wounded and missing, were 389 officers and 5,795 other ranks.‡ The

---

*R.C.A.F. squadrons made up about half the strength of No. 83 Group, which normally supported the Second British Army.

†During the advance to Falaise, troops of First Canadian Army had twice been bombed in error by Allied heavy bombers.

‡These casualties, and the still heavier ones earlier (total Canadian losses in Normandy from 6 June through 23 August were over 18,000), explain the reinforcement crisis of that summer and autumn (below, **254-257**).

loss of these gallant officers and men was the price of a most serious reverse inflicted upon the enemy.

19. The results obtained reflect the greatest credit on all formations of First Canadian Army, but particularly on those formations which had had little or no experience of battle previous to the opening of this campaign. The success of these divisions testifies to the soundness of the training which they received in England.

20. Throughout the operations, the prompt and effective cooperation of the British and United States Air Forces was a fundamental element in success. Their assistance enabled our troops to attain their objectives at a much smaller cost in casualties than could otherwise have been the case; and without their intervention the losses inflicted upon the enemy would have been much less serious than they actually were.

6. Manpower and Conscription

Although the parallel between the conscription controversies of the First and Second World Wars is striking, in the second, as already noted, the conflict took a less violent form. The basic reason was that in 1939-45 the national government, led by Mackenzie King, was heavily dependent on the support of Quebec and was determined not to adopt overseas conscription — anathema in that province — except in the last extremity. See André Laurendeau, *La Crise de la conscription, 1942* (Montreal, 1962); R. MacG. Dawson, *The Conscription Crisis of 1944* (Toronto, 1961), a book that should be used with care; Pickersgill and Forster, *The Mackenzie King Record*, I and II; Swettenham, *McNaughton*, III; Wade, *The French Canadians*, II; J. L. Granatstein, *Conscription in the Second World War, 1939-1945* (Toronto, 1969), a well-informed outline; and Stacey, *Arms, Men and Governments*.

252. The National Resources Mobilization Act, 1940

(4 George VI, Chap. 13)

This Act reflects the alarm caused by the defeat in France and Flanders and the collapse of France. It may be said to mark the beginning of a new phase in the Canadian war effort: the abandonment of the concept of limited liability (above, p. 596) except in the field of manpower. Section 2 is clearly modelled upon section 1 of the United Kingdom's Emergency Powers (Defence) Act (3 & 4 Geo. 6, Chap. 20, 22 May 1940). The Act had the effect of authorizing compulsory military service, which however, in accordance with the government's pledges (above, **189, 190** and **239**) was limited to home defence. After the plebiscite taken on 27 April 1942 (below, p. 631), the Act was amended by 6 George VI, Chap. 29 (1 August 1942) which struck out the first eight words of section 2 and repealed section 3.

(Assented to 21st June, 1940)

WHEREAS by reason of developments since the outbreak of the present war a special emergency has arisen and the national safety of Canada has become endangered; and

Whereas it is, therefore, expedient to confer upon the Governor in Council special emergency powers to permit of the mobilization of all of the effective resources of the nation, both human and material, for the purpose of the defence and security of Canada, and

Whereas it is expedient that the said powers should be conferred upon the Governor in Council during the continuation of the state of war now existing:

Therefore His Majesty, by and with the advice and consent of the Senate and the House of Commons of Canada enacts as follows: – ...

2. Subject to the provisions of section three hereof, the Governor in Council may do and authorize such acts and things, and make from time to time such orders and regulations, requiring persons to place themselves, their services and their property at the disposal of His Majesty in the right of Canada, as may be deemed necessary or expedient for securing the public safety, the defence of Canada, the maintenance of public order, or the efficient prosecution of the war, or for maintaining supplies or services essential to the life of the community.

3. The powers conferred by the next preceding section may not be exercised for the purpose of requiring persons to serve in the military, naval or air forces outside of Canada and the territorial waters thereof.

4. The powers conferred by this Act shall remain in force only during the continuation of the state of war now existing. ... *

---

*Sections 5 and 6 deal respectively with the tabling in Parliament of orders and regulations made under the Act, and with penalties for violation of such orders and regulations. The latter were not to exceed a fine of $5,000 or imprisonment for five years, or both fine and imprisonment.

253. The Plebiscite: Manifesto of the *Ligue pour la défense du Canada*, 1942

(*L'Action nationale*, January 1942)

After the Japanese attack on Pearl Harbor brought the United States into the war, the Canadian government came under greater pressure to authorize unlimited conscription. Mackenzie King decided to ask the public in a plebiscite to release the government from its pledge against overseas conscription — not with a view to introducing such a measure, but in the hope of laying the issue to rest. This produced the war's first serious rift between French-speaking and English-speaking Canada. The *Ligue pour la défense du Canada* was formed to organize opposition to release, and found much support in Quebec. Its approach, in the words of its secretary, André Laurendeau, was "conscientiously bourassiste"; it attempted, ineffectively, as Bourassa had once done, to appeal to the country as a whole. In the vote on 27 April 1942 Quebec, alone among the nine provinces, voted "No" — 993,663 to 376,188. The vote in the country at large was 2,945,514 "Yes" against 1,643,006 "No."

(*Translation*)
MANIFESTO TO THE PEOPLE OF CANADA

In the form of a plebiscite, the Ottawa government will soon place before the voters of this country a serious question: "Are you in favour of releasing the Government from any obligation arising out of any past commitments restricting the methods of raising men for military service?"

The *Ligue pour la Défense du Canada* demands that the answer to this question be: *No!* A *No* polite but firm and unequivocal. Let no one speak of an inappropriate or hasty manoeuvre. In order to obtain release from its obligations, the government has felt it necessary to resort to a popular referendum. Thus it is the right of every free citizen to influence opinion and to respond to the plebiscite, according to his judgement and his conscience, without being accused of lack of patriotism or dangerous agitation. To defend oneself and one's country is not to challenge anyone nor protest improperly. The *Ligue* thinks, rather, that in this threat-laden hour, no province and no racial group can withdraw and be silent, because of tactics or fear, without failing in an important duty and without committing itself equally to political suicide.

The reply to the plebiscite must be: *No*. Why? Because nobody asks to be freed of an obligation if he does not already have the temptation to violate it, and because, of all the promises he has made to the people of Canada, there remains only one which King would prefer not to be obliged to keep: the promise not to conscript men for overseas.

Now we do not want conscription for overseas:

— Because, in the opinion of our political and military leaders, Canada is more and more threatened by the enemy, and our chief and supreme duty is to defend our own country first;

— Because, according to the statistics given by the recruiting officials and the government itself, the voluntary system is still supplying, in February 1942, twice as many men as our different services can absorb;

— Because a small country, of eleven million inhabitants, which is claimed to be the granary and arsenal of the democracies and the allies, cannot be simultaneously an inexhaustible reservoir of fighting men;

— Because Canada has already reached and even passed the limit of her military effort, and because, in victory, we do not want to be in a worse situation than those defeated;

— Because, considering her population and financial resources, Canada has already given the allied cause as much, at least, as any of the great nations at war;

— Because none of these great nations has yet — so far as we know — undertaken to destroy its internal structure, and Canada, in no way responsible for the present war, has no right nor even duty to destroy itself.

So it is not as a province nor as an ethnic group that we take our stand. If we refuse to release the government from its pledges of 1939 and 1940, we act as Canadians, placing the interest of Canada above everything else. There is in this country, we think, a majority of Canadians for whom Canada is home, and for whom the motto *Canada d'abord* or *Canada first* has never been a mere electoral slogan, but the expression of a profound feeling and a supreme belief of the spirit. We appeal to all of these. We ask them to place the motherland above racial spirit or partisan loyalty. Do they wish to take an action that will stop the rush to the abyss and that bears strong witness to the voice of the majority from one ocean to the other? Then let them reply to Mr. King's plebiscite, with all the serene strength of free men, with a resounding NO.

God save our country! Long live Canada!

THE LEAGUE FOR THE DEFENCE OF CANADA
By its directors,

(Signed) Dr. J.-B. PRINCE, President
Maxime RAYMOND,
Georges PELLETIER,
J.-Alfred BERNIER,
L.-Athanase FRECHETTE,
Philippe GIRARD,
Gérard FILION,
Jean DRAPEAU,
Roger VARIN,
André LAURENDEAU, Secretary.

254. Crisis, 1944: General Stuart Asks for 15,000 Men

(Stacey, *Arms, Men and Governments*, p. 444)

Colonel J. L. Ralston, Minister of National Defence, had warned Mackenzie King at intervals since 1941 that the time might come when he would feel obliged to ask for overseas conscription. In 1942 King's attitude after the amendment of the National Resources Mobilization Act (above, **252**) led Ralston to resign; he was prevailed on to remain, but the letter of resignation was never withdrawn. In 1944, after the heavy casualties of the summer campaign (above, **251**), Ralston, during a visit overseas, became convinced that the future needs of the field army could only be met by overseas conscription. He brought back with him Lieut.-General Kenneth Stuart, Chief of Staff at Canadian Military Headquarters, London, and a former Chief of the General Staff. At a Cabinet War Committee meeting on 19 October Ralston read this memorandum from Stuart, which calculated that by 31 December there would be "little or no infantry" available as reinforcements unless there was a change of policy.

... The only solution that I can see is to find an additional 15,000 infantry to add to our reinforcement pool on or before 31 Dec 44, and to ask that replacements sent monthly from Canada in 1945 shall be increased to 5300, of whom 4300 should be infantry. The above addition to the pool will give us one month's holding in each theatre [Italy and Northwest Europe] and one month in the U.K. for each theatre.

It is apparent, of course, that I am leading up to a recommendation that the future effective maintenance of our Canadian forces in two theatres requires that additional personnel be made available from Canada for service overseas. Actually such is my belief today.

I can assure you that I am not anxious to make the recommendation implied above. On the other hand, I consider that, as Chief of Staff, C.M.H.Q., one of my major responsibilities is to ensure that formations in the field are supplied with adequate and well-trained reinforcements. . . . I am not satisfied, and I have attempted to express my reasons in this letter, that anticipated reinforcements will be adequate to meet future requirements of this war against Germany.

I recommend, therefore, if the numbers required cannot be found from General Service personnel in Canada, that the terms of service of N.R.M.A. [National Resources Mobilization Act] personnel be extended to include overseas service in any theatre.

255. Crisis, 1944: Mackenzie King Gets Himself a New Defence Minister

(McNaughton Papers, P.A.C.)

After nearly a fortnight of nerve-racking Cabinet discussions with Ralston, who was prepared to resign if his recommendation was not accepted, King seems to have convinced himself that there was within the Cabinet a conspiracy against himself centring around Ralston. Although the Defence Minister was still ready to seek a compromise, King privately resolved to dismiss him; and he ascertained that General A. G. L. McNaughton, the former commander of the First Canadian Army (above, p. 611) was willing to accept the Defence portfolio. This document is McNaughton's hand-written memorandum of a telephone call from King received during the Cabinet meeting on 1 November at which King sprang his mine and, referring to the fact that his 1942 resignation (above, p. 633) had never been withdrawn, expelled Ralston from the Cabinet. See Stacey, *Arms, Men and Governments*, pp. 453-58.

At 5.00 PM on Wed. 1 Nov 1944 Mr King called me by Phone. . . .

Mr King said that the Discussions were taking longer than he had expected. That the (Officers of the Dept)? [*sic*] were showing more willingness to meet the situation. It may be late before the meeting is over. He had just called me to let me know so that I would not be waiting without news.

I said that my only desire was to get a proper solution. If it can be done peacefully without a cabinet split all the better. And something more to the effect that he was not to consider himself under any obligation to me.

Mr King said his particular differences with the Minister (Ralston) will come at the last he was keeping it to the end. He said something to the effect that he was trying to establish the greatest measure of agreement in the Cabinet before hand.

I said I would continue to hold myself available.

256. Crisis, 1944: The Coming of Overseas Conscription

(Order in Council P.C. 8891, *Debates, House of Commons*, 23 November 1944)

Dropping Ralston did not prevent overseas conscription, though it may have helped convince Quebec that Mackenzie King was ready to go to almost any length to avoid it. For three weeks McNaughton tried unsuccessfully to prevail on the conscripts ("zombies") to volunteer for general service, while Ralston's friends and fellow-conscriptionists still in the Cabinet fumed and public opinion became more and more troubled. By 22 November things had reached a state where six conscriptionist ministers (including C. D. Howe and the Minister of Finance, J. L. Ilsley) met and agreed to make a mass resignation. King did not actually know of this, but it was clear to him that the government was about to break up and that only a change of policy could avert this disaster. A recommendation from the Army Council to McNaughton gave him the excuse, and on the afternoon of 23 November this order in council was tabled in the House of Commons.

Whereas it is essential in the national interest and for the efficient prosecution of the war to provide for the adequate reinforcement of the Canadian forces overseas;

And whereas it has now become necessary, in order to ensure provision of adequate reserves to meet requirements for the reinforcement of the Canadian forces fighting in Europe and in the Mediterranean, to extend the locality of service of certain personnel who have been called out for training, service or duty, pursuant to the provisions of the National Resources Mobilization Act, 1940;

Now therefore, His Excellency the Governor General in Council, on the recommendation of the Minister of National Defence and under and by virtue of the provisions of the National Resources Mobilization Act, 1940, and the War Measures Act, is pleased to order and doth hereby order as follows:

Notwithstanding the provisions of any other statute, law, regulation or order, the Minister of National Defence is hereby authorized and directed to dispatch to the following localities of service, namely: the United Kingdom and/or to European and/or Mediterranean operational theatres such personnel, in such numbers as may be approved by the governor in council (the number hereby approved being sixteen thousand) who are serving by reason of their having been called out for training, service or duty pursuant to the provisions of the National Resources Mobilization Act, 1940, as are or may from time to time hereafter be required, in the opinion of the said minister, for training, service or duty within the said localities of service; such personnel to be detailed from such units, depots and establishments as may be designated by the said minister; and the Minister of National Defence is hereby authorized and directed to issue or cause to be issued all orders and to take all steps necessary to give effect to this authorization and direction; and all personnel so dispatched or to be dispatched are respectively hereby required (in addition to all other obligations for training, service or duty) to perform while in the said localities of service such training, service or duty as may be ordered by any superior officer.

Further, all personnel so dispatched or who may at any time be dispatched are, pursuant to section 64 of the Militia Act, hereby placed on active service beyond Canada for the defence thereof.

257. Louis St. Laurent Expresses His Convictions

(Debates, House of Commons, 6 December 1944)

The tabling of P.C. 8891 (above, **256**) was followed by a long debate in the Commons on what amounted to a motion of confidence in the government. The attitude of French-Canadian members was crucial, and a high point was the short speech of Louis St. Laurent, whom Mackenzie King had brought into the Cabinet after the death of Ernest Lapointe in 1941. In the end, 34 French-speaking Liberals voted against the Liberal government, but King got an overall majority of 73, whereas he had expected only 30.

Hon. L. S. St. LAURENT (Minister of Justice): . . .
I believe that Canada's participation in this terrible war to the magnificent extent to which it has been and is being realized was absolutely essential to the survival of this nation as a nation of free men. I believe that had it not been for the heroic and obstinate and successful resistance of the people of England, Scotland and Wales during 1940 and 1941, we here in Canada would now be either dead or slaves of nazi victors and masters. . . . I believe that this nation must continue to contribute its full share to the joint efforts of that gallant company of free nations pledged and determined to achieve and to consolidate . . . victory.

I believe that our Canadian men in our navy, our army and our air force, who have fought and are fighting in that gallant company, have done so and are doing so at our instance, for us. . . .

It is for us, for you and for me, Mr. Speaker, and for our colleagues in this house and for those whom we represent that these men are enduring, are bleeding, are perhaps dying this very day, while we are here talking and debating as to how best we can act so that the numbers of them who become casualties shall not be increased.

Up to the evening of November 22 I sincerely believed that that object could be best achieved by adhering to the voluntary system, the system under which over 900,000 of our bravest and best have offered their services in this great cause. . . . The Prime Minister (Mr. Mackenzie King) has told the house that on November 22 General McNaughton himself, in conference with his staff, had come to certain conclusions and had presented them to the government on the evening of that day. As a result of that presentation I had to bring my mind to bear upon two different aspects of the problem. . . .

One was, that without adequate infantry units equal to any tasks which the fortune of battle might at any time bring into being, none of our troops could venture into the fighting line and our whole fighting effort would remain paralyzed. . . . I readily imagined what use nazi propaganda might make of this appearance that the Canadian forces were no longer in the fight. Would it not have been used to the dreadful purpose of stiffening resistance and promising the German people that it was an example which other allied forces might soon be disposed to follow and that all they had to do was to hold on long enough and they would wear us all out? Who can tell what prolongation of this terrible conflict that might have meant?

The other aspect I had to consider was the possible psychological effect of adequate reinforcement pools in the battle areas and in England. I was impressed by the consideration that the possible inadequacy of such pools might affect the morale of the men in the fighting line to an extent that would make them more vulnerable in battle; this in turn might mean casualties that would not otherwise be incurred. . . .

On November 22 it appeared that for the reasons which have already been discussed, or at least for some reasons good or bad, the numbers required for these substantial reserves might be larger than were apt to be provided in time by voluntary conversion of trained and fit personnel in our N.R.M.A. forces and general service, and no one but a fit and already trained man could meet those requirements. I therefore heeded the passionate appeal which the Prime Minister has told you he made to every one of his colleagues. I fully realized the possible and probable reactions among a great many in my province to my conduct in accepting to go on when any measure whatsoever of compulsion is added to the voluntary system for service overseas as the policy of the government. But I came here to do a war job, and because it was felt by the Prime Minister, rightly or wrongly, that I could be of some help, I feel I must still go on, whatever may be the increase in the difficulties of the task, so long as it is made apparent to me that these difficulties arise out of facts which have a bearing on the security of the men who are doing so much more for us than anything we can do for them.

I still felt and I hoped that compulsion might not be necessary to secure in time the required number of fit and trained men. . . . But no chance could be taken about it, and I decided that I would stand or fall with the Prime Minister. I may add that I have taken and I still take both comfort and pride in that decision. . . .

The all-important fact is that the reinforcements will be neither insufficient nor delayed. . . .

The will of the majority must be respected and it must prevail. But I trust that, here in Canada, the majority will always, as it is doing in this case, assert that will only after giving due consideration to the feelings and views of the minority and to the reasons for such feelings and views, and then only to the extent to which the majority is sincerely convinced that the general interests of the whole body politic require that it be thus asserted. . . .

Believing as I do that the majority in this house, after giving its best consideration to the facts which have been brought to light in this long and earnest debate, is sincerely convinced that the passing of this order in council P.C. 8891 was necessary to the proper conduct of the affairs of the Canadian body politic as a whole, and believing as I do that whenever the majority, after full consultation and mature deliberation, reaches a conclusion of that kind, it is proper the minority should accept it and loyally assist in carrying it out, I appeal to all the members of this house, whatever may have been their individual views — whether to do more or to do less than the order in council provides — to unite and to assert to the men overseas that this nation, from one ocean to the other, stands pledged to a victory that will be decisive and that will endure. . . .

258. Intake of Men into the Armed Forces, by Provinces, 1939-1945

(Stacey, *Arms, Men and Governments,* Appendix "R")

This table may be compared with **220**, above, for the First World War. In the absence of enlistment figures for the various "ethnic groups" of the population, it is probably the best guide available to the general scale of the military effort of the regions of Canada. Obviously many considerations, including varying regional health standards, prevent these figures from being strictly comparable. But the difference between the statistics for Quebec and those for other provinces is clearly significant.

Intake into the Canadian Armed Forces, Second World War, by Provinces

Officers, Other Ranks and Ratings
Excluding WRCNS, CWAC and RCAF (WD)*

Place of Permanent Residence on enrolment	Male (1) Population 18 to 45	RCN	Army(2) GS(3)	Army(2) NRMA	Army(2) Total	RCAF	Total three services	Percentage of Total Intake to Male Population 18 to 45
Prince Edward Island	19,000	1,448	5,961	372	6,333	1,528	9,309	48.18
Nova Scotia	123,000	6,837	42,462	2,558	45,020	7,498	59,355	48.31
New Brunswick	94,000	2,737	32,326	3,621	35,947	6,453	45,137	48.17
Quebec	699,000	12,404	94,446	43,823	138,269	24,768	175,441	25.69
Ontario	830,000	40,353	243,615	23,322	266,937	90,518	397,808	47.77
Manitoba	159,000	7,782	42,627	5,915	48,542	20,120	76,444	48.12
Saskatchewan	191,000	6,472	44,213(4)	8,093(4)	52,306	21,827	80,605	42.38
Alberta	178,000	7,360	44,775	6,069	50,844	19,499	77,703	43.11
British Columbia	181,000	11,925	52,620(5)	5,626(5)	58,246	20,805(6)	90,976	50.47
Outside Canada		893	5,892	8	5,900	9,485	16,278	
Not stated		263	191		191		454	
Total	2,474,000	98,474	609,128	99,407	708,535	222,501	1,029,510	41.15

Notes:
(1) Estimates from summaries 1941 Census
(2) 22,046 GS & NRMA members transferred to the RCN or RCAF, and are included with the Army intake
(3) 68,434 NRMA members volunteered for GS; they are included with GS, and not with NRMA
(4) Including N.W.T.
(5) Including Yukon
(6) Including N.W.T. and Yukon.

*The women's services. GS=General Service. NRMA=National Resources Mobilization Act (i.e., conscripts).

7. Economic Effort and Controls

As already noted, the Canadian effort on the economic fronts in 1939-45 was larger and much more varied than in 1914-18. Only a few representative documents on these matters can be presented here.

259. A Program for Munitions and Supply

(E. P. Taylor to C. D. Howe, 25 June 1940, Howe Papers, P.A.C.)

For some nine months after the outbreak of war in 1939, next to nothing was done to provide for the manufacture of army weapons in Canada. The main reason seems to have been that it was not considered economic to produce for the Canadian Army alone, and orders from Britain were not forthcoming. But after the French collapse Britain suddenly became anxious for equipment from Canada and the whole situation changed. This letter, written to the Minister of Munitions and Supply on behalf of the Executive Committee of his department, reflects the change of atmosphere and amounts to a sketch for the main operations of the department during the war. See Stacey, *Arms, Men and Governments*, Part VIII.

Dear Mr. Minister:

Our enquiries have led us to understand that the following are the principal weapons which Canada should have for home defence and/or for use abroad:

Small Arms

Lee Enfield Rifles
Sub Machine Guns
Bren Machine Guns
Vickers Machine Guns
Browning Aircraft Machine Guns

Artillery

25 pounders
4.5" Guns and/or Howitzers
3.7" Anti Aircraft Guns
40mm. Bofors Anti Aircraft Guns
Anti Tank Guns
Mortars

Ammunition for the above
Aerial Bombs
   250, 500 and 1,000 pounds.

Naval Mines and Depth Charges
Tanks
   Light
   Medium

Equipment for Minesweepers now under construction

Of the foregoing, arrangements have been completed to produce only the following:
   25 Pounders
   Bren Machine Guns
   Medium Tanks
   Aerial Bombs (now in negotiation)
   Ammunition for some of the above

It is contended that all of the equipment should be produced in Canada. Every week in which a decision is not made will mean a month's delay in getting into production due to the increasing scarcity of machine tools. . . .

If this Department is given the authority, we can organize at once to deliver all the weapons listed on the first page of this memorandum with minimum delay. If another month is lost, it is almost certain that deliveries, in quantity, could not be promised until 1942.

To tool up for such a programme would probably cost $100,000,000. The major part of this investment would be in machine tools. It is submitted that this is a relatively small sum in view of the dangers of the present situation and the money being spent in other ways. There will be more than 200,000 Canadian troops in training by the fall of this year, and it would seem only proper that to eventually make them effective they should have all the weapons and equipment necessary to fighting a modern war.

It is suggested that the best way to bring this matter to a head would be to arrange a conference between you and the members of the Executive Committee, of this Department, and the Ministers of National Defence — Militia and Naval Services and Air Services — with their principal advisers.*

Submitted on behalf of the
Executive Committee,
(signed) E. P. Taylor

*It is an indication of the new urgency in the war effort that the meeting thus recommended took place the same night. The Cabinet War Committee had

260. An Act to Amend the Department of Munitions and Supply Act, 1940

(4 George VI, Chap. 31)

The Department of Munitions and Supply was authorized by a hastily drafted statute (3 George VI, Chap. 3) which received the royal assent on 13 September 1939. The Department was actually set up only in April 1940, with C. D. Howe as its Minister. In the summer of 1940 what was virtually a new Act was passed. The excerpts given here relate to the enormous powers given to the Minister and to the valuable and flexible instrument known as the Crown company, which was used for a wide variety of purposes.

... *(Assented to 7th August, 1940)*

6. (1) The Minister may,

(*a*) buy or otherwise acquire, manufacture or otherwise produce, finish, assemble, store and transport, and sell, exchange or otherwise dispose of, munitions of war and supplies....

(*e*) mobilize, control, restrict or regulate to such extent as the Minister may, in his absolute discretion, deem necessary, any branch of trade or industry in Canada or any munitions of war or supplies;

(*f*) with the specific or general authorization of the Governor in Council, from time to time, make, issue, amend and repeal all such orders, rules, regulations, permits and licences, as the Minister, in his discretion, may consider necessary or expedient for the exercise of any of the powers conferred upon him by this Act or by the Governor in Council and any such order, rule, regulation, permit or licence may be of general or particular application and failure to comply therewith shall constitute an offence under this Act....

(3) (*a*) The Minister may, if he considers that the carrying out of any of the purposes or provisions of this Act is likely to be facilitated thereby, procure the incorporation of any one or more companies or corporations under the provisions of *The Companies Act, 1934*, or under the provisions of any Act of any province of Canada relating to the incorporation of companies, for the purpose of exercising and performing in Canada or elsewhere any of

---

already decided (14 June) that Canada should undertake production of all items of armament and equipment for her troops overseas which character or quantity indicated could be economically manufactured in Canada; and Mr. Howe had told the Committee on 5 June that the British government proposed to order in Canada the equipment for ten divisions.

the powers conferred or the duties imposed on the Minister by this Act or by the Governor in Council and may delegate to any such company or corporation any of the powers and duties conferred or imposed upon the Minister under this Act or any Order in Council. . . .

7. The Minister, exclusively, may buy or otherwise acquire, manufacture or otherwise produce, munitions of war or supplies and construct or carry out defence projects required by the Department of National Defence, excepting, however: —

(i) munitions of war or supplies manufactured in an arsenal or factory owned or operated by His Majesty the King in right of Canada;*

(ii) defence projects constructed or carried out by persons in the employ of His Majesty the King in right of Canada;

(iii) such munitions of war or supplies as, for reasons of practicability or otherwise, the Minister or Deputy Minister, at the instance of or with the approval of the Minister of National Defence, may request the Department of National Defence, by either a specific or general request, to procure, purchase or acquire; and

(iv) such defence projects as, for reasons of practicability or otherwise, the Minister or Deputy Minister, at the instance of or with the approval of the Minister of National Defence, may request the Department of National Defence, by either a specific or general request, to construct or carry out. . . .

261. Extracts from Reports of the Wartime Prices and Trade Board, 1945 and 1946

A great apparatus of controls over materials and economic activities came into existence during the war. Many of the control agencies worked under the Department of Munitions and Supply. What was probably the most important, however, the Wartime Prices and Trade Board, established as early as 3 September 1939, was responsible to

*Within a few weeks of the passage of this Act, the Dominion Arsenals were in fact transferred from the control of the Department of National Defence to that of the Department of Munitions and Supply.

the Minister of Finance. Its control of prices was generally regarded as one of the more effective features of Canadian war organization.

Report for 1 January–31 December 1945
. . .

By December, 1945, Canadian wholesale prices had risen 34 per cent over the average level for the five pre-war years, 1935 to 1939. The increase in prices in the United States over a comparable period was slightly less, amounting to about 33 per cent. When account is taken, however, of the fact that the Canadian dollar in 1945 stood at a discount of about 9 per cent as compared with the base period, and of certain technical differences in the two indexes, it can be said that the Canadian price level at the end of 1945 was lower than that of the United States in terms of the pre-war relationship. It will also be noted that the cost of living index in Canada shows a considerably smaller wartime increase than the United States index.*

Report for 1 January–31 December 1946
. . .

During the six years of war from August, 1939 to August, 1945, the cost of living index in Canada was held to an advance of about 19 per cent, while general wholesale prices increased 44 per cent. This trend compared very favourably with price increases over the four year period of war during the first world war, when living costs rose 54 per cent and wholesale prices, 106 per cent. . . .

262. Some Statistics of Canadian War Production, 1939-1945

(Compiled from Kennedy, *History of the Department of Munitions and Supply*; and "Canadian War Data," Reference Paper No. 4, Canadian Information Service, Department of External Affairs, 15 May 1946)

This table, which is highly selective, should be compared with **230**, above, for the First World War, and with E. P. Taylor's letter of 25 June

*On the basis of prices in 1935-39 equalling 100, the cost of living index in Canada in August 1939 was 100.8, that in the U.S. 98.6. In December 1945 the respective figures were 120.1 and 129.9.

1940 (above, **259**). Normally Kennedy has been followed, but where his figures are not adequate (e.g., tanks are not shown separately from other armoured fighting vehicles) the other source is used. The two sources sometimes differ widely.

Vehicles

Tanks and self-propelled mounts*	6,590
Other armoured fighting vehicles	44,464
Mechanical transport vehicles	815,729

Guns†

4-inch naval	1,749
25-pounder field (standard and self-propelled)	3,781
40-mm. anti-aircraft	4,352
3.7-inch anti-aircraft	1,735

Small Arms

Rifles (No. 4)	905,731
Pistols (9-mm.)	71,995
Bren light machine guns	186,000
Sten machine carbines	126,703
Browning aircraft machine guns	32,678

Ships

Merchant

10,000 tons	348
4,700 tons	43
Others	19
	410

Naval‡

Frigates	70
Corvettes	122
Algerine Minesweepers	62

*The S.P. mounts are presumably duplicated below under 25-pounder field guns.
† Great numbers of spare barrels made for various types of gun are not listed here.
‡ Minor naval vessels (landing craft, etc.) were also built in great numbers.

Aircraft

Service types	5,874
Advanced trainers	6,757
Elementary trainers	3,787
	16,418

8. Atomic Energy

Canada was a very junior partner in the Anglo-American effort that produced the atomic bomb in 1945, though the United States obtained Canadian raw material—uranium—in large quantities. In 1944 however the construction of a "heavy water pilot pile" in Canada was authorized as an Allied project. The establishment at Chalk River, Ontario, which resulted was completed much too late to affect the course of the war, but it launched both Britain and Canada into the atomic age. See Wilfrid Eggleston, *Canada's Nuclear Story* (Toronto, 1965); Margaret Gowing, *Britain and Atomic Energy, 1939-1945* (London, 1964); George C. Laurence, "Canada's Participation in Atomic Energy Development," *Bulletin of the Atomic Scientists*, November 1947.

263. C. J. Mackenzie, Acting President, National Research Council, to C. D. Howe, 10 April 1944

(Howe Papers, P.A.C.)

*PERSONAL AND
MOST SECRET*
... In December 1938 and January 1939 in France and Germany *a discovery was made* that certain elements, chiefly uranium, could be made to "burst" (scientific term "fission"). Since 1941 active research in the United Kingdom, the United States and Canada has been carried out and it is now certain a bomb can and will be made that will be, if not a million times, at least hundreds of times more powerful than anything yet known. It is also certain that power units will be made in the future for aeroplanes, ships and submarines that will

drive planes thousands of miles and carry ships across the ocean on a few pounds of fuel.

In 1943 the United Kingdom effort was combined with that of Canada and transferred to Montreal. The American effort has been enormous: expenditures and commitments to date are over two billion dollars.

Time and military urgency demand that every possible avenue be explored. The United States has six separate projects underway — a seventh depending on heavy water, while most important and proving, could not be started until plants to manufacture heavy water were constructed. These plants, built in America at a cost of perhaps a hundred million dollars, are now coming into production.

The present proposal is to build the pilot plant for this important phase of the project in Canada as a joint United States, United Kingdom and Canadian effort. Our ownership of uranium ores, our early interest in the production of heavy water at Trail and the presence of a highly expert group of workers in Canada give us a special interest and facility for this work.

In my opinion Canada has a unique opportunity to become intimately associated in a project which is not only of the greatest immediate military importance, but which may revolutionize the future world in the same degree as did the invention of the steam engine and the discovery of electricity. It is an opportunity Canada as a nation cannot afford to turn down.

264. Extract from Minutes of Combined Policy Committee, Washington, 13 April 1944

(Howe Papers, P.A.C.)

TOP SECRET
...
4. MONTREAL PROJECT

Major-General [Leslie R.] Groves [U.S.A.] reported on behalf of the Special Subcommittee, appointed at the meeting of 17th February, 1944 to study a proposed joint development of a heavy water pile in Canada. He summarized its Report to the Combined Policy Committee, which had been circulated previously to all members of the Committee, emphasising the premises from which conclusions had been derived and setting out the recommendations made therein.

Mr. Howe stated that Canada was prepared to accept the recommendation and, indeed, was willing to accept the cost of the development now planned. . . .

Field Marshal Sir John Dill referred to anxiety which had been shown in Great Britain that the services of the team of scientists now in Montreal should be used to the full. He expressed relief that a programme of work could now be envisaged which, with adequate priorities and exchange of information, would make that possible.

Major-General Groves stated that he foresaw no difficulties with regard to American priorities required by the proposed work in Canada. He also explained that whatever information from American sources was required for the successful prosecution of the work in Canada would be forthcoming. He thought the group in Canada should be given full support and should operate under the same security restrictions as a similar group working in the U.S.A.

Mr. Howe stated that the project would be given top priority in Canada. He agreed that there should be no difficulty over priorities on materials necessarily to be obtained in the United States. Mr. Howe felt these matters could be cleared easily through machinery already established in Canada for dealing with Canadian and American priorities.

The Committee adopted unanimously the Recommendations of the Special Subcommittee.

In fulfillment of recommendation (f), the Committee unanimously agreed that Dr. James Chadwick, Major-General L. R. Groves and Dean C. J. Mackenzie, who had constituted the investigating Special Subcommittee, should continue to act as a Subcommittee of the Combined Policy Committee to supervise, on behalf and under the general supervision of the Committee, the carrying out in Canada of this joint American-British-Canadian project in accordance with the Recommendations now adopted. . . .

9. Rapprochement with the United States

The period immediately before the outbreak of war in 1939 witnessed the beginning of a rapprochement between Canada and the United States. It was marked publicly by speeches by President Roosevelt and Mackenzie King and by trade agreements (above, p. 208) and privately by limited but unprecedented military conversations between the two countries' Chiefs of Staff, as well as by consultations on such occasions as the visit of King George VI and Queen Elizabeth (accompanied by Mackenzie King) to the United States in June 1939.

After the Allied disaster in France and Flanders early in the summer of 1940, fears on both sides of the border produced much closer co-operation. Mackenzie King exulted in the special relationship which he felt he had brought into being between himself and Canada and the President. Roosevelt clearly (and inevitably) attached less importance to it (see, e.g., **241** above), but 1940 undoubtedly marked a turning point of great significance in Canadian-American relations. Only the fundamental documents can be reproduced here. See Stanley W. Dziuban, *Military Relations between the United States and Canada* (Washington, 1959); R. Warren James, *Wartime Economic Co-operation: A Study of Relations between Canada and the United States* (Toronto, 1949) and Stacey, *Arms, Men and Governments*, particularly Part VI.

265. The Ogdensburg Declaration, 18 August 1940

(Canada, *Treaty Series*, 1940, No. 14)

Note that this document, so famous and significant in Canadian-American relations, was not a treaty or signed agreement. It was nothing more than a press release, though the Canadian government, no doubt with a view to giving it the highest possible formal status, published it in its *Treaty Series*.

Declaration by the Prime Minister of Canada and the President of the United States of America regarding the establishing of a Permanent Joint Board on Defence made on August 18, 1940. *

The Prime Minister and the President have discussed the mutual problems of defence in relation to the safety of Canada and the United States.

It has been agreed that a Permanent Joint Board on Defence shall be set up at once by the two countries.

This Permanent Joint Board on Defence shall commence immediate studies relating to sea, land, and air problems including personnel and material.

It will consider in the broad sense the defence of the north half of the Western Hemisphere.

*At the conclusion of conversations held at Ogdensburg, in the State of New York, U.S.A. [Note in original.]

The Permanent Joint Board on Defence will consist of four or five members from each country, most of them from the services. It will meet shortly.

266. The Hyde Park Declaration, 20 April 1941

(Canada, *Treaty Series*, 1941, No. 14)

The international status of this paper (which unlike the Ogdensburg one, above, **265**, was the result of Canadian initiative) was no higher than that of the Ogdensburg Declaration. But although it did not have quite the sweeping effects which its terms might suggest, it was immediately acted upon by the United States, and it may be said to have solved Canada's U.S. dollar problem for the duration of the war.

*Declaration by the Prime Minister of Canada and the
President of the United States of America
regarding co-operation for war
production made on
April 20, 1941**

Among other important matters, the President and the Prime Minister discussed measures by which the most prompt and effective utilization might be made of the productive facilities of North America for the purposes both of local and hemisphere defence and of the assistance which in addition to their own programs both Canada and the United States are rendering to Great Britain and the other democracies.

It was agreed as a general principle that in mobilizing the resources of this continent each country should provide the other with the defence articles which it is best able to produce, and, above all, produce quickly, and that production programs should be co-ordinated to this end.

While Canada has expanded its productive capacity manifold since the beginning of the war, there are still numerous defence articles which it must obtain in the United States, and purchases of this character by Canada will be even greater in the coming year than in the past. On the other hand, there is existing and potential capacity in Canada for the speedy production of certain kinds of munitions, strategic materials, aluminum, and ships, which are urgently required

*At the conclusion of conversations held at Hyde Park, in the State of New York, U.S.A. [Note in original.]

by the United States for its own purposes.

While exact estimates cannot yet be made, it is hoped that during the next twelve months Canada can supply the United States with between $200,000,000 and $300,000,000 worth of such defence articles. This sum is a small fraction of the total defence program of the United States, but many of the articles to be provided are of vital importance. In addition, it is of great importance to the economic and financial relations between the two countries that payment by the United States for these supplies will materially assist Canada in meeting part of the cost of Canadian defence purchases in the United States.

In so far as Canada's defence purchases in the United States consist of component parts to be used in equipment and munitions which Canada is producing for Great Britain, it was also agreed that Great Britain will obtain these parts under the Lease-Lend Act and forward them to Canada for inclusion in the finished articles.

The technical and financial details will be worked out as soon as possible in accordance with the general principles which have been agreed upon between the President and the Prime Minister.

Index

This is mainly, but not exclusively, an index of personal names, and should be used in conjunction with the detailed Table of Contents. Figures in italics refer to page numbers, all other figures to document numbers.